A Note on the Author

BEN MACINTYRE is a columnist and Associate Editor on *The Times*. He has worked as the newspaper's correspondent in New York, Paris and Washington. He is the author of ten previous books, including the *Sunday Times* bestsellers *Double Cross* and *A Spy Among Friends*. His most recent book is *SAS Rogue Heroes*, the first authorised biography of the SAS.

benmacintyre.com

THE
BEN MACINTYRE
COLLECTION

AGENT ZIGZAG
&
OPERATION MINCEMEAT

Two Thrilling True Tales from
World War II

Ben Macintyre

BLOOMSBURY
LONDON · OXFORD · NEW YORK · NEW DELHI · SYDNEY

Bloomsbury Publishing
An imprint of Bloomsbury Publishing Plc

50 Bedford Square
London
WC1B 3DP
UK

1385 Broadway
New York
NY 10018
USA

www.bloomsbury.com

Agent Zigzag was first published in Great Britain 2007
Operation Mincemeat was first published in Great Britain 2010
This edition first published in 2017

© Ben Macintyre, 2007, 2010
Map by Duncan Stewart

British Library Cataloguing-in-Publication Data
A catalogue record for this book is available from the British Library.

ISBN: 978-1-4088-9376-0

2 4 6 8 10 9 7 5 3 1

MIX
Paper from
responsible sources
FSC® C019777

Typeset by Hewer Text UK Ltd, Edinburgh
Printed and bound in Great Britain by CPI Group (UK) Ltd, Croydon CR0 4YY

To find out more about our authors and books visit www.bloomsbury.com.
Here you will find extracts, author interviews, details of forthcoming events
and the option to sign up for our newsletters.

Agent Zigzag

CONTENTS

AUTHOR'S NOTE

The true story that follows is based on official papers, letters, diaries, newspaper reports, contemporary accounts and memoirs.

I was first alerted to the existence of the Englishman Eddie Chapman by his obituary in *The Times*. Among the lives of the great and good, here was a character who had achieved a certain greatness, but in ways that were far from conventionally good. The obituary was intriguing as much for what it did not say – and could not know – about Chapman's exploits in the Second World War, since those details remained under seal in MI5's secret archives. At that time, it seemed the full story of Eddie Chapman would never be told.

But then, under a new policy of openness, MI5 began the selective release of hitherto classified information that could not embarrass the living or damage national security. The first 'Zigzag files' were released to the National Archives in 2001. These declassified archives contain more than 1,700 pages of documents relating to Chapman's case: transcripts of interrogations, detailed wireless intercepts, reports, descriptions, diagrams, internal memos, minutes, letters and photographs. The files are extraordinarily detailed, describing not only events and people but also the minutiae of a spy's life, his changing moods and feelings, his hopes, fears and contradictions. Chapman's diligent case officers set out to paint a complete picture of the man, with a meticulous (sometimes hour-by-hour) account of his actions. I am particularly grateful to MI5 for agreeing to my request to declassify additional files relating to the case, and to Howard Davies of the National Archives for helping to facilitate those supplementary releases.

Eddie Chapman's memoirs were published after the war, but the Official Secrets Act prevented him from describing his exploits as a double agent, and his own version of events was often more entertaining than reliable. As his handlers noted, he had no sense of chronology whatsoever. All quotations are cited in the endnotes, but for clarity I have standardised spelling and have selectively used reported speech as direct speech. Chapman's story has also emerged from the memories of the living, people touched, directly or indirectly, by the individuals and events described, and I am grateful to the dozens of interviewees in Britain, France, Germany and Norway – including Betty Chapman – who were willing to talk to me for so many hours, recalling a past now more than half a century old. For obvious reasons, some of those involved in the more clandestine areas of Chapman's life have requested anonymity.

Just weeks before this book was due to go to press, MI5 discovered an entire secret file, overlooked in previous transfers to the public archives, and generously provided me with full access to its contents. That file (which will now become available at the National Archives) gives extraordinary psychological insights into Chapman's character, as seen by his case officers. It is, perhaps, the last missing piece in the Zigzag puzzle.

Zigzag. *n, adj, adv* and *vb*: '. . . a pattern made up of many small corners at an acute angle, tracing a path between two parallel lines; it can be described as both jagged and fairly regular'.

'It is essential to seek out enemy agents who have come to conduct espionage against you and to bribe them to serve you. Give them instructions and care for them. Thus double agents are recruited and used.'

Sun Tzu, *The Art of War*

'War makes thieves and peace hangs them.'

George Herbert

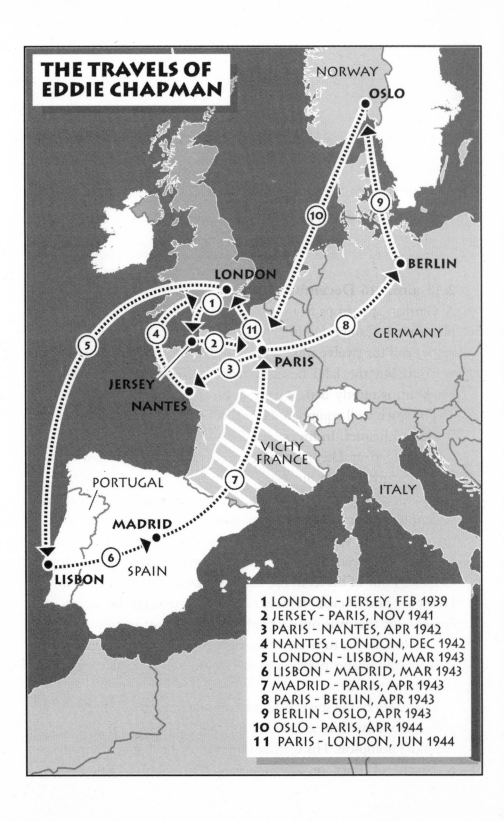

THE TRAVELS OF EDDIE CHAPMAN

NORWAY

OSLO

LONDON

GERMANY

BERLIN

JERSEY

NANTES

PARIS

VICHY
FRANCE

ITALY

PORTUGAL

MADRID

LISBON

SPAIN

1 LONDON – JERSEY, FEB 1939
2 JERSEY – PARIS, NOV 1941
3 PARIS – NANTES, APR 1942
4 NANTES – LONDON, DEC 1942
5 LONDON – LISBON, MAR 1943
6 LISBON – MADRID, MAR 1943
7 MADRID – PARIS, APR 1943
8 PARIS – BERLIN, APR 1943
9 BERLIN – OSLO, APR 1943
10 OSLO – PARIS, APR 1944
11 PARIS – LONDON, JUN 1944

Prologue

2.13 a.m., 16 December 1942

A German spy drops from a black Focke-Wulf reconnaissance plane over Cambridgeshire. His silk parachute opens with a rustle, and for twelve minutes he floats silently down. The stars are out, but the land beneath his feet, swaddled in wartime blackout, is utterly dark. His nose bleeds copiously.

The spy is well equipped. He wears British-issue army landing boots and helmet. In his pocket is a wallet taken from a British soldier killed at Dieppe four months earlier: inside are two identity cards, which are fake, and a letter from his girlfriend Betty, which is genuine. His pack contains matches impregnated with quinine for 'secret writing', a wireless receiver, a military map, £990 in used notes of various denominations, a Colt revolver, an entrenching tool, and some plain-glass spectacles for disguise. Four of his teeth are made from new gold, paid for by Hitler's Third Reich. Beneath his flying overalls he wears a civilian suit that was once of fashionable cut but is now somewhat worn. In the turn-up of the right trouser leg has been sewn a small cellophane package containing a single suicide pill of potassium cyanide.

The name of the spy is Edward Arnold Chapman. The British police also know him as Edward Edwards, Edward Simpson and Arnold Thompson. His German spymasters have given him the codename of 'Fritz' or, affectionately, 'Fritzchen' – Little Fritz.

The British secret services, as yet, have no name for him. That evening the Chief Constable of Cambridgeshire, after an urgent call from a gentleman in Whitehall, has instructed all his officers to be on the lookout for an individual referred to only as 'Agent X'.

Eddie Chapman lands in a freshly ploughed field at 2.25 a.m., and immediately falls face-first into the sodden soil. Dazed, he releases his parachute, then climbs out of his blood-spattered flying suit and buries the bundle. He shoves the revolver into a pocket and digs into the pack for a map and torch. The map has gone. He must have dropped it in the dark. On hands and knees he searches. He curses and sits on the cold earth, in the deep darkness, and wonders where he is, who he is, and whose side he is on.

The Hotel de la Plage

Spring came early to the island of Jersey in 1939, and the sun that poured through the dining-room window of the Hotel de la Plage formed a dazzling halo around the man sitting opposite Betty Farmer with his back to the sea, laughing as he tucked into the six-shilling Sunday Roast Special 'with all the trimmings'. Betty, eighteen, a farm girl newly escaped from the Shropshire countryside, knew this man was quite unlike any she had met before.

Beyond that, her knowledge of Eddie Chapman was somewhat limited. She knew that he was twenty-four years old, tall and handsome, with a thin moustache – just like Errol Flynn in *The Charge of the Light Brigade* – and deep hazel eyes. His voice was strong but high-pitched with a hint of a north-eastern accent. He was 'bubbly', full of laughter and mischief. She knew he must be rich because he was 'in the film business' and drove a Bentley. He wore expensive suits, a gold ring and a cashmere overcoat with mink collar. Today he wore a natty yellow spotted tie and a sleeveless pullover. They had met at a club in Kensington Church Street, and although at first she had declined his invitation to dance, she soon relented. Eddie had become her first lover, but then he vanished, saying he had urgent business in Scotland. 'I shall go,' he told her. 'But I shall always come back.'

Good as his word, Eddie had suddenly reappeared at the door of her lodgings, grinning and breathless. 'How would you like to go to Jersey, then possibly to the south of France?' he asked. Betty had rushed off to pack.

It was a surprise to discover they would be travelling with company. In the front seat of the waiting Bentley sat two men: the driver a huge, ugly brute with a crumpled face; the other small, thin and dark. The pair did not seem ideal companions for a romantic holiday. The driver gunned the engine and they set off at thrilling speed through the London streets, screeching into Croydon airport, parking behind the hangar, just in time to catch the Jersey Airways plane.

That evening they had checked into the seafront hotel. Eddie told the receptionist they were in Jersey to make a film. They had signed the register as Mr and Mrs Farmer of Torquay. After dinner they moved on to West Park Pavilion, a nightclub on the pier, where they danced, played roulette, and drank some more. For Betty, it had been a day of unprecedented glamour and decadence.

War was coming, everyone said so, but the dining room of the Hotel de la Plage was a place of pure peace that sunny Sunday. Beyond the golden beach, the waves flickered among a scatter of tiny islands, as Eddie and Betty ate trifle off plates with smart blue crests. Eddie was half way through telling another funny story, when he froze. A group of men in overcoats and brown hats had entered the restaurant and one was now in urgent conversation with the head waiter. Before Betty could speak, Eddie stood up, bent down to kiss her once, and then jumped through the window, which was closed. There was a storm of broken glass, tumbling crockery, screaming women and shouting waiters: Betty Farmer caught a last glimpse of Eddie Chapman sprinting off down the beach with two overcoated men in pursuit.

Here are just some of the things Betty did not know about Eddie Chapman: he was married; another woman was pregnant with his child; and he was a crook. Not some halfpenny bag-snatcher, but a dedicated professional criminal, a 'prince of the under-world', in his own estimation.

For Chapman, breaking the law was a vocation. In later years, when some sort of motive for his choice of career seemed to be called for, he claimed that the early death of his mother, in the TB ward of a pauper's hospital, had sent him 'off the rails' and turned him against society. Sometimes he blamed the grinding poverty and unemployment in northern England during the Depression for forcing him into a life of crime. But in truth, crime came naturally to him.

Edward Chapman was born in Burnopfield, a tiny village in the Durham coalfields, on 16 November 1914, a few months into the First World War. His father, a marine engineer and too old to fight, had ended up running The Clippership, a dingy pub in Roker, and drinking a large portion of the stock. For Eddie, the eldest of three children, there was no money, not much love, little in the way of guidance and only a cursory education. He soon developed a talent for misbehaviour, and a distaste of authority. Intelligent but lazy, insolent and easily bored, the young Chapman skipped school often, preferring to scour the beach for lemonade bottles, redeemable at a penny a piece, and then while away afternoons at the cinema in Sunderland: *The Scarlet Pimpernel*, and the Alfred Hitchcock films *Blackmail* and spy drama *The Man Who Knew Too Much*.

At the age of seventeen, after a brief and unsatisfactory stint as an unpaid apprentice at a Sunderland engineering firm, Chapman joined the army, although underage, and enlisted in the Second Battalion of the Coldstream Guards. Early in his training at Caterham he slipped while playing handball and badly gashed his knee: the resulting scar would provide police with a useful distinguishing feature. The bearskin hat and smart red uniform made the girls gawp and giggle, but he found sentry duty outside the Tower of London tedious, and the city beyond beckoned.

Chapman had worn the guardsman's uniform for nine months when he was granted six days' leave. He told the sergeant major that he was going home. Instead, in the company of an older guardsman, he wandered around Soho and the West End, hungrily eyeing the elegant women draped over the arms of men in sharp suits. In a café in Marble Arch he noticed a pretty, dark-haired girl, and she spotted him. They danced at Smokey Joe's in Soho. That night he lost his virginity. She persuaded him to stay another night: he stayed for two months, until they had spent all his pay. Chapman may have forgotten about the army, but the army had not forgotten about him. He was sure the dark-haired girl told the police. Chapman was arrested for going absent without leave, placed in the military prison in Aldershot – the 'glasshouse' – and made to scrub out bedpans for eighty-four days. Release and a dishonourable discharge brought to an end his first prison sentence, and his last regular job. Chapman took a bus to London with £3 in his pocket, a fraying suit and a 'jail-crop haircut', and headed straight for Soho.

Soho in the 1930s was a den of notorious vice, and spectacular fun. This was the crossroads of London society where the rich and feckless met the criminal and reckless, a place of seamy, raucous glamour. Chapman found work as a barman, then as a film extra, earning £3 for 'three days doing crowd work'; he worked as a masseur, a dancer, and eventually as an amateur boxer and wrestler. He was a fine wrestler, physically strong, and lithe as a cat, with a 'wire and whipcord body'. This was a world of pimps and racecourse touts, pickpockets and con artists; late nights at Smokey Joe's and early champagne breakfasts at Quaglino's. 'I mixed with all types of tricky people,' Chapman wrote later. 'Racecourse crooks, thieves, prostitutes, and the flotsam of the night-life of a great city.' For the young Chapman, life in this seething, seedy enclave was thrilling. But it was also expensive. He acquired a taste for cognac and the gaming tables and was soon penniless.

The thievery started in a small way: a forged cheque here, a snatched suitcase there, a little light burglary. His early crimes were unremarkable, the first faltering steps of an apprentice.

In January 1935, he was caught in the back garden of a house in Mayfair, and fined £10. A month later he was found guilty of stealing a cheque and obtaining credit by fraud. This time the court was less lenient, and Chapman was given two months' hard labour in Wormwood Scrubs. A few weeks after his release, he was back inside, this time in Wandsworth Prison on a three-month sentence for trespassing and attempted housebreaking.

Chapman branched out into crimes of a more lurid nature. Early in 1936 he was found guilty of 'behaving in a manner likely to offend the public' in Hyde Park. Exactly how he was likely to have offended the public was not specified, but he was almost certainly discovered in flagrante delicto with a prostitute. He was fined £4 and made to pay a fee of 15 shillings 9d to the doctor who examined him for venereal disease. Two weeks later he was charged with fraud after he tried to evade payment of a hotel bill.

One contemporary remembers a young man 'with good looks, a quick brain, high spirits and something desperate in him which made him attractive to men and dangerous to women'. Desperation may have led him to use the attraction of men for profit, for he once hinted at an early homosexual encounter. Women seemed to find him irresistible. According to one account, he made money by seducing 'women on the fringes of society', blackmailing them with compromising photographs taken by an accomplice and then threatening to show their husbands. It was even said that having 'infected a girl of 18 with VD, he blackmailed her by threatening to tell her parents that she had given it to him'.

Chapman was on a predictable downward spiral of petty crime, prostitution, blackmail and lengthening prison terms – punctuated by episodes of wild extravagance in Soho – when a scientific breakthrough in the criminal world abruptly altered his fortunes.

In the early 1930s British crooks discovered gelignite. At about the same time, during one of his stints inside, Chapman discovered James Wells Hunt – the 'best cracksman in London' – a 'cool, self-possessed, determined character' who had perfected a technique for taking apart safes by drilling a hole in the lock and

inserting a 'French letter' stuffed with gelignite and water. Jimmy
Hunt and Chapman went into partnership and were soon joined
by Antony Latt, alias Darrington, alias 'Darry', a nerveless half-
Burmese burglar whose father, he claimed, had been a native
judge. A young felon named Hugh Anson was recruited to drive
their getaway car.

The newly formed 'Jelly Gang' selected, as its first target,
Isobel's, a chic furrier in Harrogate. Hunt and Darry broke in and
stole five minks, two fox-fur capes and £200 from the safe.
Chapman remained in the car 'shivering with fear and unable to
help'. The next was a pawnbroker's in Grimsby. While Anson
revved the Bentley outside to cover the sound of the explosions,
Chapman and Hunt broke into an empty house next door, cut
their way through the wall, and then blew open four safes. The
proceeds, sold through a fence in the West End, netted £15,000.
This was followed by a break-in at the Swiss Cottage Odeon
cinema using an iron bar, a hit on Express Dairies, and a smash-
and-grab raid on a shop in Oxford Street. Escaping from the
latter scene, Anson drove the stolen getaway car into a lamppost.
As the gang fled, a crowd of onlookers gathered around the
smoking vehicle; one, who happened to be a small-time thief,
made the mistake of putting his hand on the bonnet. When his
fingerprints were matched with Scotland Yard records, he was
sentenced to four years in prison. The Jelly Gang found this most
amusing.

Chapman was no longer a reckless petty pilferer, but a
criminal of means, spending money as fast as he could steal it,
mixing with the underworld aristocracy, the gambling playboys,
roué actors, alcoholic journalists, insomniac writers and dodgy
politicians drawn to the demimonde. He became friendly with
Noel Coward, Ivor Novello, Marlene Dietrich and the young
filmmaker Terence Young (who would go on to direct the first
James Bond film). Young was a suave figure who prided himself
on his elegant clothes, his knowledge of fine wine and his
reputation as a Lothario. Perhaps in imitation of his new friend,

Chapman also began buying suits in Savile Row, and driving a fast car. He kept a table reserved at The Nest in Kingly Street, where he held court, surrounded by bottles and girls. Young remarked: 'He was able to talk on almost any subject. Most of us knew that he was a crook, but nevertheless we liked him for his manner and personality.'

Young found Chapman intriguing: he made no secret of his trade, yet there was an upright side to his character that the filmmaker found curious. 'He is a crook and will always be one,' Young observed to a lawyer friend. 'But he probably has more principles and honesty of character than either of us.' Chapman would steal the money from your pocket, even as he bought you a drink, but he never deserted a friend, nor hurt a soul. In a brutal business, he was a pacifist. 'I don't go along with the use of violence,' he declared many years later. 'I always made more than a good living out of crime without it.'

Chapman − careless, guiltless and Godless − revelled in his underworld notoriety. He pasted press clippings describing his crimes into a scrapbook. He was particularly delighted when it was reported that police suspected American gangs were behind the recent spate of safe-cracking because chewing gum had been found at the crime scenes (the Jelly Gang had merely used chewing gum to stick the gelignite to the safes). By the summer of 1935, they had stolen so much money that Chapman and Darry decided to rent a house in Bridport on the Dorset coast for an extended holiday; but after six weeks they grew bored and 'went back to "work"'. Chapman disguised himself as an inspector from the Metropolitan Water Board, gained access to a house in the Edgware Road, smashed a hole through the wall into the shop next door and extracted the safe. This was carried out of the front door, loaded into the Bentley and taken to Hunt's garage at 39, St Luke's Mews, Notting Hill, where the safe door was blown off.

Mixing with authors and actors, Chapman became conscious of his lack of education. He announced that he intended to become a writer, and began reading widely, plundering English literature in search of knowledge and direction. When asked what he did for a living, Chapman would reply, with a wink, that he was a 'professional dancer'. He danced from club to club, from job to job, from book to book, and from woman to woman. Late in 1935, he announced he was getting married, to Vera Freidberg, an exotic young woman with a Russian mother and a German-Jewish father. From her, Chapman picked up a grounding in the German language. But within a few months he had moved into a boarding house in Shepherd's Bush with another woman, Freda Stevenson, a stage dancer from Southend who was five years his junior. He loved Freda, she was vivacious and sassy; yet when he met Betty Farmer – his 'Shropshire Lass' – in the Nite Lite Club, he loved her too.

The Jelly Gang might mock the dozy coppers studying their abandoned chewing gum for clues, but Scotland Yard was beginning to take a keen interest in the activities of Edward Chapman. A 'gelignite' squad was formed. In 1938, the *Police Gazette* published Chapman's mugshot, along with those of Hunt and Darry, as suspects in a recent spate of cinema safe-breaks. Aware that the police were closing in, early in 1939 the gang loaded several golf bags packed with gelignite into the boot of the Bentley, and headed north. Having checked into an expensive hotel, they broke into the offices of the Edinburgh Co-operative Society, and emptied the safe. As Chapman was climbing out through a skylight, he smashed a pane of glass. A passing policeman heard it, and blew his whistle. The thieves fled over the back wall, and onto a railway line; one of the gang slipped, breaking an ankle, and was left behind. The others met up with car and driver and immediately headed south, but were intercepted by a police car, siren screaming. Chapman fled over a wall, but was caught. The four burglars were thrown into Edinburgh prison, but then, for reasons no-one can explain, Chapman was granted fourteen days bail at £150.

When Case Number Seventeen came before the Edinburgh

High Court, it was found that Chapman and his accomplices had absconded. A general bulletin was issued, photographs were distributed, and every police force in Britain was told to be on the lookout for Eddie Chapman – crook, jailbird, adulterer, blackmailer, safe-cracker, Soho denizen and now among Britain's most wanted men. On 4 February 1939, the gang extracted £476 and 3 shillings from a Co-op store in Bournemouth. Darry had sent a letter to his girlfriend hinting that the gang was heading for Jersey; police intercepted it and a warning went out that the suspects might make for the Channel Islands, and then the Continent: 'Be prepared for trouble as one at least of the men might be armed and all are prepared to put up a fight to resist arrest.'

Which is how Eddie Chapman came to be pounding down a Jersey beach leaving in his wake two plain-clothes policemen, a distraught young woman, and half a sherry trifle.

Jersey Gaol

The Evening Post.

Monday, 13 February 1939

STARTLING SCENE AT JERSEY HOTEL

~~~

POLICE SWOOP AT LUNCH HOUR

~~~

Two Guests Handcuffed
Thief Gets Away through Window
Alleged Dangerous Gang of Safe Breakers

A letter sent to a girl in Bournemouth led yesterday to the arrest of two members of a gelignite gang wanted for the 'blowing' of a safe at a co-operative store and the theft of £470. A third man got wind of the impending police swoop on the Hotel de la Plage, Havre-le-Pas, and escaped.

Residents at La Plage Hotel were at lunch when Centenier C. G. Grant of St Helier, and six members of the paid police in civilian clothing entered and, before most of the lunchers knew what had happened, two men had been handcuffed and chase was being given to the third man, alleged to be the leader of the gang. One of them, apparently more alert than the others, made his escape by way of the windows of the dining room overlooking the promenade and got clean away.

The third man, for whom active search still continues, is described as: – Edward Chapman, alias Arnold Edward Chapman, Edward Arnold Chapman, Edward Edwards and Thompson, a professional dancer, slim build, six feet in height, fresh complexion, small moustache, dressed in white shirt, yellow spotted tie, blue sleeveless pullover, grey flannels and brown sandals and no socks. He is believed to be a dangerous character. He may, by now, have obtained a jacket or an overcoat from somewhere as he has money in his possession.

The search for Chapman goes on and all ships are being watched. Anyone who may see this man or who may know anything of his whereabouts is requested to inform the Police Station immediately.

Although the police soon abandoned the chase, Chapman continued running for a mile or so up the beach before doubling back, and then cutting across the island. He found a school, empty on a Sunday, and hid inside. That evening he strolled back into Havre-le-Pas wearing a mackintosh he had found on a peg, the collar turned up. On the edge of town he checked into a tatty boarding house and shaved off his moustache with a soapy penknife. When he came downstairs, the landlady, Mrs Corfield, demanded cash up-front. Chapman gave her what he had in his pocket, and said he would pay the balance in the morning. Without money he was trapped. He would need to steal some more.

In the darkness, Chapman re-emerged and set off towards the West Park Pavilion nightclub, where the gang had spent the previous night. As soon as her lodger was gone, Mrs Corfield put on her bonnet, and headed down to the police station.

Chapman found the Pavilion deserted. He broke in through a window in the gents' lavatory, discovered the office safe, and carried it to the basement. Turning it upside down, he worked off the bottom with a pickaxe and a pair of pincers from the boiler room of the building. Inside lay £15, 13 shillings and 9d in silver, several pounds in coppers, and twelve ten-shilling notes. Chapman returned to the boarding house, his pockets laden, and went to sleep, resolving to steal or bribe his way onto a boat the next morning.

The Evening Post.

Tuesday, 14 February 1939

ALLEGED SAFE BREAKER BEFORE COURT

~~~

WANTED MAN ARRESTED IN BED CHARGED WITH BREAKING INTO WEST PARK PAVILION ACCUSED APPEALS FOR 'GIRL FRIEND'

~~~

The island-wide search for the man Chapman, who escaped when police raided the Hotel de la Plage, is at an end. Chapman, through information received by the St Helier Police, was found last night in bed in a lodging house in Sand Street, and admitted his identity to police constables. He also admitted breaking into West Park Pavilion last night.

Chapman gave the police no trouble and made a voluntary statement that he had 'done in' the safe.

This morning Chapman appeared before the magistrate, and after being remanded asked if his girlfriend could be allowed to leave the island. 'I have a girlfriend here,' he

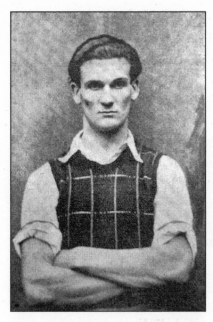

been cross-examined by police and watched and I would like to ask if these investigations might cease as she knows nothing of why we are here.'

The Magistrate: 'If she had been wise she would have gone already. We do not want her here. There is nothing against her and she is free to leave the island when she likes.'

The accused was then removed to the cells and his 'girl friend', an attractive blonde with blue eyes and a long said, speaking in a cultured page-boy bob, whose name is tone, 'and she is in a very em- said to be Betty Farmer, also barrassing position. She has left the court.'

Betty had suffered many indignities in the preceding forty-eight hours: being searched by the manageress at the Hotel de la Plage, being grilled by those horrible detectives and then having to move to the smaller, cheaper and far scruffier Royal Yacht Hotel. As Chapman was led from the court in handcuffs, she handed one of his guards a love note to pass to him, written on headed hotel paper. He put it in his pocket, grinned and waved.

Breaking into the West Park Pavilion nightclub had been an act of astonishing foolishness but also, on the face of it, an immense stroke of luck. Darry and Anson had already been shipped back to the mainland to face multiple charges at the Central Criminal Court in London. Chapman, however, had broken the law in Jersey, with its ancient legal code and traditions of self-government, and would now have to face island justice.

On 11 March 1939, Edward Chapman appeared before the Royal Court of Jersey and pleaded guilty to charges of house-breaking and larceny. The Attorney General of Jersey, prosecuting, cited Chapman's extensive criminal record and pointed out that the safe-breaking at the nightclub had been 'done with deliberation and skill which showed considerable experience and showed he was determined to rely on this sort of conduct for a living'. He demanded that this 'dangerous criminal who had failed to accept certain chances that had been given to him' receive the maximum sentence of two years' hard labour. The jury agreed.

Jersey Gaol, Chapman soon discovered, was a 'dreary little cage' where the handful of prisoners stuffed mattresses for eight hours a day and slept on planks raised a few feet off the concrete floor. The prison regime was remarkably lax. The governor, Captain Thomas Charles Foster, a retired soldier, regarded prisoners as an inconvenience in an otherwise pleasant life that revolved around visiting his neighbours, sunbathing and fishing. Foster took a shine to the new inmate when Chapman explained he had been a soldier, and he was soon put to work as the governor's personal batman, weeding the garden and cleaning his house, which backed onto the hospital block.

On the sunny afternoon of 7 July, Captain Foster, Mrs Foster, and their eighteen-year-old son, Andrew, climbed into the family car and headed down the coast to St Brelade to attend the Jersey Scottish Society's annual summer fête, a highlight of the island's social calendar. Chapman was instructed to clean the governor's kitchen in his absence. Chief Warder Briard had taken the day off, leaving Warder Packer to mind the shop. Packer unlocked the front gate to allow the governor's car through. Captain Thomas, resplendent in his kilt, muttered as he motored off that Packer should 'keep an eye on Chapman'.

As the sound of the governor's car faded, Chapman downed his mop, and darted upstairs to the empty bedroom of Andrew

Foster. From the young man's wardrobe Chapman extracted a grey pinstripe suit, brown shoes, a brown trilby, and two checked caps made by Leach & Justice of Perth. The suit was a little tight under the arms, but a reasonable fit. He also found a suitcase, into which he packed the governor's spectacles, a jar of sixpences Mrs Foster had been saving, £13 from the governor's desk drawer, a torch and a poker from the fireplace. Climbing through a skylight, he scrambled over the roof, dropped into the hospital compound, scaled a wall topped with glass, and walked away. Mrs Hamon, who worked in the laundry, noticed a figure on the roof, but assumed he must be a workman.

An hour later, Warder Packer – who had been busy flirting with the matron's daughter, Miss Lesbird – casually wandered into the governor's kitchen to see how Chapman was progressing with his chores. He did not worry unduly to find the house empty. 'At that moment,' he recalled, 'I still thought Chapman was playing a joke, and was hiding in the prison.' He searched the garden and the outhouse; then he summoned the other warders to help search the prison. Then he panicked. It took a full two hours to track down Captain Foster at the Scottish Society fete. The Chief Constable was unearthed in the golf club, and a posse led by young Andrew Foster was dispatched to watch the airport. Hotels and boarding houses were scoured, boats were prevented from leaving harbour, and every policeman and volunteer on the island was mobilised for the greatest manhunt in island memory.

Walter Picard, resident of Five Mile Road, was one of the few people on the island unaware that a prisoner had escaped. He had spent the evening under a hedge with a woman who was not Mrs Walter Picard. After this encounter, Picard and his girlfriend were strolling back to his car in the darkness when they were surprised to see a man in an ill-fitting suit bending over the open bonnet of the car, apparently attempting to jump-start it.

The man looked startled, but declared: 'Do you know who I am? I'm a member of the police.' Picard launched himself at the 'car thief'. His girlfriend screamed. A scuffle ensued: Picard was upended and thrown over a wall and Chapman vanished into the night. On the passenger seat of his car, the shaken Picard found a brown trilby, a torch and three sticks of gelignite.

Chapman had passed a most eventful day. Barely a mile from the prison, Mr A.A. Pitcher had obligingly offered him a lift in his car, and driven him to a public telephone box where he had telephoned the airport, only to be told the last plane for the mainland had departed. Pitcher dropped him off at the pier. After a meal at the Milano Café, Chapman had checked into La Pulente Hotel, and ordered a taxi. Telling the Luxicab driver he was 'interested in quarries', Chapman took a tour of the island's mines, and selected his target. That afternoon, when the workers had left L'Etacq Quarry on the western edge of Jersey, Chapman scaled the gate, found the small, reinforced bunker that served as the explosives storehouse, and prised open the door with a crowbar from the quarry tool shed. He emerged with 5lbs of gelignite and 200 detonators. It was while walking down Five Mile Road with his explosive loot that evening that Chapman spotted Walter Picard's parked car and decided to steal it.

Knowing the encounter would be reported immediately, Chapman walked on until he came across an empty bungalow belonging to Frank Le Quesne. He broke in, made himself a cup of tea (using enough tea bags 'for about fifty people', the owner later complained) and fell asleep.

In the meantime, Walter Picard made an edited report to the police, stating that:

> He was driving his car on his way home when he was hailed by a young woman, whom he did not recognise, who asked him for a lift as far as a bungalow on the Five Mile Road. He replied that he would take her as far as his house; he did so but she then persuaded him to drive her further on and some little distance along the road his lights failed for no apparent

reason. He stopped the car and his passenger then told him that the bungalow she wished to get to was fairly close and asked him to walk as far with her. After some demur he complied with her requests, but only went half way and then, turning round, saw the lights of his car had come on again. He approached the car and saw a tall man bending over the ignition. The stranger turned round and struck him and then made off.

Even the police found Picard's elaborate story 'strange', and what Mrs Picard made of it can only be imagined.

Early next morning, a fisherman carrying a large shrimping net could be seen striding purposefully along Plémont beach. Closer inspection would have revealed that beneath the fishing overalls the man was wearing business attire, and beneath that, a striped bathing suit belonging to Frank Le Quesne. Chapman had calculated that with holidaymakers enjoying the summer sun, a bathing suit might be a good disguise. In his pockets he carried enough explosives to wage a small war.

Later that morning, the divinely named Mrs Gordon Bennet reported that a man more or less fitting the description of the escaped prisoner had visited her tearooms on the cliff overlooking the beach. Centenier Percy Laurie, a volunteer policeman, and Police Constable William Golding were sent to investigate. Both were in plain clothes. Golding decided to explore the beach, while Laurie searched the caves in the cliffside. On the sand some holidaymakers were playing football, observed, from a short distance, by a tall fisherman with a net. Golding approached the spectator. 'Your name is Chapman,' he said.

'My name is not Chapman,' said the fisherman, backing off. 'You are making a great mistake.'

'Are you coming quietly?'

'You had better take me,' he replied. As Golding seized his arm, Chapman shouted that he was being assaulted, and called on the footballers to come to his aid. Laurie emerged from the caves, and ran to help, several spectators weighed in, and a free-for-all ensued, with the policemen trying to get the handcuffs on Chapman as they, in turn, were attacked by a crowd of semi-naked holidaymakers. The fracas ended when Golding managed to land a punch to Chapman's midriff. 'This appeared to distress him,' said Golding. Chapman's distress also doubtless came from the knowledge that he had eight sticks of gelignite and fifteen detonators in his pockets; a blow in the wrong place would have destroyed him, the policemen, the footballers and most of Plémont beach.

The Evening Post.

Friday, 6 July 1939

PRISONER'S ESCAPE FROM GAOL

~~~

DRAMATIC STORY OF ISLAND-WIDE SEARCH

~~~

ALLEGED ATTACK ON MOTORIST

~~~

GELIGNITE STOLEN FROM QUARRY STORE

~~~

CAPTURED AFTER FIGHT ON BEACH WITH POLICE CONSTABLE

After having been at liberty less than 24 hours, a prisoner who escaped from the public prison was recaptured. Every available police officer in the island had been on duty continuously in an island-wide search.

The missing man was Edward Chapman, possessor of several aliases and a record of previous convictions. He was described as a dangerous man and associate of thieves and dangerous characters and an expert in the use of dynamite.

Chapman was arrested at two o'clock this afternoon after a stand-up fight with a police constable on the sands at Plémont.

When the prison van arrived a large crowd waited to catch a glimpse of Chapman. He appeared perfectly composed and looked around with interest at the people, a smile flitting across his face.

Later, the constable of St Helier expressed his warm appreciation of all ranks of the police who had assisted in the most thrilling man-hunt which has taken place in Jersey for some years.

Captain Foster, the prison governor, was both enraged and humiliated. The prison board castigated him for his 'gross misconduct [in] permitting a prisoner with such deplorable criminal antecedents as Chapman so much unsupervised liberty'. Foster took out his anger on the warders, the prisoners and above all on Chapman, who was brought back to the prison and harangued by the governor, who bitterly accused him of inventing a military past to ingratiate himself: 'You have never been a soldier as you informed me, you are therefore a liar and you deserve a flogging,' he bawled. 'Why did you do it?' Chapman thought for a moment, and gave the only honest reply. 'One, I don't like prison discipline; and two, since I am sure of more imprisonment on completion of my present sentence in England, I thought I would make one job of the lot.'

Back in his cell, Chapman made a bleak calculation. On his release he would be sent back to the mainland and tried on a string of charges, just like Darry and Anson, who were now in Dartmoor. Depending on what Scotland Yard could prove, Chapman reckoned he would be in one prison or another for the next fourteen years.

The Jersey community was close knit and law abiding, and the legal authorities took a dim view of this convict who dared to steal from its prison governor, throw its inhabitants over walls, and provoke pitched battles with its policemen.

On 6 September 1939, Chapman was brought before the Criminal Assizes and sentenced to a further year in prison, to run consecutively with his earlier conviction. The news of his sentencing, somewhat to Chapman's irritation, merited only a single paragraph in the *Evening Post*, for by now the people of Jersey had other concerns. Three days earlier, Britain had declared war on Germany.

Island at War

All wars – but this war in particular – tend to be seen in monochrome: good and evil, winner and loser, champion and coward, loyalist and traitor. For most people, the reality of war is not like that, but rather a monotonous grey of discomforts and compromises, with occasional flashes of violent colour. War is too messy to produce easy heroes and villains; there are always brave people on the wrong side, and evil men among the victors, and a mass of perfectly ordinary people struggling to survive and understand in between. Away from the battlefields, war forces individuals to make impossible choices in circumstances they did not create, and could never have expected. Most accommodate, some collaborate, and a very few find an internal compass they never knew they had, pointing to the right path.

News of the war barely penetrated the granite walls of Jersey prison. The prison slop, always repulsive, grew ever nastier with rationing. Some of the warders left to join up, and those that remained provided fragmentary, unreliable information. The Nazi Blitzkrieg, first the invasion of Denmark and Norway in April 1940, then France, Belgium, Luxembourg and the Netherlands, did not touch Chapman; his was a world just 6-feet square. When the Germans entered Paris on 14 June 1940, he was barely midway through his three-year sentence.

Chapman read all 200 books in the prison library, and then reread them. With some aged grammar books, he set about teaching himself French and improving his German. He memorised the poems of Tennyson, and read H.G. Wells's *Outline of History*, a textbook purporting to describe the past but imbued with that writer's philosophy. He was particularly struck by Wells's idea of a 'federal world state' in which all nations would work in harmony: 'Nationalism as a God must follow the tribal gods to limbo. Our true nationality is mankind,' Wells had written. Meanwhile, the evil god of National Socialism marched ever closer.

Chapman read and reread Betty's love-note on the Royal Yacht Hotel letterhead. But soon another letter arrived that temporarily extinguished thoughts of Betty. From an address in Southend-on-Sea, Freda Stevenson, the dancer with whom he had been living in Shepherd's Bush, wrote to inform Chapman that he was now the father of a one-year-old girl, born in Southend Municipal hospital in July 1939, whom she had christened Diane Shayne. She enclosed a photograph of mother and child. Freda explained that she was desperately poor, barely surviving on wartime rations, and asked Chapman to send money. Chapman asked for permission to write to her but Captain Foster refused, out of spite. Freda's unanswered letters became increasingly anguished, then angry. Frustrated at his inability to help Freda or hold his first child, and cut off from the rest of humanity in a sea-bound prison, Chapman sank into bleak depression.

The Evening Post.

Saturday, 29 June 1940

FIERCE AIR RAIDS ON CHANNEL ISLANDS HARBOURS BOMBED

HEAVY CASUALTIES IN BOTH ISLANDS

Nine people are known to have been killed and many injured in a bombing and machine gun attack carried out by at

least three German aircraft   struck the pier, causing con-
over Jersey last night.   siderable damage to prop-
    The Harbour was the   erty belonging solely to
chief objective and a bomb   civilians . . .

Chapman was lying on his plank bed when he heard the first
Luftwaffe planes droning overhead. Three days later, the Channel Islands earned the unhappy distinction of becoming the only
part of Britain to be occupied by Germany during the Second
World War. There was no resistance, for the last defending
troops had pulled out. Most of the population opted to remain.
Chapman was not offered a choice. Idly, he wondered whether a
bomb might hit the prison, offering either death or the chance of
escape. The British inhabitants of Jersey were instructed to offer
no resistance and the bailiff, Alexander Moncrieff Coutanche,
who had presided over Chapman's trial, told them to obey
German orders, return home and fly the white flag of surrender.
Hitler had decided Jersey would make an ideal holiday camp,
once Germany had won the war.

    With German occupation, the Jersey prison service was
simply absorbed into the Nazi administration, along with
the police. Sealed away behind stone and iron, the prisoners
were forgotten. The prison food became more meagre than
ever, as the free inhabitants of Jersey competed for the few
resources allowed them by the German invaders. There were
no more letters from Freda. Chapman consoled himself with
the reflection that as long as the Germans controlled Jersey
when he was finally released, they could not send him back to
the waiting manacles.

    The Germans ran their own courts, parallel to the civil
judiciary. In December 1940, a young dishwasher from the
Miramar Hotel, named Anthony Charles Faramus, fell foul of
both. A Jersey islander with a reputation as a tearaway, twenty-
year-old Faramus was sentenced to six months by the Jersey
court for obtaining £9 under false pretenses by claiming an

allowance for a non-existent dependent. The German field court slapped on a further month after Faramus was found to be carrying an anti-German propaganda leaflet.

A furtive, delicate man, with a pencil moustache and darting grey eyes, Faramus was a strange but likeable fellow. He was a hopeless crook, Chapman reflected. He blushed easily, and exuded a 'sort of dispossessed gentleness', though he possessed a sharp, obscene wit. Tall and slender, he looked as if a puff of wind might carry him off. He had worked as a hairdresser in a salon in St Helier, before taking a job at the hotel. Chapman and Faramus became cellmates, and firm friends.

On 15 October 1941, a few weeks short of his twenty-sixth birthday, Chapman was finally released. Gaunt and paper-faced, his weight had fallen to just nine stone. Faramus, released a few months earlier, was waiting for him at the prison gates. Chapman knew nothing of the Nazi invasion of Greece and Yugoslavia, the sinking of the Bismarck or the siege of Leningrad, but the effects of war were visible in the transformation of Jersey. On his last day of freedom, Chapman had wandered a beach thronged with happy, well-fed holidaymakers. Now, it was an island ground down by occupation, exhausted and hungry, beset by all the moral confusion that comes from the choice between resistance, acquiescence or collaboration.

Faramus had rented a small shop on Broad Street in St Helier, and with a few chairs, some old mirrors, scissors and razors, he and Chapman opened what they referred to, rather grandly, as a hairdressing salon. Their clientele mainly comprised German officers, since the Channel Islands – Hitler's stepping stone to Britain – were now a vast, heavily defended barracks, home to the largest infantry regiment in the German army.

Faramus shaved German beards and cut German hair, while Chapman made polite conversation in basic German. One of the few British regulars was a middle-aged former bookmaker from Birmingham by the name of Douglas Stirling. An opportunist of the sort produced by every war, Stirling was a black-marketeer, buying cigarettes, tea and alcohol from the Germans, and then selling these on at a profit to local people. The barber's shop was the ideal front for what soon became a thriving trade that combined illegal profiteering with grooming the enemy.

One morning, setting out on his bicycle from the flat he shared with Faramus above the shop, Chapman momentarily forgot that a new German law required everyone to drive on the right and rode straight into a German motorcycle dispatch rider hurtling around a corner. Neither man was hurt, but the German was furious. Chapman was duly summoned to the police station and interrogated by three officers of the Feldgendarmerie, the German military police. One of these, a small man who spoke good English, eyed Chapman unpleasantly and said: 'Look, we've reason to believe you've got some German arms. Now, where is the German rifle?'

'I haven't got any German rifles,' Chapman replied, bemused.

'Have you any arms?'

'No'

'Now look, we've got our eyes on you, so if you try any trouble, we'll make trouble too. I'm only warning you.'

'Thanks for the warning,' Chapman replied, and left swiftly.

This was no warning; it was a threat. He was fined eighty Reichsmarks for the traffic violation, but more worryingly the interview seemed to suggest he had been singled out as a suspected member of the resistance, or even a saboteur. The run-in with the Feldgendarmerie had unsettled him, and set Chapman thinking of another plan to get him off this island prison. He outlined his idea to Faramus and Douglas Stirling. What if they offered to work as spies for the Nazis? If they were accepted there was surely a chance they might be sent over to mainland Britain, undercover. At the very least it would break the monotony. Stirling was enthusiastic, saying that he would suggest the ruse to his son. Faramus was more cautious, but agreed the plan was worth a shot.

Peering back with many years of hindsight, Chapman

admitted that his motives in 1941 were hazy and confused. He would later claim that the offer to spy for Germany was prompted by the simple and sincere desire to escape and be united with Diane, the child he had never seen: 'If I could work a bluff with the Germans, I could probably be sent over to Britain,' he wrote. But Chapman understood his own nature well enough to know that there was more to his decision than this. 'It all sounds fine talk, now,' he later admitted. 'Perhaps it was phony talk even then, and I don't pretend there were no other motives in the plans I began to turn over in my mind. They did not occur to me, either, in one moment, or in one mood.' He felt a genuine animus towards the British establishment. Like many justly imprisoned criminals, he saw himself as the victim of cruel discrimination. Moreover, he was impressed by the discipline and general politeness of the Germans in their smart uniforms. Nazi propaganda relentlessly insisted that their forces were invincible, and the occupation permanent. Chapman was hungry, he was bored, and he longed for excitement. In his Soho days he had mixed with film stars, and he had long imagined himself as the central character in his own drama. He had played the part of a high-rolling gangster. Now, he recast himself in the glamorous role of spy. There was little thought, if any, given to whether such a course was right or wrong. That would come later.

Chapman and Faramus composed a letter in carefully wrought German, and sent it to the German Command post in St Helier, addressed to General Otto von Stulpnägel, the senior officer in command of the occupation forces in France and the Channel Islands. A few days later Faramus and Chapman were summoned to the office of a German major, where Chapman blithely explained that he and his friend would like to join the German secret service. He listed his crimes, stressed the outstanding warrants he faced in Britain, emphasised his expertise with explosives, and concluded with a spirited anti-British rant. 'His whole theme was revenge,' Faramus wrote later. 'He said he had no time for the English ruling class, and sought only a chance to get even with them.' The major nodded blandly, while a secretary took notes and wrote down the young men's names and addresses. The matter, said the major, would be discussed with 'senior officers'.

After that, nothing seemed to happen. Over the next few days Chapman made a point every time a German came into the shop of reciting a 'tale of loathing for the society that had hounded him, and his hatred for the English and all their works', in the hope that word would filter back to the German authorities. But the days passed, and still no word came from the General von Stulpnägel. Clearly their application had been rejected, or merely ignored, on the longstanding principle that anyone who applies to join an espionage service should be rejected.

Chapman had all but forgotten the plan – and was busy hatching a fresh scheme to open up a nightclub serving black-market alcohol – when, one damp evening in December, he and Faramus were roused from their beds by a furious hammering at the door and the sound of raised German voices. On the doorstep stood two German officers. Chapman's immediate assumption was that the application to spy for Germany had borne fruit. He could not have been more wrong. These were not members of the German intelligence service, but the Gestapo. Chapman and Faramus were not being recruited, but arrested. They were handcuffed, bundled into a Vauxhall waiting in the drizzle, and driven to the dock. The senior officer, a captain, or *Hauptmann*, brusquely informed the pair that they were now prisoners, and if they attempted to escape they would be shot. From the car they were marched onto a small landing barge and manacled to an iron bar bolted to the wheelhouse. The boat engine roared and swung out of the port, heading due south, with the coast of France faintly visible through the drizzle. The Gestapo officers sat in the warmth below decks, while Chapman and Faramus shivered in the biting rain.

The next few hours passed in a miasmic rush of fear and

movement: the port at St Malo in the chill dawn; two hours handcuffed to a bench in the police station where a gendarme slipped them a baguette and some stale cheese; locked inside a compartment on the train to Paris; and finally, arrival at the Gare du Nord, where a military truck and armed escort awaited them. The German guards would not speak and shrugged off every question. Faramus was white with terror, moaning gently, his head in his hands, as they sped with their silent Gestapo escort through the broad boulevards of the occupied French capital. Finally, the truck passed through a broad gateway with iron gates draped in huge ringlets of barbed wire, and into another prison.

Much later, Chapman discovered what had happened. In the weeks before his arrest, several telephone wires on the island had been cut, the latest in a series of small acts of sabotage. The German authorities had consulted the Jersey police, some of whom were now active collaborators. These immediately pointed the finger at Chapman and Faramus, the most notorious of the usual suspects. Chapman reflected ruefully: 'The British police told them that if there was any trouble, I was probably in it.'

For the young criminal this was an entirely new experience: he had been arrested for a crime he had not committed.

Romainville

The Fort de Romainville glowers over the eastern suburbs of Paris. A brutal stone giant, by 1941 it had been made into another Nazi vision of hell. Built in the 1830s on a low hill, the hulking bastion was part of the defensive ring constructed around Paris to protect the city from foreign attack, but it also held troops who could be deployed in the event of popular insurrection – a bloated, moated, impregnable monstrosity. For the Nazis, the ancient fort served a similar psychological purpose, as a hostage camp, a place of interrogation, torture and summary execution, and a visible symbol of intimidation, inescapable in every way. Romainville was 'death's waiting room', a prison for civilians – resistance fighters, political prisoners, prominent Jews, communists and intellectuals, suspected spies, political subversives and 'trouble-makers', as well as those who had simply failed to show sufficient deference to the new rulers of France.

This shifting prison population formed an important element in the brutal arithmetic of Nazi occupation: in reprisal for each act of resistance a number of prisoners would be selected from the cells, and shot. An attack on German soldiers at the Rex Cinema in Paris, for example, was calculated to be worth the lives of 116 Romainville hostages. The more serious the incident of defiance, the higher the death toll at the hostage depot. Sometimes, hostages were told which specific act had cost them their lives. Mostly, they were not.

Chapman and Faramus, political prisoners and suspected saboteurs, were stripped, clad in prison overalls, and then taken before the camp commandant, Kapitan Brüchenbach, a stocky little man with thick glasses and eyes 'like two bullet holes in a metal door'. Brüchenbach grunted that he had orders from the Gestapo to detain them until further notice. The fastidious Faramus noted that the man 'stank of drink'.

They were then marched to a barrack building surrounded by a 12-foot barbed-wire fence, and guarded at either end by sentries with searchlights and machine guns. The men were pushed into a room, unheated and lit by a single bulb, containing half a dozen empty bunks, and locked inside. As they lay on rotting straw mattresses, the friends discussed their chances of survival, one with brittle optimism, the other in deepest gloom.

'How would you like to be shot, Eddie?' asked Faramus.

'I don't think I'd mind so terribly as all that,' came the self-deluding reply. 'I've had a pretty good life.'

The next morning, as they filed into the courtyard, Chapman and Faramus learned from the whispers of their fellow prisoners that sixteen people had been executed that morning, in retaliation for the assassination of a German officer in Nantes by members of the resistance. On the door of each cell was a warning: 'Alles Verboten', everything is forbidden. This was no exaggeration. The writing and receiving of letters was not permitted. Red Cross and Quaker parcels were intercepted. The beatings were ferocious, and unexplained. Denied contact with the world outside, the inmates measured time by the movements of the guards and the traffic in the distant Paris streets. Rations were strict and unvarying: a pint of watery vegetable soup, four ounces of black bread and an ounce of rancid margarine or cheese. At first, the two newcomers fished the maggots out of the soup; after a few days they, like everyone else, sucked it all down.

The male and female inmates were allowed to mix in the fort's giant courtyard but sexual relations were strictly forbidden, as one of the guards made clear on their first day with an elaborate, multilingual charade: 'Madame prisonniers. Parler, promenade, ja! Aber NIX, verboten, fig-fig – Nix!' And then, in case of any lingering confusion on the matter, he added: 'NIX. Keine fig-fig!' To Chapman, this sounded like a challenge.

The inmates of Fort Romainville were a peculiar assortment: rich and poor, brave and treacherous, guilty and innocent. Chapman and Faramus were the only Englishmen. There was Paulette, a blonde woman who had been arrested for espionage; Ginette, whose husband had already been executed for spying. Other women were being held as hostages for husbands or fathers who had joined the Free French, or were known to be active in the resistance. There was Kahn, a wealthy German-Jewish banker, along with Michelin – the tyre magnate – two Belgian diamond merchants, and a mysterious individual called Leutsch, a German-speaking Swiss journalist who wore horn-rimmed spectacles and claimed to have worked for British intelligence. Among the French prisoners were the former Minister of Information and a radio journalist named Le François, jailed for refusing to broadcast German propaganda. One woman, a waitress from a café in Montparnasse, was there, she claimed, because she had slapped an SS officer who had fondled her. One old fellow named Weiss, a multilingual eccentric with a pathological fear of water, had been arrested for writing an article discussing how a defeated Germany should be partitioned. Many had simply fallen foul of the invaders. Some claimed to have no idea why they were there.

Every inmate had a different story, yet all guarded their words; some declined to reveal their identities beyond a first name. For the prison was also riddled with informers, stoolpigeons whose task it was to winkle the truth from spies and agitators, and then expose them. Among the inmates, suspicion fell heavily on a Belgian named Bossuet. He claimed to have been born in Cardiff, and could spoke English well, though laced with slang. At first Chapman had warmed to the Belgian, only to be told that Bossuet was a 'professional denouncer', a *mouchard*, who had earned himself the nickname 'Black Diamond'. It was rumoured that his betrayals had sent twenty-two prisoners to their deaths. Most inmates shunned him and some attacked him when the guards were not looking. Eventually Bossuet was removed from the prison. This was seen as proof of Bossuet's guilt, but it was part of the regime of neurosis at Romainville that prisoners arrived and were removed without warning or explanation. A middle-aged man called Dreyfus, a Jewish descendant of the other famous victim of anti-semitism, was briefly held, and then inexplicably released. Immediately it was assumed that he must have turned traitor. 'It wasn't safe to talk to anyone,' Chapman reflected. 'No one knew who was who. No one would talk.'

Yet alongside the corrosive atmosphere of fear and distrust existed an equally powerful urge for intimacy. The ban on sex between prisoners was not just ignored, but violated with abandon. Men and women sought every opportunity: in the washrooms, under the stairs, in the coal store and the darker corners of the courtyard. The barrack rooms had not been designed as cells, and the locks were simple to pick. Elaborate plans were hatched by the inmates to find sexual release. No one ever escaped from Romainville, but here was a way to escape, briefly. Within weeks of arriving in Romainville, Chapman had paired off with the blonde Paulette, who was some ten years his senior, while Faramus had begun a sexual relationship with another female inmate named Lucy. Looking back, both men certainly exaggerated the extent of their 'conquests'. Chapman, more worldly than his partner, seemed to accept the strange merging of sex and fear as the natural order but Faramus, a sexual ingénue, was insistent that these 'were real love affairs, passionate and sincere'. In this closed and treacherous society, where death came without warning or explanation, sexual expression was the only remaining liberty.

While Chapman and Faramus were devising complicated trysts with the female prisoners, their offer to spy for Germany, now long forgotten by them, was slowly progressing through the German military bureaucracy. From Jersey their letter had passed to Berlin, then on to the branch of the German secret service at Hamburg, then back to Jersey again. Chapman was serving two weeks' solitary confinement in the fort dungeons when the letter finally caught up with him, in December 1941. Chapman had been consigned to the *cachots*, the underground cells, after a fight with the hated Bossuet. Prisoners in solitary received one meal of bread and soup every three days. Chapman's cell was lightless, freezing and sodden. In an effort to conserve his body heat, he scraped the gravel from the floor and covered himself with it up to the neck.

Chapman was a week into his sentence in solitary, when he was pulled from the dungeon, escorted under guard to Brüchenbach's office, and locked in a back room. Moments later he was confronted by an SS officer who carefully locked the door behind him. The visitor was tall and spare, with pale blue eyes and hollow cheeks, streaked with broken red veins. He stood looking at Chapman for several moments before he spoke. Then, in perfect English, without a hint of accent, he introduced himself as Oberleutnant Walter Thomas. Without preamble or explanation, he sat down at a desk and began to interrogate Chapman about his past crimes, his experience with explosives, his imprisonment in Jersey, and his proficiency in German. Occasionally he referred to a file. He seemed to know every detail of Chapman's criminal record, not only the crimes for which he had been sentenced, but those for which he was only suspected. The officer spoke with familiarity of Britain, of Chapman's years in Soho, his arrest in Edinburgh and his flight to Jersey; as he spoke, he twined the long fingers of his hands. His expression did not change, but he seemed satisfied by Chapman's answers. Chapman reflected later that his interrogator seemed 'the scholarly, staid' type. After an hour the man indicated that the meeting was over, and Chapman was escorted from the office, not back to the punishment dungeon, but to the barrack room.

'What happened?' Faramus asked, astonished by Chapman's early release from solitary.

Chapman swore him to secrecy and then described his encounter with the SS officer. It must mean, he continued, that their offer to work for Germany had provoked a response at last. 'All right for you,' said Faramus, suddenly fearful. 'They're sure to make use of you. But what about me? What am I worth to them?' Chapman tried to reassure the younger man, but both knew Faramus was right. The Nazis might conceivably find a use for a fit, wily and experienced criminal, with a long record and a convincing reason for hating the British establishment. But what use could the Third Reich find for a slight, twenty-year-old hairdresser whose sole crime had been a failed attempt to acquire £9 by deceit?

Further evidence of the Nazis' interest in Chapman surfaced a few days later, in the form of a military photographer with a Leica camera, who took dozens of pictures of the prisoner, full face and in profile, and then departed.

In early January 1942, Chapman was once more summoned to the Kommandant's office. This time his interrogator could not have been more different to the dead-eyed Oberleutnant Thomas. Arranged across the Kommandant's armchair was a vision of female loveliness: with large brown eyes, long red-painted fingernails, and an expensive black lambswool coat by her side she looked, to Chapman's mind, as if she had just stepped off a film set. Chapman was momentarily stunned by the apparition. Standing alongside her was a man in civilian clothes. Chapman noted his athletic physique and suntanned face; with their elegant apparel and faintly bored expressions, they might have been modelling for a fashion shoot.

The man asked questions in German, which the woman translated into English, with an American accent. There was no attempt to disguise why they had come. Chapman was peppered with questions about what work he thought he could do for the German secret service, and his motives for offering to do so. They demanded to know how much he expected to be paid, and what he would be prepared to do if sent back to Britain undercover. The woman smoked cigarette after cigarette from a long black holder. 'Supposing you didn't feel like coming back to us?' she asked suddenly.

'You'd have to trust me,' Chapman replied.

As the woman picked up her coat to leave, Chapman spotted the label inside: Schiaparelli, the Italian designer. Clearly, he reflected, Nazi spies – if that is what this couple were – could afford the height of fashion.

For a few weeks, normal prison routine resumed, broken only by the ferocious RAF bombardment of the huge Renault factory at Boulogne-Billancourt directly across the Seine from Romainville. The factory was now part of the Nazi munitions machine, making lorries for the German army. On 3 March, the RAF launched 235 low-level bombers at the plant, the largest number of aircraft aimed at a single target during the war. From the barrack windows, Chapman and Faramus saw flares, tracer and flak light up the night, felt the crump of explosive tremble through air, and watched as the city sky turned an evil orange. Chapman could sense his companion's fear. 'They'll probably send you to a civilian internee camp,' he said. 'Or maybe keep you here – if they accept me. Listen Tony, don't worry: leave it to me. Trust me.'

The two Englishmen had been in Romainville for almost four months when Chapman was taken to Brüchenbach's office for what would be the last time. Waiting for him was Oberleutnant Thomas, but this time accompanied by a more senior officer, dressed in the uniform of a cavalry Rittmeister, the equivalent of a captain. At his throat he wore the Iron Cross. Oberleutnant Thomas introduced him as 'Herr Doktor Stephan Graumann'. With an almost courtly gesture, Graumann invited Chapman to be seated, and then began to interrogate him in precise, old-fashioned English, in a soft voice with an upper-class British accent. He asked how Chapman had been treated in Romainville. When the Englishman described his time in the *cachots* on Brüchenbach's orders, Graumann sneered and remarked that the Kommandant was 'simply a trained brute'.

Graumann had a lofty, yet benevolent air, and Chapman found himself warming to the man. He often smiled to himself, as if enjoying a private joke. He would consider Chapman's answers carefully, leaning back in his chair, the index finger of one hand hooked into the side pocket of his uniform, the other stroking his thinning hair. From time to time he would don thick-rimmed spectacles and peer at the open file in front of him. Chapman decided he must be a 'a man of understanding and tolerance'.

Graumann quizzed Chapman once more about his past: his catalogue of crimes, his grasp of German and French, the members of the Jelly Gang and their current whereabouts. Time after time he returned to the question of whether Chapman was motivated more by hatred of Britain or by the promise of financial gain. Chapman responded that both were factors in his desire to spy for Germany. The interrogation continued for three hours.

Finally Graumann fixed Chapman with his watery blue eyes and came to the point. If Chapman would agree to be trained in sabotage, wireless telegraphy and intelligence work and then undertake a mission to Britain, he could promise him a substantial financial reward on his return. Chapman agreed on the spot. He then asked whether Tony Faramus would be coming too. Graumann's reply was blunt. Faramus was 'no use' to the German secret service. Graumann picked his words carefully: 'In times of war we must be careful, and one of you must remain here.' Though his language was opaque, Graumann's meaning was obvious: Faramus would remain behind, as a hostage for Chapman's good behaviour.

As they shook hands, Chapman noticed the fat gold ring with five black dots on Graumann's little finger, and remarked to himself on the softness of his hands. These were hands that had never known manual labour. The voice, the hands, the signet ring: clearly, the man must be some sort of aristocrat. If Chapman could avoid getting into any more trouble, Graumann remarked in the doorway, he would be out of Romainville in two weeks.

Chapman returned to his barrack-cell elated, but also troubled by the veiled 'half-threat' to Faramus. He did not relate the German's words to his cell-mate, but the news that Chapman would soon be leaving alone left the younger man in no doubt that his position was perilous. 'Supposing you slip up,' Faramus pointed out. 'Then I'll be the one to get it in the neck. What if once you have set foot in England, you don't want to come back, Eddie? I don't fancy being shot. Besides, I'm too young to die.'

Chapman tried to reassure him. 'Look here, Tony, let me play this my way. I am gambling with my own life, too, don't forget.' The truth of the remark was undeniable: their fates were now linked. Most Romainville victims never discovered why they had been chosen for death. If Faramus was shot, he would know he had been betrayed by Eddie Chapman. Privately, Faramus reflected that 'agreeing to play Eddie's game might cost me my life'. Could this 'bold bluff' possibly succeed? 'Desperately and fearfully,' Faramus wrote, 'I hoped so, for my sake as well as his.'

On 18 April 1942, Chapman was escorted from his cell. 'Goodbye and good luck,' he said, slapping Faramus on the back and grinning. 'Look me up in London after the war!'

'Goodbye and good luck,' replied the Jerseyman, as brightly as he could.

Chapman was met in the Kommandant's office by Oberleutnant Thomas. The few possessions he had brought from Jersey were returned to him, along with his civilian clothes, while Brüchenbach signed the release papers. Chapman walked out of Romainville gates, and was ushered by Thomas into a waiting car. He was free. But as Thomas observed, as they settled into the back seat and the driver headed west, this was freedom of a very particular sort. 'You are among friends and we are going to help you,' said the German officer, in his clipped, precise English. 'So please do not try anything silly like attempting to escape, because I am armed.' From now on, Thomas added, when in public, Chapman should speak only German.

At Gare Montparnasse, the duo transferred to a reserved first-class compartment on the train for Nantes. In the dining car, Chapman gorged himself. The ascetic-looking Thomas ate little, so Chapman finished his supper for him.

It was evening when the train pulled into Nantes, France's western port where the great Loire flows towards the Atlantic. A burly young man in civilian clothes with an impressively broken nose was waiting on the platform. He introduced himself as 'Leo', picked up Oberleutnant Thomas's suitcase and Chapman's bag of belongings, and led the way to where a large Mercedes awaited them.

Chapman sank into the leather upholstery, as Leo drove the car at high speed through Nante's winding cobbled streets, and then out into open countryside, heading northwest, past neat farms and meadows dotted with Limousin cows. At a roadside village café, a handful of peasants watched expressionless, as the Mercedes sped past. After some seven kilometres, Leo slowed and turned right. They passed what appeared to be a factory and crossed over a railway bridge, before coming to a stop in front of a pair of green iron gates with a high wall on either side. A thick screen of poplar trees shielded from view whatever was behind the wall. Leo hailed the uniformed sentry, who unlocked the gates.

Down a short drive, the car came to rest before a large stone mansion. Chapman was led inside and upstairs to a book-lined study. Here a familiar figure in a three-piece pinstriped suit sat hunched writing over a desk. 'Welcome to the Villa de la Bretonnière,' said Dr Graumann, rising to shake Chapman's hand. 'Come and have a glass of really good brandy.'

Villa de la Bretonnière

After Romainville, the Villa de la Bretonnière was paradise. The three-storey building had been built in the 1830s, the same decade as the Paris prison, but it could not have been more of a contrast. It was what the French describe as a *maison de maître*, larger than a mansion, but smaller than a château. It boasted all the hallmarks of a rich man's retreat: oak floors, huge marble fireplaces, crystal chandeliers, and double doors opening onto a large and well-tended garden. The house had belonged to a wealthy Jew, a cinema owner in Nantes, before it was requisitioned and its owner 'relocated'. The building, surrounded by trees and a high wall, suited Nazi intelligence purposes exactly.

That evening, elated by the brandy and Graumann's welcome, Chapman was shown to a room on the top floor. For the first time in four years, the door was not locked behind him. He slept in crisp linen sheets, and woke to the sound of a cock crowing. Chapman thought he had never seen anywhere so beautiful. To the west, the land sloped gently through woodland and fields to the River Erdre. Waterfowl splashed in an ornamental pond, while a litter of Alsatian puppies played on the lawn.

Chapman was escorted to breakfast by Oberleutnant Thomas. In the dining room, Graumann sat at the head of the table, reading a copy of *The Times* and eating a boiled egg. He nodded to Chapman, but did not speak. (The aristocrat, Chapman would

soon learn, did not hold with conversation during breakfast.)
Around the table, half a dozen men were tucking into a feast of
toast, eggs, butter, honey and fresh coffee, all served on the
former owner's best china. Chapman recognised Leo, the
chauffeur with the flattened nose, who grinned back through
broken teeth.

A French maidservant cleared away breakfast, cigarettes were
offered around, and Thomas introduced the other members of
the household. Each man, though Chapman could not know it,
proffered a false name. A ruddy-faced, well-built fellow with a
pearl tie-pin was presented as 'Hermann Wojch'; followed by
'Robert Keller', a slight, blond man in his early twenties,
alongside 'Albert', a balding, middle-aged man with a cheery
countenance. To Chapman's astonishment, the next person to
step forward, wearing plus fours and a gold wristwatch, greeted
him in English with a broad Cockney accent. He gave his name
as 'Franz Schmidt'.

Later, upstairs in the study, Graumann adopted his habitual
posture, with one finger hooked in his waistcoat, and explained
that Chapman was now part of the Abwehr – the German
foreign intelligence gathering and espionage service – and that he
was attached to the Nantes section, 'one of the most important
sabotage training centres of the German Secret Service in
Europe'.

For the next three months, Graumann continued, Chapman
would undergo rigorous training, under his direction: Keller
would be his wireless instructor; Wojch and Schmidt would
teach him sabotage and espionage techniques; Leo would show
him how to jump with a parachute. If he passed certain tests he
would be sent to Britain on a mission and, if successful, he would
be handsomely rewarded. There was no word as to what would
happen if Chapman failed these tests.

Meanwhile, he was free to explore the grounds of La Bretonnière, but Thomas would accompany him at all times. He
should avoid fraternizing with the locals and under no circum-

stances should he bring women back to the house. In the presence of French people he must speak only German, and if any Germans quizzed him, he should explain that he was German by birth but had lived most of his life in America. Officially, he was now part of the Baustelle Kerstang, a military engineering unit repairing roads and buildings in occupied France.

Chapman would need a spyname, Graumann declared, to protect his real identity. What was the name that the English routinely attached to Germans? Fritz? This, he chuckled, would be the codename for the new Abwehr spy number V-6523.

As he struggled to take in the flood of information, Chapman reflected that Dr Graumann, with his pinstriped suit, looked more like a 'respectable business man' than a spymaster. His tone was brisk but benign, and his eyes under heavy lids twinkled. Each time he spoke, his head jerked slightly, back and forth. His voice struck Chapman as being 'surprisingly soft, for a German', but the tone hardened very slightly as the German observed: 'Look, you will see a good many things, but you must realise that with our section things must be kept secret. I'm asking you not to be too nosey.'

For months, the Abwehr had been searching for an English-man who could be trained as a spy and saboteur and dropped into Britain. The man must be without scruple, adept at con-cealment, intelligent, ruthless and mercenary. Chapman's arrival at La Bretonnière was not some accident of fate. Rather, he represented the latest, boldest stroke in a war between the secret services of Britain and Germany that had raged, unseen but unceasing, for the previous two years.

Before the outbreak of the Second World War, the Abwehr (literally meaning 'defence') was reputed to be the most efficient intelligence service in Europe. An early appraisal by MI5, the security service controlling counter-espionage in the United Kingdom and throughout the British empire, described the Abwehr as an 'absolutely first-class organisation in training and personnel'. This assessment was overly flattering. One of the most striking aspects of the countries' intelligence services was just how little each side knew about the other. In 1939, SIS, the British Secret Intelligence Service (also known as MI6, and operating in all areas outside British territory) did not know what the German military intelligence service was called, or even who ran it. In a frank self-assessment written after the end of the Second World War, MI5 conceded that 'by the time of the fall of France the organisation of the Security Service as a whole was in a state which can only be described as chaotic . . . attempting to evolve means of detecting German agents without any inside knowledge of the German organisation'.

The Abwehr was equally ill prepared. Hitler had neither expected nor wanted to go to war with Britain, and most Nazi intelligence operations had been directed eastwards. The Abwehr intelligence network in Britain was virtually non-existent. As Britain and Germany squared up for conflict, a strange shadow dance took place between their rival intelligence services: both frantically began building up spy networks, almost from scratch, for immediate deployment against one another. Each credited the other with extreme efficiency and advanced preparations, and both were wrong.

The first serious skirmish took place over a diminutive, dubious and extremely aggravating Welsh electrician called Alfred Owens. A manufacturer of battery accumulators, Owens had made frequent business trips to Germany in the 1930s, bringing back small items of technical and military information which he passed to the Admiralty. In 1936, he was formally enrolled in British intelligence as agent 'Snow' (a partial anagram of Owens). At the same time, however, Owens had secretly made contact with the Abwehr. MI6 intercepted his mail, but when confronted with evidence of his double game, Owens insisted he was working for British interests. MI6 accepted his explanation, for the time being. On instructions from Germany, Owens picked up a wireless transmitter from the left-luggage office at Victoria Station, providing valuable technical information on German radio construction. Then he vanished to Hamburg, and it was assumed he had 'gone bad'.

The day after Britain declared war on Germany, the Welshman resurfaced and telephoned Special Branch to arrange a meeting. At Wandsworth Prison Owens was offered the choice between execution and working as a double agent; once again, he pledged loyalty to Britain. In September 1939, he travelled to Holland, this time accompanied by a retired police inspector, Gwilym Williams, posing as a Welsh nationalist eager to throw off the English yoke. There they met up with Abwehr officer Nikolaus Ritter, and returned to London with valuable information including the keys to various Abwehr radio codes.

The British still had doubts about Agent Snow, and these deepened after an extraordinary series of events in the North Sea. Ritter had asked Owens to recruit another agent for training in Germany, and agreed to send a submarine to pick them up south of Dogger Bank. MI6, obviously eager to plant a double agent within the Abwehr, duly located a reformed conman and thief called Sam McCarthy, who agreed to play the part. As they motored to the rendezvous in a trawler, McCarthy and Owens each became convinced that the other was, in fact, a German spy. Two days before the meeting, McCarthy locked Owens in his cabin and they steamed home. When Owens was searched he was found to be carrying a report describing the operations of the British intelligence services. This was traced to a Piccadilly restaurant manager and sometime MI5 informer called William Rolph. Confronted with the evidence, Rolph admitted he had been recruited by Owens to spy for Germany. As soon as the interrogators had left, he committed suicide by putting his head in a gas oven.

Owens spent the rest of the war in prison, and to this day it is uncertain whether he was a patriot, a traitor, or both. But the Snow case had shown the extraordinary value of running a double agent, and had furnished some vital technical and cryptological clues. The farce in the North Sea demonstrated that the Abwehr was looking to recruit disaffected British citizens, even criminals, as German agents.

Meanwhile, mounting fears of a German invasion prompted a spy scare in Britain of epidemic proportions. The collapse of one European country after another before the Nazi Blitzkrieg could only have one explanation: in each country there must have been a network of German agents behind the lines, aiding the German advance. A similar network, it was assumed, must exist in Britain, plotting to undermine the state. The myth of the German fifth column was born on a most un-British wave of public hysteria, stoked by the press and politicians. 'There is a well-defined class of people prone to spy mania,' wrote Churchill, who was not immune to the mania himself. 'War is the heyday of these worthy folk.'

German spies were spotted everywhere, and nowhere. Police were deluged with reports of strange figures in disguise, lights flashing at night, burning haystacks, and paranoid neighbours hearing strange tapping through the walls. One avid amateur spycatcher reported seeing a man with a 'typically Prussian neck'; Baden-Powell, the original scoutmaster, insisted you could spot a German spy from the way he walked. Anyone and everyone might be a spy. Evelyn Waugh lampooned the frenzy: 'Suspect everyone – the vicar, the village grocer, the farmer whose family have lived here for a hundred years, all the most unlikely people.' The spies were said to be spreading newspaper on the ground to give secret signals to airborne Germans, poisoning chocolate, infiltrating the police, recruiting lunatics from asylums to act in a suicide squad, and sending out murderous agents into the British countryside disguised as women hitchhikers.

Vast energy and resources were devoted to following up the reports, with a complete lack of success. The most grievous outcome of the panic was the internment of 27,000 Germans, Italians and other 'enemy aliens', most of whom were not only innocent, but also strongly opposed to Nazism. The failure to uncover the plotters merely redoubled the conviction that they must be agents of the highest quality. The secret service, wrote an insider, 'was left with the very uncomfortable feeling that there must be agents in this country whom it was unable to discover'.

The simple truth was that, apart from Arthur Owens and his band of imaginary Welsh extremists, the Abwehr had utterly failed to recruit an effective team of spies in Britain before the war. But as Operation Sealion, the plan for the German invasion of Britain, took shape, the German secret service set about rectifying this failure with a vengeance. From late 1940, as the air-duel between the RAF and Luftwaffe intensified, the Abwehr began pouring agents into Britain: they came by rubber dinghy, U-boat, seaplane and parachute; they came disguised as refugees and seamen. Some came armed with the latest wireless transmitters and carefully forged identity documents; others arrived with nothing more than the clothes they stood up in. Between September and November 1940, it is estimated that at least twenty-one Abwehr agents were despatched to Britain, with instructions to report on troop movements, identify and sabotage targets vital to British defence, prepare for the imminent invasion, and then mingle with the retreating British army. A list of prominent Britons to be arrested by the Gestapo was drawn up, and at the Abwehr headquarters in Berlin there was little doubt that Hitler's stormtroopers would soon be marching down Whitehall.

The Abwehr spies were a mixed bag. Some were Nazi ideologues, but most were the human jetsam that tends to float towards the spy world: opportunists, criminals and a handful of fantasists. The vast majority of the 'invasion spies' had one thing in common though: they were amateurs. Many spoke English badly, or not at all. Few had received more than rudimentary training. They were poorly briefed and often ignorant of English life. One was arrested after he tried to pay £10 and six shillings for a train ticket costing 'ten and six'.

The Abwehr would never find out that its entire espionage programme in Britain had been discovered, dismantled and turned against it. Many of its agents, it is true, seemed to vanish without trace, but this was only to be expected. Several had begun sending messages by wireless and secret ink, and a few seemed to be flourishing undercover. That, at least, is what Hitler was told. Yet the more professional and experienced German intelligence officers knew that the calibre of spies being sent to Britain was pitifully low. The little information coming out of Britain was low-grade stuff. No sabotage operation of any note had been carried out.

The Abwehr leadership decided that in order to penetrate Britain's intelligence defences they would need to look beyond the eager amateurs deployed so far. An altogether superior sort of spy was needed: someone handpicked and properly trained by professionals for a specific, highly dangerous mission. This individual should be dedicated, ruthless and, if possible, British. For this purpose, in March 1942, the Nantes section (or *Dienststelle*) of the Abwehr was established as an elite espionage training centre. A *Rittmeister* who was also a rising star within the Abwehr was appointed to run the new spy school, and provided with money, expert trainers, staff, and a spacious mansion just outside the city in the little village of St Joseph. The unit would be answerable to the Abwehr headquarters in Paris, but largely independent.

A young English-speaking Abwehr officer named Walter Praetorius had been appointed to find a renegade Englishman worthy of training as a top-class spy. Praetorius was a committed Nazi in his politics, but a confirmed anglophile in his tastes. His maternal great-grandfather, Henry Thoms [*sic*], had been a Scottish flax merchant who emigrated from Dundee to the Baltic port of Riga, and married a German woman. Praetorius was fiercely proud of his British blood, and liked to remind anyone who would listen that he was a scion of the 'Chiefly line of Clan McThomas'.

The young Praetorius had graduated from Berlin University, and in 1933, aged twenty-two, spent a year at Southampton University improving his English as part of an Anglo-German student-exchange scheme. He intended to become a teacher. In England, Praetorius played the flute, rowed for the university, and began to sport the clothes and airs of an English gentleman. But above all, he danced. The most lasting legacy from his year in Britain was an unlikely but intense passion for English country dancing. He learned the reels and sword dances of his Scottish ancestors, but above all he fell in love with Morris dancing. The English tend to mock Morris dancing, but Praetorius found the dancers with their odd hats and peculiar rituals quite captivating. During the vacation, he cycled around England, photographing folk dances and analysing the dance steps. After months of careful study, he pronounced that Morris dancing was the root of all dancing in the world, and therefore a foundation of world culture (a remarkable theory never proposed by anyone else, before or since).

Praetorius was popular at Southampton, where he was nick-named 'Rusty' by his contemporaries on account of the reddish tinge to his receding hair, and remembered as a 'kind, gentle type of personality'. But he was also deeply impressionable, one of nature's extremists and liable to fits of excessive and irrational enthusiasm. When he returned to Germany in 1936, his obsession with folk dancing was soon replaced by an even more extreme passion for fascism. According to British police files, his mother was already a 'rabid Nazi', and young Walter embraced the new creed with characteristic fervour and naivety, rising swiftly through the ranks of the Hitler Youth. The 'superiority of the German and Anglo-Saxon races over all others' became an article of faith, and the outbreak of war an opportunity to demonstrate German strength in the ranks of the SS. The death of his only brother, Hans, in Poland in the early days of the war served merely to inflame him further. Rusty, the gentle flautist with the passion for country dancing, had become a committed, unquestioning Nazi.

SS Oberleutnant Praetorius, adopting the spy name 'Walter Thomas' in honour of his Scottish forebears, set to work diligently trawling through paperwork and scouring prisons, refugee centres and POW camps in search of ideal spy material. He travelled to Jersey in search of collaborators, and stayed at the Almadoux Hotel. He interviewed criminals and deserters, British citizens trapped in the occupied territories and even IRA sympathisers, Irishmen who might be recruited to fight against Britain. None would suffice. Then, in late March 1942, Praetorius sent an excited message to the newly appointed chief of the Nantes Abwehr station (or Abwehrstelle), reporting that he had located an English thief in a Paris prison who 'might be trained for sabotage work', and was going to interview him at once.

Dr Graumann

Chapman began to explore his new home, with Praetorius (alias 'Thomas') as his guide and guard. Chapman's bedroom, on the top floor of La Bretonnière, was directly above that of Graumann, whose suite occupied most of the first floor. Next door to Chapman slept Keller, whose bedroom was also the radio room. Wojch and Schmidt shared a room, and Praetorius occupied the bedroom next to Graumann. The ground floor consisted of the dining room, an elegant smoking room with wall panels painted in the style of Fragonard, and a large study with desks around the walls and a steel safe in the corner. A pretty gardener's cottage stood alongside the main building, the ground floor of which had been converted into a chemical laboratory for making explosives, with pestles and mortars, scales, and rows of sinister-looking bottles lining the walls.

La Bretonnière had a full contingent of domestic staff: thirty-year-old Odette did the cooking and housekeeping, aided by Jeanette, a teenager. Two gardeners – one a released prisoner – came daily to cut the grass, tend the flower beds, weed the vegetable patch, and feed the chickens, goats and pigs housed in the grounds.

Chapman's training began at once. A Morse set was produced and under the tuition of Keller and Praetorius he was taught to distinguish between a dot and a dash. From there he graduated to the letters with two elements, then three, and finally the entire alphabet in German. He was taught elementary radio shorthand, tricks for memorizing sequences of letters and how to assemble a radio set.

Three days after his arrival, the gardeners were sent home early and Wojch set off a timed explosion in the garden, followed by a demonstration of 'chemical mixing' in the laboratory. The red-faced saboteur handled the volatile compounds with extraordinary dexterity and Chapman, who prided himself on his knowledge of explosives, was impressed: 'He just got hold of the stuff, looked at it, tasted it, and started mixing. I don't think he was a chemist, he'd simply been very well trained.' Every day, Chapman and Wojch would work in the laboratory, making homemade bombs and incendiary devices from simple ingredients such as sugar, oil and potassium chlorate. Chapman was set to work memorizing formulae.

Leo began teaching him how to jump and roll in preparation for his parachute drop. A ladder was erected against the tallest beech tree in the garden, and the height of Chapman's jumps gradually increased, until he could leap from 30 feet without hurting himself. After the years of imprisonment he was in poor physical shape, so Leo devised a strict exercise regime: Chapman would chop wood until his shoulders ached, and every morning Praetorius would accompany him on a four-mile run along the banks of the Erdre. Chapman was deeply affected by 'the beauty of the river near Nantes', reflecting that it was only since leaving prison 'that he had begun to realise how much beauty there was in the world'.

For Chapman these were strangely idyllic days. A bell would summon the men to breakfast at 8.30, and at 10.00 Chapman would practise sending radio messages to the other Abwehr posts in Paris and Bordeaux. The rest of the morning might be taken up with sabotage work, coding exercises, or parachute practice. Lunch was at 12.30, followed by a siesta until 3.00 or 3.30, followed by more training. In the evening they might play bridge, or bowls on the lawn, or walk up the road to the Café des Pêcheurs, a small wood-panelled bar in the village, and watch the sun go down over the river, drinking beer at 3 francs a glass. Sometimes, accompanied by other members of the team, Chapman would drive out into the countryside to purchase black-market food: fresh eggs, bread, hams and wine. The negotiating was done by one of the drivers, a Belgian named Jean, for the French farmers would charge a German more. The food was expensive – a ham could cost as much 2,500 francs – but there seemed to be no shortage of money.

At La Bretonnière, the alcohol flowed copiously. Dr Graumann's drinking was particularly spectacular: Chapman calculated that the chief put away at least two bottles of wine a night, followed by glass after glass of brandy. It seemed to have no effect on him whatever. On Saturdays, the household would climb into the unit's four cars, each with French registration and an SS pass, and drive into Nantes, where they would dine at Chez Elle, dance at the Café de Paris, or visit the cabaret, Le Coucou, where black-market champagne cost 300 francs a bottle. Chapman paid for nothing, and was issued with as much 'pocket money' as he desired. On these trips in to town, Chapman spotted 'V-signs', the mark of the French resistance, chalked on walls in public places. Some diligent Nazi had inserted a swastika inside each V, 'thus reversing the propaganda'. A few of the men visited the German-controlled brothel in town – pug-faced Albert was a regular at the establishment, and extolled the charms of *les jolies filles* there with such gusto that the others nicknamed him *Joli Albert*, a most inapt description.

Chapman found Wojch to be particularly good company: 'He liked life, he always had plenty of money, [he was] rather flashy, liked the girls and the drink.' He too was a former boxer and formidably strong. He would challenge the others to a form of wrestling match in which each contestant would clasp his opponent's hand and then try to force him to his knees. Wojch invariably won.

Chapman began to imagine these men as his friends. He never doubted that the names he knew them by were real. He once heard Thomas referred to as Praetorius, but simply assumed this must be a nickname.

But for all their bibulous bonhomie, his new companions were guarded in their words, furtive in their behaviour, and secretive in their activities outside the walls of the compound. From time to time Wojch or Schmidt would disappear, for a week or longer. When they returned, Chapman would discreetly inquire where they had been. The conversation, he recalled, tended to follow the same pattern:

'Had a good trip?'

'Yes. Not too bad.'

'Where did you go?'

'Oh, out of the country.'

Chapman learned never to demand a direct answer. Once, when drunk, he asked Wojch whether he had ever been to America. Wojch's smile was cold: 'What do you want to ask questions like that for?'

Beneath a veneer of informality, security was tight. All important documents were held in the office safe. From time to time Chapman would observe Graumann go into the garden with a secret document or letter, 'take it out and light a cigarette [with it] and burn the whole envelope'. At night, two ferocious Alsatians roamed the grounds, keeping intruders out and Chapman in. One morning Keller found Chapman alone in the radio room, and brusquely ordered him to leave. The door was always locked after that, and rigged with an electric alarm. When Graumann discovered that Chapman had taken to swimming in the Erdre in the early morning, he assembled the staff for a ferocious roasting: 'Good God! Is he going out alone? He has no papers on him. What if the French police pick him up?'

Later, the chief took Chapman aside, and gently explained: 'Look here, if you are going out swimming, take one of the boys along with you. If ever you want to go out, they have orders that you have only to ask, and one of the boys will go with you.'

Inevitably, however, Chapman began to glean snippets of information from his housemates. Leo, Wojch and Schmidt were 'more or less reckless, the lads of the village'. Wojch boasted that he had been an Olympic boxer before the war. He plainly knew London well, and he waxed sentimental over a former girlfriend, an Irish chambermaid in the Hyde Park Hotel. From casual remarks, Chapman picked up that Wojch had been involved in the dynamiting of a Paris hotel before the invasion of France, an attack in which many Allied officers died. Small but telling details emerged about their earlier lives. Thomas wore his English university boating tie at every opportunity, and boasted that he had been the best oarsman at Southampton. Albert revealed that before the war he had been an agent for a German firm in Liberia. Leo had been a boxer and prizefighter.

When Chapman asked Schmidt where he got his Cockney accent from, he explained that before the war he had worked as a waiter in Frascati's, the London restaurant. He had visited several of Chapman's old Soho haunts, including Smokey Joe's and The Nest, and recalled the tea dances at the Regal Theatre near Marble Arch. Slowly it dawned on Chapman that these men must be more than mere instructors; they were experienced, active spies and saboteurs, who had been deployed in France and Britain since before the outbreak of war.

But if some of 'the boys' were coming into sharper focus, their leader concealed his past behind steel shutters of politeness. For wireless practice, Graumann would set Chapman the task of transmitting English nursery rhymes such as 'Mary had a little lamb', and 'This little piggie went to Market'. 'These were things,' Chapman reflected, 'which I thought only an Englishman would know'; but Graumann claimed to have visited England only once. When Chapman remarked to Graumann on his 'terribly English accent', he batted away the implied question, saying he had been taught by a 'very good private tutor'.

One night, over dinner, the conversation turned to dogs. 'I'll show you a photograph of my dog,' said Graumann, rising from the table. Several minutes later he returned with a torn photo-graph. The dog was visible, but the face of whoever was holding it had been torn away.

'Doctor Stephan Graumann' was, in reality, nothing of the sort. His name was Stephan Albert Heinrich von Gröning. He was an aristocrat of impeccable breeding, great wealth and luxurious tastes: indeed, the 'really good brandy' he had poured down Chapman on his first evening was a fitting leitmotif for his life.

The Von Grönings had been the first family in the northern city of Bremen for some eight centuries, amassing a vast fortune through trading well and marrying better. Over the years the powerful clan had supplied seventeen members of the Bremen parliament and one notable eighteenth-century diplomat, Georg, who studied with Goethe at Leipzig and then served as ambassador to the court of Napoleon. In recognition of this achievement, he was awarded the aristocratic title 'von', and the Von Grönings had been getting steadily richer, and grander, ever since.

Born in 1898, Stephan had been brought up in circumstances of extreme privilege. His mother was an American heiress of German extraction named Helena Graue (hence his *nom d'espion*: 'Graumann'). At home, the Von Grönings spoke English, with an upper-class accent. Home was a enormous town house in the main square of Bremen, a self-satisfied statement in stucco and stone with five storeys, a fabled library, several old master portraits and an army of servants to wait on young Stephan: someone polished his shoes, someone cooked his meals, some-one else drove him to an exclusive private school in a carriage with glass windows and the family crest.

Von Gröning's pampered life very nearly came to a premature end in 1914 when the First World War erupted, and he joined the army. But not for young Stephan some dowdy and un-comfortable billet in the trenches; he was commissioned as an Oberleutnant in the legendary White Dragoons, perhaps the most elite cavalry regiment in the imperial army. Von Gröning took part in one of the last cavalry charges in history, during which most of the regiment was annihilated by British machine-gun fire. He survived, and was awarded the Iron Cross, second class, for bravery. Von Gröning's war was a short one. He contracted pneumonia, then tuberculosis, and was invalided out of the army. His mother sent him to recuperate at Davos, the fashionable health spa in Switzerland, where he met and fell in love with a Welsh woman named Gladys Nott Gillard, who was also tubercular and high-born, but penniless. They married in St Luke's church, Davos, on 19 December 1923.

The Von Grönings rented a large mansion in Davos, called the Villa Baby, and then set off travelling, back to Bremen, to Hamburg, and finally to Bavaria. Along the way Von Gröning acquired a coffee business – Gröning and Schilling – which almost immediately went bust; he began gambling on the stock exchange, and lost a lot more money. Had he not considered it vulgar to count one's wealth, he might have realised that apart from the great house at Bremen and some fine oil paintings, he was heading for bankruptcy.

Charming, brave, intellectually gifted but indolent, at the end of the war Von Gröning found himself at something of a loose end, which is where he remained for the next seventeen years. He had no desire to study. He collected etchings by Rubens and Rembrandt. He travelled a little, drank a lot and took no physical exercise of any kind (he rode a bicycle only once in his life, but declared the experience 'uncomfortable', and never repeated it). After his failed coffee enterprise, Von Gröning would have nothing more to do with business or trade, and fully occupied his time behaving as if he was rich, which he blithely assumed he was. 'He was delightful company, and very clever,' as one member of the family put it, 'but he never actually *did* anything at all.'

Stephan and his wife shared an interest in lap dogs, strong drink, and spending money they did not have; but not much else. They divorced in 1932, on the grounds of Von Gröning's 'illicit association with another woman'. He was required to provide alimony of 250 marks a month, which was paid by his mother. He then agreed to pay Gladys a lump sum of 4,000 marks, but somehow failed to pay that either. Gladys was reduced to teaching English at a school in Hamburg, while her ex-husband would lie on the sofa in the library of the family home for days on end, reading books in German, English and French, and smoking cigars. But they remained friends. Von Gröning did not make enemies easily.

Von Gröning had observed the rise of fascism from a lofty distance. He was a patriotic monarchist and an old-fashioned aristocrat from an earlier age. He had little time for the posturing Brownshirts with their extreme ideas. He regarded anti-semitism as vulgar, and Hitler as an upstart Austrian 'oik' (though at the time he kept that opinion to himself).

The outbreak of the Second World War gave new purpose to Von Gröning's dilettante existence. He rejoined the German cavalry – a very different organisation from the elegant lancers of his youth – and served on the Eastern Front as a staff officer attached to Oberkommando 4 Heeresgruppe Mitte. After a year he applied to join the Abwehr. The secret military intelligence service of the German High Command was something of an ideological anomaly: it contained its share of Nazi fanatics, but alongside them were many men of Von Gröning's stamp – officers of the old school, determined to win the war, but opposed to Nazism. The Abwehr was epitomised by its leader, Admiral Wilhelm Canaris, a spy of great subtlety who ran the Abwehr as a personal fiefdom. Hitler never trusted Canaris, rightly, for the admiral may eventually have put out feelers to Britain, seeking to negotiate an end to the war by removing the Führer.

Espionage appealed to Von Gröning, intellectually and ideologically, while his command of languages and knowledge of English and American culture made him a valuable asset in the secret service. The years spent lounging in the library at Bremen had not been entirely wasted: behind the hooded eyes and jovial manner was a practised and cynical student of human nature. His outwardly affable demeanour encouraged others to confide in him, but as a Von Gröning of Bremen, he always maintained his distance. 'He could mix in any company, but he always knew who he was.' He was swiftly spotted as the coming man within the Abwehr, and when Canaris was looking for someone to run his new Nantes spy school, Von Gröning seemed the obvious person to appoint.

Von Gröning liked Chapman. He admired the sheer energy of the man, so different from his own aristocratic languor. And he knew he could turn him into a powerful secret weapon.

The photograph he handed Chapman had once shown Gladys hugging their pet dog, a Sealyham terrier. But before coming downstairs, he had carefully torn Gladys out of the picture. Von Gröning was not going to run the risk, however small, that Chapman might recognise his British ex-wife, and thus obtain a clue to the real identity of 'Dr Graumann'.

Von Gröning bound Chapman ever closer to the team. The psychology was simple, but effective. The Englishman was flattered and spoiled, drawn into an intense atmosphere of secretive camaraderie. Like many brutal men, including Hitler himself, the members of the Nantes Abwehr section could also be sentimental and nostalgic. Von Gröning set up a 'Home corner' – on the bureau in the smoking room, where the men were encouraged to display pictures of their hometowns, and somehow obtained a photograph of Berwick-on-Tweed, the nearest town he could find to Chapman's birthplace of Burnopfield. Birthdays were celebrated with cakes, gifts and torrents of drink. Von Gröning encouraged informality, and allowed the men to daub graffiti on the walls of the unused attics. One drew a caricature of Hitler as a carrot. It was surely Chapman who carefully etched the picture of a blonde woman with a strong resemblance to Betty Farmer.

Von Gröning was privately amused to see the Führer mocked as a vegetable, but he took pains to remind Chapman that he was now part of a victorious German army that had conquered half of Europe and would soon bring Britain and Russia to their knees. Praetorius, as the most committed Nazi in the group, kept up a steady stream of Nazi jingoism.

Inevitably, the combination of healthy living, good food, group bonding and propaganda began to have the desired effect. Chapman felt himself drawn to what he called the 'German spirit', his vanity fed by the belief that this training school, staffed by hard and hard-drinking men, had been established for him alone. Every meal began with the chorus of 'Heil Hitler!', with the Englishman joining in. When Thomas declared that Britain was losing the war, Chapman believed him, though such 'gloating' left him feeling 'sick at heart'.

At the end of a boozy evening, the trainee spy could be found lustily singing *Lili Marlene* with the rest of the crew. *Lili Marlene*, he declared, was his favourite song, expressing 'the hopes of every man who has left his girl behind'.

Chapman's head was being turned by all the attention. But it was not turning nearly so far as Von Gröning imagined.

It is impossible to say when Chapman decided to start spying on his German spymasters. Many years later, he candidly admitted that he did not know quite when, or even why, he began to collect information. Perhaps he was merely taking out an insurance policy against an uncertain future. The instincts of the spy and the thief are not so different: both trade in stolen goods, on similar principles. The value of information depends on the buyer's hunger, but it is a seller's market. Slowly at first, and with great care, Chapman began to build up a stock of secrets that would be of supreme interest to British intelligence.

He noticed the way that Von Gröning assiduously read the personal advertisements in *The Times*, and sometimes the *Manchester Guardian*, occasionally underlining passages and taking notes. He overheard that Wojch had been on a sabotage mission to Spain during one of his unexplained absences, and when the door to the small anteroom off the study was left open, he spotted at least 50 lbs of gelignite in neat stacks. Inside a cupboard in Von Gröning's bedroom he saw racks of German military uniforms 'of every kind in different lockers with all kinds of numbers'. He noted how Von Gröning took the codebooks after radio practice and carefully locked them in the safe. Given the opportunity and some gelignite, Chapman knew he could open that safe.

Chapman would later claim to have manufactured a set of skeleton keys to open and snoop inside various locked drawers around the house. This seems unlikely, given how closely he was monitored, but he certainly eavesdropped on his companions, literally, by boring a small hole under the eaves of his bedroom into Von Gröning's bathroom. (If challenged, he planned to say he was putting down chemicals from the lab, to poison the rats that ran behind the panelling and kept him awake at night.) By pressing his ear to the hole, he could faintly hear the conversation taking place below, though he learned nothing of interest. He began to make notes: of crystal frequencies, code words and the times of radio transmission between Nantes, Paris and Bordeaux. He noted the position of the anti-aircraft gun emplacements in the area, and the German military headquarters at the château on the other side of the river, camouflaged with netting. Although he had been instructed not to, he carefully wrote down the chemical formula of each bomb.

As the training gathered pace, senior officials in the Abwehr began to take an interest in Von Gröning's protégé, and Chapman found himself being inspected and tested, like a prize exhibit at a country fair. In May, Praetorius escorted him to an apartment in the Rue de Luynes in Paris to meet a fat man with a red face, who drank champagne and told English jokes, but who asked a series of penetrating questions. From his demeanour Chapman assumed he must be 'a fairly high bug' in the organisation. Von Gröning would say only that this individual was 'one of our best men'.

Soon afterwards a German in civilian clothes arrived from Angers in a chauffeur-driven car. The stranger was extraordinarily ugly and quite bald, save for a fringe of hair at the back of his head, with discoloured, gold-filled teeth. He wore a thick coat, carried a leather portfolio and smoked cigars continuously. Von Gröning treated him with exaggerated respect. Chapman thought he looked 'like a gigolo'. The bald man grilled Chapman about codes and sabotage. After he had left, Praetorius let slip that the visitor was 'an old Gestapo man', the head of counter-espionage in western France, responsible for catching enemy spies with a team of radio interceptors working around the clock in shifts to pick up 'black senders', clandestine wireless operators sending messages to Britain. The Angers spycatcher had asked that Chapman be transferred to his team for a month, to act as a 'stool pigeon amongst Allied agents in the Germans' hands, and as a general aid in counter-espionage work' – a request Von Gröning had indignantly refused. 'Fritz' was his personal asset, and Von Gröning was not about to relinquish him.

In June 1942, Chapman was taken to Paris for his first real parachute jump. He would start at 900 feet, he was told, and gradually increase to 1,500 feet. After a night at the Grand Hotel and dinner at Poccardi's Italian restaurant on the Left Bank, he was driven to a small airfield near Le Bourget airport, northeast of Paris, where Charles Lindbergh had landed after his transatlantic flight fifteen years earlier. Chapman and his parachute were loaded aboard a Junkers bomber, and minutes later he was floating down over the French countryside. His first jump was a complete success; his second, immediately afterwards, was very nearly his last. The parachute failed to open properly, buckling in a gust of wind when he was 50 feet from the ground. He was swung high into the air, and then smashed down, face first, onto the airfield tarmac. Chapman lost consciousness, one front tooth, one canine, and several molars. A German doctor patched him up and, back in Nantes, Von Gröning sent him to the best local dentist, one Dr Bijet, who set about reconstructing Chapman's battered face. After two weeks of operations, Chapman had a natty new set of gold teeth to replace those he had lost, and the Abwehr had a bill for 9,500 francs. The expense of Chapman's dental work would prompt the first of several heated exchanges between Von Gröning and his Paris superiors.

Chapman's wireless skills steadily improved. Praetorius timed him with a stopwatch, and announced he had attained a speed of seventy-five letters a minute, using a hand cipher (as distinct from one encoded on the Enigma machine) based on the single code word: BUTTERMILK. Without the code word, Praetorius assured him, the code was 'unbreakable'. As he gained in confidence, like most radio operators, Chapman began to develop his own 'fist' – individual characteristics that another wireless operator or receiver could become familiar with. Chapman always ended his transmissions with a 'laughing out' sign: 'HE HU HO HA', or some variation thereof. He called these flourishes 'my little mottoes'.

Soon he graduated from the German transmitter to a radio of British manufacture, apparently seized from a British agent in France. Usually the practice messages were coded from German, but he was also required to transmit in English and French. He sent poems, rhymes, proverbs and sayings. One day he tapped out a message: 'It is very cold here but better than in Russia.' He sent Maurice, the long-suffering chief radio operator in Paris, a message asking him to buy Odette, their housekeeper, a wedding present on his behalf. A little while later he tried out an English joke: 'A man went into a shop and asked the price of the ties displayed. The customer was astonished when he heard the high price and said one could buy a pair of shoes for that price. You would look funny, said the shopkeeper, wearing a pair of shoes round your neck. Fritz.' It was not a good joke, but then the Paris operators seemed to have had no sense of humour at all. 'What silly business is this?' the Paris station responded.

As spring turned to summer, La Bretonnière was a place of quiet contentment, save for the occasional deafening explosion in the back garden. When neighbours complained, they were told that the German engineers were detonating mines found during road construction. In July, Von Gröning reported to Paris that Fritz had passed a series of tests, and was responding well to training. The chief of the Nantes spy school was enjoying himself. Managing La Bretonnière was a little like running an exclusive, intensely private men's club, even if the guests were a trifle uncouth.

Chapman was also happy. 'I had everything I wanted,' he reflected. He also had a new companion. On a black-market expedition in the countryside, Chapman had bought and adopted a young pig, which he christened Bobby. The name was probably a reference to his previous life. The British bobbies (also, less affectionately, referred to as 'pigs') had chased Chapman for years; now Bobby the Pig followed him everywhere. An intelligent and affectionate animal, Bobby lived in the grounds of the house. At Chapman's whistle he would come running, like a well-trained dog, and then lie with his trotters in the air to have his stomach scratched. When Chapman went swimming in the Erdre (Von Gröning had by now relaxed his rules on unaccompanied bathing), Bobby would join him, flopping around in the muddy shallows. Then the Englishman and his faithful pig would walk happily home together through the cowslips and yellow irises.

Codebreakers

In the summer of 1942, the analysts of Bletchley Park – the secret code and cipher centre hidden deep in the Buckinghamshire countryside – decoded one of the most bizarre messages of the entire war. It had been sent from the Abwehr station at Nantes to the Abwehr headquarters in Paris, and it read: 'Dear France. Your friend Bobby the Pig grows fatter every day. He is gorging now like a king, roars like a lion and shits like an elephant. Fritz.' (The refined codebreaking ladies of Bletchley did not hold with vulgarity: they substituted the word 'shits' with a series of asterisks.) Britain's wartime cipher experts had penetrated Nazi Germany's most sophisticated codes and read its most secret messages, but this one was, quite simply, incomprehensible.

For several months, Britain's codebreakers and spycatchers had been following the Fritz traffic with avid interest, and mounting anxiety. They knew when this new, highly prized German spy had arrived in Nantes, and when he went to Paris; they knew how many teeth he had knocked out, and what the dentistry had cost; they knew he spoke English, and that he might even be an Englishman. And they knew he was heading for Britain.

The unravelling of Germany's top-secret codes by a peculiar collection of mathematical savants in an English country house was perhaps the most spectacular espionage coup of this, or any other, war. The Radio Security Service began picking up Abwehr signals in August 1940. The wireless set and codes

obtained through Arthur Owens, 'Agent Snow', had provided
the codebreakers with a valuable head start, and the cryptographers at Bletchley Park ('Station X') were soon reading the
Abwehr's principal hand cipher, the old-fashioned manual code.
By December another team, under the leadership of the in-
spirationally eccentric Dillwyn 'Dilly' Knox, had also broken the
code used on Abwehr Enigma machines, the portable cypher
machine used to encrypt and decrypt secret communications.
From that moment until the end of the war, British intelligence
continuously intercepted and read the wireless traffic of the
German secret service.

One member of the team put the success down to 'brilliant
guesswork and a good slice of luck', but it also came through the
application of raw intellectual muscle and sheer hard work. The
Abwehr's messages had to be intercepted, sent to Bletchley Park,
sorted, distributed, the daily machine and message settings worked
out, and finally deciphered and despatched to the intelligence
services. This extraordinary feat was usually performed by Dilly
Knox and his team of large ladies (for some reason he employed
only women, and only tall ones) within twenty-four hours. Knox
himself frequently went about his work clad in pyjamas and
dressing gown; to relax, he would then go for a terrifyingly fast
drive in the country lanes around Bletchley. Knox was one of the
greatest cryptographers, and the worst drivers, Britain has ever
produced. One day he returned from motoring through the
countryside and remarked casually: 'It's amazing how people
smile, and apologise to you, when you knock them over.'

The successful deciphering of the secret German codes, codenamed Ultra, was the best-kept secret of the war. Its value to the
war effort was almost incalculable. Churchill called the intercepts
'My Golden Eggs', and guarded them jealously. The Abwehr
never suspected that its messages were being read on a daily basis,
and persisted in the mistaken belief that its codes were unbreakable. The wealth of intelligence produced by Ultra decrypts was
referred to only as the 'Most Secret Sources'.

For the purposes of counter-espionage, the Most Secret Sources gave early warning of which spies were arriving in Britain, where, and when. As a consequence, most of the 'invasion spies' were picked up the moment they arrived in Britain, and swiftly imprisoned. Several were executed. The Abwehr's attempt to build a wartime spy network in Britain was an unmitigated failure. Crucially, the German intelligence service never realised this, thanks to one soldier, one Oxford academic, and one inspired idea.

At the height of the invasion scare, Major (later Colonel) Tommy Robertson, the MI5 officer who had handled the Snow case, approached his commanding officer, Dick White, and pointed out an obvious truth: a dead enemy spy can do no more harm, but neither can he (or she) do any good. A captured spy, however, could be persuaded to double-cross his German employers in exchange for his life, and then work for his British captors. Snow had already demonstrated the potential value of the controlled double agent, who could persuade the enemy to believe he was active and loyal when he was nothing of the sort. More importantly, over time, the double agent could be used to feed vital disinformation to the enemy. Thanks to the Most Secret Sources, British intelligence could even check whether the ruse was working. Robertson was insistent: instead of putting enemy agents in prison or on the end of a rope, they should be put to work.

Robertson's suggestion was forwarded to Guy Liddell, the subtle-minded, cello-playing director of 'B Division', the branch of MI5 devoted to counter-intelligence. Liddell gave his blessing at once, and, with Cabinet approval, Robertson was duly appointed chief of a new section for catching enemy spies, turning them, and then running them as double agents. The new outfit was given the innocuously invisible name B1A. At the same time, another linked organisation was established, with senior representatives of all the military intelligence services, the Home Forces and Home Defence, to assess the information, true and false, to be sent back via the double agents. The monitoring group was named the 'Twenty Committee', because the two Xs of a double-cross make twenty in Roman numerals. This was precisely the sort of dry classical witticism favoured by the man now appointed chairman of the Twenty Committee: Major (and later Sir) John Cecil Masterman, a distinguished Oxford history don, all-round sportsman, successful thriller-writer and jail-bird.

Masterman and Robertson formed the lynchpins of the double-cross operation, and they ran it with such dazzling success that after the war Masterman could justifiably claim: 'By means of the double-cross agent system *we actively ran and controlled the German espionage system in this country.*' (The italics are his, and deserved.) Theirs was a partnership of equals, and opposites: Robertson was a professional, dealing with the nuts and bolts of running the double agents, while Masterman liaised with the top brass; Robertson was the technician, while Masterman was to become the great theoretician of the double-cross.

Thomas Argyll Robertson was universally known as 'Tar', on account of his initials. Born in Sumatra to colonial parents, Tar had spent much of childhood parked with an aunt in Tunbridge Wells, an experience that was lonely but formative, for it left him with an ability to chat to complete strangers with disarming frankness. He passed through Charterhouse and Sandhurst without, in his own estimation, learning very much, and became, briefly, an officer in the Seaforth Highlanders, and then, even more briefly, a bank clerk. In 1933, at the age of twenty-four, at the invitation of Vernon Kell, the first director general of MI5, he had given up the staid world of banking to become a full-time intelligence officer, initially dealing with political subversion, arms trafficking, and counter-espionage. 'Immensely personable and monstrously good looking', he had the rare knack of being able to talk to anyone, anywhere, about anything. Bishops, admirals, whores, crooks and revolutionaries all found it equally easy to confide in Tar Robertson. Masterman pointed out, a touch acidulously, that 'Tar was in no sense an intellectual'. Tar was no bookworm. Instead he read people. He excelled in a job that 'involved a great deal of conversing with suspect people in pubs . . . meeting, greeting, chatting, charming, chuckling, listening, offering another drink, observing, probing a little, listening some more and ending up with all sorts of confidences the other person never thought he would utter'. He continued to wear the distinctive McKenzie tartan trews of the Seaforth Highlanders, a strangely conspicuous choice of attire for someone running one of the most secret organisations in the world. (The tartan trousers earned him another, more appropriately colourful nickname: 'Passion Pants'.)

John Masterman was cut from very different cloth. It is easiest to imagine him as the antithesis, in every conceivable way, of Eddie Chapman. He was highly intellectual, intensely conventional, and faintly priggish, with a granite sense of moral duty. Masterman was the embodiment of the British Establishment: he belonged to all the right clubs, played tennis at Wimbledon, hockey for England, and cricket whenever possible. Spare and athletic, his face was hard and handsome, as if carved out of marble. He neither smoked nor drank, and lived in a world of High Tables and elevated scholarship, exclusively inhabited by wealthy, privileged, intelligent English men.

A confirmed bachelor, he might have been homosexual, but if so, in a wholly repressed and contented English way. Women were simply invisible to him; in the 384 pages of his autobiography, only one woman is mentioned with affection, and that is his mother, with whom he lived in Eastbourne during the university vacations. In his spare time, he wrote detective thrillers set in an imaginary Oxford college and starring an amateur British sleuth in the Sherlock Holmes mould. These are somewhat dry and unemotional books, more intellectual puzzles than novels, but that was how this clever, desiccated man regarded human nature – as a conundrum to be unpicked by reason. He seems a peculiar creature today, but John Masterman represented English traits that were once considered virtues: *noblessse oblige*, hard work, and unquestioning obedience to the norms of society. By his own account, he was 'almost obsessively anxious to conform to accepted standards', just as Chapman was equally determined to defy them.

Yet Masterman had one thing in common with Chapman: he had spent four years in a prison. By a stroke of terrible ill fortune, as a newly elected fellow of Christ Church in 1914, he was sent on a study course in Germany, and was trapped by the outbreak of the First World War. Masterman was interned in Ruhleben prison with a strange assortment of equally unlucky Britons: sailors, businessmen, academics, jockeys from the Berlin race-course, sportsmen, workmen, tourists and one Nobel Prize winner, Sir James Chadwick, who lectured his fellow prisoners on the mysteries of radioactivity. The young Masterman emerged after four years without visible scars, but weighed down by what he considered to be an inferiority complex. Almost all his friends and contemporaries had perished on the battlefields. 'My predominant feeling was one of shame,' he wrote. 'I had played no part in the greatest struggle in our national history.'

Masterman was already in his fiftieth year when the longed-for opportunity to play his part finally arrived with the offer to work in MI5. He seized it gratefully, and it was Britain's great good fortune that he did, for no man was better suited to the job. If Tar Robertson was the 'real genius' of the double-cross system, as the historian Hugh Trevor-Roper put it, then John Masterman was its moral conscience, meticulously analysing the motivations of men, patiently solving the riddle of the double cross, like a vast and complicated crossword puzzle.

Recruitment to MI5 was through the informal old-boy net-work, and Robertson, with the help of his deputy, a London solicitor named John Marriott, swiftly began putting together a team of gifted amateurs. Section B1A, when finally assembled, included lawyers, academics, an industrialist, a circus owner, at least one artist, an art dealer and a poet. Tar himself was the only professional in the organisation, which started its life in a requisitioned corner of Wormwood Scrubs prison before moving to a large and elegant house at 58, St James's Street, in the heart of London clubland. The team's in-house poet, Cyril Harvey, memorialised the building in camp verse:

> At 58, St James's Street
> The door is open wide
> Yet all who seek to enter here
> Must make their motives crystal clear
> Before they step inside,
> That none may probe with fell intent
> The Secrets of the Government.

Intercepted German spies were first interrogated at a secret military prison, Camp 020. Only then, if suitable for double-agent work, would they be handed over to Tar Robertson and his case officers. If they refused to collaborate, they were either imprisoned, or executed. Sometimes the death threat was overt. Masterman was unsentimental on this score. 'Some had to perish, both to satisfy the public that the security of the country was being maintained, and also to convince the Germans that the others were working properly and were not under control.' All but the most fanatical Nazis agreed to co-operate when faced with this choice, but their motives did not follow any established pattern. Some were merely terrified, desperate to save their skins, but there were also, Masterman found, 'certain persons who have a natural predilection to live in that curious world of espionage and deceit, and who attach themselves with equal facility to one side or the other, so long as their craving for adventure of a rather macabre type is satisfied'.

If the intercepted spy was considered suitable, then the hard work began, starting with a strenuous exercise of the imagination. In Masterman's words, the case officer must penetrate the world of his adopted spy, to 'see with the eyes and hear with the ears of his agent', and create for him a life as close as possible to the one he was pretending to live. If, say, the double agent was claiming to transmit from Aylesbury, then he needed to know what Aylesbury was like and, if possible, to be physically in or very near Aylesbury, since it was suspected that the Germans could pinpoint transmissions, perhaps to within a one-mile radius.

The logistical challenge was immense. Each double agent required a safe house and a staff of at least five people: a case officer, a wireless operator to monitor or transmit his messages, two guards on twelve-hour shifts to ensure he did not run away, and a trusted housekeeper to look after and feed the group. Meanwhile, the case officer had to establish what his agent had been sent to find out, and then reproduce a fake facsimile of it, but without damaging the war effort. An agent who transmitted useless information would be seen as a failure by the Abwehr, and dropped. To maintain German confidence, the double agent must send a mixture of true but essentially harmless information known as 'chickenfeed', extraneous facts, and undetectably false titbits, along with whatever disinformation was agreed upon.

Deciding what could or could not be sent to the enemy was the delicate task of the Twenty Committee. Meanwhile the double agent must be kept busy and happy, because if he turned bad, and somehow managed to inform his German spymasters that he was under British control, then the entire system would be jeopardised. Every double agent, Masterman observed, 'is prone to be vain, moody and introspective, and therefore idleness, which begets brooding, should be of all things most carefully avoided'. Tar Robertson swiftly discovered that, in order to keep these agents sweet, it was sensible to reward them, and not just with their lives. The 'principle of generosity' was thus established, and agents who had brought over cash, as many did, were often allowed to keep a percentage.

The ideal case officer needed to be a combination of guard, friend, psychologist, radio technician, paymaster, entertainments organiser and private nursemaid. It helped if he or she was also a saint, since the individual being cosseted and coaxed in this way was quite likely to be extremely unpleasant, greedy, paranoid, treacherous and, at least initially, an enemy of Britain. Finally, all of the above had to be performed at breakneck speed, because the longer a spy took to make contact with the enemy, the more likely his German spymaster would suspect that he had been captured and turned.

The results show just how brilliantly Tar Robertson chose the men and women 'of high intelligence and clearly defined purpose' who made up his team. Some 480 suspected enemy spies were detained in Britain in the course of the war. Just seventy-seven of these were German. The rest were, in descending order of magnitude, Belgian, French, Norwegian and Dutch, and then just about every conceivable race and nationality, including several who were stateless. After 1940, very few were British. Of the total intercepted, around a quarter were subsequently used as double agents, of whom perhaps forty made a significant contribution. Some of these lasted only a short time before their cases were terminated; a few continued to delude their German handlers until the end of the war. A tiny handful, the very best, were involved in the greatest strategic deception of all, Operation Fortitude, by which the Germans were persuaded to believe that the Allied invasion of France would be concentrated on the Pas de Calais, and not Normandy.

As early as 1942, Tar Robertson's team could be justly proud of its efforts. Scores of spies had been rounded up with the aid of the Most Secret Sources, and many had been recruited as double agents. Yet the B1A team remained in a state of deep anxiety, beset by the possibility that a spy could slip through the mesh, attempt to contact an agent already operating in Britain, discover that he was being controlled, and then blow the entire double-cross network.

Those fears were exacerbated when the body of a man named Englebertus Fukken, alias William Ter Braak, was discovered in

Cambridge. A Dutch agent, Ter Braak had parachuted into Britain in November 1940 but five months later, after running out of money, he had climbed into a public air-raid shelter and shot himself in the head with his German pistol. If Ter Braak could survive undetected in Britain for so long, then other German agents must be at large. Masterman voiced the nagging fear of every wartime spycatcher: 'We were obsessed by the idea that there might be a large body of spies over and above those whom we controlled.'

Moreover, MI5 could not ignore the exceptionally low grade of the spies it had caught. Indeed, the level of ineptitude among the captured spies was such that some in the intelligence service wondered if they were being deliberately planted as decoys: 'Could any intelligence service let alone one run by the super-efficient Germans, be so incompetent?' wondered Ewen Montagu, the naval intelligence officer on the Twenty Committee. Perhaps the Germans were training up a troop of super-spies to follow the dubious duds they had sent over to date. Perhaps an altogether better class of spy was already lurking undetected in Britain, or on the way?

Tar Robertson's spy-hunters therefore pricked up their ears when, early in February 1942, a reference to a hitherto unknown agent, codenamed Fritz, was picked up by British interceptors, decoded by Bletchley Park, and passed to the intelligence services. To judge from the intercepts, the Germans were taking a great deal of trouble over Fritz, who was also referred to as 'C', and sometimes as 'E'. In May, the Paris branch of the Abwehr was instructed to buy a new set of clothes for Fritz. The following week, Nantes demanded a new wireless set from the stocks of captured British equipment. In June, the listeners discovered, some 9,500 francs had been spent on his teeth, damaged during a failed parachute jump – more money than most German spies were allocated for an entire mission.

The Nantes Abwehr began to refer to Fritz as Fritzchen, the diminutive form of the name, suggesting a certain intimacy with this new recruit. From the Most Secret Sources it appeared that Stephan von Gröning, already identified by British intelligence as head of the Nantes Abwehr branch, was particularly taken with Fritz. In June he boasted to Paris that Fritz could 'now prepare sabotage material unaided'. In July he insisted that Fritz was utterly loyal, declaring that 'any connection with the enemy is out of the question'. Paris, more sceptical, replied by wondering if the word 'not' had been accidentally omitted from Von Gröning's message.

Meanwhile, the Radio Security Service reported that Fritz, plainly a novice wireless operator, was practising Morse from the Nantes Abwehr branch, using a variation of the Vigenère code known as Gronsfeld. At first his transmissions had been clumsy, and when he tried to transmit faster he merely succeeded 'in making corrupt characters and in fumbling', but he was improving rapidly. 'When he arrives in this country,' the Radio Security Service reported, 'he will send his messages in English.' After listening to Fritz 'practically every day for several weeks' the interceptor had 'learned to recognise his unmistakable style and to record its peculiarities', the telltale 'fist'. His messages sometimes ended with a cheery '73', shorthand for 'Best regards', or 'FF', meaning 'Is my message decipherable?'; he routinely signed off with the laughing sign, 'HU HU HA HO', then the insulting '99', meaning 'go to hell', or words to that effect. Fritz was turning into a first-rate radio operator, even if his messages were rather peculiar, and sometimes positively offensive.

By late summer, MI5 had assembled a thick dossier on Fritz. But they still did not know his real name, his mission, or the date and time of his planned arrival in Britain. And as for the identity of this shadowy associate nicknamed Bobby the Pig, with the regal appetite and the elephantine toilet habits, that, too, remained a mystery.

The Mosquito

One morning, Von Gröning handed Chapman a gun: a shiny American Colt revolver, with a loaded chamber. Chapman had never held a gun before. When he asked why he needed this weapon, Von Gröning replied vaguely that he might want it 'to shoot his way out of any difficulties he might encounter'. Leo taught him how to aim and fire it, using a target erected in the grounds of La Bretonnière, and soon he claimed he could hit a franc coin from 50 feet away.

The revolver was just one sign of Von Gröning's growing trust. The cadaverous Praetorius no longer shadowed his every step, and he was allowed to take walks alone with Bobby, though instructed to remain close to the villa. He was permitted to move out of his top-floor room (having carefully disguised the holes in the wainscoting) and into a bedroom in the gardener's cottage, so that he could practise mixing explosives and incendiary mixtures in the laboratory whenever he desired. The homemade bombs were getting bigger, and more sophisticated. He practised making underwater fuses, and tossing them into the duckpond. There were various tree stumps in the grounds, and Chapman was encouraged to try blowing them up. On one occasion he packed too much dynamite into a large oak stump, which exploded with such force that chunks of burning wood were blasted into the garden of the house next door, narrowly missing a neighbour. Von Gröning was livid. Chapman was not

quite the explosives expert he thought he was. While attempting
to construct a sulphuric acid fuse, the volatile mixture exploded,
burning his hand, singeing off a hank of hair and covering his
face with smuts. A French doctor bandaged the hand, and
Chapman took to his bed. 'I was suffering more from shock
than anything,' he wrote later.

Visitors continued to arrive at La Bretonnière, some to inspect
Chapman's progress, others to talk to Von Gröning or to
undergo training. One of these was a Frenchman referred to
only as 'Pierre', a collaborator with round glasses who, in
Chapman's words, 'made all the right Heil Hitler noises'. Pierre
belonged to a Breton separatist group, 'Bretagne pour les
Bretons', and he was undergoing training as a fifth columnist
in case an Allied invasion forced a German withdrawal. On
another occasion Chapman was allowed to be present during a
meeting with two men, one of whom was introduced as
'Monsieur Ferdinand' and the other, a lad of about eighteen,
who appeared quite petrified. These were members of a Gaullist
cell, apparently planning to leave France via an established escape
route and join the Free French in London. Monsieur Ferdinand,
it seemed, was prepared to smuggle Chapman along with them,
for the right price. Von Gröning was clearly exploring alternative
ways to get Chapman into Britain.

Von Gröning and his protégé grew closer. Chapman's own
father had been distant, when he wasn't absent entirely, and he
had not seen him now for a decade. Von Gröning, avuncular and
apparently kindly, stepped into the role. The affection was not
feigned on either part. In the evenings, while Von Gröning
soaked up the brandy, Chapman would listen rapt as the older
man talked of art, music and literature. They discovered a shared
pleasure in the novels of H.G. Wells and the poetry of Tennyson. Very occasionally Von Gröning would stray into politics or
military matters. He remained convinced that Germany would
win the war, and that any attempt by the Allies to invade France
would result in 'a tremendous bloodbath'; but his was the

assessment of an experienced soldier, not a statement of ideology. To Chapman's surprise, he praised the tactical skill of the Allied invasion of North Africa, and described the British raid on nearby St Nazaire as 'very cleverly planned and excellently carried out'. In August the Allies launched the disastrous Dieppe raid on France's northern coast, with the loss of 4,000 men killed, wounded, or captured. The German victory was celebrated with a party at La Bretonnière, but Von Gröning also raised a toast to the 'courage and daring' of the Allied commandos.

If Von Gröning's view of the war was nuanced and balanced, then that of his deputy was precisely the opposite. Praetorius and Von Gröning had never warmed to one another. Praetorius regarded his boss as the snobbish remnant of an old world, while the younger man was altogether too enthralled by Hitler for Von Gröning's liberal tastes. The young Nazi insisted the scale of Russian losses meant victory on the Eastern Front was imminent. Stalingrad would fall in 1943, to be followed by a 'full-scale attack on Britain with all main forces from Europe and the Russian Front'. Rommel would conquer all, he insisted, while the prospect of a 'terrific Blitz' on Britain, the land he so admired, sent Praetorius into spasms of delight: 'You can imagine what it would be like with all of our Stukas and all of the men who have been trained and hardened and toughened,' Praetorius exclaimed. 'What could the Americans do?' Chapman was beginning to find him extremely irritating.

One morning in mid-summer, Von Gröning instructed Chapman to pack his bags: he was going to Berlin with 'Thomas' for the next phase of his training. In the early hours of a foggy morning, the train from Paris pulled up in a small railway station on the outskirts of the German capital. A car was waiting for them. Chapman asked where they were heading. Praetorius seemed tense and embarrassed. 'It is rather awkward at the present moment because if anyone realises you are British we should both be shot without any questions being asked.' He then

added politely: 'Would you mind not asking any more questions?' They seemed to be passing through densely wooded
suburbs, but it was still dark outside and the driver had deliberately dimmed his headlights, so that Chapman could see almost
nothing. From the faint shimmer of dawn on the horizon, he
judged they were heading north.

After a drive of twenty-five minutes, they passed through a
pair of iron gates guarded by three sentries in military uniform,
down a long drive lined with flower beds and through a high
stone arch, before pulling up in front of a small *Schloss* with a
tower, surrounded by trees, a high stone wall and barbed wire
fences. At the door stood a man in early middle age, short but
athletically built, with a dignified air. His wife, rather taller,
hovered anxiously in the background; pictures of their children
were arranged in the hall. The little man introduced himself as
'Herr Doktor'. He explained that Chapman was free to wander
the castle grounds between lessons, but should on no account try
to leave the estate.

Wojch had been a skilled teacher of practical sabotage, but
Chapman's new tutor was in a different league. Over the next
week Chapman would be given an intensive course in the very
latest explosive technology, by a master of the subject. MI5 later
identified him as one Dr Ackerman, a professional chemist, and
one of the most knowledgeable explosives experts in Germany.
Chapman was shown into a laboratory, with rows of cork-
stopped glass bottles, test tubes, thermos flasks, measuring scales,
pestles and mortars. Patiently, painstakingly, the expert introduced Chapman to an unimagined universe of lethal science, the
arcane secrets of explosives, burning mixtures, booby traps and
delayed sabotage.

He taught Chapman how to make a time-fuse from a cheap
wristwatch, by inserting a small screw with two nuts on it into
the celluloid face and then attaching one end of electrical wire
connected to a torch battery via the winding mechanism; when
the small hand touched the screw, a charge would pass from the

battery into a fuse and ignite the explosion. Next he took an alarm clock, and demonstrated how to delay an explosion for up to fourteen hours, by linking the detonator to the winding spring. If no clock or watch was available, he could make a fuse by filling an ink bottle with sulphuric acid, and placing a strip of cardboard between glass and lid; the acid would slowly eat away the cardboard, finally making contact with the fuse screwed into the lid, where the heat of the reaction would detonate the explosive charge.

Next, he took a large lump of coal from the scuttle, and showed Chapman how to drill a hole in it 6-inches deep and pack this with explosives and detonator, disguising the hole with plasticine, boot polish and coal dust. Placed in the coalbunkers of a ship or train, the device would be invisible and inert, until shovelled into the furnace where the heat would ignite the explosion.

Chapman was taught how to dynamite munitions trains and petrol dumps, how to pack an attaché case with explosives and then place pyjamas or a towel on top, to muffle the alarm–clock fuse inside. He learned how to construct a booby trap from a package that exploded when the string around a parcel was cut: inside the string were two strands of wire insulated from one another, so that when cut with scissors an electric circuit was completed, setting off the explosion. Ackerman drew diagrams showing how to connect a series of linked explosives with dynamite wire and detonating fuse, and explained the formula for calculating how much high explosive would be needed to bring down a bridge (*length x breadth x depth x 2 = number of grams of explosive required*). Some of Ackerman's techniques were diabolically cunning: placing a dead butterfly over the wire detonator attached to a railway line would ensure the casual observer would never spot the device, and when the train passed over, the charge would explode, derailing the locomotive.

The little explosives teacher neither smoked nor drank, and paused only for meals. Chapman decided he was a perfectionist:

'He insisted on exact proportions, never hurrying, grinding everything very small and mixing it very carefully.' The ingredients needed to create a bomb could be bought over the counter at British chemists, Ackerman explained: potassium chlorate was a common slug killer, potassium nitrate, a fertiliser, potassium permanganate, a throat gargle; the British used ferric oxide as a floor stain, and ground aluminium as a silver paint powder. The lectures ran on late into the evening. After supper, Ackerman would pull up a chair beside the fire and continue his tutorials, sometimes calling on Praetorius to help translate technical terms.

After five days, the doctor finally seemed satisfied, and Chapman was exhausted. He and Praetorius were picked up by the same driver in the middle of the night, and driven back to the station in darkness.

Back at La Bretonnière, Chapman was warmly greeted by Von Gröning, who announced that he had devised a small test for him. A friend, one Major Meier, was responsible for security in the local factories, including the nearby Battignolle locomotive works. Von Gröning had boasted to Meier that he was training up a sabotage agent, a former burglar who could break into anything; he bet he could even place a dummy bomb in the locomotive factory. Major Meier had accepted the wager. A few nights later, Chapman and Leo hauled themselves over the barbed wire surrounding the factory, slipped passed the slumbering guard and placed a package, addressed to Major Meier, alongside the main office. Von Gröning was delighted; with the money from the wager he threw yet another party in honour of 'Fritz'.

Chapman went back to his mephitic potions in the gardener's cottage. The successful raid on the locomotive works had been enjoyable, but after nearly five months in La Bretonnière, he was growing bored, and frustrated by the enforced chastity. Leaving aside the whores of Nantes, he had barely seen a woman. The others laughed about the lack of female company, joking that they lived 'like bloody monks'.

One evening, Chapman, Albert and Wojch went out on a 'spree' in Nantes, where they picked up some girls in one of the official cars. Unluckily, a Gestapo officer spotted the women climbing into their car and an official complaint was filed. When it reached Von Gröning's desk, he exploded. 'There was a hell of a lot of trouble,' Chapman wrote. Wojch suffered the brunt of Von Gröning's fury: the rotund saboteur with the pearl tie-pin was banished to a unit of the Wachkommando based in distant Rocquencourt near Paris. Chapman never saw him again. In a message to his bosses, Von Gröning noted primly that Fritz, though ideal in every other respect, was apparently prone to what he called 'undesirable emotional activity'.

As always, when bored and sexually stymied, Chapman lapsed into what he called his 'nihilistic' frame of mind. His mood darkened still further when he raised a subject that had been troubling him ever since leaving Romainville, and asked for permission to write to Tony Faramus. Von Gröning refused, but said he would send the young man a food parcel. A little later, Chapman inquired once more: 'Could something be done for him?' Von Gröning told him that this was 'impossible', and changed the subject. Chapman now descended into a dark depression. He would lie on his bed for hours, smoking, and staring at the ceiling. At one point he even asked 'if he could return to the camp at Romainville'. Von Gröning realised that unless he moved fast, and put Chapman to work, he might lose this mercurial young spy prodigy altogether.

On 29 August 1942, Chapman was summoned to Von Gröning's study and presented with a typed sheet of paper. He was told to read it and, if he agreed with the terms, to sign it. The document was a contract, a formally executed agreement to spy on his own country that is surely unique in the annals of legal history. The first section was a list of prohibitions: Chapman must never divulge to anyone the names of his German contacts in Jersey, France or Germany, the places he had been, or the things he had learned. The penalty for violating any of these clauses would be death. Chapman would undertake to spy in the interests of the German High Command, and faithfully perform whatever mission he was set by the Abwehr. As compensation, he would be paid the following sums: while in France he would receive 12,000 francs a month; from the date of his departure, he would be paid 300 Reichsmarks a month, and payment would continue should he be captured; on his return, having completed his mission to the satisfaction of the Abwehr, he would receive the sum of 150,000 Reichsmarks. Chapman estimated this was the equivalent of about £15,000 – in fact, the value was nearer to £250, or around £7,300 at today's prices. The contract was not with the German government, but a personal legal agreement between Chapman and his spymaster: Von Gröning had already signed it, in the name S. Graumann (Doktor).

The final clause was a triumph of German bureaucratic thinking: Chapman would be legally obliged to pay all relevant taxes on these sums in France. The German secret service was about to send Chapman on a mission of treachery in which it was likely he would be killed or executed, and they were worrying about his tax return.

As Chapman was digesting the terms of this extraordinary deal, the German spymaster asked him a question. If Scotland Yard caught him, approximately how many years could Chapman expect to spend in prison? Chapman had considered that question many times himself. He replied that he would probably receive a sentence of between fifteen and twenty years. The older man then turned to Praetorius and observed: 'I don't suppose there would be much danger of him surrendering to the police then.'

Chapman signed the contract, but later found himself pondering that apparently offhand comment. Graumann, a man he had come to admire, had chosen him not because he was special, but because he was a criminal with a past so crooked he would never dare run to the authorities. Chapman had always known that was part of the German calculation, but the remark stung, and it stuck.

Filing away the signed contract, Von Gröning began, for the first time, to outline Chapman's mission: in a few weeks he would be parachuted into Britain with a wireless and enough money to survive for a long period. He would then find a place to hide out and gather a quantity of explosives, with help from his criminal associates if needed. There were many important tasks Chapman could perform in Britain, but his primary target was to sabotage the aircraft factory manufacturing the Mosquito bomber in Hatfield, Hertfordshire.

The De Havilland Mosquito – or *Anopheles de Havillandus* as military wags liked to call it – had proved a lethal nuisance to the Nazis ever since it went into production in 1940. Indeed, its effect on the German High Command was positively malarial. Designed and built at the De Havilland Aircraft Company factory outside London, it was a revolutionary military aircraft. Constructed almost entirely of wood, with a two-man crew and no defensive guns, the little plane could carry 4,000 lbs of bombs to Berlin. With two Rolls-Royce Merlin engines and a top speed of 400 mph it could usually outrun enemy fighters. The Mosquito, nicknamed 'the Wooden Wonder', could be assembled, cheaply, by cabinetmakers and carpenters. It could be used for photo-reconnaissance, night-fighting, U-boat killing, mine-laying and transport, but its main task was target bombing, and being so light and accurate it could destroy a single building with minimal harm to civilians. In the course of the war, Mosquitoes would pick off the Gestapo Headquarters in Oslo, Shell House in Copenhagen, and Amiens Jail.

Reichsmarschall Hermann Göring, Head of the Luftwaffe, was particularly infuriated by the persistent little Mosquito; the mere mention of the plane could send him into a rage. 'It makes me furious when I see the Mosquito,' he once ranted. 'I turn green and yellow with envy. The British, who can afford aluminium better than we can, knock together a beautiful wooden aircraft that every piano factory over there is building, and they give it a speed that they have now increased yet again. What do you make of that? There is nothing the British do not have. They have the geniuses and we have the nincompoops. After the war is over I'm going to buy a British radio set – then at least I'll own *something* that has always worked.'

For reasons therefore both military and political, the Abwehr had been devising a plan to combat the Mosquito for months. If the De Havilland production line could be stopped, by crippling the factory boilers and generator, this could tip the air war in Germany's favour, demonstrate the worth of Von Gröning's new agent, and boost the Abwehr's reputation. It might also mollify the irascible Reichsmarschall.

That afternoon, Von Gröning sent an exultant wireless message to Paris, reporting that he had conducted 'preliminary detailed discussions' with Fritz, and persuaded him to sign a contract. The message was picked up in Britain, where the MI5 officer monitoring the Fritz traffic remarked ominously: 'Things seem at last to be coming to a head.'

9

Under Unseen Eyes

The contract in Chapman's hands may have been legally un-enforceable, signed with a false name, and frankly absurd, but it had the desired psychological effect. The prospect of adventure sent Chapman's spirits soaring once more. The drunken camaraderie of La Bretonnière was pleasant, to be sure, but at the back of his mind was Freda and the baby in England; also Betty; also Vera, his ex-wife; and, if none of the aforementioned worked out, then any number of Soho sirens.

The days accumulated in a succession of tests, trials, details and delays. The ugly spycatcher from Angers returned, in a 'terrific Chrysler with a wireless', to witness a demonstration of Chapman's sabotage and shooting skills: he shot a line of wine glasses from fifteen paces, one after the other, and set off an acid fuse. The next performance was for a colonel from a Panzer division, who appeared in a Mercedes: Chapman blew up a tree stump in a timed explosion using batteries and a wristwatch. The same evening Von Gröning announced that he had tickets for the Folies-Bergère, the music hall that was still playing to full houses in occupied Paris. Chapman was excited at the prospect of a night out in Paris, although his pleasure palled somewhat when he overheard Von Gröning remark on the train that 'the chief wanted to see him'. Chapman was not being taken to enjoy the spectacle; once again, he *was* the spectacle.

That evening, as they entered the famous opera house in the 9th Arrondissement, Chapman heard his spymaster whisper to Thomas: 'Let Fritz go first, and *he* will just sit behind.' The show was already underway in a froth of petticoated dancers doing the can-can, when two men in civilian clothes quietly entered and sat directly behind them. One had a moustache and a pronounced limp: 'He kept looking at me the whole time, sort of behind his programme,' Chapman recalled. This individual was most probably Rudolf Bamler, head of Abwehr counter-intelligence and one of the few die-hard Nazis in the organisation. After the show Von Gröning left by taxi, while Praetorius and Thomas walked back to the hotel, pausing to look in the shop windows: 'Each time I looked,' wrote Chapman. 'I saw these two men very carefully studying me.'

Chapman was relieved to get back to the Grand Hotel. As he and Praetorius walked to their rooms, he heard American voices coming from Von Gröning's suite. He turned to his minder: 'Americans?'

'No, it's just two of our fellows having a game,' said Praetorius, quickly. But that evening, by opening a cupboard door and pressing his ear to the folding partition that separated his room from that of Von Gröning, he was sure he could hear his chief talking to two Americans. One of them was saying: 'Well, we would like to see the guy.' Chapman felt certain the 'guy' was him; he recalled that Graumann had remarked that if the De Havilland sabotage was successful, he would be sent on 'a big mission to America'.

La Bretonnière had offered a brief feeling of freedom, but now he had the sensation of being watched and monitored as surely as if he had been back in prison with the warders spying through the slot in the iron door. Everyone, it seemed, was keeping an eye on Chapman: his comrades in Nantes, senior Nazi officials, American spies and even, perhaps, his own countrymen.

One night, in the Café de France in Nantes, Chapman caught sight of a young man regarding him intently from a corner table.

Von Gröning had warned that he was 'in all probability being watched by the British', and had shown him some photographs of suspected agents, none of whom he recognised. Now he was convinced he was being tailed. The fellow was in his twenties, well built, with a side parting, a grey suit and a 'West End' look to him that seemed oddly familiar. Chapman looked away, disconcerted, and when he looked back a moment later, the man had vanished. Chapman did not mention the incident to Von Gröning, but the urge to escape grew stronger: he must get to Britain, before the British got to him.

In September, Chapman was escorted back to Ackerman's *Schloss* in Berlin, arriving once more in the dead of night. 'You have remembered everything,' the little German chemist declared, after he had thoroughly tested his pupil. 'I am highly satisfied with you.' The scientist then launched into a detailed disquisition on exactly how to blow up the De Havilland plant. If the boilers were linked, he should explode the central one using 15 kilograms of dynamite packed into an attaché case and a delay fuse of at least half an hour. The blast should wreck the other two, and three 80-ton boilers, the scientist explained, would mean 240 tons of matter 'exploding in all directions', which should destroy the generator at the same time.

The chemist departed, to be replaced by an older man in civilian clothes, who announced, in English, that he had come to instruct Fritz in the use of 'secret ink'. From a briefcase, he produced a sheet of white paper, and what appeared to be a matchstick with a white head. Chapman was instructed to place the writing paper on a newspaper, and then clean the paper on both sides for ten minutes using a wad of cotton wool wiped 'in a rotary motion'. The paper was placed on a sheet of glass, and Chapman was shown how to sketch a message in block capitals using the matchstick, each word separated by dashes. The stick left no visible mark. Chapman was told he could now write in pencil on both sides of the paper, or in ink on the reverse side from the secret writing, as if it was an ordinary letter. The man then vanished, taking the scribbled sheets. When he returned a few hours later, the paper had been immersed in some sort of chemical solution and the secret message had emerged, 'a faint greeny colour', behind the scrawled pencil. The Professor (as Chapman now christened him) handed over two more matchstick pens, and told him to practise his secret writing twice a week. The letters would be forwarded to him, and he would assess their proficiency.

Chapman returned to Nantes by plane and parachute. After taking off from Le Bourget, a Junkers bomber dropped him in a field near the town airfield. The Nantes unit had been deployed in the area as a reception committee, but Chapman made his own way to the airfield and announced himself to the sentry as 'Fritz'.

Back at la Bretonnière, Von Gröning covered the dining table with hundreds of aerial photographs of potential landing spots – Britain spread out 'like a mosaic'. They agreed that the village of Mundford, north of Thetford in Norfolk, would be ideal, being rural and sparsely populated, but still reasonably near London. He was then shown aerial photographs of the De Havilland factory in Hatfield, pinpointing the precise location of the boiler room.

In preparation for blending in to a country he had not seen for three years, Chapman listened to the BBC at night, and studied the English newspapers along with a London guidebook to refresh his memory of the city streets. Leo was sent to Dieppe to obtain British equipment left over from the raid, while Von Gröning travelled to Berlin in person to collect English paper currency. Chapman was photographed, in a studio in Nantes, to obtain images for his fake identity cards. In it he is leaning forward towards the camera, in matinee idol pose, an oddly intense look on his face. You can almost see the strain of waiting behind his eyes.

The arrangements seemed to gather pace, the final threads weaving together. But then one evening, to Chapman's astonishment, he was taken aside by his German spymaster and asked if he wanted to back out of the mission altogether. 'Look, don't think we're forcing you to go to England, because we have other work if you don't want to go.'

'No,' Chapman replied, momentarily stunned. 'I want to go to England.'

Von Gröning continued: 'If you feel you're not confident that you can do these things, don't go. There's plenty of other work for you here, we can use you on other things.'

Chapman protested that he was ready and able: 'I think I can do what I was set out to do.'

Von Gröning's next suggestion was even more disquieting: would Chapman like Leo to accompany him on this assignment? Chapman had to think fast. With Leo as a minder, his freedom of action would be seriously curtailed, and if the toothless little thug suspected Chapman's motives, he would kill him, on the spot, possibly with his bare hands.

'I don't think that would advisable,' he said quickly. 'Probably one could get through whereas two wouldn't, especially as Leo doesn't speak English.'

Von Gröning dropped the subject, but it had been an unsettling exchange. Was the German warning him, or trying to protect him? He need not have worried; it was another test of his resolve. On 24 September, Von Gröning sent a message to Paris headquarters: 'Fritz is spiritually and physically undoubtedly absolutely fit.'

Like every sprawling bureaucracy, the Abwehr combined nitpicking with inefficiency: first they obtained the wrong type of parachute; then the Luftwaffe seemed unable to locate the correct plane. A bomber was too noisy for a nighttime drop, so inquiries were made for a transport plane from Russia, or the Middle East. The repeated delays frayed everybody's nerves. Finally a Focke-Wulf reconnaissance plane was located, at which point somebody pointed out that several agents had been injured during parachute jumps, so perhaps Fritz should instead be taken to the coast by boat, and then rowed to shore in a rubber dinghy. But what sort of boat?

After much argument, it was agreed to send Fritz by plane. That decision soon became bogged down in a new debate over the drop zone. If Fritz aimed for Thetford, it was argued, the plane might be shot down by night fighters operating around London. The Cambrian Mountains were suggested as an alternative by someone who had plainly never been there. Paris duly instructed Nantes: 'Show Fritz photos of the Cambrian Mountains.' Chapman took one look at these, and dug in his heels. Being dropped over the flatlands of Norfolk was alarming enough, but landing on a frozen Welsh hillside in the middle of winter was a different prospect altogether. Finally, grudgingly, he backed down, and said that if the Abwehr really believed these mountains were 'safer than anywhere else', then so be it. The Welsh hills became the 'new operational objective' and Paris ordered that Fritz be 'made familiar in every detail with conditions in the Cambrian Mountains and means of getting from there to London'. But a few days later the Paris Abwehr chief, exercising every boss's right of irrational self-contradiction, reverted to the original idea, and Mundford was again selected as the target.

Then, in November, just as it seemed all the wrinkles had been ironed out, the entire mission was put on hold. The war lurched into a new phase, Hitler decided to occupy the whole of France, and Chapman was suddenly drafted into the German army.

For several months, the Nazi leadership had been observing the Vichy regime with mounting concern. Since the French collapse in 1940, the collaborationist French government in Vichy, under Henri Philippe Pétain, had been allowed to rule the unoccupied portion of southern France as a puppet-state under Nazi control. But after the Vichy Admiral François Darlan signed an armistice with the Allies in Algeria, Hitler decided to violate the 1940 agreement by invading the zone under Vichy control, in an operation codenamed 'Case Anton'. Every available man would be drafted in to aid the new military occupation, including Eddie Chapman.

The member of the Nantes Abwehr section, now Truppe 3292 of Abwehrkommando 306, were formally attached to an SS division and ordered to head south. The spies donned military clothing: Von Gröning wore the full regalia of a cavalry officer, with double-breasted leather trench coat and forage cap, Praetorius his SS uniform, and the others a variety of military outfits. They looked like the cast of a Gilbert and Sullivan opera. Chapman himself was ordered to dress up in the field green uniform of a lance corporal in the German marines, with a gold-trimmed collar and a yellow swastika armband. He was faintly disappointed that his uniform had no epaulettes, but he was allowed to carry his gun.

On 12 November 1942, Thomas and the others climbed into the Mercedes, while Chapman travelled with Von Gröning in a second car, along with spare tins of petrol, food, and an arsenal of automatic weapons. As they sped south, Chapman passed lines of SS soldiers heading in the same direction and a column of troop-laden trucks that stretched for five miles. French men and women watched from the roadside. To Chapman, some of the bystanders seemed 'shocked, frightened and resentful' but most appeared 'apathetic'. 'There were no scenes or anything,' he noted, 'they just refused to speak and looked very surly as we drove past.' At crossroads and checkpoints, the French gendarmes waved them through and saluted smartly, greeting an occupation they could do nothing to prevent. Several times, the Abwehrkommandos stopped for refreshments, and by the time they reached Limoges, Von Gröning's little war party was, as always, well oiled.

In Limoges, the troop took up billets in a small hotel and linked up with another unit under the command of one Major Reile, a Gestapo officer, who informed them they would be raiding the homes of suspected enemy agents. Armed with pistols and submachine guns, Chapman and the men followed Von Gröning to an apartment building, where they knocked down the door of a flat belonging to one Captaine le Saffre. The suspect had fled, leaving papers strewn everywhere. While the men ransacked the flat, Chapman picked up a handful of papers and stuffed them in his pocket.

At the next house, the troop broke in to find two terrified old ladies cowering under a bed. Von Gröning was dismayed, and even more embarrassed when the women stammered that the man they were looking for had been dead for two years. The German aristocrat had no taste for Gestapo work. By the end of the evening, his troop had raided a dozen houses, most of them empty or occupied by the wrong person, and gathered a grand total of five French suspects, including a seventeen-year-old boy. The terrified Frenchmen, protesting their innocence, were locked in a hotel bedroom without their trousers. Von Gröning later released them all. 'Why should I send them to a concentration camp?' he said. 'They may be guilty, but they may be innocent.' Back at the hotel, Chapman inspected the papers he had gathered from the flat, which appeared to be notes from a diary, 'Rendez-vous with so-and-so at such and such an hour . . .'. He carefully destroyed them.

Truppe 3292's contribution to the occupation had been insignificant: they had netted some 'very small fry' and let them go, looted some booze, and frightened two old women. This still merited a slap-up dinner in celebration. It was Chapman's twenty-eighth birthday. On the way back to Nantes he wondered if his inclusion in the invasion had merely been another part of his training: 'I think it was to see what reaction I would have to the raid.' His reaction was a peculiar one: he had thoroughly enjoyed himself. It was perhaps a sign of his moral confusion, and the effect of living among Nazis for so long, that he would later recall this episode – the midnight raids, the smashing down of doors, the terrified people dragged from their beds, the wearing of his first swastika – as 'a lovely little trip'.

The Drop

The invasion of Vichy was Chapman's final test. Having dithered for so long, the Abwehr now swung into action with bewildering speed: Von Gröning announced that Chapman would be leaving for Britain within days. He reported that Fritz seemed 'visibly relieved' by the news. Paris had sent a questionnaire, a detailed list of the intelligence he might usefully supply from Britain, and together they rehearsed the details of his imminent mission.

He would be dropped over Mundford at around two in the morning. Simultaneously, a bombing raid would be carried out 'some place further inland' to draw off any night fighters. On landing he should dig a hole in an inconspicuous spot, and bury his parachute, overalls, helmet, jumping boots, leggings and entrenching tool. Every item would be British-made. Wearing his civilian clothes (they discussed obtaining a British army uniform, but rejected the idea) he should hide out somewhere until dawn and then, using a compass and map, make his way the thirty or so miles to Norwich and take a train to London. Once there, he should make contact with his old accomplice, the notorious Jimmy Hunt, and send his first transmission three days after landing, between 9.45 and 10.15 a.m.. Paris, Nantes and Bordeaux would all be listening out for his signal. Von Gröning here remarked that 'British red tape' would probably mean that if he were captured, it would take some time before British intelligence got around to using him for deception purposes. If there was a long delay, said Von Gröning, he would suspect the worst.

Most importantly his first message, and all subsequent messages, should be preceded by five Fs. This was his 'control sign', the agreed signal that he was operating of his own free will. If the message did not start FFFFF, Von Gröning would realise he had been caught and was transmitting under duress. Naturally, if someone was pretending to be Chapman, they would not know the agreed 'control sign', and Von Gröning would again conclude that he had been captured. Likewise, if a message was preceded by PPPPP, that would be an emergency warning that he was being watched by the security services or tailed by the police.

Thereafter, Chapman would be expected to transmit every morning between 9.45 and 10.15, on an all-mains transmitter of British manufacture taken from a captured British agent, which could be operated inside a room without an external aerial. He should transmit at a set frequency, and take five radio crystals in case of difficulties. All messages should be in English, using the same cipher system but a new code word: CONSTANTINOPLE.* If, for any reason, he could not use his transmitter, he was to insert the following advertisement in the personal column of *The Times*: 'Young couple require small country cottage near Elstree or Watford with modern conveniences.' He would then send messages, using the secret ink, to a safe house in neutral Portugal, addressed to:

Francisco Lopez Da Fonseca
Rua Sao Mamede 50-51
Lisbon

These would be picked up by a German agent in Lisbon, and forwarded to Von Gröning.

* See Appendix 1

The sabotage of the De Havilland aircraft factory (codenamed 'Walter', a reference to Praetorius/Thomas) was Chapman's primary mission, but not his sole objective. He should also gather and send information on US troop movements, particularly convoys, and note destination labels attached to railway freight cars, divisional signs, evidence of shipbuilding and any other military intelligence he could glean. He should also send weather reports to aid bombing raids, specifically describing cloud height, temperature, wind direction and strength, and visibility. To some extent, Chapman could use his own initiative. If the De Havilland premises proved impregnable, he might attack the aircraft propeller factory at Weybridge in Surrey, or sugar and rubber refineries, or merely do 'nuisance work' by leaving bombs in attaché cases in tube station luggage lockers. Von Gröning was reassuring: 'Take your time. Think of things very quietly. It doesn't matter if you don't succeed. Don't run any unnecessary risks. If you can come back we have something else for you to acquit, some other valuable task.' He could, if he wished, recruit more members of the Jelly Gang as accomplices.

In order to pay his criminal contacts, obtain the necessary explosives, and live generally, Chapman would be given £1,000 in used notes (worth approximately £33,000 today). That should be 'enough to be going on with', said Von Gröning, adding that more cash, if needed, could be provided through agents already in Britain. Von Gröning refused to identify these individuals, saying that contact would be arranged by radio. 'Of course our agents are there. We have them, we have the connections, but we have to be very, very careful not to take any risks.' Chapman wondered if Wojch had already been sent ahead to wait for him, help him, or, quite possibly, to spy on him.

Von Gröning continued his briefing. The day before Chapman was ready to carry out the sabotage he should send a message stating: 'Walter is ready to go,' and the time of the planned explosion. Reconnaissance planes would then monitor the effectiveness of the attack.

If Chapman was unlucky enough to fall into the hands of the British secret services, said Von Gröning, he should 'give as little information as possible, offer his services, and ask to be sent back to France'. Then he should immediately contact the Abwehr, which would employ him as a triple agent, after staging 'a number of small acts of sabotage' to convince the British of his bona fides.

Chapman's mission would last three months, after which he was to make his way back to France, in any one of three ways: a U-boat could be sent to pick him up off the English or Scottish coast, at a location to be arranged by wireless; alternatively, he could travel to the Republic of Ireland, where there were 'various people who would assist him to return'. The third and, Von Gröning stressed, the best escape route, would be to go to neutral Portugal. Once in Lisbon, he could make his way to the safe house on Rua Sao Mamede, introduce himself as Fritz to Senhor Fonseca, and give the password: 'Joli Albert'. Chapman's safe passage would then be arranged through the German consulate. Once back in France, he would receive his money, and a hero's welcome.

Von Gröning painted a tantalising picture of the financial and other rewards Chapman could expect from a grateful Third Reich. After making a report in Berlin, he would be sent on an extended 'holiday', with visits to all the major cities in Germany. He might be asked to carry out an important mission in the US, but he could be posted wherever he wished, and perhaps even receive his own Abwehr command. Chapman had once remarked that he would like to attend one of the great Berlin rallies where Hitler addressed the rapt crowds. Von Gröning promised that this could be arranged. Indeed, he would do more: he would get Chapman a good seat 'in the first or second row' even if it meant dressing him in the uniform of a high official. Von Gröning had never shown much enthusiasm for Hitler himself, but seemed only too happy to smuggle Chapman into a Nazi rally and place his spy as close as possible to the Führer.

Chapman judged this a good moment to raise, once again, the subject of Faramus in Romainville. Von Gröning was soothing. 'Don't you worry,' he said, 'we're going to send Faramus a parcel. I haven't had news from him myself but I'm going to look up the question and see what's happening about him – he'll be well looked after.'

If Chapman was reassured, he should not have been, for poor Faramus had by now been swallowed up by the Holocaust. No longer a hostage for Chapman's good behaviour, he was now but a mote in the toils of a murderous bureaucracy. Chapman believed that he still held his friend's life in his hands; in fact, even if he had failed or defected, no one would have remembered to kill Tony Faramus. He had been selected for death already. At the moment Chapman was packing his bags in Nantes, Faramus was being transported by cattle car to the Nazi concentration camp at Buchenwald.

Faramus had been summoned from his cell in Romainville without explanation, taken to a transit camp at Compiègne, and then loaded onto a cattle train with 120 other prisoners, in a truck intended for eight animals. Death came slowly, by suffocation, dysentery, thirst. After a few days, 'it was hard to tell the living from the dead, so small had become the margin between them'. The living stood shoulder to shoulder with the dead, for there was no room to fall. Five days after leaving Compiège, the death train drew up at Buchenwald, near Weimar. Of the 120 people packed into the truck, sixty-five were still alive, and those barely. Among the survivors was little Tony Faramus, who pondered, as he was led away to slavery: 'It was hard to believe that such carnage was the work of man.'

On 12 December 1942, Von Gröning threw a farewell party at la Bretonnière. A goose was killed and roasted, and toast after toast was drunk to the success of Chapman, Fritz, Little Fritz. Everyone sang *Lili Marlene*. Von Gröning, who had drunk to excess even by his own extreme standards, was in an ebullient mood: 'If you do this for us, you will have nothing more to worry about. Your whole future will be made when you come back. Don't you worry, it will be quite alright. I'll have another bottle of champagne with you.'

Praetorius ushered Chapman to one side. He seemed uncomfortable, fidgeting and twitching even more than usual, and whispered: 'I have rather an embarrassing thing to do, but for every agent we do it, but it is only matter of form and I hope you won't be insulted.'

'What is it?'

Praetorius explained that before heading to Britain, Chapman must be thoroughly searched, for any labels, receipts, tickets or other items from France or Germany that might indicate he was a spy from occupied territory. Chapman could not be allowed to leave with 'anything which could possibly be recognised as coming from us'.

'You don't mind?' Praetorius asked.

'Of course not.'

So far from objecting, Chapman was grateful for the inadvertent warning from 'Thomas'. When everyone else had staggered drunkenly to bed, Chapman took all the notes he had made, the radio frequencies, formulae, codes and names, and burned every scrap.

In the morning, a doctor arrived to give Chapman a full medical examination, and then, with Praetorius and Von Gröning standing over him, he packed his British canvas rucksack with everything that a German spy might possibly need in enemy territory, and much that he might not:

1 entrenching tool
1 wireless
1 Colt revolver, loaded, with spare chamber
2 handkerchiefs
12 detonators, carefully packed in sawdust in case he hit the ground hard
chocolate

grape jelly

1 hat

1 razor

1 compass

1 matchbox, with 'matches' for secret writing

1 pair spectacles (clear glass)

2 clean shirts

1 British army map

1 ID card in the name of George Clarke of Hammersmith

1 ID card in the name of Morgan O'Bryan of Dublin, electrical engineer.

Every item was either of British manufacture, or made to appear so. Even his wallet was filled with everyday items, taken from the dead at Dieppe: two deck-chair tickets, one Torquay golf club ticket, one YMCA hostel receipt, and family photographs, all of people Chapman had never met. Here, too, was Betty's love note on Royal Yacht Hotel headed paper, now badly creased and frayed – the only authentic item among the frauds.

With a peculiar expression, Von Gröning now handed Chapman a single brown pill, wrapped in a tiny cellophane package, explaining that Chapman could swallow it 'if there was any trouble'. The word 'trouble' did not need defining. Both men knew what happened to captured German spies; what might be done to a spy who was also British did not require elaboration.

Chapman bade farewell to the men of the unit, to Bobby the Pig, and to La Bretonnière, the only 'home', as he put it, he had known in ten years. He had found 'genuine comradeship' here, albeit with some remarkably nasty people. Before leaving, he handed Praetorius 500 francs, and told him to buy a drink for the boys.

That night Chapman, Von Gröning and Praetorius stayed at the Hôtel des Ambassadeurs in Paris. In the morning, Prateorius searched him as promised, and then handed over a canvas bag sealed with oilskin containing £990 in used notes of varying denominations. Had Chapman looked inside the moneybag, he might have spotted that the wads of money were held together by bands stamped 'Reichsbank, Berlin', with 'England' written on them in pencil. In an unbelievable act of thoughtlessness, the Abwehr had given Chapman a cash package that immediately identified him as a German spy. Having checked every inch of his clothing for clues, Praetorius had handed Chapman a death sentence in used notes.

Waiting at Le Bourget airfield was a Luftwaffe colonel whom Chapman recognised from his parachute practice. The colonel seemed to know all about Chapman's mission, for he discussed with him the merits of the Mosquito bomber, and the importance of halting its production. 'You have beautiful planes,' he added.

The colonel introduced a pilot, a tall, blond young man wearing an Iron Cross and struck Chapman as 'extremely shy', who then led Chapman across the tarmac towards a sleek black plane, 25-feet long with twin engines and machine guns mounted on each side. This, the pilot explained with pride, was a Focke-Wulf of the latest design, adapted for parachuting. A square section had been cut from the floor of the fuselage, and replaced by a wooden panel, wedged tight with packing material. Pulling a release handle caused the trap door to drop away. Chapman would be taken across the Channel by a three-man crew: the young pilot, Leutnant Fritz Schlichting, Überleutnant Karl Ischinger, the navigator and commander, and an *Unteroffizier* as wireless operator and gunner. They would be communicating by an intercom 'of the larynx type'. Chapman noticed that the pilot appeared to be deliberately standing in front of the control panel, as if to prevent his passenger from inspecting it.

At the hut, Chapman slipped his flying overalls on top of his civilian clothes, the old suit that he had taken to Jersey all those years ago. As he buttoned up the flying suit, strapped on his kneepads and laced up his landing boots, Chapman noticed that his hands were shaking.

There was a delay as they waited for a weather report from

Britain. Chapman smoked cigarette after cigarette. To make conversation, Chapman asked what the chances were of being shot down by flak or night fighters. The young pilot laughed, and said they could 'evade attack' using a device to deflect sound: from the ground the plane would appear to be at least one kilometre behind its actual position. Chapman realised that none of the crew was wearing a parachute, and felt a tiny surge of reassurance.

Shortly after 11 p.m. the pilot beckoned Chapman towards the plane. Von Gröning and the Luftwaffe colonel walked alongside as he clomped over the tarmac. It was slow going, encumbered by the knee pads and landing boots, the parachute and bulky kitbag strapped to his back. Chapman shook hands with the friend whose real name he did not know, who declared that the moment he received the first message from Fritz he would break out the champagne at La Bretonnière. 'We shall be waiting, the Colonel and I,' said Von Gröning. 'We shall definitely be waiting.'

Chapman squeezed through the cockpit hatch, and the pilot instructed him to kneel over the floor hole, facing the rear of the plane. The gunner was already seated at the rear. The navigator scrambled in behind.

At 11.25 the Focke-Wulf soared upwards from Le Bourget into the darkness. The sole illumination inside the cockpit was a tiny hand torch held by the wireless operator. As the plane banked, Chapman caught glimpses of many small lights in the distance. They climbed higher. He thought he could smell sea air. Suddenly the cockpit was freezing, despite the meagre warmth from a heater. The wireless man indicated that Chapman should strap on his oxygen mask. From time to time the navigator would write something on a small piece of paper, and hand it over his head to the pilot. If Chapman lay face down, the pack squeezed the breath out of him. On his knees, he was unable to straighten his back or turn around. Chapman felt cramp creeping up his body. Something warm and tickling ran over his chin. He had failed to strap the mask tightly enough;

blood was seeping from his nose. As they crossed over the English coast north of Skegness, he saw searchlights slicing the sky. The plane seemed to spiral down, the engines in a fighting scream, and then rose again. Passing over the Cambridgeshire fens, the Focke-Wulf performed a strange figure-of-eight dance in the sky. Chapman fastened his helmet and tied his parachute cord to a bolt overhead. The crew seemed unperturbed: 'Far from being nervous or apprehensive, they laughed and joked,' as if on a joy ride.

Chapman felt the pilot tap him on the back. He tore off the oxygen mask, got to his knees, and yanked the release handle. The trap door vanished beneath him, and he jolted downwards, but instead of falling through air, he was suspended, head down, on the underside of the plane, the air rushing past him, tearing his breath away. His outsized pack had caught on the sides of the hatch. He dangled, helpless, for what seemed like an age, but was in truth no more than ten seconds. Then he felt a blow in the small of his back – the boot of the wireless operator – and he was somersaulting down. A loud crack, a jolt, and the parachute obediently fluttered open above him. Suddenly it was utterly quiet. The blood dripped off his chin. In the far distance, he saw searchlights jousting in the dark. Below he heard the wail of a siren, signalling the all-clear. For a strange moment he wondered if that might be France down there, and not England. Could this be another of Von Gröning's tests? For twelve minutes, he drifted down through the still, windless night, towards a spot in the darkness below, which was at least twenty miles from where he was supposed to be.

11

Martha's Exciting Night

At 1.48 on the morning of 16 December, Sergeant Joseph Vail of the Littleport Police heard what he thought must be two separate planes, or one with two very powerful engines, over the west side of the town. An alert was immediately relayed to every police station in the area: 'Keep a close watch in area Wisbech – Downham Market – Ely as a plane has been spotted circling in the neighbourhood having come south from the Lincolnshire coast. Suggest it might be Nightcap, although not in expected area.' Another telephone call was made to a number in Whitehall, then another to the home of Major Tar Robertson, who got up, and put on his tartan trousers. At this point, Eddie Chapman's feet had not yet touched the ground.

Operation Nightcap was the codename for MI5's 'Fritz-trap'. As early as October a message had been intercepted revealing that Fritz would 'very soon be going on his holiday', and a warning had been sent to security service liaison officers in three different areas of the country to expect the arrival of an enemy agent:

Agent X is probably under 30 and about six feet tall. He may use the name Chapman. He speaks English, French and German. He is a trained wireless operator. It is possible that Agent X may be supplied with means of committing suicide e.g. poison tablets. On arrest he should therefore be

immediately searched, detained pending inquiries and sent
up to London under escort.

For months, British radio interceptors had monitored every
dot and dash of the Fritz traffic, until they imagined they knew
the man intimately. From the Most Secret Sources, the counter-
espionage team had obtained a broad idea of Fritz's mission,
although not of the plan to target the De Havilland Mosquito
factory. The traffic suggested that there were three possible drop-
zones: Mundford, North Norfolk, and the Cambrian Mountains, with the last-named regarded as the most probable.
Robertson had even discovered Fritz's real surname, although
this initially proved more of a red herring since MI5 had spent
several fruitless days investigating the entirely innocent Robert
William Chapman, a soldier who had been reported missing in
the Western Desert and who might, it was surmised, have been
recruited by the Abwehr while a prisoner of war.

The spycatchers of B1A knew the details of Fritz's dentistry,
the names on his fake ID cards, and even the approximate length
of his hair after the Most Secret Sources reported: 'It may be of
intelligence interest that Fritzchen said in clear at 1300 GMT
today that he "could not keep his schedule this morning as he
was having a hair cut".' They knew that his password was 'Joli
Albert', the colour of his boots, and the poisonous contents of his
turn-ups.

But MI5 also knew that the chance of catching Fritz, even
with the information from the Most Secret Sources, was slim.

There had been much debate within B-Division, the counter-
espionage branch of MI5, about the best way to ensnare him. A
full police dragnet, with roadblocks and house-to-house
searches, was rejected on the grounds that it offered 'too many
possibilities of leakage and subsequent press notices'. If an enemy
agent was alerted to the hunt, the Germans might realise that
their messages were being read, and the Most Secret Sources
must be protected at all costs. Another option was to prepare a

'flying column' of Field Security Police – or FSPs – the military police attached to the security service, which could be mobilised to the drop-zone at short notice. This, too, was rejected, since it might 'cause problems with local police and offer only a small chance of success'.

Finally, it was decided to set up a combination of traps, and hope that at least one was sprung. As soon as the Most Secret Sources received an indication that Fritz was on his way, Operation Nightcap would be mobilised, Dick White would be called at his private telephone number in London, and regional liaison officers and Fighter Command would be placed on alert. An intelligence officer stationed at Fighter Command would track incoming planes, and if an enemy aircraft was spotted that seemed to be heading for one of the three target areas, he would alert the night-duty officer at MI5, who would then contact the chief constable in the area with instructions to scour the countryside, but discreetly. If the plane was shot down, the parachutist would bail out and could then be picked up. If, however, the spy managed to land undetected, the police should 'comb out' boarding houses and hotels. Participants in Nightcap were told sternly: 'Whatever you do you should emphasise to all your collaborators the vital necessity of keeping the search as quiet as possible . . . the public must *not* be told that a parachute agent is being looked for.' If the police were asked why they were whacking every bush and looking up every tree, they should 'pretend to be looking for a deserter'.

Despite the elaborate preparations, MI5 was well aware that its net was full of holes. This was clearly a well-trained agent, a 'fully fledged saboteur . . . capable of operating his W/T set perfectly'. Being English, Fritz was equipped with the finest camouflage a spy could have, and he was about to be dropped in any one of three remote, sparsely-populated areas, each up to twelve miles in diameter: he had money, a gun and, to judge from the Most Secret Sources, plenty of gumption. MI5 was realistic: 'We quite realise that our plans do not offer more than a 40% chance of finding our man if he keeps his head and plays his part well.'

Fighter Command did pick up the Focke-Wulf, and six fighters from Number 12 Fighter Group were sent in pursuit. One of these got within range but then 'the instruments of the plane packed up for no understandable reason'. The German plane got away, and only Sergeant Vail's vigilance ensured that Operation Nightcap happened at all. Because Chapman had struggled for vital moments to extricate himself from a plane flying at 350 miles per hour, he had landed well outside the expected drop-zone. In the end, the person who ensured the capture of Agent X was Eddie Chapman.

Martha Convine could not sleep. She had been woken by a plane, droning loudly overhead, and lay wondering whether it was German. She was getting drowsy, when the all-clear siren had woken her up again. Her husband George, foreman of Apes Hall Farm, Ely, was snoring steadily of course, because George could sleep through the Battle of Britain, and recently had. Martha was finally dropping off, when she heard a loud banging on the door.

Martha shook George awake, put on her dressing gown, and peered out of the window into the darkness. 'Who is it?' A man's voice replied: 'A British airman, had an accident.'

It was 3.30 in the morning. For the last hour, Chapman had been stumbling around the wet celery fields in the darkness, dazed and still traumatised from being dangled out of an aircraft at terrifying speed. He had almost hit an empty barn on the way down, and he seemed to have lost his map. Finally he had found the eighteenth-century stone farmhouse, and shone his torch through the window in the door. On the hall table lay an English telephone book — a relief since it meant, of course, that the glutinous mud that had been steadily caking his boots for the last hour was British, and not French.

While George sleepily lit the lamp, Mrs Convine went

downstairs and opened the door. The figure on the doorstep might have emerged from a swamp. Martha 'noticed he had blood on his face'. He was also wearing a lounge suit. You can't be too careful in wartime, so Martha asked him where his plane was. He gestured vaguely at the surrounding countryside: 'Across the fields,' he said, mumbling that he had come down by parachute.

'I thought I heard a "Jerry",' said Martha.

'Yes,' the man said, nonsensically. 'That would be a cover plane for ours.'

Indeed, he really did not start making sense until he was sitting by the range in the kitchen with a cup of tea in his hand. He had asked to use the telephone and George, who was a special constable and knew the number by heart, dialled the police station at Ely for him. The man spoke very quietly into the mouthpiece, but Martha distinctly heard him say that he had 'just arrived from France', which was thrilling.

By the time Sergeants Vail and Hutchings arrived in the police car with two constables it was 4.30, the parachutist had drunk three cups of tea and eaten four slices of toast, and was evidently feeling much better, even cheery.

Convine led the policemen to the living room, where the man was chatting with Martha. Vail reported that: 'He shook hands with us and appeared agitated, but pleased to see us.' He then reached into his pocket and pulled out a pistol, saying: 'I expect the first thing you want is this.' He unloaded the gun and handed it to Vail, along with another loaded magazine.

When Vail asked where he had arrived from, the man replied: 'France, I want to get in touch with the British Intelligence Service. It is a case for them. I'm afraid I can't tell you much.'

An oblong parcel, sewn in sacking, lay on one of the living-room chairs. The man explained that it contained his 'radio transmitter, chocolate and shirts'. When Vail asked if he had any money, he stripped off his shirt to reveal 'a small package strapped to his back between his shoulder blades', which he removed and handed over. Inside, the astonished officer glimpsed wads of bank notes. He also produced his wallet, with an identity card for 'George Clarke'.

'Is that your real name?' asked Vail. The man just 'shook his head and smiled.'

While the constables went to find his parachute, the man became 'extremely talkative', boasting about the senior German officers he knew and declaring, apropos of nothing at all, that the only way to invade Europe was from Africa via Italy. Vail wondered if he might be 'dazed' from his descent. The man smelled slightly of celery.

The exotic visitor and his police escort departed in the police car. George said he was going back to bed, as there was work to do tomorrow. But Martha sat in the kitchen as dawn came up, thinking about the strange events of the last few hours. Later that morning, while doing the dusting, she found a British army reconnaissance map down the back of the sofa, which must have fallen out of the man's pocket. When she spread it out on the kitchen table, she saw that Mundford was circled in red crayon. The man had been 'very polite', Martha Convine thought, and underneath all that mud and blood he was probably rather handsome. She could not wait to tell her neighbour, but knew she could not. Sergeant Vail had said they must not breathe a word of what had happened to anyone, which was also thrilling.

At police divisional headquarters Chapman was stripped, body-searched, issued with a new set of clothing and brought before the Deputy Chief Constable, who shook his hand in a friendly manner. Chapman was wary: he did not like being inside a police station and he was not in the habit of telling the truth to policemen. His answers were cagey.

'Name?'

'George Clarke will do, for now.'

'Trade or profession?'

'Well, put me down as independent.'

The Chief Constable picked up the canvas bag containing the

radio. 'That should not be opened except by the Intelligence Service,' Chapman snapped.

The brown pill had been found in his turn-up. Did he have any more?: 'They had better have a look.'

Chapman gave a most selective account of his story, starting in Jersey and ending with the 'very terrifying experience' of being suspended upside down from a German plane.

Why had had he gone to the Channel Islands? 'For a holiday.'

Why was he imprisoned in Romainville? 'For political reasons.'

Then he clammed up. 'I have had a rough passage,' he said. 'I need to speak to the British secret services, when I will have a very interesting story to tell.'

The secret services were just as keen to hear Fritz's story. Two men in civilian clothes arrived in a Black Maria. Papers were signed, and Chapman was driven through the morning traffic to London and the Royal Patriotic School in Wandsworth, where he was formally detained under article 1A of the 'Arrival from Enemy Territory Order'. Then he was loaded back into the car. He did not know, and hardly cared, where he was going. The excitement, fear and exhaustion of the previous twenty-four hours had drained him. He barely noticed the sandbagged doorways of the city at war. After half an hour, they turned through a gate in a high wooden fence, topped by double rolls of barbed wire, and drew up in front of large and ugly Victorian mansion.

Two men in gym shoes led Chapman to a room in the basement, with a bench and two blankets, and locked him inside. A man with a monocle opened the door, peered hawkishly at him, said nothing, and then went away. He was stripped again, and ordered to put on flannel prison trousers and a coat, with a 6-inch white diamond shape sewn on the back. A doctor appeared, and ordered him to open his mouth. The medic spent several minutes probing and tapping at his teeth, particularly the new dental work. Then he tested Chapman's heart, listened to his lungs, and declared him to be in the peak of condition, though 'mentally and physically spent'. A man with a camera arrived and took photographs from the front and in profile.

Chapman fought to keep his head up. With a supreme effort he stared into the lens. The face in the picture is drained by fatigue and stress. There is caked mud in the tangled hair, and a trace of dried blood in the moustache. But there is something else in the face. Behind the drooping eyelids and stubble lies the very faint trace of a smile.

Camp 020

Lieutenant Colonel Robin 'Tin Eye' Stephens, the commander of Camp O20, Britain's secret interrogation centre for captured enemy spies, had a very specialised skill: he broke people. He crushed them, psychologically, into very small pieces and then, if he thought it worthwhile, he would put them back together again. He considered this to be an art, and not one that could be learned. 'A breaker is born and not made,' he said. 'There must be certain inherent qualities: an implacable hatred of the enemy, a certain aggressive approach, a disinclination to believe, and above all a relentless determination to break down the spy, however hopeless the odds, however many the difficulties, however long the process may take.' In photographs, Stephens might be the caricature Gestapo interrogator, with the glinting monocle and '*vays* of making you talk'. He certainly did have ways of making people talk, but they were not the brutal, obvious ways of the Gestapo. Behind the tin eye was an instinctive and inspired amateur psychologist.

Born in Egypt in 1900, Stephens had joined the Gurkhas, the legendarily tough Nepalese troops, before moving to the security service in 1939. He spoke Urdu, Arabic, Somali, Amharic, French, German and Italian. This multilingualism should not be taken to indicate that Stephens was broadminded about other races and nations. He was ragingly xenophobic, and given to making remarks such as: 'Italy is a country populated by undersized, posturing folk.' He disliked 'weeping and romantic fat

Belgians', 'shifty Polish Jews' and 'unintelligent' Icelanders. He also detested homosexuals. Above all, he hated Germans.

In 1940 the government set up a permanent centre for the interrogation and imprisonment of suspected spies, subversives and enemy aliens in Latchmere House, a large and gloomy Victorian house near Ham Common in West London. Latchmere House had been a military hospital in the First World War, specialising in the treatment of shell-shocked soldiers. In Stephens's words, it had 'lunatic cells ready made for a prison'. Secluded, forbidding and surrounded by multiple barbed wire fences, the interrogation centre was codenamed Camp 020. Colonel Stephens, extrovert and short-tempered, terrified his underlings almost as much as the prisoners. He never removed his monocle (he was said to sleep in it) and though everyone called him 'Tin Eye' as a consequence, very few dared do so to his face. But there was another side to this bristling martinet. He was a superb judge of character and situation; he never lost his temper with a prisoner, and he condemned the use of violence or torture as barbaric and counter-productive. Anyone who resorted to the third degree was immediately banned from Camp 020.

Away from the interrogation cells, Tin Eye could be charming and very funny. He was a frustrated writer, as can be seen from his reports, which have a delightful literary flourish; some of his more extreme statements of prejudice were simply intended to shock or amuse. He thought of himself as a master of the interrogative arts. Some of his colleagues thought he was quite mad. What few disputed was that he was outstanding at his job: establishing the guilt of the enemy spy, breaking down his resistance, extracting vital information, scaring him witless, winning his trust and then, finally, turning him over to Tar Robertson for use as a double agent. No one could turn a spy like Tin Eye.

At 9.30 on the morning of 17 December, Eddie Chapman found himself in Interrogation Room 3 of Camp 020, facing this strange, angry-looking man with the uniform of a Gurkha and the eye of a basilisk. Stephens was flanked by two other officers, Captains Short and Goodacre. The three officers made a grim and forbidding tribunal. That was part of Tin Eye's technique. 'No chivalry. No gossip. No cigarettes . . . a spy in war should be at the point of a bayonet. It is a question of atmosphere. The room is like a court and he is made to stand up and answer questions as before a judge.'

The room was bugged. In another part of Camp 020, a stenographer recorded every word. 'Your name is Chapman, is it?' barked Tin Eye.

'Yes, Sir.'

'I am not saying this in any sense of a threat, but you are here in a British Secret Service prison at the present time and it's our job in wartime to see that we get your whole story from you. Do you see?'

The threat didn't need to be made. Chapman told him every-thing, in a great tumbling torrent of confession. He told Stephens about his dismissal from the Coldstream Guards, his criminal past, his time in Jersey prison, the months in Romainville, his recruit-ment, his training in Nantes and Berlin, and the parachute drop. He told him about the codes he knew, the sabotage techniques he had learned, the secret writing, the passwords, codewords and wireless frequencies. He told him about Graumann and Thomas, Wojch and Schmidt, and the ugly man from Angers with the gold teeth. He explained how he had gathered information, and then destroyed it at the last moment.

When Chapman began to describe his decision to take up full-time crime, the interrogation veered close to farce.

'Well, then it gets rather difficult, Sir. I started running around with a mob of gangsters.'

'What do you mean?'

'I can't say exactly how I drifted in.'

'What made you turn over to these curious people?'

'It's rather difficult to say.'

When he described his mission to blow up the machine room of the De Havilland aircraft factory, Stephens interrupted.

'Pretty hazardous undertaking, isn't it?'

'Yes.'

'You were rather a favourite. Did they trust you?'

'Yes.'

'They said they thought rather highly of you, that you could get in anywhere and do virtually anything?'

'Yes, I could.'

Stephens turned the discussion to the contents of Chapman's kitbag. He pointed out that the cash had come wrapped in bands that immediately identified it as German, and 'would have cost him his neck' when they were spotted.

'The man who was supposed to search you, proceeds to identify your currency with a German label?' asked Stephens, incredulously.

'That's the fault of Thomas,' said Chapman, equally astonished. 'In the excitement he probably forgot to take it off.'

Stephens made a note. The process of distancing Chapman from his German handlers, by undermining his faith in their efficiency, had begun. So when Chapman recalled the conversation with Von Gröning, in which the older man had laughingly said that Chapman would never dare betray them because the British police would lock him up, Stephens again interjected. 'That was plain, unvarnished blackmail,' he said, in mock outrage, and was delighted when Chapman, 'with some bitterness, said he felt that all along'.

After two hours of interrogation, Stephens left Chapman in the company of Captain Short, a rotund, owlish figure, as cheery as his boss was menacing. Today this technique would be called 'good cop–bad cop'; in his secret guide to interrogation techniques, Stephens called it: 'blow hot–blow cold'.

'They treated you pretty well, didn't they?' said Short, in a sympathetic tone.

'Yes, I had a very good time there.'

'Particularly after having been in prison in Jersey and the other concentration camp.'

'How long have I to remain in this one? I mean, I've taken quite a lot of risks getting information which I thought would be of value, and [it is] valuable I think.'

Stephens had Chapman exactly where he wanted him. The spy seemed keen to tell all, with apparent honesty. He wanted to tell more. He wanted to please his captors. And he wanted to get out of prison.

In his office, Stephens took a telephone call from the policeman who had accompanied Chapman back to London: 'I don't know what this man may tell you, Sir. He came with a German parachute, but I recognised him at once – he was in my platoon some years ago.' By an odd coincidence, the two men had been in the Coldstream Guards together, and the policeman now related how Chapman had gone AWOL and was then cashiered. The information tallied precisely with the story Chapman had told: so far, then, he was telling the truth.

The interrogators began to turn up the heat. Chapman was allowed a break, and some food, but then they were back, probing, deliberately misrepresenting what he had already said, worrying away at any fissures in his story to find out if he was lying, or holding something back. In Stephens's mind, 'No spy, however astute, is proof against relentless interrogation.' The MI5 officers worked in shifts, late into the night. 'Physically and mentally it will wear down the strongest constitution in the end,' Stephens predicted.

The information continued to pour out of Chapman: in the course of forty-eight hours he gave more than fifty descriptions of separate individuals, from Graumann the spymaster to Odette the cook. Chapman described things of vital importance and utter triviality; he described the flak emplacements at Nantes, the location of the Paris Abwehr headquarters, his part in the occupation of Vichy France, and the price of black-market butter. He described the Breton nationalists, the treacherous Gaullists and the sundry other dodgy characters that had passed through Nantes. He told them some things they knew, such as the wireless codes they had already broken, which allowed them to test Chapman's truthfulness; but he also told them much that was new, and priceless, creating an astonishingly detailed picture of German espionage methods. He seemed not only eager to impart information, but offered suggestions as to how it might be used. Surely, said Chapman, by acting on this intelligence, Britain could break the Abwehr code and intercept messages between the various units.

The interrogators offered a vague response, but inside they rejoiced, for Chapman's suggestion showed that the Most Secret Sources were still intact: 'It is quite clear from his remarks that he has not the slightest idea that we have been breaking the messages which have passed between these stations during the last few months,' wrote the interrogators. It swiftly became apparent that Chapman would not have to be cajoled into acting as a double agent for Britain, but was itching to get to work. One motive for his willingness became clear when he described what had happened to Tony Faramus.

'He is a hostage for my good behaviour,' explained Chapman.

'For your good behaviour in France, or here?'

'Here. The idea was to use him as a kind of lever to make me do my work here.' If Chapman could convince his German masters that he was doing their bidding, then, he explained, his friend's life might yet be saved. Stephens made another note.

While Chapman's memory was scoured for valuable information, his luggage was simultaneously being searched for clues. The matches for secret writing and the evil-looking brown pill were sent for scientific analysis; the bank notes were individually examined, their serial numbers noted, to try to establish where they had come from; the fake identity cards were subjected to ultra-violet light scanning by HM Stationery Office, their precise chemical composition and typography analysed and compared to the genuine article; the wireless was sent to the Special Operations Executive (responsible for sabotage and espionage behind enemy lines) to find out if it had come from a British agent operating in France, and if so, which one. Chapman was quizzed about every item in his wallet. He explained that only one was really his own: 'That was a private letter written by a girlfriend to me – a girlfriend of mine before the war – I brought that back with me.'

Chapman's every statement was compared to the evidence in the Most Secret Sources, to try to catch him in a lie. When Chapman's chronology was erroneous, as it frequently was, they would go over the times and dates again and again, until satisfied that any errors were 'natural inexactitudes', not deliberate distortions. Scotland Yard was asked to provide details of his criminal record, to check out his extravagant claims of villainy; when the record arrived, it was found that many of the crimes Chapman had admitted to were not on it.

Stephens later claimed that Chapman had also 'confessed to an experiment in sodomy' during his Soho years. It is hard to know what to make of this: there is no trace of this confession in the interrogation transcripts. Tin Eye, moreover, was an extreme homophobe, who prided himself on his ability to identify and expose experimental sodomites. Chapman may have had a homosexual affair earlier in his youth but it is certain that he had been heterosexual, to an almost pathological degree, for many years. By way of recommendation, Stephens noted approvingly: 'Today there is no trace of sodomy and gone is any predilection for living on women on the fringes of society.'

With the evidence Chapman was providing, British intelligence was swiftly building up a picture of the entire Abwehr system in France. The German secret service had been so certain of its unbreakable code that the personnel at the various units often used their own names in wireless correspondence. That information was now merged with Chapman's descriptions, allowing them to identify the different players in the organisation. Chapman would have been astonished.

British intelligence had long ago established that the head and deputy head of the Nantes Abwehr section were Rittmeister Stephan von Gröning and Oberleutnant Walter Praetorius. But the man Chapman knew as 'Wojch' was really Feldwebel Horst Barton, while 'Schmidt' was Franz Stoetzner, both suspected saboteurs who had come to England before the war to work as waiters sponsored by an association of British restaurateurs and hoteliers. 'Leo' was a known German criminal named Leo Kreusch, and 'Albert' a former travelling salesman named Albert Schael. The Gestapo officer from Angers who had tried to recruit Chapman was probably Dernbach, 'one the principal counter-espionage agents in France'. Piece by piece, they began to put faces to names: even the pilot of the Focke-Wulf and the beautiful translator at Romainville were identified. Tar Robertson was impressed at the way Chapman had been kept in the dark over the identities of his German comrades: 'On no occasion has anyone's real name become apparent to him,' he wrote. When one of the interrogators casually dropped the name 'Von Gröning' into the conversation, Chapman's failure to react proved he had never heard it before.

Establishing a complete picture of Chapman's life in France would take time, but time was already running out. The day after his arrival at Camp 020, Chapman scribbled a message for Colonel Stephens, pointing out that 'today was the supposed start of my transmission' and recalling Von Gröning's observation about British red tape.

'It is important that we have a connection with the "Boche"

at earliest possible moment,' he wrote, perhaps deliberately deploying the sort of language favoured by Stephens. 'Dr Graumann especially stressed the point. He may suspect we may be arranging something. He probably thinks it would take much longer for me to commence, if I was arranging anything with yourselves.'

The same day, the Radio Security Service began to pick up the German reply station in Paris. Every three minutes, starting at 9.45 a.m., Maurice sent out a message, calling for Fritz to respond. MI5 now faced a quandary. If contact was delayed, Von Gröning would suspect something had gone wrong; but if they responded without being absolutely certain that Chapman was playing straight, then the results could be catastrophic. It was decided to wait a day or two, in order to get Chapman, and his motives, 'in sharper focus'.

By evening, Chapman had still received no response from Stephens. He had been interrogated now for forty-eight hours with only brief intermissions; he was tired and anxious. Unless contact was made soon the consequences could be dire. He was also torn: between the affection he still felt for Von Gröning and the urgent need to betray him; by the desire to save his own skin, and that of Tony Faramus; between self interest and some greater good, as yet undefined; between loyalty to his friends, and duty to his country. He wrote another, much longer letter to Stephens. It is an extraordinary document, a combination of self-pity, self-examination and self-assertion, reflecting the internal agony of the spy. It is the statement of a man groping his way through moral darkness towards the light:

Mon Commandant,
One does not expect gratitude from one's own country – but allow me to draw your attention to a few facts. For thirteen months now I have been under German rule. During this time even when undergoing detention I was treated with strict fairness and friendli-

ness. I made many friends – people who I respect and who I think came to like me – unfortunately for them and for me.

I set out from the first day to try to mass together a series of facts, places, dates etc. concerning the German organization, which I think would be a task fairly formidable even for one of your trained experts. From the start I was very much handicapped, my knowledge of German was slight, my French even less – two languages most essential for this work. I studied French until I mastered it, even learning the slang. I read it now as fluently as English. Then, sir, for nine months I listened to every conversation I could hear. I opened many drawers containing documents 'gehein' [secret] written on all of them. I bored very small holes from the bathroom to the room of Dr Graumann, a man very much my friend.

Don't think I'm asking for any friendship now, it's a little late – on the other hand this strange thing patriotism. I laugh a little cynically when I think of it sometimes. I have fought the fight and my country won (why I can't explain). I wish like hell there had been no war – I begin to wish I had never started this affair. To spy and cheat on one's friends it's not nice it's dirty. However, I started this affair and I will finish it. Don't think I ask anything for this, I don't. It seems very strange to be working for two different governments – one offers me the chance of money, success and a career. The other offers me a prison cell.

There is not a great deal of time left to arrange things.
Yours sincerely,
Eddie

While Chapman was penning this heartfelt note, Stephens was gathering together his four interrogators for a conference on what to do with this remarkable and potentially very valuable crook. As Stephens pointed out, Chapman had accepted that he was in a strange position, wanted by the British police but offering – pleading – to work for British intelligence. 'If Chapman is to be believed, he offered to work for the Germans as a means of escape [and] on landing he immediately put himself at the disposal of the British authorities to work against the Germans.' The preliminary psychological profile indicated that Chapman's motives, despite his personal affection for Graumann, were 'hatred for the Hun coupled with a sense of adventure. There is no woman in the case and no bargain for rehabilitation. He is possessed of courage and nerve.'

But there was plainly a problem. If Chapman was allowed his liberty, he would surely be picked up by the police. He had even remarked on it to Stephens: 'As I figure it out, with my brilliant past, I am due for a stretch of something like fourteen years.' Worse, he might link up with his criminal gang again. But if he was kept under guard in Camp 020, Stephens predicted, 'he will go sour and might attempt a break'. The only way to operate him safely would be to place him at half-liberty, under surveillance but not in prison, 'under control in a quiet, country place'.

'My opinion,' Stephens declared, 'is that Chapman should be used for XX [Double Cross] purposes . . . and then sent back to France to join a party of saboteurs already in training to be sent to America for a really big job.'

The interrogation team unanimously agreed. There was a risk in sending Chapman back into France. He might be exposed by the Germans, or he might confess all to them; he might even change sides again. But the potential benefits of having a spy at the heart of the German secret service outweighed the dangers. That evening Camp 020 sent a message to the Double Cross team in St James's Street: 'In our opinion, Chapman should be used to the fullest extent . . . he genuinely means to work for the British against the Germans. By his courage and resourcefulness he is ideally fitted to be an agent.'

Tar Robertson had been following every twist of the developing case and agreed to send one of his case officers to take a look at Chapman the next day. Before Chapman could be inducted into the XX fold, he would need a codename. By convention, the names of agents should be plucked from thin air, mere handles that did not connect in any way with their real identities. But the convention was constantly flouted. 'Snow' of course was a partial anagram of Owens; another double agent was called 'Tate' because Robertson thought he looked like the comedian Harry Tate; it was said that Dusko Popov, a rather louche Yugoslavian agent, had been named 'Tricycle' because of his taste for three-in-a-bed sex. The name selected for Edward Chapman could not have been more apt.

On the evening of 18 December, Tar sent a message to all B1A personnel: 'We have chosen the name of Zigzag for Fritzchen.'

35, Crespigny Road

The man despatched by Tar Robertson to handle Zigzag was Captain Ronnie Reed, a young, unobtrusive radio expert, and an inspired choice. A thin-faced man with a spindly moustache, spectacles and a pipe, he looked like an archetypal, middle-ranking army officer. Indeed, he looked so much like an archetypal, middle-ranking army officer that when Tar Robertson needed a photograph to put on a fake identity card for Operation Mincemeat – in which a dead body, dressed in army uniform and carrying misleading information, was deliberately washed up on the coast of Spain – he chose a picture of Ronnie Reed. Reed looked just like everybody else, and nobody at all.

Reed's father, a waiter at the Trocadero restaurant, had died in the Battle of the Somme in 1916, and his mother brought him up in a tenement in King's Cross. From the Saint Pancras Church of England School, he had won a scholarship to the Regent's Park Polytechnic School, where he studied engineering and developed a passion for radios. He could build a wireless from scratch and with his schoolfriend Charlie Chilton (who went on to become a celebrated radio presenter and producer) he would broadcast to the world from his bedroom with a homemade transmitter: Ronnie would sing a warbling rendition of Bing Crosby's *Dancing in the Dark* while Charlie strummed the guitar.

The outbreak of war found Reed working as a BBC radio engineer by day, and flying through the ether by night with the call-sign G2RX. One night, Reed and his mother had taken cover during an air raid, when a police car drew up. Reed was summoned from the shelter and driven, through the falling bombs, to Wormwood Scrubs. A man was standing at the prison gate. 'Ah, Mr Reed, we've been waiting for you. Come in,' he said. He was led through dimly lit corridors to a cell on the first floor.

Inside the cell, flanked by two guards, was a man in flying uniform, his face covered in blood.

'This man is a parachutist,' said an officer with red tabs on his uniform, who had entered the cell behind Reed. 'He's supposed to transmit tonight back to Germany. We want you to go out into a field in Cambridge, and transmit, and make sure he sends the message we have prepared.'

That night, Reed and the parachutist, Gösta Caroli, soon to become double agent 'Summer', sat in a pigsty in a Cambridge-shire field and sent a Morse code message to Hamburg: : 'I'm going underground for a few days, while I sort out some accommodation, and I've arrived safely.'

So began Reed's career in the secret service.

Shy, gentle and reserved, Reed was easy to overlook, but he was the 'humble genius' of wartime wireless work, perfectly tuned to the arcane mysteries of the radio. He also had the knack of identifying the 'fist' of another operator, and then of being able to imitate it precisely – he was probably the best Morse-code mimic in Britain. Reed's skills made him indispensable to Robertson's team, and soon he was monitoring all double agent radio traffic. One of his tasks was to stand over agents as they transmitted back to the Abwehr, to ensure they were not inserting coded messages. If an agent was unwilling or unable to transmit then Reed would send the message himself, com-plete with the agent's telltale 'fingerprint'. But Ronnie Reed was more than just an accomplished radio ham; under Robertson's guidance, he was developing into a first-rate intelligence officer, incisive, sympathetic, and virtually invisible.

In Chapman's cell, Reed shook hands with his new charge for the first time. The young officer had planned to take an instant dislike to this unrepentant criminal with the 'lurid past'. But like most people, and against his will, he found himself charmed.

Reed frankly explained that if Chapman was to work for MI5 he would need to live a hermit-like existence. Any contact with the police, the Bohemians of Soho or the criminal fraternity would be forbidden. Instead, Reed explained, 'he would have to work for us under strict supervision in almost complete isolation from other members of the community'. Chapman laughed and said that after all the recent excitement a quiet life would be most welcome. Reed said he would return the following day to make the first transmission to Germany, and left Chapman to draft a message, using the Constantinople code and the FFFFF control sign. Reed would then check it, and sit beside him as he transmitted it.

As changeable as ever, Chapman seems to have been buoyed by his conversation with Reed, for he now sent another letter to Stephens. Gone was the peevish, introverted tone. Now he was positively chatty:

Mon Commandant,
Merci pour votre bonté. As we have little time to get to know each other — let me start and give you a little explanation. At the present moment my story is very difficult to tell. My mind is such a frenzied mass of names, formulas, descriptions, places, times, explosions, radio telegraphy and parachute jumping, small but important conversations, intrigue playing against intrigue. On top of this you must try and imagine a brain — weakened by three years of imprisonment and many months in the punishment cell . . . some-times in trying to put facts together I really thought I was going mad . . . these things are not untrue, they have all passed — but dates, names, times, are all jumbled in my head higgledy-piggledy, like some giant jigsaw puzzle . . . To conclude Mon Commandant. Be a little patient with me if my places and dates and times don't

coincide . . . I'm afraid that whole thing has rather passed like a dream: it's for you to try and make it a realisation.

Eddie

Tin Eye Stephens was accustomed to intimidating new arrivals at Camp 020. He was not used to being addressed in this facetious tone or told what to do, let alone by an oikish young burglar in prison garb. But instead of exploding, as he might have done, Stephens just chuckled, and tucked the note in the Zigzag file.

The next morning, Chapman was picked up by Reed and two burly Field Security Policemen in a Blue Maria, and driven 150 yards from the front gate of Latchmere House to the Equestrian Club, a small concert hall within the grounds used as a club-house, with a 25-foot flagpole that Reed thought would serve as an aerial. The place was deserted. While the FSPs stood guard, Reed set up Chapman's wireless.

At 10.02 a.m., under Reed's vigilant gaze, Chapman tried to contact his Abwehr controllers. At 10.06 the reply station responded that it was receiving him 'rather weakly' and with interference, but gave the go-ahead. Agent Zigzag then tapped out his first message as a double agent: 'FFFFF HAVE ARRIVED. AM WELL WITH FRIENDS. OK.' He added his usual laughing coda: 'HI HU HA.'

In the afternoon, the Most Secret Sources reported that the Abwehr stations in France had confirmed that this message was 'definitely Fritz' because they 'recognised his style of sending and especially the method he adopts for signing off his messages'. The deception was up and running.

The following morning, Reed and Chapman found it impossible to renew the contact with Paris. It appeared that the transmissions were being picked up in Nantes, but not at the main receiving station in the capital. A second message was sent 'blind': 'FFFFF GET MORRIS [*sic*] BRING YOUR SET

NEARER COAST. MUST HAVE BETTER RECEPTION.
F. OK'

By late December they received the first direct message from
Von Gröning: 'THANKS FOR MESSAGE. WISH GOOD
RESULTS. OK.'

So far the double-cross seemed to be working, although it
would be two weeks before the problems of reception and
transmission could be ironed out. The radio traffic was codenamed ZINC, and filed alphabetically alongside Zigzag.

Chapman seemed more than co-operative, Reed reported,
and was still producing a steady stream of valuable intelligence:
'Zigzag's powers of observation are extremely good and he is
being quite truthful in whatever he tells us.' (Reading that
assessment, John Masterman noted that he was sceptical that
such a man even understood the concept of complete honesty.)

Special Branch set about tracing the rest of the Jelly Gang.
Jimmy Hunt, it transpired, had been convicted of warehouse
breaking and larceny in 1938; Darry was still in Dartmoor, on a
seven-year stretch; the others were all either deserters, doing
time, or dead. This was ideal. There was no chance of accidental
contact, and with the members of the gang safely out of the way
they could be brought into the story with no danger that they
might turn up unannounced. Chapman had been instructed to
contact his old chums, and perhaps bring one back. Hunt seemed
the ideal candidate. As Masterman pointed out, 'the Germans
had not a photograph of Hunt, but only a general description,
[so] it would be possible to impersonate him by someone with a
Cockney accent'. Hunt the safebreaker would play a central role
in the coming drama, without once leaving his prison cell.

Gradually it was starting to dawn on Chapman's handlers that
they had obtained a double agent of potentially huge value.
When Camp 020 mistakenly passed the identity of Zigzag to
another branch of the intelligence service, there was a loud
squeal of protest from Masterman, the master of the double-
cross, at this 'gratuitous' sharing of information. B1A was jealous

of its new treasure, and while Tar was happy to pass on his intelligence findings, he was not about to share Zigzag with anyone.

The forensic investigations confirmed how highly the Germans prized Agent Fritz. The quality of his equipment was declared to be first class. The cash he had brought was genuine British currency, not the forged stuff that the Abwehr had often palmed off on lesser agents. The match heads were impregnated with quinine, which the boffins in the science department described as 'a very good means of secret writing'. The brown pill was potassium cyanide, instantaneously lethal. The wireless was traced to a British SOE agent. Only in the matter of the forged ID cards did the Abwehr seem to have cut corners. The Stationery Office dismissed them as amateur forgeries and liable to be spotted as such by any observant policeman. 'It does seem rather extraordinary that the Germans should not take a little more trouble in constructing their documents,' Tar complained, as if miffed that the Germans were not trying hard enough. One unsolved mystery was how the Focke-Wulf had managed to escape the pursuing RAF fighters: the Air Ministry could only conclude that 'something queer was taking place in connection with the plane and the radio beams associated with it'.

Camp 020 was no place to run a double agent. If Zigzag was to be effective, he must be kept happy, and that would require creature comforts at least comparable to those of La Bretonnière. Chapman had been pampered by the Germans: 'They pandered to his vanity, granted him liberty and treated him with respect.' MI5 must now try to find a red carpet, or the nearest equivalent, and roll it out for Zigzag.

Corporal Paul Backwell and Lance Corporal Allan Tooth were, by common agreement, the two best Field Security Policemen in British intelligence. Both had been policemen before the war, and would enjoy successful careers in the intelligence corps after it. They were bright, well educated and good-natured; they were also large and, when they wanted to be, extremely intimidating. Tar Robertson summoned Back-well and Tooth to his office and told them to take a car to Camp 020, where they would pick up one 'Edward Simpson', 'a dangerous criminal who is wanted by police and who has been released in order to carry out an operation of an extremely hazardous character'. They should accompany this man to a safe house in north London where they would live with him until further notice. Robertson was in deadly earnest: 'The success of this operation depends upon the utmost degree of secrecy.' A photographic pass would be issued in the name Simpson, indicating that he was performing 'special duties for the War Office', which could be produced if they were ever challenged by officials.

'There is no reason to doubt Simpson's loyalty to this country and you are not therefore to regard yourselves as his guards,' Robertson continued. 'You should look upon yourselves rather as chaperones, whose duty it is to prevent him getting into trouble with the police and with his old criminal associates, to act as a screen between him and the outside world.' 'Simpson' should never be left alone, day or night. He should not com-municate with anyone, use the telephone or send letters. If he attempted to escape, Tooth and Backwell should not hesitate to 'place him under restraint' and then contact either Reed or Masterman. Both policemen would be issued with firearms.

At the same time, they should provide him with companion-ship. 'This regime is bound to be irksome,' said Tar, 'and you must therefore do your best to make his life as agreeable as is possible in the circumstances.' They could take him to the local pub of an evening: each officer would receive £5 as a beer float, and Simpson would also be provided with cash in order to be able to 'stand his round'. Having gained his confidence, the policemen should note down anything he said of importance, and encourage him to talk about his past. In short, they should guard him, befriend him, and then spy on him. If Backwell and Tooth thought it strange that they were being expected to keep a known crook out of the hands of the police, they were much too discreet to say so.

Days before Christmas, Backwell and Tooth, in plain clothes, arrived at Camp 020, collected Chapman's personal property, and escorted him from his cell. Chapman, without preamble, asked Backwell if he might borrow a pound, as he wanted to give a tip to the sergeant 'who had looked after him so well'. (Only Chapman would swan out of Camp 020 as if checking out of a smart hotel.) They drove north. In the car, Chapman's chaperones introduced themselves as 'Allan' and 'Paul' and explained they would now be his 'permanent companions, friends who were protecting him from police and his previous criminal associates'. Chapman said little as they drove. 'Conversation was strained,' Backwell reported.

No one paid any attention to the three men who climbed out of the car and walked up the garden path of 35, Crespigny Road – a nondescript detached house, on a quiet street, in the unremarkable north London borough of Hendon. A few of the neighbours were 'digging for victory' in their front gardens, but none looked up. It would have taken a neighbour of exceptional inquisitiveness to spot that Number 35 never took down its blackout curtains (many people did not bother), or that the locks had been changed, or that a man with a thin moustache had arrived that very morning to erect an aerial on the back roof.

Inside Number 35, Backwell locked the door, and the three housemates began, in his words, to 'settle in'. Reed had set up the radio room on the upper floor; Chapman's bedroom was next door, while the two FSPs shared the third bedroom. The housekeeper, Mrs West, would not be arriving for a few days, so the policemen divided up the chores: Tooth would do the shopping and Backwell the cooking. When Chapman was out of earshot, they divvied up their other task: 'Allan and I agreed to concentrate on different aspects of Eddie. Allan studied his character, likes and dislikes, while I kept to the factual side and noted everything of interest that he said in conversation.'

Chapman was anxious. He complained of sleeping badly, and showed no inclination to leave the house. Like a couple of burly mother hens, Tooth and Backwell set about 'making Eddie feel at home'. Backwell asked Chapman what reading material he enjoyed, and was astonished to discover his love of serious literature. 'His taste was unusual for anyone who had lived his kind of life,' thought Backwell, who bought him some German novels, the works of Alfred Tennyson, and the plays of Pierre Corneille, in French.

Gradually, Chapman seemed to relax. His days were filled with further interrogations, sending wireless messages under Reed's supervision, and making plans. In the evenings, he read, smoked, listened to the radio and chatted with his amiable guards. Privately, Backwell and Tooth compared notes on their ward. They were struck that German propaganda seemed to have had an 'enormous' effect on him; at first he dismissed BBC reports of Allied advances, claiming that he knew Germany was winning the war, that Russia was exhausted. The Allies, he insisted, would never succeed in invading France. Backwell decided to mount his own propaganda campaign, by exposing him to such patriotic literature as *I, James Blunt*, H.V. Morton's novel imagining a Britain under Nazi rule. 'Gradually we made him realise that German propaganda, however convincing it had been, was far from the truth.'

After a few days of communal living, Backwell and Tooth reported that Chapman now appeared 'quite happy', and 'a mine of information'. Their companion seemed to know all about sabotage, and 'often speaks of various methods of destroying pylons, bridges, petrol tanks, etc'. Often he insisted on conversing in French. The policemen agreed they were living with a most peculiar fellow. One moment he was reading classical literature in the original French and quoting Tennyson, and the next he would be discussing the best way to blow up a train.

One night, as they were relaxing after dinner, Chapman wondered aloud 'what it was that made him leave Germany to come over here'. He continued musing in the same vein: 'In Germany he could have lived well, both now and after the war. He was not forced to come.' The two policemen pondered the same question. His politics seemed to be based on a close reading of H.G. Wells: 'He has no sympathy with nationalism and in the post-war reconstruction he would like to see a world federation.' Tooth decided that, in his heart, Chapman was a patriot: 'He is proud to be British and wants us to win the war.' On the other hand, he was apparently impelled by some internal recklessness. 'It seems that he is a man to whom the presence of danger is essential,' Tooth wrote. 'I feel that it is for this reason that he would be undertaking his return to France, for he is virtually a man without a country.'

Some days later, Chapman let slip that he had a private plan of his own, but then he changed the subject, remarking: 'It is such a wild scheme it would not be thought feasible.' Tooth duly reported Chapman's remarks to Reed and Robertson, adding: 'I can only glean that the success of these plans depends entirely on Dr Graumann keeping a promise that he should visit Berlin, when I gather something of great importance was to take place.'

Chapman showed no remorse for his past, and regaled his new companions with extravagant tales of his own villainy, such as the time he broke into the Grimsby pawnbrokers and the raid on Express Dairies. The information was duly added to MI5's growing list of Chapman's undetected crimes. 'I think we should keep these new adventures entirely to ourselves, but have it on record,' wrote Reed.

The interrogators, spycatchers and double-crossers of MI5 (Reed excepted) were usually upper class and the products of English public schools. Most had never encountered a man like Chapman before, and their first instinct was to despise this uncouth fellow with his flamboyant manner. Yet in almost every case they came first to like, and then to respect him, though never entirely without misgivings.

As Christmas approached, espionage experts all over London

wondered what to do about Eddie Chapman, and what made him tick.

When he was not thinking up new ways to deceive and double-cross Nazi Germany, John Masterman, historian and athlete, liked to think about cricket. Sometimes he thought about espionage and cricket at the same time. 'Running a team of double agents,' he reflected, 'is very much like running a club cricket side. Older players lose their form and are gradually replaced by newcomers. It is not always easy to pick the best players to put into the field. Some of the players required a good deal of net practice before they were really fit to play in a match.' In Chapman he seemed to have discovered a batsman of astonishing natural ability, who needed no additional training and who might well knock up a fantastic innings. If, that is, he did not stalk off the pitch, and then reappear to open the bowling for the other side.

Masterman entertained these thoughts as he lay on the floor of the barber's shop in the Reform Club on Pall Mall. At the start of the war he had resided in the United University Club; then when a bomb blew the roof off, he had moved in to the Oxford and Cambridge. Not long after that, the barber at the Reform Club had died and his salon had closed; Masterman was invited to make his digs there instead, an offer he readily accepted since the club was only a few minutes walk from B1A headquarters. And so now he spent his nights on the floor where the hair clippings of 'great and clubbable' men had fallen ever since 1841.

Sleeping on a thin mattress on the hard tiles was not easy. The cook at the Reform did his best with the rations, but the food was seldom anything but grim. The electricity shut down with monotonous irregularity. Baths were doled out in strict rotation, and were always cold. But Masterman loved living at the Reform: 'I had, with my memories of my uselessness in the First War, a kind of unconscious wish for trials and discomfort.' He watched his fellow men at war (the women were, as ever, invisible to him) and reflected on their stoicism. One night the

Carlton Club was hit by a bomb. The members of the surrounding clubs, in pyjamas and slippers, formed long lines to save the
library from the flames, passing books from hand to hand and
discussing the merits of each as they passed. Such people,
thought Masterman, 'made defeat seem impossible'. This strange
warrior monk would spend the rest of his war in this masculine
world of institutional food, hard floors and cold baths. And now,
with a new, intensely fit, first-class batsman to send to the crease,
John Masterman was as happy as he had ever been in his life.

On the other side of London, in Latchmere House, the
commandant of Camp 020 was also thinking about Agent
Zigzag. Tin Eye Stephens regarded most enemy spies as 'the
rabble of the universe, their treachery not matched by their
courage'. But Chapman was different – the 'most fascinating
case' to date. Unlike every other captured agent, he had not
displayed even a flicker of fear. He seemed to crave excitement,
and very little else. 'What manner of man is the spy?' Stephens
pondered. 'Is he patriotic, brave? Is he of the underworld, a
subject of blackmail? Is he just a mercenary? Spies who work for
money alone are few, but they are dangerous.' For a crook, he
observed, Chapman was strangely uninterested in money. He
seemed genuinely patriotic, but not in the Hun-bashing, jin-
goistic way that Stephens epitomised. What Chapman seemed to
want was another breathless episode in the unfolding drama of
his own life. If MI5 could stage-manage the next act with
enough flair, Tin Eye reflected, then Zigzag might be their
biggest star yet.

On Christmas Eve, Maurice, the German wireless operator in
Paris, sent a message to Agent Fritz: 'PLEASE COME AT NINE
FORTY FIVE AND FIVE PM QRQ.' (The sign 'qrq' was ham
shorthand for 'send more quickly'.) The Germans were still
apparently having difficulty picking up Chapman's transmissions.
Ronnie Reed had fiddled with Chapman's radio and could find
no fault, but he was not too alarmed. The patchy link would buy
them some more time.

Far more worrying was something that Chapman had said. Soon after arriving in Crespigny Road, he asked Reed to find Freda Stevenson, his former lover and the mother of his child. Chapman had only vaguely alluded to Freda before. Now he explained that he had never held his own daughter, now three-years old, that he was still in love with Freda, and that he wanted to see them both, urgently. Reed said he would try to find her.

Freda was an unknown quantity. Allowing Chapman to contact her might lift his spirits, Reed reflected, but it would complicate the case. If Chapman was serious about his feelings for a woman he had not seen for years and a child he had never met, would that affect his willingness to return to France? Perhaps Freda had remarried; perhaps she had given the child up for adoption. Reed concluded: 'We should know the exact situation concerning them before Zigzag visited them, rather than run his neck into what might be an extremely awkward situation.' But as the days passed, Chapman's requests to see Freda and Diane grew more urgent. Reed stalled, and every time he did so, Chapman's face would fall, and he would shuffle off to his room. Backwell and Tooth treated him like a particularly fractious and unpredictable teenager. 'Eddie had moods,' wrote Backwell. 'If things did not go as he planned, he would go upstairs to bed and stay there for hours on end and refuse to eat. He never got annoyed with Allan and me on these occasions. But we left him alone when he felt like this.'

Chapman's deteriorating temperament cast a pall over the Christmas celebrations at 35, Crespigny Road. Backwell roasted a chicken with sausages. Tooth took some photographs around the Formica-topped kitchen table: the series offers a strange reflection of Chapman's volatile mood swings: in one snap he is drinking beer and grinning at the camera, in the next he appears sunk in misery.

Another reason for Chapman's frustration was the continuing difficulty in communicating with his German spymasters. His wireless could pick up messages sent from France, but he was unable to make direct contact and had to send his replies 'blind'. Soon after Christmas, Reed announced that he had solved the problem. Chapman had casually remarked that during his time in La Bretonnière he had noticed a loose switch on the wireless, which he had fixed by soldering it with a hot poker. This, noted Reed primly, is 'a method not calculated to provide a really satisfactory electrical connection'. He took the machine home, mended the switch himself, and returned the next morning saying he was sure it would now work.

Chapman had written and encoded a simple message overnight. Reed checked it over, approved it, and switched on the wireless. At 9.45, a connection was made with the Paris receiving station. Everything was working perfectly. But in their haste and excitement to see if the repair had worked, they made a mistake. It was the first error of the entire case, but it was also the very worst mistake they could have made. At 9.47 on 27 December, Chapman tapped out the following message: 'CALL AT 1000 IF PARIS UNABLE RECEIVE ME. OK FRITZ. HU HA HU HO.' The acknowledgement came back that the message had been clearly received. Reed and Chapman were jubilant.

Ten minutes later, they were sitting over a cup of tea in the kitchen when Chapman suddenly turned pale, and stammered: 'My God, I believe I forgot the Fs.'

14

What a Way Out

The wrath of Tar Robertson was terrifying to behold. Tin Eye Stephens was so angry so much of the time that his underlings had become used to it; but Tar practically never lost his temper. 'He was non-judgemental,' said one friend. 'He saw the best in everyone.' On the morning of 28 December, when Reed stutteringly informed his boss that he had just sent a message on the Zinc traffic without the agreed 'all OK' sign, Robertson did not see the best in Reed. He saw red.

By omitting the five Fs from the start of the message Chapman and Reed had accidentally indicated to Von Gröning that Fritz was being controlled by British intelligence. Not only had this probably scuppered one of the most promising double agents of the war, there was a risk it could tip off the Abwehr to the fact that other supposedly loyal agents were being similarly controlled. The entire Double Cross system might be in danger.

Reed was crippled with embarrassment and contrition. For a wireless operator of his experience, this was a mistake so elementary as to be almost unforgivable. Part of Reed's job was to watch for so-called 'control signs' which an agent might surreptitiously insert into his traffic to alert a German handler that he was working under duress. Sometimes these tip-offs were minuscule: omitting a word of greeting, the addition (or omission) of an X or a full stop. But Chapman's agreed sign, to indicate that he was still a free agent, was obvious and unmistakable; MI5 knew what it was; it had been used in each of Zigzag's messages to date.

Young Reed fired off a volley of painful excuses. 'From the fact that both Zigzag and I completely forgot about them [the five Fs], it can be seen that they are a very easy thing to omit,' he grovelled. He pointed out that Chapman would 'undoubtedly have done the same thing if he had been operating as a free agent', which was hardly the point. He also claimed that since 'Zigzag has already sent two messages including the five Fs, I personally do not feel that this omission is as bad as it would have been had it occurred earlier during his traffic'. This was the flailing shame of a man desperately trying to mollify his incandescent boss.

The same evening, at the second agreed receiving window of 5.00 p.m., Chapman and Reed sent another message, this time making no mistake. 'FFFFF SORRY DRUNK OVER XMAS FORGOT FFFFF. HAPPY XMAS. F.'

'They may forget about the inclusion of the five F's themselves,' wrote Reed, with a confidence he did not feel. For the next twenty-four hours MI5 anxiously scanned the Most Secret Sources, expecting to see a flurry of transmissions indicating that Von Gröning now knew that his agent had been caught and was transmitting under British control. Finally, the interceptors picked up a laconic message: 'Message of 14 letters from Fritzchen deciphered. It was found that this did not begin with 5 enciphered F's.' Von Gröning had believed the second message. A stupid mistake on one side had been cancelled out by an equally foolish error on the other, and poor, frazzled Reed could breathe again. Much later, he would claim the mistake was merely 'annoying'. At the time it was mortifying.

Chapman was relieved, but increasingly restless. A life of domesticity locked up in a suburban house with two ex-policemen was not quite how he had envisaged the role of a spy. He began to agitate for a decision about what would be done with him. He drew up a note, under the heading: 'Work I could possibly do in France', and gave it to Reed:

> Preparations should now be put in running order for my return. I have been given to understand that my liberty is to be given to me on my return to France – It has been suggested by Dr Graumann I should make a tour of Germany. But of course I think I can also stay in Paris. There are many points which could be attacked and I can give fairly good schemes for attacking them . . . I can supply detonators and a small quantity of dynamite and details of places to be attacked. If I were given two or three good men and allowed to train them myself, allowed to fix things up for them in France, allowed a free hand in my own methods, I am sure I can accomplish good work. On the other hand if we only want information then again I must be trained more thoroughly in German as my knowledge is not enough and also in different army and navy specialities. This is rather a long job and if the people who are preparing the things for my departure will come and see me and take down my ideas I am sure good results will be obtained.

Laurie Marshall, Reed's deputy, was duly dispatched to Crespigny Road to hear Chapman's ideas, which ranged from the simple and effective to the dramatic and bizarre. If he was returned to Nantes, Chapman explained, he could conceal coded information in the 'silly joking messages' he sent in his radio transmissions; more ambitiously, if the British sent out a sabotage team, he could try to supply them with explosives and detonators from the stock in Graumann's office in La Bretonnière. 'The men must be very resolute and prepared to lose their lives,' Chapman insisted. Among the possible targets would be Gestapo offices, Abwehr HQs and SS officers. Chapman had noticed that senior Abwehr officers often sent one another cases of cognac as gifts; it would be comparatively easy to make a booby trap from one of these, and pack it with 'sufficient explosive to destroy a whole building'. Marshall found Chapman's enthusiasm 'a little sinister', but reported that the discussion had provided 'an excellent indication of the way Zigzag's mind is working'.

There was no sign, as yet, that the Abwehr suspected anything was amiss, but to sustain Von Gröning's faith in his agent some sort of demonstration of Chapman's skills would soon be required. 'We should do all that we can to arrange a speedy and spectacular explosion of some kind at the De Havilland works,' wrote Masterman. This staged act of sabotage should then be widely reported in the press, and certainly in *The Times* – Von Gröning's British newspaper of choice.

It was an article of faith among the Double Cross team that a double agent should, as far as possible, live the life the Germans believed he was living, and do the things he claimed to be doing. Masterman called this 'the principle of verisimilitude, the imperative necessity of making the agent actually experience all that he professes to have done'. It is far easier, under interrogation, to tell part of the truth than to sustain a latticework of pure lies. If Chapman was going to pretend to have blown up the De Havilland factory, then he must go and case the joint, precisely as he would if he were genuinely bent on sabotage.

Chapman and Backwell made the 10-mile journey to Hatfield by bus, and got off at the stop just beyond the factory. Chapman carefully surveyed the target as they walked slowly around the perimeter fence. Near the main entrance, as arranged, Backwell stopped and stood with his back to the plant, while Chapman looked over his shoulder and described, while pretending to chat with his friend, everything in sight: the gate appeared to be manned by a single police guard, and inside the compound Chapman thought he could see three possible powerhouses. In the field he counted twenty-five aircraft, Chapman's first sight of the sleek wooden Mosquitoes. Even to the eyes of an amateur they were beautiful little planes, which 'also conveyed an air of warlike viciousness'. A little further along, the fence ran behind the garden of The Comet public house. Next door to the pub was a small café. The morning shift was just arriving, and the guard plainly knew all the factory workers by sight, for he nodded to each as they passed, entering the names on a list.

Chapman and Backwell repaired to the café for a cup of tea. In the corner of the tearoom sat a man in uniform, a lance corporal, who stared at them but said nothing. Could he be an Abwehr spy, sent to see if Fritz was performing his mission? Or was he just a vigilant serviceman on leave, wondering why two men were chatting in undertones next to an important military factory in the middle of a war? Would he give the alarm and have them arrested? Backwell rejected the thought: 'He seemed more nervous than suspicious.' Perhaps the corporal was just late back from leave.

That night, with the agreement of the factory owner, who had been brought into the plot by MI5, Backwell and Chapman returned and inspected the area more thoroughly. Four large transformers were housed inside a walled yard. Nearby was a building beside an empty swimming pool. In their reconnaissance photographs the Germans had incorrectly identified this as a subsidiary powerhouse, when it contained only an old boiler and pump for the disused swimming pool. At night, the main entrance was still guarded, but a smaller gate, alongside the pub, was simply left locked. Chapman explained that, if he was really trying to cripple the factory, he would climb over this small gate in the middle of the night, clipping the barbed wire on top and using the pub as cover. He would then plant two suitcases, each filled with 30 lbs of explosives: one under the main bank of transformers, and the other in the supposed subsidiary power-house. Each of these would be primed with a wristwatch fuse on a one-hour delay. If such an attack were mounted in reality, it 'would completely ruin the output of the whole factory'. Of course, not even a super-spy would be able to lug 60 lbs of explosive and two suitcases over a barbed-wire gate on his own:

for this fictional feat of sabotage, Chapman would need an equally imaginary accomplice. Jimmy Hunt would be the ideal man for the job, and since he was still firmly incarcerated, he was in no position to object.

On New Year's Eve, Chapman sent a message to Von Gröning: 'FFFFF WENT DOWN AND SAW WALTER. IT IS VERY DIFFICULT JOB. IT CAN BE DONE. I HAVE CLOTHES TICKETS ETC.'

The inside of the De Havilland plant was only one picture Chapman would have to be able to paint with confidence on his return to France. If he was to convince Von Gröning that he had reestablished contact with his Soho criminal friends, then he would have to go to Soho; if he was going to claim that he had landed near Ely and then taken the morning train to London, he would have to be able to describe what the place looked like in daylight. His German spymaster had asked for additional information such as troop movements and defensive measures, and if he was going to maintain his credibility he would have to start delivering – or at least appearing to deliver – what they wanted. Clearly, he could not do this cooped up in Hendon. He would need to go and do some snooping; John Masterman and the censors on the Twenty Committee could then decide what could be safely sent to Von Gröning.

MI5 sensed that the Abwehr was becoming impatient. Fritz had been in Britain for three weeks when a message arrived demanding: 'PLEASE SEND SPECIFIC INFO ON MAIN GOVERNMENT AND WAR OFFICES.' A few days later another message landed: 'PLEASE GIVE NAME PLACE AND SHORT DESCRIPTION OF YOUR ARRIVAL.'

Chapman swiftly replied: 'FFFFF LANDED TWO MILES NORTH OF ELY AND BURIED GEAR. TOOK TRAIN NEXT DAY WITH TRANSMITTER TO LONDON AND LATER CONTACTED FRIENDS. ALL OK. FRITZ.' But Von Gröning had plainly had enough of cheery but vague reassurances. He wanted some particulars. So Backwell and Tooth now instituted a series of day trips for their housemate. They took him back to Ely, to the spot where he had landed, and traced his notional walk to Wisbech railway station, where they ate fish and chips. They visited the spots that a German spy might visit: they walked around the Hendon aerodrome, the London railway termini, and the parts of the City of London that had suffered recent bomb damage. They began to drop in more often at the Hendon Way pub, where the three men became 'well known and accepted'. No one asked them questions; there was something about the two older men, sitting in front of their beer in the corner of the snug that did not invite familiarity.

They went clothes shopping in the West End, keeping a lookout for military transport vehicles, American army signs, bomb damage, government offices and criminals who might recognise Chapman. 'Eddie soon began to regain his confidence,' Backwell reported; 'In spite of this he never tried to lose either Allan or myself, and seemed nervous if we were away from him for a short time.' Such trips were vital background for Chapman's cover story, but more than that they 'helped to keep his mind occupied'. As Backwell and Tooth were discovering, Chapman's mind, when left unoccupied, tended to turn to dark thoughts, dwelling on Freda and his daughter, and his own sexual frustration.

Chapman seemed 'terribly restless'. He remarked that he did not know how to translate the technical German words used in bomb-making, so a German teacher, Mrs Barton, was sent to Crespigny Road to provide personal tuition. John Masterman, like a don with a demanding student, suggested he be given the four-volume Muret Saunders German dictionary, to study in bed. More books and magazines were provided, but Chapman could not sit still for more than a few minutes. One night he confessed to Tooth that he had 'feelings of nihilism – when he feels his life is empty and nothing really matters'. Reed was becoming increasingly alarmed by Chapman's depressive outbursts, his fidgety impatience and repeated references to sex. 'His inherent boisterousness and vitality soon turned to the path of the inevitable feminine relaxation . . . Many attempts were made to sublimate these emotions and direct his energy into more profitable channels.'

Reed, Tar Robertson and John Masterman held a planning meeting and agreed that Chapman's restlessness made it 'quite impossible to run him as a long term double agent in this country', for he was temperamentally unsuited to the 'cloistered life'. A broad strategy was laid out: the sabotage of the De Havilland factory would be faked, as elaborately, loudly and convincingly as possible; Chapman would claim credit with his German spymasters, and then return to occupied France, probably via Lisbon; he should not take back accomplices, or contact other Allied agents in France, but carry out intelligence and perhaps sabotage work on behalf of Britain, to be specified at a later date.

That evening, Reed visited Crespigny Road to explain the decisions that had been made. Chapman was sitting in a chair looking 'very pale'. Tooth explained in an undertone that he had been listening to the radio, when Chapman had walked in and heard a 'reference to secret inks and troop movements'. The news referred to some entirely unconnected event, but for a ghastly moment Chapman – as ever assuming a central role in any drama – had thought the report must be about himself, and was still in shock

Reed initiated a general conversation about the future. He pointed out that if the simulated attack on the De Havilland plant worked out as hoped, then the Germans would be delighted and might want to keep him in Britain. Would Chapman be prepared to stay, and perhaps carry out other, faked acts of sabotage?

Chapman shook his head. 'I have another, more personal matter to conduct on my return, in Berlin.'

'Any individual enterprise, on your part, no matter how

commendable, would probably be less satisfactory than our recommendations,' said Reed.

Chapman was tart: 'Since you don't know my plans, how can you judge?'

'I think you should tell us exactly what you propose to do.'

'I will not do that. You would think it absurd and impossible. As I am the sole judge of whether I can pull it off, it is best if I keep it to myself.'

Chapman was stubborn, but with 'a great amount of patience and sympathy', Reed pressed him, again and again, to say what was on his mind. Finally, Chapman relented, and took a deep breath.

'Dr Graumann has always kept his promises to me, and I believe he will keep the promises he made about what will happen when I return. He believes I am pro-Nazi. I always said "Heil Hitler!" in the presence of groups of people and expressed admiration for Hitler as a man and for the Nazi philosophy. Whenever Hitler was speaking on the radio, I always listened with rapt attention, and I told Dr Graumann how much I would like to be present at a Nazi rally where Hitler spoke.' Graumann had promised to obtain Chapman a seat near the podium, 'in the first or second row' . . . even if it meant dressing him in the uniform of a high official.

'I believe Dr Graumann will keep his promise.' Chapman paused. 'Then I will assassinate Hitler.'

Reed sat in stunned silence, but Chapman was still talking. 'I am not sure yet exactly how I will do it, but with my knowledge of explosives and incendiary material it should be possible.'

Reed recovered his composure sufficiently to protest that it would be extremely difficult to get close enough to the Führer to throw a bomb. 'Whether or not you succeeded, you would be liquidated immediately.'

Chapman grinned. 'Ah, but what a way out.'

Reed did not try to dissuade him. Late into the evening they discussed the possibilities. Chapman explained that he could never lead a normal life in Britain, given his past; nor could he remain in occupied France forever. Here was an opportunity to give meaning to his life, albeit by forfeiting it.

Writing up his report that night, Reed tried to divine what drove this latest, extraordinary twist in the Zigzag affair. In part, the offer to assassinate Hitler seemed to spring from the suicidal nihilism that sometimes weighed on Chapman. But he was also hungry for fame, seeking 'the big way out'. Reed remembered how Chapman had once hoarded newspaper clippings of his crimes: 'He can think of no better way of leaving this life than to have his name prominently featured throughout the world's press, and to be immortalised in history books for all time – this would crown his final gesture.' There was something desperate about this self-appointed mission; a crooked man's offer to assassinate a truly evil one. Yet there was also something else, a strange spark of heroism, a sense of moral obligation in a person whose only duty, hitherto, had been to himself. Reed was moved. 'I believe he has a considerable amount of loyalty towards Great Britain.'

Eddie Chapman, 16 December 1942.
Photographed at Camp 020, MI5's secret wartime interrogation centre, in
the hours following Chapman's landing by parachute in Cambridgeshire.

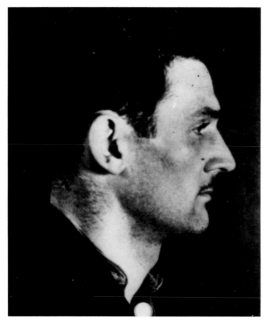

Chapman at Camp 020, muddy-faced after landing in a damp celery field.

Chapman eating Christmas dinner, 1942, at the MI5 safe house, 35, Crespigny Road. The photograph was taken by Allan Tooth, his police minder.

While the previous photograph shows Chapman grinning merrily, another reveals the spy looking more morose – a reflection, perhaps, of his violent mood swings.

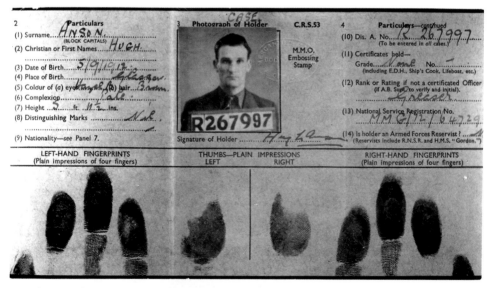

An Irish identity pass for Chapman created by Nazi forgers, one of two fake ID cards he carried with him in 1942. The photograph, taken in a studio in Nantes, shows Chapman in typical matinée-idol pose.

The merchant seaman's pass forged for Chapman by MI5 in the name of 'Hugh Anson', a former member of his criminal gang.

Jersey under Occupation: a British police sergeant takes orders from a Nazi officer.

Norway under Occupation: Vidkun Quisling, collaborator-in-chief and Nazi puppet, inspects the 'Viking Regiment' composed of Norwegian Nazi volunteers.

The entrance to Fort de Romainville, the nineteenth-century Paris fortress which was transformed into a Nazi concentration camp.

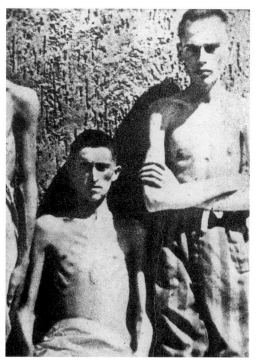

Faramus (*right*), aged about twenty-three, in the Mauthausen-Gusen death camp.

Anthony Charles Faramus playing a POW in the 1955 film *The Colditz Story*.

The Mosquito bomber under construction at the De Havilland aircraft factory in Hatfield, Hertfordshire.

A Mosquito – the 'Wooden Wonder' – being prepared for a bombing run over Germany.

The De Havilland aircraft factory, with Mosquitoes on the airfield behind.
The two men leaning against the wall may be Allan Tooth and Paul Backwell,
Chapman's MI5 minders.

The faked sabotage of the De Havilland plant: tarpaulins have been draped over
the buildings, painted to simulate damage from an explosion, while debris has been
spread around the area.

The *City of Lancaster*, the 3,000 ton merchant vessel, commanded by Captain Reginald Kearon, which carried Chapman to Lisbon.

The coal bomb constructed by Nazi engineers in Lisbon which Chapman agreed to take on board the *City of Lancaster*.

An X-ray of the coal bomb showing a block of explosive with cylindrical fuse, encased in moulded plastic and painted to resemble a lump of Welsh coal.

The doctored photograph sent to Lisbon in 1944 for the Operation Squid deception. The ruler is eighteen inches long but appears to be only six inches, thus making the depth charge appear to be one-third of its real size.

Freda and Diane

Where was Freda? Chapman's inquiries were persistent. What had been a request was now a demand. He was petulant, and becoming confrontational. One night he confided to Backwell that the care of Freda and Diane was the only thing that now mattered to him. He must make amends. The policeman reported: 'He wants to provide for the [child] in whom, he has said, his one interest lies.' He even spoke of taking custody of Diane, if Freda was in difficulty, but conceded that this was 'impossible' in the current circumstances. He asked Tooth, in the event of his death, to give Diane the complete works of H.G. Wells on her sixteenth birthday. But at the same time he wondered if it would be better for his daughter never to 'know of his existence, [since] he would only handicap her and cause her pain and trouble'.

'Personal matters occupy a great deal of his attention,' Backwell reported. If killing Hitler was one self-appointed mission for Chapman, then caring for Freda and Diane was the other.

One night, he lost his temper and scribbled a furious note to Tar Robertson: 'My sources of information have practically run dry. I can be of no further service here, and for many, many personal reasons I don't wish to stay here one day longer.' Backwell passed on the letter, with an accompanying note: 'He feels his present position is intolerable, being in the country again, and yet unable to see old acquaintances and do as he pleases . . . E is essentially a man of action who cannot by nature follow a stereotypical form of living.' Backwell was convinced that only a meeting with his former lover and their daughter would put Chapman back into a reasonable frame of mind. 'The question of Freda always seems to be at the back of his mind,' he wrote. 'The arrangement of a meeting with Freda would almost completely solve his problems.'

Reed was doubtful. There was no telling how Freda might react to a reunion. The security risk was too great, since 'if she bore any malice and realised Zigzag was back in the country she would probably go to the police and cause an embarrassing situation'. Even if a reunion went well, Freda would somehow have to be incorporated into Chapman's cover story, possibly putting her and the child at risk. He told Chapman that the police were still trying to trace Freda while the 'authorities' considered his request. Chapman reacted badly. He became even more 'truculent and moody', and took to his bed. Reed was now alarmed. Chapman plainly believed MI5 had already found Freda, but was deliberately keeping them apart. And he was right.

Police had tracked down Freda Elsie Louise Stevenson almost immediately, because for some years Freda had been trying to find Eddie Chapman 'in connection with an application for a maintenance allowance'. She was now living with her daughter in a boarding house at 17 Cossington Road, Westcliffe-on-Sea, Essex.

Freda's life had grown steadily bleaker in the years since Chapman left her at the age of nineteen. She had been living in the flat in Shepherd's Bush when he vanished in 1939, a few weeks before she discovered she was pregnant with Diane. She had tried to find Eddie, first through a parade of Soho barmen, then by asking around his criminal associates, and finally by going to the police. This was how she learned that he was in Jersey, in prison. She sent letters, and photographs. There was never any reply. Then came the invasion, and there was no longer any point in writing. A rumour went around the London underworld that Chapman had been shot by the Germans while trying to escape from Jersey.

Freda moved on. She had trained as a dancer, but when war started there was less and less dancing to be done. She moved to Southend, to be near her mother. A pale, frail creature, with large brown eyes and a small, down-turned mouth, she was trusting and gentle by nature; but also astonishingly resilient, and a ferociously protective mother. Her father, a bus driver, had died before she was born, so she, too, had been raised fatherless. She did not ask, or expect, much from life, and with what little life gave her, she made do. In August 1941, she had met and married a much older man called Keith Butchart, the manager of a balloon works. The marriage foundered almost immediately. One night, when Butchart was out drinking, Freda gathered up little Diane, burned her new husband's suit in the fire, and moved out.

She was living in a boarding house, and working part time as a firewoman, when the two officers from Special Branch arrived. In the front parlour, they asked her lots of questions about Eddie Chapman. When they went away, Freda hugged Diane, and felt a small glimmering of hope.

Back at Crespigny Road, Tooth and Backwell found that their role had expanded to include the care and maintenance of Chapman's libido. Not only did they have to cook, clean and find entertainment for their ward, they were now expected to help him find women of easy virtue. The two policemen accepted this new duty with cheerful resignation. Up to now MI5 had sought to steer Chapman away from what Reed had delicately termed 'feminine relaxation'. Now they were instructed that if Chapman wanted to relax, he should be encouraged to do so.

On 15 January, after dinner at the Landsdowne pub, Chapman and Backwell went to a part of New Bond Street known to be a red-light area. After a hurried negotiation in a doorway,

Chapman picked up a prostitute, who took him to a flat above a shop. 'Luckily there was a pub just opposite,' reported Backwell, 'and he promised to meet me there in about half an hour. He was as good as his word.' A few days later, the crook and the policemen went out 'relaxing' together. In Lyons Corner House, they met two girls, Doris and Helen, and invited them out to dinner. The men agreed beforehand that if anyone asked what Chapman did they would say he was a member of the armed forces 'just back from abroad' – a cover story that would also explain why he was so unfamiliar with life in wartime Britain. He had last lived in London in 1939, and it took weeks before he adapted to a world of coupons and rationing, blackouts and bomb shelters.

The visit to New Bond Street, perhaps inevitably, afforded only temporary relief. Soon Chapman was more depressed than ever. His minders came up with more elaborate diversions. One night, with Chapman wrapped up in coat, hat and scarf, they took him to see the stirring wartime film epic *In Which We Serve,* starring Noel Coward, Chapman's old acquaintance from his earlier life. Chapman was warned to be alert, and if he saw anyone he knew to make himself scarce and then meet his minders at a pre-arranged place. For a while the system worked well, and several times Chapman was able to spot former associates before they saw him. 'There was one amazing thing about Eddie,' Backwell reported. 'When it came to faces and descriptions he was superb. Often in London he would single out faces that he had seen before in a quite different place.'

But Chapman's own features were also distinctive. One evening, at the entrance to Prince's restaurant in the West End, Chapman came face to face with a 'cat-burglar' in a brown, double-breasted suit, whom he had known before the war. Flushed and 'slightly drunk', the man thrust out a hand and said: 'Hullo, stranger, fancy seeing you.' Tooth prepared to intervene, but Chapman 'looked hard at the man, said a formal "Hullo", and continued down the stairs.' The man followed, apologising for his mistake but still insisting that Chapman was the 'split [*sic*] image of someone he knew'. Chapman now broke into French – 'some jocular remark about having a twin' – and left the astonished man in the doorway. Backwell believed the bluff had worked: 'The man apologised and left, somewhat bewildered but, I think, fairly sure he had made a mistake.' Chapman claimed he had forgotten the man's name; none of his minders believed him. 'I suppose it is natural for Zigzag not to reveal the identity of this cat-burglar out of a sense of loyalty to his previous criminal associates,' reflected Reed. 'After all, it is really not our concern.'

The incident merely served to reinforce Chapman's frustration with his semi-captivity, in which he could observe the London he knew, but never be a part of it. He demanded to see Winston, his younger brother who he believed to be in the army, but was told (falsely) that 'so far our inquiries indicated that his brother was in India'. One night he contemplated climbing out the window at Crespigny Road and heading to the West End, but a flash of conscience stopped him, the realisation that 'it was not in the interests of his work or of his companions'. Yet he hankered for his old friends, and asked Reed to find Betty Farmer. Reed was not certain whether this was for amorous purposes, or to apologise for having abandoned her so spectacularly in a Jersey hotel dining room three years earlier. As always, Chapman's motives were hard to read: here was a man who kept every option open, who seemed congenitally incapable of taking a bet without hedging it. The last trace of Betty Farmer was her tearful statement to the Jersey police back in 1939. She had vanished. Reed thought this was just as well. Chapman's emotional life was already complicated enough.

It was decided to arrange a meeting with one of the very few people of Chapman's acquaintance who could be trusted: Terence Young, the film-maker, who was now an intelligence officer attached to the Field Security Section, Guards Armoured Division, in the Home Forces. In the intervening years, Young had become something of a celebrity as an up-and-coming film director and there were moves afoot to take him out of uniform to make propaganda films. Churchill was said to have taken a 'personal interest' in the project. Young was approached by Marshall of B1A, and asked, over tea at Claridge's, whether he would meet Chapman, in conditions of strict secrecy, to 'talk to him about some of his old friends' and 'build up his morale'. Young was delighted to agree, saying he had often wondered what had happened to his wicked old friend. 'He said that Zigzag was a crook and would always be one,' Marshall reported, 'but an extraordinary fellow.'

Young went on to describe the glamorous, roué world Chapman had inhabited before the war, the people he knew from 'the film, theatrical, literary, and semi-political and diplomatic worlds', and his popularity, 'especially among women'. Could Chapman be trusted with intelligence work, Marshall inquired? Young was adamant: 'One could give him the most difficult of missions knowing that he would carry it out and that he would never betray the official who sent him, but that it was highly probable that he would, incidentally, rob the official who sent him out . . . He would then carry out his [mission] and return to the official whom he had robbed to report.' In short, he could be relied on to do whatever was asked of him, while being utterly untrustworthy in almost every other respect.

Chapman and Young were reunited over a late dinner in a discreet corner booth at the Savoy, with Marshall as chaperone. They seemed 'delighted to see each other and conversation was very animated', Marshall reported. As the drink flowed, however, the discussion turned to the war, and Young expressed the view that an Allied victory was 'inevitable'. Chapman shot back that this was 'smug and complacent', before launching into a paean about 'Hitler's idealism and the strength and efficiency of the German soldier'. Despite the re-education efforts of Tooth and Backwell, the effects of living among Nazis for so long still lingered. On the way home to Crespigny Road, Marshall warned Chapman of the 'folly of expressing such views, no matter how true they might be'.

Chapman's faith in German military efficiency was being undermined in another way: the Abwehr was still having technical difficulty with its wireless receivers. The Most Secret Sources revealed that a new radio station, codenamed 'Horst' and manned by a full-time operator identified as Leutnant Vogy, had been set up specifically to receive Fritz's messages at St Jean de Luz. But on 14 January, Maurice sent a message saying Chapman should continue to send his messages 'blind', because the new aerial had blown down. This new proof of ineptitude offered an opportunity to put the Germans on the defensive. The next message from Fritz to Von Gröning was, in Chapman's words, 'a stinker': 'FFFFF DISGUSTED AND WORRIED BY LACK OF RECEPTION. THIS IS A HOPELESS BUNGLE. HAVE BEEN PROMISED FULL SUPPORT AND MUST HAVE IT. WORK GOING SPLENDIDLY. HAVE FULL LIST OF ALL YOU WANT. YOU MUST DO SOME-THING TO CLEAR UP THE TROUBLE. F.'

For the next few days, Abwehr radio traffic was studied to gauge the effects of this broadside. There was nothing. Plainly, the radio operator had simply decided to suppress the irate message in order, in Reed's words, 'not to reap the wrath' of Von Gröning. Not for the first time (or last) the smaller cogs in a large machine took a unilateral decision to prevent the boss from finding out about their own incompetence. A few days later, Maurice sent a meek message saying that the aerial had been fixed and 'new arrangements have been made'. From that moment on, transmission and reception worked perfectly.

Backwell took Chapman shopping, for bombs. If Chapman was going to convince the Germans he had wrecked the De Havilland factory with explosives, then he must test whether it was possible, in reality, to obtain the necessary ingredients. It was astonishingly easy. At Timothy Whites they bought potassium chlorate in the shape of weed killer. At Boots in Harrow they picked up potassium permanganate and nitrate of saltpeter; J.W. Quibell in the Finchley Road was happy to sell Chapman sulphur powder, moth crystals and aluminium powder in the form of silver paint; flour and sugar could be bought, for a price, at any grocer. Britain might be in the grip of rationing, but buying the materials for a homemade bomb was a piece of cake. (In fact, obtaining the ingredients for a decent cake would have been rather harder.) Chapman's shopping list was never queried: when he mistakenly asked for 'Kalium' (the German for potassium), a pharmacist's assistant merely thought he was being asked for calcium. Back at Crespigny Road, Chapman experimented 'on a small scale' with mixing various explosives. This time he did not practise blowing anything up: unlike the neighbours at La Bretonnière, the good people of Hendon would certainly not have tolerated lumps of burning tree-stump whizzing around their back gardens. 'This kept Eddie busy,' wrote Backwell, but 'he was terribly restless, and could not concentrate for long on any one thing.'

Perhaps Chapman should have been content, making bombs, brushing up his German, meeting old friends, sending sharp little notes to his German masters and gathering together the strands of a cover story, but he was miserable. His longing to see Freda and the child had become an obsession. He talked of little else. Reed realised that a problem was about to ignite a crisis: 'In this frame of mind he might easily have gone bad on us when he returned, and revealed to the enemy his association with us. Even if this did not happen he would probably have been unwilling to carry out any of our instructions and would have acted entirely on impulse and his own fancies.'

Marshall, Reed's deputy, was sent to Crespigny Road to have a heart-to-heart with Chapman over a bottle of whisky. Marshall was a sympathetic character, and an excellent listener. As they drank and talked, Chapman began to open up as never before. He spoke entirely in French, which 'tends to break down his natural reserve and to lead him to express his innermost thoughts', Marshall noted. Chapman talked of his harsh child-hood, his resentment at his lack of education, his impatience and his desire to make amends for the past, and of his desire to find a rationale for living, or dying.

They talked until 3.00 in the morning. Marshall's nine-page account of this 'serious and intimate' conversation is one of the most revealing documents in the Zigzag files: a complete character study of a man wrestling with differing elements in his own nature.

'He is endeavouring, perhaps for the first time, to understand himself and the meaning of life,' wrote Marshall. 'During the last three years he has discovered thought, H.G. Wells, literature, altruistic motives and beauty. Although he does not regret his past life he feels he has no place in society and it would be better if he dies – but not needlessly. He wishes to make retribution for the bad things he has done. He cannot be satisfied that he has done something of value unless he actually performs some concrete action himself.'

He confessed that he was torn between patriotism and egotism, and 'fighting against himself'. Hitherto, he had always 'acted for himself and had done what he wanted to do'; but he had changed. 'Now he had realised that he must consider other people and he was finding it very difficult.' At one stage Chapman turned to his companion with a pained expression and asked: 'Do you consider that personal life is more important than one's country or ideals?'

Marshall replied that he did not.

The next question was still more profound: 'What do you think is the purpose of life?'

This time Marshall had his answer: 'I said that I believed that man was climbing to some high destiny, that he had struggled from his ape-like existence to his present state of civilisation, that he was gradually climbing and that it was the duty of every one of us to help man onwards in his ascent.'

Realising how high-minded this must sound, Marshall added

quickly: 'This does not necessarily mean we have to be "goody-goody". War is a bestiality.'

Chapman pondered Marshall's words, and remarked that this credo was similar to that of H.G. Wells and, insofar as he had one, his own philosophy. They spoke of socialism and capitalism, patriotism and duty. 'It rather seemed,' thought Marshall, 'as if he had come on these things for the first time, and thought them great discoveries, as indeed they are.'

Now it was Marshall's turn to ask a question: 'What personal part do you propose to play in helping man in his struggle?'

Chapman's reply was bleak: 'My life is of little value and it would be better for me to die – not to throw my life away needlessly, but to do something by which I could make retribution [sic] for the wrongs I have committed.'

Marshall shot back that this was 'the coward's way out. If you cause yourself to die now, that is an admission of defeat. You are now a thinking man. Man must progress, and you must play your part in making that progress possible. It is for you to decide whether a British victory would help mankind in his upwards progress, or whether it would be better if Nazi principles prevail.'

Chapman replied that he had already made his mind up on that score: 'England cannot be allowed to lose the war.'

Marshall reflected that Chapman 'has seen too much brutality and horror, the cowed French population [and] the brutality of the Gestapo,' to be able to stand aside. Marshall made his way home from Crespigny Road in the freezing London dawn, convinced that Chapman would now 'play his part'.

Reed was fascinated by Marshall's report of his evening with Chapman, describing it as 'a most valuable character study'. It revealed a man anxious to do his duty, but also determined to find some sort of resolution to his inner turmoil. Finding Chapman's 'higher destiny' in the war against Hitler would not be possible until he had made peace closer to home. It was time to unleash Operation Freda.

On 26 January 1943, Freda and Diane were driven up to London, and lodged at the Brent Bridge Hotel. The reunion took place that night. Backwell and Tooth, such gentle jailers, provided flowers, a bottle of champagne and babysitting services. While Freda Stevenson and Eddie Chapman got reacquainted in an upstairs room, the policemen played with three-year-old Diane in the hotel lobby. Eddie had been coached to tell Freda that he had escaped from Jersey, and that in return the police had dropped all charges. 'He would now join the army and be posted overseas.' She accepted the explanation without question. The following day, Freda and Diane moved into Crespigny Road, to become, in Backwell's words, 'part of the household' now comprising one crook and double agent, one dancer-turned-firewoman, one energetic toddler and two long-suffering policemen.

Freda had re-entered Chapman's life as abruptly and completely as he had left hers, almost four years earlier. In this bizarre parody of domesticity, Chapman no longer demanded trips to the West End or meetings with his former cronies, but seemed 'quite content to limit himself to our own circle'. Of an evening the young couple would walk, arm in arm, to the Hendon Way, while one policeman followed at a discreet distance, and the other looked after Diane and did the chores.

Of course, the twin tasks of running an expanded household while operating an untested double agent did present logistical challenges. Freda had moved into Chapman's bedroom. The challenge was, therefore, 'to get Freda up, dressed and downstairs before 9.45 am, as the tapping of the key could be heard in the bathroom or on the stairs'. There was the additional difficulty that Mrs West, the cleaner, came in during the mornings, but had to be prevented from operating her vacuum cleaner when Chapman was transmitting.

One evening, at around 7.00, Chapman announced that he and Freda were retiring to bed. 'Eddie, we're on the air at 9 o'clock,' whispered Reed as the couple left. 'Don't forget.'

At 8.00, Reed tiptoed up the stairs and knocked gently on the door. 'You've got an hour, Eddie.' There was no reply.

At 8.45, Reed banged on the door. 'You've only got fifteen minutes, Eddie.'

Chapman poked his head around the door. 'Oh no, not just fifteen minutes,' he said, and vanished inside again.

Reed was wondering whether he would have to go in and insist on *coitus interruptus* himself when, with minutes to spare, a tousled Freda finally emerged.

Freda responded to the subterfuge with an impressive lack of curiosity. Her lover was seldom out of sight of one, and usually two, burly men, who monitored his every move. More men, usually in civilian clothes but including one with striking tartan trousers, came and went at odd times of day, and Freda was often told to take a long walk with the toddler. Sometimes Eddie could be heard practising German nouns. There were some very odd-looking chemicals in the kitchen cupboard. 'Freda must have got very used to the strange happenings,' Backwell reflected. 'But she never asked any questions.' When she and Chapman had lived together in Sterndale Road, there had been strange comings and goings and peculiar men whose presence and business was never explained, so it may have seemed just like old times. 'Although she knew very little of what was going on, she accepted things without question and became quite accustomed to the three of us always being together,' wrote Tooth.

The transformation in Chapman's mood was immediate. 'Since he has seen Freda and the child, E has been in very good spirits and says that his whole outlook towards the future has changed. He now has a "raison d'être". He has lost interest in other women and in going to the West End, and says he is quite prepared to remain in this neighbourhood, working on his cover story and preparations for his return to France.' In place of the gloomy grouch of before, the new Chapman seemed positively ebullient. He doted on his daughter, a bubbly child whose vitality and noise filled the house. Chapman's black nihilism gave way to an equally extreme optimism, and exaggerated self-confidence. He even began to discuss what he might do when the war ended, something he had never done before. He talked of moving to Poland with Freda, and setting up a cabaret, or simply returning to crime since he doubted 'his capacity to live a law-abiding life'. But he also wondered whether there might be a place for him in the secret services, as this 'would fulfil his need for excitement'.

Tooth privately doubted very much whether MI5 would welcome Chapman as a permanent addition to its ranks, but noted that at least the young man was feeling positive: 'Previously, he had no faith in the existence of a future for him, and had little desire for it.' Having achieved one mission – reuniting with Freda and his child – Chapman was now eager to complete the next, the fake sabotage of the De Havilland factory.

'What a man!' wrote Ronnie Reed, on learning that Operation Freda had succeeded beyond all expectations. 'It is extraordinary how obvious a course of action seems after it has been taken. The introduction of a specific woman into the case overcame nearly all difficulty and re-orientated the whole picture of his emotional problems and his attitude to life.' By an odd coincidence, it was discovered that Chapman's divorce from Vera Freiberg had been made absolute during his time in prison. He promptly proposed to Freda, who sensibly suggested that they might wait until after he had returned from active service.

There was more than mere altruism in MI5's pleasure at the turn of events: an Eddie Chapman with a fiancée and child in Britain was far less likely to defect to Germany. Given his previous record, Chapman's marriage proposal today might well be forgotten tomorrow, but as Reed noted sagely 'this resolution provides a strong incentive for him to return to Allied Territory'. Chapman's British spymasters were, on the whole, honourable and upright men, but they knew a useful lever when they saw one. Just as the Germans held Faramus as a hostage for

Chapman's loyalty, so MI5 could now be expected to look after Freda, just so long as Chapman behaved himself. Of course, the matter was never expressed in such bald terms. There was no need to be so vulgar.

As for Freda, perhaps she genuinely never realised her pivotal role in the unfolding drama, nor imagined that the polite gentleman visitors who treated her so courteously had an ulterior motive; maybe she never asked any questions because she really never suspected a thing. But then again, Freda was a born survivor, and if she did understand the part she was playing, she was far too canny to say so.

Abracadabra

Persuading the Germans that the De Havilland aircraft factory had been wrecked, without causing any real damage, would require some powerful magic. So a magician was summoned. Enter, Jasper Maskelyne: professional conjuror, star of the West End, and Britain's most flamboyant secret weapon. Maskelyne came from a long line of magicians, alchemists and astronomers (his grandfather had been a celebrated stage conjurer in Victorian Britain) and by the 1930s he was already well known as a master-illusionist, specialising in sleight of hand and exposing the fraudulent claims of spiritualists. He was also a skilled inventor (one of his most lasting gifts to humanity is the coin-operated toilet door. When you 'spend a penny', you owe it to Jasper Maskelyne). He looked as a conjurer ought, with lacquered centre-parting, film-star moustache, top hat and magic wand. He was very clever, and insufferably vain.

When he first offered to contribute his magical skills to the war effort he was dismissed as a showman (which he was) and put to work entertaining the troops. But eventually General Archibald Wavell, the imaginative commander of British forces in North Africa, realised that Maskelyne's talents might be applied to the battlefield. Maskelyne was sent to the Western Desert, where he assembled 'The Magic Gang', possibly the most eccentric military unit ever formed, whose members included an analytical chemist, a cartoonist, a criminal, a stage-designer, a

picture restorer, a carpenter and a lone professional soldier to fill
out the military paperwork. The gang set about bamboozling the
enemy. They built fake submarines and Spitfires, disguised tanks
as trucks, and successfully hid part of the Suez Canal using a
system of revolving mirrors and searchlights that created a
blinding vortex in the sky nine miles wide.

For his greatest trick, Maskelyne helped to win the Battle of
El Alamein by creating an entire array of 'tricks, swindles and
devices' to convince Erwin Rommel that the British counterattack was coming from the south, rather than the north. In
1942, the Magic Gang built over two thousand dummy tanks
and constructed a bogus water pipeline to water this phony
army. The half-built pipeline was easily spotted from the air,
and the slow progress of its construction seems to have
convinced the Germans that no attack was possible before
November. Rommel went home on leave, and the attack
started on 23 October. After the victory, Churchill praised the
'marvellous system of camouflage' that had helped to make it
possible.

This, then, was the ideal person to help make the De Havilland factory disappear in a puff of smoke. According to Charles
Fraser-Smith, a supplier of military gadgets to the secret services
who would later be immortalised as 'Q' in the James Bond
novels, Maskelyne was called in to make it 'look, from the air, as
if the place had been blown to Kingdom Come'. In consultation
with Tar Robertson and Colonel Sir John Turner, head of the
Air Ministry camouflage section, a plan for faking the sabotage of
the factory began to take shape.

At first the planners contemplated laying asbestos sheets across
the roof, and then simply starting a large fire which would surely
be spotted by German reconnaissance. Masterman vetoed this
idea, pointing out that the flames would make a very tempting
target for the Luftwaffe, with the 'danger that the Germans may
try to bomb the factory while the fire is burning'. Instead, it was
decided to erect a veil of camouflage so convincing that it would

seem, from the ground as well as from the air, as if a very large bomb had exploded inside the factory power plant.

The camouflage technicians constructed four replicas of sub-transformers out of wood and papier-mâché, painted a metallic grey. Two of these would be rolled over, as if blown sideways by the force of the blast. Meanwhile the real transformers would be covered with netting and corrugated iron sheets painted to look, from high above, like a 'vast hole' in the ground. On the night of the deception, the large green wooden gates to the transformer building would be replaced by a pair of mangled and broken green gates. The walls of the smaller building would be draped with tarpaulins, painted to look like the half-demolished remnants of a brick wall, while the other walls would be covered in soot, as if blackened from an explosion. Rubble and debris would be spread around the compound to a radius of 100 feet. Colonel Turner assured Tar that the reconnaissance pilots, as well as any German agent sent to inspect the damage, would be utterly fooled.

Chapman tapped out a message to Von Gröning: 'FFFFF WALTER READY TO GO. BEGIN PREPARATIONS FOR MY RETURN. F'

Military meteorologists studied the weather forecast and the passage of the moon, and decreed that the attack would be best staged on the night of 29/30 January, when there should be little cloud cover (allowing the Germans to see what had been done) but long hours of darkness. That night, the moon would not rise until 2.30 in the morning, giving the conjurers at least three hours of darkness in which to perform.

Building a convincing stage-set was only one half of the production. To convince the Germans, the press reviews would have to be fixed as well, and for that only one newspaper would suffice: *The Times* – 'The Thunderer', the organ of the British establishment. Chapman had arranged to send Stephan von Gröning messages through *The Times*; MI5 would now employ the same direct method of communication to feed him a lie.

The editor of *The Times* was Robert Barrington-Ward, a pillar of press probity who shared the same alma mater as John Masterman. Even so, Masterman warned that getting Barrington-Ward to play ball might be 'extremely difficult'. Masterman briefly laid the situation before him, emphasised the importance of the deception, and then asked if the newspaper would agree to 'publish a small paragraph on the Saturday morning following the incident'. Barrington-Ward refused, politely, regretfully and adamantly, observing that 'though he would like to help, the suggestion that he should insert what was in fact a bogus notice in *The Times* cut across his whole policy. Not only the reputation but the public utility of *The Times* depended entirely on the principle that it should never insert any items of news which it did not believe to be true.' Masterman remonstrated. The single paragraph deception was such 'a small thing in itself'. But Barrington-Ward did not budge: 'The answer is respectfully no'.

The editor of *The Times* was technically right: when an independent newspaper, even in wartime, deliberately publishes falsehoods, it ceases to be either independent, or a newspaper. Barrington-Ward also dissuaded Masterman from trying to 'plant' the false story in the press via the Ministry of Information, since this would either involve lying to the newspapers or, worse, letting journalists in on the ruse, a strategy certain to end in disaster since most hacks are, by nature, incapable of keeping a secret. Instead, Barrington-Ward advised Masterman to make a 'private approach' to others of his profession who might adhere to less firm ethical principles: the *Daily Telegraph*, perhaps, or the *Daily Express*. Masterman was not used to being lectured on ethics. Somewhat embarrassed, the two men shook hands and agreed they would both regard the negotiation as 'not having taken place'.

Arthur Christiansen, editor of the *Express*, was either less fastidious, or more patriotic, or both. He, too, pointed out that the hoax 'meant him deliberately publishing something in the paper which he knew was not true', but he was happy to oblige. Indeed, he relished the idea of pulling the wool over German eyes but pointed out that under wartime censorship rules he was not supposed to publish anything likely to encourage the enemy. Reporting the destruction of a vital aircraft factory was firmly in the category of unprintable news and if he did so, 'the censors, as soon as they saw the paragraph, would be shouting down his 'phone'. They struck a compromise: Christiansen would publish the fake report, but only in his earliest edition, which was sent to Lisbon, from whence it would be distributed, via the German consulate, to Germany and the occupied territories. If the Germans ever discovered that the notice had appeared only in the first edition they would simply conclude the censor had spotted it and forced the editor to cut it out of later editions. Masterman drafted a one-paragraph account of a news event that had not happened, and never would. Christiansen, chuckling, translated it into journalese.

Chapman sent a message alerting Von Gröning to the planned date of the sabotage: 'FFFFF ARRANGEMENTS FOR WAL-TER ARE NOW COMPLETE. OBJECTIVES ARE SUB-STATIONS'.

The last elements of the elaborate deception were slotted into place. Fighter Command was instructed to watch out for reconnaissance planes over the Hatfield area, but on no account to attack them. If any factory employees asked about the painted tarpaulins, the factory owner would say that this was part of a test 'to see if high altitude photography can pick up minor damage'. If the press turned up they should be told that 'something had occurred, but very small and not worthwhile reporting'. That should get the rumour-mill grinding.

As darkness fell, a team of camouflage experts from the Royal Engineers, including a number of stage designers who had worked at the Old Vic, slipped into the De Havilland aircraft factory and set about perpetrating the fraud. It seems likely that

Maskelyne led the team, though he may simply have watched from the wings. That was typical of the man: now you saw him, and now you didn't. This was prestidigitation on an industrial scale, yet in a few hours the camouflage team was finished, and Ronnie Reed watched them disappear into the 'inky blackness'. Shortly before midnight the people of Hatfield were woken by a loud explosion.

Dawn broke on a panorama of devastation. The site of the bogus blast was 'surrounded by chaos', in Reed's words. Brick, rubble, bent iron, lumps of concrete and splintered wood were spread around the substation courtyard. From the side, the smaller building appeared to have been struck with a giant mallet, while the dummy transformers lay smashed among the debris, like the guts of some vast disembowelled animal. Even the boiler-room operator was convinced, for he arrived at the factory office 'in a state of great excitement', shouting that the building had been struck by a bomb. A screen was swiftly erected, as if to keep out prying eyes.

Tar Robertson surveyed the conjurer's handiwork, and professed himself delighted. 'The whole picture was very convincing,' wrote Reed. 'Aerial photography from any height above 2,000 feet would show considerable devastation without creating any suspicion.' The weather conditions were not ideal, with thick cloud cover, but if 'the other side paid a visit' they would witness a 'scene of destruction', a con trick painted on canvas. This, wrote Fraser-Smith, was 'Maskelyne's master-piece'.

Chapman dispatched a triumphant wireless message: 'FFFFF WALTER BLOWN IN TWO PLACES.' That night, an exultant Stephan von Gröning ordered 'champagne all round' at La Bretonnière. A reply duly arrived: 'CONGRATULA-TIONS ON GOOD RESULT OF WALTER. PLEASE SEND INFO ON NEWSPAPER REPORTS. WILL DO ALL WE CAN ARRANGE YOUR RETURN. STATE PROPOSITIONS.'

DAILY EXPRESS

Monday, 1 February 1943
First edition

FACTORY EXPLOSION

Investigations are being made into the cause of an explosion at a factory on the outskirts of London. It is understood that the damage was slight and there was no loss of life.

The very terseness of the newspaper report was designed to imply there was more to the story. The first edition was printed at 5.00 a.m., and copies were dispatched, as usual, to Lisbon.

By a pleasing coincidence, the day after the bombing, Hermann Göring, who had boasted that no enemy aircraft could fly unscathed over Berlin, was due to address a military parade in the German capital. Before he had begun speaking, Mosquitoes from 105 Squadron droned overhead, and began pounding the city, disrupting the procession and enraging the head of the Luftwaffe. The same afternoon, Mosquitoes from 139 Squadron inflicted similar indignity on a parade being addressed by Dr Goebbels. Once more the Mosquito had demonstrated its worth. With what satisfaction the German High Command must have received the news that the Mosquito factory was now in ruins, thanks to a German sabotage agent.

The tone of Von Gröning's congratulatory message to Agent Fritz suggested that the Abwehr was in no hurry to bring him back, given the excellent results achieved so far. MI5, however, wanted to return Chapman to France as soon as possible, before the police found out that they were sheltering a known criminal. As Tar remarked: 'The Security Service is, as matters stand, compounding two felonies at least, and a great many more which it believes to have been committed.' Chapman, buoyed with new-found confidence, was just as keen to get to work, as a spy, a saboteur or an assassin.

Chapman's offer to kill Hitler was rejected, without fanfare or explanation. MI5's files are suspiciously silent on the subject. Although the proposition must have been debated at the highest levels, in the declassified documents there remains no trace of this. The official report on the Zigzag case describes in detail Chapman's proposal to blow up the Führer, but the passage immediately following – which presumably records the response to the offer – has been blanked out by MI5's internal censor.★ Perhaps the veto came from Churchill himself. In May 1942, British-trained Czech partisans had killed Reinhard Heydrich, Hitler's potential successor and the head of Reich security, but the hideous wave of reprisals that followed had persuaded the British Cabinet to rule out further assassination attempts. Perhaps Chapman was too loose a cannon to be fired at such a moving target. It is equally possible that Chapman, now he had discovered love and fatherhood, was no longer so keen 'to depart in a blaze of glory'.

Reed believed Von Gröning's promise to send Chapman to a Nazi rally had been 'vague'. On the contrary, it had been most specific. Despite his own reservations about Hitler, Von Gröning had responded enthusiastically to the idea of placing Chapman in close proximity to the Führer, even if that meant disguising him as a German officer. This raises another, intriguing possibility. Von Gröning, like many members of the Abwehr, was fundamentally opposed to the Nazi regime. Some Abwehr officers had been plotting to bring down Hitler since 1938, and the July plot to assassinate the Führer the following year would lead to the abolition of the Abwehr and the execution of Canaris himself. Had Von Gröning seen in Chapman a potential tool for assassinating Hitler? Did the German aristocrat himself cherish an ambition 'to be immortalised in history books for all time'?

★ See National Archives, File KV2/459. Document 254 B, paragraph 50.

Had he divined that his prize spy, for all his apparent commitment, might have an ulterior motive for wanting to get alongside
the Nazi leader? Were Chapman and Von Gröning secretly
working together to this end? The answers will probably never
be known, because British intelligence quietly quashed the idea.
John Masterman seldom made, and almost never admitted, a
mistake. Yet after the war he still wondered if a grave error had
been made when MI5 'declined to encourage' Chapman's
proposal to kill Hitler: 'Perhaps we missed an opportunity,
for Zigzag was an enterprising and practical criminal.'

Within MI5, debate still raged over what to make of Chapman. Reed, Masterman and Robertson were certain that he was
'frank and straightforward', though mercurial. 'His sincerity can
hardly be doubted,' insisted Reed. The Cockney scholarship boy
from the tenements of King's Cross understood Chapman's
harsh background, and could speak his language. Others were
unconvinced. Captain Shanks, one of Reed's brother case
officers, decided Chapman was a fraud, 'a man whose stock-
in-trade is the attractive, suave and agreeable manner, a superficial elegance . . . He gives the impression of the rolling stone
who has gathered no moss, but acquired a certain amount of
polish.' Shanks thought it 'possible' that Chapman's character
contained 'a spark of decency', but he was doubtful. Here was a
profiteer and a pirate who had agreed to work for the Germans
out of pure self-interest, and was now offering his services to
Britain with the same base motives. 'Chapman is no fool, he may
have decided to run with the hare and hunt with the hounds. It is
difficult to accept that a man who has all his life been an enemy
of society should be actuated by any patriotic sentiments.' Shanks
conceded that 'whether a patriot or opportunist, Chapman has
undoubtedly done this country a service', but he could not
conceal his distaste.

Such observations were partly true, but they also reflected the
gulf between the predominantly upper-class and well-educated
doyens of the secret services, and the working-class, unschooled

crook with whom they were now in league. It had not escaped the notice of the more snobbish case officers that Chapman tried to cover up his North Eastern accent with 'a refined manner of speaking', but that he struggled to sound educated. 'His natural and instinctive speech is at times ungrammatical,' noted one interrogator. 'But I think it is to be admired that a man of his background and character should have acquired even the rudimentary culture which he has.'

In no instance was the social gulf wider than between Eddie Chapman and Victor, Lord Rothschild – peer, millionaire, scientist, and the head of B1C, MI5's explosives and sabotage section.

Lord Rothschild was the product of Eton, Cambridge, Clubland and the topmost drawer of British society. He had an inherited title, everything money could buy, and an IQ of 184. Malcolm Muggeridge, the journalist and writer who worked in intelligence during the war, found him unbearable, suffused with 'the bogus certainties of science, and the equally bogus respect, accorded and expected, on account of his wealth and famous name'. But he was also oddly shy, and entirely fearless, with a boyish love of explosions. As head of B1C (with a staff of exactly two secretaries) Rothschild's role was anti-sabotage: to identify parts of Britain's war effort vulnerable to attack, and to defeat German sabotage plots. One of his tasks was to ensure that Winston Churchill's cigars were not booby-trapped. Another, far less amusing, was to dismantle German bombs: explosives concealed in coat hangers, bombs disguised as horse droppings, Thermos flasks packed with TNT. This he did with astonishing coolness in a private laboratory paid for out of his own capacious pocket. 'When one takes a fuse to pieces,' he wrote, 'there is no time to be frightened.' Most people were happy to take Lord Rothschild's word for this.

As a trained German sabotage agent, Chapman obviously needed to be dismantled and examined by Lord Rothschild as carefully as any bomb. They met twice, talked for hours, and got on famously: the crook and the peer, two men with nothing in common save a shared interest in loud bangs. They discussed booby traps and incendiary devices, coal bombs, train bombs and the various ways to scuttle a ship. Chapman explained German techniques for making fuses out of wristwatches, ink bottles, and electric bulb filaments. He showed Lord Rothschild how to conceal a rail bomb with a butterfly, how to hide dynamite in blocks of marzipan, and how to make a detonator from a patented stomach medicine called Urotropin.

Rothschild absorbed it all with astonishment and admiration: 'I think it's terrific what you've kept in your mind. It's a hell of a sweat committing things to memory.'

'I've had quite a lot of experience of setting these things,' Chapman replied.

'Of course you knew a certain amount about this business before, didn't you?'

'I've had quite a little experience getting into places.'

'Are you an expert on electrical matters?'

'Not an expert, but I did start my hectic career as an electrical engineer.'

'The trouble about you is that you're too good at this sort of thing . . . I mean the average chap who presumably the Germans would get hold of wouldn't be so skilled with his fingers as you are.'

And thus they burbled on, delighting in one another's expertise, a highly trained scientist and an equally well-trained burglar.

'How do you open a safe then?' asked Rothschild.

'Well, you stick the dynamite in the keyhole and you don't damage the safe, only sometimes you put a little too much in and blow the safe door up, but other times you're lucky and the safe just comes open.'

Thus the scion of a great banking dynasty learned how to rob a bank.

When the conversation turned to the faked sabotage of the De Havilland factory, Rothschild grew wistful. 'I'd like to have done it with you,' His Lordship sighed. 'It would have been fun, wouldn't it?'

When they had finished with the past, they turned to the future.

'What are you going to do when you go back?' Rothschild asked.

'Well, I'm rather waiting for suggestions. I mean if I can be of any help, I want to do everything I can to assist.'

Rothschild had a suggestion: he would like to get his hands on some German bombs, detonators, and other gizmos: 'I think they ought to provide us with a little equipment.'

'Well, what would you like?'

'Some of their gadgets. If you do ever think of paying us a visit again, we'd rather like to have some German equipment instead of our own, you know. It's more interesting in some ways, isn't it?'

When Ronnie Reed appeared, in the middle of a discussion about how to make a bomb out of a piece of coal, Rothschild turned to him with all the enthusiasm of a child: 'We were just saying that we two would rather like to do a little show together – blow something up.'

Finally, with reluctance, Lord Rothschild wound up an interrogation that reads like a chat between two old friends with a shared hobby: 'We've been gassing away for a hell of a long time,' he said happily.

Chapman rose and shook hands with the chubby, beaming peer he knew as 'Mr Fisher'. 'Well, many thanks, goodbye,' said His Lordship. 'And good luck in case I don't see you again before you go off on one of your trips.' He might have been sending Chapman off on a jolly holiday, instead of a mission into the heart of Nazi Germany.

The Greater the Adventure

Major Tar Robertson came in person to congratulate Chapman on the success of the fake sabotage operation. They sat in the front room of 35, Crespigny Road, while Backwell and Tooth busied themselves in the kitchen, and Freda took Diane for a walk, again.

'I consider you to be a very brave man,' Tar declared. 'Especially in view of the fact that you are prepared to go back to France and carry on working for us.' Of the many spies that had passed through Camp 020, only a 'few, a very few', could be considered genuinely stout-hearted. Chapman, he said, was the bravest so far.

Tar then set out the broad lines of his mission. Once Chapman had learned his cover story, he would be returning to occupied France as a long-term counter-intelligence agent with the principal aim of acquiring information about the Abwehr. He should accept any mission offered to him by the Germans, and then contact Allied intelligence as opportunities arose. Chapman would not be provided with a wireless, since this could too easily lead to his exposure, and nor would he be put in contact with British agents operating in France, being 'far too valuable to risk by any such link-ups'. Arrangements would be made to enable him to pass on messages, but he should not attempt to communicate, unless he had information of the highest urgency, until contact was safely re-established.

'I am not at all keen for you to take any action in France which might get you into trouble with the German authorities, and I am most anxious for you not to undertake any wild sabotage enterprises,' Robertson declared. Killing Hitler was not on the agenda.

Before Tar could continue, Chapman raised a question that had been troubling him since his conversation with Lord Rothschild. If he returned with an accomplice – Leo, say, or Wojch – 'people for whom he had a certain liking', then presumably he would be expected to hand them over to the police on arrival, 'knowing that in doing so these people would be sentenced to death'. He was not sure he could do that. He had never betrayed an accomplice yet. Tar responded that although this was a matter for the law, he was 'pretty certain that we would take every possible step to see that his wishes were granted'. Chapman would not have to deliver his friends to the hangman.

Tar resumed: 'We are preparing a cover story as near to the truth as possible so that if you are cross-examined in detail by the Germans, you need only tell them the truth.' The chief of Double Cross had studied German interrogation techniques, he knew the dangers Chapman would be facing, and he had even drawn up a checklist of ways to withstand the pressure: 'Always speak slowly, this enables hesitation to be covered when necessary; create the impression of being vague; do not appear to be observant; give the impression of being bewildered, frightened or stupid; feign drunkenness or tiredness long before they actually occur.' Chapman might well face physical torture, drugs, or anaesthetic, Tar warned, but German interrogators generally preferred to get results by 'procuring *mental* breakdown . . . by making the witness uncertain, uncomfortable, ridiculous or embarrassed, by stripping him naked or dressing him in women's underwear, making him stand facing the wall, making him sit on a three-legged chair so that it is a constant effort to keep his balance'. Chapman would probably face two interrogators: 'one with a brutal manner, the other suave'. Above all, he should stick to his cover story, and never tell an unnecessary lie.

For all his expert advice, Robertson also knew that if Chapman fell into the hands of the Gestapo, and they chose to disbelieve him, they would break him. And then they would kill him.

The first task was to get Chapman back behind enemy lines, but the Abwehr seemed in no hurry to remove him. Despite Chapman's request to be picked up, the Most Secret Sources revealed that the matter was not even being discussed across the Channel. In response to the request for 'propositions', Chapman sent a message: 'FFFFF PICK UP BY SUBMARINE OR SPEEDBOAT. WILL FIND SUITABLE POINT ON COAST. TRYING TO GET SHIPS PAPERS. SEE BACK PAGE EXPRESS FEB 1.'

The response, a few days later, was blunt: 'IMPOSSIBLE PICK YOU UP BY SUBMARINE'. Instead, it said, Chapman must return by the 'NORMAL' way, in other words by ship to Lisbon. This had always been Von Gröning's preferred route, but there was nothing normal about booking a passage to neutral Portugal in the middle of a war. 'The suggestion was absurd,' said Reed, 'for Zigzag, being in the possession only of a poor identity card, aged 28 and having no business whatsoever, could not possibly go as a passenger.' The Germans probably knew this, and the suggestion was merely a ruse to keep him profitably in place. It was clear, said Reed, that 'any attempt to return to occupied territory would have to be made by Zigzag alone'. To Chapman's way of thinking, the refusal to send a U-boat was evidence that his German bosses were 'not over-anxious to pay him the £15,000 they had promised'.

Masterman believed there was a chance the Germans might eventually send a submarine but was 'not prepared to offer any odds', and trying to keep Chapman out of trouble while awaiting that distant possibility was an 'unenviable and practically impossible task'. Chapman must make his own way to Lisbon, with the help of MI5. Reed asked an MI5 agent in

Liverpool to find out how a man might be shipped, under a false identity, as a crewman aboard a British merchant vessel sailing to Portugal. The agent reported that such a scheme was feasible, 'provided the man could look and behave like a seaman'.

While Reed began planning Zigzag's departure, Chapman made his own preparations. A handwritten note duly arrived on Tar's desk under the heading, 'Points I would like to have done'. It was his last will and testament. 'The Germans have given me a contract for £15,000' he wrote,

> this contract is at present in Berlin. I am to be given the money on my return to France. If anything happens to me I want the things which I have arranged for my daughter Dianne [sic] Chapman to be carried on – for this I appoint two of my friends – Allan and Laurie [Tooth and Marshall] to see what I want doing is carried out. Freda Stevenson is to divide the money equally between herself and daughter. If it is not possible for me to get the money out of the country, then I hope that when the Allies enter Germany they will make the Germans pay up 'Quoi meme'. This I have explained to Ronny [Reed]. In return I offer to do my best and obey any instructions given to me.

Some £350 had already been made over to Chapman from the money he had brought from France: from this, he asked that Freda be paid a regular weekly stipend of £5. When the money ran out, he hoped that MI5 would continue to pay the money until he was 'in a position to repay and continue the payments'. If he came by additional cash in France, he would try to channel the money back to Freda via a watchmaker he knew in Nantes who made regular trips to neutral Switzerland, whence money could be transferred to Britain.

'Zigzag is fully convinced that the Germans will pay him,' wrote Laurie Marshall. 'He does not ask the British authorities to pay any money to him or to his descendants.'

This was all most confusing for the more literal-minded members of MI5. Here was a grasping thief who seemed to have no interest in money for himself. Backwell had also noted that while Chapman was keen 'to get as much money as he can from the Germans, he does not seem very interested in the financial side of the undertaking'. He was scrupulous in paying his share of expenses, and once remarked wryly that with the cash he had brought over, he was 'paying for his stay' at Crespigny Road.

Under Masterman's 'principle of generosity', double agents should be compensated. But how much? Laurie Marshall, an accountant in peacetime, now began totting up Chapman's net worth as a spy. First, there was 'the risk to his life which he will incur on our behalf: he will do his utmost not to betray us [but] if his betrayal of the Germans is discovered he will pay with his life'. An additional factor was the value of the information he might obtain in the future: 'If Zigzag successfully reinstates himself with the Germans, he will be in a unique position to give us full information on the activities of the German SS in France, as soon as we are able to catch up with him.' Yet there was also an entry on the other side of the ledger: 'We cannot be absolutely certain that Zigzag, once returned to his friends in Nantes, will maintain 100% loyalty to us, nor can it be sure that he will fully carry out the mission given to him – he may carry out some individual task of his own. It is not considered that he will fail us, but we cannot have complete certainty.'

The equation was therefore: Chapman's life plus the value of his intelligence, minus the possibility that he might turn traitor, fail, or head off on some wild freelance mission. The accountant carefully added it all up and advised that: 'Substantial payment be made now to Zigzag [and] a further substantial payment should be promised after the successful completion of his mission or our obtaining information that although he had worked loyally for us, his mission had been unsuccessful owing to his being suspected by the Germans.' The money should be added to the cash already paid over, and if Chapman failed to return the total would automatically be paid to Freda and her daughter. In the meantime, a savings account would be opened, and the money invested in a 3 per cent war loan. That way the man being sought by British police and employed by two rival secret services would not only be profiting from the war, but investing in it. The money would be held in the London Co-Operative Society. Chapman had always favoured Co-Ops, though more for what he might take out of them than for what he could put into them.

So far, Zigzag's double-cross had gone without a hitch and that, to Reed's cautious mind, was a cause for concern: 'It was almost too good to be true and much more reasonable that arrangements should go a little wrong.' Chapman agreed: everything was 'going rather too smoothly'. Von Gröning would surely appreciate him even more if matters appeared to go slightly awry. Jimmy Hunt, or his fictional doppelgänger, would be the fall guy.

Chapman had already informed the Germans that he had recruited Hunt as an accomplice, and that he owed him £15,000 for his notional part in the De Havilland factory sabotage. Since it had been decided that Chapman would be returning alone, the fictional Hunt now needed to be disposed of, preferably in such a way as to put the wind up the Germans.

On the morning of 9 February, midway through sending a message to France, Chapman and Reed deliberately broke off the transmission with 'PPPPP', the agreed danger signal. Once again, the Germans failed to spot the warning. Reed was incensed: 'After making such careful arrangements for Zigzag to indicate that the police were on his track, they had failed him in practice.' The stakes would have to be raised.

The following day another message was sent: 'FFFFF DANGEROUS TO CONTINUE TRANSMITTING. THINGS GETTING AWKWARD. ESSENTIAL COME BACK WITH JIMMY. HAVE IMPORTANT DOCUMENTS. SHIPS PAPERS HARD TO OBTAIN.'

The story Chapman would tell the Germans was this: Jimmy Hunt had seen the German message refusing to send a submarine and, suspecting that he might not be paid, had begun to make trouble, demanding that he accompany Chapman back to France; the PPPPP signal had been sent, he would explain, because Jimmy had spotted a police car, which they suspected might be intercepting radio transmissions.

Once again, the German reply was complacent, ignoring the 'awkwardness' Chapman had referred to and requesting more information on the bombing of the factory. Chapman sent a terse message saying that the substations at the factory had been 'completely destroyed' by placing '60 lbs of gelignite under the transformers'. This was followed by another message saying he had 'seen a chance to return to Lisbon and asking if preparations had been made to receive him'. To this, there was no reply. Clearly, the Germans must be made to sit up and pay more attention.

On 12 February, the *Evening Standard* carried a news item under the headline 'Gelignite Inquiries' on the front page: 'A man was questioned at Shepherd's Bush police station last night in connection with the possession of gelignite.' The *News Chronicle* carried a similar story, reporting that '185 names have been taken during a club raid in Hammersmith'. Both stories were, of course, fake, placed in the newspapers with the connivance of their editors.

Chapman now sent his last wireless message: 'FFFFF JIMMY ARRESTED. SEE EVENING STANDARD FEBRUARY 12TH FRONT PAGE. CLOSING TRANSMITTER AT ONCE. WILL TRY AND GET TO LISBON. FRITZ'. In an internal memo, Reed ordered: 'No further transmissions are to be made on Zigzag's transmitter.' The fictional Jimmy Hunt had served his purpose, and could now be liquidated. The ZINC traffic was ended.

Chapman's last, panicky message seemed to have the desired effect. The Most Secret Sources picked up a worried transmission from Von Gröning, ordering radio operators in Paris and Bordeaux to continue scanning the airwaves for any word from his agent; to do anything else, he said, would be 'absolutely inexcusable'.

In a single blow, MI5 had convinced the Germans that a prize agent was now in mortal danger, Hunt had been removed from the picture, and a little more time had been bought in which to prepare Chapman's return trip to the Abwehr.

For a month, Chapman had been allowed, in Reed's words, 'to live as man and wife with Freda and his illegitimate child'. Now the time had come to break up the strange domestic arrangements at Crespigny Road. Backwell and Tooth were almost as sorry to see Freda and Diane leave as Chapman himself. Theirs had been a strange, homely world, a cocoon from the grim realities of the war. Tar Robertson arranged for Eddie and Freda to spend their last night together, not in Crespigny Road, but in the grander surroundings of a bedroom in the St James headquarters. There is an oddly touching exchange in the transcript of one of Lord Rothschild's interviews with Chapman. The two men were in the middle of a complicated discussion about detonators, when Ronnie Reed interrupted:

'Victor, do you mind if Eddie just has a word with Freda on the telephone?'

'No, rather not, of course not.'

When Chapman had left the room, Reed explained to Rothschild: 'As it's her last night in London we thought it would be advisable for her to spend her last night here. He's just getting her to bring some clothes.'

'Beautiful,' said Lord Victor.

It *was* rather beautiful.

'Freda returned home,' wrote Backwell in his diary, 'and we settled down to some concentrated grilling.'

Chapman's life would depend on his ability to tell his cover story 'unhesitatingly'. Hour after hour, day after day, Chapman was coached on every detail of the tale he must tell the Germans, from the instant he landed to the moment of Hunt's 'arrest'. After a week of this, a Field Security Policeman named Hale was brought in to play the part of a German interrogator: he aggressively pummelled Chapman with questions: where had he lived, who had he seen, how had he obtained explosives, and what had he discovered? Hale repeatedly tried to trip him up with strange questions such as: 'What shoes was Jimmy Hunt wearing?' He tried to bluff him, accusing him of being a British spy, and alarming him by claiming that there had been a German observer at the factory on the night of the explosion whom they would shortly produce. Chapman was 'not shaken in any way'. When Hale demanded to know what had happened to the members of the Jelly Gang, Chapman did not miss a beat: 'Poor Freddy Sampson, he was taken as a deserter by the RAF; Tommy Lay is still serving four years in Wandsworth and Darry is doing seven years in Dartmoor. I am not sure what George Sherrard is up to, but he is living in Kilburn and probably mixed up in some monkey business.' As for Hunt, Chapman would say he had been released on bail after his arrest on explosives charges.

Reed, who monitored the trial interrogation, was pleased at the way Chapman had withstood the bullying tactics. He was a natural liar: 'We can rely upon his ingenuity to fill in small details and incidents of an amusing character which always give an added basis for believing that a man's story is true . . . Zigzag is not easily rattled during an interrogation and unless the enemy have some knowledge of his having worked for the British Intelligence during his stay in this country (something which is highly unlikely) I do not believe he will experience any real difficulty in persuading them that he has carried out his mission to their satisfaction.'

Part of that mission had been to collect military and other information. If Chapman was to convince his German bosses of his bona fides, he must not only tell a convincing story, but also bring back some goodies. Chapman drew up a list of all the things he had seen that the Abwehr might be remotely interested in; from this, Reed removed anything that might be useful to the enemy; then they added some additional information, interesting but essentially harmless; and finally some believable fictions, that would set the Abwehr guessing. The resulting mixture – chickenfeed garnished with grains of truth – was approved by the Twenty Committee, and then written out on fourteen sheets of plain writing paper with the secret ink matchsticks. Chapman sketched out a series of army divisional signs, some accurate, some imaginary: 'Blue starfish with curling tentacles on yellow background', 'blue hands and white clouds over top of shield', and so on; he revealed that Llandudno was home to the Inland Revenue office (a building even MI5 officers might be happy to see bombed), and that the Ministry of Agriculture had a branch at Africa House, Kingsway; he sketched a map of the military aerodrome at Hendon, and described the defences around Green Park and Hyde Park in central London: 'AA guns camouflaged and concreted. Few lorries or troops. Piquet guards, ATS, some huts. Four masts, possibly radio, near trees, approx 24 rockets stand and iron and stone ammunition shelters, empty.' Reed calculated there was information here of sufficient interest to persuade the Abwehr that Chapman was in earnest, and in sufficient quantity to show he was keen.

Among themselves, the officers of MI5 discussed what additional information Chapman might reveal to the Germans if he was exposed as a double agent or, worse, turned traitor. Chapman had always been driven in and out of Camp 020 and other sensitive military installations at night. Stephens thought he might have 'picked up the names of officers or warders', but nothing of any great value. Robertson was also sanguine: 'There is no information in Zigzag's possession which we should in the least mind him imparting to the Germans should he be disposed to go bad on us,' he wrote, adding quickly: 'we do not in fact consider that he would go bad.'

There was one secret, above all others, that Chapman must never know. 'It is imperative that no hint should be given to him about Most Secret Sources,' wrote Reed. Chapman had no inkling that the Abwehr codes had been broken. But in some ways, his information had been *too* good: he had provided clues that he believed would help Britain to break those codes – which indeed they would have done, had the codes not be broken already. If he was forced to reveal what he had told MI5, then the Abwehr might conclude that its codes were now vulnerable and change them, providing Bletchley with a new headache. Chapman must be made to believe the Abwehr codes were still invulnerable, by painting a 'gloomy picture . . . regarding the capabilities of our interception organisation to pick up and decode radio messages'. Reed told Chapman that MI5 could gather German wireless transmissions, but found it difficult to trace enemy agents transmitting in Britain, and almost impossible to crack German codes without 'a vast number of intercepts'. Even with the information Chapman had provided, Reed said sadly, 'the successful solving of any cipher must take a very long time'. This was all untrue, but Chapman replied that Reed's assessment confirmed what he had been told by Von Gröning 'that the code in use by their radio stations was a most difficult one and practically impossible to break'. If he was exposed, Chapman could be relied on to confirm the Abwehr's belief that its wireless transmissions were secure. Ultra was safe in Zigzag's hands: the deception agent was effectively deceived.

Having recited his cover story until he was bored stiff, Chapman was set to work memorising a questionnaire listing all the information he might usefully acquire when back in occupied territory. This, too, had to be carefully vetted. MI5 interrogators had gathered much useful information from the questionnaires of captured German spies, since these often revealed gaps in Abwehr knowledge and areas of particular concern. Tar Robertson was insistent: Chapman must only be given 'instructions which, if he were captured and forced to reveal them to the other side, would not convey information to the enemy'. Chapman's questionnaire was astonishingly broad, covering just about every aspect of the Abwehr organisation including its codes, personnel, buildings, relations with the Gestapo, favourite hotels, and plans in the event of an Allied invasion. SOE wanted to know about counter-espionage techniques, most notably the wireless interception station run by Dernbach – the bald spycatcher of Angers. Rothschild asked if Chapman would be kind enough to dig up information on sabotage targets in the UK, chemicals used by saboteurs, and camouflage techniques.

Chapman agreed to all the requests, even the impossible ones, for he was in the highest of spirits. The prospect of peril seemed to work on him like a drug, with Backwell noting that: 'In spite of the fact that he has quieted down in many ways, it seems that he is a man to whom the presence of danger is essential.' Robertson agreed, reflecting that this 'deep-seated liking for adventure, movement and activity is more likely to be the cause, than the effect, of his criminal career'.

The mission was to be open-ended, in time as well as content, for as Rothschild observed: 'You may see lots of openings, which at the moment are a closed book.' He might bring back a team of saboteurs, or go to America, or volunteer to train a team of German fifth columnists to remain in France in the wake of an Allied invasion and German retreat: 'Obviously if he were to gain control of such an organisation the value to the Allied cause would be immense,' wrote Reed. Chapman should use his own initiative: 'It all depends on the opportunities that you see presented to you when you go back,' Rothschild told him. MI6, as the service operating outside British territory, might have had a claim to Chapman's services, but MI5 was already running Agent Zigzag, and intended to continue doing so.

For reasons both practical and personal, the B1A team was confident that Chapman would not turn traitor, not least because of the rekindled emotional bond with Freda, and their daughter. Soon after they parted, Freda sent Chapman a passionate letter, which MI5 intercepted and copied, before passing it on. 'You will see that the incentive for him to return to this country is quite strong,' Reed remarked, as he showed the letter to his boss. Then there was the money: he might be about to be rewarded with a small fortune by the Germans, but his first priority was providing for his family in Britain, and that would depend on remaining loyal. But most important was the character of Chapman himself. Robertson believed him to be 'genuinely inspired with patriotism', and though he might be a criminal, the potential intelligence windfall from having a spy at the heart of the German secret service was an opportunity too good to squander on the basis of mere morality. Tar concluded that given 'the excellent personal relations which Zigzag appears to enjoy with various officers, it would be of the greatest possible value to get him back into those circles with the added prestige of having successfully completed a mission on their behalf'. Reed was emphatic: 'He will be greeted as a hero.'

As the hour of departure loomed, the case officer reported that Chapman was as ready as an agent could be. 'Zigzag is confident that he can put over his story and his morale is extremely good . . . While his interrogation in Berlin may be arduous, after the first few days he should have no difficulty in continuing the old life he used to lead before coming here.'

If, 'by some unhappy chance', his collaboration with the British was uncovered, he could probably survive by playing triple agent. But to do that, he would have to explain why he had included the FFFFF message, the sign that he was acting freely, *from the outset*. In Tar's words, 'it is very important to have an alternative cover story for a final emergency, which satisfactorily explains the deliberate untruth of the primary cover story'. Reed came up with an ingenious solution.

If Chapman was exposed, he should say that MI5 'had detained Freda as a hostage and had forced him to return to France' by threatening to 'shoot this woman'. As proof that he had tried to warn Von Gröning he was under control, he could point to the message, sent after Christmas, in which he had omitted the FFFFF signal. He could claim that the British had then spotted the omission, and forced him to include it thereafter. In this way, a mistake might just be turned to Chapman's advantage. Reed admitted that this explanation was a long shot, to be deployed as 'a very last resort', but if Chapman found himself backed into a corner, it 'might possibly enable him to escape with his life'.

The safe house on Crespigny Road, Chapman's unextraordinary home for three extraordinary months, was packed up. His wireless set was stacked away in a cupboard – he planned to tell Von Gröning he had buried it – along with the fake ID cards, the cash, and the poison pill. He solemnly shook hands with Paul Backwell, before climbing into the waiting Black Maria with Reed and Tooth, who would accompany him to Liverpool for the next stage. Tar had told him: 'Except in special circumstances we do not expect to hear from you, if at all, for a considerable time.' What Tar did not say, and both men knew, was that there was a strong likelihood, once he left British shores, that they would never hear from Zigzag again.

It fell to Colonel Stephens to write the final report that sent Chapman on his way, and he rose to the occasion magnificently, pulling out all the literary stops. Tin Eye wrote with professional pride and frank admiration, in prose of the deepest purple:

> The story of many a spy is commonplace and drab. It would not pass muster in fiction. The subject is a failure in life. The motive is sordid. Fear is present. Patriotism is absent. Silence is not the equipment of a brave man, rather it is the reaction to a dread of consequence. High adventure just means nothing at all.

> The story of Chapman is different. In fiction it would be rejected as improbable. The subject is a crook, but as a crook he is by no means a failure. His career in crime has been progressive, from Army desertion to indecency, from

women to blackmail, from robbery to the blowing of safes. Latterly his rewards have been large, and no doubt he despises himself for his petty beginnings. The man, essentially vain, has grown in stature and, in his own estimation, is something of a prince of the underworld. He has no scruples and will stop at nothing. He makes no bargain with society and money is a means to an end. Of fear, he knows nothing, and he certainly has a deep-rooted hatred of the Hun. In a word, adventure to Chapman is the breath of life. Given adventure, he has the courage to achieve the unbelievable. His very recklessness is his standby. Today he is a German parachute spy; tomorrow he will undertake a desperate hazard as an active double agent, the stake for which is his life. Without adventure, he would rebel; in the ultimate he will have recourse again to crime in search of the unusual. The risk is considerable, but so long as there is a chance of success I think the risk should be taken.

For Chapman, only one thing is certain, the greater the adventure, the greater is the chance of success.

Stowaway Spy

Captain Reginald Sanderson Kearon, master of the merchant ship the MV *City of Lancaster*, had spent his war being shot at by German torpedoes. He had taken command of the MV *Assyrian* in 1940, only to have it sunk under him by a U-boat. Then he took the helm of the MV *Belgravian*, until that was also torpedoed. On both occasions he had been the last man to leave his sinking ships.

Kearon was one of thousands of unsung heroes of the Merchant Navy who continued to ply the oceans throughout the war transporting vital supplies. The merchant ships travelled in convoys, often under-gunned and ill-defended. This was not like other forms of warfare: it was dirty, often boring, and enormously dangerous. The enemy was usually invisible.

The 3,000-ton *City of Lancaster* had been built by Palmers of Jarrow in 1924 as a coal ship; now she carried food, building supplies, munitions, and anything else needed to sustain the war effort, wherever the Empire required it. Her thirty-man crew were mostly Liverpudlian Irishmen, hard men who worked their hearts out at sea and drank themselves incapable on shore. The *Lancaster* was as battle-scarred as her captain. She had evacuated 2,500 people from St Nazaire in 1940, and seen the ship alongside her bombed and sunk with all hands. She had been stalked by German U-boats and attacked by Heinkel bombers, and she had fought back with her 10- and 12-pounders, two anti-aircraft guns and a pair of machine guns, fore and aft. No one pretended it was a fair fight.

A big, bluff Irishman born in Arklow on the coast of County Wicklow in 1905, Kearon looked like Neptune in uniform. His hair had gone grey but the edges of his wide beard were still rust-red, as if corroded by salt spray. A strong mixture of sea water, rum and rage ran in his veins, making him entirely fearless, beloved and feared by his crew in equal measure, and apparently unsinkable. Having spent three years as a floating target, and had two ships sunk under him, this sea dog was longing to bite back.

The *City of Lancaster*, bound for Freetown in Sierra Leone via Lisbon, was at Liverpool docks taking on a cargo of pipes, mail and parcels for POWs, when Captain Kearon was summoned to the shipping office on the quay. Waiting for him was a thin, slight man in civilian clothes with an inadequate moustache. He introduced himself as Major Ronald Reed (he had been promoted). Politely, but authoritatively, the little man explained that he worked for British intelligence. Captain Kearon, he said, would soon be taking on a new crew member, one Hugh Anson, as an assistant steward. This man was a double agent, performing a vital secret mission for the British government, and Kearon would be responsible for his wellbeing on board. In Lisbon he would jump ship. The desertion would leave the *City of Lancaster* short-handed, Reed said, but this was unavoidable. Kearon should report the incident as normal, just as he would for any other crew member. The crew should be told that Anson was a former criminal who had served five years in prison in Lewes, but who had been released early, with the help of the Prisoner's Aid Society, on condition that he join either the Merchant Navy or the armed forces. His cover – as 'a man who had a bad record but who it was thought had turned over a new leaf' – would help explain his lack of nautical experience, and when he vanished in Lisbon, it would simply be assumed that he had turned over an old leaf.

Reed was grave: 'From now on this man's life is in your hands.

It is absolutely essential that no word of his mission should become known to the crew.' Finally he produced a large bulky envelope, tied with string, sealed with a blue seal and stamped 'OHMS', On His Majesty's Service. The package should be locked in the ship's safe, and then handed to 'Anson' on arrival in Lisbon. Inside was Chapman's Colt revolver with a spare loaded chamber, fifty £1 notes, and a ration book and clothing book made out in the name of Hugh Anson. There were also press clippings, describing an explosion at a factory in north London.

Back in his hotel room, Reed wrote that Captain Kearon 'impressed me as being discreet'. Reginald Kearon, in truth, was thrilled to have a British spy on board his ship.

Chapman and Tooth had checked in to the Washington Hotel. Reed was staying at the rather more comfortable Adelphi. Even in the secret world, the officer class had privileges and it was safer that the three conspirators not be seen together, just in case anyone was watching.

Hugh Anson was the name of the petty criminal who had been the driver of the Jelly Gang's getaway car. In his cover story, Chapman would explain to the Germans that he had paid Anson £100 for all his identity cards, and had then substituted his own photograph for that of Anson, who agreed to 'lie low' for two months before reporting the missing documents. Chapman would claim that he had obtained his seaman's papers by bribing one Frani Daniels, a criminal contact at the shipping office. The real arrangements for shipping out Chapman had proved far more intricate. The MI5 counterfeiters had put together a 'complete set of forged civilian papers', including a National Service registration form, a National Health Insurance card and an unemployment book. But obtaining the correct seaman's papers was proving a 'vast and complicated' business. Finally, with the help of a local MI5 operative named Hobbes, Reed decided to steal a selection card from the catering department of the Merchant Navy. Hobbes walked into the Liverpool shipping office pretending to be inspecting the fire precautions, and walked out with the necessary papers – which Reed then fraudulently filled out over a beer in the corner of the Flying Dutchman pub next door. 'This course, though morally in-correct, was practically suitable,' Reed reported.

That evening was spent going over arrangements for com-municating with Britain when and if Chapman gained access to a German radio. Reed decided that the best way to send messages was by means of a simple code embedded in Chapman's 'ham chat', the little flourishes he had always added to his messages, notably his 'laughing out' signs.

The message QLF is a jocular sign meaning 'please send with your left foot', and 99 means something a little more insulting. If Chapman sent 'QLF', it would indicate that his German spy-masters were 'completely satisfied'; if he sent '99', it would mean they were 'suspicious'. More complex messages could be sent using the various combinations of the laughing sign:

HU HU HU: no information to impart
HA HA HA: Nantes Abwehr unit is closing down
HI HA HU: I am going to Berlin
HA HU HI: I am going to Paris
HU HI HA: I am going to Angers
HE HE HE: I am going to America
HE HE HE HA: A group of Americans have gone to the USA and are operating there

'The "laughing out" sign occurred throughout Zigzag's traffic [and] it is not thought that any question will be raised by the enemy,' wrote Reed.

If he gained unsupervised access to a wireless, he should send messages in the usual way but encoded on the word DELIGHT-FUL. Chapman had been invited by the Germans to invent a code word for his first mission, and had come up with CON-STANTINOPLE. If, in the future, he was asked by the Germans to think up another code word, it was agreed that he would select POLITENESS. Unbeknownst to Chapman, Bletchley Park could already read any message he sent, but having the codeword beforehand would make the lives of the codebreakers even simpler. 'We shall not have the bother of having to attempt to solve his messages but will be able to do so immediately,' wrote Reed.

Von Gröning had always passed on his copies of *The Times* to Chapman. When a message from Zigzag had been safely received, Reed would post a message in the personal columns of the newspaper, on either the Tuesday or Thursday after receipt, stating: 'Mrs West thanks the anonymous donor of the gift of £11'. The second digit of the number would describe the number of the message received. So if MI5 had picked up six messages, Mrs West would thank her unknown benefactor for £46. With luck, the fictional Mrs West (a small tribute to the housekeeper at Crespigny Road) should end up a wealthy woman.

Finally, Reed and Chapman laid an 'elephant trap'. Chapman was instructed to tell his Abwehr masters that, before leaving Britain, he had made arrangements 'that if any other members of the German secret service require assistance', they could contact the safecracker Jimmy Hunt at the telephone number: Gerrard 4850. When the telephone was answered, the caller should say: 'It is Lew Leibich speaking, and I would like to speak to Jimmy.' The number would be directly linked to a telephone on Ronnie Reed's desk at B1A, who would arrange an appropriate reception committee.

With a map of Lisbon, Reed and Chapman located the German safe house on the Rua Mamede, and the German consulate. Reed also made Chapman memorise a Lisbon telephone number, to be called in case of emergency. Ralph Jarvis, the MI6 representative in Lisbon, had already been alerted that an important agent was en route. The Radio Security Service and Bletchley Park were instructed to keep a watch for any reference to Fritz in the Most Secret Sources.

At the end of the evening, Chapman announced that he wished to write a farewell letter to Freda. Reed suggested he send it via Laurie Marshall, who would forward it. The letter was copied and duly sent on to Freda. The letter of adieu remains classified, but the covering letter to Marshall reads: 'Goodbye for the present, I shall soon be back with you at 35 – thank you for your kindness to me – please give or forward this letter to Freda.' This was not the tone of a man in fear for his life.

The following day, Chapman presented himself at the Board of Trade office. The clerk accepted the forged paperwork without demur, merely remarking that the shipping company had sent another assistant steward to the *City of Lancaster* and clearly 'did not know what they were doing'. Chapman was told to report to the ship, and prepare to sail the following day. They returned to the hotel, where Tooth packed Chapman's belongings, including two new white steward's uniforms and fourteen sheets of what, to the naked eye, appeared to be plain, white writing paper, and searched his clothing for anything that might betray him, just as Praetorius had done so many months before. Chapman then set off for the docks, Reed reported, 'in the approved style with kitbag over his shoulder'.

Tooth and Reed followed 'at a very respectable distance'. Possibly the distance was too respectable, for 'somehow or other, after trudging for a number of miles around the docks, Zigzag disappeared'. One moment he had been walking ahead, doing a very reasonable impression of a jolly jack tar, and the next he had vanished. Reed wondered if Chapman had suddenly had second thoughts and absconded. With rising anxiety they searched the docks but could find neither Chapman nor, infuriatingly, the *City of Lancaster*. Finally, they gave up, and began walking dejectedly back to the hotel. They had told Chapman to meet them at the Adelphi, but 'some sort of feminine intuition' told Reed that his spy might just have returned to his own, less classy hotel: 'Sure enough Zigzag was in the bar, with a prostitute.'

They decided not to interrupt him, but tiptoed away, leaving him to finish his negotiations. From the Adelphi, they called the bar of the Washington and got Chapman on the line, who cheerfully reported that he had found the boat, left his kit on board, and been instructed to return the next morning at 8.00 a.m. 'He did not wish to dine with us as he was "busy",' Reed reported, delicately. They agreed to rendezvous in Reed's room at the Adelphi at 9.00 p.m.

Reed and Tooth dined at the hotel, and just before the appointed hour climbed the stairs to Reed's suite. On opening the door, they found Chapman inside: 'Zigzag had, in some way, managed to obtain entry and was reclining on the bed awaiting dinner which he had ordered on my telephone, together with a number of bottles of beer.' In the space of a few hours Chapman had confirmed all the qualities that made him a great crook, a superb spy, and a most fickle man: he had written a love letter to the mother of his child, vanished, slept with a prostitute, broken into a locked room, and helped himself to room service at someone else's expense. He had also, it emerged, stolen Reed's gold-plated scissors and nail file, 'which he had coveted for a time'. This was all as Young had once predicted: Chapman would do his duty, while merrily picking your pocket.

Reed could not bring himself to be angry. Indeed, the incident deepened his affection for this strange young man he had known for all of eight weeks. 'Zigzag is himself a most absorbing person. Reckless and impetuous, moody and senti-mental, he becomes on acquaintance an extraordinarily likeable character. It is difficult for anyone who has been associated with him for any continuous period to describe him in an unbiased and dispassionate way. It was difficult to credit that the man had a despicable past. His crimes of burglary and fraud, his association with "moral degenerates", and his description as a "dangerous criminal" by Scotland Yard is difficult to reconcile with more recent behaviour.'

Chapman's past *was* despicable; his recent actions had been almost heroic (with lapses); but his future remained quite unknowable. At the docks, Chapman waved, and headed up the gangplank of the *City of Lancaster*, leaving Reed to reflect: 'The case of Zigzag has not yet ended. Indeed, time may well prove that it has only just begun.'

Joli Albert

On 15 March 1943, the *City of Lancaster* steamed out of the Mersey to join the convoy assembling in the Irish Sea, forty-three merchant vessels in all, escorted by three destroyers and four more lightly armed corvettes. The ships formed into lines, with the escorts on either side, ahead and astern, like sheepdogs, moving the flock forward, wary for predators. Hugh Anson, the new assistant steward, was told to find a berth with the gunners and then report to the Captain's cabin. As the convoy sailed south, Chapman and Kearon held a hushed and hurried consultation. The Captain, 'fearing prying fingers', offered to safeguard any of his passenger's secret spy equipment, and was rather disappointed to be handed some ordinary sheets of writing paper. He locked them away in the safe, being careful not to get his fingerprints on them. Kearon explained that he would treat Chapman like any member of the crew, but in the course of the passage he would expect him to behave in an unruly fashion, since this would confirm his cover story as a 'bad lad' and help explain his disappearance when they reached Lisbon.

If they reached Lisbon. That afternoon, a lone German bomber streaked out of the sky and released its payload, narrowly missing a 5,000-ton cargo boat carrying explosives and ammunition. High above, the Focke-Wulf reconnaissance planes circled. 'Nervous expectancy showed on every face', and Chapman noticed that the crew slept fully clothed. Not that he had time to notice much, as Snellgrove, the chief steward, put him to work scrubbing out, serving meals, and generally doing the dogsbody work expected of a rookie. Chapman complained, loudly. Snellgrove noted that 'Anson was seasick most of the time and quite useless at his job'.

That night, as the convoy headed into the Atlantic, Chapman was woken from a queasy sleep by the ship's alarm. On deck, still fumbling with his lifebelt, he was sent staggering by a huge explosion, followed by another. Two merchant ships and a tanker were burning furiously, and by the light of the flames Chapman could make out the dark shapes of the other ships. A torpedo had struck the ammunition ship. Captain Kearon shut down the engines, and starbursts lit up the sky. The U-boats, it seemed, had slunk away again. The windows of the ship's bridge had been blown out, and glass lay around the deck. There was no further attack that night, but Chapman could not sleep.

The next morning Captain Kearon told him that seven ships were missing from the convoy, three of which had been sunk by collisions during the night, or from damage incurred by the exploding munitions ship. Chapman reflected that this was just the sort of information he might usefully pass on to the Germans in Lisbon, since it would confirm what they already knew, but demonstrate keenness on his part. For the same reason Chapman began making daily notes of the ship's position and course. Since German reconnaissance planes were already tracking the ships, 'no harm would be done by giving the position of the convoy to the enemy'. The Captain agreed, and offered to let Chapman see the ship's log-book in order to chart their exact position. With his remaining secret ink, Chapman carefully wrote down the information on a sheet of writing paper.

Captain Kearon was relishing his new role as spy's assistant. But the rest of the crew did not know quite what to make of the new steward. Word of Anson's prison record spread quickly, and it was agreed he was clearly 'a high-class burglar'. He seemed to have plenty of money, a gold monogrammed cigarette case and he wore an expensive wristwatch. Anson's nickname in Soho, he confided, was 'Stripey', on account of the time he had spent in striped prison garb. But for a crook, he was surprisingly polite and cultured; he read books in French 'for pleasure'. 'Several members of the crew were impressed by his good education,' Kearon later reported. 'The gunlayer summed up the general opinion that he was man of good family gone wrong.' One evening, Chapman astonished the ship's company by announcing that he would compose a poem, there and then. With a pencil and an envelope he set to work, and then declaimed the result. The eight-line poem, which survives in MI5's archives, was plainly intended to be autobiographical, the story of Stripey, who lives hard, survives on his own cunning, and has multiple girlfriends. It ends:

> Happy go lucky, come what may
> Three cheers for Stripey, hip hip Hooray.

As poetry goes, this little spasm of doggerel may not have been up to much, but to the ears of Chapman's messmates it was Shakespeare, further evidence that they were in the presence of a genuine gentleman robber. Anson was certainly bolshy enough to be a poet, for he grumbled unceasingly. The Captain duly noted down his poor attitude in the ship's log: 'He said he did not like sea life as no one did their share of work, he said he did most of the work. This is definitely untrue, as I, master, have observed.'

On the 18th the *City of Lancaster* steamed into the Tagus, and tied up at Santos Quay. Portugal was still neutral, though its dictator was inclining to the Nazis, and Lisbon was a boiling cauldron of espionage, awash with refugees, smugglers, spies, hustlers, arms dealers, wheeler-dealers, middlemen, deserters, profiteers and prostitutes. It was Chapman's kind of town. John Masterman described Lisbon in his post-war novel, *The Case of the Four Friends*, as a 'sort of international clearing ground, a busy

ant heap of spies and agents, where political and military secrets
and information – true and false, but mainly false – were bought
and sold and where men's brains were pitted against each other'.
The Allied and Axis powers maintained safe houses, dead drops,
fleets of informants and small armies of competing spies, as well
as official consulates and embassies, all under the thin veneer of
neutrality. The Abwehr even ran its own bars and brothels, for
the express purpose of extracting information from sex-starved
and drunken British sailors.

The crew of the *City of Lancaster* assembled on deck for a
lecture about avoiding strong drink and loose women while on
shore. The bosun, Valsamas, distinctly overheard Anson whisper:
'Pay no attention. That's just a lot of bullshit.'

On land, the assistant steward joined four of his crewmates at
the British Seamen's Institute in Rua da Moeda, where all
proceeded to get loudly drunk, in the traditional manner. Anson
declared that he would pay, but after an hour of steady drinking
at MI5's expense, the new assistant steward told one of the
gunners he had 'business to attend to' in town with an old
acquaintance.

'If I find this friend I am well away,' he confided.

When Gunner Humphries pressed him about the identity of
his friend, Chapman merely winked and remarked mysteriously:
'No names, no packdrill.' He agreed to meet them later at
George's, a brothel-bar on the dockside.

A few days earlier, Bletchley Park had decoded an Abwehr
message to another double agent, codenamed 'Father', indicating that the safe house at 50, Rua Sao Mamede had been 'brûlé',
or burned. MI5 had no way of warning Agent Zigzag that his
contact address had metaphorically gone up in smoke.

Chapman's taxi dropped him at a large, dirty building, deep in
the working-class district of the city. The door was answered by
a young girl, who fetched her mother. '*Joli Albert*,' said Chapman
brightly, and then in halting Portuguese: 'My name is Fritz. May
I see Senhor Fonseca?' This declaration was met with 'blank

faces'. He tried again in German, English and French. Finally he
wrote the name 'Fonseca' on a piece of paper. This provoked a
flicker of recognition, and from the ensuing mime he understood that Senhor Fonseca was not in. He wrote down the word
'telephone'. After some more gesticulating, the girl led him to a
nearby café, dialed a number, and handed the receiver to
Chapman. A man's voice answered. *'Joli Albert'* said Chapman.
The password was no more effective, but at least the man spoke a
form of French. He agreed to meet Chapman at the café next
door. With deep misgivings, Chapman waited, smoking heavily
and drinking foul Portuguese brandy. Finally a slim young man
in his late twenties appeared, with a much older man, who spoke
German. Once more Chapman gave his password, and explained
that he needed to see a senior Abwehr officer. Their alarmed
expressions indicated how badly the plan had gone awry. Clearly
they 'did not know anything about the matter', and with every
word he uttered, Chapman was putting himself in greater peril.
He apologised for his mistake and told the two men to 'forget
the whole business'. Then he ran.

Back at George's Bar, the party was in full swing. Chapman
slipped into throng of sailors and tarts, his return almost unnoticed, and was soon in conversation with an English-speaking
Portuguese barmaid called Anita. She was twenty-six, thin, with
a dark complexion, wavy black hair and deep brown eyes; she
was also a prostitute and a paid MI6 informant. She would later
tell British intelligence that the man everyone knew as Anson
had confided that his real name was Reed. Ronnie would have
been scandalised.

Chapman spent the night with Anita in a small hotel near the
harbour, wondering if the Germans had given up on him,
whether he was heading into a trap, and whether his career
as a double agent was already over.

Early next morning, Chapman entered the smart lobby of the
German Legation on Rua do Pau de Bandeira, and told the
sleepy man at the front desk that his name was Fritz, he was a

German agent, and he would like to see the senior Abwehr officer. The man yawned, and told him to come back in two hours. When he returned, the receptionist was markedly more alert, even attentive. An official of some sort appeared, and told Chapman to go to a house in the nearby Rua Bueno Aires. Outside the address he had been given, a Fiat car was waiting with the engine running and two civilians in the front seat. Chapman was told to sit in the back and was driven in silence to yet another address, a flat at 25, Rua Borges Carniero. There he was escorted upstairs, where the two men politely invited him to explain his business: Chapman told the story he knew by heart, for the first of what would be many recitations. The taller of the two, clearly senior, nodded and occasionally asked questions, while the other, a small, fat man, took notes. When Chapman had finished, the tall man thanked him politely, told him to remain on board his ship, but to kindly return to this address the following day.

That evening Captain Kearon could be heard roasting Steward Anson for spending a night ashore without permission, and warning him bluntly about the perils of venereal disease. When Anson told the Captain to 'mind his own business', Kearon exploded and told him 'any future offence must entail prosecution at home'. The crew agreed: Anson was on very thin ice.

Though Captain Kearon put on a grand show of fury, the master of the *City of Lancaster* was deeply relieved to see Chapman return. When they were alone, Chapman described how he had spent two days being ferried and shunted from place to place, and added that if and when he came to make a report to MI5, he could tell them the Abwehr is a bureaucratic nightmare. Kearon would later state: 'He instructed me to report that the organisation worked just the same as it does in London. He said Ronnie would be pleased to hear that!' Kearon made a suggestion: when Chapman was ready to leave the ship, he should start a fight. This would allow the Captain to punish him, and provide the obvious rationale that Anson had jumped ship to avoid another prison sentence in Britain.

When Chapman returned the next day to Rua Borges Carniero, he was ushered into the presence of an elegant young man in horn-rimmed spectacles, who introduced himself as 'Baumann' in excellent English, and 'apologised for the inconvenience' of the previous day and Germany's failure to welcome him with due fanfare. The man offered Chapman a cigar and a glass of brandy, and invited him to tell his story once more. The identity of Chapman's suave interrogator is uncertain: MI5 would later identify Baumann, alias Blaum, alias Bodo, as an officer who had served as chief of the Abwehr sabotage section in Lisbon since 1942. But it is equally possible that Baumann was Major Kremer von Auenrode, alias Ludovico von Kartsthoff, the head of the Lisbon Abwehr station. Chapman himself believed that Baumann was 'connected with Johnny', the German codename for agent Snow. Owens's German controller had been a Major Nikolaus Ritter, alias Doktor Rantzau. Whoever he was, Baumann seemed to know a great deal about Chapman's time in France, his mission and its results.

Chapman handed over the sheets of paper with secret writing, and then made Baumann an offer he had been mulling over since setting sail for Lisbon. During his sabotage training in Berlin, Chapman explained, he had learned how to construct a coal bomb by drilling a cavity into a large lump of coal, and then packing it with high explosive. Placed in the bunkers of a ship, the device would remain unnoticed until shovelled into the furnace, whereupon it would explode, sinking the vessel.

If Baumann would provide him with such a bomb, said Chapman, he would hide it among the coal on the *City of Lancaster*, then jump ship as planned, and send the boat, her captain and crew to the bottom of the Atlantic Ocean.

Tar Robertson was unflappable. But when the latest batch of wireless intercepts arrived from the Most Secret Sources on the morning of 21 January, he almost took flight. Agent Zigzag had been in Lisbon two days, and already he seemed to be contemplating an act of gross treachery by offering to sink the ship that had taken him there.

In a top-secret message, the Abwehr station in Lisbon had informed Admiral Wilhelm Canaris that Agent Fritz was in a position to sabotage a British merchant vessel with a coal bomb, and requested authorisation to proceed. The operation required permission from the Abwehr chief himself, since it 'contravened the established policy of the Abwehr not to undertake sabotage in or from Portugal'. To make matters worse, the same message described the precise route to Lisbon taken by the *City of Lancaster*, and how many ships had been sunk in the attack on the convoy: this information could only come from Chapman. At the very least he had 'told the Germans more about his convoy than he should have done'. At worst, it was further evidence of treachery.

Robertson convened a crisis meeting, and drew up a series of aims, in order of priority. First, to protect the ship and its crew; second, to preserve the Ultra secret and the Most Secret Sources; and finally, 'not to interrupt Zigzag's mission unless he was, or it seemed probable that he was, double-crossing us'.

Reed could not believe that Chapman would turn traitor so swiftly. Had he been forced or instructed to carry out the sabotage, or was it his own idea? 'Whatever view we took of Zigzag's character and patriotism we could not run the risk of taking it for granted that he would not, in fact, commit the sabotage,' he wrote. While the meeting was still in progress, Berlin sent a message approving the sabotage of the *City of Lancaster*.

MI6 had also read the cables, and offered to use its own people in Lisbon to neutralise Zigzag. Robertson told them to wait. The *City of Lancaster* was not due to leave port for a few days, and since Chapman was planning to jump ship just before she set sail, there was probably still time to intercept him, and the coal bomb.

Major Reed, wrote Tar, was 'acquainted with the relevant facts and considerations'. Moreover, 'the master and Zigzag both know Mr Reed and it is therefore easier for him to approach them with less chance of arousing German suspicion'. Reed must fly to Lisbon at once, where he should find Chapman and interrogate him immediately. Unless Chapman volunteered information about the sabotage plot, freely and without prompting, he should be arrested at gunpoint and 'brought back in irons'. Chapman might be surprised to see Reed pop up in Lisbon, but there was no reason he should deduce that the Abwehr's messages had been intercepted: 'It would be quite natural for us to send Mr Reed out to ascertain if he had contacted the Germans and what they had said.'

Little Ronnie Reed, the radio ham who had joined up because he liked to play with wirelesses, was about to find himself a leading player in a rapidly unfolding drama that might require him to bring a known criminal back to justice at the point of a gun.

While Reed was scrambling to catch the next passenger flight to Lisbon, Chapman went back to Rua Borges Carniero to pick up the bombs. A few days earlier he had handed Baumann a sample lump of coal from the ship's bunkers. Welsh coal has a distinctive grain and colour, and the German forgers had achieved remarkable results. Baumann now presented him with two irregular black lumps about 6-inches square – in shape, weight and texture indistinguishable from real Welsh coal. Rather than drill out an existing piece of coal, as the Doctor had done, in order to pack in more explosive Baumann's engineers had taken a canister of explosive with a fuse attached, and moulded a plastic covering around it, which had been painted and covered in coal dust. The only clue to the lethal contents was 'a small aperture, the diameter of a pencil, in one face'.

Chapman was impressed: the bombs, he declared, 'could not possibly be detected'. He told Baumann he would plant them in the bunkers that night, and jump ship the following morning. Baumann confirmed that all the necessary paperwork was ready to get him out of the country, including a new passport with a photograph taken in Lisbon two days earlier.

That evening, Chapman walked up the gangplank of the *City of Lancaster*, somewhat gingerly, with two large coal bombs in a rucksack strapped to his back. He did not know that Ronnie Reed was hurtling towards Portugal as fast as wartime air travel could carry him; nor did he know that Captain Jarvis of MI6 had posted an agent to watch the ship, and was standing by for orders to seize and, if necessary, kill him.

But Chapman was not going anywhere near the furnace, and he had no intention of blowing up the ship. He was simply using his initiative, as instructed. His friend and fellow bomb-enthusiast, that courtly and well-bred 'Mr Fisher', had asked him to obtain some German sabotage 'toys', and that was precisely what he intended to do. Mr Fisher, he reflected, would be thrilled to get his hands on the two beauties in his backpack.

Once on board, Chapman carefully stashed the rucksack in his locker. He then approached a large gunner by the name of Dermot O'Connor, who was dozing on his bunk, and punched him hard on the nose. The brawny Irishman had been identified by Chapman as the crewmember most likely to be goaded into a brawl without asking awkward questions. This conjecture was proven entirely accurate.

O'Connor erupted from his berth like a surfacing killer whale, and the two men set about thumping one another with enthusiasm, noise and any weaponry that came to hand. There are two versions of how the fight ended: according to Chapman's self-flattering account, he finished off O'Connor by whacking him on the head with a half-empty bottle of whisky; according to Captain Kearon (and every other witness), O'Connor neatly felled Chapman by head-butting him in the eye. Chapman was carried off to the sick bay, bleeding profusely and shouting that the Irishman had violated 'the Queensberry rules'. When they had been patched up, both men were fined half-a-day's pay by Captain Kearon, who loudly told Chapman that he was now in serious trouble.

A farcical staged scene followed:

Captain Kearon: 'Have you met a better man at last?'

Anson: 'After fighting him fairly and beating him by the Marquis of Queensberry rules he head-butted me in the face. The people on this ship are hooligans.'

Kearon: 'Are you the only decent one on board then?'

Anson: 'Yes.'

At dawn the next day, Assistant Steward Anson, the left side of his face cut and badly bruised, was detailed to take Captain Kearon his early morning tea. Chapman knocked on the door of the Captain's cabin and slipped inside, carrying a tea tray in one hand, and a rucksack with two large bombs in the other. Chapman had earlier explained to Kearon that he was 'trying to get a special bomb on board for transport to home', and he now thrust the coal bombs into the Captain's hands, explaining that 'he had put to them the proposition that he should sabotage the *City of Lancaster* and the enemy had agreed'. Kearon was no shrinking violet, but even he quailed at being handed 10 lbs of high explosive in his bed by a man with a face that seemed to have gone through a meat grinder. He announced that he would weigh anchor immediately and head home. Chapman insisted that the bombs were safe unless heated, and that any change of plan would only attract German suspicion. The Captain was eventually 'persuaded to carry on his usual route and act as though nothing had happened'. Now wide awake, Kearon opened the safe, extracted Chapman's package, pushed the two evil-looking bombs inside, and shut the door, quickly. Chapman stuffed the papers and money in his rucksack and handed the revolver back to the Captain, 'as a present'. In return, the Captain gave Anson the address of his sister-in-law, Doris, who lived in Oporto, just in case he had any trouble. They shook hands, and Chapman slipped away into the dawn.

Captain Kearon's cameo role in British military espionage was over. The British spy had acted his part superbly, the Captain reflected. 'He lived up to his reputation as a jail-bird very realistically.' This was not, perhaps, entirely surprising.

That afternoon the Most Secret Sources picked up a message from the Lisbon Abwehr station confirming that Fritz had completed his mission. The news was relayed by Captain Ralph Jarvis of MI6 to Ronnie Reed of MI5 when he arrived at Lisbon airport at 5.30 p.m. on Tuesday, 23 January, travelling under the name Johnson, an official with the Ministry of War Transport. Reed's heart sank. If Chapman had planted the bomb he was a traitor guilty of attempted murder, and the tons of coal in the ship's bunkers would somehow have to be sorted through, piece by piece. Jarvis explained that Captain Kearon had been interviewed by his agents at the shipping office and 'denied emphatically that Hugh Anson had any connection whatsoever with British intelligence'. Reed replied that the Captain probably thought he was protecting a British agent, and obeying orders to 'tell absolutely no one about the connection'.

Captain Kearon and Ronnie Reed met, alone, at the Royal British Club in Lisbon. The MI5 case officer could tell immediately from the Captain's buoyant and conspiratorial expression that his fears were unfounded. Kearon explained that Chapman had 'behaved magnificently', that the 'plot' to sabotage the ship had been a ruse to obtain the bombs, and that two lumps of exploding coal were now sitting in the safe of his ship, which he would be only too happy to pass on as soon as possible. Anson had specifically told him that 'the coal was High Explosive and was to be given to Ronnie', and had suggested that MI5 should stage some sort of fake explosion on board, 'in order to send up his prestige' with the Germans.

Kearon also described how he and Chapman had agreed that the ship's course and the attack on the convoy could be reported to the Germans without endangering British shipping, and how

Chapman had valiantly allowed himself to be flattened by a large Irish gunner for the sake of his cover story. When the waiter was not looking, he passed over the names and addresses in Lisbon Chapman had left with him, and a revolver.

Reed sent a jubilant telegram to Tar Robertson: 'Convinced Z playing straight with us.'

The relief was shared in London. Not only had Chapman demonstrated his loyalty, but British intelligence now had two intact bombs of a type they had never seen before. 'This is typical of the risks that Chapman has been prepared to undertake on our behalf,' wrote Tin Eye Stephens. He had offered to carry out a sabotage mission knowing that when the *City of Lancaster* did not sink at sea, he would inevitably be suspected of double-dealing, 'with possibly fatal results to himself'. Yet he had been prepared to take the chance. 'He thought that the value to the British of getting examples of the devices used by the Germans justified the risk to himself.'

Slightly less thrilled by the outcome was MI6. Relations between the sister services were often strained, and the men of external espionage did not appreciate the men of internal security encroaching on their patch. MI6 flatly refused to contemplate staging a fake sabotage of the *City of Lancaster* in Lisbon, pointing out that this would be 'politically complicated'.

Jarvis of MI6, in civilian life a merchant banker, put the wind up poor Ronnie Reed by pointing out that the coal bombs might be activated by a delay fuse rather than heat, and could explode at any moment. Reed did not share Lord Rothschild's insouciant approach to high explosive. He thought better of packing the bombs in his luggage: 'It would be most unfortunate if an explosion were to take place in the plane on my return journey home, both for the plane, the political consequences, and myself . . .'.

Rothschild instructed that the bombs should be photo-graphed, x-rayed, placed in a heavy iron box padded with cork, and then sent to Gibraltar on the next British vessel, addressed to

'Mr Fisher' c/o ANI, Whitehall. In Gibraltar, the package would be picked up from Captain Kearon by an MI5 agent who would say: 'I come from Ronnie'. Rothschild was insistent on one point: the bombs should be sent 'if possible intact and not sawn in half'. Only someone like Rothschild could imagine that anyone else would *want* to saw up a lump of coal packed with high explosive.

Damp Squib

No one paid much attention to the Norwegian sailor with the livid black eye who boarded the afternoon flight from Lisbon to Madrid, and sat quietly at the end of the aeroplane. He carried a Norwegian passport in the name of Olaf Christiansson, describing him as a seaman, born in Oslo. There was a party of Norwegians on board, but their quiet compatriot did not engage them in conversation. Indeed, he could not, because he did not speak a single word of Norwegian.

At Madrid airport, a stocky little man with rosy cheeks emerged from the waiting crowd. 'Are you Fritz?' he whispered. 'Yes,' said Chapman, '*Joli Albert*'. At the Hotel Florida, Chapman dined on roast pork, drank a bottle of sticky Spanish wine, and slept for twelve hours. The next five days passed in a blur. Chapman lost count of the nameless German visitors who came and went, asking the same questions, or very slightly different questions. Sometimes the interrogations took place in his hotel room, or in the lounge, or nearby cafés. The rosy-cheeked German gave him 3,000 pesetas and told him he might want to stock up on clothes, tea and coffee and 'other articles difficult to obtain in Occupied Europe'. So he was going back to France. Through the Madrid streets, Chapman was followed, discreetly, by a smiling little shadow.

The man who had first interviewed him in Lisbon, later identified by MI5 as Abwehr officer Konrad Weisner, reappeared at the Hotel Florida and announced he would be accompanying Chapman to Paris. In a private sleeper compartment, Chapman lay awake as the stations rumbled by in the darkness: San Sebastian, Irun, Hendaye, Bordeaux. At dawn on 28 March, the train pulled into the Gare d'Orsay: waiting on the platform was Albert Schael, Chapman's moon-faced drinking companion from Nantes, the original *Joli Albert* and the first familiar face he had seen. They embraced like old friends, and as they drove to the Abwehr apartment on the Rue Luynes, Chapman asked where Doctor Graumann was. Albert, speaking in an undertone so the driver could not hear, hissed that he had been sent to the Eastern Front 'in disgrace'.

The cause of Von Gröning's banishment is unclear. Chapman later learned that his spymaster had quarrelled with the head of the Paris Branch on an issue of 'policy', and Von Gröning's prodigious intake of alcohol had then been used as an excuse for removing him. Von Gröning later claimed that he had wanted to send a U-boat to pick up Chapman but had been overruled, sparking a furious disagreement. It is equally possible that, like other members of the Abwehr, Von Gröning's loyalty to Hitler had come under suspicion. Whatever the cause, Von Gröning had been stripped of his post in Nantes, and ordered to rejoin his old unit, the Heeresgruppe Mitte, in Russia.

Chapman considered Dr Graumann an 'old friend', but more than that, he was a protector and patron. If anyone could shield Chapman from the Gestapo, it was Dr Graumann. His disappearance was a serious blow. The interrogations continued: the Luftwaffe colonel who had seen him off at Le Bourget airport and the pilot, Leutnant Schlichting, quizzed him about his jump and landing. They were followed by an army officer, unnamed and unfriendly, and then a civilian, who rattled off a series of 'about 50' technical questions about British military installations and weapons, none of which Chapman could answer. Whenever Chapman inquired after Dr Graumann he would receive 'vague replies' to the effect that he was 'somewhere on the Eastern Front'. Finally,

Chapman screwed up his courage to announce that he wanted to see Dr Graumann immediately and that he 'would not give his story or work for anyone else'. The request, and accompanying fit of pique, was ignored, or so it seemed.

The general tenor of the questions was affable, but persistent. Chapman was allowed to 'amuse himself' in the evenings, but always accompanied by Albert and at least one other minder. But his request for an 'advance' on the money owed him was flatly rejected. After an angry protest, he was given 10,000 francs to spend, which was later increased, with evident reluctance, to 20,000. This was not the hero's reception and untold riches he had been hoping for. The disagreement left Chapman feeling distinctly uncomfortable.

Chapman memorised the faces of his interrogators, and the few names he could glean. But most of his mental energy was devoted to telling and retelling the story, half truth, half fiction, that had been seared into his memory over the days and weeks in Crespigny Road. The story never altered, and Chapman never faltered, though he was careful to offer only vague timings and dates, mindful of Tar Robertson's warning: 'Timing is the essential factor to conceal, the cover story must not be too precise.' He knew the story so well that, at times, he believed it himself. We know the story, because a verbatim transcript survives:

I landed at about 2.30, in a ploughed field. I was at first stunned by my descent, but on recovering my sense I buried my parachute under some bushes by a small stream running along the edge of the field. I undid the package which had been strapped to my shoulders, taking with me the transmitter and putting the detonators in my pockets. I could see a small barn not far away and, after approaching this cautiously, I realised that it was deserted and entering through a window I climbed up into the loft and slept until daybreak. I was not aware of the time I awoke, because my watch had stopped. It had apparently been broken by my descent. I left this barn and walked along a small road and on to the main road, travelling in a southerly direction, until I saw a signpost which said Wisbech. A study of my map showed me I must be somewhere near Littleport, and when I arrived in the village I saw the name on the railway station. Inspection of the times of trains to London showed that one was leaving at 10.15. I caught this and arrived at Liverpool Street at about a quarter to one. I entered the buffet there, had a drink and bought some cigarettes and, after staying for a few minutes, went to a telephone booth in the station and called Jimmy Hunt at the Hammersmith Working Men's Club. Whoever answered the phone said that Jimmy would be in at about 6 o'clock, so I took the underground train to the West End and went to the New Gallery Cinema, where I saw 'In Which We Serve'. I thought it best not to walk about the West End in daylight so soon after arriving.

I stayed at the cinema until blackout time and then phoned Jimmy again at the Club. He was very surprised to hear my voice, but arranged to meet me at the underground station at Hyde Park. When he arrived we went into a nearby public house and I told Jimmy that I had managed to escape from Jersey and that I had so many things to talk over I thought it would be better if we could go somewhere quieter. I was especially anxious that the police should not know that I was back in the country, so Jimmy said that we had better go to one of his cover addresses in Sackville Street where he was living with a girl. I told him I did not want anyone else to see me, so he phoned her and told her to go out for a time as he had a business friend calling on him. She was used to disappearing when Jimmy had 'shady' business to transact so this did not appear unusual.

On arrival at the flat in Sackville Street I explained the whole thing to Jimmy. I told him that when I was imprisoned in

Jersey I had decided to work for German Intelligence; that
they had treated me extremely well and had promised me a
considerable amount of money if I would carry out a mission
in Britain. I had brought £1,000 with me and had been
promised £15,000 if I succeeded in sabotaging De Havillands. It was an invaluable opportunity for Jimmy to obtain
quite a lot of money and the protection of the German
government to get him out of the country. I showed him the
radio transmitter I had brought with me and said that I
required some place where I could work this. Jimmy told me
that the police had been after him quite a lot lately and that
he had been considering renting a house in Hendon. Meanwhile, however, it would be advisable for me to stay at the
flat in Sackville Street and keep pretty quiet.

I went along to the house in Hendon on Saturday and I
transmitted from there for the first time on Sunday morning.

I explained to Jimmy how necessary it was for me to start
straight away and obtain the materials for my sabotage at De
Havillands. We agreed it would be unwise for me to go out
very much, in case the police were on my track, but Jimmy
said that there remained some gelignite at St Luke's Mews
which we had used on jobs before the war.

I went to De Havillands with Jimmy one day round about
the new year, and we surveyed the whole factory from the
road nearby. We saw that there were three places which we
thought should be our primary objectives. We decided to
hold a reconnaissance at night time and entered by an
unguarded gate, which had only a small amount of barbed
wire attached to it. Near the boiler house, we came across six
huge power transformers in a yard. By climbing over a wall,
it was possible to gain access, and we realised that an
explosive charge under one, or perhaps two of the trans-

formers would completely ruin the output of the whole factory. We looked around and found another subsidiary power house near a building which was by the swimming pool; it was bounded by a high fence and contained two more transformers which obviously handled considerable power. We decided it would be necessary to place about 30 lbs of explosive under each transformer, and thought it would be possible to fit this into two suitcases.

On the night arranged we went up there at about 7 o'clock and parked the car behind a garage in the front of the factory. We had some coffee at a place nearby and then crept through the gardens of a house at the back of the 'Comet' and slipped through the barbed wire at the unguarded gate. Jimmy made for the transformers near the swimming pool and I tackled the one near the power house. We left one hour's delay on each of our explosive mixtures, and stopped our car on the bypass about two miles away from De Havillands. Fifty-five minutes after, we heard two immense explosions, about 30 seconds apart. As soon as this occurred we came straight back to London.

The day after we had arranged for the sabotage, I had arranged to meet a girl at The Hendon Way called Wendy Hammond, who worked at a subsidiary of De Havillands. She told me that there had been an awful mess and that people at the factory were trying to hush it up and say that nothing had occurred. It was clear that there had been considerable damage, and some people were injured, but no one wanted to admit it.

Jimmy was often with me in the bedroom when I transmitted and he took a great deal of interest in the radio messages which we received. He was especially interested to know whether there was any chance of receiving his

£15,000 and when you sent the message to say that it was
impossible to pick me up by submarine he became somewhat truculent and thought that the chances of receiving the
money were extremely remote. He said that he would come
back with me to Lisbon and see that he was paid. Unfortunately, as you know, he was arrested on suspicion of
possessing gelignite, and later the Hammersmith Club was
raided to see if he had any other confederates. He was
released by the police after he had been detained for about a
week, but I did not have very much contact with him after
that. Owing to the arrest of Jimmy it was not possible for
him to come with me, and it would have been very much
more difficult to obtain two sets of documents to get out of
the country, so of course I had to come alone.

Sticking to the broad lines of the cover story was easy enough;
the challenge was to remain alert while seeming relaxed, to
maintain consistency, to anticipate the thrust of the interrogation
and stay one question ahead. What was it Robertson had said?
Speak slowly, be vague, never tell an unnecessary lie. The rules
were all very well in the living room at Crespigny Road, but
under the relentless probing of expert Abwehr interrogators
Chapman could feel his grip slipping, as the truth and lies
merged. The donnish Masterman had warned him: 'The life
of a secret agent is dangerous enough, but the life of the double
agent is infinitely more precarious. If anyone balances on a
swinging tightrope it is he, and a single slip can send him crashing
to destruction.' No one could balance forever, with so many
hands tugging at the rope.

After ten gruelling days in Paris, Chapman was told he would
be travelling to Berlin. The journey would take him to the heart
of Nazism, but something also led him to suspect it 'would bring
him nearer to Graumann'. That suspicion was confirmed when
Albert took him aside, and suggested that whatever might
happen in Berlin, he should 'reserve the more interesting details

of his experiences in England for the time when he might meet Graumann'. The ingratiating Albert asked Chapman to put in a good word for him with Dr Graumann.

The train to Berlin was packed with soldiers, but a first-class compartment had been reserved for Chapman and his new minder, an officer he knew as 'Wolf'. When an army major insisted on taking a seat in the reserved carriage, Wolf summoned the train police and the furious man was ejected, shouting that he would report the offence to Himmler himself.

From Berlin station, he was whisked to a small hotel, La Petite Stephanie, off the Kurfürstendamm. The grilling continued. Chapman was getting tired. The anxiety was fraying his confidence. He slipped. An interviewer, apparently from Abwehr headquarters, casually asked him to describe how he had constructed the suitcase bomb used in the De Havilland sabotage. Chapman explained again how torch batteries attached to a detonator had been strapped to the right side of the suitcase using adhesive tape. The man pounced: in earlier interviews, in Paris and Madrid, Chapman had described how he had attached batteries to the *left* side. Chapman forced himself to think quickly but answer slowly, as Tar had instructed: 'I had two suitcases – one set of batteries was fixed to the right side, and one to the left.' A sweaty moment passed.

The next day, a tall, slim naval officer appeared at La Petite Stephanie, introduced himself as Müller, and presented Chapman with a brand new German passport made out in the name 'Fritz Graumann'; place of birth: New York; father's name: Stephan Graumann. It was the strongest hint yet that his old spymaster was back in the game. Müller told Chapman to pack and be ready to leave in an hour: they were going to Norway.

Back in Bletchley, the codebreakers charted Zigzag's meandering route as he criss-crossed Europe from south to north: they passed on Chapman's new passport names, Norwegian and German, and noted that the supposed sabotage of the

City of Lancaster had 'certainly raised his stock' with his German bosses.

There was only one hitch: the bombs had not gone off, and though the Germans did not appear to suspect Chapman, they were becoming impatient. 'The Germans have shown the greatest interest in the *City of Lancaster* and are naturally anxious to discover if the act of sabotage actually took place,' Masterman warned. Anita, the prostitute from George's Bar, reported that Jack, an indigent black beachcomber who lived under a nearby bridge, had been approached by two Germans who offered him 2,000 escudos for information about sailors from the British ship. The Abwehr had broken all the rules to smuggle the bombs aboard the *City of Lancaster*, but the ship was still intact: Canaris wanted results. Ewen Montagu, the naval representative on the Twenty Committee, issued a warning: 'There must either be an explosion or Zigzag is blown.'

Some sort of incident would have to be staged on board the ship: Operation Damp Squib was born.

Victor, Lord Rothschild was a little disappointed to be told he could not blow up a 'perfectly good merchant ship', but settled for 'as big a bang as possible, together with a lot of smoke'. The prospect of even a moderate explosion aboard the *City of Lancaster* sent his blue blood racing: 'A good decent bang would be a good idea. I do not know how much of a bang one can make without doing damage. I suppose it depends where the bang takes place.'

Together Rothschild and Reed cooked up an elaborate scenario. When the ship docked in Britain, Reed would go aboard, disguised as a customs officer, accompanied by another agent in similar disguise carrying an explosive device in an attaché case. This agent, 'who will previously have been to MI5 head office for tuition in working the bomb', would pretend to search for contraband, plant the bomb in the bunker, light the fuse, and then get out of the way, quick. When he heard the explosion, the agent would 'fall down and pretend he has hurt his arm, which will be bandaged by the master'. He would then explain that 'he was poking the coal in the bunker when there was a hissing noise, followed by an explosion which blew him over'. The crew would then be interrogated and sailors' gossip would do the rest. 'The story of the sabotage will get back to the enemy through some members of the crew,' Reed predicted.

The operation required a special bomb that would make plenty of noise and smoke without killing the MI5 agent who set it off, igniting the coal, or sinking the ship. Rothschild turned to his friend and fellow explosives-enthusiast, Lieutenant Colonel Leslie Wood of the War Office Experimental Station, who duly produced a device guaranteed to make a 'sharp explosion, accompanied by a puff of reddish smoke, approximately three minutes after ignition'. Wood sent a parcel to Rothschild by courier: 'Herewith your three toys: one for you to try yourself, not in the house! The other two for your friend to play with.'

Operation Damp Squib was a very silly plan. It was complicated, risky and involved far too much play-acting ('binding up a notional injury is fortuitously introducing unnecessary "business" of a dangerous kind', warned Masterman). Damp Squib was vetoed, much to Rothschild's annoyance, and he vented his frustration by blowing up all three toys himself.

Instead the bomb would have to be 'discovered' when the ship reached Glasgow; this would be followed by a full interrogation of everyone on board: 'When the *City of Lancaster* next touches at Lisbon, German sub agents will certainly try to get in touch with members of the crew and will get the impression (probably in most cases from some intoxicated seaman) that something curious had happened on the voyage because there was a formidable inquiry when the ship returned to the UK. This is all that is necessary in order to build up Zigzag.'

Sure enough, when the ship put in at Rothesay docks on 25 April, a small army of Field Security Police clambered aboard and began rummaging through the coal bunkers, tossing the coal over the side, piece by piece. The gawping crew noticed that 'as each piece of coal was thrown into the dock they all ducked'. Finally, after some five hours, an officer, 'who was very dirty and smothered in coal dust', was seen emerging from the bunkers, triumphantly 'holding in his hand an object which looked like a lump of coal'. Every member of the crew was then interrogated, with particular emphasis on the voyage to Lisbon and the disappearance of Assistant Steward Hugh Anson.

Auto-suggestion worked its magic: sailors who had noticed nothing out of the ordinary about their former shipmate, now declared that they had suspected Anson was a German spy from the moment he came on board. They recalled his gold cigarette case, his wads of cash and 'swanking' manner, his general incompetence at sea, his good manners, and his apparent educa- tion 'beyond his station'. Under interrogation all sorts of sinister details emerged: the way he had boasted of his crimes, bought drinks for everyone, and then slipped away from George's Bar. Why, he even wrote poetry and read books in French. One of the crew produced Chapman's poem as conclusive proof of the man's fiendish brilliance. 'The standard of the poetry does not come up to the flattering adulation of the crew,' one of the interrogators remarked dryly, but to the men of the *Lancaster*, the accumulated evidence pointed to one conclusion: Anson was a multilingual, highly educated Nazi spy who had tried to murder them all with an 'infernal machine' hidden in the bunkers.

As 'a spur to rumour-spreading', the crew was solemnly sworn to secrecy. The gossip raged through Glasgow docks like a brushfire, to Reed's delight: 'Approximately 50 people now regard Zigzag as an enemy agent and know about this bomb business, and it will grow in the telling, which is precisely the result [we] wish to have.' The rumour was passed to other seamen, and from there, through countless bars, to different ships, other ports, and from thence across the seas. It even reached the ears of the owner of the *City of Lancaster*, who was livid: 'He has no objection to helping put agents on board, but he thinks it is going a bit far when they leave explosives around on the ship.'

From the lowest bars of Europe, the story of how a top German spy had tried to sabotage a British ship, reached German High Command, the FBI, and the highest levels of the British government. A copy of the Zigzag file was sent to Duff Cooper, the former Minister of Information who now supervised covert operations as Chancellor of the Duchy of Lancaster, who in turn showed it to Winston Churchill. Cooper reported that he had 'discussed Zigzag at some length with the prime minister who is showing considerable interest in the case'. MI5 was instructed to give the case the highest priority and to inform Churchill immediately 'if and when contact is reestablished with Zigzag'.

J. Edgar Hoover, the FBI chief, was also watching Zigzag's trail. Through John A. Cimperman, the FBI liaison officer based at the American embassy in London, Reed and Rothschild channelled 'comprehensive memoranda' on the Chapman case to the American government. 'I promised Mr Hoover that I would let him have appreciations of the sabotage aspects in return for their co-operative attitude,' wrote Rothschild. Chapman was fast becoming a secret star worldwide: in Washington and Whitehall, in Berlin and Paris, his exploits, real and unreal, were discussed, admired and wondered at.

It was at this moment that Zigzag-Fritz, the most secret spy in the Most Secret Sources, vanished from the wireless traffic, abruptly and completely.

The Ice Front

Stephan von Gröning never spoke of the horrors he witnessed during his second stint on the Eastern Front, but he was 'deeply affected' by the experience. He recalled one episode only: being sent to reopen a church that had been closed by the Communists, in some small town that the Germans had overrun. He remembered how the village people entered the building and fell to their knees. Von Gröning was not a religious man, but he had been moved by the expression of profound piety in the midst of a pitiless war. In the last few months he had aged by several years. His hair was now grey, the face more sallow and drooping. His hands shook until stilled by the first drink of the morning. Much of his dissipated hauteur had dissolved in the freezing winds of Russia. At the age of forty-five, Von Gröning had begun to look like an old man.

But the erect figure in the military greatcoat waiting behind the barrier at Oslo airport was still instantly recognisable. 'Thank God you are back,' said Von Gröning. 'He appeared really moved.' As for Chapman, he was genuinely delighted to see 'the old man', his affection undimmed by the months he had spent betraying him, and his intention to continue doing so. Von Gröning introduced the chubby, balding figure in naval uniform beside him as Kapitan Johnny Holst – his real name, for once. The man grinned cheerily, and welcomed Chapman to Norway in execrable English.

As they drove into the city, Von Gröning explained that Chapman would soon be free to 'enjoy a well-earned holiday', but before that, he must be interrogated one last time, and a full, definitive report had to be sent to Berlin.

Von Gröning had arrived only a few days earlier and taken up residence in a smart 'bachelor flat' at 8, Grønnegate near the presidential palace, where he now opened a bottle of Norwegian aquavit to celebrate Chapman's safe arrival. The party began. An attractive young woman named Molli was the first guest to arrive, then a tough and shrewd-looking German called Peter Hiller and finally Max, a Pole with long hair and flashy jewellery. Chapman remembered little of his first night in Oslo, but he recalled that the guests seemed 'pleased to see him and were very enthusiastic about his success in England' and none more so than Von Gröning. When Chapman asked for news of the rest of the Nantes team, the German was vague. Walter Thomas, he said, was currently in Berlin, and would shortly be travelling to Oslo to resume his duties as Chapman's 'companion'. Inwardly, Chapman groaned: the young Nazi with the passion for English country dancing was such grim and earnest company. The 'hard-drinking Holst', currently dissolving into the sofa to the strains of a German drinking song, seemed a far more jovial chum. Soon afterwards, a fight broke out between Holst and Hiller over Molli's charms, and Chapman passed out.

The interrogation started the next morning, despite the seismic hangovers of both interviewer and interviewee. Von Gröning was a masterful inquisitor. For a start, he knew his subject intimately and the best ways to feed Chapman's vanity, ignite his anger and prick his pride. Behind the heavy lids he seemed half-asleep at times, but then he would dart a question under Chapman's guard that would leave him scrambling. The interrogation continued for two weeks with every word re-corded and transcribed by Molli Stirl, the woman at the party who was secretary of the Oslo Abwehr station. Von Gröning was unrelenting and meticulous, but there was something different

about the way he questioned Chapman, something far removed
from the harsh grilling in Spain, France and Berlin. Von Gröning
wanted Chapman to get it right: when he made an error, of
chronology or fact, he would gently lead him back, iron out the
inconsistency, and then move on again. Von Gröning was on
Chapman's side; he was willing him to succeed, for Chapman's
sake, but also for his own.

Chapman sensed the shift in their relationship. In Nantes, he
had been dependant on Von Gröning's goodwill, eager for his
praise, flattered by his attention. The roles had not quite been
reversed, but equalised. Chapman needed Von Gröning to
believe him, and Von Gröning needed Chapman to succeed,
forging a strange, unspoken complicity. At times, the older man
seemed almost 'pathetically grateful' to Chapman, without
whom he might still be wading through the slush and blood
of the Eastern Front. Von Gröning was 'proud of his protégé',
but he was also reliant on him, and that, Chapman reflected, was
his 'best security'. Von Gröning's status had plummeted when
Chapman disappeared; his return had raised Von Gröning's stock
in the Abwehr once more. Chapman was more than just another
spy: he was a career investment, the 'man who had "made" him
in the German Secret Service', and they both knew it.

The mutual dependence of spy and spymaster was not peculiar
to Chapman and Von Gröning; it was the central defining flaw of
the German secret service. The Abwehr's decentralised structure
allowed individual officers to control their own networks of spies.
Wilhelm Canaris sat in judgment over all, but the separate
branches, and even individual officers within the same branch,
operated with a degree of independence, and in competition. In
the British secret services case officers shared responsibility since a
spymaster whose self-interest was bound up with the success of his
own agent could never see that agent clearly. 'Absolute personal
integrity and the exclusion of all personal considerations is the first
and fundamental condition of success,' insisted Masterman. In the
Abwehr, by contrast, each spymaster was ambitious for his own

spy to the point where he might suppress his own suspicions and insist on the loyalty or efficiency of an agent despite evidence to the contrary. Even when a spy was useless, or worse, the spymaster would be unwilling to admit the failure, on the assumption, logical but fatal, that it was 'better for selfish reasons to have corrupt or disloyal agents than to have no agents at all'.

Did Von Gröning see Chapman clearly through those watery blue eyes? Several times Chapman noticed his 'watchful' expression and wondered if his yarn had been unravelled by this man who knew him better than any other. As one associate put it: 'Stephan made up his own opinion, he was secretive, and he did not tell people what he was thinking unless they asked.' If Von Gröning suspected he was being lied to, that the entire tale of sabotage, heroism and escape was a monstrous fabrication, he said nothing, and the heavy-lidded eyes chose not to see.

Chapman was installed at Forbunds, a large and comfortable wood-built hotel in Oslo city centre, which had been commandeered by the Abwehr and the Luftwaffe. Von Gröning handed over 500 Kroner as spending money, and told him he could have more 'as and when he required it'. The reward would be paid when the report had been written up, taken to Berlin, and approved.

Chapman came face to face with the war of occupation for the first time. In France he had mixed with a handful of tarts, collaborators and black-marketeers, but had little contact with other French citizens. In London his conversations outside the security service had been few, and strictly supervised. Now, he observed Nazi rule at unpleasantly close proximity.

The invasion of Norway, in April 1940, had been swift and devastating. The nation was decapitated, and King Haakon fled into exile in London. The Norwegian Nazis, led by Vidkun Quisling, assumed office as a puppet government under German rule. Hitler had simple ambitions for Norway: to defend it against the expected British counter-invasion, to bleed the

country white, and convert it to Nazism. The Norwegian
people, however, declined to be bullied into fascism. Pressure
and threats gave way to outright coercion. In spring 1942,
Goebbels declared of the recalcitrant Norwegians: 'If they will
not learn to love us, they shall at least learn to fear us.' Many had
learned to fear the Nazis in the ensuing Gestapo-led terror, but
more had learned to hate them. A few collaborated, as a few
always will; the more extreme or ambitious joined the Norwegian Nazi party, or volunteered for the 'Viking Regiment' – the
Norwegian legion deployed by Hitler on the Eastern Front.
Quisling, vague, inefficient and fanatical, won the rare distinction of being so closely associated with a single characteristic –
treachery – that a noun was created in his name. At the opposite
moral pole an active Norwegian resistance movement organised
protests, strikes, sabotage and even assassinations.

Between the extremes of collaboration and resistance, the
majority of Norwegians maintained a sullen, insolent loathing
for the German occupiers. As a mark of opposition many wore
paperclips in their lapels. The paperclip is a Norwegian invention: the little twist of metal became a symbol of unity, a society
binding together against oppression. Their anger blew cold in a
series of small rebellions and acts of incivility. Waiters in
restaurants would always serve their countrymen first; Norwegians would cross the street to avoid eye contact with a German
and speak only in Norwegian; on buses no one would sit beside a
German, even when the vehicle was jam-packed, a form of
passive disobedience so infuriating to the Nazi occupiers that it
became illegal to stand on a bus if a seat was available. Collaborators were shunned by former friends, neighbours and family,
seldom openly rebuked, but socially ostracised. The resistance
groups called this the 'Ice Front', Norwegian society's collective
cold shoulder, intended to freeze out the enemy.

The Germans and their Norwegian collaborators sought
refuge from the hostility in a handful of places where they could
socialise, such as the Ritz Hotel and a large restaurant renamed

Löwenbräu, which admitted only Germans and collaborators. But even here, Chapman recalled, sealed off from the rest of Norway, 'It was an uneasy feeling.' Norwegians assumed Chapman was German and avoided him. They answered in monosyllables, or eyed him with ill-veiled contempt from behind what he called a 'wall of hatred'. He had experienced none of this antagonism in France. A naturally sociable man, Chapman was learning what it feels like to be loathed.

Chapman's discomfort was compounded by the sensation that his German handlers also regarded him with some distrust. The grinning Johnny Holst accompanied him everywhere, friendly but vigilant. The German officials who came and went at the Forbunds Hotel 'appeared somewhat suspicious and were not communicative'. His disingenuous questions about intelligence operations met with silence. Von Gröning had promised him 'complete freedom'. Both knew that Chapman's freedom was far from complete. The Abwehr officials he met never gave their names. Not once did he cross the threshold of Abwehr headquarters, a large block of flats at Klingenberggate. Von Gröning instructed him to relax and 'not to work'. He had assumed this was a reward, but gradually the realisation dawned that this enforced leisure was a security precaution, a way of keeping him at arm's length.

He was told to carry a pistol, to report if he felt he was being followed, and to ensure that he was never photographed. British agents were doubtless watching him, Von Gröning warned, and might even target him. But the Germans were also watching him. And so were the Norwegians.

Chapman had been in Oslo a few days when Praetorius, the man he knew as Walter Thomas, finally arrived, dirty, dishevelled after a three-day train journey via Sweden and more than usually grumpy. Praetorius, newly married to Friederike, his childhood sweetheart, had been undergoing training in Berlin for officers intended for the Eastern Front. He was furious at being ordered to babysit Chapman instead. Unlike Von Gröning, who had been only too delighted to escape the carnage, Praetorius saw himself as a knightly warrior in the old tradition: an ardent Nazi and anti-Communist, he was itching, he said, to do 'battle against the Reds' and was determined to win himself an Iron Cross. (Chapman concluded that Thomas had a 'hero complex'.) Alternately spouting Nazi propaganda and practising his English country dancing steps, Praetorius was once again a constant presence, eccentric, humourless and profoundly aggravating. After just a few days, Chapman begged Von Gröning to make him go away, but the spymaster, who found Praetorius no less annoying, said he had no choice: Berlin had specifically ordered that the young Nazi should be present at the debriefing and act as Chapman's 'companion'. Unbeknownst to either of them, Praetorius was compiling his own report.

After two solid weeks of interrogation, Von Gröning boarded the plane to Berlin with the final version of Chapman's story, neatly typed up by Molli Stirl, in his briefcase. Chapman could finally relax, unaware that his fate was being furiously debated at Abwehr headquarters in Berlin where one faction of the German secret service wanted him rewarded, and another wanted him eliminated. The argument can be partially reconstructed from post-war interrogations of Abwehr personnel. Von Gröning, naturally, led the supporters' club, pointing out that Chapman had performed 'the only successful sabotage ever carried out' by the sabotage branch of the Paris Abwehr. His most vigorous opponent was the officer newly appointed to head the Paris station, Von Eschwege, who insisted that Fritz was either 'controlled by the British' or a fraud who, so far from carrying out a successful mission, 'when he went to England did nothing, and lied about his activities'.

The argument was complicated by an internal turf war and a personality clash. According to an Abwehr officer present during the debate, Von Eschwege 'apparently had the idea, which is not unknown to any of us, that nothing which had been done before was any good'. Von Gröning, on the other hand, was described as 'one of those "don't-tell-me-what-to-do-I-know"' types'. The dispute raged for five days until finally, judgment was passed, presumably by Canaris himself. The Abwehr needed a success story; there was nothing to prove that Chapman was double-dealing, and there was plenty of evidence, including English newspaper reports, to back up his account. He had shown exemplary bravery in the service of Germany and should be rewarded, congratulated, pampered, and closely watched.

Von Gröning returned to Oslo 'beaming with pleasure'. The Abwehr, he announced, had decided to award Chapman the sum of 110,000 Reichsmarks: 100,000 for his 'good work in England', and an additional 10,000 for the plot to sabotage the *City of Lancaster*. This was some 27 per cent less than the 150,000 Reichsmarks he had been promised in the original contract, but it was still a large sum, and an accurate reflection of circumstances: the Abwehr was only about 73 per cent sure Chapman was telling the truth. Like any experienced contract-criminal, Chapman asked to be paid 'in notes', but Von Gröning said that the money would be held for him 'in credit' at the Oslo Abwehr headquarters, where Chapman could 'draw on it when necessary'. He did not need to add that this way Chapman would be less tempted to abscond with the cash. He would also receive a monthly wage of 400 Kroner. Chapman signed a receipt, which was countersigned by Von Gröning – now not only his spymaster, but his private banker.

The scene that followed marked perhaps the oddest moment in the entire saga. According to Chapman, Von Gröning then rose 'solemnly' to his feet, and handed him a small leather case. Inside, on a red, white and black ribbon, was an Iron Cross – *das Eiserne Kreuz*, the highest symbol of bravery. First awarded in 1813 to Prussian troops during the Napoleonic wars, the Iron Cross was revived by the Kaiser in the First World War and by the Second World War had become a central element of Nazi iconography, the stark symbol of Aryan courage. Hitler himself proudly displayed the Iron Cross he was awarded as a corporal in

1914. Göring won two, one in each war. The mystique of the cross was such that postcards of the most famous recipients were printed and avidly collected by children and adults alike. The medal, Von Gröning said, was in recognition of Chapman's 'outstanding zeal and success'. No other British citizen has ever received the Iron Cross.

Chapman was astonished and privately amused by this extra-ordinary presentation. He reflected wryly to himself: 'If I stay with this mob long enough, I might end up a Reichsmarschall . . .'

As the Nazi occupation weighed ever more heavily on Norway, Chapman, under orders to enjoy himself, lived a lotus life: 'You are free to explore the countryside,' Von Gröning told him. 'Go yachting and bathing.' Chapman did what he was told. During the day he was left to explore his new home, always with Johnny Holst or Walter Praetorius in tow. At night they would go drinking at the Löwenbräu or the Ritz. It was hinted that his next mission might involve a sea crossing, and so Holst 'was put at his disposal to teach him yachting, whenever he needed him'. Holst was a wireless instructor, yet he was available to go sailing or drinking at a moment's notice, 'postponing classes whenever he felt so inclined'. Chapman's new companion was a strange man, cultured and refined in many ways, but a slob in others. He spoke Danish and Norwegian, loved music and the sea. When very drunk (which he was much of the time) he could be belligerent and morose; when merely tipsy (which he was the rest of the time) he was sentimental and lachrymose. He suffered from acute delirium tremens, and his hands shook violently. Holst was having an affair with another of the Abwehr secre-taries, a German woman named Irene Merkl who had been a fifth columnist in Norway before the invasion. 'If the British ever come to Norway, she would be shot,' Holst would remark with pride.

Von Gröning, aware of Chapman's propensity for boredom, told him to 'brush up on his Morse', and so he was escorted one morning to the wireless training school, lodged in a large Oslo town house, the upstairs rooms of which had been divided into cubicles, each with a locked door. Trainee spies were brought in at different times, and locked in, to ensure they never spotted one another. Chapman's telegraphy was tested, and declared to be good, though 'rusty'. He was then 'hustled' out. Plainly, he could not be trusted to be left alone with a radio.

Life in Oslo drifted pleasantly by. Chapman, it seemed, was not expected to learn, or do, anything very much. A photographer named Rotkagel, the former manager of a Leica factory, was detailed to teach him photography, and he was issued with his own camera and film. Chapman found it strange to be 'regarded as an expert'; from time to time he was consulted on matters of sabotage, 'asked to give advice as a result of his exploits', and presented to visiting German dignitaries by a proud Von Gröning, as 'the man who has already been over there for us'.

One day, Chapman half-jokingly declared to Von Gröning that he wanted 'to buy a boat'. Instead of dismissing the idea, the German promptly produced a wad of cash. From Evanson's yard, with Holst's help and advice, he purchased a Swedish yawl, an elegant little sailing vessel with a small cabin, ideal for navigating through the fjords. As the days passed, the surveillance regime seemed to relax; Holst and Thomas no longer dogged his every step. He was even allowed to sail alone, with consequences that were almost disastrous when he put out into the Oslo fjord against Holst's advice and lost his sails in a storm. He was towed back to harbour, but instead of being mocked for his foolishness, this escape only seemed to 'enhance his stock' among the Germans.

Chapman was fêted, a free captive, rich and idle; he should have been happy. But the Ice Front had chilled him. The wintry stares of the Norwegians, the sense of unreality, compounded by his own double-dealing, had wrought a change. In Nantes, he had been content to take advantage of the situation but now, living a life of fake bonhomie and stolen luxury with his German companions, he found himself affected by the oppressive contempt of the Norwegians, a 'truly brave, patriotic people'.

The Ritz Hotel, a classical-fronted, cream-painted building with wrought iron balconies in the exclusive Skillebekk neighbourhood, had once been the preserve of Oslo's wealthy; now it was the chosen retreat of a different elite composed of occupiers and collaborators. Every evening, officers of the SS, the Gestapo and the Abwehr mingled with recruits to the Viking Regiment and members of the Quisling government.

One evening in late April, Chapman was drinking at the mahogany bar of the Ritz, when he spotted two young women at a corner table, laughing together. When one of them took out a cigarette, Chapman sauntered over and offered a light. '*Bitteschon*' – the girl shook her head, shot a glance of acid disdain, and lit her own cigarette. Chapman noticed that up close she was 'most attractive', with delicate features and large eyes with almost colourless pupils. Undaunted, Chapman drew up a chair. He was French, he lied, a journalist writing an article for a Paris newspaper. He bought more drinks; he made the girls laugh. Holst joined the group, and began chatting to the other girl in Norwegian, whose name was Mary Larsen, while Chapman set about charming her blonde friend, in French and English. Finally, she conceded that her name was Dagmar. Slowly, almost imperceptibly, the ice began to thaw. Chapman invited her to dinner. She refused point blank. Chapman persisted. Finally, she relented.

Only much later did Chapman pause to wonder why a beautiful girl who hated Germans should choose to drink in the city's most notorious Nazi hangout.

The Girl at the Ritz

Dagmar Mohne Hansen Lahlum was born in Eidsvoll, a small, rural town in south-east Norway where the Norwegian constitution was signed in 1814. The daughter of a shoemaker, Dagmar was anything but strait-laced and from an early age she was regarded by local gossips as altogether too pretty and opinionated for their respectable town. The neighbours muttered that she had fancy airs and would come to no good. Dagmar loathed living in Eidsvoll, claiming, with some justification, that nothing interesting had happened there since 1814. She would pore over magazines sent to her by an aunt in Oslo and try to reproduce the latest fashions with her needle and thread, while dreaming of escape: 'She was young, she wanted to explore the world, to learn English, and dance.'

Shortly before the war, at the age of seventeen, Dagmar packed up her few belongings, headed for the city and found work as a receptionist in a hotel in the capital. She enrolled in evening modelling classes and learned to sashay and swivel her hips. She had watched, appalled and a little excited, as the solid ranks of invading German troops marched down Karl Johanns Gate, but at first the occupation hardly touched her. At night, in her tiny flat at Frydenlundsgate, she read books about art and poetry, and painted elaborate clothing designs. 'She wanted to improve herself.' She, like Chapman, 'wanted adventure'.

Her first she quickly regretted. She met a much older man

named Johanssen who seemed worldly and sophisticated and married him with a 20,000 Kroner dowry from her father. Johanssen expected Dagmar to cook and clean like an obedient Hausfrau, which was not what Dagmar had in mind at all. She left him, and demanded her dowry back; Johanssen refused. On the night she met Chapman, Dagmar was celebrating her twenty-first birthday with her best friend Mary, and toasting the start of her divorce proceedings.

Dagmar would be the grand passion of Chapman's war, but few love affairs can have started more inauspiciously. She thought Chapman was an enemy invader, though conceded he was charming. With her Craven 'A' cigarettes, long ebony holder, high heels and fashionably risqué dresses he imagined she was just a good-time girl. Both were utterly mistaken. For Dagmar Lahlum, model and dressmaker, was also secretly working as an agent for Milorg, the spreading Norwegian resistance network. Though neither knew it, Eddie Chapman and his 'beautiful and adorable' new lover were fighting on the same side.

Chapman quickly became infatuated. He adjusted his lie, dropped the pretence of being a French journalist, and claimed to be German, born and raised in the US. He wined and dined Dagmar with every luxury that occupied Oslo could supply. No longer did she sew her own clothes, for he bought her anything she desired. He took her sailing on the fjords; they swam naked in the icy water, and made love in the woods. As always, Chapman's love and loyalty moved on the shifting tide of his moods. He was loyal to Britain, but happy to be courted by the Nazis; he was loyal to his MI5 spymasters, but considered his truest friend to be Von Gröning, the man he was betraying; he was still betrothed to Freda, but besotted with Dagmar. Von Gröning observed the blooming love affair with shrewd approval. A spy in love was a spy who might be manipulated, and Dagmar – of whom they had no suspicion – might be a most useful bargaining chip. It was precisely the same calculation MI5 had made over Freda.

Though Dagmar seemed to be in love, Chapman sensed tension and a little fear in her, something private and alert. She plainly disbelieved his claim to be German-American, and often asked how he had developed such a strange accent. She refused to accompany him to restaurants used by Norwegians. In the street, her fellow countrymen would stare at them, a Norwegian girl holding hands with a German, and she would blush deeply. The gossips noted sourly how Dagmar smoked black-market American cigarettes and sported an expensive new wardrobe. 'Because she had nice clothes everyone assumed she was Nazi. It was the rule: if you had money, you must be collaborating.' Chapman saw how her compatriots subtly slighted Dagmar; he sensed her hurt and embarrassment, and bristled on her behalf. One night, in the Löwenbräu, a legionnaire from the Viking Regiment made a barbed remark about Dagmar within earshot. The next moment the Norwegian was flat on his back, with Chapman beating the glue out of him for this 'fancied slight'. Johnny Holst had to drag him off. From her comments it was obvious that Dagmar was 'anti-Quisling', but he knew that behind her back the Norwegians called her a 'Nazi's tart'. Trapped in his tangle of lies, Chapman longed to tell her the truth, but held back, knowing the truth could kill them both.

The precariousness of the situation was underlined when Chapman was summoned to Von Gröning's flat one evening and presented to a tall, grey-haired man in an expensive-looking English suit. He introduced himself as 'Doktor König', in excellent English with an American accent, and he seemed to know Chapman's story alarmingly well. There was something about the intensity of his clinical manner and 'hawk-like' gaze that was deeply unnerving. Chapman concluded he must be 'some kind of psychologist'. Without preamble, König launched into a detailed interrogation that had clearly been prepared 'with a view to testing his reliability'. Chapman was being hunted.

König: 'Where could you leave a valuable package safely in London?'

Chapman: 'The Eagle Club, Soho.'

'Who would you leave it with?'

'Milly Blackwood,' said Chapman, thinking quickly. Milly had indeed been the owner of the Eagle, but she was now, he knew, safely dead.

'Where would you conceal a secret message for another agent?'

'In a telephone booth or a public lavatory.'

'Where did you leave your wireless?'

'I have the address of a house, in the garden of which, near a certain tree, I buried it.'

The interrogator paused, and gave Chapman a long look: 'I am in charge of an agent who will shortly be going to England on a mission. The agent might need the wireless.'

Suddenly, with a lurch, Chapman sensed the trap. The wireless, of course, was stashed away in a cupboard in Whitehall, and he had no way of contacting his British handlers to arrange for it to be buried. He could give an invented address for the hiding place, but if the Germans did send an agent to find it and turned up nothing, his entire story would unravel. No one in MI5 had spotted this flaw in his story. Even Von Gröning had missed it, or chosen to overlook it. Was it a bluff? Dare he counter-bluff? He was first vague, and then petulant, complaining it was 'unfair' to give his radio to another agent. 'I myself expect one day to be sent back to England,' he blustered. It was hardly a convincing argument. The Abwehr could easily find him another transmitter. The grey-haired interrogator eyed him coldly. It was, Chapman said with thumping understatement, an 'uncomfortable moment'.

That evening, the grey-haired man escorted Chapman to a quiet restaurant and began to ply him with cognac, while 'periodically asking awkward questions'. Chapman got drunk, but not nearly as drunk as he appeared. By the end of the evening, hawk-face was also slurring his words and seemed more 'benign', but as Chapman staggered to his feet, the man fixed him with an unblinking look. 'You are not absolutely sincere,' he said.

Chapman held the stare for a second, and then grinned: 'I know I am not.'

When Chapman returned to the flat in Grønnegate the next morning, the grey-haired visitor had vanished, and Von Gröning was in buoyant mood. 'The doctor was quite satisfied with your answers and information,' he said breezily. 'You passed the test.'

There were other tests. A few nights later, Chapman was sitting alone in the Löwenbräu, waiting for Dagmar, when a Norwegian woman aged about forty-five sat down beside him, and introduced herself as Anne. They began chatting in German. Anne remarked on his accent. Chapman replied that he had been raised in America. They switched to English, which she spoke perfectly. In an undertone, she began to complain about the occupation, the lack of food and the swaggering German soldiers. Chapman listened, but said nothing. She invited him to dinner. He politely declined. As soon as Dagmar arrived, Chapman rose swiftly and announced they were leaving. A few nights later he saw Anne again at the Löwenbräu. She was very drunk. Chapman looked away but she spotted him, weaved up, and hissed: 'I think you are a British spy.' The remark was loud enough to be heard at the next table. When Chapman related the incident to Von Gröning, the German remarked simply: 'Leave it to me.' Chapman told himself that this Anne must have been an *agent provocateur* for the Germans; but perhaps she had been a genuine member of the resistance, testing his loyalties, and he had exposed her. He never saw her again.

The underground war raged. One afternoon, as Chapman and Dagmar drank a cup of tea in his room, a shattering explosion rocked the hotel. Chapman stuffed his few belongings into a suitcase and he and Dagmar clattered down the staircase to join the throng in the street, staring in wonder as the top floor of the hotel blazed. The Norwegian fire brigade arrived and began putting out the fire, as slowly and inefficiently as possible, spraying water everywhere while the Norwegian crowd jeered and cheered. Chapman thought the scene worthy of a Marx Brothers script. By the time the firemen had completed their leisurely work, Forbunds Hotel was in ruins. Dagmar disappeared from Chapman's side and returned a few moments later: 'It is the work of the British,' she whispered.

Chapman and his minders moved in to new quarters, Kapelveien 15, a safe house in the northern suburb of Grafsin that would become the Oslo equivalent of Crespigny Road, with Holst and Praetorius playing the parts of Backwell and Tooth. In an echo of the domestic arrangements with Freda, Chapman urged Dagmar to live there too. At first she resisted. Her countrymen would spurn her even more as a 'kept woman', and who would pay the rent? Chapman laughed, explaining that there was 'sufficient money for them both'. Dagmar moved in.

The money was indeed plentiful, but not endless, and Chapman was burning through it at an astonishing rate. Von Gröning was only too happy to dole out cash on demand; indeed he encouraged Chapman to spend as much as possible, to host parties, buy Dagmar whatever she wanted and foot the bill for every occasion. There was a method to Von Gröning's profligacy by proxy. Once Chapman had spent his money, he would need to go back to work; an impecunious spy, like a spy in love, was easier to handle.

Chapman, typically, had no idea how much money was left, but he was not so careless that he failed to spot another aspect of Von Gröning's financial arrangements: the German was skimming his cut. If Chapman asked for, say, 10,000 Kroner, Von Gröning would agree, give him a chit to sign, but then hand over perhaps half that sum. However much he requested, Von Gröning always produced less, and 'pocketed the balance'. Von Gröning's speculations on the stock market had been disastrous, but in Chapman he had found an investment offering a substantial return, and not just in terms of career development. Hitherto, Chapman had regarded Von Gröning as his mentor, upright, aristocratic and unassailable. Now he had demonstrated that he was also an embezzler, but Chapman was happy to let his spymaster 'help himself'. Neither man alluded to what each knew was going on, their tacit understanding forming yet another strand in the web of complicity.

Kapelveien 15 could have been an illustratration from a Nordic book of fairy tales – a large wooden house set back off the road in a large garden dotted with fruit trees and currant bushes. Roses clambered over the roof. 'It was a delightful spot,' Chapman reflected. On the door was a nameplate: 'Feltman'. Like La Bretonnière, his new home had once had Jewish owners. Idly, Chapman wondered what had happened to them.

Joshua and Rachel Feltman had emigrated to Norway from Russia in the 1920s. They had opened a barber's shop, and then a clothes shop. They had done well. In 1927, Joshua bought the house at Grafsin. Rachel could have no children of her own, but she adopted a nephew, Herman, and raised him as her son. The neighbours welcomed them. Then came the horror.

Like everyone else, the Feltmans witnessed the invasion with mounting disbelief and deepening fear. Joshua was a big, placid man who believed the best of everyone. The Nazis were human too, he said. At first it seemed he might be right. But then, early in 1942, the Feltmans were summarily ordered to leave their home. They moved into a flat above the shop. Herman, now twenty-four years old, urged his parents to take refuge in neutral Sweden: the Germans were beginning to round up Jews and tales of frightful atrocities had begun to filter northwards from Europe. Joshua hesitated, and Herman decided to go alone, to prepare the way for his mother and father. With a Jewish friend he boarded a train for Stockholm. As the border approached, Nazi soldiers climbed aboard and began demanding documents. Herman's papers declared him to be Jewish. He jumped from the moving train, broke an arm and fractured his spine. He was still in hospital when the Germans arrested him, and shipped him to Poland.

Unaware of their son's fate, still Joshua and Rachel wavered, but then, when the Nazis began to corral the small community of Norwegian Jews, they ran. Milorg offered to help smuggle them to Sweden: a group of partisans would take them, on foot, to the border, and see them safely across. Joshua loaded their possessions onto his back, and they set off. No one knows exactly what happened next. Perhaps the partisans coveted the few chattels in Joshua's sack. Perhaps their guides were secret collaborators. Soon after Chapman and Dagmar moved into Kapelveien 15, the dead bodies of the Feltmans were found in woods near the Swedish border. A few weeks later, their only son Herman was gassed and cremated in Auschwitz.

Seventeen-year-old Leife Myhre, who lived at Number 13, watched the new neighbours move in. He had run errands on Saturday mornings for Joshua Feltman, and Rachel Feltman had given him biscuits. He liked the Feltmans, 'they were fair, hardworking, straightforward people', and he hated the Germans. At first some German officers had moved into Number 15, but now a new set of neighbours had taken their place. They wore civilian clothes, and over the fence he heard them speaking English. They had big parties, and afterwards they would line up the bottles and shoot them, one by one. Sometimes they shot rats in the garden. 'They were in extremely good physical condition. One day the telephone rang, and I saw one of them run all the way up the garden and then dive straight through an open widow to answer it.' Leife was impressed, in spite of himself. He never spoke to anyone in the house, except once, after the Norwegian woman moved in. 'She was very attractive, and not much older than me. Once, when I saw her on the street, I stopped her and said: "You shouldn't be mixing with these Germans you know." She looked around and blushed and then she whispered to me: "I am not working for them, you know".'

There was something in her expression – embarrassment, defiance, fear – that Leife never forgot.

Chapman, his lover, and his minders settled happily into the pretty house stolen from the murdered Feltmans. Chapman took photographs of the domesticated evening scene: Dagmar sewing a button on his jacket in the living room, her face shyly, or perhaps intentionally, averted; Holst, unconscious from drink on the sofa, his hand thrust down his trousers, wearing a smile of stupefaction. Chapman invariably won the shooting competitions in the back garden because Holst could not hold a gun straight on account of the DTs. Meanwhile, Praetorius would practise English country-dance steps on the back porch. Sometimes Von Gröning would come to dinner. Dagmar was told that the paunchy visitor was a Belgian journalist.

One morning Von Gröning appeared at the house and told Chapman they would be leaving for Berlin in a few hours, to see 'certain people, connected with sabotage organisation, [who] were interested in his story'. That evening they checked into the Hotel Alexandria in Mittelstrasse, and then drove on to a flat where three men were waiting: a Hauptmann in Wehrmacht uniform, a Luftwaffe lieutenant colonel and an SS officer in civilian clothes who was plainly drunk and 'applied himself freely to a bottle of cognac' throughout the meeting. They asked Chapman some vague questions about the De Havilland plant and other potential sabotage targets in Britain, in particular the location of 'vital machinery, requiring replacement from America'. Chapman pointed out, sensibly, that any such military factory would be heavily guarded. While the panel absorbed this sobering thought, another bottle of brandy was opened. When that was finished, the meeting broke up.

Von Gröning was livid, declaring he was 'disgusted with the whole affair'. The colonel was a fool, and the SS man was plastered, he said. Chapman was also somewhat baffled by the strange encounter, but the meeting had provided one useful piece of intelligence: the higher powers were evidently planning to send him on another mission to Britain. If that were the case, he would need something to present to MI5 on his return.

Chapman had not been entirely idle during those lazy days on the fjords, for as he cruised around Oslo he had been quietly filling out the questionnaire he had brought in his head. He noted down possible RAF targets – ammunition dumps, the huge tanks where the Luftwaffe stored petrol on the Eckberg isthmus, the harbours where the U-boats docked and refuelled. He memorised the faces of the officials he met, the names he picked up, the addresses of key German administration buildings and descriptions of the informers and collaborators who milled around the bars. 'It all depends on the opportunities that you see presented to you,' Rothschild had told him. Slowly, surreptitiously, Chapman drew a mental map of the German occupation of Oslo.

One afternoon after his return from Berlin, Chapman and Dagmar untied the little yawl from its mooring and set sail, slipping out under the shadow of Akershus castle and heading into the expanse of Oslo fjord. With Chapman at the tiller, they sailed past the Aker shipyards towards the Bygdøy peninsula, the finger of land that curls into Oslo bay like a question mark. A mile from the harbour, Chapman dropped anchor and they waded onto a small, pebble beach, empty except for some deserted fishing huts.

Bygdøy was Norway's most exclusive preserve, a gated, guarded enclave divided into a series of estates, including one of the royal properties. Now it was the home of Vidkun Quisling. The pair climbed through a patch of dense woodland, and found a path leading to the hilltop on which stood a huge stone mansion, once home to a Norwegian millionaire, and now Quisling's private fortress and administrative headquarters. He had named it Gimli, after the great hall in Norse mythology where righteous souls dwell for eternity. Leading Dagmar by the hand, Chapman kept to the woods skirting the estate until they came in sight of a machine-gun tower guarding a gated entrance.

Beyond it, an avenue of lime trees led to the villa; he measured the barbed-wire fences and counted the armed guards.

Back on board, Chapman opened a bottle of cognac, set sail, and as they scudded through the waves he gave the helm to Dagmar, while he sketched a map of the Quisling estate and its defences; Tar Robertson would be most interested. Chapman could never explain when, or even quite why, he decided to confess his true identity to Dagmar. Perhaps he simply could not bear to lie any more. He later denied that he had been 'under the influence of drink at the time', which suggests that he was at least a little tipsy. Undoubtedly, the Ice Front played a part. Dagmar had been ostracised by her own people as a 'Nazi whore': she, Chapman, and a handful of others within the Norwegian resistance knew otherwise, but he could see the effect it was having on her. Chapman knew that 'he risked losing her if he continued to impersonate a German', and holding on to Dagmar seemed more important than anything else.

Further down the coast, Chapman anchored the little yawl. At dusk, with Dagmar in his arms, he made his declaration: he told her he was a British spy, that the Germans believed him to be a German agent, and that he would shortly be returning to Britain on a mission. Dagmar was intrigued: she had always suspected that he was not German. Above all, she was relieved, for the discovery gave her a means to untangle her own motives and feelings. She had allowed herself to be picked up by a man she believed to be German because she thought he might have information useful to the resistance, but also because he was handsome, charming and generous. Now, having discovered his real identity, she could love him without shame. She was curious to learn the 'details of Chapman's work for the British', but Chapman insisted that she should know as little as possible. He swore her to silence. She agreed, and took his secret to the grave.

Thus was Dagmar Lahlum recruited, unofficially, into the British secret service. 'You could be of use,' Chapman told her. Von Gröning seemed to like her; she should take every opportunity to be 'alone with him' and get him to talk freely; she could also help to gather information on the other members of the Oslo Abwehr.

Chapman's declaration to Dagmar was an act of faith, but it was also a wild gamble. Her hatred of the Germans seemed as genuine as her feelings for him; he did not believe that she had been planted by the Germans at the Ritz as a honey-trap. But he could not be certain. He set her a small test: to locate the Oslo headquarters of the Abwehr, which Chapman already knew. If she found the Abwehr HQ, it would be proof of her commitment; and if she failed it, well, he would probably already be in a Gestapo prison, or dead. Dagmar accepted the challenge with gusto.

The next few days were anxious ones. Chapman deliberately left Dagmar alone in the company of Praetorius, Holst or Von Gröning, and then carefully studied their faces for any 'change of attitude' that might indicate a betrayal. He detected not a flicker of suspicion. Two days after his confession, Dagmar whispered that she had found the information he wanted: the Abwehr headquarters was at 8, Klingenberggate, and the head of station was a naval officer, with four rings on his sleeve. Chapman began to breathe easier. Not only was Dagmar apparently faithful; she might prove a first-class sub-agent, a formidable new branch of Agent Zigzag.

Dagmar seemed to be privy to all sort of interesting information; moreover, she was a vital prop. A man taking a photograph of a military installation would arouse suspicion, but what could be more natural than a young man taking snapshots of his Norwegian girlfriend? Von Gröning threw a party for Chapman's twenty-ninth birthday at his flat: Thomas gave him a radio, Holst an ivory ashtray, and Von Gröning, a Van Gogh print. Dagmar baked a cake, and took lots of photographs of the revellers, as souvenirs. That night, Chapman climbed into the attic of Kapelveien 15, peeled back the metal sheet that protected the wooden girder next to the chimney stack, and hid the film inside: here was a complete photographic record of the Oslo Abwehr team, 'obtained discreetly' by a vague, pretty Norwegian girl no one could ever suspect of spying.

The espionage partnership of Eddie Chapman and Dagmar Lahlum was also an alliance, at one remove, between the British secret services and the Norwegian underground. Dagmar had hinted at her links with the resistance movement, which subsequent events confirmed. One evening they found themselves near the university: a student demonstration was taking place, protesting against the latest attempt to Nazify the education system. Suddenly the police attacked, and began hauling off the student leaders. Dagmar pointed to a young man being led away, and whispered that he was a member of Jossings, an underground resistance group. Brandishing his SS pass, Chapman intervened and 'obtained the immediate release of Dagmar's young friend' but not before a loud 'argument with a German soldier and a German officer in the street'.

On 10 July 1943, as they were walking arm in arm through Oslo, Dagmar told Chapman to wait in the street, and then darted into a tobacconist. She returned a few minutes later, empty handed, looking flushed and excited, and whispered the news: 'The Allies have invaded Sicily.' The news of the invasion had not been broadcast on Norwegian radio, and Dagmar could only have obtained the information through the underground. Under Chapman's questioning, 'she intimated, without revealing the names of any of her contacts, that this information came through the patriotic Norwegian Jossings'.

Not for the last time, Chapman wondered who had caught whose eye at the Ritz bar.

Sabotage Consultant

At the end of summer, 1943, with the first chill settling on the fjords, Chapman was summoned to Von Gröning's flat and presented with a contract for 'new sabotage work' in Britain. Chapman should sign on the dotted line, the German blandly declared, shoving a piece of paper across the desk and unscrewing the lid of his silver fountain pen. The contract was similar to the first, and promised the same financial reward. Chapman read it carefully, and handed it back, politely observing that he 'did not consider the proposition of sufficient importance', and had plenty of money already.

Von Gröning was astonished, and then enraged. A furious row erupted, with the German bitterly pointing out that without his support Chapman would still be rotting in Romainville prison, or dead. Chapman declined to budge, saying the job was too imprecise, that mere sabotage was an unworthy task, and that the money was insufficient. His refusal was partly a ruse to buy time and delay the parting from Dagmar, but also a bid for a more explicit mission that he could take back to his British spymasters. Robertson's instructions had been clear: find out what the Germans desire, and we will know what they lack. Von Gröning's authority had been fatally compromised by his dependence on Chapman, and this was a defining moment in the relationship between patron and protégé. Von Gröning now needed his spy more than Chapman needed his spymaster. The older man raged and spluttered, threatening all manner of punishment, until his face had turned an alarming scarlet and the veins stood out on his neck. Finally, he dismissed Chapman, telling him that his allowance would be cut. Chapman shrugged: if his own income was reduced, then Von Gröning would also find himself out of pocket.

The 'deadlock' persisted for a week. One by one, the other members of the station, Praetorius, Holst, and even the secretaries, approached Chapman and told him of Von Gröning's fury, and the dire consequences of his refusal to sign the contract. Chapman held fast, insisting he was 'after some bigger and better job and would not accept anything so vague'. When Von Gröning cut off his funds altogether, Chapman responded with an angry letter, saying that if he persisted, then he was prepared to go back to Romainville and face his fate.

Von Gröning caved in, as Chapman knew he must. The German flew to Berlin, and returned the following day in 'good spirits'. The Abwehr chiefs had earmarked an important new espionage mission for Chapman, for which 'there would be a large reward'. Chapman would be sent back to Britain to find out why the enemy was winning the war under the sea.

For the first three years of the conflict, Germany's U-boats had ravaged Allied shipping with brutal success. Prowling in 'wolf packs', the submarines struck with terrifying efficiency, as Chapman knew from personal experience, before gliding away unseen and often unscathed. Recently however, the balance of the conflict had altered, and U-boats were being attacked and sunk at an alarming rate. The Germans remained ignorant that the Enigma code had been broken. Rather, Berlin decided that the British must have developed some sophisticated form of submarine-detection system that enabled them to track U-boats from the surface, and then take action, evasive or aggressive. Chapman's mission was to identify this submarine detector, find out how it worked, photograph it, steal it if possible, and then bring it back. For this he would be rewarded with 600,000

Reichsmarks, an additional 200,000 marks converted into the currency of his choice, and his own Abwehr command in occupied Europe.

Here was an almost unbelievable fortune, a prize for a virtually unattainable mission, and a ringing declaration of German faith in Chapman's abilities and loyalty. At first he hesitated, pointing out that he knew nothing of the technicalities involved and would 'need coaching in what he was to look for'. This would all be arranged, said Von Gröning, with the complaisance of a man whose investment might be about to produce a quite astonishing dividend.

To find this fabled weapon, Chapman would be exposed to the deepest secrets of Germany's underwater war. A document arrived from Berlin containing all the information, 'known or surmised', about this supposed submarine detector. A few days later he was escorted by Holst and Von Gröning to the Norwegian port of Trondheim, where three, intensely suspicious officers of the marine Abwehr reluctantly described what little they knew about Britain's submarine-tracking capability. The British, they explained, seemed to be using some sort of parabolic reflector with a 'rebounding ray' to pick up the submarines; the detonators used on British depth-charges also appeared to have an inbuilt device for measuring the distance from the target, and thus exploded with maximum devastation. Quite how the British asdic (later sonar) system worked was a mystery to them: perhaps, they speculated, it used an 'ultra-red ray device', or television, or a technique for detecting and measuring heat from the U-boat exhaust.

Chapman was left with the 'impression that these people knew very little about our U-boat detection devices', and were 'extremely worried' about this secret weapon able to track a submarine, night or day, from a distance of 'up to 200 miles'. One U-boat, they said, had been 'attacked in bad weather in thick fog', something hitherto thought impossible. U-boat casualties were 'extremely high', and mounting. The officers conceded they had no idea where the device came from, but offered 'the address of an engineering depot in Kensington that might be making it'. Throughout the interview, as Chapman took notes, the senior naval intelligence officer 'continually stared at him and remarked that he had seen him somewhere before'.

Back in Oslo, Chapman was summoned to see Kapitan-zur-See Reimar von Bonin, the chief of the Abwehr in occupied Norway. It was the first and only time that they would meet. Over lunch at Von Bonin's grand apartments in Munthesgate, the balding German officer, clad in full naval uniform with four gold bars on his sleeve, explained that the British anti-submarine device was so sensitive it could detect a U-boat lying on the seabed with its engines off, and surmised that the British must be using 'x–ray apparatus of some sort'.

The mission was scheduled for March 1944. As before, Chapman would be parachuted into a remote area of Britain with all the necessary equipment. When he had identified or, better still, obtained the device, he should steal a small fishing boat from the south coast of England, and sail ten miles out to sea, where he would be 'picked up by five seaplanes and escorted to the coast of Europe'. The Abwehr apparently believed that Chapman would be able simply to steal a boat, in the middle of a war, and set sail: this was either a measure of ignorance, or faith in Chapman's criminal talents, or both. He was taken to Bergen, and spent three days being trained by the harbour master in 'the use of a compass on a small fishing cutter'.

The preparations to pitch Chapman into the war at sea were interrupted, however, by a slightly different outbreak of hostilities: another turf war, this time within the German High Command. In December, a senior German air force officer arrived from Berlin declaring that 'Chapman was just the type of man the Luftwaffe was looking for to send on a mission'. The Luftwaffe had its own plans for the celebrated British spy, and its own paranoia. A second, rival mission was now unveiled: just as

Germany's U-boats were suffering from some new detection device, so British night-fighters seemed to be winning the war in the air with secret new technology. British aircraft had been downed containing a hitherto unknown radar system: not enough hardware had survived the crashes to reconstruct the equipment, but there was sufficient to alert the Luftwaffe that it was facing a dangerous new weapon. The technology in question was probably the American-designed radar system the AI 10 (Airborne Interceptor Mark 10), in use by British fighters and bombers, most notably the Mosquito, since late 1943. 'No reward would be too great if he could obtain a photograph or the plans of this device,' Chapman was told.

A few months earlier, Chapman had been the object of profound suspicion. Now, it seemed, with Nazi Germany on the defensive, he was the golden boy of the Abwehr, courted by both navy and air force, 'each wanting their part of the mission to have priority'. Von Gröning intervened in the internal tussle: the naval mission would take precedence (and the navy would pay for the operation); the night-fighter radar would be a subsidiary target.

Chapman found his skills being put to practical use: like some emeritus lecturer in espionage, he gave seminars as a 'kind of honorary consultant in sabotage methods' to a select audience of spooks, using the fictional attack on the De Havilland plant as a text-book case. Before he had been kept away from wireless operations, but now he was asked to teach telegraphy to two young Icelanders, Hjalti Bjornsson and Sigurdur Nordmann Juliusson. Germany believed Iceland might become the launch-pad for an Allied invasion of the Continent, and so the Abwehr had begun to forge an Icelandic espionage network. Bjornsson and Juliusson had been recruited in Denmark by one Gubrandur Hlidar, a slightly peculiar Icelandic vet who was 'more interested in practising artificial insemination, in which he was a specialist, than espionage, in which he was not'. Hlidar's recruitment of Bjornsson and Juliusson suggests he should have stuck to his test tubes, for these two were not the stuff of spies: though thoroughly willing, they were also remarkably dense. Several weeks of intensive instruction was needed before they had mastered the most basic wireless techniques.

The last remants of the La Bretonnière gang began to break up. The relationship between Von Gröning and Praetorius, never friendly, was steadily deteriorating, with Praetorius, neurotic and touchy, accusing Von Gröning of plotting to keep him in Oslo to deny him the heroic military future he craved. Finally, after repeated lobbying to higher authorities to deploy him elsewhere, he got his wish. Praetorius was delighted with his new appointment, although his new position is not one normally associated with the fearsome Nazi war machine, let alone the Teutonic heroes of old: Praetorius had long been convinced of the therapeutic physical and cultural effects of English folk dancing. Somehow he had persuaded the German authorities of this, and was duly appointed dance instructor to the Wehrmacht.

When Chapman asked where the young Nazi had gone, Von Gröning said, with a look of disgust, that he was 'touring Germany instructing the German forces in sword-dancing, reels etc, which he had learned when in England'. Von Gröning was amused but amazed: the decision to deploy his deputy on the dance floor was yet further proof that the German High Command was in the hands of fools. A few weeks later, Praetorius sent a photograph of himself giving a dance lesson to the troops (sadly, this has not survived). The man Chapman knew as Thomas had been an irritating and pedantic companion, but a fund of entertaining eccentricities. Chapman felt a flicker of regret as the Nazi-dancer packed his white suit and dancing shoes, and twirled out of his life forever.

Alone in the evenings, Chapman and Von Gröning plotted the future; not the details of espionage but the sort of plans old friends make together to boost morale in bad times. They agreed to set up a club or a bar together in Paris: Chapman would act as

the manager, and Dagmar could be the hostess. Such an establishment, Von Gröning hinted, would make 'useful background
for carrying on his activities' after the war. They both knew it
was make-believe. With Praetorius out of the way, Von Gröning relaxed and became more outspoken. He no longer seemed
obliged to proclaim a jingoism he did not feel, nor to conceal his
feelings about Nazism: 'Hitler is by no means in charge of the
direction of military operations any longer,' he said. 'It is entirely
in the hands of the German general staff, and one no longer reads
"I, Hitler, command . . ." on army orders . . .'. He confided in
Chapman that he had always admired Churchill, and that he
secretly listened to the BBC every night in bed. When it was
reported that a number of British officers had been shot in Stalag
3, he openly 'expressed disgust'. He even 'aired his anti-Hitler
views in public', and told Chapman of his revulsion at the mass-
murder of European Jews. His sister Dorothea, he revealed, had
recently adopted a Jewish girl to save her from the gas chambers.

Von Gröning was an old-fashioned German patriot, committed to winning the war, but equally determined to oppose
the horrors of Nazism. Such views were not uncommon within
the Abwehr. Wilhelm Canaris had made sure to appoint men
who were loyal to him rather than to the Nazi party, and there is
evidence that from an early date he and others within the
Abwehr were actively conspiring against Hitler. Canaris had
employed Jews in the Abwehr, aided others to escape, and is
believed to have provided intelligence to the Allies revealing
German intentions. The intense rivalry between the Abwehr and
the SS had been steadily building, amid accusations that Canaris
was defeatist, if not actively treacherous. The Abwehr chief was
extracted from actual command, and would soon fall foul of
Nazi loyalists in dramatic fashion.

As the day of departure approached, Chapman and Dagmar
also made plans. From the moment he had confessed to her on
the boat, Dagmar 'knew he would one day leave her to return
to England'. They too built fantasies out of the future,

imagining the club they would run in Paris, the children they would have and the places they would go after the war. Dagmar should continue to act as his agent after he had gone, Chapman told her. She should maintain contact with the various members of the Abwehr, and generally 'keep her eyes and ears open for information that might later be of interest'. He would arrange for the British to make contact with her as soon as it was safe, but she should 'trust nobody unless she was approached by somebody who gave, as a password, her full name – Dagmar Mohne Hansen Lahlum'. Since she would be working as a British agent, Chapman grandly announced, Dagmar must be paid.

Just as he had left instructions for MI5 on looking after Freda, Chapman now set about making provision for Dagmar. Through Von Gröning, she should be paid a monthly allowance of 600 Kroner from his account until further notice. She should also be provided with somewhere to live. Von Gröning readily agreed: so long as Dagmar was under German protection, then Chapman's loyalty might be assured. Holst was sent to find suitable accommodation, and Dagmar was duly lodged in a comfortable little flat at 4a Tulensgate. Chapman now had two different women, under the protection of two different secret services, on opposing sides of the war.

On 8 March 1944, eleven months after coming to Norway, Chapman boarded a plane bound for Berlin, the first stop en route to Paris, and England. His parting from Dagmar was agonising. Chapman faced an uncertain future, but he left Dagmar in multiple jeopardy, employed and secretly paid as an unoffical British agent, but ostensibly 'kept' by the German Abwehr. If Chapman's betrayal was discovered then she, too, would fall under German suspicion. If Germany lost the war, her countrymen might seek reprisals against her for 'fraternising'. Dagmar wept, but insisted she was not afraid. If Norwegians mocked her, she would tell them to 'mind their own business'; if the 'Mrs Gossips' back in Eidsvoll wanted to cluck and mutter in their kitchens, then they could. They exchanged promises: she would keep her word, and he would come back for her, one day.

As they sped towards Berlin, Von Gröning and Chapman went over the details of the mission. His code, as before, would be the 'double transposition operation type', based on the code word ANTICHURCHDISESTABLISHMENTARIANISM (Chapman was never one to make life easy for the German receivers). The days and times of transmission would be worked out using a formula based on a fragment of a line from the First World War song *Take Me Back to Dear Old Blighty* – 'Liverpool, Leeds or Birmingham, I don't [care] . . .' All that remained was to establish a control signal, a word or phrase that would indicate he was operating freely. Chapman had already made his choice. Free messages would always contain the word DAGMAR, the equivalent of the FFFFF sign used on his first mission. Von Gröning duly informed Paris and Berlin: 'If the message does not include the word Dagmar, the agent is operating under control.'

Encoded in Chapman's control signal was a warning to his German handlers: if anything should happen to Dagmar, then all bets were off.

Lunch at the Lutétia

Zigzag had vanished, and was presumed dead. There had been a brief surge of hope when the Most Secret Sources reported that the Lisbon Abwehr station had been asked to 'provide a cover address for Fritzchen at Berlin's request'. But the request was never followed up, and there was no further mention of Fritzchen. The radio-listeners and codebreakers of Bletchley continued to scour the airwaves for any trace of the agent. Churchill himself demanded to be informed if and when he resurfaced. But there was nothing: nothing from Chapman himself, no indication from the Most Secret Sources that the German agent 'Fritz' was still operative, and no sightings reported by the network of SOE spies spread throughout occupied France. The Nantes station seemed to have closed down, and Von Gröning's name no longer appeared in Abwehr wireless traffic. Chapman had probably broken under interrogation. Perhaps the failure to blow up the *City of Lancaster* had brought him under suspicion, or perhaps he had been betrayed by a British mole. Men like Masterman and Robertson were not sentimental, yet the thought of what Chapman may have endured before execution gave them pause for thought.

One freezing spring morning on the rocky coast of Iceland, a seal hunter spotted three men 'whose appearance and activities seemed to him suspicious': they did not look like seal hunters, they were not hunting seals, and no other sane person would be trudging through the snowy dawn at ten degrees below zero. The hunter informed the local sheriff, who told the American commander stationed nearby, who sent out an expedition 'into the wastelands' to investigate. They found the three men quickly, which was just as well, for they had almost frozen to death. The leader of the luckless little band was German, and the other two were Icelanders who admitted, after some 'guttural protestations of innocence', that their names were Bjornsson and Juliusson.

The German, Ernst Christoph Fresnius, claimed to be gathering meteorological information for a German shipping institute, but it did not take long to persuade the bovine Bjornsson to confess that they had hidden a radio transmitter and a pedal-operated generator in a nearby cave. All three were shipped to Camp 020 in London, where Stephens swiftly extracted the truth, playing Fresnius off against his 'unsubtle retainers'. It was only a matter of hours before Stephens learned that the trio had been sent to monitor and report on troop movements, confirming that the Germans were 'worried still about the possible use of Iceland as a base for continental invasion'.

So far the case seemed predictable, but when Bjornsson and Juliusson began to describe their training at a spy school in Norway, Stephens suddenly sat up and paid attention. The wireless instructor in Oslo, they said, had been a 'mysterious figure, speaking bad German in a rather loud high-pitched voice, clad in a pepper-and-salt summer suit, displaying two gold teeth and enjoying the amenities of a private yacht'. There was only one person in the world with that combination of dentistry and sartorial taste. Photographs of Chapman were produced, and Bjornsson and Juliusson identified their Oslo radio instructor without hesitation. The Double Cross team was overjoyed. Even dry, hard John Masterman, from his monkish cell at the Reform Club, hailed the return of 'an old friend'. Zigzag had darted back onto MI5's radar. But what – with his sharp new suit and private yacht – was he up to?

Since Chapman's last trip to Berlin, the German capital had been thrashed and crushed by repeated and ferocious aerial bombardment. The city was barely recognisable as he and Von Gröning drove down shattered streets through 'mountains of rubble', rank with the stench of leaking gas, smoke and putrefaction. 'The whole city reeked of fire. It was like the ruins of Pompeii,' Chapman reflected. The faces of the Berliners were gouged with 'resignation and misery'.

Chapman and Von Gröning checked into the Metropol Hotel on Friedrichstrasse, and after a meagre meal of tinned meat, they were driven, past the bombed remnants of the Berlin Bank and the Kaiserhof Hotel, to the Luftwaffe headquarters – a huge concrete monolith of a building on Leipzigerstrasse. On the fifth floor a Luftwaffe captain displayed fragments of electrical instruments retrieved from British aircraft, including a dashboard-mounted screen with which, he explained, the enemy could apparently 'locate our night fighters and bombers with the greatest of ease'. The intelligence officer had only a vague notion of where these machines might be found, suggesting that Chapman might try 'Cossors of Hammersmith', the military manufacturer, or else locate a fighter base in England and obtain the device by theft or bribery.

Again Chapman was struck by the faith in his criminal talents: 'The Germans left it entirely to [my] sagacity to get through, with the aid of former pals.' Moreover, with every official he met, the scope of his mission to England expanded. He was introduced to another officer who explained that the Luftwaffe command believed bombers at certain British airfields were assigned to bomb specific German cities. As a subsidiary mission Chapman, or one of his gang, should spy on the airbases in Cambridgeshire and try to ascertain the bombing schedule. A civilian named Weiss then gave Chapman a four-hour lecture on

'radio-controlled rockets and flying bombs'. This was the first
Chapman had heard of these terrifying pilotless bombs intended
to blast Britain, finally, into submission. All countries were now
racing to deploy these weapons, Weiss explained, in what would
be the war's fiery finale. Chapman's task would be to find out if
Britain had yet produced flying bombs, and when it intended to
use them.

That night, in the hotel on Friedrichstrasse, Chapman and Von
Gröning gazed out of the window of the Metropol Hotel, the only
building in the neighbourhood still standing, 'an island in a sea of
rubble'. From the exhaustion on the faces of Berliners, the appalling
wreckage of the city, and the fantastical expectations pinned to
Chapman's assignment, both men had reached the same conclusion: Germany was facing defeat and desperately attempting to turn
the tide before the imminent continental invasion. Von Gröning
now 'made no secret of the fact that he expected Germany to lose
the war', and he confided that he had begun 'converting much of
his money into articles of value' – assets that could be moved easily
in the unpredictable aftermath of defeat – and stashing them in his
mansion in Bremen. The flying bombs represented a last reckless
gamble, Von Gröning said, but the Nazi propaganda machine was
still predicting total victory. 'If their weapons are not successful,' he
added soberly, 'the reaction will be enormous.'

Chapman and Von Gröning were ordered to proceed to Paris
and await instructions: Chapman was lodged once more at the
Grand Hotel, while Von Gröning stayed at the Lutétia, the SS
headquarters on the Boulevard Raspail. Agonising suspense
followed. The delay, Von Gröning explained with frustration,
was 'due to the inability or reluctance of the Luftwaffe to find a
plane'. Chapman wandered the streets of Paris, and beheld a city
broken in morale and spirit. There was growing French resentment at the Allied bombing raids that killed Germans and
ordinary civilians indiscriminately, and little enthusiasm for
the expected invasion. In the cafés, people muttered: 'Life under
the Germans is preferable to having no homes.'

Rittmeister Stephan von Gröning (alias Doctor Graumann), Chapman's aristocratic German spymaster.

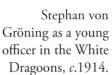

Stephan von Gröning as a young officer in the White Dragoons, c.1914.

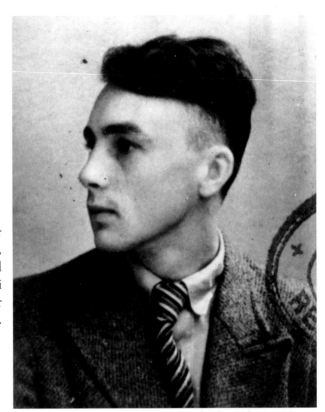

Oberleutnant Walter Praetorius (alias Thomas), Chapman's principal German minder – a Nazi fanatic with a taste for English folk-dancing.

Franz Stoetzner (alias Franz Schmidt), the German agent with the cockney accent who spied in Britain before the war while working as a London waiter.

Karl Barton (alias Hermann Wojch), the principal sabotage instructor at La Bretonnière.

Colonel Robin 'Tin Eye' Stephens, commander of Camp 020: interrogator, martinet and inspired amateur psychologist.

Victor, Lord Rothschild: peer, millionaire, scientist, and head of MI5's wartime explosives and sabotage section. Rothschild and Chapman discovered a shared passion for blowing things up.

John Cecil Masterman: Oxford academic, thriller writer, sportsman and spymaster; the intellectual behind the Double Cross operation.

Jasper Maskelyne, the professional conjuror employed by the War Office to baffle and deceive the Germans.

Major Ronnie Reed, an unobtrusively brilliant BBC radio engineer who became Chapman's first case officer.

Reed operating Chapman's German radio set.

Dagmar Lahlum, the Norwegian girlfriend unofficially recruited by Chapman into MI5.

Freda Stevenson, pictured here with baby Diane, her daughter fathered by Chapman. This was possibly the image sent to Chapman in Jersey prison.

Betty Farmer, the woman Chapman abandoned at the Hotel de la Plage in 1938. 'I shall leave, but I will always come back.'

Graffiti in the attic at La Bretonnière, the German spy school in Nantes, including what appears to be a likeness of Betty Farmer, Chapman's girlfriend, probably drawn by the apprentice spy himself.

Hitler caricatured as a carrot in the attics of La Bretonnière: evidence that Von Gröning may have actively encouraged a disrespectful attitude towards the Führer.

La Bretonnière. This photograph, taken by Stephan von Gröning in 1942, remained in his wallet for the rest of his life.

Chapman after his return to Britain in 1944.

Chapman pictured in a West End drinking den with Billy Hill, crime baron and self-styled 'King of Soho', and the boxer George Walker (*right*).

Chapman protesting in 1953 after his attempts to serialise his memoirs in a newspaper were stymied under the Official Secrets Act.

Hamming it up for the camera in full SS uniform, an outfit he never wore in real life.

The Iron Cross awarded to Eddie Chapman by a grateful Führer for his 'outstanding success'. No other British citizen has ever received the medal.

Chapman in his pomp, posing with his Rolls-Royce. As honorary crime correspondent for the *Sunday Telegraph*, Chapman specialised in warning readers to steer clear of people like himself.

In mid-April, word came through that Chapman would fly from Brussels. He and Von Gröning scrambled to Belgium by train, only to learn that the flight had been called off 'owing to the danger of interception by night-fighters'. They trailed disconsolately back to Paris. In May there was a fresh flurry, when Chapman was informed he would be dropped near Plymouth during a German bombing sortie, but again he was stood down. The Allied invasion could begin any day, Von Gröning told him, and 'if he landed in England before it started, his first and most important mission would be to discover the date and place [of the attack]'. Although Von Gröning expected Germany to lose the war eventually, he, along with most Germans in occupied France, remained airily confident that Germany's Channel defences could 'repel any attack'.

Adding to the tension, Chapman had been allocated a new 'shadow', in the shape of a young, slightly built man from the Lutétia known as Kraus, or Krausner. Von Gröning warned Chapman that Kraus, a homosexual who frequented the Paris underworld, had a reputation as a spycatcher and had trapped more enemy agents than anyone else in German counterespionage and was 'astute in posing off-hand questions'. Like every other German officer, he had a task for Chapman – the delivery of a camera and money to an agent already established in Britain.

One evening after dinner, Kraus asked nonchalantly if Chapman knew Dennis Wheatley, the British thriller writer. Chapman said he had met him. 'Is he working for British Intelligence?' asked Kraus.

Chapman pretended to be indignant: 'How the hell should I know?' Chapman did not know, as Kraus evidently did, that Wheatley had become a key member of the London Controlling Section, the top-secret nerve centre organising strategic deception under the direction of Lieutenant-Colonel John Bevan.

On Sunday morning in the Place Pigalle, Chapman recognised a fellow former hostage from Romainville, a young

Algerian named Amalou. That evening, in a café in the Latin
Quarter called Le Refuge, Amalou explained that he had been
released from the prison after Chapman; he didn't know why,
nor why he had been arrested in the first place. When Chapman
asked for news of Anthony Faramus, Amalou shrugged sadly:
Faramus had been taken from the prison a few months after
Chapman; no one knew if he was alive or dead.

Faramus was now in Mauthausen concentration camp. At
Buchenwald, he had been starved, frozen in his ersatz tunic and
wood-soled shoes, beaten, and worked in the slave gangs until
he collapsed. 'If and when I come to my end,' he had reflected,
'the remains of my body will be dragged across the muck to the
outside and dumped at a spot from which, later on, the
crematorium wagon will come to fetch it.' Faramus had calculated that he might have 'approximately six months of natural life
left' when, for no reason he could discern, he was loaded on to
another train, and transferred to Mauthausen, the vast labour
camp in upper Austria.

Here conditions were, if anything, worse than in Buchenwald, for this was truly, in the words of Faramus, 'an extermination camp, a boneyard'. The Mauthausen-Gusen complex of
camps was intended to be the most hideous of all: here the
'Enemies of the Reich', the intelligentsia and others could be
exterminated by lethal labour. Disease, violence, brutality and
the gas chambers killed relentlessly. Over 56,000 people perished
at Buchenwald; as many as 300,000 may have died at Mauthausen. Some workers sought death: skeleton-slaves working in the
quarries at Mauthausen would wait for their guards to be
distracted, find the heaviest boulder they could lift and hurl
themselves off the cliff sides. Others, like Tony Faramus, his leg
ulcerated and poisoned, his body riddled by disease, waited
listlessly for the end. While Chapman wondered what had
happened to his friend, Faramus was also racked by wonder:
'All the time, I wondered – why? Why such bestiality? What was
the purpose of it all?'

A few days after the meeting with Amalou, Kraus casually remarked to Chapman that he would like to visit Le Refuge in the Latin Quarter. Chapman was stunned. He began 'to think furiously'. Had he been followed to the café? Had he said anything to Amalou that could expose him? Had he put himself, or Faramus, in deeper danger by inquiring after his friend? Was Amalou an informer? Chapman suggested they go to the Lido instead, and an unpleasantly 'knowing' smile darted across the face of Kraus.

Shortly afterwards, a letter from Dagmar arrived saying she was 'having a good time and had met a certain Sturmbann-führer', the agreed code that she was still being paid and was not under suspicion. Chapman noticed that the letter had already been opened.

On 6 June, the Allies invaded northern France in the largest seaborne invasion ever launched. Operation Overlord was supported by Operation Fortitude, the deception carried out by the Double Cross team. For months the double agents of B1A had been feeding disinformation to the Germans indicating that the invasion would be aimed at the Pas-de-Calais region. Allied troops poured into Normandy, wrong-footing the enemy in one of the most successful wartime deceptions ever achieved.

D-Day changed everything, including Chapman's mission. MI5 had come to believe Chapman could achieve 'the un-believable'; in parts of the Abwehr, there seems to have been a growing belief that he could work miracles. In the fervid days following the invasion, the German spy chiefs even discussed infiltrating Fritz into the Normandy beachhead to operate behind the lines, with 'any uniform he liked (that of a padre was suggested), any money he wanted and the assistance of other agents'. Berlin sent instructions that he should find the code used in transmissions between ships 'for the shelling of coastal towns by the navy in support of the land forces'. The plan foundered when it was pointed out that even a spy of Chapman's resource would find it hard to swim out to a ship in the middle of a bloody conflict disguised as a military chaplain, and then steal top-secret codes.

It was agreed that Chapman should instead train a team of fifth columnists to be left behind in Paris if the Germans retreated. He was set to work teaching Morse to two women volunteers who proved entirely unsuited to the task: one, an excitable Italian ballet dancer called Monica, the other a former typist named Gisella. Chapman noted with admiration Monica's 'dimples', but began to suspect that he was now marooned within the frantic German military bureaucracy.

Von Gröning was also depressed. He told Chapman he was convinced he would 'never leave', but had other reasons to worry: the Abwehr was no more. Following yet further evidence linking Abwehr officers to anti-Nazi activities, Hitler had pounced. He had summoned Canaris and accused him of allowing the secret service to 'fall to bits'. Canaris had shot back that this was hardly surprising as Germany was losing the war. Hitler fired Canaris immediately, shifting him to a meaningless position. The Abwehr was abolished, and its operations absorbed into the RSHA – or Reichssicherheitshauptamt 'Reich Security Main Office' – under Himmler's SS. Von Gröning found himself no longer working for the liberal Canaris but under the control of Walter Schellenberg, chief of the SS foreign intelligence service.

In his gloom, Von Gröning even contemplated his own spy mission, declaring he would volunteer to stay behind in the event of a retreat and pose as a French antiques salesman to coordinate the fifth column. Chapman put this plan down to an 'excess of brandy'. Chapman tried to cheer him up, and for his birthday bought him an engraved ivory statuette as a memento of their stay in Paris.

In June Germany produced its long-feared counterpunch, unleashing on London the first of its 'flying bombs' or V-1s (the 'V' standing for Vergeltungswaffe – 'reprisal weapon'). 'Terrible devastation will ensue,' Von Gröning predicted, 'since nothing could survive the explosion within a 4,000 metre radius.' The destruction would be such that if Chapman ever did reach Britain, he might be unable to use his radio since all power plants would be destroyed. On the 13th, the first day of the flying bomb barrage, the German and the Englishman tuned in to the BBC to hear the reports of the damage. Von Gröning's face fell: the bombing was the last item of news, the reference to Hitler's new weapon 'slight', even nonchalant. There had been 'few casualties'. The broadcaster was lying (more than 6,000 British civilians would die from V-1 attacks over the next nine months) but it was a fine piece of propaganda. Von Gröning dismissed it as such, but he admitted that the flying bombs would prove 'a flop' unless their effectiveness could be properly assessed.

Chapman had finally convinced himself that Germany would lose the war without his help when, once again, the spymasters sprang into unexpected action, and a message arrived from the new bosses in Berlin announcing that a plane was now 'at Chapman's disposal'; he would fly from Holland on 27 June. The reason for the sudden activity lay in the flying-bomb campaign. Uncertain of the effects of its mighty barrage due to the fog of British propaganda, Germany needed reliable eyes and ears on the ground: Chapman's new mission was to assess the destruction caused by the V-1s and send back details, along with weather reports and barometric readings. He would act as target spotter and damage assessor, to enable the gunners to aim their flying bombs from launch pads in northern France with greater precision.

In the panelled splendour of the Lutétia Hotel, Von Gröning ran through Chapman's mission. In order of priority, his tasks were: to obtain details of Britain's U-boat tracking apparatus; to locate and steal the device used in night fighter aircraft; to report on the effects of the V-1s, giving precise timings and the resulting damage; to provide weather reports; to locate the various US air bases in Britain; to identify which German cities were being targeted by each air base, and to employ another member of his gang to monitor them and report using a second radio.

The sheer complexity of Chapman's multiple mission reflected a mounting desperation on the part of German intelligence, a realisation that only a truly spectacular breakthrough could affect the momentum of the war. The Germans, unaware that their entire spy network had been turned against them, believed they had several active agents in Britain. Some of these were held in high regard. None had ever been asked to undertake a mission of such difficulty and danger. Fritz had attained near-mythical status, and somewhere in the upper echelons of German High Command it was believed, in a triumph of wishful thinking, that this lone British spy could yet help win the war for Germany.

For this exalted purpose, Chapman was issued with the best espionage kit Germany could provide, including a miniature Wetzlar camera, a Leica camera (to be passed on to the unnamed spy in Britain), a Leitz range-finder and exposure meter, and six rolls of film. No longer was there talk of Chapman unearthing his old radio in Britain: he now had two brand new sets complete with aerials, headphones, five crystals, and a bakelite Morse code key. For self-defence, and possible self-destruction, Chapman was handed a Colt revolver with seven rounds, and an aluminium phial containing a white liquid and several pills, poison with instant effects that 'might come in useful, should anything go wrong'. Finally, Chapman was presented with a bulky canvas bag containing £6,001 in used notes of various denominations (the equivalent of almost £200,000 today), separated into envelopes – the most money Chapman had seen since the smash-and-grab raids of the 1930s. As part of his cover, he carried two fake letters, one addressed to Mr James Hunt of St Luke's Mews, London; the other signed by 'Betty' and filled with 'harmless chatter'.

★   ★   ★

The Abwehr might have been disbanded, a failed organisation in many ways, but nobody could fault its officers' hospitality and sense of occasion. Von Gröning announced that a farewell luncheon would be held at the Lutétia Hotel for the departing Fritz, spy number V-6523. With every hour the Allies drew closer to Paris, but in Von Gröning's convivial universe, there was always time for a party.

And so, on 25 June 1944, a celebrated German spy and secret British double agent was guest of honour at a lunch party at the SS headquarters in occupied Paris. The guests were Von Gröning, the sinister Kraus, two attractive secretaries from the typing pool, and an intelligence officer from Bremen who was a friend of Von Gröning. In a panelled private dining room, around a table loaded with food and wine, the guests drank to Chapman's health and wished him good luck. Even Chapman found the occasion 'unreal'. Midway through the main course, the telephone rang and he was handed the receiver: it was a senior SS officer, conferring his personal best wishes and sending up 'two bottles of cognac and cigarettes for the party'. Von Gröning rose tipsily to his feet and gave a farewell speech, extolling Chapman's past exploits and predicting that his mission would have 'a profound effect on the war'. Was there, perhaps, just a glimmer of irony in Von Gröning's voice when he raised a glass to Chapman's future 'triumph'? Chapman noticed that Kraus wore his unnerving 'half-smile' throughout.

The bibulous farewell party spilled onto the pavement of the Boulevard Raspail, as Von Gröning, Chapman, and a large leather suitcase containing his equipment were loaded into a waiting car. 'The last glimpse I had of the chiefs of the Lutétia was the group of them standing waving from the front steps as we drove away.'

25

The Prodigal Crook

As a blustery dawn rose over Cambridgeshire on the morning of 29 June, three weeks after D-Day, a man in civilian clothes could be seen walking, unsteadily, down Six Mile Bottom Road, with a large leather suitcase balanced on his head, swearing to himself. Chapman was in a spectacularly bad mood. In the last twenty-four hours he had been wined and dined, shot at, and hurled out of a plane at nearly 4,000 feet; he had thrown up over his parachute overalls, and banged his head on a hard East Anglian road. And now he had been screamed at by a farmer's wife, who threatened to set the dogs on him.

A few hours earlier, after shaking hands with Von Gröning, Chapman had been strapped into a harness in the back of a German Junkers 88, at Soesterberg airfield, near Utrecht in Holland. The bomber pilot was a fresh-faced lad of about twenty-one. Schlichting, the pilot on his earlier flight, had, it seemed, been shot down in his 'invisible' Focke-Wulf. This was not news to inspire confidence. Shortly before midnight the bomber had climbed into the sky, crossed the North Sea at an altitude of just 50 feet, and then flew parallel to the coast, keeping 'out of the direct light of the rising moon'.

Once over the coast, the Junkers had come under attack from night fighters and anti-aircraft batteries. The engines screamed as the pilot took evasive action, spiralling up to 4,000 feet, and then plunging back down again – Chapman's stomach rolled with every twist. His guts lurched again as flak thudded into the plane's tail.

Over the drop zone, Chapman tumbled out of the hatch into the darkness, and drifted to earth for a dozen or so hideous minutes, buffeted by a strong wind and desperately trying to cling on to a large suitcase filled with radio and photographic equipment. Somewhere over Cambridge, clutching his cumbersome luggage, he had vomited the remains of the banquet from the Lutétia.

Chapman's second landing had been even worse than his first. Swinging wildly in the wind, he had narrowly avoided a hedge, and then landed hard on a country road between Cambridge and Newmarket, knocking himself out. For fifteen minutes he lay stunned, before staggering to his feet. Groggily, he cut loose his pack, wrapped his overalls, gloves, knee pads, belt and entrenching tool into the parachute, and hid the bundle under a hedge. Still dazed, he had knocked at the door of a nearby cottage and explained to the woman who answered it that he had just made a forced landing. The woman took one look at his civilian clothes, screeched in terror, and slammed the door in his face. Chapman had set off as fast as his jellied legs would carry him, fearful of a shotgun blast in the back. This was not the welcome he had been hoping for.

At a smallholding, Chapman steeled himself to try again. This time the reception was more cordial. He telephoned the nearest police station, and got through to the night-duty officer, who began, with plodding precision, to take down 'the details': name, place of birth, date of birth, married or single . . .

'Peeved,' Chapman brusquely instructed the man to contact his chief constable immediately and explain that a British double agent had landed. 'Don't be silly,' said the policeman on the other end. 'Go to bed.'

Enraged, Chapman shouted: 'That's exactly what they told me last time. Ring up your station in Wisbech. They'll remember me.'

Finally, a sleepy Ronnie Reed was roused from his bed by a ringing telephone. 'It's Eddie,'said a familiar, high-pitched voice. 'I'm back, with a new task.'

Two hours later, Chapman found himself back in Camp 020, staring at his own reflection in the glinting monocle of Tin Eye Stephens. Two weeks earlier, the Most Secret Sources had intercepted a message from Paris to Berlin, signed by Von Gröning, asking 'whether operation possible?'. B1A was alerted: if Von Gröning was back in business, then perhaps Zigzag was also about to resurface. An agent in Paris reported seeing a British man in the Lutétia Hotel answering to Chapman's description, 'a wiry type, a pure adventurer'.

And here, to Stephens's delight, was the rogue himself, 'expansive in his conceit', relating an almost impossible tale of survival, and describing the 'splendid time' he had had in occupied Norway. 'The courageous and ruthless Chapman has given satisfaction to his no less ruthless German employers,' wrote Stephens. 'He has survived who knows what tests. He was apparently able to match their best drinkers without giving the show away, and to lead a life as hard as any of them.'

After an hour of conversation, Chapman was 'tired beyond the point of useful investigation', but even a cursory interrogation suggested 'he will have a vast amount of intelligence of the highest order to impart'. Chapman was put to bed in a safe house in Hill Street in Mayfair, and fell into an exhausted sleep. Stephens, however, remained awake, writing and pondering. Tin Eye was possibly the least sentimental officer in the entire secret services, and Chapman scored highly in the three categories of human being he most despised, as a spy, a spiv and a 'moral degenerate'. Yet he was impressed, even moved, by this strange young man: 'The outstanding feature of the case is the courage of Chapman. Yet there is something more to the story than that, for Chapman has faced the searching inquiries of the German secret service with infinite resource. He has rendered, and may still render his country great service. For that, in return,

Chapman deserves well of his country, and a pardon for his crimes.' A general instruction was circulated to all MI5 officers connected with the case stating that Zigzag should be 'greeted as a returned friend to whom we owe much and who is no way under suspicion or supervision of any kind'.

The next morning Chapman was driven to the Naval and Military Club, where he was reunited with Tar Robertson and Ronnie Reed over a substantial breakfast. The warmth of their welcome could not have been more heartfelt. Reed was particularly delighted to see his friend 'back safely, and roaring like a lion'. For the second time in two years, Chapman unburdened himself to his British spymasters. But this time his story was not the incoherent torrent of half-remembered facts he had brought from La Bretonnière, but the detailed, precise, minutely memorised dossier of a trained agent. He produced an undeveloped roll of film with photos of senior Abwehr officials, and a scrap of rice paper on which he had noted the codeword used by Oslo for radio traffic – PRESSEMOTTAGELSETRONDHEIMS-VEIEN – and the various crystal frequencies. He described in detail the people he had met, the places he had seen, and the various sensitive military sites he had identified as potential bombing targets. His observations were as meticulous and precise as his earlier reports had been vague and inchoate, offering a complete picture of the German occupying force: the location of the SS, Luftwaffe, and Abwehr headquarters in Oslo, tank depots, the U–Boat signals centre, air supply bases, naval yards, German divisional signs and flak defences. From memory, he sketched a map locating Vidkun Quisling's mansion in Bygdøy and described how he had 'purposely put ashore there whilst yachting to view the house'.

After breakfast, Chapman was given a medical examination by Dr Harold Dearden, the psychiatrist at Camp 020, who pronounced him 'mentally quite fit though physically tired'. At first his listeners were inclined to believe he was stretching the truth, but as the information poured out of Chapman, all scepticism evaporated. 'All the evidence appears to prove his complete innocence affirmatively and conclusively,' wrote Stephens. 'It is inconceivable [that], if he had revealed any part of the truth concerning his adventures in this country on the occasion of his previous visit, the Germans would have allowed him his freedom, still less have rewarded him with the very large sums of money which they paid him and even still less that they would now have sent him over once more.'

There was a simple way to check whether he was telling the whole truth. MI5 knew he had been involved in training Bjornsson and Juliusson, but Chapman himself had no idea that the two hopeless Icelandic spies had been caught. If he volunteered information about the Icelanders without prompting, wrote Stephens, 'it would be a first-rate check on his good faith'. Chapman did precisely that, offering a detailed account of the spies, their appearance and training, that tallied exactly with what his interrogators already knew. 'I think this goes far to indicate that Chapman is playing straight,' wrote Stephens. Chapman was genuine; even the suicide potions he brought were the real thing – pills of potassium cyanide made by Laroche of Paris, and also in liquid form: 'The only safe place for it is down the drain and well washed away,' concluded MI5's scientific department.

Another indication of Chapman's good faith lay in the revelation that the Leica camera and £1,000 from the fund he had brought were intended for another German spy in Britain, 'a man whom they undoubtedly believe to be one of the most valuable agents they have operating in this country'. Chapman's spymasters had taken pains to ensure that he did not discover the name of this other spy. But MI5 knew it: his name was Brutus.

Roman Garby-Czerniawski, alias Armand Walenty, was a Polish fighter pilot who had operated a secret anti-Nazi group in France until he was captured by the Germans in 1941. After eight months in prison, the Germans believed they had turned him, and allowed him to 'escape' in order to forge a Polish fifth column in Britain. Garby-Czerniawski had turned himself in, and was now being operated, very successfully, as Double Agent 'Brutus'.

For some time, Garby-Czerniawski's German handlers had been promising to supply him with more money and better photographic equipment. Shortly before Chapman landed, the Most Secret Sources had picked up an Abwehr message between Paris and Weisbaden saying that Fritz had been given 'money and a Leica' to pass to 'Hubert', the German codename for Brutus. When Chapman announced he was acting as a courier, he was merely confirming what MI5 already knew.

Here was fresh evidence that Chapman was 'safe'. But the supposed handover of the equipment from Zigzag to Brutus could pose a serious headache: it would require stage-managing and correlating not one, but two separate streams of false information, and the two agents would no longer be able to operate independently thereafter. 'Zigzag will be given, and will have to appear to carry out, instructions which would link Zigzag to Brutus. It does not suit us to have these two agents linked, but it is going to be very difficult to avoid.'

The extraordinary breadth of Chapman's mission offered much scope for deceiving the Germans once again, but MI5 was cautious. 'Although no one thinks for a moment that [Chapman] might be double crossing us, if he is to be used for any form of deception, this issue must, of course, be placed beyond all possible doubt.'

There were just two aspects of Chapman's story that troubled the meticulous Stephens: Chapman's loyalty to his German spymaster, Von Gröning, the man he called Dr Graumann, and Chapman's relationship with Dagmar Lahlum.

Chapman friendship with Von Gröning had intensified in the intervening months, and Chapman's loyalty to Britain might be tempered by his affection. 'It must always be borne in mind that he had a very close connection and high regard for Graumann,' wrote Stephens. 'He regards him as being anti-Nazi and liberal in his outlook.' Chapman was quick to defend Graumann, insisting he was 'a very able man, cautious and resourceful, but was handicapped by the poor material in the way of personnel that he had at his disposal'. He also pointed out that his spymaster's sister had adopted a Jewish child, although the more cynical heads in MI5 wondered whether, if true, this was simply 'a form of insurance for the future'.

Stephens had to consider the possibility that Von Gröning and Chapman might be in league together. There was always something unknowable and fickle in Chapman's makeup. The opportunist and the man of principle were one, for as Stephens observed: 'Chapman is a difficult subject and a certain percentage of his loyalties is still for Germany. One cannot escape the thought that, had Germany been winning the war, he could quite easily have stayed abroad. In England, he has no social standing; in Germany, among thugs, he is accepted. It is not easy to judge the workings of Chapman's mind: he is bound to make comparisons between his life of luxury among the Germans, where he is almost a law unto himself, and his treatment here, where he still has the law to fear.' Those doubts were echoed by Len Burt, the head of Special Branch and the senior police officer liaising with MI5 who, on the basis of Chapman's past record, remained 'quite convinced that Zigzag is a man without scruples who will blackmail anyone if he thinks it worth his while and will not stop even at selling out to the opposition if he thinks there is anything to be gained out of it'.

The riddle could not be solved immediately. Chapman must be watched, his relationship with Von Gröning probed: he should be handled with kid gloves. MI5 could not match the munificence of his Nazis handlers, but they could try: 'Although we do not propose to and cannot supply him with champagne for his meals, this is the sort of thing with which we have to compete.'

Of greater concern was Chapman's relationship with Dagmar Lahlum — 'the inevitable girlfriend', as one MI5 officer sighed.

By confiding in this untested woman, Zigzag had, in Stephens's view, 'blundered badly'. She could betray him at any moment with disastrous consequences: if Von Gröning realised he was being double-crossed, any information Chapman sent to Germany would then be interpreted, rightly, as the opposite of the truth. Zigzag would then be providing real, not false, intelligence to the enemy.

Chapman insisted, loudly and repeatedly, that Dagmar was not only loyal to him, but a skilled spy in her own right and vigorously anti-German. He described how he had wooed her, and how he had debated with himself for months before telling her the truth. 'She is not a "fast" girl,' he protested, 'and I am quite satisfied that she was not "planted" by the Germans in the café when I first met her.' If she had betrayed him to the Germans, 'he would have at once observed a change of attitude of the Germans towards him'. If the Germans had suspected Dagmar, or himself, they would not have agreed to provide her with a free apartment and a monthly stipend. Dagmar had his 'complete confidence'. But for Chapman's British handlers, 'the unofficial introduction of this girl into the service of the British government' added an unexpected and unwelcome complication.

Chapman's interrogators noted that he was 'anxious at every opportunity to talk about Dagmar Lahlum'. He returned to the subject again and again, insisting that he had made a promise to 'ensure her financial position', and clear her name after the war: 'One of his objects will be to reinstate her with her compatriots by asserting that she had double-crossed the Germans.' Chapman's passion seemed genuine enough, but then MI5 had not forgotten Freda Stevenson, who was still being supported by the British secret services. 'There was some sort of understanding, of which ZZ has by now doubtless repented, that if he ever came back he would marry Freda,' noted a sceptical interrogator.

As his trump card, Chapman described how Dagmar had

learned of the Sicily landings through the Norwegian underground, and how she was linked to the resistance movement.
What better proof could there be of her bona fides? MI5 did not
quite see it that way. British intelligence services were in contact
with Milorg, the main Norwegian resistance group, but regarded
the organisation as inefficient and unwieldy, and prone to leaks.
That Dagmar was apparently part of Milorg and may have told
them of Chapman's real identity only served to muddy the
waters further. Dagmar was working for one secret organisation,
in league with another, and being paid by a third: from the
British point of view, the lady had too many suitors for comfort:
'Dagmar is in contact with the Norwegian underground movement, at the same time has the confidence of a British Secret
Service Agent, and is at present being maintained by the German
Secret Service.'

Stephens's faith in Chapman was undimmed, but he urged
caution: 'I do not wish to be held wanting in admiration of a
brave man [but] I must issue a warning about this strange
character. In England, he is wanted for crime. In Germany
he is admired and treated royally by the German Secret Service.
It is not unnatural, therefore, in the years, that he has come to
dislike the English in many respects and to admire the Germans.
Indeed, there is more than admiration, there is a genuine
affection for his spymaster Graumann. His present ambition is
to settle down with Dagmar Lahlum in Paris at the end of the
war. Where do the loyalties of Chapman lie? Personally, I think
they are in fine balance.'

Chapman's supporters, including Tar Robertson, pointed out
that he had thoroughly demonstrated his loyalty already. But set
against this was his criminal past, his affection for Von Gröning,
and now the problem of yet another romantic entanglement.
After long debate, the spymasters agreed. There would be a final
installment in 'one of the most fascinating chapters of contra-
espionage history in the war'. Chapman would be given one
more chance to prove his mettle.

On 30 June, two days after landing, Chapman sent his first radio message to Von Gröning, while Ronnie Reed looked on approvingly: 'HARD LANDING BUT ALL OK. FINDING BETTER PLACE. COMING AGAIN THURSDAY. DAGMAR.'

26

Doodlebugs

Britain, pummelled and pounded for so long, was braced for Hitler's flying bombs. Nazi propaganda had given early warning of a new weapon that would wreak vengeance for the bombing of the Fatherland and finally crush British resistance. Early in 1944, the Germans began instructing their agents that they should soon evacuate London for their own safety. The first robot bombs, powered by a jet engine, with a crude guidance system, had whined over the city on the night of 13 June. The bombs, each carrying 1,800 lbs of explosive, flew at around 400 mph with a buzzing drone like a venomous insect that would abruptly stop when the fuel ran out, leaving an eerie, empty silence as the bomb plummeted to earth, followed by the explosion.

At first the flying bombs came in ones and twos; then in swarms. On the night of 15 June, 217 missiles hammered into Britain, with forty-five dropping on central London. Unpredictable and hard to shoot down, the V-1s gave a horrible new twist of uncertainty to civilian life. People on the ground would stop to listen anxiously to the engine overhead, waiting for the sudden silence. Typically, the British found a comic nickname to blunt the fear of these atrocious weapons – 'doodlebugs'.

The bombs flew blind, and this was both a strength and a weakness. There was no-one to report where the payload had been dropped, and no way to aim them with confidence. A pattern emerged in London. The German gunners appeared to be targetting the heart of the city, but most of the bombs were dropping two or three miles short of Trafalgar Square. John Masterman made the obvious deduction: 'It was clear that the Germans could only correct their aim and secure results by adjustments based on experiment, and that their data must rest in the main upon reports from this country.' If those reports could be doctored, then the V-1s could be diverted to where they would do less damage.

By the time Chapman arrived in Britain with orders to report on the flying bombs, a rudimentary deception plan was in place. If the double agent's reports exaggerated the number of bombs in the north and west of London, but minimised those in the south and east, the Germans at the launchpads would logically assume that they were over-shooting, and reduce the range. The flying bombs were already falling short, and with a careful stream of false reports they might be lured even further south and east, away from the densely populated areas of central London and even into countryside where they would fall mainly in fields and woods. Clearly there were limits to this form of deception: 'If St Paul's was hit, it was useless and harmful to report that the bomb had descended upon a cinema in Islington,' since the Germans would swiftly discover the truth, and the credibility of the double agent would be compromised. Masterman ruled that the Twenty Committee must 'decide what measure of useful deception was possible without blowing the agents'.

To the hard-headed men of military intelligence, the plan was clear and logical, but persuading the British Cabinet that it should authorise a ruse that would spare some Londoners but might condemn others to death was far harder. The politicians argued, somewhat bizarrely, that public morale would be damaged if the flying bombs were diverted to new, hitherto un-scathed areas of the country since the bomb-scarred residents of central London had 'learned to live' (and die) with the devastation and they were best able to cope with a fresh bombardment.

The ministers baulked at the 'terrible responsibility . . . for directing the attack against any part of London'. Despite their qualms, the deception went ahead.

The barrage intensified. By the end of June some 660 V–1s had landed on London. The Germans seemed to be aiming for the Charing Cross area, but the mean point of impact was calculated to be Dulwich station in south London. Juan Pujol, the celebrated Spanish double agent codenamed 'Garbo' by the British, had volunteered to provide his German spymasters with accurate information about where the bombs were landing: 'I might take on the work of making daily observations . . . and let you have by radio an exact report on objectives hit so that you will be able to correct any possible errors of fire.' Garbo spiced up his reports with characteristic eruptions of Nazi fervour: 'I am certain you will be able to terrify this very pusillanimous people who will never admit that they are beaten.'

The Germans were hungry for more, and the arrival of Zigzag, with specific instructions to monitor bomb damage, was the clearest indication that the Germans were short of accurate intelligence, and thus vulnerable. Chapman also brought evidence of Berlin's faith in a weapon that 'his German masters confidently believe has reduced London and the South coast to a shambles'.

Chapman sent his first report, misrepresenting the location, timing and damage inflicted by the bombs, on 1 July. He continued to transmit disinformation in a steady stream for a month. The data had to be carefully coordinated so the double agents involved – most notably Zigzag and Garbo – 'should report actual incidents in North West London but give as the times of those incidents the actual times of incidents in South East London. If this is done skilfully it is hoped the enemy will identify the bomb which fell in South East London with the incident in North West London and plot it there.' The Germans must be persuaded that they were consistently overshooting. In the words of Dr Reginald Jones, the brilliant physicist assigned to

Air Intelligence: 'We could give correct points of impact for bombs that tended to have a longer range than usual, but couple these with the times of bombs that had actually fallen short.' When the enemy corrected their aim, they would therefore 'reduce the average range'. The resulting disinformation then had to be carefully vetted, before being sent over on Zigzag's wireless. All this took time. 'It is essential,' wrote Chapman's handler, 'that it should not be apparent to recipients that there is always a substantial time lag.' The gamble was huge. If Chapman was rumbled, then instead of taking his reports at face value the Germans would read them for what they were: the obverse of the truth, and instead of shortening their aim they would extend it. Rather than draw the flying bombs away from the target, Zigzag might inadvertently lead them to it.

To bolster Chapman's credibility, photographs were taken of the doodlebug damage at various points around London, so that he could send these on to the Germans via Lisbon. But Air Intelligence vetoed the move: 'I am afraid we cannot approve of their being sent over, since they would be of considerable value to the enemy, and naturally those that would be of no value to the enemy would stand Zigzag himself in very little stead.' Here was the essential dilemma of running a double agent: how to send information that appeared accurate, but could do no harm.

Chapman had been instructed to provide daily weather reports with barometric readings. MI5 asked the Twenty Committee whether he might send these without compromising security? Chapman had been provided with more than enough money to buy a barometer, after all, and therefore had little excuse not to send the readings to his German masters. Reluctantly, the authorities agreed. Chapman could send barometer readings but with 'slight errors introduced'.

Chapman's deception messages have survived only in fragments. MI5 was careful to destroy the traffic, aware of the potential repercussions if the inhabitants of south London realised they were being sacrificed to protect the centre of the city.

German intelligence in Oslo picked up Chapman's coded messages every morning, and Paris in the evening. At first reception was poor and patchy, but it improved after Chapman sent a volley of abuse. 'The outgoing traffic, apart from complaints of poor service, has consisted almost entirely of reports on the times and places of impact of flying bombs,' reported Chapman's case officer. There was no hint in the Most Secret Sources that Chapman's bomb reports were regarded with suspicion. His British handlers were delighted: 'The Zigzag channel was considered indispensable to the bomb damage deception scheme.'

The success of that scheme is still debated. At the very least, the Germans never corrected their range, and the bombs continued to fall short, in the suburbs and countryside, where they killed and destroyed, to be sure, but on a far lesser scale. Chapman has 'held his place in German confidence', wrote John Masterman. Masterman knew what it was like to be bombed. He had lain awake on the floor of the barber's shop at the Reform Club, listening to the doodlebugs overhead, and wondering, in the thudding silence, if the next one would destroy him. 'I was as frightened as the next man of the bombing,' he admitted. But the 'shambles' predicted by German propaganda had not materialised. St Paul's Cathedral, the Reform Club, and Masterman himself all survived the onslaught of the doodlebugs, and owed their survival, in some measure, to a double agent tapping out lies in Morse code on a German wireless.

Masterman was exultant: 'The deception was a very real triumph . . . saving many thousands of lives.'

On 25 July, the bomb deception scheme was suspended. Evening papers had begun to print maps showing where bombs had fallen, potentially threatening the deception. But in any case, radar-controlled anti-aircraft batteries from the US had begun to shoot down V-1s in large numbers, and a month later the threat had effectively been neutralised, though the bombs had killed

6,184 people. Chapman told his German handlers he was going in search of the 'secret equipment for which he was promised high reward'. Chapman's low boredom threshold was well known, as was his venality: the announcement that he was going in search of more lucrative espionage targets appears to have aroused no German suspicion.

Chapman had spent a month in his safe house, dutifully 'tapping out such messages as the Air Ministry want to put over', but he was becoming restive: 'If this state of affairs continues he will go bad on us,' wrote his case officer. 'He will turn his tortuous mind to working out schemes for making more money, which will almost certainly bring him to the notice of the Police. It would be extremely embarrassing for us if he should be arrested while still on our hands.' As ever, Chapman's libido was in constant need of exercise. One evening Reed accompanied him to a notorious pick-up bar in Cork Street and handed him a £20 note: 'Take your pick! But be back in half an hour.'

Chapman still could not walk the city's streets alone in case he was arrested, for Scotland Yard had a long memory. MI5 wondered whether that memory should now be erased. 'I do feel his exploits to date have amply earned him a pardon for the various outstanding crimes he is alleged to have committed,' wrote John Marriott, one of MI5's lawyers and Robertson's deputy. 'I agree,' wrote Tar. Under constitutional law no one may be pardoned for a crime unless already tried and convicted. Instead, police forces around the country with an interest in prosecuting Eddie Chapman were simply informed through Special Branch that the Home Secretary 'desired that no such proceedings should be brought'. This was a pardon in effect, if not in name. 'No action should be taken against him, at least not without prior consultation with us,' MI5 insisted. Chapman, however, was not informed that his slate had been wiped clean: the threat of prosecution remained a useful leash.

The spy chiefs now debated how best to employ Zigzag. Chapman himself volunteered to return to France, saying he could help 'comb out any German underground movement which may have been left behind'. That idea was vetoed: Chapman was too valuable as a double agent in Britain, feeding lies to the enemy. 'Any question of Zigzag's return to the Germans at this stage of the war is out of the question,' his handlers decided. Ronnie Reed took him to lunch at the RAC Club, and marvelled at his guiltless internal contradictions. In one breath Chapman would be describing his love for Dagmar, but in the next proclaiming he was 'anxious to write to Freda to tell her he was back in London'. Reed agreed to pass on the message, but advised Chapman to tell her he was 'very busy and would communicate with her in a few days time'. More worryingly, Chapman was talking about writing up his adventures as an 'autobiography', an idea that MI5 quashed immediately, pointing out that it would be 'impossible for him to disclose during the war, and in all probability for a long time thereafter, anything about his work for the Germans or for ourselves'. Chapman grumpily replied that he still wanted to write up an account 'while it was still fresh'. He promised to confine his reminiscences to 'his old criminal activities'. MI5 was not convinced.

Chapman had brought ample evidence of German anxieties over the vulnerability of its U-boat fleet. Tar concluded that the best way to 'stimulate Zigzag's interest', and baffle the enemy, would be to exploit those fears by sending over 'deceptive material about anti-submarine devices'. A new plan was formed: Chapman would dispatch a message to his handlers saying he had located the factory in the north of England where a new submarine detection device was being manufactured, but had been unable to obtain the device itself because the factory was 'in continual active operation'. He would then claim that he had managed to 'steal a document and photographs from an office in the building': the document could be transcribed and sent over by wireless, and the photographs sent via Lisbon. Both, needless to say, would be fake.

Through the Most Secret Sources and traditional espionage, the British knew that the German Navy was alarmed by the rising U-boat toll, and that they feared some new weapon must be in use. In fact, the Germans were wrong. As Ewen Montagu of Naval Intelligence observed, 'the increasing number of U-boat kills was due to other devices, most notably the Mark XXIV mine, and by intercepting and decoding U-boat signals using Ultra'. The single most important British weapon in the under-water war was the ability to pick up and read the U-boat radio traffic. However, if the Germans believed there was some other new and powerful underwater weapon in use, that fear should be encouraged, and expanded. As always when practising to de-ceive, MI5 stuck as close to the truth as possible while planting a deception.

British destroyers, frigates and corvettes had recently been fitted with a device called a 'hedgehog', a mortar bomb that exploded on contact with a submarine. The Most Secret Sources revealed that German intelligence had found out about the hedgehog through 'careless talk by merchant seamen'. Since they knew something about the weapons already, a great deal of misinformation could be loaded onto a little information: 'While we should not disclose details of their design and construction, we should notionally increase their range and explosive effect and, more important, try to convince [the Germans] that they were fitted with proximity fuses which would go off on a near miss without actual impact.' This 'proximity fuse' would suppo-sedly trigger other depth charges once it had located the sub-marine. There was, of course, no such thing, but by making the humble hedgehog appear to be a beast of terrifying ferocity, Naval Intelligence hoped to further erode German morale, and make the U-boat fleet more wary of attacking convoys. Most importantly, if U-boat commanders feared that the Royal Navy had a rocket-propelled device that could hunt them at the bottom of the ocean, then they would be less likely to dive deep: nearer the surface, they were easier to kill.

Chapman duly sent out a message saying that he had heard about this 'proximity fuse', smaller than a normal depth charge and developed by Cossor's to attack deeply submerged U-boats. The response was encouraging: 'After passing the information on to the German navy, the Abwehr [*sic*] came back to Zigzag with much praise and an insistent demand that he should get more details.' Chapman reported (incorrectly) that 'all secret manufacture by Cossor's is now done in St Helens', and announced that he was heading north to try to gather more information. The stage was set for Operation Squid.

While the Admiralty worked out the details, Chapman was encouraged to enjoy himself. Agent Zigzag was still 'worth keeping sweet', yet a distinct sourness had begun to creep into the relationship between Chapman and the British secret services, for reasons that had little to do with the war and everything to do with personality – the warp and weft of espionage.

Ronnie Reed's role in the Zigzag case came to a sudden end when he was posted to the American forces as intelligence liaison officer in France. Reed's reputation (and, for that matter, his moustache) had grown over the previous two years, and he had eagerly embraced the 'wonderful experience' of seeing France for the first time. For Chapman, however, Reed's departure was a heavy blow. The two men had grown deeply fond of one another, sharing so many anxious moments hunched over the wireless. On the day of Reed's departure, Chapman presented his departing case officer with a small parcel, wrapped in tissue paper: inside, still in its leather case, was Chapman's Iron Cross. It was a typically spontaneous gesture of admiration and friendship. Reed was profoundly touched.

To replace Reed as the Zigzag case officer, in a rare but calamitous misjudgement, Tar Robertson appointed a man who could not have been more different, or less to Chapman's taste.

Major Michael Ryde was a crisp, by-the-book professional, with an overdeveloped sense of moral rectitude, an under-developed sense of humour, and a drink problem. The son and grandson of chartered surveyors, Ryde had married the only daughter of Sir Joseph Ball, a notorious political fixer and the head of MI5's investigative branch. Ball had steered his son-in-law into the security services just before the outbreak of war, and for three years Ryde had performed an exceptionally boring desk job as regional security liaison officer in Reading. Newly promoted to B1A, he was clever, fastidious and moralising; Ryde could be charming when sober, but was invariably unpleasant when drunk. He and Chapman loathed one another on sight. In the tangle of Chapman's loyalties, there was now an ironic symmetry. His closest friend, a German spymaster, must be betrayed out of a duty to his country; but the man who should have been his ally in that enterprise, would soon become his sworn enemy.

Ryde regarded his vulgar new ward as an encumbrance and an embarrassment, and within hours of taking on the case he had made it his personal goal to expel Chapman from the British secret services at the first opportunity.

Michael Ryde.

27

Going to the Dogs

As the war staggered towards its finale, the British secret services looked to the future and began to see their spy networks in a new light. Wartime espionage was a dirty business, and Chapman was by no means the only person of dubious character to find a home in MI5. But with victory in prospect, an element in the intelligence hierarchy now wondered whether there ever could – or rather should – be a place in it for a scoundrel like Eddie Chapman.

Chapman's new case officer, Major Ryde, was now his constant companion. It was torture for both, for few partnerships were more ill-matched than the roistering crook and his patrician shadow. Chapman insisted on going out on the town at every opportunity and MI5's expense. The £80 spending money and fifty clothing coupons he had been given on arrival evaporated in a few days. Chapman demanded more, pointing out that he had brought £6,001 in his suitcase when he parachuted into Britain the month before. Ryde tartly informed him that the £10 notes were out of date and unusable. Chapman was 'disagreeably surprised' but quite unabashed, and demanded that he should be allowed to keep the rest of the cash he had brought. MI5 watched the money pour into the hands of various Soho casino owners, and barmen 'with some apprehension'.

Ryde trailed after him resentfully. 'I have spent a good deal of time with Zigzag at the cost of a certain amount of boredom and a certain amount of money expended on entertaining him,' he complained. Ryde had nothing against strong drink; indeed, quite the reverse. He just did not want to drink in the company of men like Eddie Chapman.

Early in August, Ryde called a meeting with Tar Robertson to discuss the Zigzag case and, if possible, to end it. Ryde reported that Chapman seemed 'most discontented at the moment'; he was expensive, moody and entirely disreputable. 'He has been keeping the bad company of some professional pugilist with whom he has been hitting the high spots' and was 'always in the company of beautiful women' – a fact that seems to have vexed Ryde in a way that suggests envy more than disapproval. The case officer wrote a report, ending with the conclusion: 'The Zigzag case must be closed down at the earliest possible moment.' Ryde was immediately slapped into line by his superiors. John Masterman insisted that the word 'earliest' be replaced by 'latest', and Tar agreed: the case should be closed only when it was 'convenient' to do so. Stung, Ryde backed off: but he was now gunning for Chapman, and collecting all the ammunition he could.

Robertson took Chapman to lunch at his club, and found him in a state of seething resentment towards Ryde, complaining bitterly about 'the way his case was being run'. When asked about his future plans. Chapman 'did not seem to have any very clear ideas on the subject', Tar reported, though he spoke vaguely of setting up a club, or running a pub, or working for MI5 after the war. 'He is quite clearly restless and is likely to be so, as long as he is asked to perform the rather humdrum business of tapping a key at our instructions.'

Relations between Chapman and Ryde might be reaching crisis point, but in other respects the Zigzag case was ticking along most satisfactorily. The Germans seemed as devoutly trusting as ever. Early in August, Von Gröning had sent a message asking Chapman to suggest a method for delivering the camera and money to his fellow spy, and instructing him to find 'a suitable person' who could monitor bomber formations at airfields in East Anglia. The Air Ministry had vetoed any deception in this latter area, so Chapman stalled, saying he was still searching for a recruit since 'the friends he hoped to employ for this purpose are in prison or otherwise not available'.

Operation Squid, the plan to convince the Germans that Britain had some new and devastating weapon able to detect and destroy U-boats, moved into its next phase. The deception would take two forms. The first was a 'stolen' photograph purporting to show an underwater anti-submarine 'proximity fuse' which did not, of course, exist. This would have to be smuggled to the Germans via Lisbon. A real hedgehog depth charge was photographed alongside a ruler a foot and a half in length, which had been adapted to appear as if it was only six inches long, thus making the weapon appear one-third of its actual size. Chapman would tell the Germans he had bribed a merchant seaman bound for Lisbon to act as a 'mule', by hiding the photo 'in a French letter in a tin of Epsom Salts', and that he would convince the sailor he was smuggling drugs. In reality MI6 in Lisbon simply acted as 'postman', and arranged for the fake photograph in its tin to be delivered to the Germans by one of their agents disguised as a seaman. The German reaction was precisely as hoped: 'After they had received the photo the Abwehr were avid for full details of the fuse,' wrote Ewen Montagu.

Zigzag duly obliged. With the help of Professor Geoffrey J. Gollin, the brilliant scientific adviser to the Naval Intelligence Division, Montagu drew up a bogus letter from Professor A.B. Wood, an expert in underwater acoustics at the Admiralty Research Laboratory at Teddington, to a scientist at Cossor's munitions factory named Fleming. In it he extolled the virtues of a new, top-secret anti-submarine device. Chapman told his German handlers he had found the letter in the Manchester offices of Cossor's, and had copied it. He now sent the fake letter by radio, verbatim:

Dear Fleming,

I feel sure that you will be as pleased as I was to hear the results of the latest squid trials.

A standard deviation of plus or minus 15 feet is a wonderful improvement on the old method of depth-find-ing and my only regret is that our present target is incapable of greater speeds. Doubtless 13 knots is as much as the enemy is likely to reach in this war but we must always keep a 'jump' ahead, preferably two jumps!

I thought you might like the enclosed photos of the standard remote setting depth charge fuse for coupling direct to the squid Mk J indicator controller (as suggested by the late Captain Walker).

I hope to visit Manchester again soon and am looking forward to having another of our discussions which have proved so fruitful during the last three years.

Yours sincerely,

A.B. Wood

Professor

There was no Captain Walker, no 'Mk J indicator controller' and certainly no depth charge capable of detecting a submarine at a distance of 15 feet and then pursuing it at a speed of 13 knots. There was, however, a Fleming, Ian Fleming – the future creator of James Bond – who was then working in Naval Intelligence. Fleming may have been party to this subterfuge, designed to breed maximum anxiety among German U-boat commanders and keep them as close as possible to the surface. Ewen Montagu proclaimed the operation a triumph. 'We never found out what the assessment of this information by the German navy was, but the actions of the Abwehr made it seem that they must have been very favourable.'

Despite the success of Operation Squid, Ryde did his best to undermine the achievement. 'I do not myself believe there is any substantial chance of these photographs reaching Berlin,' he wrote. 'Unless the Admiralty press us to carry on the case, I am convinced that we ought to close it down and part company with Zigzag as soon as possible, giving him such financial bonus, if any, as he is thought to deserve . . .' Ryde seemed more determined than ever to expel Chapman, and the preparations for handing over the camera to Brutus offered an opportunity. It was decided that Zigzag would arrange to leave the money and camera in a marked package at a railway-station cloakroom, but while the handover was being organised, the Germans sent a radio message hinting at doubts over Chapman's loyalty. Brutus's German handler wrote that he did not wish his agent to make direct contact with Fritz, since the latter was, in his opinion, 'not quite reliable'. This may have reflected no more than internal rivalry, one spymaster questioning the dependability of another's agent, but it was enough for Ryde to declare that the Germans were 'dubious about Zigzag's integrity'.

German suspicions, Ryde wrote, may have been further stoked by widely reported statements made in Parliament about the V–1s by Duncan Sandys, the minister who chaired the War Cabinet committee on flying bombs. Sandys had let slip certain crucial details about bomb-damaged parts of London. 'The messages sent by Zigzag, if compared in detail with the recent speech made by Duncan Sandys in the House, show very serious discrepancies, and there is a possibility that the case will be blown on these grounds.' Then there was the question of Dagmar. 'Zigzag is liable to be compromised through the girlfriend he left behind in Oslo,' wrote Ryde, slowly but implacably chipping away at his own agent's credibility. When it was mooted that Chapman might continue to work for MI5 after the war, Ryde was scornful: 'It is unlikely that his private life will be such that he will remain suitable for employment.' He also pointed out that Chapman's value was dependent on his relationship with Von Gröning and that this link would become worthless with the end of the war.

Chapman, unaware of Ryde's machinations, had discovered a new and lucrative pastime. Through some of his old criminal contacts, he learned that dog races in south London were being 'fixed'. With the connivance of the owners, certain dogs were being fed meatballs laced with Luminal, an anti-epileptic drug. A mild hypnotic, the Luminal had no visible effect until the animal, usually the favourite, had run some distance, when it would slow down. For a consideration, Chapman arranged to receive a tip-off when a dog had been knobbled; he then bet heavily on the second favourite and usually collected a tidy profit, which he would split with his criminal informant.

One evening in August 1944, Chapman turned up at his safe house several hours late for an appointment to transmit to Germany, and explained casually that he had been at the dog track. 'Zigzag himself is going to the dogs,' his case officer puffed, gleeful to have been provided with such a convenient double entendre. Chapman, Ryde reported, was 'making quite large sums of money by backing the winners of races which have already been fixed'. When confronted, Chapman angrily insisted that he was merely profiting through information gathered from his contacts, a technique not so very far removed from espionage. Ryde, of course, did not see it that way. 'To take advantage of other people's dirty work to fleece the bookmakers cannot be regarded as a desirable occupation,' he sniffed.

Reluctantly, and under intense pressure, Masterman and Robertson accepted that Chapman might soon have 'served his purpose'. Yet they baulked at cutting him adrift. Tar insisted that Chapman had 'done an extremely good and brave job', and if the case was shut down then he should be properly looked after 'by giving him a fairly substantial sum of money'. With the avuncular concern he had always shown, Robertson wondered whether Chapman might be coaxed towards the straight and narrow by means of a legitimate job. Chapman was duly told that 'if he could put up some firm business proposition it might not be impossible for us to help him with the capital'. He had seemed enthusiastic, and talked of running a club in the West End or a hotel in Southend (The Ship Hope Hotel was for sale, he said), in order to be near Freda and Diane. Ryde declared that it would be a 'waste of money' for someone with such a long criminal record to open licensed premises, since the police would simply 'close them down as soon as they find out that he is in fact behind the business'. The only way to set up Chapman as an hotelier would be to alert the local chief constable, and explain the situation: 'If the latter, notwithstanding Zigzag's past record, appears willing to give his venture a fair chance so long as the hotel was properly conducted, then it might be worthwhile for Zigzag to go on with it.' Ryde doubted that any chief constable would agree to this proposition, or that Chapman would keep his nose clean: 'It is obvious that we cannot assist him financially if his idea of business is to work the dogs.'

Just as Ryde had predicted, Chapman was drifting back to his old haunts – the Shim-Sham club and the Nite Lite – and his old ways. The pull of the criminal brotherhood was growing stronger, yet his years as a secret agent had changed him: his primary allegiance was still to Britain, and the other secret fraternity of which he was now a part. When Ryde hinted that Chapman's days as an agent might be numbered, he had responded crossly, declaring that 'if we no longer require his services' he would 'get in touch with the Americans'.

Safe from prosecution thanks to the Home Secretary's un-official 'pardon', Chapman was allowed to move around London more freely, though Ryde followed at a distance, tutting, watching and gathering evidence. The spy manager was now actively spying on his spy: 'I have seen Zigzag walk up to a Norwegian and address him in Norwegian, I have seen him in the company of highly undesirable characters, speaking to a German Jewess in German, a Frenchman in French. I have heard him discussing with a man with a known criminal record conditions in Paris in such a way that it must have been apparent that he has been there within the last few months.' Chapman, Ryde reported to his superiors, was keen to write a memoir of his exploits: how soon before his natural swagger got the better of him, and he bragged to his nasty friends, he speculated? 'I am able to curb these indiscretions when I happen to be present,' he wrote, 'but there is no knowing what form these conversations take when I am not there.'

Ryde was overruled again. Whatever his personal behaviour, Chapman was still a trusted asset: 'The war may end at any moment and all contact with the Germans be lost and his case may die a natural death.' If this happened, Chapman should be let go with tact and generosity, and told that 'the necessity of closing the case was no reflection on him, but forced upon us by the war situation'.

Ryde grumbled and plotted: 'It is becoming increasingly clear to me that there are a number of serious security dangers which, in the case of a character like Zigzag, it is impossible to avoid.' Zigzag was proving harder to kill off than Ryde anticipated: every time he believed he had Chapman on the ropes, the man would bounce back with another demonstration of his worth. Von Gröning continued to send messages of support, demanding ever more intelligence: 'Try to get latest editions of monthly anti-submarine report issued by anti-submarine warfare division of Admiralty . . . Very important.' Von Gröning repeatedly congratulated Fritz on his performance: 'General report [is of] great interest.'

On 8 September, Germany launched its first V-2 attacks against Paris and London. The V-2 was a quite different creature from its predecessor: an early ballistic missile driven by liquid oxygen and alcohol, the rocket bomb had a range of 200 miles, flew at ten times the speed of the V-1 and carried a nose cone with a ton of high explosive. Chapman had learned of these weapons back in France, and warned British intelligence of a 'radio controlled rocket which will be bigger, very costly in fuel and not at all economical in construction'. Von Gröning instructed Chapman to act, once again, as a target locator for the new bombs: 'Continue giving data about place and time of explosions. Are they more frequent now?' The V-2 attacks were often devastating – 160 people were killed in a single explosion when a bomb fell on a Woolworth's department store in south London – but Chapman sent a reply down-playing the effects: 'Heard many rumours of explosions of gas works and mains but no information of the cause. Making inquiries.'

During his visit to the Luftwaffe headquarters in Berlin, Chapman had been shown fragments of British night-fighter radar equipment, and noticed that the pieces had serial numbers. He now asked Von Gröning to transmit a complete list of those serial numbers, notionally so that he could steal the correct device, but in fact to give the Air Ministry a clear idea of exactly what the Germans had salvaged. It was also decided that a display of petulance would keep Von Gröning keen. Chapman sent an angry message, complaining that he was not receiving sufficient backup and urgently needed more money. He also asked, pointedly, whether the German secret service intended to support him when the war was over.

Chapman could not have known it, but during his absence Hitler had destroyed the remains of the Abwehr. On 20 July, Claus von Stauffenberg, a German officer, tried and failed to assassinate Hitler by planting a bomb in an attaché case in the conference room at Hitler's 'Wolf's Lair' – his command post for the Eastern Front in Rastenburg, Prussia. The device exploded against the heavy leg of an oak table which probably shielded the Führer from the full force of the blast. Chapman would not have made such an elementary mistake. Five thousand members of the German military were arrested in the aftermath of the failed 20 July plot, including Canaris and his deputy, Hans Oster. They were tried, convicted of treason, and then hanged. Von Gröning does not appear to have been implicated in the plot, but as an Abwehr officer of the old school with anti-Nazi views, he was undoubtedly under suspicion.

Von Gröning's response to Chapman's complaint arrived after a gap of several days. It was an odd, and oddly moving message, the statement of a proud man whose world was falling apart:

WAR SITUATION NEED NOT AND WILL NOT
AFFECT YOUR RETURN YOU MUST MAKE
SUGGESTIONS IN GOOD TIME AND YOU WILL
HAVE EVERY SUPPORT WHATEVER HAPPENS.
WAS HOME, MY HOUSE DESTROYED BY BOMBS,
OTHERWISE   WOULD   HAVE   ANSWERED
SOONER. GRAUMANN.

The Von Gröning family home in Bremen, that great five-
storey symbol of aristocratic eminence, had been flattened by
Allied bombers. The house had been empty: the cook, chauffeur, valet, gardener, maids and other servants had been laid off
long before. The gilded carriage had been stolen, the family cars
commandeered. Von Gröning's pictures, antiques, china, silver,
and other valuable *objets d'art* – the remains of his great in-
heritance – had been stored in the attic. All had been destroyed.
The only item of value recovered from the rubble was a singed
silver plate engraved with the names of his fallen comrades in the
White Dragoons.

28

Case Dismissed

Chapman imagined his old friend, sitting in the bombed-out wreckage of a privileged life, drinking himself into amnesia. He was touched by Von Gröning's plight: 'SORRY YOUR BAD NEWS DON'T DRINK TOO MUCH. AM GOING TO MANCHESTER TO DO JOB. WHAT ABOUT PICKUP OFF NE COAST? CAN YOU LEAVE ME COVER AD-DRESS IN FRANCE ALSO RADIO POSSIBILITY FOR JIMMY OR MYSELF TO GO THERE. NEED FRENCH MONEY ALSO. DAGMAR.'

Von Gröning's message had hinted at a plan to continue espionage operations with Chapman, 'whatever happens'. The Allies were acutely conscious of the danger of Nazi resistance groups emerging in Germany to fight on after the war was over. Indeed, at Himmler's instigation diehard SS fanatics were already forming a partisan group, the so-called 'Werewolf' organisation, to continue a guerrilla campaign in Germany in the event of an occupation. Ryde grudgingly conceded that the message put the Zigzag case in a different light: it showed that the German spymaster 'has a post-war plan in mind and there is now a real purpose in keeping the case running' in order to find out 'whether Graumann intends to continue to work after the complete and final German collapse'. If Chapman could 'get the Germans to lay on an expedition to meet him somewhere in the North Sea,' Ryde reported, then an ambush might be staged.

As promised, the next day, Von Gröning sent over a complete list of all the serial numbers obtained from the equipment in downed British aircraft, 'a collection of words, figures, stops and dashes', that added up to another intelligence bonanza. The Air Ministry set about identifying the various bits of machinery. Montagu of Naval Intelligence was overjoyed: 'The Germans have told the Agent highly secret information about the state of their knowledge . . . there are also points in it of which we did not, in fact, know that the Germans were aware, even from our knowledge gained from Most Secret Sources.' A proposal to launch yet another deception plan based on the night-fighter intelligence was ruled out, however, on the grounds that 'German knowledge is too near the knuckle for us to try to tamper with it at this stage'.

Ryde fumed. Chapman had escaped again, and to make matters worse, Robertson had instructed him to discuss compensation with this unpleasant young man and decide whether 'we should out of our own funds supplement what ZZ has received from the Germans'. The money was disappearing fast. 'I still maintain that we are bound to give Zigzag a square deal,' wrote Tar, 'as he has done a very considerable service for this country.' The sum of £5,000 was suggested, as a 'settlement of our indebtedness to him [and] to impress upon Zigzag that we value the work which he has done for us at least as high as the Germans value that which he has done for them'.

One evening, in strained conversation with Ryde, Chapman remarked that he expected to be 'dealt with fairly' by the secret services.

'Could you give me some idea of what you have in mind?' Ryde asked, through gritted teeth.

'Well, the Germans gave me £6,000 when I came back here,' Chapman replied.

Ryde responded that 'of the £6,000 he had brought with him, £1,000 was for someone else and that being the case he had £5,000 from the Germans.'

Ryde could hardly believe that he was having to haggle with such an individual. He pointed out that Chapman had also kept the money from his first mission, and should be grateful. 'This argument did not seem to impress Zigzag,' who tersely pointed out that the entire case had so far 'only cost the British government about £200.'

'I think that is a matter about which you should feel gratified,' said Ryde, with all the considerable pomposity at his disposal. But Chapman was 'not at all impressed'. The discussion ended in deadlock, acrimony, and even deeper mutual antipathy.

The Germans, it seemed, were in a much more generous mood. Chapman had sent a message demanding 'at least £6,000 to be delivered to him by parachute'. In reply, the Germans had said that they would rather send the money through Lisbon, perhaps via the 'reliable sailor' who had delivered the photographs. But if that proved impossible, then they pledged to drop the money by air. 'Such promises are generally empty,' insisted Ryde, at the same time scenting another opportunity to put an end to his agent.

The Abwehr had often made a practice, in the past, of providing agents with forged British currency. This was an economy measure, but a foolish one, since several Nazi spies were uncovered trying to spend the fake cash. 'I think it would be important in closing the Zigzag case to destroy his faith in the Germans,' wrote Ryde. 'Zigzag's only interest in the case is the money he can make out of it, and if we were able to get the money and then prove to him that it was forged, we shall have gone a long way towards shattering the very high esteem which he undoubtedly has for Graumann and others . . . If the money is in fact counterfeit, Zigzag will probably send an unprintable message, closing the case himself.'

In the meantime Chapman sent a message to Von Gröning saying he was heading to the Liverpool docks to try to find a courier to bring the money back.

Ryde wanted to sack Chapman without a penny. He wanted

to see him off the premises in such a way that he could never come back, never demand anything else of the intelligence services, and never work as a spy again. For this he needed to demolish his credibility. Just one serious blunder would bring Chapman down. In the end, Ryde discovered two, furnished by Chapman's closest allies: Von Gröning, the newly homeless aristocrat, and Jimmy Hunt, a newly released convict.

Ryde was intrigued by the close relationship between Chapman and Von Gröning: 'Zigzag has always spoken of Graumann in the highest terms and has expressed something akin to affection for "the old man".' But there was something more to the mutual admiration in this case, something about Von Gröning he felt that Chapman was holding back. Ryde was a prig and a snob, but he was also a talented spy, with the intuitive ability to spot a lie.

One morning in the safe house, after Chapman had transmitted his morning message to Germany, Ryde deftly steered the conversation towards 'Dr Graumann', and wondered 'whether the Germans have any suspicion that he was being worked under control'. Before Chapman could answer, Ryde continued, as if thinking aloud: 'If Graumann did suspect this, it is unlikely that he would reveal his suspicions as it is in his own personal interests to keep the case going as long as possible.' Chapman agreed, 'without a moment's hesitation'.

'Graumann is my best security,' he added.

'What do you mean?' asked Ryde.

'He has made a great deal of money out of the case. For example when I ask for £6,000, Graumann probably draws £12,000 and pockets the change.'

Slowly it dawned on Ryde that Chapman was putting out enough rope to hang himself. If Chapman and Von Gröning were in league embezzling money from their German masters, then it was also probable that Chapman had confided that he was working for the British. If so, then Von Gröning, for reasons of greed and ambition, was betraying his own country with an agent he knew to be false. This evidence of financial collusion, wrote Ryde, 'increases my suspicion that he has at least told Graumann, his German spymaster, of his connection with us in this country'.

Seeing Ryde's expression, Chapman changed the subject. 'My impression was that Zigzag knew perfectly well what was in my mind but was not going to admit it, and my earlier suspicions were strengthened.'

Ryde conceded that the possible risks from a joint conspiracy involving Zigzag and his German boss might be limited, since Von Gröning's self-interest would probably ensure that he kept Chapman's secret. 'If it is true that Graumann is aware of Zigzag's position in this country it is very unlikely that anyone other than Graumann knows and there is probably little danger to us at present.' But more important to Ryde's campaign, if Chapman had revealed himself to his German spymaster but had kept the fact from the British, this was a major security breach, proof that he had lied. Ryde was elated: 'It may show that Zigzag has withheld from us this very important piece of information and it is against our principles to run a case with anyone who is found not to be absolutely open with us.'

If Chapman had told Von Gröning he was working for British intelligence, then who else had he let in on the secret? The question was soon answered.

Ryde was still debating how best to deploy this new evidence of Chapman's unreliability, when Jimmy Hunt accidentally administered the *coup de grâce*. One late October evening Ryde's deputy, an MI5 officer called Reisen, paid an unannounced visit to Chapman's flat, and found a debauched scene. Chapman was throwing a party. Characters from his seedy past and increasingly dubious present were ranged around the sitting room in various states of inebriation, including the boxer George Walker, a jobbing journalist named Frank Owens, and sundry other denizens of the Soho underworld. As Reisen entered the room, a large individual with the pallor of long-term imprisonment rose unsteadily to his feet. Here was Jimmy Hunt, the safe-cracker who had played such a crucial role in Chapman's early criminal life and then, as a figment of MI5's imagination, in his second career as a spy.

'I suppose you have come to take Eddie away on a job,' Hunt grinned knowingly. Reisen made a non-committal reply, determined not to betray his astonishment 'in the presence of so many others'. The implication of Hunt's remark was clear, and Reisen was 'quite certain that Hunt knew the nature of the job to which he referred'. Chapman had not merely spilled the beans: he had spilled them to a newly liberated, extremely drunk convict, and in so doing he had served up his own head, on a plate.

Ryde, delighted and vindictive, marshalled his evidence and moved in for the kill, as remorseless as if he had been terminating an enemy spy. Chapman had faced so many inquisitors in the past: Tin Eye Stevens, Praetorius, Von Gröning, Dernbach and a beautiful woman in a designer coat in Romainville jail; he had survived interrogations by the Gestapo, the Abwehr, and MI5; an *agent provocateur* in an Oslo bar, an inquisitive SS spy-catcher in Paris, and any number of agents posing as spies had all tried to trip him up. But it was the bean counter of Whitehall who trapped him in the end.

Ryde's denunciation was a masterpiece. 'I have long suspected that Zigzag has no regard whatever for the necessity of observing complete silence regarding his connection with us,' he wrote; by confiding in Hunt, Chapman had 'broken the most elementary security rules'. With malice aforethought, Ryde methodically laid out the case for the prosecution: Chapman had already confided in one unauthorised individual, Dagmar Lahlum, and was probably in league with his German spymaster; he had attempted to extract money from MI5, gambled in fixed dog races, and kept the company of professional criminals; he had threatened to work for a rival secret service, and he was costing a small fortune to maintain in a lifestyle of champagne and loose women. Leaving aside Von Gröning, who clearly had a vested interest in his success, the Germans were uncertain of their spy's loyalty, and the speech by Duncan Sandys had probably undermined his credibility anyway. Finally, and fatally, he had bragged to a known criminal about his work for the British secret services. 'This act of Zigzag's does of course provide a first-class excuse for closing the case with him in the wrong and for administering a very firm rebuke,' said Ryde, with relish. 'In view of the inflammable situation caused by Zigzag's indiscretions to his very doubtful friend . . . it seems to me that we should dismiss him, explaining that he has broken his side of the bargain and that from now on he need expect no assistance from us in any trouble he may find himself in the future.'

Nor should he be allowed to work as an intelligence agent for anyone else: 'We should impress upon Zigzag that we would take the strongest possible exception to any approach which he might feel inclined to make to the Americans or French or any other government.' In Ryde's view, Chapman should not receive another penny: 'I should be opposed to paying him any further money, for once we do this we lay ourselves open to further approaches . . . We can now say to Zigzag that he can expect no further assistance, either financial or legal, we have obtained for him from the police a clean sheet, and he has a large sum of money which he would never have obtained without assistance. He has now let us down badly.'

Ryde advised against continuing the Zigzag traffic with Germany without Chapman himself, arguing that any attempt to impersonate his radio technique would pose a 'considerable risk, because Zigzag has a distinctive style'. The case should simply be shut down in a clean break, leaving the Germans to believe that Chapman had been caught: 'As far as the Germans are concerned Zigzag is away contacting a courier. Should he never reappear on the air again the assumption will be that he has been arrested.'

Faced with Ryde's damning dossier, the MI5 chiefs had little choice but to agree. The Admiralty, with reluctance, acquiesced, although Operation Squid was still underway. 'My feeling,' wrote Masterman, 'is that his case should be closed now, that we should pay Zigzag nothing and that the Yard should be informed.' Tar Robertson did not object: 'We should close it now.' On 2 November 1944, Chapman was presented with a copy of the Official Secrets Act. Unaware of what was coming, he signed it, thereby stating: 'I understand that any disclosure by me, whether during or after the present war, of facts relating to the undertaking upon which I have been engaged . . . will be an offence punishable by imprisonment.' Having gagged Chapman, MI5 then sacked him.

Ryde was authorised to dismiss Chapman, which he did, 'as forcibly as possible', throwing him out of the Hill Street flat after a fierce lecture on the error of his ways and warning him that if he dared to reveal what he had done during the war he would be prosecuted. Ryde was exultant and ungenerous in victory and washed MI5's hands of Chapman with a flourish, and a threat: 'He must understand that he must now stand on his own feet, and should he make any approach we, the office, will consider whether he should not be interned or otherwise disposed of.'

Chapman had repeatedly risked his life for the British secret services; he had provided invaluable intelligence for the Allied war effort, he had penetrated the upper echelons of the German secret service, and helped disrupt V-weapon attacks on central London; even now, German intelligence officers were poring over documents, furnished by Zigzag, describing a non-existent anti-submarine weapon; he had extracted some £7,000 from the Nazi exchequer, £230,000 at modern prices, and cost the British government almost nothing. But he was also a criminal, expendable, and quite the wrong sort of person, in the eyes of many, to be hailed as a hero. This was the man MI5 would now 'dispose of', if he dared to bother them again.

The Zigzag case was closed, and at the age of thirty, Chapman's career as a secret agent came to an abrupt and permanent end. That evening, over dinner at his club with fellow officers, Major Ryde reviewed the fall of Eddie Chapman with placid self-satisfaction, concluding that: 'Zigzag should be thankful we are not going to lock him up.'

Tin Eye Stephens, however, saw Zigzag differently: Chapman was the worst of men, in whom war had brought out the best. Years later, Stephens wrote: 'Fiction has not, and probably never will, produce an espionage story to rival in fascination and improbability the true story of Edward Chapman, whom only war could invest with virtue, and that only for its duration.' In Germany, Stephan von Gröning waited in vain for a message from his agent and friend. When the Nazis retreated, he continued to listen and hope, and as Hitler's regime crumbled around him, he was listening still.

Chapman, by rights and inclination, might have been expected to react to his sacking with indignation. But in truth, MI5's ungrateful farewell had set him free at last. He was no longer in thrall to either the German or the British secret services. He had money and a medal from the former, and an informal pardon from the latter: no other secret agent could claim to have been rewarded in this way by *both* sides. MI5 had threatened dire reprisals if he revealed his story, but he knew that one day it would be told.

Chapman returned to what he knew best, for Britain at the end of the war was a criminal cornucopia. Through his old networks, he came into contact with Billy Hill, a nightclub owner and underworld boss who styled himself the 'King of Soho'. Hill had spent the war setting up some profitable black market and protection rackets. He was a 'hard character with considerable dash and more verve', in Chapman's view, and the ideal ally. Making money by drugging greyhounds was strictly a pastime. New money-making schemes beckoned. Chapman and Hill went into partnership.

Dismissal from his country's service also left Chapman free to pursue matters of the heart once more, for he had conceived yet another romantic quest. This time the focus was not Dagmar (who waited in Oslo), nor Freda (who continued to draw her stipend from MI5), nor his ex-wife Vera, nor Anita, the Portuguese prostitute from George's bar. Chapman was now determined to find Betty Farmer, the girl he had left behind at the Hotel de la Plage, six years earlier. Perhaps she was dead; perhaps she was married, or had moved away. But Chapman knew that if he could find Betty, and she would let him, he could make amends.

Chapman contacted Paul Backwell and Allan Tooth, the two former policemen who had served as his minders, and asked for their help. He also recruited a private detective, Doughy Baker. The search began to obsess Chapman, driving out every other thought, and every other woman: 'Uppermost in my mind was the desire to find Betty, my girl, whom I had last seen when I dived through a hotel window before my arrest.' Backwell and Tooth traced Betty only as far as a hotel on the Isle of Man in 1943. Her family thought she was working in a factory somewhere near London. A friend said Betty had been walking out with a Spitfire pilot, who was shot down in the sea off Margate.

Chapman arranged a summit meeting to discuss the search for Betty Farmer. Over lunch at the fashionable Berkeley Hotel (Chapman was as profligate and generous as ever), the ex-policemen explained that searching for a single woman in the chaos of wartime Britain was no easy task, particularly without a photograph: 'Is there anyone here who looks like her at all?' Chapman looked around the dining room, with its lunchtime clientele of debs and guardsmen, bankers and mobsters. He pointed to a slim woman with blonde hair, seated at a corner table, her back to the room. 'That girl,' he said, 'looks exactly like her from the back.' At that moment, the woman turned around.

'Jesus!' exclaimed Chapman. 'It *is* Betty. Excuse me gentlemen.'

Backwell and Tooth, discreet to the last, slipped away, as a waiter swept up the remains of a coffee cup that had dropped from Betty Farmer's astonished fingers when a man she had last seen in a Jersey courtroom tapped her on the shoulder. Chapman pulled up a chair.

'I shall go,' he had told her – in the distant days before the war – 'but I shall always come back.'

Aftermath

With the end of the war, the Double Cross team was quietly disbanded. It would be decades before anyone outside the Most Secret circle knew it had existed. A few eventually emerged from the shadows of British intelligence to tell their stories and reap some glory, but most did not.

Tommy 'Tar' Robertson gave up the spy game, and spent the rest of his life farming sheep in Worcestershire. The 'real genius' of the double-cross operation was awarded the US Legion of Merit by Harry Truman, the Royal Order of the Yugoslav Crown by King Peter in a bizarre ceremony at Claridge's, and an OBE from Britain for work too secret to be described. John Masterman, muscle-bound by duty, considered Tar's early retirement to be 'one of the greatest losses which MI5 ever suffered', but Robertson was entirely happy tending his sheep. He stopped wearing tartan trousers, but he continued to talk to strange characters in pubs. When Tar died in 1994, a small poem was offered as an epitaph to the spymaster who never lost the knack of listening:

> Blessed are they with cheery smile
> Who stop to chat for a little while.
> Blessed are they who never say:
> 'You've told me that story twice today.'

John Cecil Masterman, who liked lecturing more than listening, was knighted, feted and awarded the OBE. He returned to Oxford, his clubs, his cricket and his mystery novels. He became provost of Worcester College, and also Vice Chancellor of Oxford. In 1957 he published another detective novel *The Case of the Four Friends,* featuring a character called Chapman, which discussed the nature of the criminal mind: 'To work out the crime before it is committed, to foresee how it will be arranged, and then prevent it! That's a triumph indeed.' He sat on industrial boards and accepted governorships at the major public schools, a stalwart member of the great and good. 'Everything which is good in this curious world owes its origin to privileged persons,' he maintained.

But in 1970, for the first time in his life, Masterman broke ranks with the ruling classes by publishing a book about the Double Cross organisation. His account had been written immediately after the war, strictly for internal MI5 reading, but he had secretly kept a copy for himself. The spy scandals of the 1960s had shattered the morale of the British intelligence community, and Masterman was determined to restore some of its confidence by relating this story of unalloyed success. Roger Hollis, the head of MI5, and Alec Douglas-Home, the Prime Minister, refused to authorise publication, so Masterman published *The Double Cross System in the War of 1939-45* in the United States, where the Official Secrets Act could not stifle it. Many establishment figures, including some of Masterman's former colleagues in MI5, were scandalised; John Marriott never spoke to him again. In 1972, the British government bowed, and the book was published, subject to the removal of a number of contentious passages. 'How strange it was,' wrote Masterman, 'that I, who all my life, had been a supporter of the Establishment, should become, at eighty, a successful rebel.'

Others followed suit: Ewen Montagu published his account of Operation Mincemeat, the successful deception plan that had convinced the Germans the Allies intended to invade the

Balkans and Sardinia rather then Sicily. Montagu, by then Judge Advocate of the Fleet, even played a cameo role in the 1956 film *The Man Who Never Was*.

Paul Backwell, Chapman's wartime minder, became a captain in the Intelligence Corps, and Allan Tooth remained a senior NCO in the Field Security Service.

Ronnie Reed accepted a job with MI5 after the war as senior technical adviser to the security service. Between 1951 and 1957, he headed the counter-espionage section, responsible for investigating Soviet moles in Britain, including the Burgess, McLean and Philby cases. Reed officially retired in 1977, but was invited to stay on in MI5 as a senior advisor. He later wrote the definitive monograph on wartime radio work, which was published as an appendix to the official account of British Intelligence in the Second World War. Reed was much too self-effacing to put his name to it. He died in 1995, at the age of seventy-eight. The Iron Cross presented to Chapman by Von Gröning for services to the Third Reich and then passed on to Reed as a souvenir of their friendship, remains in the possession of the Reed family.

Victor, Lord Rothschild won the George Medal for his wartime work with explosives, joined the Zoology Department of Cambridge University, and went on to become security advisor to Margaret Thatcher. His student membership of the Cambridge Apostles, and his links with the KGB spies Guy Burgess and Anthony Blunt, led to allegations that he was the 'Fifth Man' in the Cambridge Spy Ring. He furiously denied the charges, and published an open letter to British newspapers in 1986 stating: 'I am not, and never have been, a Soviet agent.'

Michael Ryde, Chapman's last case officer, left MI5 soon after the war and rejoined the family firm of chartered accountants. He soon drank himself out of a job, however, and began a sad decent into alcoholism. One marriage disintegrated, and he walked out of the next, leaving two young children. In the

pub, to general disbelief, Ryde would boast of his role in the case
of Eddie Chapman, a man he had despised.

Terence Young survived the Battle of Arnhem to become a
highly successful film-maker, and directed the first and second
James Bond films, *Dr No* and *From Russia with Love* (in which a
Russian spy develops a plan to kill Bond and steal a coding
machine). The persona of the world's most famous secret agent
was probably based on Young himself, with some cast members
remarking that 'Sean Connery was simply doing a Terence
Young impression'.

Jasper Maskelyne the conjuror virtually vanished after the war,
to his intense irritation. He received no decoration, no formal
recognition for his deception schemes, and official accounts of
the North African campaign barely mentioned him. The audi-
ences for his magic shows grew smaller, and the venues steadily
less glamorous. Embittered, he gave up magic, emigrated to
Kenya, set up a successful driving school, took part in the
campaign against the Mau Mau rebels, and died in 1973.

Reginald Kearon, Captain of the *City of Lancaster*, went on to
take command of five more merchant vessels in the course of the
war. He was awarded the OBE for war service and the Lloyd's
War Medal. The sea kept trying, and failing, to claim him: in
1948, unsinkable Reg Kearon went on a solo pleasure cruise in
the Mediterranean and was later found 'drifting on a wreck in
Haifa Bay'. He retired in 1954, the same year that the *City of
Lancaster* (renamed *Lancastrian*) was broken up.

From 1945 Robin 'Tin Eye' Stephens ran Bad Nenndorf, the
Combined Services Detailed Interrogation Centre (CSDIC)
near Hanover, a secret prison set up following the British
occupation of north-west Germany. This was the German
version of Camp 020, where Tin Eye was charged with flushing
the truth out of the numerous intelligence officers and spies
picked up as the Allies pushed into Germany, including Himmler's assistant Walter Schellenburg, and Ernst Kaltenbrünner,
Heydrich's successor as head of the RSHA, (a 'giant of evil' in

Stephens's view). Tin Eye was accused of using brutal methods to extract confessions, but he was acquitted of all charges, having damned his accusers as 'degenerates, most of them diseased by VD [and] pathological liars'.

Stephan von Gröning was arrested by American forces, and held in a prison camp outside Bremen. Homeless, he had been staying with his sister Dorothea and her adopted Jewish daughter when the soldiers arrived. The Americans got lost escorting him to the prison, so half-American Von Gröning showed them the way, in perfect English, with an upper-class accent. He was allowed to send one card a month to relatives. The man whose linen had always been ironed by servants, found himself pleading for handkerchiefs and toothpaste. He was released after six months and discovered, to his intense annoyance, that in order to obtain a ration book, and thus to eat, he had to get a job. Through family friends, he was found nominal employment at the Bremen Museum, but he rarely turned up for work.

The money may have all gone, but Von Gröning lived on his name, 'loyal to his own class' to the end. He married a much younger woman named Ingeborg, and though she worked, he did not. He would lie for long hours on the sofa, reading borrowed books. Von Gröning seldom spoke of the war. He believed Eddie Chapman had been captured, exposed as a spy and executed. He kept a photograph of La Bretonnière in his wallet.

Walter Praetorius, alias Thomas, the Nazi who loved folk dancing, was arrested, transferred to Bad Nenndorf and interrogated by Tin Eye Stephens. Stephens considered the camp inmates to be 'invariably foul', but Praetorius impressed him, perhaps because his Anglomania chimed with Tin-Eye's raw jingoism. Praetorius was released after several months of interrogation, with the verdict that he had 'had a long and possibly creditable record of service as a permanent official of the German Secret Service'. Praetorius settled in Goslar, West Germany, where he returned to teaching, and dancing.

On 5 May 1945, troops of the 41st US Cavalry liberated Mauthausen-Gusen concentration camp, and found a scene from Hell – human skeletons staggering through an abandoned factory of death. Among the emaciated ghosts was Anthony Faramus. He had lost a lung and seven ribs, his body had been racked by diphtheria, scarlet fever, gangrene and dysentery. But somehow the frail Jersey boy who blushed so easily had survived. Back in Britain, he was treated in an RAF hospital, and then discharged with £16 in cash, and a weekly allowance of £2. He arranged to meet up with Eddie Chapman through the journalist Frank Owens, who witnessed their 'awkward' meeting:

'I thought you were dead,' said Chapman.

'I thought so too, sometimes.'

'How did you make out?'

'Not so good.'

'I was always worried about how you got on.'

'I often felt the same way about you, Eddie, and wondered whether you'd make the grade. That was certainly a tricky game you were playing.'

There was an embarrassed silence.

'Where did you go?' asked Chapman.

'Many places so bad, Eddie, that I was sometimes even tempted to give your game away to the Jerries. Anyway, rather than do those swine a favour, I kept quiet.'

There was another long pause, before Chapman said: 'You know, Tony, if it hadn't been for me you wouldn't have had to go through all that.'

Faramus had never betrayed Chapman, and Chapman had maintained the confidence of the Germans, in part, he believed, to protect Faramus. They went to a nearby pub, and got very drunk. 'Millions died without being able to utter a single word,' Chapman reflected to his friend. 'We at least have lived to tell our stories.'

Faramus wrote a harrowing memoir, and obtained work as a film extra. In a painfully ironic piece of casting, he played the part of a prisoner of war in the film *Colditz* – the inhabitants of Colditz may have suffered, but never as he had done.

Faramus emigrated to Hollywood – and ended up as Clark Gable's butler.

Dagmar Lahlum waited in vain for Chapman to come back, while Norway carried out a grim accounting. Vidkun Quisling was arrested at his mansion Gimli, tried for treason, and executed by firing squad. Two members of the Norwegian resistance were tried for the murder of the Feltmans, but acquitted. Dagmar's neighbours back in Eidsvoll whispered behind her back, and called her a 'German tart'; she heard them, but said nothing. She never told her neighbours or family that she had assisted the British secret services during the war. To get away from the 'Mrs Gossips', she took a job as an assistant nurse aboard the cruise ship, *Stvanger Fjord*, which sailed between Oslo, New York and Nova Scotia. She and Chapman had both learned to love the sea and, like him, 'she was always restless'. She worked in a bookshop, then as a hairdresser and finally as an accountant. Dagmar still wore the most fashionable clothes, and smoked Craven 'A' cigarettes. She never married, never had children, and never lost her looks. In old age she wore makeup and leopard skin hats, and once her niece caught her dancing alone in front of the mirror. When Dagmar died of Parkinson's disease in 1999, her niece found a box of letters, carefully written out in English, on sheet after sheet of airmail paper. They were addressed to Eddie Chapman. None had ever been sent. Dagmar's niece burned them all.

Freda Stevenson, rightly, saw no point in waiting. She became a shorthand typist, and in 1949, she married a bank clerk five years her junior. Four years later, she had become a newsagent's clerk, divorced her first husband, and married a wealthy garage proprietor called Abercrombie. Though the security service was careful to destroy the agreement under which she was to be paid £5 a month until further notice and removed all references from the files, Freda may have continued to receive cheques from the London Co-operative Society, the fruits of Chapman's deal with MI5, until the day she died. Like Faramus, Freda was a survivor.

At the Berkeley Hotel, Eddie Chapman and Betty Farmer talked for hours, and got married shortly thereafter. It was a happy, enduring marriage, even though Chapman's eye wandered more or less continuously for the next fifty years. He left often, but he always came back. A daughter, Suzanne, was born in October 1954.

Zigzag never did go straight. After the war, he returned to the demimonde of London's West End, where the wastrels welcomed him home. During the 1950s, he smuggled gold across the Mediterranean. After buying a share in Billy Hill's motor yacht, *The Flamingo*, a former mine-sweeper, Chapman and a like-minded crew sailed to Morocco where they became involved in a ludicrous plot to smuggle 850,000 packets of cigarettes and kidnap the deposed sultan: the plan collapsed when the villainous crew got into a dockside brawl, and they were expelled from Tangiers, hotly pursued by a reporter from the *Sunday Chronicle* whom they invited on board, and then locked in his cabin. *The Flamingo* caught fire in Toulon harbour, possibly for insurance purposes, giving rise to suspicions that Chapman's sabotage skills had not deserted him. Soon after, the Hill gang knocked off a post-office van, escaping with £250,000. During the 1960s, Eddie and Betty Chapman moved to Africa's Gold Coast. Chapman became involved in a complicated building contract. There was a corruption inquiry, but by then he had come home.

Tin Eye Stephens had wondered 'what will happen when Chapman, embroiled again in crime, as he inevitably will be, stands up in court and pleads leniency on the grounds of highly secret wartime service?' He duly found out. Chapman would appear in court repeatedly over the next twenty years, but he never returned to prison. When he was charged with passing forged currency in 1948, he produced a character reference from an unnamed 'senior officer of the War office' stating that he was 'one of the bravest men who served in the last war'. The referee was almost certainly Ronnie Reed. MI5 had not entirely welched on its debt. Again, in 1974, he was found not guilty of hitting a man on the head with a glass during a dance party at the Watersplash Hotel in the New Forest. The fight was over a young woman named Theresa Chin. Chapman told the court: 'I was trained in unarmed combat for my wartime activities and I didn't need a glass to defend myself in a pub brawl. I could have killed him with my bare hands.' When he was acquitted, he offered to buy the jury a drink.

Chapman still mixed with blackmailers, high-rollers and low thieves. He drove a Rolls-Royce (though he never passed a driving test) and wore fur-collared coats. The newspapers loved him – 'Eddie Chapman, the gentleman crook'. He was even, for a time, the 'honorary crime correspondent' of the *Sunday Telegraph*, 'whose readers he proceeded to warn against the attentions of people like him'. In 1960, a reporter asked him if he missed the old days of crime. 'I do a bit,' he said wistfully. 'I've no regrets. No conscience about anything I've done. I like to think I was an honest villain.'

John Masterman once wrote: 'Sometimes in life you feel that there is something which you *must* do, and in which you must trust your own judgment and not that of any other person. Some call it conscience and some plain obstinacy. Well, you can take your choice.' War, briefly, brought out in Chapman an obstinate conscience. His vices were as extreme as his virtues, and to the end of his life, it was never clear whether he was on the side of the angels or the devils, whether he deceived the deceivers, or whether he had made a pact with his German spymaster. He died of heart failure in 1997, at the age of eighty-three: he may have ascended heavenwards; or perhaps he headed in the opposite direction. He is probably zigzagging still.

Chapman tried to publish an account of his wartime exploits, but like John Masterman he was blocked by MI5. He wrote a bowdlerised version of events which appeared in a French newspaper, *L'Etoile*, and then in the *News of the World* in 1953, but when Chapman strayed into official secrets the government lawyers stepped in. He was fined £50 and an entire edition of the newspaper had to be pulped. A second attempt at publication was thwarted by D–Notice. Eventually, a ghosted and semi-fictionalised memoir, *The Eddie Chapman Story*, which described his time in Germany but not his MI5 work, appeared in 1954. 'What is the truth about Eddie Chapman?' one paper demanded. 'Why, if these astounding claims are true, was he not arrested and convicted as a traitor to his country?'

Finally, in 1966, Chapman was allowed to publish another version, *The Real Eddie Chapman Story*, which referred, without giving details, to his work for MI5. This provided the basis for a rather poor film, *Triple Cross,* directed by Terence Young and starring Christopher Plummer as Chapman. The film bears only a superficial relation to the truth. Chapman was disappointed by it. He never received the recognition he thought he deserved; but then, Chapman could probably only have achieved *that* level of recognition by assassinating Hitler. Somehow, he became rather rich, and for a while owned a castle in Ireland and a health farm in Hertfordshire, not far from the De Havilland Mosquito plant.

In 1974, in a London bar, Chapman bumped into Leo Kreusch, the toothless German prizefighter who had taught him to shoot in La Bretonnière. Leo told Chapman the real name of the man he had always known as Graumann, revealing that he had survived the war and that he was now living in Bremen. Chapman wrote Von Gröning a letter, in which he recalled, with affection, the times they had spent together in Nantes, Paris and Oslo. He inquired whether his old friend knew what had happened to the Norwegian sailing yawl purchased with his reward money, and whether he remembered Dagmar Lahlum. 'I suppose she is married now,' he reflected nostalgically. Chapman described his properties, enclosing a photograph

of the ancient Irish castle he had acquired, and invited Von
Gröning to come and stay: 'What delightful memories we could
exchange . . . I remember how much you used to like castles.'

This was not, perhaps, the most tactful approach, but Eddie
could not know that Von Gröning was no longer a wealthy man.

Suzanne Chapman was married in 1979 at Shenley Lodge, the
thirty-two room health spa owned by Eddie and Betty. Among
the wedding guests that day was an elderly, short-sighted German gentleman who amused the children by reciting old-
fashioned English nursery rhymes. When the party wound
down, Eddie Chapman and Stephan von Gröning linked arms
and wandered off together, deep in reminiscence. Betty was
surprised and moved by the enduring bond between the spy and
his spymaster: 'They were like brothers.' As the last wedding
guests departed, laughter and singing could be heard drifting
from the garden: the faint strains of *Lili Marlene*.

HI HU HA HA HA

Postscript

A few weeks after the publication of *Agent Zigzag*, I received a telephone call from the German Ambassador to London, Wolfgang Ischinger. 'I have just finished your book,' he said. 'You describe how Eddie Chapman was flown across the Channel by the Luftwaffe and then parachuted into Britain. I thought you might be interested to know that the man who commanded that flight was my father. Both he and the pilot, Fritz Schlichting, are still very much alive.'

Leutnant Fritz Schlichting, the young pilot
who flew Chapman to Britain in 1942.

Schlichting had been the tall, shy pilot with the Iron Cross at the controls of the Focke-Wulf reconnaissance plane in 1942, while Karl 'Charlie' Ischinger was his commanding officer and navigator, described by Chapman as a 'small, thickset young man of about twenty-eight, with steady blue eyes'. Chapman himself had believed these men were dead: 'The whole crew had been shot down and killed over England on their sixtieth sortie,' he wrote.

The discovery that the pilot and navigator had not only outlived the war, but survived still, led to a meeting with Fritz Schlichting at his home in Detmold, Germany. At the age of eighty-four, charming and hospitable, the former pilot recalled that day as if he had stepped off the runway at Le Bourget last week, rather than a long lifetime ago.

'We were the Luftwaffe Reconnaissance Squadron number 123 stationed in the Château du Buc, outside Versailles. We flew night flights over Britain, photographing the effects of bombing raids and helping to identify targets. It was dangerous work. I lost

Uberleutnant Karl 'Charlie' Ischinger, commander of the Luftwaffe plane that flew Chapman to Britain in 1942, reporting to Major Armin Göbel, chief of Reconnaissance Squadron 123.

more than eighty comrades. The average number of flights before being shot down was about forty. I flew eighty-seven in all.

'One day my commanding officer, Major Gobin, told Charlie [Ischinger] and me that we had been chosen for a special mission. He told us to dress in civilian clothing, and go to Paris. We met the English spy and his handlers in a restaurant for dinner: we knew him only as "Fritz", like me. Much later I discovered his real name. He was delightful, excellent company. We all got on famously.

'We all met a few weeks later at Le Bourget airfield, and I showed him over the plane. Chapman seemed quite calm, although he asked lots of questions. On the way over the Channel we sang songs. There was a bad moment when Chapman was preparing to jump, and we realised that his parachute cord was not properly tied. If he had jumped like that, he would have fallen to his death. Charlie gave the signal, and Chapman opened the hatch. He had this huge pack on his back – heaven knows what was in it – and as he jumped it got wedged in the hole. He was struggling, but it wouldn't budge, so Charlie got out of his seat and gave him a big boot in the back.

'That was the last we saw of Chapman for about four months, but we heard that his mission had been successful. Everyone was very pleased with him. It never occurred to anyone that he might be working for the British. We met up with him again in Paris. It was a great reunion. Chapman handed Charlie and me two packages, containing a big box of chocolates and a pound of coffee which he had bought in Madrid on his way back. It was real coffee beans, not the fake stuff, so we were delighted.

'After the Chapman mission, as a reward, we were each presented with a special engraved silver goblet. I have always treasured it. Charlie is my still my best friend. He is ninety-seven now, and his health is not good, but we still have get-togethers when we remember the extraordinary night we dropped the English spy into Britain.'

★　　★　　★

The courtly Luftwaffe pilot was only one of several people to emerge from Chapman's past, adding fresh myths and memories, some affectionate, and some decidedly less so. An elderly, rather refined female voice came on the telephone at *The Times*, and without giving her name declared angrily: 'He was an absolute shit, you know. The handsomest man I ever met. But a prize shit.' Then she rang off. In Norway, another of Chapman's wronged women finally won recognition for her heroism. The Norwegian media picked up the Chapman story, and the national newspaper *Aftenposten* ran a front-page story with the headline: 'She died a German collaborator, but she was really a British spy.' It emerged that Dagmar had been brought before a war-crimes tribunal after the war, imprisoned for six months, and agreed to acknowledge her own guilt in lieu of a formal conviction. Reviled and ostracised by her countrymen, Dagmar had kept her promise to Chapman, and never revealed her wartime links with the British Secret Service.

John Williams, a friend of Chapman's, recalled the first time they had met, when Shenley Lodge was being run as a country club with bar and roulette table before its more respectable incarnation as a health farm: 'I arrived at the impressive front entrance of Shenley only to hear the most fearsome of noises from the roof of the mansion. It was on this roof I met Eddie, strapped into a Vickers machine gun firing at a sheet draped between two oak trees half a mile away!' Another acquaintance, the journalist Peter Kinsley, wrote a letter to *The Times* after *Agent Zigzag* was serialised: 'Eddie would have loved the publicity. His old friends said he should have worn a T-shirt emblazoned "I am a spy for MI5". The last time I met him he described how he had missed a fortune in ermine (to be used in Coronation robes) during a furs robbery, because he thought it was rabbit. He also said he successfully convinced a German au pair girl that he was a Post Office telephone engineer, and robbed the wall safe. He was also once visited by an income tax inspector, and produced a doctor's certificate that he had a weak heart and could not be "caused stress". Ten minutes later, he drove, in a Rolls-Royce, past the inspector waiting in the rain at a bus stop, and gave him a little wave.'

I received a mournful letter from Brian Simpson, a collector of wartime medals who had lived near Shenley Lodge in the 1980s. Simpson had heard of Chapman's adventures though a mutual friend, and asked if he could buy his Iron Cross. Sure enough, a few weeks later, Chapman duly produced the German medal; indeed, he produced two, saying that he had been given another one by Hitler himself. A deal was struck: Eddie Chapman took the money, and a delighted Simpson took the medals. Two decades later, on reading this book, the collector realised he had been conned. Chapman, of course, had given his own Iron Cross to Ronnie Reed many years earlier. Those in Simpson's possession were replicas. 'Your book came as quite a shock,' wrote Simpson. 'It now seems that Eddie had the last laugh. My wife was also offered a small jewelled dagger which Eddie said was

Tommy 'Tar' Robertson, head of Section B1A,
wearing the tartan trews of the Seaforth Highlanders
that earned him the nickname 'Passion Pants'.

given to him by Hermann Göring. She declined to take it.' Chapman, needless to say, had never laid eyes on Göring.

One after another, Chapman's former associates, ex-lovers and victims emerged from the past, to add their stories – some true, some the legacy of Chapman's self-mythologizing. But then, to my astonishment, there reappeared the only person who really knew the truth about Eddie Chapman: Eddie Chapman himself.

John Dixon, an independent film-maker, called me to say that he had six hours of footage of Chapman talking about his life, not one second of which had ever been broadcast. Dixon had shot the film in 1996, the year before Chapman died, with a view to making a documentary that never happened. He had kept the film safe, thinking that one day Chapman's story would be told. He now offered to show it to me.

Sitting in a small screening room in Soho, meeting Chapman for the first time from beyond the grave, was one of the strangest experiences of my life. Chapman was old and already ill when the film was made, but still vital. He exudes a feral charm, as he lounges in an armchair, reminiscing, smoking, chuckling, winking and flirting with the camera. He describes parachuting into Britain, his relationship with Von Gröning, the faked bombing of the de Havilland aircraft, and his life in Jersey, France, Lisbon and Oslo. His criminal exploits are remembered with airy pride.

But there is a valedictory tone to his words: this is the last testament of a man talking to posterity, and setting the record straight or, in some instances, bent. Because at the age of eighty-two, Chapman is still a shameless liar. In one passage, for example, he describes being taken to see Winston Churchill in 1943 and sharing a bottle of brandy with the Prime Minister while the latter sat in bed in his dressing gown. It is a splendid story. It is also completely untrue.

Chapman could never have imagined that MI5 would decide

to release its records, and that the truth about his wartime service would one day be revealed. His own death is imminent, but here is Eddie Chapman still playing by his own rules: a grinning villain, spinning a yarn, looking you straight in the eye, and picking your pocket.

Ben Macintyre
April 2007

Eddie Chapman is reunited with his MI5 handlers at the Savoy, October 1980.
Chapman, back row, third from right; Tommy 'Tar' Robertson, back row, third from left;
Roman Garby-Czerniawski, double agent 'Brutus', front row, third from left.

APPENDIX

This is an exact copy of the explanation of Chapman's code, contained in the MI5 archives (KV2/455):

MULTIPLICATION CODE
Given to
An English Parachutist

This code is based on the word: 'CONSTANTINOPLE' which is agreed upon before the agent's departure. Constantinople is then given its numerical position in the alphabet in the following manner and multiplied by the date on which the transmission takes place. In this case the 8th has been chosen.

C	O	N	S	T	A	N	T	I	N	O	P	L	E
2	9	6	12	13	1	7	14	4	8	10	11	5	3
													8
23	6	8	97	05	3	7	15	8	4	80	92	2	4

The next procedure:
Write out the alphabet in full, giving each letter its numerical position.

a b c d e f g h i j k l m n o p q r s t u v w x y z
1 2 3 4 5 6 7 8 9 10 11 12 13 14 15 16 17 18 19 20 21 22 23 24 25 26

The result of the multiplication is then written out and the message to be transmitted – in this case:

'I HAVE ARRIVED AND IN GOOD HEALTH'

is written below.

It will be noticed that the first five letters are 'f's. This is the agreed sign between the agent and his German Control that he is operating of his own free will. Should he be forced to transmit, the omission of the five 'f's would immediately disclose to the German Control that he had been apprehended.

The Method of Coding:

Add 'f' (which is the 6th letter) to the 2 above it, making 8, and selecting the 8th letter in the alphabet – 'h' –

In the second instance 'f' again (the 6th letter in the alphabet), added to 3, making 9 which is – 'i' –

This method is continued throughout the message including the signature 'FRITZ'.

2	3	6	8	9	7	0	5	3	7	1	5	8	4	8	0	9	2	2	4
f	f	f	f	f	I	H	A		V	E	x	A	R	R		I	V	E	D	A	N
h	i	l	n	o	p	h	f	y	f	y	f	z	v	q	v	n	f	c	r
D		I	N	G	O	O	D	H		E	A	L	T	H	x	F	R		I	T	Z	x
f	l	t	o	x	v	d	m	h	h	m	y	p	b	n	r	r	v	b	b

The Groups of 5

are then read off horizontally instead of vertically as in other cases.

Thus:

HILNO PHFYL YFZVQ VNFCR FLTOX VDMHH MYPBN
RRVBB

Note: It is always necessary to include the exact number of letters in the code before commencing the coded groups of five.

NOTES

The KV2 series is located at The National Archives, Kew.

Unless otherwise noted all interrogations are of Chapman by the MI5 officer named.

Newspapers extracts reproduced in the text have been edited.

Where three or more subsequent note entries refer to the same source only the first and last entries from the main text are shown as prompts.

1. The Hotel de la Plage

3 **with all the trimmings** Interview with Leonard Maxie, former waiter at Hotel de la Plage, Jersey, July 2006.

3 **in the film business** Interview with Betty Chapman, Amersham, 25.11.05.

3 **I shall go** Ibid.

3 **How would you like** Edward Chapman, *The Real Eddie Chapman Story*, (London, 1966), p. 32. Henceforth: *Chapman*.

4 **prince of the underworld** Robin Stephens, 7.1.42, KV2 457.

5 **off the rails** Interview with Betty Chapman, 25.11.05.

6 **jail-crop haircut** *Chapman*, p. 27.

6 **three days** Report by Laurie. C. Marshall, 15.1.43; MI5 ref. 133B. This file, newly released by MI5, has been allocated to KV2 457. Material in this file, henceforth: 'KV2 457 (additional)'.

6 **wire and whipcord body** Frank Owens, introduction to ibid., p. 9.

6 **I mixed with all types** Ibid., p. 27

7 **behaving in a manner** Police record, KV2 455.

7 **with good looks** Owens in *Chapman*, p. 9.

7 **women on the fringes** R. Stephens, *Camp 020: MI5 and the Nazi Spies* (London, 2000), p. 218. Henceforth: *Camp 020*.

7 **infected a girl of 18** Ibid.

7 **best cracksman** KV2 457.

7 **cool, self-possessed** *Chapman*, p. 28.

8 **shivering with fear** Interrogation by Ronald Reed, 7.1.43, KV2 457.
9 **He was able** Interview with Terence Young, 22.1.43, KV2 458.
9 **He is a crook** Ibid.
9 **I don't go along** *Sunday Telegraph*, 23 March 1963.
9 **went back to 'work'** Paul Backwell's report, KV2 456.
11 **Be prepared for trouble** *Jersey Evening Post*, 13.2.39.

2. Jersey Gaol

16 **done with deliberation** *Jersey Evening Post*, 14.2.39.
16 **dangerous criminal who** Ibid.
16 **dreary little cage** Anthony Faramus, *The Faramus Story* (London, no date stated, 1954?), p. 12. Henceforth: *Faramus*.
16 **dangerous criminal** Ibid.
16 **batman** Minutes of the Jersey prison board, Jersey Historical Archive.
16 **keep an eye on Chapman** Ibid.
17 **At that moment** Warder Packer's evidence to Jersey prison board, Jersey Historical Archive.
17 **Do you know** *Jersey Evening Post*, 6.7.39.
18 **interested in quarries** to **Your name is Chapman** Ibid.
20 **free-for-all** *Daily Express*, 8.7.39.
20 **This appeared to** *Jersey Evening Post*, 6.7.39.
21 **gross misconduct** Minutes of the Jersey prison board, Jersey Historical Archive.
21 **You have never** Ibid.

3. Island at War

24 **Nationalism as a God** H.G. Wells, *Outline of History* (London, 1920), p. 209.
26 **sort of dispossessed** *Faramus*, p. 10.
27 **Look we've reason** Interrogation, 1.1.43, KV2 456.
28 **If I could work a bluff** Interrogation, 17.12.42, KV2 455.
28 **It all sounds fine talk** *Chapman*, p. 48–9.
28 **His whole theme** *Faramus*, p. 29.
29 **tale of loathing** Ibid., p. 30.
30 **The British police** Interrogation, 17.12.42, KV2 455.

4. Romainville

32 **stank of drink** *Faramus*, p. 39.
32 **How would you** Ibid., p. 36.
32 **Alles verboten** *The Trial of German Major War Criminals*, vol. 6 (London, 1946), p. 141.
33 **Madame prisonniers** *Faramus*, p. 40.
34 **professional denouncer** Interrogation by E. Goodacre, 18.12.42, KV2 455.
34 **It wasn't safe to talk** Interrogation by Goodacre, 17.12.42, KV2 455.

34 **were real love affairs** *Faramus*, p. 43.
35 **the scholarly, staid** Interrogation by Victor Rothschild, 28.1.43, KV2 458.
36 **What happened?** *Faramus*, p. 48.
36 **All right for you** Ibid., p. 37.
37 **Supposing you didn't** *Faramus*, p. 49.
37 **You'd have to trust** Ibid.
37 **They'll probably send** Ibid.,p. 37.
38 **simply a trained brute** *Chapman*, p. 62.
38 **a man of understanding** Ibid., p. 62.
38 **no use** Interrogation by Stephens, 7.1.42, KV2 457.
38 **In times of war** Interrogation by Stephens, 17.12.42, KV2 455.
39 **half-threat** Ibid.
39 **Supposing you slip** *Faramus*, p. 37.
39 **Goodbye and good luck** Ibid., p. 49.
39 **You are among friends** *Chapman*, p. 64.
49 **Welcome to the Villa** Ibid., p. 66.

5. Villa de la Bretonnière

42 **one of the most important** Interrogation by Stephens, 17.12.42, KV2 455.
43 **respectable business man** Ibid.
43 **surprisingly soft** Ibid.
43 **Look, you will see** Interrogation by Rothschild, 2.1.43, KV2 456.
43 **absolutely first class** T.A. Robertson (attrib), report of SOE training course, KV4 172.
44 **by the time of the fall** John Curry, *The Security Service 1908–1945: The Official History* (London, 1999), KV4 1–3.
46 **There is a well-defined** Cited in Emily Jane Wilson, *The War in the Dark: The Security Service and the Abwehr 1940–1944*, PhD thesis (Cambridge, 2003)
46 **typically Prussian neck** Ibid.
46 **Suspect everyone** Evelyn Waugh, cited in ibid.
47 **was left with the** Curry, op. cit.
48 **Chiefly line of Clan** Letter by Walter Praetorius, 1979, on Thomas Family website.
49 **kind, gentle type** Walter Praetorius file, KV 2 524.
49 **rabid Nazi** Ibid.
49 **superiority of the German** Ibid.
50 **might be trained** ISOS intercept, 2.2.42, KV2 456.

6. Dr Graumann

52 **He just got hold** Interrogation, 1.1.43, KV2 456.
53 **pocket money** Ibid.
53 **He liked life** Interrogation by Rothschild, 2.1.43, KV2 456.
54 **Had a good trip?** Interrogation, 1.1.43, KV2 456.
54 **What do you want** Interrogation by Rothschild, 2.1.43, KV2 456.
54 **take it out and light** Interrogation by Goodacre, 17.12.42, KV2 455.
54 **Good God!** Interrogation by Stephens, 17.12.42, KV2 455.

54 **Look here, if you**　Ibid.
55 **more or less reckless**　Interrogation by Rothschild 28.1.43, KV2 458.
55 **Mary had a little**　Interrogation by Rothschild, 2.1.43, KV2 456.
55 **which I thought**　Ibid.
55 **terribly English accent**　Interrogation by Stephens, 3.1.43, KV2 456.
55 **very good private tutor**　Interrogation by Reed, 21.12.43, KV2 456.
55 **I'll show you a photograph**　Interrogation by Stephens, 3.1.43, KV2 456.
56 **really good brandy**　*Chapman*, p. 66.
57 **uncomfortable**　Interview with Ingeborg von Gröning, Bremen, 22.05.06.
57 **He was delightful**　Ibid.
58 **illicit association**　Gladys von Gröning, immigration file, HO 405/16169.
59 **He could mix in**　Interview with Ingeborg von Gröning, Bremen, 22.05.06.
59 **Home corner**　*Chapman*, p. 73.
60 **German spirit**　Ibid., p. 71.
60 **Heil Hitler**　Ibid., p. 69.
60 **the hopes of every**　Ibid., p. 72.
61 **of every kind**　Interrogation by Stephens, 17.12.42, KV2 455.
61 **a fairly high bug**　Interrogation by Stephens, 19.12.42, KV2 455.
62 **one of our best**　Ibid.
62 **like a gigolo**　Report by Reed, 1.1.43, KV2 457.
62 **an old Gestapo man**　Interrogation by Goodacre, 17 12 42, KV2 455.
62 **black senders**　Ibid.
63 **unbreakable**　Reed report, 15.3.43, KV2 459.
63 **my little mottoes**　Interrogation, 1.1.43, KV2 456.
63 **It is very cold**　ISOS intercept, 20.10.42, KV2 460.
63 **A man went**　Ibid., 23.10.42.
64 **What silly business**　Ibid., 14.10.42.
64 **I had everything**　Interrogation by Stephens, 17.12.42, KV2 455.

7. Codebreakers

65 **Dear France . . .**　ISOS intercept, 13.10.42, KV2 460.
66 **brilliant guesswork**　Peter Twinn, in F.H. Hinsley and Alan Stripp (eds.), *Codebreakers: The Inside Story of Bletchley Park* (Oxford, 2001).
66 **It's amazing how**　Cited in Penelope Fitzgerald, *The Knox Brothers*, (London, 2001), p. 98.
66 **My Golden Eggs**　Cited in Wilson, op cit
68 **By means of the**　J.C. Masterman, *The Double Cross System in the War 1939–1945* (London, 1972), p. 3.
68 **Immensely personable**　Address by Christopher Harmer at memorial service for T.A. Robertson, 1909–94, at Pershore Abbey, in papers of Lieutenant Colonel T.A. Robertson, courtesy of the Trustees of the Liddell Hart Centre for Military Archives, King's College, London.
68 **Tar was in no sense**　J. C. Masterman, *On the Chariot Wheel: An Autobiography* (Oxford, 1975), p. 219.
69 **involved a great**　Harmer, op. cit.
69 **Passion Pants**　Ibid.
70 **almost obsessively anxious**　Masterman, *On the Chariot Wheel*, p. 108.
70 **My predominant feeling**　Ibid., p. 114.
70 **real genius**　Cited in Wilson, op. cit.

71 **At 58 St James's Street** Masterman, *On the Chariot Wheel*, p. 377.
71 **Some had to perish** Masterman, *The Double Cross System*, p. 54.
71 **certain persons who** Ibid., p. 1.
71 **see with the eyes** Ibid., p. 22.
72 **is prone to be** Ibid., p. 24.
72 **principle of generosity** Ibid., p. 25.
73 **of high intelligence** Masterman, *On the Chariot Wheel*, p. 219.
74 **We were obsessed** Ibid.
74 **Could any intelligence** Ewen Montagu, *Beyond Top Secret Ultra* (London, 1977), p. 134.
75 **now prepare sabotage** Reed notes of ISOS intercepts, 30.6.42, KV2 456.
75 **any connection with the** Ibid., 28.7.42.
75 **he merely succeeded** Reed report, 20.8.41, KV2 455.
75 **When he arrives** RSS report, 19.9.41, KV2 455.
75 **practically every day** Memo, KV2 455.
75 **learned to recognise** Ibid.
75 **Is my message** Reed report, 20.8.41, KV2 455.

8. The Mosquito

76 **to shoot his** Reed report, 8.2.42, KV2 458.
77 **I was suffering more** Interrogation by Rothschild, 2.1.43, KV2 456.
77 **made all the right** Interrogation by Goodacre, 17.12.42, KV2 455.
77 **Monsieur Ferdinand** Ibid.
77 **a tremendous bloodbath** Interrogation by Major D.B. 'Stimmy' Stimson,17.12.42, KV2 455.
78 **very cleverly planned** Ibid.
78 **courage and daring** KV2 457.
78 **full-scale attack** Backwell report, 30.12.42, KV2 456.
78 **terrific Blitz** Interrogation by Stephens, 17.12.42, KV2 455.
78 **You can imagine** Ibid.
78 **It is rather awkward** Interrogation by Rothschild, 2.1.43, KV2 456.
81 **He insisted on exact** Ibid.
81 **like bloody monks** Interrogation, 1.1.43, KV2 456.
82 **There was a hell** Ibid.
82 **undesirable emotional** ISOS intercept, 2.10.42, KV2 460.
82 **nihilistic** Backwell notes, KV2 456.
82 **Could something be** Interrogation by Goodacre, 18.12.42, KV2 455.
82 **impossible** Ibid.
82 **if he could return** Backwell notes, KV2 456.
83 **I don't suppose there** Memo, KV2 456.
84 **It makes me furious** See *A Short History of the DH98 Mosquito*, bbc.co.uk
85 **preliminary detailed** ISOS intercepts, 12.10.42, KV2 460.
85 **Things seem at last** Memo, 24.9.42, KV2 456.

9. Under Unseen Eyes

86 **terrific Chrysler** Interrogation by Goodacre, 17.12.42, KV2 455.
86 **the chief wanted** Interrogation by Stephens, 17.12.42, KV2 455.

87 **Let Fritz go first** to **Each time I looked** Ibid.
87 **Americans?** Interrogation by Rothschild, 2.1.43, KV2 456.
87 **No, it's just two** Ibid.
87 **Well, we would** Ibid.
87 **a big mission** Interrogation by Stephens, 17.12.42, KV2 455.
88 **in all probability** Memo, KV2 456.
88 **West End** Ibid.
88 **You have remembered** Interrogation by Stephens, 3.1.43, KV2 456.
88 **I am highly** Ibid.
88 **exploding in all directions** Interrogation by Rothschild, 2.1.43, KV2 456.
88 **in a rotary motion** Interrogation by R. Short, 18.12.42, KV2 455.
89 **a faint greeny colour** Ibid.
89 **like a mosaic** Interrogation by Stephens, 3.1.43, KV2 456.
90 **Look, don't think** Interrogation by Rothschild, 2.1.43, KV2 456.
90 **If you feel you're** to **I don't think** Ibid.
90 **Fritz is spiritually** ISOS intercepts, 26.9.42, KV2 460.
91 **Show Fritz photos** Memo, KV2 456.
91 **safer than anywhere else** Ibid.
91 **new operational objective** Reed note, ISOS Intercept, 7.12.42, KV2 456.
91 **made familiar in every** ISOS intercepts, 7.12.42, KV2 460.
92 **apathetic** Interrogation, 1.1.43, KV2 456.
92 **There were no scenes** Interrogation by Stephens, 17.12 42, KV2 455.
93 **Why should I send** *Chapman,* p. 103.
93 **Rendez-vous with** Interrogation by Goodacre, 18.12.42, KV2 455.
93 **very small fry** Ibid.
94 **I think it was** Interrogation by Stephens, 17.12 42, KV2 455.

10. The Drop

95 **visibly relieved** Reed's note, ISOS Intercept, 10.12.42, KV2 456.
95 **some place further** Interrogation by Goodacre, 17 12 42, KV2 455.
95 **British red tape** Chapman statement, 18.12.42, KV2 455.
96 **Young couple require** Memo, KV2 455.
97 **nuisance work** Interrogation by Rothschild, 2.1.43, KV2 456.
97 **Take your time** Interrogation by Stephens, 17.12.42, KV2 455.
97 **Of course our agents** Ibid.
97 **Walter is ready to go** Interrogation by Stephens, 7.1.42, KV2 457.
98 **give as little information** Interrogation by Goodacre, 18.12.42, KV2 455.
98 **a number of small** Ibid.
98 **various people who** Interrogation by Stephens, 17.12.42, KV2 455.
98 **Joli Albert** Ibid.
98 **holiday** Camp 020 report, 11.7.44, KV2 459.
98 **in the first or second** Reed report, 1.1.43, KV2 456.
99 **Don't you worry** Interrogation by Goodacre, 18.12.42, KV2 455.
99 **it was hard to tell** *Faramus,* p. 74.
99 **It was hard** Ibid., p. 78.
99 **If you do this** Interrogation by Stephens, 17.12.42, KV2 455.
100 **I have rather** Ibid.
100 **anything which could** Interrogation by Rothschild, 2.1.43, KV2 456.
100 **You don't mind** Ibid.
101 **if there was any** Interrogation by Stephens, 7.1.42, KV2 457.

101 **home** *Chapman*, p. 107.
101 **genuine comradeship** Ibid.
102 **Reichsbank, Berlin** Interrogation by Stephens, 7.1.42, KV2 457.
102 **England** Ibid.
102 **You have beautiful** Interrogation by Stephens, 17.12.42, KV2 455.
102 **of the larynx type** Interrogation by Stimson, 17.12.42, KV2 455.
103 **evade attack** Ibid.
103 **We shall be waiting** Interrogation by Stephens, 17.12.42, KV2 455.
104 **Far from being nervous** Interrogation by Stimson, 17.12.42, KV2 455.

11. Martha's Exciting Night

105 **Keep a close watch** Memo, KV2 455.
105 **very soon be going** Reed notes on ISOS intercepts, KV2 456.
105 **Agent X is probably** Memo, KV2 455.
106 **It may be of intelligence** RSS memo, 8.10.42, KV2 455.
106 **too many possibilities** Memo, KV2 455.
107 **flying column** to **pretend to be looking** Ibid.
107 **fully fledged saboteur** Memo, 1.10.42, KV2 455.
107 **We quite realise** Memo, 4.10.42, KV2 455.
108 **Who is it** Police report, KV2 455.
108 **A British airman** to **Yes** Ibid.
109 **just arrived from** Report of Sgt J. Vail, KV2 455.
109 **He shook hands** to **very polite** Ibid.
110 **George Clarke will** Report of Deputy Chief Constable Ely, KV2 455.
112 **mentally and physically** Stephens report, 17.12.42, KV2 455.

12. Camp 020

113 **A breaker is born** *Camp 020*, p. 107.
113 **There must be certain** Ibid.
113 **Italy is a country** Ibid., p. KV4 14, p. 306.
113 **weeping and romantic** *Camp 020*, p. 54.
114 **shifty Polish Jews** Ibid., p. 73.
114 **unintelligent** Ibid., p 295.
114 **lunatic cells ready** Ibid., p. 40.
115 **No chivalry** Ibid.,p 19.
115 **It is a question** Ibid., p. 71.
115 **Your name is Chapman** Interrogation by Stephens, 17.12.42, KV2 455.
116 **That was plain** Stephens report, 18.12.42, KV2 544.
116 **with some bitterness** Ibid.
117 **blow hot-blow cold** *Camp 020*, p. 109.
117 **They treated you** See interrogation by Stephens, 17.12.42, KV2 455.
117 **I don't know what** Cited in Montagu, op. cit., p. 108.
117 **No spy, however astute** *Camp 020*, p. 105.
117 **Physically and mentally** Ibid., p. 58.
118 **It is quite clear** Reed memo, 21.12.42, KV2 456.
118 **He is a hostage** Interrogation by Goodacre, 18.12.42, KV2 455.
119 **That was a private** Interrogation by Stephens, 17.12.42, KV2 455.

119 **natural inexactitudes** Stephens memo, KV2 455.
119 **confessed to an** *Camp 020*, p. 218.
119 **Today there is no** Stephens report, 7.1.42, KV2 457.
120 **one the principal** Reed notes on ISOS intercepts, 28.7.42, KV2 456.
120 **On no occasion** Robertson memo, 24.12.42, KV2 456.
120 **today was the supposed** Chapman statement, 18.12.42, KV2 455.
120 **It is important** Ibid.
121 **Dr Graumann especially** Ibid.
121 **in sharper focus** Reed report, 15.3.43, KV2 459.
121 **Mon Commandant** Chapman to Stephens, 18.12.42, KV2 455.
122 **If Chapman is** Stephens report, 7.1.42, KV2 457.
123 **hatred for the Hun** Ibid.
123 **As I figure it** Stephens report, 18.12.42, KV2 455.
123 **he will go sour** to **My opinion** Ibid.
123 **In our opinion** Joint statement by interrogators, 18.12.42, KV2 455.
124 **We have chosen** Robertson memo, 18.12.42, KV2 455.

13. 35, Crespigny Road

126 **Ah, Mr Reed** to **I'm going** Transcript of videotaped interview with Ronnie Reed, 1994, courtesy of Nicholas Reed.
126 **humble genius** Interview with Charles Chilton, 5.10.06.
127 **lurid past** Reed memo, 19.12.42, KV2 455.
127 **he would have** Ibid.
127 **Mon Commandant** Chapman to Stephens, 19.12.42, KV2 455.
128 **rather weakly** Reed report, 20.12.42, KV2 455.
128 **FFFFF HAVE ARRIVED** Ibid.
128 **definitely Fritz** ISOS intercepts, 20.9.42, KV2 460.
128 **recognised his style** Reed notes on ISOS intercepts, KV2 456.
128 **GET MORRIS** Reed notes, KV2 456, and ISOS intercepts, 21.12.42, KV2 460.
129 **THANKS FOR** Reed notes, KV2 456.
129 **Zigzag's powers of** Reed report, KV2 458.
129 **the Germans had** Memo, KV2 456.
129 **gratuitous** Memo Masterman to Robertson, 17.12.42, KV2 455.
130 **a very good** Report, 19.12.42, KV2 455.
130 **It does seem** Robertson memo, 30.1.43., KV2 458.
130 **something queer was** Air ministry report, 7.2.43, KV2 458.
130 **They pandered to** Stephens report, 7.1.42, KV2 457.
131 **a dangerous criminal** Robertson briefing, 21.12.42, KV2 456.
131 **The success of this** to **stand his round** Ibid.
132 **who had looked** Note, KV2 456.
132 **permanent companions** Ibid.
132 **Conversation was strained** Backwell notes, KV2 458.
132 **settle in** to **a mine of information** Ibid.
133 **often speaks of** Backwell notes, KV2 456.
133 **what it was that** Tooth notes, KV2 456.
134 **In Germany he** to **I can only glean** Ibid.
134 **I think we should** Reed memo, 26.12.42, KV2 456.
135 **Running a team** Masterman, *The Double Cross System,* p. 90.
135 **I had, with my memories** Masterman, *On the Chariot Wheel*, p. 212.

136 **made defeat seem** Ibid.
136 **the rabble of the universe** Stephens report, 7.1.42, KV2 457.
136 **most fascinating case** Ibid.
136 **what manner of man** *Camp 020*, p. 105.
136 **PLEASE COME AT** Reed report, KV2 456.
137 **We should know** Reed report, 1.1.43, KV2 456.
137 **Eddie had moods** Backwell notes, KV2 458.
138 **a method not calculated** Reed memo 23.12.42, KV2 456.
138 **CALL AT 1000** Reed report, 10.2.42, KV2 458.
138 **My God, I believe** Reed report, 28.12.42, KV2 456.

14. What a Way Out

139 **He was non-judgemental** Harmer, op. cit.
140 **From the fact** Reed report, 28.12.42, KV2 456.
140 **undoubtedly have** to **They may forget** Ibid.
140 **Message of 14 letters** ISOS intercepts, 27.12.42, KV2 460.
140 **annoying** Reed report, 28.12.42, KV2 456.
141 **Preparations should now** Undated note, KV2 456.
141 **silly joking messages** Marshall interrogation, 24.12.42, KV2 456.
141–2 **The men must** to **a little sinister** Ibid.
142 **We should do all** Masterman memo, 26.12.42, KV2 456.
142 **the principle of** Masterman, *The Double Cross System*, p. 19.
142 **also conveyed** Frank Ruskell, cited in *Short History of the DH98 Mosquito*, op. cit.
143 **He seemed more** Backwell report, 30.12.42, KV2 456.
143 **would completely ruin** Cover story narrative, KV2 459.
144 **FFFFF WENT DOWN** Memo, KV2 456.
144 **PLEASE SEND SPECIFIC** Reed report, 10.2.42, KV2 458.
144 **PLEASE GIVE NAME** Memo 5.1.43, KV2 456.
144 **LANDED TWO MILES** Ibid.
145 **well known and accepted** Backwell notes, KV2 458.
145 **Eddie soon began** to **terribly restless** Ibid.
145 **feelings of nihilism** Tooth notes, KV2 456.
146 **His inherent boisterousness** Reed report 15.3.43, KV2 459.
146 **quite impossible** Minutes of meeting, 31.12.42, KV2 456.
146 **cloistered life** Robertson report, 11.1.43, KV2 457.
146 **very pale** Tooth notes, KV2 456.
146 **reference to secret** Ibid.
146 **I have another** Reed report, 1.1.43, KV2 456.
146–8 **Any individual enterprise** to **I believe he has** Ibid.

15. Freda and Diane

149 **He wants to provide** Backwell report, KV2 456.
149 **impossible** Ibid.
149 **know of his existence** Marshall report, 15.1.43, MI5 ref. 133B, KV2 457 (additional).
149 **Personal matters** Backwell report, KV2 456.

149 **My sources of information**   Handwritten note, accompanying Backwell note of 12.1.43, KV2 457 (additional).

149 **He feels his present**   Backwell note, 12.1.43, KV2 457 (additional).

150 **The question of Freda**   Ibid.

150 **if she bore any**   Reed Report, 15.3.43, KV2 459. Document 254 B.

150–1 **truculent and moody** to **feminine relaxation**   Ibid.

152 **Luckily there was**   Backwell report, KV2 458.

152 **just back from abroad**   Ibid.

152 **There was one**   Ibid.

152 **cat-burglar**   Marshall report, 7.1.43, KV2 457 (additional).

152 **slightly drunk**   Tooth notes, 7.1.43, KV2 457 (additional).

152 **Hullo, stranger** to **some jocular remark**   Ibid.

153 **The man apologised**   Backwell report, KV2 458.

153 **I suppose it is natural**   Reed report, 7.1.43, KV2 457 (additional).

153 **so far our inquiries**   Reed memo, 13.1.43, KV2 457 (additional).

153 **it was not in the interests**   Marshall report, 15.1.43, MI5 ref. 133B, KV2 457 (additional).

154 **talk to him about**   Marshall report, 23.1.43, KV2 458.

154 **build up his morale** to **folly of expressing**   Ibid.

155 **FFFFF DISGUSTED**   Reed report, 15.3.43, KV2 459. Document 254 B.

155 **not to reap**   Ibid.

155 **new arrangements**   Ibid.

156 **Kalium**   Interrogation by Rothschild, 2.1.43, KV2 456.

156 **This kept Eddie busy**   Backwell notes, KV2 458.

156 **In this frame of mind**   Reed report, 15.3.43, KV2 459. Document 254 B.

156 **tends to break down**   Marshall report, 15.1.43., MI5 ref. 133B, KV2 457 (additional).

157 **serious and intimate** to **Do you consider**   Ibid.

158 **a most valuable character**   Reed handwritten note on ibid.

159 **He would now**   Reed report, 1.1.43, KV2 456.

159 **part of the household**   Backwell notes, KV2 458.

159 **quite content to limit** to **to get Freda up**   Ibid.

159–60 **Eddie, we're on** to **Oh no, not just**   Interview with Ronnie Reed, 1994, Nicholas Reed

160 **Freda must have**   Backwell notes, KV2 458.

160 **Although she knew**   Ibid.

160 **Since he has**   Tooth notes, 26.1.43, KV2 458.

161 **his capacity to live**   Tooth notes, KV2 456.

161 **would fulfil his**   Ibid.

161 **Previously, he had**   Tooth notes, 26.1.43, KV2 458.

161 **What a man!**   Reed handwritten note on ibid.

161 **It is extraordinary**   Reed report, 15.3.43, KV2 459. Document 254 B.

161 **this resolution provides**   Ibid.

16. Abracadabra

164 **look, from the air**   Charles Fraser-Smith, *The Secret War of Charles Fraser-Smith* (London, 1981), p. 121.

164 **danger that the**   Masterman handwritten note on Reed memo, 7.1.43, KV2 457.

165 **vast hole**   Fraser-Smith, op. cit.

165 **FFFFF WALTER READY** Reed report, 15.3.43, KV2 459.
166 **extremely difficult** Masterman memo, 27.1.43, KV2 458.
166 **publish a small paragraph** to **not having taken place** Ibid.
166 **meant him deliberately** Masterman memo, 27.1.43, KV2 458.
167 **the censors** Ibid.
167 **FFFFF ARRANGEMENTS** Reed report, KV2 458.
167 **to see if high** Colonel Sir John Turner memo, KV2 458.
167 **something had occurred** Reed memo, KV2 458.
168 **inky blackness** Reed report, 31.1.43, KV2 458.
168 **in a state of great** to **scene of destruction** Ibid
168 **masterpiece** *Fraser-Smith*, op. cit.
168 **FFFFF WALTER BLOWN** Reed report, 15.3.43, KV2 459. Document 254 B.
168 **champagne all round** Stephen report, 7.1.42, KV2 457.
168 **CONGRATULATIONS** Reed report, 15.3.43, KV2 459. Document 254 B.
169 **The Security Service** Robertson memo, 11.1.43, KV2 457.
170 **to depart in** Reed Report, 15.3.43, KV2 459. Document 254 B.
170 **vague** Ibid.
170 **to be immortalised** Ibid.
171 **declined to encourage** Masterman, *The Double Cross System*, p. 132.
171 **Perhaps we missed** Ibid.
171 **frank and straightforward** Reed report, 13.3.43, KV2 459.
171 **a man whose** Shanks report. 6.1.43, KV2 457.
171 **a spark of decency** to **whether a patriot or** Ibid.
172 **a refined manner** Marshall report, 15.1.43, MI5 ref. 133B, KV2 457 (additional).
172 **His natural and instinctive** Ibid.
172 **the bogus certainties** Malcolm Muggeridge, *Chronicles of Wasted Time*, vol. II, (London, 1979), p. 222.
172 **When one takes** Cited in Kenneth Rose, *Elusive Rothschild: The Life of Victor, Third Baron* (London, 2003), p. 67.
173 **I think it's terrific (ff)** Interrogation by Rothschild, 2.1.43, KV2 456.

17. The Greater the Adventure

175 **I consider you** Robertson report, 2.2.43, KV2 458.
175 **few, a very few** *Camp 020*, p. 176.
175 **far too valuable** Reed note, KV2 456.
176 **I am not at all** Robertson report, 2.2.43, KV2 458.
176 **people for whom** to **We are preparing** Ibid.
176 **Always speak slowly** Robertson (attrib.), report of SOE training course, KV4 172.
176 **procuring** *mental* Ibid.
176–7 **one with a brutal** Ibid.
177 **FFFFF PICK UP BY** Reed notes on ISOS intercepts, KV2 456.
177 **IMPOSSIBLE PICK** Reed report, 13.3.43., KV2 459.
177 **NORMAL** Ibid.
177 **The suggestion was** Reed report, 15.3.43, KV2 459. Document 254 B.
177 **any attempt to return** Ibid.
177 **not over-anxious** Reed report, 13.3.43, KV2 459.

177 **not prepared to offer** Robertson memo, KV2 457.

177 **unenviable and practically** Reed report, 13.3.43, KV2 459.

178 **provided the man** Memo, KV2 457.

178 **Points I would** Chapman undated note, KV2 458.

178 **in a position** Marshall report, 2.2.43, KV2 456.

178 **Zigzag is fully** Ibid.

179 **to get as much** Ibid.

179 **paying for his stay** Tooth notes, KV2 456.

179 **principle of generosity** Masterman, *The Double Cross System,* p. 18.

179 **the risk to his** Marshall report, 2.2.43, KV2 456.

179 **If Zigzag successfully** to **Substantial payment** Ibid.

180 **It was almost** Reed report, 15.3.43, KV2 459. Document 254 B.

180 **going rather too** Reed memo, 10.2.43, KV2 458.

180 **After making such** Reed report, 15.3.43, KV2 459. Document 254 B.

180 **FFFFF DANGEROUS TO** Reed memo, 10.2.43, KV2 458.

181 **awkwardness** to **seen a chance** Ibid.

181 **Gelignite Inquiries** *Evening Standard,* 12.2.43.

181 **A man was questioned** Ibid.

181 **185 names have** *News Chronicle,* 10.2.43.

181 **FFFFF JIMMY** Reed memo, 10.2.43, KV2 458.

181 **No further transmissions** Ibid.

182 **absolutely inexcusable** Reed report, 15.3.43, KV2 459. Document 254 B.

182 **to live as man** Reed report, 8.2.43, KV2 458.

182 **Victor, do you** Interrogation by Rothschild, 28.1.43, KV2 458.

182 **Freda returned home** Backwell notes, KV2 458.

182 **unhesitatingly** Ibid.

183 **What shoes** Reed notes, 10.2.43, KV2 458.

183 **not shaken in** Reed memo, 10.2.43, KV2 458.

183 **Poor Freddy Sampson** Backwell notes, KV2 458.

183 **We can rely** Reed report, 8.2.43, KV2 458.

184 **Blue starfish** Reed report, 15.3.43, KV2 459. Document 254 B.

184 **AA guns camouflaged** Ibid.

184 **picked up the** Stephens notes, KV2 456.

184 **There is no information** Robertson, 11.1.43, KV2 457.

184 **It is imperative** Reed memo, 10.2.43, KV2 458.

185 **gloomy picture** Reed report, 15.3.43, KV2 459. Document 254 B.

185 **a vast number** to **that the code in** Ibid.

185 **instructions which** Robertson note, KV2 457.

186 **In spite of the** Backwell report, KV2 456.

186 **deep-seated liking** Robertson memo, 11.1.43, KV2 457.

186 **You may see lots** Interrogation by Rothschild, 28.1.43, KV2 458.

186 **Obviously if he were** Reed report, 13.3.43, KV2 459.

186 **It all depends on** Interrogation by Rothschild, 28.1.43, KV2 458.

186 **You will see that** Reed report, 15.3.43, KV2 459. Document 254 B.

187 **genuinely inspired** Robertson memo, 11.1.43, KV2 457.

187 **the excellent personal** Ibid.

187 **He will be greeted** Reed report, 8.2.43., KV2 458.

187 **Zigzag is confident** to **might possibly** Ibid.

188 **Except in special** Robertson memo, 11.1.43, KV2 457.

188 **The story of many** Stephens report, 7.1.42, KV2 457.

18 Stowaway Spy

191 **a man who had** Reed report, 3.3.43, KV2 458.
191 **From now on this** ibid.
192 **impressed me as** ibid.
192 **lie low** Reed memo, 10.2.43, KV2 458.
192 **complete set of forged** Reed report, 3.3.43, KV2 458.
192 **vast and complicated** Reed report, 15.3.43, KV2 459. Document 254 B.
193 **This course** Reed report, 3.3.43, KV2 458.
193 **ham chat** Reed notes, KV2 458.
193 **please send with** to **suspicious** Ibid.
193 **The 'laughing out'** Reed report, 15.3.43, KV2 459. Document 254 B.
194 **We shall not have** Reed notes, KV2 458.
194 **Mrs West thanks** Reed report, 15.3.43, KV2 459. Document 254 B.
194 **that if any other** Ibid.
194 **It is Lew Leibich** Ibid.
195 **Goodbye for the present** Handwritten note to Marshall, 3.3.43, KV2 458.
195 **did not know what** Reed report, 3.3.43, KV2 458.
195–6 **in the approved** to **which he had coveted** Ibid.
196 **Zigzag is himself** Reed report, 15.3.43, KV2 459. Document 254 B.
197 **The case of Zigzag** Ibid.

19. Joli Albert

198 **fearing prying fingers** Reed report, 26.3.43, KV2 459.
198 **bad lad** Ibid.
198 **Nervous expectancy** *Chapman*, p. 137.
199 **Anson was seasick** Reed report, 18.4.43, KV2 461.
199 **no harm would** Reed report, 26.3.43, KV2 459.
199 **a high-class burglar** Major R.L. Brown report, 26.4.43, KV2 461.
200 **for pleasure** Ibid.
200 **Several members** Reed report, 26.3.43, KV2 459.
200 **The gunlayer summed** Ibid.
200 **Happy go lucky** Brown report, 26.4.43, KV2 461.
200 **He said he did** Extracts from ship's log, *City of Lancaster*, KV2 459.
201 **sort of international** Masterman, *The Case of the Four Friends*, (London, 1961), p. 19.
201 **Pay no attention** Major R.L. Brown report, 26.4.43, KV2 461.
201 **If I find this** Ibid.
201 **No names** Ibid.
201 **'brûlé'** Reed report, 15.3.43, KV2 459. Document 254 B.
202 ***Joli Albert*** Camp 020 report, 11.7.44, KV2 459.
202 **blank faces** Stephens report, 29.6.44, KV2 459.
202 **'telephone'** Camp 020 report, 11.7.44, KV2 459.
202 **did not know** Ibid.
202 **forget the whole** Ibid.
203 **mind his own** Extracts from ship's log, *City of Lancaster*, KV2 459.
203 **any future offence** Ibid.
203 **He instructed me** Reed report, 26.3.43, KV2 459.
204 **apologised for the** Camp 020 report, 11.7.44, KV2 459.

204 'connected with Johnny' Stephens report, 29.6.44, KV2 459.
205 contravened the ISOS intercept, 27.5.45, KV2 459.
205 told the Germans Memo, 23.3.43, KV2 459.
205 not to interrupt Report of meeting, 22.3.43, KV2 459.
205 Whatever view we Ibid.
206 acquainted with the Ibid.
206 brought back in irons Ibid.
206 It would be quite Ibid.
206 a small aperture Memo, undated, KV2 459.
207 could not possibly Ibid.
208 the Queensberry rules Extracts from ship's log, *City of Lancaster*, KV2 459.
208 Have you met Ibid.
208 trying to get a Reed report, 26.3.43, KV2 459.
268–9 he had put to to in order to send Ibid.
210 Convinced Z playing Telegram, KV2 459.
210 This is typical of Stephens report, 27.6.43, KV2 460.
210 with possibly fatal Ibid.
210 He thought that Ibid.
210 politically complicated Reed report, 26.3.43, KV2 459.
210 It would be most Ibid.
211 I come from Ronnie Rothschild memo, 28.3.43, KV2 461.
211 if possible intact Ibid.

20. Damp Squib

212 Are you Fritz? Camp 020 report, 11.7.44, KV2 459.
212 other articles difficult Ibid.
213 in disgrace Ibid.
213 old friend Major Michael Ryde report, 24.10.44, KV2 460.
213 about 50 Camp 020 report, 11.7.44, KV2 459.
213–14 vague replies to advance Ibid.
214 Timing is the essential Robertson (attrib.), report of SOE training course, KV4 172.
214 I landed at about Reed report, 15.3.43, KV2 459. Document 254 B.
218 The life of a secret Masterman, *The Double Cross System*, p. 32.
218 would bring him Camp 020 report, 11.7.44, KV2 459.
218 reserve the more Ibid.
219 I had two suitcases *Chapman*, p. 158.
220 certainly raised his Camp 020 report, 11.7.44, KV2 459.
220 The Germans have shown Masterman memo, 18.4.43, KV2 461.
220 There must either Montagu memo, 18.4.43, KV2 461.
220 perfectly good Rothschild memo, 25.4.43, KV2 461.
220 as big a bang Ibid.
220 A good decent bang Ibid.
220 who will previously Rothschild, 'Plan Damp Squib', KV2 461.
220–1 fall down and pretend to The story of the sabotage Ibid.
221 sharp explosion Letter, Colonel Leslie Wood to Rothschild, KV2 461.
221 Herewith your three toys Ibid.
221 binding up a notional Masterman, handwritten note attached to Rothschild, 'Plan Damp Squib', KV2 461.

221 **When the** *City of Lancaster* Masterman memo, KV2 461.
222 **as each piece** Brown report, 26.4.43, KV2 461.
222 **who was very dirty** Reed report, 26.4.43, KV2 461.
222 **holding in his hand** Ibid.
222 **swanking** Brown report, 26.4.43, KV2 461.
222 **beyond his station** Ibid.
222 **The standard of** Reed report, 26.4.43, KV2 461
222 **infernal machine** Ibid.
222 **a spur to rumour** Rothschild, 'Plan Damp Squib', KV2 461.
222 **Approximately 50 people** Memo, 26.4.43, KV2 461.
222 **He has no objection** Reed report, 26.4.43, KV2 461.
223 **discussed Zigzag at** Duff Cooper to Dick White, 5.5.43, KV2 459.
223 **if and when contact** Ibid.
223 **comprehensive memoranda** Rothschild memo, 6.12.43, KV2 461.
223 **I promised Mr Hoover** Ibid.

21. The Ice Front

224 **deeply affected** Interview with Ingeborg von Gröning, Bremen, 22.05.06.
224 **Thank God you** *Chapman,* p. 161.
224 **the old man** Ryde report 24.10.44, KV2 460.
225 **enjoy a well-earned** Camp 020 report, 11.7.44, KV2 459.
225 **bachelor flat** to **companion** Ibid.
226 **pathetically grateful** *Chapman,* p.164.
226 **proud of his protégé** Camp 020 report, 11.7.44, KV2 459.
226 **best security** Ryde report, 24.10.44, KV2 460.
226 **man who had** Camp 020 report, 11.7.44, KV2 459.
226 **Absolute personal** Masterman, *The Double Cross System,* p. 187.
227 **better for selfish** Ibid., p. 72.
227 **watchful** Interview with Ingeborg von Gröning, Bremen, 22.05.06.
227 **Stephan made up** Ibid.
227 **as and when he** Camp 020 report, 11.7.44, KV2 459.
228 **If they will not** Olav Riste and Berit Nökleby, *Norway 1940–45: The Resistance Movement* (Oslo, 2004), p. 51.
229 **It was an uneasy** *Chapman,* p. 171.
229 **wall of hatred** Ibid.
229 **appeared somewhat** Camp 020 report, 11.7.44, KV2 459.
229 **complete freedom** Stephens report, 29.6.44, KV2 459.
230 **not to work** Camp 020 report, 11.7.44, KV2 459.
230 **battle against the** *Chapman,* p. 172.
230 **hero complex** Ibid.
230 **companion** Camp 020 report, 11.7.44, KV2 459.
230 **the only successful** Rothschild interview with Agent JIGGER (Von Schoenich), Paris, 8.11.44, KV2 460.
230–1 **controlled by the** to **one of those** Ibid.
231 **beaming with pleasure** *Chapman,* p. 174.
231 **good work in England** Camp 020 report 11.7.44, KV2 459.
231 **in notes** to **draw on it when** Ibid.
231–2 **solemnly** to **If I stay with** *Chapman,* p. 175.
232 **You are free** Camp 020 report, 11.7.44, KV2 459.

232–2 **Go yachting** to **to buy a boat** Ibid.
  233 **enhance his stock** Camp 020 report, 11.7.44, KV2 459.
  234 **truly brave** *Chapman*, p. 171.
  234 *Bitte schön* Ibid., p. 176.
  234 **most attractive** Ibid.

22. The Girl at the Ritz

  235 **She was young** Interview with Bibbi Røset, Oslo, 15.6.06.
  235 **She wanted to** Ibid.
  235 **wanted adventure** Ibid.
  236 **beautiful and adorable** Camp 020 report, 11.7.44, KV2 459.
  237 **Because she had** Interview with Bibbi Røset, Oslo, 15.6.06.
  237 **fancied slight** Camp 020 report, 11.7.44, KV2 459.
  237 **anti-Quisling** *Chapman*, p. 177.
  237 **Nazi's tart** Interview with Bibbi Røset, Oslo, 15.6.06.
  237 **hawk-like** *Chapman*, p. 178.
  237 **some kind of psychologist** Stephens report, 29.6.44, KV2 459.
  237 **with a view to** Camp 020 report, 11.7.44, KV2 459.
  237 **Where could you (ff)** Ibid.
  238 **I myself expect** Ibid.
  238 **uncomfortable moment** Stephens report, 29.6.44, KV2 459.
  238 **periodically asking** Ibid.
  238 **benign** *Chapman*, p. 179.
  239 **You are not** Camp 020 report 11.7.44, KV2 459.
  239 **I know I am not** Ibid.
  239 **The doctor was** Ibid.
  239 **I think you are** *Chapman*, p. 180.
  239 **Leave it to** Ibid.
  240 **It is the work** Camp 020 report, 11.7.44, KV2 459.
  240 **kept woman** Ibid.
  240 **sufficient money** Ibid.
  240 **pocketed the balance** Ryde report, 24.10.44, KV2 460.
  241 **help himself** Ibid.
  241 **It was a delightful** *Chapman*, p. 196.
  242 **they were fair** Interview with Leife Myhre, Oslo, 16.6.06.
  242 **They were in** to **I am not working** Ibid.
  243 **certain people** Camp 020 report, 11.7.44, KV2 459.
  243 **applied himself** to **disgusted with the** Ibid.
  244 **It all depends** Interrogation by Rothschild, 28.1.43, KV2 458.
  245 **under the influence** Camp 020 report, 11.7.44, KV2 459.
  245 **Nazi whore** Interview with Bibbi Røset, Oslo, 15.6.06.
  245 **he risked losing** Camp 020 report, 11.7.44, KV2 459.
245–7 **details of Chapman's** to **she intimated** Ibid.

23. Sabotage Consultant

  248 **new sabotage work** Camp 020 report, 11.7.44, KV2 459.
248–50 **did not consider** to **extremely high** Ibid.

251 **the address of an** Stephens report, 29.6.44, KV2 459.

251 **continually stared at him** Camp 020 report, 11.7.44, KV2 459.

251 **x–ray apparatus** Ibid.

251 **picked up by five seaplanes** Stephens report, 29.6.44, KV2 459.

251 **the use of a compass** Camp 020 report, 11.7.44, KV2 459.

251–2 **Chapman was just** to **each wanting their part** Ibid.

252 **kind of honorary** Masterman, *The Double Cross System*, p. 171.

252 **more interested in** *Camp 020*, p. 350.

253 **touring Germany** Camp 020 report, 11.7.44, KV2 459.

254 **useful background for** Ryde report, 27.7.44, KV2 460.

254 **Hitler is by no means** Stephens report, 29.6.44, KV2 459.

254 **It is entirely** to **aired his anti–Hitler** Ibid.

254 **knew he would one** Camp 020 report, 11.7.44, KV2 459.

255 **keep her eyes and** Ibid.

255 **trust nobody unless** Ibid.

255 **mind their own** Interview with Bibbi Røset, Oslo, 15.6.06.

255 **Mrs Gossips** Ibid.

256 **double transposition** Camp 020 report, 11.7.44, KV2 459.

256 **Liverpool, Leeds or** Reed memo, 7.7.44, KV2 459.

256 **If the message does** Ibid.

24. Lunch at the Lutétia

257 **provide a cover address** ISOS intercept, 15.12.44., KV2 459

257 **whose appearance and** *Camp 020*, p. 298.

258 **into the wastelands** Ibid.

258 **guttural protestations** Ibid.

258 **unsubtle retainers** Ibid., p. 299.

258 **worried still about** Ibid.

258 **mysterious figure** Masterman, *The Double Cross System*, p. 171.

258 **an old friend** Ibid.

259 **The whole city** Camp 020 report, 11.7.44, KV2 459.

259 **resignation and misery** Ibid.

259 **locate our night** Camp 020 report, 11.7.44, KV2 459.

259–60 **Cossors of Hammersmith** to **made no secret of** Ibid.

260 **converting much of** Stephens report, 29.6.44, KV2 459.

260 **If their weapons are** to **Life under the Germans** Ibid.

261 **owing to the danger** Camp 020 report, 11.7.44, KV2 459.

261 **if he landed in England** to **astute in posing** Ibid.

261 **Is he working** *News of the World*, 25.10.53.

261 **How the hell** Ibid.

262 **If and when I come** *Faramus*, p. 93.

262 **approximately six months** Ibid., p. 100.

262 **an extermination camp** Ibid., p.136.

262 **All the time** Ibid., p.82.

263 **to think furiously** Camp 020 report, 11.7.44, KV2 459.

263 **knowing** *Chapman*, p. 241.

263 **having a good time** Camp 020 report, 11.7.44, KV2 459.

263 **any uniform he liked** Stephens report, 29.6.44, KV2 459.

263 **for the shelling of** Camp 020 report, 11.7.44, KV2 459.

264 **dimples** Stephens report, 29.6.44, KV2 459.
264 **never leave** Ibid.
264 **fall to bits** Cited in obituary of Erich Vermehren de Saventhem by Richard Bassett, *Independent*, 3.5.05.
264 **excess of brandy** *Chapman*, p. 237.
264 **Terrible devastation will** Camp 020 report, 11.7.44, KV2 459.
265 **slight** Ibid.
265 **few casualties** Ibid
265 **a flop** Report, 13.7.44, KV2 460.
265 **at Chapman's disposal** Camp 020 report, 11.7.44, KV2 459.
266 **harmless chatter** Ibid.
267 **unreal** *News of the World*, 1.11.53.
267 **two bottles of cognac** Camp 020 report, 11.7.44, KV2 459.
267 **a profound effect** *News of the World*, 1.11.53.
267 **triumph** Ibid.
267 **half-smile** *News of the World*, 25.10.53.
267 **The last glimpse** *Chapman*, p. 244.

25. The Prodigal Crook

268 **out of the direct** *News of the World*, 1.11.54.
269 **Peeved** Camp 020 report, 11.7.44, KV2 459.
269 **Don't be silly** Ibid.
269 **That's exactly what** *News of the World*, 1.11.53.
270 **It's Eddie** Interview with Ronnie Reed, 1994, Nicholas Reed.
270 **whether operation possible** ISOS intercept, 10.6.44, KV2 459.
270 **a wiry type** Memo, 25.9.44, KV2 460.
270 **expansive in his conceit** *Camp 020*, p. 224.
270 **splendid time** Memo, 28.6.44, KV2 459.
270 **The courageous and** Stephens in Camp 020 report, 11.7.44, KV2 459.
270 **tired beyond the point** Camp 020 report, 11.7.44, KV2 459.
270 **moral degenerate** *Camp 020*, p. 218.
270 **The outstanding feature** Stephens in Camp 020 report, 11.7.44, KV2 459.
271 **greeted as a returned** Milmo memo, 29.6.44, KV2 459.
271 **back safely, and** Interview with Ronnie Reed, 1994, Nicholas Reed
271 **purposely put ashore** Camp 020 report, 11.7.44, KV2 459.
271 **mentally quite fit** Dearden, cited in Stephens report, 29.6.44, KV2 459.
272 **All the evidence appears** Reed memo, 28.6.44, KV2 459.
272 **it would be a first-rate** Stephens in Camp 020 report, 11.7.44, KV2 459.
272 **I think this goes far** Ibid.
272 **The only safe place** Memo, 10.7.44, KV2 459.
272 **a man whom they** Reed memo, 28.6.44, KV2 459.
273 **escape** Thaddeus Holt, *The Deceivers: Allied Military Deception in the Second World War* (London, 2004), p. 853.
273 **money and a Leica** Reed report, 28.6.43, KV2 459.
273 **Zigzag will be given** Milmo memo, 1.8.44, KV2 460.
273 **Although no one thinks** Milmo memo, 28.6.44, KV2 459.
273 **It must always be** Memo, 29.6.44, KV2 459.
274 **a very able man** Camp 020 Report, 11.7.44, KV2 459.
274 **a form of insurance** Stephens Report, 29.6.44, KV2 459.
274 **Chapman is a difficult** Camp 020 Report, 11.7.44, KV2 459.

274 **quite convinced that** Ryde, memo of meeting, 14. 8. 44, KV2 460.
274 **Although we do not** Milmo memo, 28.6.44, KV2 459.
274 **the inevitable girlfriend** Camp 020 report, 11.7.44, KV2 459.
275 **blundered badly** Stephens report, 29.6.44, KV2 459.
275 **She is not a** Camp 020 report, 11.7.44, KV2 459.
275 **he would have at** to **One of his objects** Ibid.
275 **There was some sort** Marriott memo, 29.7.43, KV2 459.
276 **Dagmar is in contact** Camp 020 report, 11.7.44, KV2 459.
276 **I do not wish to be held** Stephens in Camp 020 report, 11.7.44, KV2 459.
276 **one of the most** Stephens report, 29.6.44, KV2 459.
277 **HARD LANDING BUT** Ibid.

26. Doodlebugs

279 **It was clear that** Masterman, *The Double Cross System*, p. 179.
279 **If St Paul's was hit** Ibid.
279 **decide what measure** Ibid.
279 **learned to live** Michael Howard, *Strategic Deception in the Second World War* (London, 1995), p. 178.
280 **terrible responsibility** to **I am certain you** Ibid.
280 **his German masters** Reed memo, 28.6.44, KV2 459.
280 **should report actual** Masterman, *The Double Cross System*, p. 181.
281 **We could give correct** Ibid.
281 **reduce the average range** Ibid.
281 **It is essential** Memo, KV2 460.
281 **I am afraid we** Note from Air Ministry, 29.8.44, KV2 460.
281 **slight errors introduced** J.A. Drew memo, 11.7.44, KV2 459.
282 **The outgoing traffic** Ryde report, 26.7.44, KV2 460.
282 **The Zigzag channel** Ryde to Robertson, 13.9.44, KV2 460.
282 **held his place** Masterman, *The Double Cross System*, p. 172.
282 **I was as frightened** Masterman, *Chariot Wheel* p. 212.
283 **secret equipment for** Memo, 1.8.44, KV2 460.
283 **tapping out such** Ryde, memo of meeting, 14.8.44, KV2 460.
283 **If this state of affairs** Ibid.
283 **Take your pick!** Interview with Ronnie Reed, 1994, Nicholas Reed.
283 **I do feel his exploits** Marriott memo, 29.7.43, KV2 459.
283 **I agree** Ibid.
283 **desired that no such** Sir Alexander Maxwell memo, 15.7.44, KV2 460.
283 **No action should** D.I. Wilson note, with ibid.
284 **comb out any German** Ryde, memo of meeting, 14.8.44, KV2 460.
284 **Any question of Zigzag's** Ibid.
284 **anxious to write to Freda** Stephens report, 29.6.44, KV2 459.
284 **very busy and would** Ibid.
284 **autobiography** Ryde memo, 26.7.44, KV2 460.
284 **impossible for him** Ryde memo 6.8.44, KV2 460.
284 **while it was still fresh** Ryde memo, 26.7.44, KV2 460.
284 **his old criminal activities** Ibid.
284 **stimulate Zigzag's interest** Ryde, memo of meeting, 14.8.44, KV2 460.
284 **deceptive material about** Memo, 1.8.44, KV2 460.
284 **in continual active** Ibid.

284 **steal a document** Ibid.
285 **the increasing number** Montagu, op. cit., p. 114.
285 **careless talk by** Ibid.
285 **While we should not** Ibid., p. 124.
286 **After passing the** Ibid., p. 125.
286 **all secret manufacture** Memo, 1.8.44, KV2 460.
286 **worth keeping sweet** Ryde memo, 6.8.44, KV2 460.
286 **wonderful experience** Interview with Ronnie Reed, 1994, Nicholas Reed

27. Going to the Dogs

288 **disagreeably surprised** Camp 020 report, 11.7.44, KV2 459.
288 **with some apprehension** Ibid.
288 **I have spent a good** Ryde report, 24.8.44, KV2 460.
289 **most discontented at** Ryde memo, 8.8.44, KV2 460.
289 **He has been keeping** *Camp 020*, p. 225.
289 **always in the company** Ibid.
289 **The Zigzag case must** Ryde, memo of meeting, 14.8.44, KV2 460.
289 **the way his case** Robertson memo, 15.8.44, KV2 460.
289 **did not seem** Ibid.
289 **He is quite clearly** Ibid.
290 **a suitable person** Memo, 1.8.44, KV2 460.
290 **the friends he hoped** Ibid.
290 **in a French letter** Montagu, op. cit., p. 126
290 **After they had received** Ibid.
291 **Dear Fleming** Fake letter from A.B. Wood, KV2 460.
291 **We never found out** Montagu, op. cit., p. 126.
291 **I do not myself** Ryde to Robertson, 13.9.44, KV2 460.
292 **not quite reliable** ISOS intercept, 25.9.44, KV2 460.
292 **dubious about Zigzag's integrity** Ryde to Robertson, 13.9.44, KV2 460.
292 **The messages sent** Ibid.
292 **Zigzag is liable** Memo, 1.8.44, KV2 460.
292 **It is unlikely that his** Ibid.
293 **Zigzag himself is** Ryde memo, 6.8.44, KV2 460.
293 **making quite large** Ibid.
293 **To take advantage** Ibid.
293 **served his purpose** Robertson memo, 15.8.44, KV2 460.
293 **done an extremely good** Ibid.
293 **by giving him** Ibid.
293 **if he could put up** Ryde memo, 6.8.44, KV2 460.
294 **waste of money** to **It is obvious that we** Ibid.
294 **if we no longer require** Ryde, memo of meeting, 14.8.44, KV2 460.
294 **I have seen Zigzag** Ryde to Robertson, 13.9.44, KV2 460.
295 **I am able to curb these** Ibid.
295 **The war may end** Ryde report, 24.8.44, KV2 460.
295 **the necessity of closing** Ryde, memo of meeting, 14.8.44, KV2 460.
295 **It is becoming increasingly** Ryde to Robertson, 13.9.44, KV2 460.
292 **Try to get latest editions** ISOS intercept, 4.9.44, KV2 460.
292 **General report great** Ibid.
292 **radio controlled rocket** Stephens Report, 29.6.44, KV2 459.

295 **Continue giving data** ISOS intercept, 4.9.44, KV2 460.
296 **Heard many rumours** Message sent 14.9.44, KV2 460.
297 **WAR SITUATION NEED NOT** ISOS intercept, 28.8.44, KV2 460.

28. Case Dismissed

298 **SORRY YOUR BAD** Ryde report, 24.8.44, KV2 460.
298 **has a post-war plan to get the Germans to lay** Ibid.
299 **a collection of words** Montagu memo, 29.8.44, KV2 460.
299 **The Germans have told** Ibid.
299 **German knowledge is** Ibid.
299 **we should out of our** Ryde memo, 6.8.44, KV2 460.
299 **I still maintain that we are** Ryde, memo of meeting, 14.8.44, KV2 460.
299 **settlement of our** Ibid.
299 **dealt with fairly (ff)** Ryde report, 24.8.44, KV2 460.
300 **at least £6,300** Ryde to Robertson, 13.9.44, KV2 460.
300 **reliable sailor** Ryde report, 19.9.44, KV2 460.
300 **Such promises are** Ryde to Robertson, 13.9.44, KV2 460.
300 **I think it would be** Ryde report, 19.9.44, KV2 460.
301 **Zigzag has always** Ryde report, 24.10.44, KV2 460.
301–4 **whether the Germans to As far as the Germans** Ibid.
305 **My feeling** Masterman, handwritten note on ibid.
305 **We should close it now** Ibid.
305 **I understand that** Signed copy of Official Secrets Act, 2.11.44, KV2 461.
305 **as forcibly as possible** Ryde report, 24.10.44, KV2 460.
305 **He must understand** Ibid.
306 **Zigzag should be thankful** Ibid.
306 **Fiction has not** *Camp 020*, p. 217.
306 **hard character with** *Sunday Chronicle*, 24.7.54.
307 **Uppermost in my mind** Eddie Chapman, *Free Agent*, p. 11.
307 **Is there anyone** Interview with Betty Chapman, 25.11.05
307 **That girl** Eddie Chapman, *Free Agent*, p. 12
307 **Jesus!** Ibid.
308 **I shall go** Interview with Betty Chapman, 25.11.05.

Aftermath

309 **real genius** Cited in Wilson, op. cit.
309 **one of the greatest** Masterman, *On the Chariot Wheel*, p. 219.
309 **Blessed are they** Address by Christopher Harmer at memorial service for T.A. Robertson at Pershore Abbey.
310 **To work out the crime** Masterman, *The Case of the Four Friends*, p. 14.
310 **Everything which is good** Masterman, *On the Chariot Wheel*, p. 371.
310 **How strange it was** Ibid., p. 361.
311 **I am not, and never** *Daily Telegraph*, 4.12.86.
312 **Sean Connery was simply** Lois Maxwell (Miss Moneypenny), cited in Wikipedia.
312 **drifting on a wreck** Lloyd's Register of Captains, National Maritime Museum.

312 **giant of evil** *Camp 020*, p. 22.

313 **degenerates, most of them** FO 371/70830 paper CG 2290/G, cited by Hoare in *Camp 020*, p. 8.

313 **loyal to his own class** Interview with Ingeborg von Gröning, Bremen, 22.05.06.

313 **invariably foul** FO 371/70830 paper CG 2290/G.

313 **had a long and possibly** *Camp 020*, p. 72.

314 **awkward** *Faramus*, p. 177.

314 **I thought you were dead (ff)** Ibid.

314 **Millions died without** Eddie Chapman's foreword to Ibid., p. 7.

315 **German tart** Interview with Bibbi Røset, Oslo, 15.6.06.

315 **Mrs Gossips** Ibid.

315 **she was always** Ibid.

316 **what will happen when** *Camp 020*, p. 226.

317 **senior officer of the** *Evening Standard*, 13.10.48.

317 **one of the bravest men** Ibid.

317 **I was trained in** *Daily Telegraph*, 10.10.74.

317 **honorary crime** *The Times*, obituary of Eddie Chapman, 26.12.97.

317 **I do a bit** *Daily Express*, 'The Sentimenal Screwsman', 21.10.60.

317 **Sometimes in life** Masterman, *Chariot Wheel*, p. 361.

318 **What is the truth** *News of the World*, 'A Traitor or a Hero?', 10.1.54.

318 **A lot of water** Chapman to Von Gröning, 1.11.74, courtesy of Ingeborg von Gröning.

319 **They were like** Interview with Betty Chapman, 25.11.05.

ACKNOWLEDGEMENTS

Dozens of people in five countries have generously contributed to the writing of this book, with research help, interviews, advice, and access to photographs, documents and memories. In Britain, I am indebted to Betty Chapman, Tony Faramus, Howard Davies and Hugh Alexander at the National Archives, Mary Teviot for her splendid genealogical sleuthing; Professor M.R.D Foot and Calder Walton for their invaluable historical expertise; Major A.J. Edwards and the late Colonel Tony Williams at the Military Intelligence Museum archive; Caroline Lamb at the Liddell Hart Centre for military archives; Dunia Garcia-Ontiveros at the National Maritime Museum; George Malcolmson, Royal Navy Submarine Museum; David Capus, Metropolitan Police Service Records Management Branch. Andrea and Edward Ryde, Sophia and Charles Kitson, Margery Barrie, Carolyn Elton, Nicholas Reed and Charles Chilton all helped me to build up a more complete picture of the various case officers. In Jersey, I am grateful to Steven Guy-Gibbens, Governor HM Prison La Moye, and Paul Matthews, Deputy Judicial Greffier, for granting me access to closed prison, police and judicial records; to Linda Romeril and Stuart Nicolle at the Jersey Historical Archives, and Jan Hadley and John Guegan of the Jersey *Evening Post*. In Norway, Alf Magnussen of *Aftenposten* was supremely helpful in tracking down memories of Dagmar through Bibbi Røset, Leife Myhre and Harald Næss (who kindly allowed me to destroy part of his roof with a crowbar in the search for

Chapman's concealed film). In America, Anne Cameron Berlin carried out useful preliminary research in the US National Archives. In Germany, I am grateful to Peter Steinkamp for his work at the Bundesarchiv-Militärarchiv in Freiburg, and to Petra and Ingeborg von Gröning for their hospitality and help. I am also grateful to Georges and Caroline Paruit, the owners of La Bretonnière in Nantes.

For a secretive organisation, MI5 has been a model of openness: not only providing access to hitherto classified files, but assisting in the search for additional material. To the other individuals who prefer not to be named: you know who you are, and how grateful I am.

Robert Thomson, Keith Blackmore, Anne Spackman, Bob Kirwin, Daniel Finkelstein and all my colleagues on *The Times* have been supportive and tolerant, and occasionally both; Michael Evans was typically generous with his expertise. Denise Reeves performed several miracles of picture research.

Michael Fishwick and Trâm-Anh Doan of Bloomsbury have been the most delightful and expert collaborators, and Kate Johnson's work on the manuscript was, as usual, superb, saving me from a multitude of embarrassments. All remaining errors are entirely the result of my own intransigence.

Finally my thanks and love to Kate Muir, as always, for her support, patience, and fine editorial judgement. This book is dedicated to her.

SELECT BIBLIOGRAPHY

Archives:

National Archives, Kew
National Martime Museum, Greenwich
undesarchiv-Militärarchiv, Freiburg
National Archives, Washington DC
British Library Newspaper Archive, Colindale
Jersey Historical Archives
Jersey Newspaper Archives, St Helier
Jersey Judicial Archives

Printed Sources:

Andrew, C., Secret *Service: The Making of the British Intelligence Community* (London, 1985)

Bennett, R., *Behind the Battle: Intelligence in the War with Germany 1939-45* (London, 1999)

Carter, M., *Anthony Blunt: His Lives* (London, 2001)

Chapman, Edward, *The Eddie Chapman Story;* foreword by Frank Owens (London, 1953)

————*Free Agent: The Further Adventures of Eddie Chapman* (London, 1955)

————*The Real Eddie Chapman Story* (London, 1966)

Curry, J., *The Security Service 1908-1945: The Official History* (London, 1999)

Farago, Ladislas, *The Game of the Foxes: The Untold Story of German Espionage in the US and Great Britain During World War Two* (New York, London, 1972)

Faramus, Anthony Charles, *The Faramus Story* (London, no edition or year stated)

———*Journey into Darkness: A True Story of Human Endurance* (London, 1990)

Foot, M.R.D., SOE: *The Special Operations Executive 1940–1946* (London, 1999)

Harris, Tomas, *Garbo: The Spy Who Saved D-Day;* Introduction by Mark Seaman (London, 2004)

Haufler, Hervie, *The Spies Who Never Were: The True Stories of the Nazi Spies Who Were Actually Double Agents* (New York, 2006)

Hesketh, R., *Fortitude: The D-Day Deception Campaign* (London, 1999)

Hinsley, F.H., *British Intelligence in the Second World War: Its Influence on Strategy and Operations* (London, 1979), Vol I.

Hinsley, F.H. and Simkins, C.A.G., *British Intelligence in the Second World War: Security and Counter-Intelligence* (London, 1990), Vol. IV.

Holt, Thaddeus, *The Deceivers: Allied Military Deception in the Second World War* (London, 2004)

Michael Howard, *Strategic Deception in the Second World War* (London, 1995)

Kahn, David, *Hitler's Spies: German Military Intelligence in World War II* (New York, 2000)

Knightley, Philip, *The Second Oldest Profession* (London 1986)

Liddell, G., *The Guy Liddell Diaries, 1939–1945,* Volumes I and II (ed. Nigel West) (London, 2005)

Macksey, Kenneth, *The Searchers: Radio Intercept in Two World Wars* (London, 2003)

Masterman, J.C., *The Double Cross System in the War 1939–1945* (London, 1972)

———*On the Chariot Wheel: An Autobiography* (Oxford, 1975)

Miller, Russell, *Codename Tricycle: The True Story of the Second World War's Most Extraordinary Double Agent* (London, 2005)

Montagu, Ewen, *Beyond Top Secret Ultra* (London 1977)

———*The Man Who Never Was* (Oxford, 1996)

Paine, Lauran, *The Abwehr: German Military Intelligence in World War II* (London, 1984)

Popov, Dusko, *Spy/Counterspy* (New York, 1974)

Rose, Kenneth, *Elusive Rothschild: The Life of Victor, Third Baron* (London, 2003)

Sebag-Montefiore, Hugh, *Enigma: The Battle for the Code* (London, 2000)

Schenk, P., *Invasion of England 1940: The Planning of Operation Sealion* (London, 1990)

Stephens, R. 'Tin Eye', *Camp 020: MI5 and the Nazi Spies;* Introduction by Oliver Hoare (London, 2000)

Stevenson, William, *A Man Called Intrepid: the Secret War of 1939–45* (London, 1976)

Waller, John H., *The Unseen War in Europe: Espionage and Conspiracy in the Second World War* (New York, London, 1996)

West, Nigel, *MI5: British Security Service Operations 1909-45* (London, 1981)

Wilson, Emily Jane, *The War in the Dark: The Security Service and the Abwehr 1940–1944*, PhD thesis (Cambridge, 2003)

Winterbotham, F.W., *The Ultra Secret* (London, 1974)

PICTURE CREDITS

Plate sections

Eddie Chapman, 16 December 1942. (*KV2 462*, © *the National Archives*)

Chapman at Camp 020. (*KV2 462*, © *the National Archives*)

Chapman eating Christmas dinner, 1942. (*KV2 462*, © *the National Archives*)

Chapman during Christmas dinner, 1942. (*KV2 462*, © *the National Archives*)

An Irish identity pass for Chapman created by Nazi forgers. (*KV2 462*, © *the National Archives*)

Jersey under Occupation. (© *Popperfoto*)

Norway under Occupation. (© *Fox photos/Getty Images*)

The entrance to Fort de Romainville. (*From the collection of Anthony Faramus, in* Journey into Darkness, *Grafton Books, 1990*)

Faramus at Mauthausen-Gusen death camp. (*From the collection of Anthony Faramus, in* Journey into Darkness, *Grafton Books, 1990*)

Faramus as a POW in *The Colditz Story*. (*From the collection of Anthony Faramus, in* Journey into Darkness, *Grafton Books, 1990*)

The Mosquito bomber under construction at the De Havilland aircraft factory. (© The Times)

A Mosquito being prepared for a bombing run over Germany. (© The Times)

The De Havilland aircraft factory. (*KV2 457*, © *the National Archives*)

The faked sabotage of the De Havilland plant. (*KV2 458*, © *the National Archives*)

The *City of Lancaster*. (© *National Maritime Museum*)

The coal bomb constructed by Nazi engineers. (*KV461*, © *the National Archives*)

An X-ray of the coal bomb. (*KV2 461*, © *the National Archives*)

The doctored photograph for the Operation Squid deception. (*KV2 460*, © *the National Archives*)

Rittmeister Stephan von Gröning (alias Doctor Graumann). (*Courtesy of Ingeborg von Gröning*)

Stephan von Gröning as a young officer. (*Courtesy of Ingeborg von Gröning*)

Oberleutnant Walter Praetorius. (© *the National Archives*)

Franz Stoetzner (alias Franz Schmidt). (*Courtesy of MI5*)

Karl Barton (alias Hermann Wojch). (*Courtesy of MI5*)

Colonel Robin 'Tin Eye' Stephens. (© *BBC*)

Victor, Lord Rothschild. (© *Topfoto*)

John Cecil Masterman. (*National Portrait Gallery, London*)

Jasper Maskelyne. (© *British Library, London*)

Major Ronnie Reed. (*Courtesy of Nicholas Reed*)

Reed operating Chapman's German radio set. (*Courtesy of Nicholas Reed*)

Dagmar Lahlum. (*Courtesy of Bibbi Røset*)

Freda Stevenson with baby Diane. (*KV2 462*, © *the National Archives*)

Betty Farmer. (© *News International Syndication*)

Graffiti in the attic at La Bretonnière. (*Author's collection*)

Hitler caricatured as a carrot in the attic at La Bretonnière. (*Author's collection*)

La Bretonnière, 1942. (*Courtesy of Ingeborg von Gröning*)

Chapman after his return to Britain in 1944. (© *News International Syndication*)

Chapman in a West End drinking den. (© *News International Syndication*)

Chapman protesting in 1953 after his attempts to serialise his memoirs in a newspaper were stymied under the Official Secrets Act. (© *Topham/AP*)

Chapman in full SS uniform. (© *Popperfoto.com*)

The Iron Cross. (*Courtesy of Nicholas Reed, photo by Richard Pohle*)

Chapman posing with his Rolls-Royce. (© *Daily Telegraph*)

Images in the text

p. 15 (*Courtesy of the Jersey Evening Post*)
p. 21 (*Courtesy of the Jersey Evening Post*)
p. 90 (*KV2 462*, © *the National Archives*)
p. 114 (© *BBC*)
p. 287 (*Courtesy of Carolyn Elton*)
p. 321 (*Courtesy of Fritz Schlichting*)
p. 322 (*Courtesy of Wolfgang Ischinger*)
p. 325 (*Courtesy of His Honour Judge David McEvoy, QC*)
p. 327 (*Courtesy of Sir James Spooner*)

INDEX

Abwehr (German intelligence service)
42–3; Nantes section 42, 48, 50,
59, 74–5, 92, 120, 257; rivalry with
British secret services 44–7; renewal
of forces with Operation Sealion
47–50; members' opposition to
Nazism 58, 170–1, 213, 254;
Stephan von Gröning's rise in 58–9;
interception of signals at Bletchley
Park 65–6; failure to build wartime
network in Britain 67; Chapman's
contract with 83; plan to combat
Mosquito 85; examples of
inefficient practices 91, 130, 300;
abolition 170, 264, 296; Lisbon
201, 204, 209; mutual dependence
of spy and spymaster 226–7; Oslo
229, 234, 246, 251; debate over
Chapman on his return 230–1;
supreme confidence in Chapman
263–4; farewell party for Chapman
267
Abwehrkommandos 92–3
Ackerman, Dr 79–81, 88–9
Admiralty 290, 295, 305
AI 10 (Airborne Interceptor Mark 10)
252
Air Intelligence 281
Air Ministry 130, 283, 290, 296, 299
Aldershot military prison 6
Amalou 262, 263
Angers spycatcher 62, 86, 120, 186
Anita (prostitute/MI6 informant) 202,
220, 307
Anson, Hugh 8, 15, 22; as assumed
identity of Chapman at sea 191,
192
Auschwitz 242

B1A *see* double-cross agent system
Backwell, Corporal Paul 130–1; as
chaperone to Chapman 131–4, 137,

142–3, 145, 149, 151–2, 155–6,
160, 175, 182, 188; on Chapman's
character 137, 149–50, 179, 186;
tracing of Betty 307; career after
the war 311
Baden-Powell, Robert 46
Bad Nenndorf (Combined Services
Detailed Interrogation Centre) 312–
13
Balkans 311
Ball, Sir Joseph 287
Bamler, Rudolf 87
Barrington-Ward, Robert 166
Barton, Mrs (German teacher) 145
Battignolle locomotive works 81
Battle of El Alamein 164
Baumann (alias Blaum, Bodo)
(sabotage chief) 204, 206–7
BBC (British Broadcasting
Corporation) 89, 125, 133, 254,
265
Belgium 261
Bennet, Mrs Gordon 19
Bergen 251
Berlin: Chapman's trip for explosives
training 78; Von Gröning's promise
that Chapman would visit 98, 134,
146–7; preparations for Chapman's
trip to Norway 218–19; Abwehr's
debate over Chapman's fate 230–1;
Luftwaffe HQ 259, 296; ruins after
aerial bombardment 259, 260
Berwick upon Tweed 59
Bevan, Lieut.-Col. John 261
Bijet, Dr (dentist) 63
Bjornsson, Hjalti 252–3, 258, 272
Blackwood, Milly 238
Bletchley Park 65–6, 74–5, 185, 194,
201, 219–20, 257
Blunt, Anthony 311
Board of Trade 195
Bobby the Pig 64, 65, 75, 76, 101

Operation Mincemeat

'Who in war will not have his laugh amid the skulls?'

– Winston Churchill, *Closing the Ring*

CONTENTS

Preface

In the early hours of 10 July 1943, British, Commonwealth and American troops stormed ashore on the coast of Sicily in the first assault against Hitler's 'Fortress Europe'. With hindsight, the invasion of the Italian island was a triumph, a pivotal moment in the war, and a vital stepping stone on the way to victory in Europe. The offensive – then the largest amphibious landing ever attempted – had been months in the planning, and although the fighting was fierce, the casualty rate among the Allies was limited. Of the 160,000 soldiers who took part in the invasion and conquest of Sicily, more than 153,000 were still alive at the end. That so many survived was due, in no small measure, to a man who had died seven months earlier. The success of the Sicilian invasion depended on overwhelming strength, logistics, secrecy and surprise. But it also relied on a wide web of deception, and one deceit in particular: a spectacular con trick dreamed up by a team of spies led by an English lawyer.

I first came across the remarkable Ewen Montagu while researching an earlier book, *Agent Zigzag*, about the wartime double agent Eddie Chapman. A barrister in civilian life, Montagu was a Naval Intelligence officer who had been one of Chapman's handlers, but he was better known as the author, in 1953, of *The Man Who Never Was*, an account of the deception plan he had masterminded in 1943 codenamed 'Operation Mincemeat'. In a later book, *Beyond Top Secret Ultra*, written in

1977, Montagu referred to 'some memoranda which, in very special circumstances and for a very particular reason, I was allowed to keep'.

That odd aside stuck in my memory. The 'special circumstances', I assumed, must refer to the writing of *The Man Who Never Was*, which was authorised and vetted by the Joint Intelligence Committee. But I could think of no other case in which a former intelligence officer had been 'allowed to keep' classified documents. Indeed, retaining top-secret material is exactly what intelligence officers are supposed not to do. And if Ewen Montagu had kept them for so many years after the war, where were they now?

Montagu died in 1985. None of the obituaries referred to his papers. I went to see his son, Jeremy Montagu, a distinguished authority on musical instruments at Oxford University. With an unmistakable twinkle, Jeremy led me to an upstairs room in his rambling home in Oxford, and pulled a large and dusty wooden trunk from under a bed. Inside were bundles of files from MI5, MI6 and the Naval Intelligence Department, some tied up with string and many of them stamped 'Top Secret'. Jeremy explained that some of his father's papers had been transferred after his death to the Imperial War Museum, where they had yet to be catalogued, but the rest were just as he had left them in the trunk: letters, memos, photographs and operational notes relating to the 1943 deception plan, as well as the original, uncensored manuscripts of his books. Here, too, was Ewen Montagu's unpublished 200-page autobiography and, perhaps most importantly, a copy of the official, classified report on 'Operation Mincemeat' – the boldest, strangest and most successful deception of the war.

If my discovery of these papers reads like something out of a spy film, that may be no accident: Montagu himself had a rich sense of the dramatic. He must have known they would be found one day.

More than half a century after publication, *The Man Who*

Never Was has lost none of the flavour of wartime intrigue, but it is, and was always intended to be, incomplete. The book was written at the behest of the Government in order to conceal certain facts; in parts, it is deliberately misleading. Now, with the relaxation of government rules surrounding official secrecy, the recently declassified files in the National Archives, and the contents of Ewen Montagu's ancient trunk, the full story of Operation Mincemeat can be told for the first time.

The plan was born in the mind of a novelist, and took shape through a most unlikely cast of characters: a brilliant barrister, a family of undertakers, a forensic pathologist, a gold prospector, an inventor, a submarine captain, a transvestite English spy master, a rally driver, a pretty secretary, a credulous Nazi, and a grumpy admiral who loved fly-fishing.

This deception operation – which underpinned the invasion of Sicily and helped to win the war – was framed around a man who never was. But the people who invented him, and those who believed in him, and those who owed their lives to him, most certainly were.

This is their story.

Ben Macintyre
London, October 2009

1

The Sardine Spotter

José Antonio Rey María had no intention of making history when he rowed out into the Atlantic from the coast of Andalucia in southwest Spain on 30 April 1943. He was merely looking for sardines.

José was proud of his reputation as the best fish-spotter in Punta Umbria. On a clear day, he could pick out the telltale iridescent flash of sardines several fathoms deep. When he saw a shoal, José would mark the place with a buoy, and then signal to Pepe Cordero and the other fishermen in the larger boat, *La Calina*, to row over swiftly with the horseshoe net.

But the weather today was bad for fish-spotting. The sky was overcast, and an onshore wind ruffled the water's surface. The fishermen of Punta Umbria had set out before dawn, but so far they had caught only anchovies and a few bream. Rowing *Ana*, his little skiff, in a wide arc, José scanned the water again, the rising sun warming his back. On the shore, he could see the little cluster of fishing huts beneath the dunes on Playa del Portil, his home. Beyond that, past the estuary where the rivers Odiel and Tinto flowed into the sea, lay the port of Huelva.

The war, now in its fourth year, had hardly touched this part of Spain. Sometimes José would come across strange flotsam in the water, fragments of charred wood, pools of oil, and other debris that told of battles somewhere out at sea. Earlier that morning, he had heard gunfire in the distance, and a loud explosion. Pepe said that the war was ruining the fishing business; no one had any money, and he might have to sell *La Calina* and *Ana*. It was rumoured that the captains on some of the larger fishing boats spied for the Germans or the British. But in most ways the hard lives of the fishermen continued as they had always done.

José had been born on the beach, in a hut made from driftwood, twenty-three years earlier. He had never travelled beyond Huelva and its waters. He had never been to school, or learned to read and write. But no one in Punta Umbria was better at spotting fish.

It was mid-morning when José noticed a 'lump' above the surface of the water. At first he thought it must be a dead porpoise, but as he rowed closer the shape grew clearer, and then unmistakable. It was a body, floating, face down, buoyed up by a yellow life jacket, the lower part of its torso invisible. It seemed to be dressed in uniform.

As he reached over the gunwale to grab the body, José caught a gust of putrefaction and found himself looking into the face of a man, or, rather, what had been the face of a man. The chin was entirely covered in green mould, while the upper part of the face was dark, as if tanned by the sun. José wondered if the dead man had been burned in some accident at sea. The skin on the nose and chin had begun to rot away.

José waved and shouted to the other fishermen. As *La Calina* drew alongside, Pepe and the crew clustered by the gunwale. José called for them to throw down a rope and haul the body aboard, but 'no one wanted to touch it'. Annoyed, José realised he would have to bring it ashore himself. Seizing a handful of sodden uniform, he hauled the corpse on to the stern, the legs trailing in the water, and rowed back to shore, trying not to breathe in the smell.

At the part of the beach called La Bota – the boot – José and Pepe dragged the body up to the dunes. A black briefcase, attached to the man by a chain, trailed in the sand behind them. They laid out the corpse in the shade of a pine tree. Children streamed out of the huts and gathered around the gruesome spectacle. The man was tall, at least six foot, dressed in a khaki tunic and trench coat, with large army boots. Seventeen-year-old Obdulia Serrano spotted a small silver chain with a cross around the dead man's neck: he must have been a Roman Catholic, she thought.

Obdulia was sent to summon the officer from the defence unit guarding that part of the coast. A dozen men of Spain's 72nd Infantry Regiment had been marching up and down the beach earlier that morning, as they did, rather pointlessly, most mornings. The soldiers were now taking a siesta under the trees. The officer ordered two of his men to stand guard over the body in case someone tried to go through the dead man's pockets, and trudged off up the beach to find his commanding officer.

The scent of the wild rosemary and jacaranda growing among the dunes could not mask the stench of decomposition. Flies buzzed around the body. The soldiers moved upwind. Somebody went to fetch a donkey to carry the body to the village of Punta Umbria four miles away. From there, it could be taken by boat across the estuary to Huelva.

José Antonio Rey María, unaware of the events he had just set in train, pushed the skiff back into the sea, and resumed his search for sardines.

Two months earlier, in a tiny, tobacco-stained basement room beneath the Admiralty building in Whitehall, two men had sat puzzling over a conundrum of their own devising: how to create a person from nothing, a man who had never been.

The younger man was tall and thin, with thick spectacles and an elaborate Air Force moustache, which he twiddled in rapt concentration. The other, elegant and languid, was dressed in naval uniform and sucked on a curved pipe that fizzed and crackled evilly. The stuffy underground cavern lacked windows, natural light and ventilation. The walls were covered in large maps, and the ceiling stained a greasy nicotine-yellow. It had once been a wine cellar. Now it was home to a section of the British Secret Service made up of four intelligence officers, seven secretaries and typists, six typewriters, a bank of locked filing cabinets, a dozen ashtrays and two scrambler telephones. Section 17M was so secret that barely twenty people outside the room even knew of its existence.

Room 13 of the Admiralty was a clearing house of secrets, lies and whispers. Every day the most lethal and valuable intelligence – decoded messages, deception plans, enemy troop movements, coded spy reports and other mysteries – poured into this little basement room, where they were analysed, assessed, and despatched to distant parts of the world – the armour and ammunition of a secret war.

The two officers – Pipe and Moustache – were also responsible for running agents and double agents, espionage and counterespionage, intelligence, fakery and fraud: they passed lies to the enemy that were damaging, as well as information that was true but harmless; they ran willing spies, reluctant spies pressed into service, and spies who did not exist at all. Now, with the war at its height, they set about creating a spy who was different from all the others and all that had come before: a secret agent who was not only fictional, but dead.

The defining feature of this spy would be his falsity. He was a pure figment of imagination, a weapon in a war far removed from the traditional battle of bombs and bullets. At its most visible, war is fought with leadership, courage, tactics and brute force; this is the conventional war of attack and counterattack, lines on a map, numbers and luck. This war is usually painted in black, white and blood red, with winners, losers and casualties: the good, the bad and the dead. Then there is the other, less visible, species of conflict, played out in shades of grey, a battle of deception, seduction and bad faith, of tricks and mirrors, in which the truth is protected, as Churchill put it, by a 'bodyguard of lies'. The combatants in this war of the imagination were seldom what they seemed, for the covert world, in which fiction and reality are sometimes enemies and sometimes allies, attracts minds that are subtle, supple, and often extremely strange.

The man lying in the dunes at Punta Umbria was a fraud. The lies he carried would fly from London to Madrid to Berlin, travelling from a freezing Scottish loch to the shores of Sicily, from fiction to reality, and from Room 13 of the Admiralty all the way to Hitler's desk.

2

Corkscrew Minds

Deceiving the enemy in wartime, thought Admiral John Godfrey, Director of Naval Intelligence, was just like fishing: specifically fly-fishing for trout. 'The Trout Fisher,' he wrote, in a top-secret memo, 'casts patiently all day. He frequently changes his venue and his lures. If he has frightened a fish he may "give the water a rest for half-an-hour", but his main endeavour, viz. to attract fish by something he sends out from his boat, is incessant.'

Godfrey's 'Trout Memo' was distributed to the other chiefs of wartime intelligence on 29 September 1939, when the war was barely three weeks old. It was issued under Godfrey's name, but it bore all the hallmarks of his personal assistant, Lieutenant Commander Ian Fleming, who would go on to write the James Bond novels. Fleming had, in Godfrey's words, a 'marked flair' for intelligence planning, and was particularly skilled, as one might expect, at dreaming up what he called 'plots' to outfox the enemy. Fleming called these plans 'romantic Red Indian daydreams', but they were deadly serious. The memo laid out numerous ideas for bamboozling the Germans at sea, the many ways that the fish might be trapped through 'deception, ruses de guerre, passing on false information and so on'. The ideas were extraordinarily imaginative and, like most of Fleming's writing, barely credible. The memo admitted as much. 'At first sight, many of these appear somewhat fantastic, but nevertheless they contain germs of some good ideas; and the more you examine them, the less fantastic they seem to appear.'

Godfrey was himself a most literal man: hard-driving, irascible and indefatigable, he was the model for 'M' in Fleming's Bond stories. There was no one in naval intelligence with a keener appreciation of the peculiar mentality needed for espionage and counterespionage. 'The business of deception, handling double agents, deliberate leakages and building up in the minds of the enemy confidence in a double agent, needed the sort of corkscrew mind which I did not possess,' he reflected. Gathering intelligence, and distributing false intelligence, was, he said, like 'pushing quicksilver through a gorse bush with a long-handled spoon'.

The Trout Memo was a masterpiece of corkscrew thinking, with fifty-one suggestions for 'introducing ideas into the heads of the Germans', ranging from the possible to the wacky. These included dropping footballs painted with luminous paint to attract submarines; distributing messages cursing Hitler's Reich in bottles from a fictitious U-boat captain; a fake 'treasure ship' packed with commandos; and sending out false information through bogus copies of *The Times* ('an unimpeachable and immaculate medium'). One of the nastier ideas envisaged setting adrift tins of explosives disguised as food, 'with instructions on the outside in many languages', in the hope that hungry enemy sailors or submariners would pick them up, try to heat the tins, and blow themselves up.

Though none of these plans ever came to fruition, buried deep in the memo was the kernel of another idea: Number 28 on the list was fantastic in every sense. Under the heading 'A Suggestion (not a very nice one)' Godfrey and Fleming wrote: 'The following suggestion is used in a book by Basil Thomson: a corpse dressed as an airman, with despatches in his pockets, could be dropped on the coast, supposedly from a parachute that had failed. I understand there is no difficulty in obtaining corpses at the Naval Hospital, but, of course, it would have to be a fresh one.'

Basil Thomson, former assistant premier of Tonga, tutor to the King of Siam, ex-governor of Dartmoor prison, policeman and novelist, had made his name as a spy catcher during the First World War. As head of Scotland Yard's Criminal Investigation Division and the Metropolitan Police Special Branch, he took credit (only partly deserved) for tracking down German spies in Britain, many of whom were caught and executed. He interviewed Mata Hari (and concluded she was innocent), and distributed the 'Black Diaries' of the Irish nationalist and revolutionary Sir Roger Casement, detailing his homosexual affairs: Casement was subsequently tried and executed for treason. Thomson was an early master of deception, and not just in his professional life. In 1925 the worthy police chief was convicted of an act of indecency with 'Miss Thelma de Lava' on a London park bench, and fined £5.

In between catching spies, carrying out surveillance of union leaders and consorting with prostitutes (for the purposes of 'research', as he explained to the court), Thomson found time to write twelve detective novels. The hero of these, Inspector Richardson, inhabits a world peopled by fragrant damsels in distress, stiff upper lips and excitable foreigners in need of British colonisation. Most of Thomson's novels, with titles such as *Death in the Bathroom* and *Richardson Scores Again*, were instantly forgettable. But in *The Milliner's Hat Mystery*, published in 1937, he planted a seed. The novel opens on a stormy night with the discovery of a dead man in a barn, carrying papers that identify him as 'John Whitaker'. By dint of some distinctly plodding detective work, Inspector Richardson discovers that every document in the pockets of the dead man has been ingeniously forged: his visiting cards, his bills, and even his passport, on which the real name has been erased using a special ink remover, and a fake one substituted. 'I know the stuff they use; they employed it a lot during the war,' says Inspector Richardson. 'It will take out ink from any document without leaving a trace.' The remainder of the novel is spent unravelling the identity of the body in the barn. 'However improbable a story sounds we are trained to investigate it,' says Inspector Richardson. 'Only that way can we arrive at the truth.' Inspector Richardson is always saying things like that.

The idea of creating a false identity for a dead body lodged in the mind of Ian Fleming, a confirmed bibliophile who owned several of Thomson's novels. From one spy and novelist it passed into the mind of another future spy-novelist and in 1939, the year that Basil Thomson died, it formally entered the thinking of Britain's spy chiefs as they embarked on a ferocious intelligence battle with the Nazis.

The trout-fishing Admiral Godfrey later wrote that the Second World War 'offers us far more interesting, amusing and subtle examples of intelligence work than any writer of spy stories can devise'. For almost four years, this 'not very nice' idea, as he called it, would lie dormant, a bright lure cast by a fisherman-spy, waiting for someone to bite.

In late September 1942, a frisson of alarm ran through British and American intelligence circles, when it seemed that the date of the planned invasion of French North Africa might have fallen into German hands. On 25 September, an RAF Catalina FP119 seaplane, flying from Plymouth to Gibraltar, crashed in a violent electrical storm off Cadiz on Spain's Atlantic coast, killing all three passengers and seven crew. Among these was Paymaster Lieutenant James Hadden Turner, a Royal Navy courier, carrying a letter to the Governor of Gibraltar informing him that the American General Dwight Eisenhower would be arriving on the rock immediately before the offensive, and that 'the target date has now been set as 4th November'. A second letter, dated 21 September, contained additional information on the forthcoming invasion of North Africa.

The bodies had washed ashore at La Barrosa, south of Cadiz, and were recovered by the Spanish authorities. After twenty-four hours Turner's body, with the letter still in his pocket, was turned over to the local British consul by the Spanish admiral in command at Cadiz. As the war raged, Spain had maintained a neutrality of sorts, with the Allies haunted by the fear that General Francisco Franco might throw in his lot with Hitler. Spanish official opinion was broadly in favour of the Axis powers; many Spanish officials were in contact with German intelligence, and the area around Cadiz, in particular, was known to be a hotbed of German spies. Was it possible that the letter, revealing the date of the Allied attack, had been passed into enemy hands? Eisenhower was said to be 'extremely worried'.

The invasion of North Africa, 'Operation Torch', had been in preparation for months. Major General George Patton was due to sail from Virginia on 23 October with the Western Task Force of 35,000 men, heading for Casablanca in French Morocco. At the same time, British forces would attack Oran in French Algeria, while a joint Allied force invaded Algiers. The Germans were certainly aware that a major offensive was being planned. If the letter had been intercepted and passed on, they would now also know the date of the assault, and that Gibraltar, the gateway to the Mediterranean and North Africa, would play a key role in it.

The Spanish authorities assured Britain that Turner's corpse had 'not been tampered with'. Scientists were flown out to Gibraltar, and the body and letter were subjected to minute examination. The four seals holding down the envelope flap had been opened, apparently by the effect of the sea water, and the writing was still 'quite legible' despite being immersed for at least twelve hours. But some forensic spycraft suggested the Allies could relax. On opening Turner's coat to take out the letter in his breast pocket, the scientists noticed that sand fell out of the eyes in the buttons and the button holes, having been rubbed into the coat when the body washed up on the beach. 'It was highly unlikely,' the British concluded, 'that any agent would have replaced the sand when rebuttoning the jacket.' The German spies operating in Spain were good, but not that good. The secret was safe.

Yet British suspicions were not without foundation. Another victim of the Catalina air crash was Louis Daniélou, an intelligence officer with the Free French forces, travelling under the name Charles Marcil, who was on a mission for the Special Operations Executive (SOE), the covert British organisation operating behind enemy lines. Daniélou had been carrying his notebook and a document, written in French and dated 22 September, which referred, albeit vaguely, to British attacks on targets in North Africa. Intercepted and decoded wireless messages indicated that this information had indeed been passed on to the Germans: 'All the documents, which included a list of prominent personalities [i.e. agents] in North Africa and possibly information with regard to our organisations there, together with a notebook, have been photostatted and come into the hands of the enemy.' An unnamed Italian agent had obtained the copied documents and handed them to the Germans, who mistakenly accorded the information 'no greater importance than any other bit of intelligence'. The Germans may also have suspected the 'documents had likely been planted as a deception'.

An important item of military intelligence had washed into the Germans' hands from the Atlantic; luckily, its significance had eluded them. 'This suggested that the Spanish could be relied on to pass on what they found, and that this unneutral habit might be turned to account.' Here was evidence of a most ingenious avenue into German thinking, an alluring fly to cast on the water.

The incident had rattled the wartime intelligence chiefs, but in the corkscrew mind of one intelligence officer it had lodged, and remained. That mind belonged to one Charles Christopher Cholmondeley, a twenty-five-year-old flight lieutenant in the Royal Air Force, seconded to MI5, the Security Service. Cholmondeley (pronounced 'Chumly') was one of nature's more notable eccentrics, but a most effective warrior in this strange and complicated war. Cholmondeley gazed at the world through thick pebble spectacles, from behind a remarkable moustache six inches long and waxed into magnificent points. Over six feet three inches tall, with size 12 feet, he never quite seemed to fit his uniform, and walked with a strange, lolloping gait, 'lifting his toes as he walked'.

Cholmondeley longed for adventure. As a schoolboy at Canford School in Dorset, he had joined the Public Schools Exploring Society on expeditions to Finland and Newfoundland, to map as yet uncharted territory. Living under canvas, he had survived on Kendal Mint Cake, discovered a new species of shrew after it died inside his sleeping bag, and enjoyed every moment. He studied geography at Oxford, joined the Officers' Training Corps, and in 1938 applied, unsuccessfully, to the Sudan Service. He briefly worked as a King's Messenger, the corps of couriers carrying messages to embassies and consulates around the world that was often seen as a stepping stone to an intelligence career. The most distinguished of Cholmondeley's ancestors was his maternal grandfather, Charles Leyland, whose gift to the world was the Leyland Cyprus, or Leylandii, cause of countless suburban hedge disputes. Cholmondeley had a more glamorous future in mind: he dreamed of becoming a spy, a soldier, or at least a colonial official in some far-flung and exotic land. One brother, Richard, died fighting at Dunkirk, further firing Charles's determination to find action, excitement and, if necessary, a hero's death.

Cholmondeley may have had the mind of an adventurer, but he had neither the body nor the luck. He was commissioned pilot officer in November 1939, but his poor eyesight meant he would never fly a plane, even if a cockpit could have been found to accommodate his ungainly shape. 'This was a terrible blow,' according to his sister. So, far from soaring heroically into the heights, as he had hoped, Cholmondeley was grounded for the duration of the war, his long legs cramped under a desk. This might have blunted the ambitions of a lesser man, but Cholmondeley instead poured his imagination and energies into covert work.

By 1942 he had risen to the rank of flight lieutenant (temporary) in the RAF's Intelligence and Security Department, seconded to MI5. Tommy Argyll Robertson (universally known as 'Tar' on account of his initials), the MI5 chief who headed the B1A section of British intelligence, which ran captured enemy spies as double agents, recruited Cholmondeley as an 'ideas man', describing him as 'extraordinary and delightful'. When off duty, Cholmondeley restored antique cars, studied the mating habits of insects, and hunted partridge with a revolver. He was courtly and correct, and almost pathologically shy and secretive. He cut a distinctive figure around Whitehall, his arms flapping when animated, hopping along the pavements like a huge, flightless, myopic bird. But, for all his peculiarities, Cholmondeley was a most remarkable espionage thinker.

Some of Cholmondeley's ideas were madcap in the extreme. He had, in the words of a fellow intelligence officer, 'one of those subtle and ingenious minds which is forever throwing up fantastic ideas – mostly so ingenious as either to be impossible of implementation or so intricate as to render their efficacy problematical, but every now and again quite brilliant in their simplicity'. Cholmondeley's role, like that of Ian Fleming at Naval Intelligence, was to imagine the unimaginable, and try to lure the truth towards it. More formally, he was secretary of the top-secret XX Committee, or Twenty Committee, the group in charge of overseeing the exploitation of double agents, so-called because the two roman numerals formed a pleasing pun as a double-cross. (The name may also have been an ironic tribute to Charlie Chaplin, whose *Great Dictator*, a film released in 1940, operates under a XX flag, mimicking a swastika.) Under the chairmanship of John Masterman, a dry and ascetic Oxford don, the Twenty Committee met every Thursday in the MI5 offices at 58 St James's Street, to discuss the double-agent system run by 'Tar' Robertson, explore new deception plans, and plot how to pass the most usefully damaging information to the enemy. Its members included representatives of Navy, Army and Air

Intelligence, as well as MI5 (the Security Service, responsible for counterespionage) and MI6 (the Secret Intelligence Service, SIS, responsible for gathering intelligence outside Britain). As secretary and MI5 representative at this weekly gathering of high-powered spooks, Cholmondeley was privy to some of the most secret plans of the war. He had read the 1939 memo from Godfrey and Fleming containing the 'not very nice' suggestion of using a dead body to convey false information. And the Catalina crash off Cadiz had demonstrated that such a plan could work.

On 31 October 1942, just one month after the retrieval of Lieutenant Turner's body from the Spanish beach, Cholmondeley presented the Twenty Committee with his own idea, under the codename 'Trojan Horse', which he described as 'a plan for introducing documents of a highly secret nature into the hands of the enemy'. It was, in essence, an expanded version of the plan outlined in the Trout Memo.

A body is obtained from one of the London hospitals (normal peacetime price £10), it is then dressed in Army, Naval or Air Force uniform of suitable rank. The lungs are filled with water and the documents are disposed in an inside pocket. The body is then dropped by a Coastal Command aircraft at a suitable position where the set of the currents will probably carry the body ashore in enemy territory. On being found, the supposition in the enemy's mind may well be that one of our aircraft has either been shot or forced down and that this is one of the passengers. Whilst the courier cannot be sure to get through, if he does succeed, information in the form of the documents can be of a far more secret nature than it would be possible to introduce through any normal B1A channel.

Human agents or double agents can be tortured or turned, forced to reveal the falsity of the information they carry. A dead body would never talk.

Like most of Cholmondeley's ideas, this one was both exquisitely simple and fiendishly problematical. Having outlined his blueprint for building a latter-day Trojan Horse, Cholmondeley now set about picking holes in it. An autopsy might reveal that the corpse had not died from drowning, and the plane carrying out 'the drop' might be intercepted. Even if a suitable body could be found, this would have to be made to 'double for an actual officer'. One member of the Twenty Committee pointed out that if a corpse was dropped out of a plane at any height, it would undoubtedly be damaged, 'and injuries inflicted after death can always be detected'. If the body was placed in a location where it would wash into enemy or enemy-occupied territory, such as Norway or France, there was every possibility of 'a full and capable postmortem' by German scientists. 'Neutral' Spain and Portugal were both leaning towards the Axis: 'Of these, Spain was clearly the country where the probability of documents being handed, or at the very least shown, to the Germans was greater.'

Cholmondeley's plan was both new, and very old. Indeed, the unsubtle choice of codename, Trojan Horse, shows how far back in history this ruse runs. Odysseus may have been the first to offer an attractive gift to the enemy containing a most unpleasant surprise, but he had many imitators. In intelligence jargon, the technique of planting misleading information by means of a faked accident even has a formal name: the 'haversack ruse'.

The haversack ruse was the brainchild of Richard Meinertzhagen, ornithologist, anti-semitic Zionist, big-game hunter, fraud and British spy. In *Seven Pillars of Wisdom*, T. E. Lawrence (of Arabia) offered a pen portrait of his contemporary Meinertzhagen as an extraordinary, and extraordinarily nasty, man. 'Meinertzhagen knew no half measures. He was logical, an idealist of the deepest, and so possessed by his convictions that he was willing to harness evil to the chariot of good. He was a strategist, a geographer, and a silent laughing masterful man;

who took as blithe a pleasure in deceiving his enemy (or his friend) by some unscrupulous jest, as in spattering the brains of a cornered mob of Germans one by one with his African knob-kerri. His instincts were abetted by an immensely powerful body and a savage brain.'

In 1917, the British Army, under General Sir Edmund Allenby, twice attacked the Turks at Gaza, but found the way to Jerusalem blocked by a strong enemy force. Allenby decided that the next offensive should come at Beersheba in the east, while hoping to fool the Turks into expecting another attack on Gaza (which was the most logical target). The officer on Allenby's intelligence staff in control of the deception was Major Richard Meinertzhagen.

Meinertzhagen knew that the key to an effective deceit is not merely to conceal what you are doing, but to persuade the other side that what you are doing is the reverse of what you are actually doing. He stuffed a haversack with false documents, personal letters, a diary and £20 in cash, and smeared it with his horse's blood. He then rode out into no-man's land until shot at by a Turkish mounted patrol, upon which he slumped in the saddle as if wounded, dropped his haversack, binoculars and rifle, and galloped back to the British lines. One of the letters (written by Meinertzhagen's sister, Mary) purported to be from the haversack owner's wife, reporting the birth of their son. It was pure Edwardian schmaltz: 'Good-bye, my darling! Nurse says I must not tire myself by writing too much . . . Baby sends a kiss to Daddy!'

Meinertzhagen now launched an operation to make it seem as if a feverish search was underway for the missing bag. A sandwich, wrapped in a daily order referring to the missing documents, was planted near enemy lines, as if dropped by a careless patrol. Meinertzhagen was ordered to appear before a (non-existent) court of inquiry to explain the lost haversack.

The Turks duly concentrated their forces at Gaza, and redeployed two divisions away from Beersheba. On 31

October 1917, the British attacked again, rolling back the thin Turkish line at Beersheba. By December, the British had taken Jerusalem. Meinertzhagen crowed that his haversack ruse had been 'easy, reliable and inexpensive'. But victory may also be attributed to another devious Meinertzhagen ploy: the dropping of hundreds of cigarettes laced with opium behind Turkish lines. Some historians have argued that the haversack ruse was not quite the success Meinertzhagen claimed. The Turks may have been fooled. Or they may just have been incredibly stoned.

The ruse was updated and deployed once more early in the Second World War. Before the Battle of Alam Halfa in 1942, a corpse clutching a map that appeared to show a 'fair going' route through the desert was placed in a blown-up scout car. It was hoped that Rommel's tanks would find the map, be misdirected into soft sand and get bogged down. In another variation on the theme, a fake defence plan of Cyprus was left with a woman in Cairo who was known to be in contact with Axis intelligence. But the most recent variant had been plotted, with pleasing symmetry, by Peter Fleming, Ian Fleming's older brother, an intelligence officer serving under General Archibald Wavell, then Supreme Allied Commander in the Far East. Peter, who shared his brother's vivid imagination and was already a successful writer, concocted his own haversack ruse, codenamed 'Error', aimed at convincing the Japanese that Wavell himself had been injured in the retreat from Burma and had left behind various important documents in an abandoned car. In April 1942, the fake documents, a photograph of Wavell's daughter, personal letters, novels and other items were placed in a green Ford sedan, and pushed over a slope at a bridge across the Irrawaddy River, just ahead of the advancing Japanese army. Operation Error may have been great fun, but 'there was never any evidence that the Japanese had paid any attention to the car, much less that they drew any conclusions from its contents'.

This was the central problem with the haversack ruse: it had become, over three decades, deeply embedded in intelligence folklore, and the source of many an after-dinner anecdote, but there was precious little proof that it had ever actually worked.

Room 13

John Masterman, the chairman of the Twenty Committee, wrote detective novels in his spare time. These featured an Oxford don, much like himself, and a sleuth in the Sherlock Holmes mould. The operation outlined by Charles Cholmondeley appealed strongly to Masterman's novelistic cast of mind, as a mystery to be constructed, scene by scene, with clues for the Germans to unravel. Despite some misgivings about its feasibility, the Twenty Committee instructed Cholmondeley to investigate the possibilities of utilising the Trojan Horse plan in one of the theatres of the Second World War.

Spies, like generals, tend to fight the last battle. Axis intelligence had failed to act on the genuine documents that had washed up with Lieutenant Turner, and so missed the opportunity to anticipate Operation Torch; they would be unlikely to make the same mistake twice. 'The Germans, having cause to regret the ease with which they had been taken by surprise by the North African landings, would not again easily dismiss strategic Allied documents if and when they came into their possession.'

Since, in Cholmondeley's outline plan, the corpse would be arriving by sea, the operation would fall principally under naval control, so the representative of the Naval Intelligence Department on the Twenty Committee, Lieutenant Commander Ewen Montagu, was assigned to help Cholmondeley flesh out the idea. Montagu had also read the Trout Memo. He 'strongly supported' the plan, and volunteered to 'go into the question of obtaining the necessary body, the medical problems and the formulation of a plan'.

The choice of Ewen Montagu as Cholmondeley's planning partner was largely accidental, but inspired. A barrister and workaholic, Montagu's organisational skills and mastery of detail perfectly complemented Cholmondeley's 'fertile brain'. Where Cholmondeley was awkward and charming, Montagu was smooth and sardonic, refined, romantic and luminously intelligent.

Ewen Edwin Samuel Montagu, aged forty-two, was the second of three sons of Baron Swaythling, the scion of a Jewish banking dynasty of quite dazzling wealth. The first half of his life had been almost uniformly pleasurable, materially and intellectually. 'My memory is of a continuous happy time,' he wrote, looking back on his early years. 'We were lucky in every way.'

Montagu's grandfather, founder of the family fortune, had changed his name from Samuel to the more aristocratic-sounding Montagu, prompting a cruel limerick by Hilaire Belloc:

> *Montagu, first Baron Swaythling he,*
> *Thus is known to you and me.*
> *But the Devil down in Hell*
> *Knows the man as Samuel.*
> *And though it may not sound the same*
> *It is the blighter's proper name.*

Ewen's father had taken over the bank, and made even more money. His uncle Edwin went into politics, becoming Secretary of State for India. The family home was a red-brick palace in the heart of Kensington, at 28 Kensington Court. The hall was panelled in old Spanish leather; the 'small dining room' seated twenty-four; for larger gatherings there was the Louis XVI drawing room, with silk-embroidered chairs, Art Deco mouldings and an 'exquisite chandelier' of unfeasible size. The Montagus entertained nightly, and lavishly: 'Statesmen (British and world), diplomats, generals, admirals etc.'. Presiding over these occasions were 'Father' (vast, bearded and stern), 'Mother' (petite, artistic and indefatigable), 'Granniemother', Dowager Lady Swaythling, who, in Ewen's estimation, looked 'like a very animated piece of Dresden China [and] like most women of her milieu never did a hand's turn for herself'.

Ewen and his brothers had been brought up surrounded by servants and treasures but, in a reflection of the ideological ferment of the time, each emerged from childhood utterly different from the others. The eldest son, Stuart, was pompous and unimaginative as only an English aristocratic heir can be; by contrast Ewen's younger brother, Ivor, rejected the family money and went on to become a committed communist, a pioneer of British table tennis, a collector of rare breeds of mice, and a radical film-maker.

The house was equipped with a hydraulic lift, which the Montagu children never entered: 'It was a *servants'* lift, to carry trays or washing baskets or themselves invisibly past the gentlemanly regions when untimely menial presence might offend convention.' There were at least twenty servants (although no one was counting), including a butler and two footmen, a cook and kitchen maids, two housemaids, Mother's personal maid, a nurse and nursemaid, a governess, a secretary, a cockney coachman, a groom, and two chauffeurs. 'Born as I was into a very rich family, the servants abounded, and made one's life entirely different,' wrote Ewen.

Ewen had attended Westminster School, where he was clad in top hat and tails, educated superbly, and beaten only infrequently. Before going on to Trinity College, Cambridge, he spent a year at Harvard, studying English composition, but mostly enjoying the Jazz Age in a way the Great Gatsby might have envied and living, in his own words, 'the sort of American social life one saw in the films'. The experience turned Montagu into a lifelong Americanophile: 'I felt a great debt of gratitude to Americans for all their kindness to me and felt that I should try to repay it in some small measure.' The war would provide that opportunity.

At Cambridge, Ewen had a personal valet and a 1910 Lancia two-seater sports car he called 'Steve'. He dabbled in Labour politics, but left the more extreme left-wing thinking to his brother Ivor, who followed him to Cambridge a year later and was already well on his way to becoming a committed Marxist. Despite their differing personalities and politics, Ewen and Ivor were close friends. 'The "spread" among us three brothers was amusing,' Ewen reflected. Stuart 'already had a banker's attitude to life', whereas Ewen and Ivor had no intention of following the family career path. 'He and I were much closer than either of us [was] with Stuart as we had many more interests in common.'

'We had nothing to do but enjoy ourselves,' Ewen reflected. 'And, from time to time, work.' They did, however, find time to 'invent' table tennis. Ivor was extremely good at 'ping pong'. The game had no real rules or regulations and so he founded the English Ping Pong Association. Jaques, the sports manufacturer, got wind of the fledgling club and stuffily pointed out that the company had copyrighted the name 'ping pong'. Ewen recalled: 'I advised him to choose another name for the game; as we bandied names at one another, one of us came up with table tennis.' Ivor would go on to found the International Table Tennis Federation in 1926, and served as its first president for the next forty-one years.

Another project initiated by the Montagu brothers at Cambridge was 'The Cheese Eaters' League'. Ivor and Ewen shared a passion for cheese, and set up a dining club to import and taste the most exotic specimens from around the world: camel's milk cheese, Middle Eastern goat cheese, cheese made from the milk of long-horned Afghan sheep. 'Our great ambition was to get whale's milk cheese,' Ewen wrote, and to this end he contacted a whaling company to arrange that 'if a mother whale was killed the milk should be "cheesed" and sent to us'.

Montagu made the most of his privileged time at Cambridge, but he was already honing the intellectual muscles that would stand him in good stead, first as a lawyer, then as an intelligence officer – most notably the ability 'to study something with little or no sleep intensively over a short period'. He was also physically tough. Once, when riding to hounds, his foot slipped out of a stirrup, which then swung up as the horse swerved, cutting a large gash in his chin and knocking out five teeth. Another huntsman picked up one of Ewen's smashed teeth. 'I put it in my pocket and rode on,' Ewen recalled. The accident left him with a lopsided smile, which he deployed charmingly, but sparingly, and a useful ledge on which to hang his pipe.

While still at university, Ewen became engaged to Iris Solomon. It was, in many ways, a perfect match. Iris was the daughter of Solomon J. Solomon, the portrait painter. She was vivacious, intelligent, and of just the right Anglo-Jewish stock. They married in 1923. A son soon arrived, followed by a daughter.

Through the 1920s and 1930s, the young lawyer and his wife lived a golden existence, in the interval between one devastating war and another. They socialised with the most powerful in the land; at weekends they repaired to Townhill, the Montagu estate near Southampton, where twenty-five gardeners tended exquisite gardens laid out by Gertrude Jekyll. Here they shot pheasants, hunted, and played table tennis. In summer they sailed Ewen's forty-five-foot yacht on the Solent; in winter they skied in Switzerland.

But most of all, Ewen (like his future boss, Admiral Godfrey) loved to fish, in the river and salmon pools at Townhill. In later life he would be described as 'one of the best fly-fishermen in the realm'; he modestly denied this, insisting he was 'never better than a mediocre if enthusiastic fisherman'. For Montagu, on the riverbank, in court and, soon, at war, there was no more satisfying experience than 'the thrill of the strike and the joy of playing the fish'.

Ivor Montagu, meanwhile, was pursuing a different career path. By the age of twenty-two he had founded the English Table Tennis Association, written a book entitled *Table Tennis Today*, created the Film Society (with Sidney Bernstein), and made two expeditions to the Soviet Union, where he perfected his Russian and searched for 'an exceedingly primitive vole' found only in the Caucasus. The experience led to a zoological monograph on *Prometheomys*, the 'Prometheus Mouse', and a lifelong faith in the Soviet machinery of state. In 1927 he had married Frances Hellstern, universally known as 'Hell' (and regarded as such by her mother-in-law) – an unmarried mother and the daughter of a bootmaker from south London. The marriage made tabloid headlines: 'Baron's Son Weds Secretary'. Queen Mary wrote to Lady Swaythling: 'Dear Gladys, I feel for you. May.' Ivor could not have cared less.

In 1929 Ivor linked up with the Soviet film director Sergey Eisenstein, and together they travelled to Hollywood, where Ivor became close friends with Charlie Chaplin, whom he taught to swear in Russian. The youngest Montagu brother would go on to work as a producer on five of Alfred Hitchcock's British films.

Ivor's politics, meanwhile, marched steadily leftward, from the Fabian Society to the British Socialist Party to the Communist Party of Great Britain. He visited Spain during the civil war, and made a series of pro-Republican documentaries. While Ewen hobnobbed with generals and ambassadors, Ivor mixed with the likes of George Bernard Shaw and H. G. Wells. While Ewen lived in Kensington, Ivor cut himself off from his father's money and moved with Hell to a terraced house in Brixton. Yet, for all their differences, the brothers remained close, and saw one another often.

After joining the bar in 1924, Ewen had developed into an exceptionally able lawyer. He learned to absorb detail, improvise, and mould the collective mind of a malleable jury. Ewen

Montagu was born to argue. He would dispute with anyone, at any hour of the day, on almost any subject, and devastatingly, since he possessed the rare ability to read an interlocutor's mind – the mark of the good lawyer, and the good liar. He became fascinated by the workings of the criminal mind, and confessed to feeling 'a certain sympathy with rogue characters'. He relished the cut and thrust of the courtroom, where victory depended on being able to 'see the point of view, and anticipate the reactions, of an equally astute opposing counsel'. Montagu was invariably kind to people below him in social status, and capable of the most 'gentle manners', but he liked to cut those in authority down to size. He could be fabulously rude. Like many defence lawyers, he enjoyed the challenge of defending the apparently defenceless, or indefensible. He had one client, a crooked solicitor, in whom he may have seen something of himself: 'If he could see a really artistic lie, a gleam would come into his eye and he would tell it.' In 1939, Montagu was made a King's Counsel.

Ewen was sailing his yacht off the coast of Brittany, six months after taking silk, when he learned that war had been declared. The sailing trip had been delightful, 'hard in the wind, in glorious weather and escorted by porpoises playing around our bow'. On hearing the prime minister's grim wireless statement that Britain was now at war, Ewen had swung the helm around and headed back to port, knowing that nothing in his gilded life would ever be as shiny again. He recalled 'looking out to sea and realising all had gone smash for me. All had been going so well, as a new Silk all looked promising, and in my family and private life all was so wonderful. And now full stop.'

Iris and the two children, Jeremy and Jennifer, would be packed off to the safety of America, away from the Luftwaffe bombs that would soon rain down on London. As one of the country's most prominent Jewish banking families, Ewen knew the Montagu clan faced special peril in the event of a Nazi invasion.

At thirty-eight, Ewen was too old for active service, but he had already volunteered for the Royal Naval Volunteer Reserve. With the outbreak of war, he was commissioned as acting lieutenant commander and swiftly came to the attention of Admiral John Godfrey, the head of Naval Intelligence. 'It is quite useless, and in fact dangerous to employ people of medium intelligence,' wrote Godfrey. 'Only men with first-class brains should be allowed to touch this stuff. If the right sort of people can't be found, better keep them out altogether.' In Montagu he knew he had the right sort of person.

Godfrey's Intelligence Department was an eclectic and unconventional body. In addition to Ian Fleming, his personal assistant, Godfrey employed 'two stockbrokers, a schoolmaster, a journalist, a collector of books on original thought, an Oxford classical don, a barrister's clerk, and an insurance agent'. This heterogeneous crew was crammed into Room 39 at the Admiralty, which was permanently wreathed in tobacco smoke and frequently echoed to the sounds of Admiral Godfrey, shouting and swearing. Fleming awarded Godfrey the heavily ironic nickname 'Uncle John', for seldom has there been a less avuncular boss. 'The permanent inhabitants who finally settled in this cave,' he wrote, 'were people of very different temperaments, ambitions, social status and home life, all with their particular irritabilities, hopes, fears, anguishes, loves, hates, animosities and blank spots.' Any and every item of intelligence relevant to the war at sea passed through Room 39 and though the atmosphere inside was often tense, Godfrey's team 'worked like ants, and their combined output was prodigious'. The ants under Godfrey were responsible not merely for gathering and disseminating secret intelligence, but for running agents and double agents, as well as developing deception and counterespionage operations.

Godfrey had identified Montagu as a natural for this sort of work, and he was swiftly promoted. Soon, he not only represented the Naval Intelligence Department on most of the important intelligence bodies, including the Twenty Committee, but ran his own subsection of the department: the top-secret Section 17M (for Montagu).

Housed in Room 13, a low-ceilinged cavern twenty feet square, Section 17M (later renamed Section 12) was responsible for dealing with all 'special intelligence' relating to naval matters, principally the so-called 'Ultra' intercepts, the enemy communications deciphered by the cryptanalysts at Bletchley Park following the breaking of the Enigma, the German cipher machine. In the early days of 17M, the Ultra signals came in dribs and drabs, but gradually the volume of secret information swelled to a torrent, with more than 200 messages arriving every day, some a few words long but others covering pages. The work of understanding, collating and disseminating this huge volume of information was like 'learning a new language' according to Montagu, whose task it was to decide which items of intelligence should pass to other intelligence agencies and which merited inclusion in the Special Intelligence Summaries, 'the cream of all intelligence', while coordinating with MI5, Bletchley Park, the intelligence departments of the other services, and the Prime Minister. Montagu became fluent at reading this traffic, which, even after decoding, could be impossibly opaque. 'The Germans have a passion for cross-references and for abbreviations, and they have an even greater passion (only equalled by their ineptitude in practice) for the use of codenames.'

Section 17M expanded. First came Joan Saunders, a young woman married to the librarian of the House of Commons, 'to do the detailed work of indexing, filing and research'. Joan – a tall, strapping, jolly-hockeysticks woman with a booming voice and a personality to match – was effectively Montagu's chief assistant. She had been a nurse in the early part of the war, and had run a nursing station during the retreat from France. She was practical, bossy, occasionally terrifying and wore a tiger-skin fur coat to work in winter. The other female staff called her

'Auntie', but never to her face. Her familiarity with dead bodies would prove most useful. 'She is extraordinarily good, very methodical but also frightfully alert,' Montagu told his wife. 'Very pleasant to work with, although not much to look at. I'm not lucky in assistants as regards looks.' Montagu was something of a connoisseur of female beauty.

By 1943, the section had swelled to fourteen people, including an artist, a yachting magazine journalist, and two 'watchkeepers' to monitor any night traffic. The working conditions were atrocious. Room 13 was 'far too small, far too cluttered with safes, steel filing cabinets, tables, chairs etc. and especially far too low, with steel girders making it even lower. There was no fresh air, only potted air [in] conditions which would have been condemned instantly by any factories inspector.' The only light came from fluorescent strips 'which made everyone look mauve'. In theory, the staff 'were not supposed to listen to what we said over the telephone or to each other'. In such a confined space, this was impossible: there were no secrets between the secret keepers of Room 13. Despite the rigours, Montagu's unit was highly effective: they were, in the words of Admiral Godfrey, 'a brilliant band of dedicated war winners'.

As he had in the courtroom, Montagu delighted in burrowing into the minds of his opponents in the field of espionage, the German saboteurs, spies, agents and spymasters whose daily wireless exchanges, eavesdropped, decoded and translated, poured into Room 13. He came to recognise individual German intelligence officers among the traffic and, like his former rivals in court, he 'began to regard some almost as friends': 'They were so kind to us unconsciously.'

In America, at Ewen's instigation, Iris had begun working for British Security Coordination, the intelligence organisation based in New York and run by William Stephenson, the spymaster who revelled in the codename 'Intrepid'. Behind a front as British Passport Control, Stephenson's team ran black propaganda against Nazi sympathisers in the US, organised espionage, and worked assiduously to prod America into the war, by fair means or foul. In a way, spying and concealment was already in Iris's blood, for her father, the painter Solomon J. Solomon, had played a part in the invention of military camouflage during the First World War. In 1916, he had built a fake nine-foot tree out of steel plates shrouded in real bark, for use as an observation post on the Western Front. This was a family that understood the pleasure and challenge of making something appear to be what it was not. Ewen was pleased that his wife was now, as he put it, 'in the racket' too. Ewen and Iris wrote to one another every day, although Montagu could never describe exactly what his day involved: 'If I am killed there are four or five people who will be able after the war to tell you the sort of things I have been doing.'

Montagu's role expanded once more when Godfrey placed him in charge of all naval deception through double agents – 'the most fascinating job in the war', in Montagu's words. By means of the Ultra intercepts and other intelligence sources, Britain captured every single spy sent to Britain by the Abwehr, the German military intelligence organisation. Many of these were used as double agents, feeding misinformation back to the enemy. Montagu found himself at the very heart of the 'Double Cross System', helping 'Tar' Robertson and John Masterman to deploy double agents wherever and whenever the Navy was involved. He worked with Eddie Chapman, the crook turned spy, codenamed 'Zigzag', to send false information about submarine weaponry; he investigated astrology to see if Hitler's apparent belief in such things could be used against him ('very entertaining but useless') and in November 1941 he travelled to the US to help establish a system for handling double agent 'Tricycle' (the Serbian playboy Dusko Popov), in the penetration of German spy rings operating in America. The Double Cross System also involved the creation of bogus spies. 'A great number who did not really exist at all in real life, but were imaginary people notionally recruited as sub-agents by double agents whom we were already working.' In order to convince the enemy that these invented characters were real, every aspect of the fake personality had to be conjured into existence.

Some of the material that crossed Montagu's desk was strange beyond belief. In October 1941, Godfrey ordered Montagu to investigate why the Germans had suddenly imported 1,000 Rhesus monkeys, as well as a troop of Barbary apes. Godfrey speculated that 'it might be an indication that the Germans intended to use gas or bacteriological warfare, or for experimental purposes'. Montagu consulted Lord Victor Rothschild, MI5's expert on explosives, booby traps, and other unconventional forms of warfare. His lordship was doubtful that the large monkey imports were sinister. 'Though I have kept a close eye on people applying for animals,' he wrote, 'those cases so far investigated have proved innocuous. For example, an advertisement in *The Times* for 500 hedgehogs proved to be in connection with the experiments being done by the foot and mouth disease research section.'

Montagu would never fight on the front line, but there was no doubting his personal bravery. When Britain was under threat of German invasion in 1940, he hit on the idea of trying to lead the invading force into a minefield, using himself as bait. The minefields off Britain's east coast had gaps in them, to allow the fishing boats in and out. The Germans knew the approximate, but not the precise, location of these channels. If a chart could be got into their hands showing channels close enough to the real gaps to be believable, yet slightly wrong, then the invading fleet might be persuaded to ram confidently up the wrong route, and, with any luck, sink. Popov – Agent Tricycle – would pass the false chart to the Germans, claiming he had obtained it from a Jewish officer in the Navy keen to curry favour with the Nazis. Popov would say that this man, a prominent lawyer in civilian life, 'had heard and believed the propaganda stories about the ill-treatment of Jews and did not want to face the risk of being handed over to the Gestapo'. The chart was his insurance policy, and he would only hand it over in return for a written guarantee that he would be safe in the event of a successful German invasion of Britain. Popov liked the plan, and asked what name he should give the Germans for this treacherous naval officer. 'I thought you had realised,' said Montagu. 'Lieutenant Commander Montagu. They can look me up in the Law List and any of the *Jewish Year Books*.'

There was considerable courage in this act, although Montagu later denied it. If the Germans had invaded, they would have swiftly realised that the chart was phoney, and Montagu would have been even more of a marked man than he was already. There was also the possibility that someone in British intelligence might hear of the chart, and the treacherous Jewish lawyer prepared to sell secrets to save his own skin: at the very least, he would have some complicated explaining to do. The plot made Montagu appear, to German eyes, to be 'an out and out traitor'. He was unconcerned: what mattered was telling a convincing story.

Before placing Montagu in charge of naval deception, Godfrey had passed him a copy of the 'Trout Memo' written with Ian Fleming. Montagu considered Fleming 'a four-letter man', and got on with him very well. ('Fleming is charming to be with, but would sell his own grandmother. I like him a lot.') Years later, when both men were long retired, Godfrey gently reminded Montagu of the debt, and the origins of the operation: 'The bare idea of the dead airman washed up on a beach was among those dozen or so notions which I gave you when 17M was formed,' he wrote. Montagu replied blandly: 'I quite honestly don't remember your passing on this suggestion to me. Of course, what you said may have been in my subconscious and may have formed the link – but I can assure you that it was not conscious which shows the strange workings of fate (or something!).'

The strange workings of fate had now thrown together, in Room 13, Montagu, the whip-smart lawyer, and Cholmondeley, the gentle, lanky, unpredictable ideas man, an ill-matched pair who would develop into the most remarkable double act in the history of deception. They had the backing of the Twenty Committee, they had plenty of precedents, and they had the outline of a plan: what they did not yet have was a clear idea of what to do with it.

4

Target Sicily

The plan of action agreed by Winston Churchill and Franklin Delano Roosevelt when they met in Casablanca in January 1943 was, in some respects, blindingly obvious: after the successful North Africa campaign, Operation Torch, the next target would be the island of Sicily.

The Nazi war machine was at last beginning to stutter and misfire. The British 8th Army under Montgomery had vanquished Rommel's invincible Afrika Korps at El Alamein. The Allied invasion of Morocco and Tunisia fatally weakened Germany's grip, and with the liberation of Tunis, the Allies would control the coast of North Africa, its ports and airfields, from Casablanca to Alexandria. The time had come to lay siege to Hitler's fortress. But where?

Sicily was the logical place from which to deliver the gut punch into what Churchill famously called the soft 'underbelly of the Axis'. The island at the toe of Italy's boot commanded the channel linking the two sides of the Mediterranean, just eighty miles from the Tunisian coast. If the combined British and American armies were to free Europe, prise Italy out of the Fascist embrace, and roll back the Nazi behemoth, they would first have to take Sicily. The British in Malta and Allied convoys had been pummelled by Luftwaffe bombers taking off from the island and, as Montagu remarked, 'no major operation could be launched, maintained, or supplied until the enemy airfields and other bases in Sicily had been obliterated so as to allow free passage through the Mediterranean'. An invasion of Sicily would open the road to Rome, draw German troops from the Eastern Front to relieve the Red Army, allow for preparations to invade France, and perhaps knock a tottering Italy out of the war. Breaking up the 'Pact of Steel' forged in 1939 by Hitler and Mussolini would shatter German morale, Churchill predicted, 'and might be the beginning of their doom'. The Americans were initially dubious, wondering if Britain harboured imperial ambitions in the Mediterranean, but eventually they compromised: Sicily would be the target, the precursor to the invasion of mainland Europe.

If the strategic importance of Sicily was clear to the Allies, it was surely equally obvious to Italy and Germany. Churchill was blunt about the choice of target: 'Everyone but a bloody fool would *know* it was Sicily.' And if the enemy was foolish enough not to see what was coming, he would surely cotton on when 160,000 British, American and Commonwealth troops and an armada of 3,200 ships began assembling for the invasion. Sicily's 500-mile coastline was already defended by seven or eight enemy divisions. If Hitler correctly anticipated the Allies' next move, then the island would be reinforced by thousands of German troops held in reserve in France. The soft underbelly would become a wall of muscle. The invasion could turn into a bloodbath.

But the logic of Sicily was immutable. On 22 January, Churchill and Roosevelt gave their joint blessing to 'Operation Husky', the invasion of Sicily, the next great set-piece offensive of the war. General Eisenhower was summoned to Casablanca, and given his orders.

All of which presented Allied intelligence chiefs with a fiendish conundrum: how to convince the enemy that the Allies were *not* going to do what anyone with an atlas could see they *ought* to do.

The previous June, Churchill had established the London Controlling Section (a deliberately vague title) under a

Controller of Deception, Lieutenant Colonel John H. Bevan, to 'prepare deception plans on a worldwide basis with the object of causing the enemy to waste his military resources'. Bevan was responsible for the overall planning, supervision, and coordination of strategic deception. Immediately after the Casablanca conference, he was instructed to draw up a new deception policy to disguise the impending invasion of Sicily. The result was 'Operation Barclay', a complex, many-layered plan that would try to convince the Germans that black was white or, at the very least, grey.

Johnnie Bevan was an Old Etonian stockbroker, an upright pillar of the Establishment whose convivial and modest temperament belied an exceedingly sharp mind. He had that rare English ability to achieve impressive feats while maintaining a permanent air of embarrassment, and he tackled the monumental task of wartime deception in the same way that he played cricket. 'When things were looking pretty bad for his side at cricket, he would shuffle in, about sixth wicket down, knock up 100 and shuffle out again looking rather ashamed of himself.' Bevan played with the straightest of straight bats, as honest and upright a team player as one could imagine: which was probably what made him such a superb deceiver.

While Bevan controlled the business of deception from within the Cabinet War Rooms, the fortified underground bunker beneath Whitehall, his counterpart in the Mediterranean was Lieutenant Colonel Dudley Wrangel Clarke, the chief of 'A' Force, the deception unit based in Cairo. Clarke was another master of strategic deception, but of a very different stamp. Unmarried, nocturnal and allergic to children, he was possessed of 'an ingenious imagination and a photographic memory', and a flair for the dramatic that invited trouble. For the Royal Tournament in 1925, he mounted a pageant depicting imperial artillery down the ages, which involved two elephants, thirty-seven guns and 'fourteen of the biggest Nigerians he could find'. He loved uniforms, disguises and dressing up. Most of one of his ears was lopped off by a German bullet when he took part in the first Commando raid on occupied France, and in 1940 he was summoned to Egypt, at the express command of General Sir Archibald Wavell, commander-in-chief in the Middle East, and ordered to set up a 'special section of intelligence for deception'.

Clarke and 'A' Force had spent the last two years baffling and bamboozling the enemy in a variety of complicated and flamboyant ways. Between them, Colonels Bevan and Clarke would construct the most elaborate wartime web of deception ever spun. Yet in its essence the aim of Operation Barclay was quite simple: to convince the Axis powers that instead of attacking Sicily in the middle of the Mediterranean, the Allies intended to invade Greece in the east, and the island of Sardinia, followed by southern France, in the west. The lie went as follows: the British 12th Army (which did not exist) would invade the Balkans in the summer of 1943, starting in Crete and the Peloponnese, bringing Turkey into the war against the Axis powers, moving against Bulgaria and Romania, linking up with the Yugoslav resistance and then finally uniting with the Soviet armies on the Eastern Front. The subsidiary lie was intended to convince the Germans that the British 8th Army planned to land on France's south coast, and then storm up the Rhône valley, once American troops under General Patton had attacked Corsica and Sardinia. Sicily would be bypassed.

If Operation Barclay succeeded, the Germans would reinforce the Balkans, Sardinia and southern France in preparation for invasions that would never materialise, while leaving Sicily only lightly defended. At the very least, enemy troops would be spread over a broad front and the German defensive shield would be weakened. By the time the real target became obvious, it would be too late to reinforce Sicily.

The deception plan played directly on Hitler's fears, for the Ultra intercepts had clearly revealed that the Führer, his staff and local commanders in Greece all feared that the Balkans represented a vulnerable point on the Nazis' southern flank.

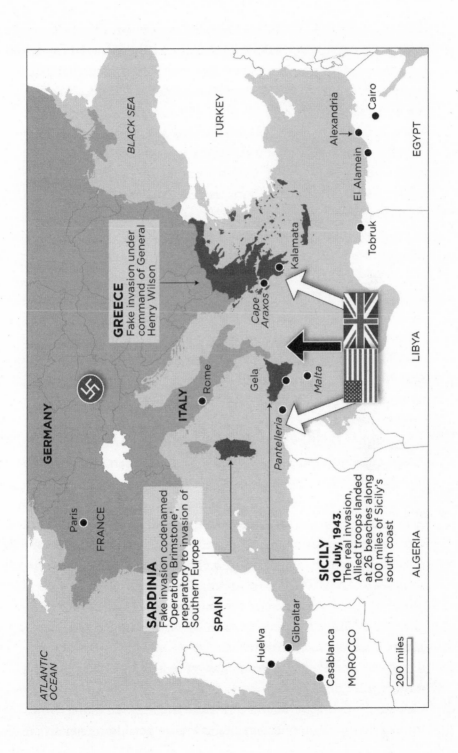

Even so, shifting German attention away from Sicily would not be easy, for the strategic importance of the island was self-evident. A German intelligence report produced in early February for the Supreme Command of the Armed Forces, the Oberkommando der Wehrmacht (OKW), was quite explicit, and accurate, about Allied intentions: 'The idea of knocking Italy out of the war after the conclusion of the African campaign, by means of air attacks and a landing operation, looms large in Anglo-Saxon deliberations . . . Sicily offers itself as the first target.' The deception operation would need to shift Hitler's mind in two different directions: reducing his fears for Sicily, while stoking his anxiety about Sardinia, Greece and the Balkans.

'Uncle' John Godfrey identified what he called 'wishfulness' and 'yesmanship' as the twin frailties of German intelligence: 'If the authorities were clamouring for reports on a certain subject, the German secret intelligence service was not above inventing reports based on what they thought probable.' The Nazi high command, at the same time, when presented with contradictory intelligence reports, was 'inclined to believe the one that fits in best with their own previously formed conceptions'. If Hitler's paranoid wishfulness and his underlings' craven yesmanship could be exploited, then Operation Barclay might work: the Germans would deceive themselves.

The deception swung into action on a range of fronts. Engineers began fabricating a bogus army in the Eastern Mediterranean; double agents started feeding false information to their Abwehr handlers; plans were drawn up for counterfeit troop movements, fake radio traffic, the recruitment of Greek interpreters and officers, and the acquisition of Greek maps and currency to indicate an impending assault on the Peloponnese.

While Bevan and Clarke began weaving together the strands of Operation Barclay, Montagu and Cholmondeley went hunting for a dead body.

In his initial plan, Cholmondeley had assumed one could simply pop into a military hospital and pick a bargain cadaver off the shelf for £10. The reality was rather different. The Second World War may have been responsible for the deaths of more people than any conflict in history, yet dead bodies of the right sort were surprisingly hard to find. People tended to be killed, or to kill themselves, in all the wrong ways. A bombing victim would never do. Suicides were more common than in peacetime, but these were usually by rope, gas or chemical means that could easily be detected in a postmortem examination. Moreover, the requirements were specific: the plan called for a fresh male body of military age, with no obvious injuries or infirmities, and cooperative next of kin who would not object when the corpse of their loved one was whisked away for unspecified purposes, to an unstipulated place, by complete strangers. Montagu turned for advice to someone who knew more about death than any man living.

Sir Bernard Spilsbury was the senior pathologist at the Home Office, an expert witness in many of the most famous trials of the age, and pioneer of the modern science of forensics. Sir Bernard collected deaths as other people collect stamps or books. For half a century, until his own mysterious demise in 1949, Spilsbury accumulated ordinary deaths and extraordinary deaths, carrying out some 25,000 autopsies: he studied death by asphyxiation, poisoning, accident and murder, and he jotted down the particulars of each case in his spidery handwriting on thousands of index cards, laying the foundations for modern crime scene investigation.

Spilsbury had come to public attention with the infamous Dr Crippen case of 1910. When Michigan-born Dr Hawley Harvey Crippen was captured attempting to flee to North America with his mistress, it was Spilsbury who identified the remains buried in his cellar in London as those of his missing wife, Cora, through distinctive scar tissue on a fragment of skin. Crippen was hanged in 1910. Over the next thirty years, Spilsbury would testify in courtrooms across the land, laying out the Crown's case in clear, precise, unarguable tones of moral rectitude. The newspapers adored him as an erect, handsome figure in the witness box, who combined scientific certainty with Edwardian upright character. As one contemporary observed, Spilsbury was a one-man instrument of retribution: 'He could achieve single-handed all the legal consequences of homicide – arrest, prosecution, conviction and final postmortem – requiring only the brief assistance of the hangman.' His courtroom manner was famously oracular and clipped, never using three words where one would suffice. 'He formed his opinion; expressed it in the clearest, most succinct manner possible; then stuck to it come hell or high water.'

Before Spilsbury, forensic pathology was widely discredited, regarded as inexact and medically dubious. However, by 1943, he had helped to transform the study of dead bodies – the 'Beastly Science' as it was known – into a branch of science both ghoulish and glamorous. Simultaneously, he acquired a reputation for experimenting on himself. Spilsbury inhaled carbon monoxide to test its effect on the body and made notes on his sensations (which were unpleasant). He climbed down a manhole in Redcross Street to check on gas that had killed a workman. When he accidentally ingested meningitis germs in a hospital laboratory, he 'just carried on'. It was said that Sir Bernard could identify the cause of death simply by smelling a corpse. In 1938, *The Washington Post* hailed him as 'England's modern Sherlock Holmes'.

But a lifetime of inhaling death, peering into cadavers, and familiarity with the darkest sides of human nature had affected the great scientist. Media attention had gone to his head. Sir Bernard was aloof, arrogant, and utterly convinced of his own infallibility. He saw the world bleakly, through a veil of cynicism and self-satisfaction, and seldom evinced a shred of sympathy for anyone, living or dead. With heavy-lidded eyes and a 'haughty, aristocratic bearing', he looked like a lizard in a lab coat, and smelled permanently of formaldehyde.

Ewen Montagu arranged to meet the famous pathologist

over a glass of lukewarm sherry at Spilsbury's club, the Junior Carlton. Spilsbury had already done macabre service for British intelligence. Captured enemy spies were offered a stark choice: either work as double agents, or face execution. Most agreed to cooperate, but a few resisted, or were deemed unusable. These, the 'unlucky sixteen' as they became known, were tried and executed. Spilsbury was brought in to carry out autopsies on these executed spies, including Josef Jakobs, shot by firing squad in the summer of 1941, the last person to be executed in the Tower of London.

Sir Bernard was sixty-six, but looked far older. Montagu was not in the habit of subservience, but he had seen Spilsbury perform in court and was deeply in awe of 'that extraordinary man'. Conscious of how odd the words sounded, the younger man explained that the Navy 'wanted the Germans and Spaniards to accept a floating body as that of a victim of an aircraft disaster'. What manner of death would fit in with the impression the Government wished to give? Spilsbury's heavy lids did not even blink at the question. Indeed, as Montagu later recorded, 'never once did he ask why I wanted to know, or what I was proposing to do'.

There was a long pause while the forensic scientist considered the question, and sipped his sherry. Finally, in his courtroom voice, 'clear, resonant, without any trace of uncertainty', he presented his verdict. The easiest way, of course, would be to find a drowned man and float him ashore in a life jacket. But failing that, any number of other causes of death would do, for the victims of air accidents at sea, Spilsbury explained, do not necessarily die from traumatic injury or drowning: 'Many die from exposure, or even from shock.'

Spilsbury returned to his laboratory at St Bartholomew's Hospital, and Montagu reported back to Cholmondeley that the hunt for a suitable corpse might be easier than they had anticipated. Even so, it was hardly possible to 'ask around' for a dead body, as gossip would undoubtedly spread and embarrassing questions would be asked. Briefly they considered whether grave robbery might be the answer, 'doing a Burke and Hare', but that idea was swiftly scotched. (In 1827, William Burke and William Hare stole the body of an army pensioner from its coffin, and sold it to the Edinburgh Medical College for £7. They went on to murder sixteen people, selling their bodies for medical dissection. Hare testified against Burke, who was hanged and publicly dissected.) It was not a happy comparison. Stealing corpses was unpleasant, immoral and illegal, and even if successful, a body that had lain in the ground for only a few days would be too decomposed for use. What was needed was a discreet and helpful individual with legal access to plenty of fresh corpses.

Montagu knew just such a man: the coroner of St Pancras in north-west London, who went by the delightfully Dickensian name of Bentley Purchase.

Under English law, the coroner, a post dating back to the eleventh century, is the government official responsible for investigating deaths, particularly those occurring under unusual circumstances, and determining their causes. When a death is unexpected, violent or unnatural, the coroner is responsible for deciding whether to hold a postmortem and, if necessary, an inquest.

Bentley Purchase was a friend and colleague of Spilsbury in the death business, but Purchase was as cheery as Sir Bernard was grim. Indeed, for a man who spent his life with the dead, Purchase was the life and soul of every occasion. He found death not only fascinating but extremely funny. No form of violent or mysterious mortality surprised or upset him. 'A depressing job?' he once said. 'Far from it. I can't imagine it getting me down.' He would offer slightly damp chocolates to guests in his private chambers, and joke: 'They were found in Auntie's bag when she was fished out of the Round Pond at Hampstead last night.' A farmer by birth, Purchase was 'rugged in appearance and character', with 'an impish sense of humour' and a finely calibrated sense of the ridiculous: he loved Gilbert and Sullivan operas, toy trains, boiled eggs, and the model piggery he ran near Ipswich. He never wore a hat, and laughed loudly and often.

Montagu knew Purchase as 'an old friend from my barrister days', and dropped him a note asking if they might meet to discuss a confidential matter. Purchase replied with directions to the St Pancras Coroner's Court, and a typically jovial postscript: 'An alternative means of getting here is, of course, to get run over.'

Purchase had fought in the First World War as a doctor attached to the Field Artillery, winning the Military Cross for 'conspicuous gallantry and devotion to duty'. He fought on until 1918, when a shell splinter removed most of his left hand. By the time war broke out again, he was nearly fifty, too old to wear uniform, but 'aching to get into the war'. Indeed, he had already demonstrated a willingness to help the intelligence services and, if necessary, 'distort the truth in the service of security'. When an Abwehr spy named William Rolph killed himself by putting his head in a gas oven in 1940, Purchase obliged with a verdict of 'heart attack'. In the same month that he received Montagu's note, Purchase had been called in to deliberate on the case of Paul Manoel, an agent of the Free French Intelligence Service who had been found hanging in a London basement following interrogation as a suspected enemy agent. Purchase's inquest was 'cursory in the extreme'.

The coroner was initially dubious when Montagu explained that he needed to find a male corpse for 'a warlike operation' but 'did not wish to disclose why a body was needed'.

'You can't get bodies just for the asking, you know,' Purchase told him. 'I should think bodies are the only commodities not in short supply at the moment [but] even with bodies all over the place, each one has to be accounted for.'

Montagu would say only that the scheme required a fresh cadaver that might appear to have drowned or died in an air accident. The matter, he added gravely, was 'of national importance'.

Still Purchase hesitated, pointing out that if word got out that the legal system for disposing of the dead was being circumvented, 'public confidence in coroners of the country would be shaken'.

'At what level has this scheme been given approval?' the coroner asked.

Montagu paused before replying, not entirely truthfully: 'The Prime Minister's.'

That was enough for Bentley Purchase, whose 'well developed sense of comedy' was now thoroughly aroused. Chortling, he explained that, as a coroner, he had 'absolute discretion' over the paperwork and that in certain circumstances a death could be concealed, and a body obtained, without getting official permission from anyone. 'A coroner,' he explained, 'could, in fact, always get rid of a corpse by a certificate that it was going to be buried outside the country – it would then be assumed that a relative was taking it home (i.e. to Ireland) for burial and the coroner could then do what he liked with it without let, hindrance or trace.'

Bodies were pouring into London morgues at an unprecedented rate: in the previous year Purchase had dealt with 1,855 cases, and held inquests into 726 sudden deaths. Many of the bodies 'remained unidentified and were in the end buried as unknowns'. One of these would surely fit the bill. The St Pancras mortuary was attached to the Coroner's Court, so Purchase offered to give Montagu a tour of the bodies currently in cold storage. 'After one or two possible corpses had been inspected and for various reasons rejected', the two men shook hands and parted, with Purchase promising to keep a lookout for a suitable candidate.

The St Pancras mortuary was without doubt the most unpleasant place Montagu had ever been: but then, his had been a life almost entirely free of unpleasant places and upsetting sights.

Ewen Montagu bemoaned 'the inevitable misery of separation' from his family. His letters to his wife Iris are filled with longing and loneliness. 'I miss you most frightfully, and life has just seemed one long, grey monotone since we have been separated.' But he had grown to enjoy his existence as a bachelor spy. 'The interest and pressure of my work managed to keep my morale up,' he wrote. 'In a way it was like a mixture of constructing a crossword puzzle and sawing a jigsaw puzzle and then waiting to see whether the recipient could and would solve the clues and place the bits together successfully.' The only drawback to living at Kensington Court was the presence of Lady Swaythling, with whom he argued constantly. He found time to get away for fishing trips on Exmoor. 'It was lovely to be far from the noise and the worry and just listening to the noise of the stream,' he told Iris. 'I haven't enjoyed anything as much since you left.' He relished the fishing most when it was hardest. 'The greatest fun is the very delicate casting into awkward places.'

Lord Swaythling had taken the Rolls-Royce with him to Townhill, so Montagu borrowed a bicycle to commute to work. In order to transport his 'super-secret papers', he bolted a large pannier on the front and chained his briefcase to it. The head of security at the Naval Intelligence Department questioned whether it was safe to cycle around with a briefcase full of secrets. What if the case was stolen? But after some argument, Montagu was given formal permission to continue with this unorthodox arrangement for transporting documents 'as long as I always wore a shoulder holster and an automatic pistol'.

On 24 January 1943, Montagu cycled as usual back to Kensington Court, where Ward the butler opened the massive front door to him. Nancy, 'one of the best cooks in London', had rustled up a fine dinner in spite of rationing, although the Dowager Lady Swaythling insisted that standards had slipped. 'Mother is too awful for words,' Ewen wrote to Iris. 'She complains that she can't get her nice chocolates "of decent quality" whereas everyone else is overjoyed at getting any at all.'

Ewen ate alone in the dining room panelled in oak from

the Place Vendôme, beneath the glowering portraits of his ancestors. There was always plenty of cheese. He then spent an hour in the great library, working on the 'crossword puzzles' in his briefcase. The Casablanca Conference had ended with the decision to invade Sicily. Cholmondeley's plan to foist a dead body on the Germans with false documents was still only on the drawing board, but the decision at Casablanca had sharply accelerated the timescale: unless Montagu found a suitable body, and fast, Trojan Horse would be, in a manner of speaking, dead in the water.

Finally, Montagu turned in, returned the papers to his briefcase, locked it, and headed to the basement bedroom where he now slept because of the air raids. Mabel the maid ('who had been in the family for more than thirty-five years') had turned down the crisp cotton sheets on the bed.

That same evening, in a grimy disused warehouse on the other side of London, a young Welshman swallowed a large dose of rat poison, ending a life which could not have been more different, in every conceivable way, from that of the Hon. Ewen Montagu.

5

The Man Who Was

Aberbargoed was a grim place a century ago, a brooding village of coal-dusted sadness and unremitting toil. The colliery opened in 1903. Before the coal was found, there was nothing at Aberbargoed, save the green valleys. With the coal came rows of pinched, terraced streets, housing hundreds of miners and their families. Without coal it was nothing. And when the coal ran out, as it eventually did, there was nothing much left. Even before the First World War, Aberbargoed was suffering, and struggling.

Into this bleak world Glyndwr Michael was born, on 4 January 1909, at 136 Commercial Street. His mother was Sarah Ann Chadwick, his father a colliery haulier named Thomas Michael. What few records have survived of this family give a flavour of their troubled lives. At the age of twenty, in 1888, Sarah had married another coalminer, George Cottrell. She signed their marriage certificate with a cross. Sarah never learned to read or write, or ever had any use for either skill. Although two daughters resulted from her marriage to Cottrell, the relationship did not last, and by 1904 she was living with Thomas Michael in a cramped house beside the railway line at Dinas. They never married. Like his father, who died of tuberculosis when Thomas was a child, Thomas Michael had been a coalminer all his life. A Welsh Baptist, born in Dinas, he worked deep in the pits, hauling coal trucks by hand through the bowels of the earth. At some point before meeting Sarah, Thomas Michael contracted syphilis, which he passed on to her, and which apparently went untreated. It is possible that when Glyndwr Michael was born, his parents bequeathed him congenital syphilis, which can cause damage to bones, eyes and brain.

When Glyn was an infant, the family moved twelve miles from Aberbargoed to Taff's Well, next to Rockwood Pit, where another child, Doris, was born two years later. Unable to pay the rent, the Michaels moved from one dingy house to another, each more decrepit than the last, first to 7 Garth Street, and then again, a few years later, to 28 Cornwall Road, Williamstown, Penygraig, in the Rhondda Valley, where Sarah gave birth to her third child by Thomas. There was little food. The children wore shoes once a week, to church. Thomas Michael drank.

Around 1919, when Glyn was nine or ten, his father's health began to decline, probably due to the delayed effects of syphilis, combined with the lung-rotting damage caused by working underground for over three decades. Soon after this, his grandmother died of 'senile decay'. Mental frailty would be a recurrent feature of the family's medical history. Thomas Michael began to cough horribly, and sweat at odd times of the day. The right side of his chest began to sink inwards.

Early in 1924, Michael was no longer able to work, and the family was forced to live on charity from the Pontypridd Union, the second largest Poor Law authority in Britain. For a time they were homeless and were forced to move into a single room at Llwynypia Homes, a charity hostel. The Pontypridd Union paid 23 shillings for a man and wife, and 2 shillings for each child. A family of five was now surviving, barely, on £1, 9 shillings a week. Thomas Michael became 'melancholic', according to a medical report which added that he was 'confused and very depressed', rapidly losing weight and had a racking, rattling cough.

Just before Christmas 1924, Thomas Michael stabbed himself in the throat with a carving knife. He was rushed to the county mental hospital in Bridgend, where the wound was cleaned and stitched up. Thomas Michael was a mental and physical wreck, coughing blood and in 'deep mental depression'. He was fifty-one years old, but looked eighty. Percy Hawkins, a nurse at the institution, described him: 'Hair is grey and thin. Pupils are somewhat irregular, they react to light and converge. Tongue has a dry white fur. Teeth very deficient and carious. He is thin and poorly nourished. Patient coughs and spits a good deal, and sweats heavily at night.' Both lungs were riddled with disease.

At first, Thomas seemed to be recovering. He began to speak quite rationally, and to notice his surroundings. But on 13 March 1925 he caught influenza, which developed into bronchial pneumonia, with 'a hectic temperature, copious and foul-smelling expectoration, very weak and depressed'. He stopped eating. On 31 March Thomas Michael died.

Glyndwr Michael, now sixteen years old, had witnessed his father turn from a vigorous coalminer into a diseased husk. He had seen him stab himself, and then watched him fall apart in a lunatic asylum. Glyn had been born poor. Now he was a pauper. He may already have been suffering from mental illness. When Thomas Michael was buried in a common grave in Trealaw cemetery, Reverend Overton presiding, Glyn Michael signed the burial register in a blotted, uncertain hand without using capital letters.

The widowed Sarah moved, with her three youngest children, into a minuscule flat in the back streets of Trealaw, now dependent entirely on alms for survival. The Pontypridd Union, however, was going bust, such was the demand for charity in the struggling South Wales coalfields. A year after Thomas Michael's death, Health Minister Neville Chamberlain told Parliament that the Pontypridd Union had run up an overdraft of £210,000, and further money would be advanced only 'on condition that the scale of relief was reduced'. As the Depression struck, the economic situation in South Wales turned from bad to catastrophic. Glyn found part-time employment as a gardener and labourer, but work was hard to come by.

At the outbreak of war in 1939, Sarah and Glyn Michael were still living at 135 Trealaw Road. Glyn's two half-sisters and his sister Doris had each married coalminers, and now had families of their own. His younger brother had left home. Glyndwr was not considered eligible for military service, which suggests that he was unfit, either physically or, more probably, mentally. On 15 January 1940, Glyn's mother died in her bed of a heart attack and an aortic aneurism. Sarah had been his only emotional support. On 16 January, Glyndwr Michael witnessed his mother's death certificate, buried her alongside his father in the Trealaw cemetery, and disappeared. A country at war had little attention to spare for a man who was homeless, destitute and most likely mentally ill.

Bentley Purchase often wondered why people came to the capital to die. More than a quarter of all the cases he examined were suicides, but many of these were not Londoners. What impulse, he mused, 'led men and women to London to end their lives? Was it because the dead from the provinces hoped that in the vastness of the capital one more tragedy would pass unnoticed? Or did they wish to spare relatives and friends the distress that would arise inevitably if they ended their lives on their own doorsteps?' Purchase was puzzled, in a detached and scientific way: 'It still surprised him how many people seemed to be utterly friendless and unwanted when they arrived in his mortuary.'

It is not clear how or when Glyndwr Michael got to London. In the winter of 1942 he was staying in 'a common lodging house' in west London, although he also appears to have been sleeping rough in disused buildings and undergoing some sort of treatment at a lunatic asylum. He was clean shaven, which suggests he owned a razor, and was living somewhere where he could use it.

On 26 January 1943, Michael was found in an abandoned warehouse near King's Cross and was taken to St Pancras

Hospital, suffering from acute chemical poisoning. As Sir Bernard Spilsbury's case notes attest, suicides in wartime Britain found an extraordinary variety of ways to poison themselves: with Lysol disinfectant, camphor, opium, carbolic, hydrochloric acid, alcohol, chloroform and coal gas. Michael ingested rat poison, probably 'Battle's Vermin Killer', a paste laced with highly toxic white phosphorus. It was assumed that Michael had killed himself intentionally. His father had attempted suicide, and self-destruction, tragically, often runs in families. But it is also possible that the poisoning was accidental. Rat poison was usually spread on stale bread and other scraps: the phosphorus made it glow in the dark, so the rodents would be attracted by both the light and smell. It is entirely possible that Michael ate rotting leftover food laced with poison because he was hungry.

Phosphorus poisoning is a horrific way to die, as acid in the digestive system reacts with the phosphide to generate the toxic gas phosphine. The pathology follows three distinct phases. Often within minutes, the victim suffers nausea and vomiting, as the phosphorus affects the gastric tract, followed by delirium, cramps, restlessness, convulsions, extreme thirst, and two particularly unpleasant symptoms peculiar to phosphorus poisoning: 'smoking stool' and 'garlic breath'. The second phase, some twenty-four hours after the initial poisoning, is one of relative calm when the symptoms appear to subside. In the third phase, the victim suffers breakdown of the central nervous system, jaundice, coma, kidney, heart and liver failure, and finally death. It took poor Glyndwr Michael more than two days to die, but he appears to have been sufficiently lucid in the second phase to tell the nurses at St Pancras who he was, and what he had eaten. He was pronounced dead on 28 January 1943.

At the age of thirty-four, Glyndwr Michael had simply slipped through the cracks of a wartime society with other concerns: a single man, illegitimate and probably illiterate, without money, friends or family, he had died unloved and unlamented, but not unnoticed.

As soon as the body of Glyndwr Michael reached St Pancras morgue, Bentley Purchase informed Ewen Montagu that a candidate for the project had arrived in his jurisdiction and would be 'kept in suitable cold storage until we were ready for it'.

Purchase carried out a swift inquest, with a foregone conclusion. In a suspected poisoning, the coroner would normally have held an autopsy, but none was ordered in this case, for obvious reasons. Purchase listed Michael as 'lunatic', which suggests that he had been certified insane and was undergoing treatment. The death certificate, based on the coroner's inquest, described him as 'labourer, no fixed abode', and gives the cause of death as 'phosphorus poisoning. Took rat poison [in a] bid [to] kill himself while of unsound mind.' Purchase informed the registrar that the body was being 'removed out of England' for burial.

In private, the coroner gave Montagu a more detailed account. The dead man, he explained, had taken 'a minimal dose' of rat poison. 'This dose was not sufficient to kill him outright, and its only effect was so to impair the functioning of the liver that he died a little time afterwards.' The human body normally contains traces of phosphorus, the coroner explained, and 'phosphorus is not one of the poisons readily traceable after long periods, such as arsenic which invades the roots of the hair, etc., or strychnine'. The rat poison would leave few clues to the cause of death, 'except possibly faint traces of chemical action in the liver'. Determining how the man had died after immersion in water would require 'a highly skilled medico-criminal chemist who would have to weigh all the chemical compositions of every organ before he could come to any conclusion'. Purchase liked a flutter, and he was willing to 'bet heavily against anyone being able to determine the cause of death with sufficient certainty to deny the presumption that the man had been drowned or killed by shock through an aeroplane crash and then been immersed in water'.

For a second, even weightier, opinion Montagu turned once more to Sir Bernard Spilsbury, the world's foremost medico-criminal chemist. They met again at the Junior Carlton Club. Sir Bernard's verdict was as dry as his sherry: 'You have nothing to fear from a Spanish postmortem; to detect that this young man had not died after an aircraft had been lost at sea would need a pathologist of my experience – and there aren't any in Spain.'

Spilsbury's answer was typical of the man. Typically self-assured, typically laconic, but also (and this was increasingly true of Sir Bernard's lofty pronouncements) typically open to question. For Sir Bernard Spilsbury was not the forensic oracle he had once been; far from infallible, he had started to make some terrible mistakes. Today, even his evidence in the Crippen case is open to doubt. Utterly convinced of his own rectitude and adamant in his prejudices, Spilsbury helped to send 110 men to the gallows. Some, with hindsight, were plainly innocent. His theories and opinions had increasingly taken precedence over the facts, most notably in the case of Norman Thorne, sentenced to death for killing his girlfriend. The woman had almost certainly committed suicide, and the evidence was at best contradictory, but Spilsbury's testimony had been unwavering, despite a rising tide of protest at the way one man's 'expertise' was sending a possibly innocent man to the gallows. 'I am a martyr to Spilsburyism,' said Thorne, shortly before his execution.

By the 1940s, Spilsbury's reputation had begun to fade; his marriage was collapsing, and his mind had started to fail. His fabled sense of smell had deserted him. He was overworked and in 1940 he suffered a small stroke. The death of a son in the Blitz affected him deeply. His answers to Montagu's questions bore all the hallmarks of the last days of Sir Bernard Spilsbury: emphatic but questionable, and potentially extremely dangerous.

Identifying whether an individual has drowned, or died by some other means, is one of the oldest and most difficult medical dilemmas. In the thirteenth century, a book by Chinese physicians entitled *The Washing Away of Wrongs* addressed the thorny issue of suspicious death by drowning. Even today, the medical community has no universally agreed diagnostic tests for drowning. Spilsbury himself had closely studied the pathology of drowning in the spectacular 'Brides in the Bath' case of 1915, when George Joseph Smith, a swindler and bigamist, was accused of killing at least three of his wives. In each case, the victim had been found in the bath. Spilsbury exhumed the bodies, and set about proving that they could not have died by natural causes. In court, it took him just twenty minutes to convince the jury that it is possible to murder someone, and leave no marks of violence, by suddenly submerging them in water while bathing. Smith was hanged.

In the course of that case, Spilsbury had become intimately acquainted with the symptoms of drowning: the fine white froth, known as *champagne de mousse*, in the lungs and on the lips; the marbled and swollen appearance of the lungs, inflated by the inhalation of water; water in the stomach; foreign material, such as vomit or sand, in the lungs; and haemorrhages in the middle ear. A drowning person dies violently, struggling, often bruising or rupturing the muscles in the neck or shoulder as he grasps and gasps for air. None of these symptoms would be present in the body of Glyndwr Michael, who had not died in water, but in a hospital bed, heavily sedated. On the other side of the coin, anyone killed by phosphorus, however small the dosage, would have yellowed skin and probably gastric burns, as well as significant traces of the chemical in the body, easily detectable with the science of 1943.

The renowned forensic scientist did not examine the body of Glyndwr Michael. Instead, Sir Bernard offered his opinion, as was his habit, *de haut en bas*, and stuck to it, come hell or high water.

Spilsbury was also wrong in his complacent avowal that Spain contained no able pathologists. If the body was examined by a country doctor, the deception might pass unnoticed; but it was intended that the body and its documents should pass into German hands: there was at least one highly trained pathologist in Spain working for German intelligence who would be able to spot the imposture as fast as Spilsbury himself, and probably faster. So far from offering certainty, Sir Bernard's opinion, accepted by Montagu, represented an enormous gamble. If it failed, then the victims of Spilsburyism could number in their thousands.

Montagu would later claim that the body used in the deception had 'died from pneumonia after exposure'; that his relatives had been contacted and told that the body was needed for a 'really worthwhile purpose'; and that permission was duly obtained 'on condition that I should never let it be known whose corpse it was'. None of this was true. Montagu and Cholmondeley certainly made 'feverish enquiries into his past and about his relatives', but only to ensure that Glyndwr Michael had no past to speak of, and no relatives likely to cause problems by asking questions. Sarah was dead. Michael had two siblings, and two half-siblings, all still living in the Welsh valleys. Apparently they had not looked after him in life; there was little chance they would care more for him after death. Anyway, they were not consulted. Indeed, they were not even located. In a draft, unpublished manuscript, Montagu wrote: 'The most careful possible enquiries, made even more carefully than usual in view of our proposals, failed to reveal any relative.' Montagu never did reveal Glyndwr Michael's identity. However, he could not remove his name from the official record, and he left personal papers which also identify him. In one letter, Montagu referred to Glyndwr Michael as 'a ne'er do well, and his relatives were not much better . . . the actual person did nothing for anyone ever – only his body did good after he was dead.' It was true that Michael's life had been a short and unhappy one: he had never done well, but then, he had never had much of an opportunity. Posthumously, the ne'er do well was about to do very well indeed.

Bentley Purchase warned that time was of the essence. The
corpse could not be frozen solid to arrest decay entirely, since
fluids in the body expand as they turn to ice, damaging fragile
soft tissue, which would be only too evident once the body
was defrosted. The mortuary at St Pancras had one 'extra-cold
refrigerator' which could be set at four degrees centigrade, cold
enough to retard decomposition substantially, but not so cold as
to prevent it entirely. The body of Glyndwr Michael was already
beginning to rot. If the corpse was to be of any use, warned
Purchase, it 'would have to be used within three months'.

Before the operation could be formally launched, it needed a
new codename. Trojan Horse had been acceptable as the initial
title, but if any German agent were to stumble across it, the
implication of some sort of hoax would be glaringly obvious.
Codenames were compiled by the Inter-Services Security
Board, covering almost every aspect of the war: nations, cities,
plans, locations, military units, military operations, diplomatic
meetings, places, individuals and spies were all disguised
under false names. In theory these codewords were neutral
and indecipherable, a shorthand for those in the picture, and
deliberately meaningless to those outside it. Random lists of
codenames were issued in alphabetical blocks of ten words, and
then selected by chance as needed; six months after it became
defunct, a codeword could be reassigned and reused, a deliberate
ploy to muddy the waters.

Churchill had a clearly defined policy on choosing codewords for major operations: 'They ought not to be given names
of a frivolous character such as "Bunnyhug" and "Ballyhoo",'
the Prime Minister decreed. 'Intelligent thought will already
supply an unlimited number of well-sounding names that do
not suggest the character of the operation and do not enable
some widow or mother to say that her son was killed in an
operation called "Bunnyhug" or "Ballyhoo".'

However, the rule requiring that codewords be devoid of
meaning was routinely ignored, by all sides, throughout the

war, for spies found the temptation to invent joking and hinting titles for their most secret projects almost irresistible. Agent 'Tate' was so-called because he looked like the music-hall performer Harry Tate; the criminal Eddie Chapman was named 'Zigzag', since no one could be certain which way he might turn; Stalin, meaning 'man of steel', was awarded the codename 'Glyptic', meaning 'an image carved from stone'. The Germans were even more culpable in this respect. The Nazis' long-range radar system was named 'Heimdall' after the Norse god with the power to see great distances; the planned invasion of Britain was codenamed 'Sealion' – a most unsubtle reference to the lions on the royal coats of arms, and the planned seaborne attack.

Montagu was particularly scathing of the Abwehr's 'stupidity' in selecting such revealing codewords: the codename for Britain, he pointed out, was 'Golfplatz', meaning golf course, while America was 'Samland', a reference to Uncle Sam. Montagu now broke his own rule that codenames be chosen so that 'no deductions could be made from them', and selected a name that had been used for a mine-laying operation in 1941, and was now up for grabs.

Plan Trojan Horse became 'Operation Mincemeat'. There was nothing haphazard about the choice. All the talk of corpses was having an effect, and Montagu's 'sense of humour having by this time become somewhat macabre', a codeword that signified dead meat seemed only too apt, and a 'good omen'. There was no danger of any grieving mother complaining that her dead son had been deployed under a frivolous and tasteless codeword because, as the planners knew very well, in the case of Glyndwr Michael, there was no one to grieve.

Even before Bentley Purchase had completed his inquest, Cholmondeley and Montagu set to work, drawing up a formal proposal to put to the intelligence chiefs. On 4 February, a week after the death of Michael and on the very day Purchase completed his inquest, they presented a draft of Operation Mincemeat to the Twenty Committee: 'This operation is proposed in view of the fact that the enemy will almost certainly get information of the preparation of any assault mounted in North Africa and will try to find out its target.'

The plan envisaged dropping the dead body, with fake documents, from a plane, to give the impression that 'a courier carrying important "hand of officer" documents was en route for Algiers in an aircraft which crashed'. The overall scheme should not only divert the Germans from the real target, but portray the real target as a 'cover target', a mere decoy. This was a brilliant piece of double bluff, for it would ensure that when the Germans found out about genuine preparations to attack Sicily, as they must, they would assume this was part of the deception plan. Sicily could not be left out of the equation altogether, for as Cholmondeley and Montagu pointed out, if 'the real target is omitted from both the "operation plan" and the "cover plan" the Germans will almost certainly suspect, as not only is Sicily a very possible target, but the Germans are believed already to anticipate it as a possible target'. Since 'the Germans will be looking with care for our cover plan as well as our real plan', Operation Mincemeat would feed them both a false real plan, and a false cover plan – which would actually be the real plan.

The outline did not go into specifics as to how this misinformation would be put across, nor where the body would be dropped, and warned that, once launched, it could not be delayed: 'The body must be dropped within twenty-four hours of its being removed from its present place in London. The flight, once laid on, must not be cancelled or postponed.' The Twenty Committee pondered only briefly, before issuing a flurry of requests to the representatives of the different services. The Air Ministry should investigate finding a suitable plane, preferably one used by SOE; the draft plan should be shown to the intelligence chiefs of the Army, Navy and RAF; Colonel Johnnie Bevan of the London Controlling Section should be asked for his approval; the Admiralty should 'find out a suitable position for dropping the body'; and the War Office should look 'into the question of providing the body with a name and necessary papers'. The naval attaché in Madrid, Captain Alan Hillgarth, should be informed of the plan so that 'he will be able to cope with any unforeseen circumstances'.

Montagu and Cholmondeley were instructed to 'continue with preparations to give MINCEMEAT his necessary clothes, papers, letters, etc. etc.'. Out of the officially nameless corpse in the mortuary they must conjure up a living person, with a new name, a personality, and a past. Operation Mincemeat began as fiction, a plot twist in a long-forgotten novel, picked up by another novelist, and approved by a committee presided over by yet another novelist. Now it was the turn of the spies to take the reality of a dead Welsh tramp, make him into a fiction, and so change reality.

A Novel Approach

Montagu and Cholmondeley had spent much of the previous three years nurturing, moulding and deploying spies who did not exist. The Twenty Committee and Section B1A of MI5 had turned the playing of double agents into an art form, but as the Double Cross System developed and expanded, more and more of the agents reporting back to Germany were purely fictional: Agent A (real) would notionally employ Agent B (unreal), who would in turn recruit other agents, C to Z (all equally imaginary). Juan Pujol García, Agent 'Garbo', the most famous double agent of them all, was eventually equipped with no fewer than twenty-seven sub-agents, each with a distinct character, friends, jobs, tastes, homes and lovers. Garbo's 'active and well-distributed team of imaginary assistants' were a motley lot, including a Welsh Aryan supremacist, a communist, a Greek waiter, a wealthy Venezuelan student, a disaffected South African serviceman and several crooks. In the words of John Masterman, the thriller-writing chairman of the Twenty Committee, 'The one-man band of Lisbon developed into an orchestra, and an orchestra which played a more and more ambitious programme.' Graham Greene, a wartime intelligence officer in West Africa, based his novel *Our Man in Havana*, about a spy who invents an entire network of bogus informants, on the Garbo story.

Masterman, writing after the war, declared that 'for deception,

"notional" or imaginary agents were on the whole preferable'
to living ones. Real agents tended to become truculent and
demanding; they needed feeding, pampering, and paying. An
imaginary agent, however, was infinitely pliable, and willing
to do the bidding of his German handlers at once, and without
question: 'The Germans could seldom resist such a fly if it was
accurately and skilfully cast,' wrote Masterman, himself a dab
hand with a fly-fishing rod.

Maintaining a small army of fake people needed concerted
attention to detail. 'How difficult it was,' wrote Montagu, 'to
remember the characteristics and life pattern of each one of a
mass of completely non-existent notional sub-agents.' These
imaginary individuals had to suffer all the vagaries of normal
life, such as getting ill, celebrating birthdays, and running out
of money. They had to remain perfectly consistent in their
behaviour, attitudes and emotions. As Montagu put it, the
imaginary agent 'must *never* step out of character'. The network
of fake agents enabled British intelligence to supply the Germans
with a steady stream of untruths and half-truths, and it lulled the
Abwehr into believing it had a large and efficient espionage
network in Britain, when it had nothing of the sort.

Creating a personality to go with the corpse in the St Pancras
morgue would require imaginative effort on an even greater
scale. In his novel *The Case of the Four Friends*, Masterman's
sleuth, Ernest Brendel, observes that the key to detective
work is anticipating the actions of the criminal: 'To work out
the crime before it is committed, to foresee how it will be
arranged, and then to prevent it! That's a triumph indeed.'
With Masterman's help, Cholmondeley and Montagu would
lay out the clues to a life that had never happened, and frame a
new death for a dead man.

The fictitious agents so far invented by the Double Cross
Team all spoke for themselves, or rather through others, in
wireless messages and letters to their handlers, but they were
never seen. In the case of Operation Mincemeat, the fraudulent

individual could communicate only through the clothes on his back, the contents of his pockets and, most importantly, the letters in his possession. He would carry official typed letters to convey the core deception, but also handwritten personal letters, to put across his personality. 'The more real he appeared, the more convincing the whole affair would be,' reflected Montagu, since 'every little detail would be studied by the Germans'.

The information he carried would have to be credible, but also legible. 'Would the ink of the manuscript letters, and the signatures on the others, not run so as to make the documents illegible?' Montagu wondered. Waterproof ink might be used, but that would 'give the game away'. They turned to MI5's scientists, and numerous tests were carried out using different inks and typewriters, and then immersing the letters in sea water for varying periods to test the effects. The results were encouraging: 'Many inks on a freshly written letter will run at once if the surface is wetted. On the other hand, a lot of quite usual inks, if thoroughly dried, will stand a fair amount of wetting even if exposed directly to the water. When a document is inside an envelope, or inside a wallet which is itself inside a pocket, well dried inks of some quite normal types will often remain legible for a surprising length of time – quite long enough for our purpose.'

The precise form of the deception would be decided in time: first they needed to create a credible courier.

It is no accident that both Montagu and Cholmondeley were both enthusiastic novel-readers. The greatest writers of spy fiction have, in almost every case, worked in intelligence before turning to writing. Somerset Maugham, John Buchan, Ian Fleming, Graham Greene, John le Carré: all had experienced the world of espionage at first hand. For the task of the spy is not so very different from that of the novelist: to create an imaginary, credible world, and then lure others into it, by words and artifice.

As if constructing a character in a novel, Montagu and

Cholmondeley, with the help of Joan Saunders in Section 17M, set about creating a personality with which to clothe their dead body. Hour after hour, in the Admiralty basement, they discussed and refined this imaginary person, his likes and dislikes, his habits and hobbies, his talents and weaknesses. In the evening, they repaired to the Gargoyle, a glamorous Soho club of which Montagu was a member, to continue the odd process of creating a man from scratch. The project reflected all the possibilities and pitfalls of fiction: if they painted his personality too brightly, or were inconsistent in the portrait, then the Germans would surely detect a hoax. But if the enemy could be made to believe in this British officer, then they were that much more likely to credit the documents he carried. Eventually, they came to believe in him themselves. 'We talked about him until we did feel that he was an old friend,' wrote Montagu. 'He became completely real to us.' They gave him a middle name, a nicotine habit, and a place of birth. They gave him a hometown, a rank, a regiment and a love of fishing. He would be furnished with a watch, a bank manager, a solicitor and cufflinks. They gave him all the things that Glyndwr Michael had lacked in his luckless life, including a supportive family, money, friends, and love.

But first he needed a name and, more importantly, a uniform. It was originally intended that the dropped body should appear to be that of an army officer ferrying important messages to the top brass in North Africa. An army officer could wear battledress, normal combat uniform, rather than a formal fitted uniform. Army officers did not carry identity cards with photographs when travelling outside England, which obviated the need to obtain a mugshot of Glyndwr Michael for a fake card. The Director of Military Intelligence, however, pointed out that if the courier were an army officer, then the discovery of the body would have to be reported to the military attaché in Madrid, and the information passed from there to London, increasing the number of people in the know, and the danger of a leak.

Since the idea had originated in Naval Intelligence, it was more sensible to make him a naval officer, thus keeping the secret within naval circles. A naval officer, however, would be unlikely to carry documents relating to the planned invasion, and such officers always travelled in full naval 'display' uniform, complete with braid and badges of rank on the sleeve. The idea of getting the corpse measured up by a tailor was too ghoulish (and too dangerous) to contemplate. The Secret Service contained men of varied talents and occupations, but no gentlemen's outfitters with experience of dressing the dead.

After much discussion, it was decided that the body would be dressed as a Royal Marine, the corps which forms the amphibious infantry of the Royal Navy. Marines always travelled in battledress, made up of beret or cap, khaki blouse and trousers, gaiters and boots. This uniform came in standard sizes.

Since the Marines, unlike the Army, travelled with photographic identity cards, one of these would have to be faked. This raised an additional problem. Although there were thousands of British Army officers currently serving, the number of Royal Marines officers was comparatively small, and their names appeared on the Navy List, of which German intelligence undoubtedly possessed a copy. One of these would need to 'lend' his name to the dead body.

Casting his eye down the list of serving naval officers, Montagu noticed a large block of men with the surname Martin. No fewer than nine of these were Royal Marines, eight lieutenants, and one captain, who had been promoted to acting major in 1941. The ferrying of important documents would be entrusted to a fairly senior officer, so Captain William Hynd Norrie Martin was unknowingly pressganged into the job. The real Norrie Martin was commissioned in 1927, becoming one of the Fleet Air Arm's best pilots. In 1943 he was instructing British aircrew at Quonset Point, Rhode Island, and thus unlikely to get wind of what was being done with his name. By pure coincidence, the real Martin had served aboard the aircraft carrier *Hermes*, which was sunk by the Japanese in April 1942, with the loss of more than 300 men. A death notice for the fake William Martin would need to be posted in the British press: the Germans would believe this referred to the body carrying the documents, but the real Major Martin's friends and colleagues would probably assume he had died in the sinking of the *Hermes*, with his death only belatedly confirmed.

Captain William 'Bill' Martin was duly issued with identity card number 148228 by the Admiralty. He was made four years younger than Glyndwr Michael, but Cardiff was chosen as his place of birth, just ten miles from Michael's birthplace in Aberbargoed. The card assigned Martin to 'Combined Operations', the force set up to harass the Germans by combined Navy and Army operations, and directed by Lord Louis Mountbatten. The identity card was suspiciously shiny, so as an added precaution it was endorsed 'issued in lieu of No. 09650 lost'. This was Montagu's own identity card number, to ensure that anyone investigating this non-existent officer with the fake identity card would eventually come to him. Losing an identity card was a serious lapse in wartime Britain, but as well as explaining its newness, the replacement card provided the first plank in the personality of Bill Martin: he was accident-prone. Montagu signed the card, the first of many occasions when he would stand in for Bill Martin.

All that was needed to complete the card was a photograph. Glyndwr Michael had never had a passport or any other form of photographic identity card, and trying to obtain a recent photograph, if such a thing existed, would have involved contacting the Michael family. Montagu and Cholmondeley repaired to the St Pancras mortuary with a camera and tape measure. While Cholmondeley measured Glyndwr for the Royal Marines battledress and boots, Montagu prepared him for his photograph. It was the first time they had seen the body: the face seemed thin and sickly, rather different from the strapping young warrior they had already framed in their minds. Still, as

Montagu remarked: 'He does not have to look like an officer
– only like a staff officer', and these were seldom the most
impressive physical specimens.

This was possibly the first time Glyndwr Michael had ever
been photographed. But the morbid modelling session was a
'complete failure'. After only a few days, the eyes of a corpse in
cold storage begin to sink into the skull, and the facial muscles
start to sag. It is simply impossible to take a photograph of the
face of a dead person that looks anything other than entirely,
unmistakably dead. Michael had been emaciated before he died.
Every day he spent in the St Pancras mortuary, he looked slightly
deader. No matter at what angle he was photographed, and
under what light, the newly named William Martin resolutely
refused to come alive for the camera.

Back in the office, and in the street, Montagu and
Cholmondeley surreptitiously scanned the faces of friends and
strangers alike, in the hope of spotting someone who might
stand in as Bill Martin's double. Glyndwr Michael's face was
unremarkable, with greying hair, thinning in front. It was not,
thought Montagu, an 'appearance that would have singled
him out in a crowd'. Yet finding someone who even vaguely
resembled him was proving extraordinarily difficult.

While Montagu searched for the right face, 'rudely staring
at anyone with whom we came into contact', Cholmondeley
went clothes shopping. Glyndwr Michael had been tall and thin,
'almost the same build' as Cholmondeley himself. Cholmondeley
first bought braces, gaiters, and standard issue military boots, size
12. Then, having obtained permission from Colonel Neville of
the Royal Marines, he presented himself at Gieves, the military
tailors in Piccadilly, to be fitted for a Royal Marines battledress,
complete with appropriate badges of rank, Royal Marines flashes
and the badge flashes of Combined Operations. The uniform
was finished off with a trench coat and beret. The clothes would
need the patina of wear, so Cholmondeley climbed into the
uniform, and wore it every day for the next three months.

Underwear was a more ticklish problem. Cholmondeley, understandably, was unwilling to surrender his own, since good underwear was hard to come by in rationed, wartime Britain. They consulted John Masterman, Oxford academic and chairman of the Twenty Committee, who came up with a scholarly solution that was also personally satisfying. 'The difficulty of obtaining underclothes, owing to the system of coupon rationing,' wrote Masterman, 'was overcome by the acceptance of a gift of thick underwear from the wardrobe of the late Warden of New College, Oxford.' Major Martin would be kitted out with the flannel vest and underpants of none other than H. A. L. Fisher, the distinguished Oxford historian and former President of the Board of Education in Lloyd George's Cabinet. John Masterman and Herbert Fisher had both taught history at Oxford in the 1920s, and had long enjoyed a fierce academic rivalry. Fisher was a figure of ponderous grandeur and gravity who ran New College, according to one colleague, as 'one enormous mausoleum'. Masterman considered him long-winded and pompous. Fisher had been run over and killed by a lorry after attending a tribunal examining the appeals of conscientious objectors, of which he was chairman. The obituaries paid resounding tribute to his intellectual and academic stature, which nettled Masterman. Putting the great man's underclothes on a dead body and floating it into German hands was just the sort of joke that appealed to his odd sense of humour. Masterman described the underwear as a 'gift'; it seems far more likely that he simply arranged for the dead don's drawers to be pressed into war service.

Montagu and Cholmondeley were both, in different ways, adapting themselves to the part of Bill Martin. Montagu had forged his signature. Cholmondeley was wearing his clothes. Slowly, the personality of Major Martin was coming into focus, a character who would have to be revealed by whatever was in his wallet, pockets and briefcase. Martin, it was decided, was the adored son of an upper-middle-class family from Wales. (His Welshness was virtually the only concession to Glyndwr Michael's real identity.)

He was a Roman Catholic. Catholic countries were believed to be averse to surgical autopsies for religious reasons, and this traditional reluctance would presumably be compounded if the body was thought to be that of a co-religionist.

The William Martin they conjured up was clever, even 'brilliant', industrious but forgetful, and inclined to the grand gesture. He liked a good time, enjoyed the theatre and dancing, and spent more than he had, relying on his father to bail him out. His mother Antonia had died some years earlier. They began to ink in his past. He had been educated, they decided, at public school and university. He was a secret writer of considerable promise, though he had never published anything. After university, he had retired to the country to write, listen to music, and to fish. He was something of a loner. With the outbreak of war, he had signed up with the Royal Marines, but found himself consigned to an office, which he disliked. 'Keen for more active and dangerous work,' he had escaped by switching to the Commandos, and had distinguished himself by his aptitude for technical matters, notably the mechanics of landing craft. He had predicted that the Dieppe raid would be a disaster, and he had been right. Martin was, they concluded, 'a thoroughly good chap', romantic and dashing, but also somewhat feckless, unpunctual, and extravagant.

The first witness to Martin's fictional character was his bank manager. Montagu approached Ernest Whitley Jones, joint general manager of Lloyds Bank, and asked him if he would be prepared to write an angry letter about an overdraft that did not exist, to a client who was also imaginary – a request that is surely unique in the annals of British banking. Whitley Jones was, perhaps predictably, a cautious man. It was not, he pointed out, normal practice for the general manager of the bank's head office to perform such a mundane task. But when Montagu explained that he would rather not 'bring in' anyone else, the manager relented. Such a letter 'could sometimes come from head office', he said, 'especially when the general manager was the personal friend of the father of a young customer whose extravagance needs some check and the father does not want to nag his son'.

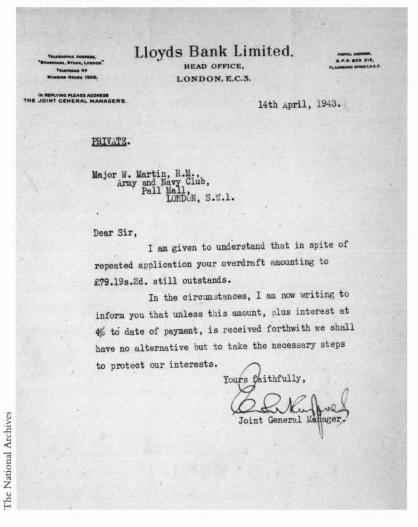

Lloyds Bank Limited.

HEAD OFFICE,

LONDON, E.C.3.

TELEGRAPHIC ADDRESS.
"BRANCHAGE, STOCK, LONDON."
TELEPHONE Nº
MANSION HOUSE 1500.

POSTAL ADDRESS.
G. P. O. BOX 215,
71, LOMBARD STREET, E.C.3.

IN REPLYING PLEASE ADDRESS
THE JOINT GENERAL MANAGERS.

14th April, 1943.

PRIVATE.

Major W. Martin, R.M.,
     Army and Navy Club,
          Pall Mall,
               LONDON, S.W.1.

Dear Sir,

          I am given to understand that in spite of
repeated application your overdraft amounting to
£79.19s.2d. still outstands.

          In the circumstances, I am now writing to
inform you that unless this amount, plus interest at
4% to date of payment, is received forthwith we shall
have no alternative but to take the necessary steps
to protect our interests.

                              Yours faithfully,

                              Joint General Manager.

The dunning letter was addressed to Major Martin at the Army and Navy Club, in Pall Mall. This, it was decided, would be Martin's home when in 'town'. Cholmondeley obtained a bill from the club, made out to Major Martin.

Having imagined Martin's father, Montagu and Cholmondeley now decided this anxious parent deserved a larger part in the unfolding drama. Enter John G. Martin, paterfamilias, 'a father of the old school' in Montagu's words, who may well have been modelled on his own father: affectionate, but formal and controlling. The letter itself was probably written by Cyril Mills, a colleague in MI5. Mills, the son of the circus impresario Bertram Mills, had taken over the circus business after his father's death in 1938, and was now one of the key operatives in the Double Cross Team. Mills knew how to put on an impressive show. The resulting letter, pompous and pedantic as only an Edwardian father could be, was 'a brilliant tour de force'.

Tel. No. 98

Black Lion Hotel
Mold
N. Wales
13th April 1943

My Dear William,

I cannot say that this hotel is any longer as comfortable as I remember it to have been in pre-war days. I am, however, staying here as the only alternative to imposing myself once more upon your aunt whose depleted staff & strict regard for fuel economy (which I agree to be necessary in wartime) has made the house almost uninhabitable to a guest, at least one of my age. I propose to be in Town for the nights of 20th & 21st of April when no doubt we shall have an opportunity to meet. I enclose the copy of a letter which I have written to Gwatkin of McKenna's about your affairs. You will see that I have asked him to lunch with me at the Carlton Grill (which I understand still to be open) at a quarter to one on Wednesday the 21st. I should be glad if you would make it possible to join us. We shall not however wait luncheon for you, so I trust that, if you are able to come, you will make a point of being punctual.

Your cousin Priscilla has asked to be remembered to you. She has grown into a sensible girl though I cannot say that her work for the Land Army has done much to improve her looks. In that respect I am afraid that she will take after her father's side of the family.

Your affectionate
Father

Cholmondeley and Montagu were now enjoying themselves, warming to the task of invention, the depth of detail, the odd plot twists: the exasperated father sorting out his son's financial affairs, resentful of his sister-in-law's rule over the family house and having to stay in a second-class hotel; niece Priscilla, sensible but chunky, with, it was implied, a slight crush on her older cousin Bill; the hints of wartime deprivation and rationing; the artful ink splodge on the first page. Montagu's acidulous sense of humour ran through every word of the forgeries.

While the larger themes of Martin's life were being sketched out, Cholmondeley also began to gather the smaller items that a wartime officer might carry in his pockets and wallet, individually unimportant but vital corroborative detail. In modern spy parlance, this is known as 'wallet litter', the little things everyone accumulates that describe who we are, and where we have been. Martin's pocket litter would include a book of stamps, two used; a silver cross on a neck chain and a St Christopher's medallion, a pencil stub, keys, a packet of Player's Navy Cut cigarettes (the traditional Navy smoke), matches, and a used twopenny bus ticket. In his wallet they inserted a pass for Combined Operations HQ which had expired, as further evidence of his lackadaisical attitude to security. The members of Section 17M, all of whom were party to the secret, added their own refinements. There was much discussion over exactly which wartime nightclub Bill might favour. Margery Boxall, Montagu's secretary, obtained an invitation to the Cabaret Club, a swinging London nightclub, as proof of Martin's taste for the high life. To this was added a small fragment of a torn letter, written to Bill from an address in Perthshire, relaying some snippet of romantic gossip: '. . . at the last moment – which was the more to be regretted since he had scarcely ever seen her before. Still, as I told him at the time . . .' The handwriting is that of John Masterman.

Two identity discs, stamped 'Major W. Martin, R.M., R/C'

(Roman Catholic), were attached to the braces that would hold

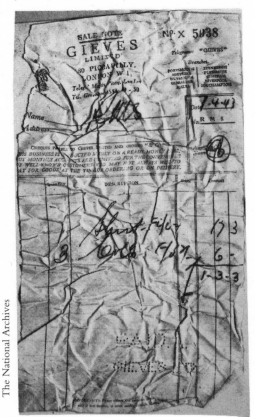

the dead man's trousers up. A bill for shirts from Gieves, paid in cash, was crumpled up in preparation for stuffing into a pocket. Bill Martin would be carrying cash on his final journey: one £5 note, three £1 notes, and some loose change. The banknote numbers were carefully noted. As with all money that might be passed to, or received from, the enemy, the currency was carefully tracked in case it might reappear somewhere significant. If the money disappeared after the body arrived in Spain, it would at least prove that the clothes had been searched.

Nothing was left to chance. Everything the body wore or carried was minutely inspected to ensure that it added to the story, on the assumption that the Germans would make every 'effort to find a flaw in Major Martin's make-up'. And yet something was missing from Martin's life. It was Joan Saunders who pointed it out: he had no love life. Bill Martin must be made to fall in love. 'We decided that a "marriage would be arranged" between Bill Martin and some girl just before he was sent abroad,' wrote Montagu. Though he referred nonchalantly to 'some girl', Montagu already had a girl firmly in mind.

Pam

Jean Leslie was just eighteen in 1941 when she joined the counterintelligence and double-agent section of MI5. Jean was beautiful, in a most English way, with alabaster skin and wavy chestnut hair. She had left school at seventeen, and then been educated by her upper-class parents in the traditional ladylike skills of typing, secretarial work and attending debutante parties. But she was far cleverer than this might suggest. She was too clever, from her widowed mother's point of view. 'What on earth are we going to do with Jean?' she worried. A family friend suggested that there might be a suitable job in the War Office. A few weeks later, Jean had found herself signing the Official Secrets Act, and then plunged into the byzantine business of MI5's top-secret paperwork. Initially, she worked in the section B1B, which gathered, filed and analysed Ultra decrypts, Abwehr messages and other intelligence to be used in running the double agents of the Double Cross System. She loved it.

The secretarial unit was headed by a sharp-tongued dragon named Hester Leggett, who demanded absolute obedience and perfect efficiency among her 'girls'. Jean's job was to sort through the 'yellow perils', yellow carbon copies of interrogations from Camp 020, the wartime internment centre in Richmond, near London, where all enemy spies were grilled. She would read the accounts given by the captured spies, and try to spot anything that required the attention of her senior (male) colleagues. It was Jean Leslie who identified the 'glaring inconsistencies' in the confession of one Johannes de Graaf, a Belgian agent. De Graaf was subsequently found to be playing a triple game. Jean was delighted with herself; and then distraught, when it appeared that De Graaf would face execution.

The all-female secretarial team was known as 'The Beavers', and the most eager beaver of all was young Jean Leslie. 'I was frightfully willing to help, always. I ran everywhere. I was so keen to please.' Hester Leggett, rather cruelly nicknamed 'The Spin', for spinster, repeatedly reprimanded her for sprinting through the hushed offices in St James's Street. 'Don't run, Miss Leslie!'

This beautiful young woman who ran everywhere had caught the eye of Ewen Montagu. Jean could not fail to notice how the friendly and undoubtedly handsome older officer seemed to pay her special attention. 'In fact, he was trailing me a bit. He was rather smitten.' Indeed he was: Montagu's writings, official and unofficial, describe her variously as 'charming', 'very attractive', and other admiring adjectives.

In mid-February, the hunt began for a suitable mate for Major Martin. 'The more attractive girls in our various offices' were asked to supply photographs for use in an identity parade. Montagu made a point of asking Miss Leslie if she would oblige. 'I think he had every intention of getting one off me somehow.' That evening, Jean, keen as ever and rather flattered by the attention, ransacked her dressing-room drawer for a recent photograph. With the bombing of London, Mrs Leslie had moved out of the capital, to a borrowed house on the Thames near Dorchester in Oxfordshire, where her daughter spent weekends. A few weeks earlier, she had gone swimming in the river at Wittenham Clumps with Tony, a Grenadier Guard on leave who, like Montagu, was smitten, and about to return to the war. 'The swimming there was horrible', but the occasion had been a happy one. Tony had taken a photograph, which he sent to her afterwards. In it, Jean has just emerged from the water in a patterned one-piece swimsuit, with towel held demurely, hair windswept, and a sweet grin on her face. In 1940s England, the image was not just attractive, but very nearly saucy, and both Jean Leslie and Ewen Montagu knew it.

The request for photographs had garnered 'quite a collection'. It was no accident that the Naval Intelligence Department contained a high ratio of particularly attractive women. 'Uncle John gave specific orders that only the prettiest girls should be employed, on the theory that then they would be less likely to boast to their boyfriends about the secret work they were doing.' Some of Montagu's female colleagues in Room 13 were distinctly put out when he selected a photograph of a woman from another department: 'We were all rather jealous,' recalled Patricia Trehearne, one of his assistants. But there was never any doubt who would win this particular beauty contest. Jean's photograph was added to the growing pile of Martin's possessions, and a new and central character was worked into the unfolding plot: this was 'Pam', his new fiancée, a vivacious young woman working in a government office, who was excitable, pretty, gentle and really quite dim. It was decided that Bill had met Pam just five weeks earlier, and had proposed to her after a whirlwind romance, buying a large and expensive diamond ring for the purpose. John Martin, his father, did not approve, suspecting Pam might be something of a gold digger. No date for the wedding had been set. Here was a typical wartime romance: sudden, thrilling and, as matters would shortly turn out, doomed.

Jean Leslie had sufficient security clearance to be partially inducted into the secret. Montagu told her that the photograph depicted a fictitious fiancée, as part of a deception plan. 'I knew it was going to be planted on a body, but I didn't know where.' Charles Cholmondeley later took Jean aside and asked her in serious tones: 'Has anybody else got that photograph? If so, you should ask for it back. If you gave it to someone and they were going out on the second front and were captured and this photograph was discovered in his possession, the consequences could be very serious.' Jean contacted Tony, the Grenadier Guard, and told him to destroy any other copies of the photograph. Hurt, Tony complied. Montagu also took Jean aside, and impressed upon her the need for absolute secrecy. Then he asked her out to dinner. She accepted.

Montagu adored his wife, Iris. 'I never realised how lonely and really empty life could be just because you weren't there,' he wrote once. His wartime letters are passionate, peppered with rude jokes, poems and stories, and haunted by the fear that they might be parted for ever: 'How ultra-happy our life was before this bloody business started . . . Bugger Hitler.' Whenever Iris's letters were delayed from New York, he would half-joke: 'You must have gone off with an American.' But he longed for female company. 'I am always the gooseberry,' he complained. He declined an invitation to a dance, although he longed to go: 'It was a question of whether there was a girl I could take, I literally couldn't think of anyone, not even anyone to try.' Jean Leslie was single, extremely pretty, and good company. Ewen did not try to conceal his first date with Jean from his wife, but he did not dwell on it either. 'I took a girl from the office to Hungaria [a restaurant] and had dinner and danced. She is an attractive child.'

Bill would need love letters to go with his photograph of Pam. The job of drafting these fell to Hester Leggett, 'The Spin', the most senior woman in the department. Jean remembered her as 'skinny and embittered'. Hester Leggett was certainly fierce and demanding. She never married, and she devoted herself utterly to the job of marshalling a huge quantity of secret paperwork. But into Pam's love letters, she poured every ounce of pathos and emotion she could muster. These letters may have been the closest Hester Leggett ever came to romance: chattering pastiches of a young woman madly in love, and with little time for grammar.

The Manor House
Ogbourne St George
Marlborough, Wiltshire
Telephone Ogbourne St George 242 *Sunday 18th*

I do think dearest that seeing people like you off at railway stations is one of the poorer forms of sport. A train going out can leave a howling great gap in ones [sic] life & one had to try madly - & quite in vain – to fill it with all the things one used to enjoy a short five weeks ago. That lovely golden day we spent together oh! I know it has been said before, but if only time could stand still for just a minute – But that line of thought is too pointless. Pull your socks up Pam & don't be a silly little fool.

Your letter made me feel slightly better – but I shall get horribly conceited if you go on saying things like that about me – they're utterly unlike ME, as I'm afraid you'll soon find out. Here I am for the weekend in this divine place with Mummy & Jane being too sweet and understanding the whole time, bored beyond words & panting for Monday so that I can get back to the old grindstone again. What an idiotic waste!

Bill darling, do let me know as soon as you get fixed & can make some more plans, & don't please let them send you off into the blue the horrible way they do nowadays — now that we've found each other out of the whole world, I don't think I could bear it.

All my love, Pam

The headed notepaper (obtained from Montagu's brother-in-law) was used on the basis that 'no German could resist the "Englishness"' of such an address. The next letter, notionally dated three days later, was on plain paper, written by 'Pam' in a frantic rush as her boss, 'The Bloodhound', threatened to return from lunch at any moment. As the official report on Operation Mincemeat acknowledged, Hester Leggett's effort 'achieved the thrill and pathos of a war engagement with great success'.

Office
Wednesday 21st

The Bloodhound has left his kennel for half an hour so here I am scribbling nonsense to you again. Your letter came this morning just as I was dashing out — madly late as usual! You do write such heavenly ones. But what are these horrible dark hints you're throwing out about being sent off somewhere — of course I won't say a word to anyone — I never do when you tell me things, but it's not abroad is it? Because I won't have it, I WON'T, tell them so from me. Darling, why did we go and meet in the middle of a war, such a silly thing for anybody to do — if it weren't for the war we might have been nearly married by now, going round together choosing curtains etc. And I wouldn't be sitting in a dreary Government office typing idiotic minutes all day long — I know the futile work I do doesn't make the war one minute shorter —

Dearest Bill, I'm so thrilled with my ring — scandalously extravagant — you know how I adore diamonds — I simply can't stop looking at it.

I'm going to a rather dreary dance tonight with Jock & Hazel, I think they've got some other man coming. You know what their friends always turn out to be like, he'll have the sweetest little Adam's apple & the shiniest bald head! How beastly and ungrateful of me, but it isn't really that – you know – don't you?

Look darling, I've got next Sunday & Monday off for Easter. I shall go home for it, of course, <u>do</u> come too if you possibly can, or even if you can't get away from London I'll dash up and we'll have an evening of gaiety – (by the way Aunt Marian said to bring you to dinner next time I was up, but I think that might wait?)

Here comes the Bloodhound, masses of love & a kiss from Pam

Hester Leggett ended the second letter with a flourish, as Pam's looping, girlish handwriting collapses into a hasty scrawl.

For good measure, Montagu and Cholmondeley added to Martin's wallet a bill for an engagement ring from S. J. Phillips of New Bond Street, for a whopping £53 0s. 6d. The ring was engraved 'P. L. from W. M. 14.4.43'.

Two more letters rounded off Martin's personal cache. The first was from his solicitor, F. A. S. Gwatkin, of McKenna & Co., referring to his will and tax affairs: 'We will insert the legacy of £50 to your batman,' wrote Mr Gwatkin, who regretted that he could not yet complete Martin's tax return for 1941/42: 'We cannot find that we have ever had these particulars and shall, therefore, be grateful if you will let us have them.' On top of everything else, Major Martin's tax return was overdue. Finally there was another letter from John Martin, this time a copy of a letter to the family solicitor, discussing the terms of his son's marriage settlement and insisting that 'since the wife's family will not be contributing to the settlement I do not think it proper that they should preserve, after William's death, a life interest in the funds which I am providing. I should agree to this course only were there children of the marriage.'

Montagu and Cholmondeley were delighted with the plot they had created, with its looming premonition of disaster, a dashing but flawed hero, a sexy, faintly dippy, heroine and a rich cast of comic supporting characters: The Bloodhound, Father, Fat Priscilla, and Whitley Jones the Bank Manager. But from a distance of nearly seventy years, the plot seems almost hackneyed. The sense of impending doom, and Pam's 'foreboding', are thumpingly melodramatic. 'Bill darling, don't please let them send you off into the blue the horrible way they do . . .'

Admiral John Godfrey was strict on the danger of 'overcooking' an espionage ruse. 'The nearer the approach to the "thriller" type of intelligence the more must both the giver, and the recipient, be on their guard. Elegant trimmings should have no place in the intelligence officer's vocabulary. On the other hand the man who cannot tell a good story is a dull dog.'

By this time, Godfrey was no longer on hand to offer his sage judgement, for in the midst of Operation Mincemeat, Montagu and Cholmondeley had lost their mentor. The admiral's sandpaper personality had finally proven too much for his superiors: he was removed from the Naval Intelligence Department, despatched to naval command in India, and replaced by Commodore (later Rear Admiral) Edmund Rushbrooke, an able administrator but an officer with little of Godfrey's fire and flair. 'He is very old and lacking in energy after that human dynamo,' wrote Montagu, whose assessment of Godfrey was equally blunt: 'He was the world's prize shit, but a genius . . . I had enormous admiration for him as an intelligence brain and organiser – the more sincere as I loathed him as a man.' The good news about Godfrey's departure was that Montagu and Cholmondeley now had 'the unhoped for benefit of an entirely free hand'. But it also meant that the 'preparation and devising of Mincemeat', in Montagu's words, 'was entirely unsupervised and unchecked'.

Godfrey was one of the few senior officers who could – and probably would – have pointed out that the story contained a surfeit of elegant trimmings. The characters seem closer to caricatures: the beastly bank manager, the bullying boss, the cheerful gal about to be socked in the eye by fate. The doomed love affair, the stiff-upper-lipped marine heading to death: these were the staples of popular culture in 1943. The Bill Martin story was the product of minds that had read too many romantic novels, and seen too many films in which the hero pulls away in the train, never to be seen again. That may have been partly intentional, for this was not supposed to be a genuine collection of people and events, aimed at convincing a British audience, but a story that a German might believe to be British. The task of the barrister, and the intelligence officer, in Montagu's estimation, was to ask: '"How will that argument or bit of evidence appeal to the hearer?" And not "How does it appeal to me?"'

In one sense, the story of Bill Martin was too perfect. There were no loose ends. A person's pockets and wallet will usually contain at least something that makes no obvious or immediate sense: an unidentified photo, an illegible note-to-self, paperclips, a button. In Martin's pockets there was nothing stray or inexplicable, nothing unlikely or meaningless. The personal letters contain no obscure allusions to third persons, or in-jokes, or spelling mistakes: none of the qualities that distinguish real, as opposed to manufactured, correspondence. Everything tied together, everything added up. There was excessive detail. Would 'Pam' really bother to identify that she worked in a 'Government office'? Bill would surely know this. In the same way, would a jeweller trouble to replicate the words engraved on a ring when sending in a bill? In the warped intelligence mentality, something that looks perfect is probably a fake.

But then, the plot was not perfect. Indeed, it contained some potentially catastrophic mistakes. Major Martin left money to his 'batman': an officer in the Royal Marines would never have referred to a batman, but rather to his Marine Officer's Attendant, or MOA. Why did he pay cash for his shirts (at a military tailor that extended the most generous credit to serving officers) when he was deeply overdrawn and owed £53 for an engagement ring?

Far more dangerously, the plot would never have stood up to scrutiny if German spies in Britain had made even the most cursory checks on it. A single telephone call to Ogbourne St George 242 would have established that no one by the name of Pam was known there. A glance at the hotel register for the Black Lion Hotel would have showed that no Mr J. C. Martin had stayed on the night of 13 April. Even a moderately competent agent could have called S. J. Phillips of New Bond Street to check when payment for the ring was due, and discovered that no such ring had been sold.

Montagu and Cholmondeley were blasé about the danger of being rumbled by an enemy agent in Britain, for the simple reason that they did not believe there were any. 'There was almost complete security,' wrote Montagu. 'We were able to put over what we liked to the enemy.' True, of the several hundred enemy spies dropped, floated or smuggled into Britain, all but one was picked up and arrested: the exception was found dead in a bunker after committing suicide. The Germans simply did not have an intelligence operation in Britain. By March 1943 there were so many double agents in the Double Cross System that 'Masterman raised the question whether we ought not to "liquidate" some of our agents, both for greater efficiency and for plausibility'. An 'execution subcommittee was formed' to bump off a fake agent 'every few months'.

Montagu would cycle home every evening, his briefcase full of secrets, complacent that he was 'the only deceptioneer in daily contact with the whole of special intelligence', and that his secrets were perfectly safe. Yet there were numerous spies living in London from supposedly neutral countries happy to furnish information to the Axis powers. Ewen Montagu never knew it, but there was one spy operating under his nose, a man with whom he shared a taste for exotic cheese and table tennis, and both parents.

Ivor Montagu was addicted to founding, and joining, different clubs. From the Cheese Eaters' League and the English Table Tennis Association, he had graduated to the Association of Cine Technicians, the Zoological Society, Marylebone Cricket Club, the editorial board of *Labour Monthly*, the World Council of Peace, the Friends of the Soviet Union, Southampton United Football Club, the Society for Cultural Relations with Soviet Russia, and Chairmanship of the Woolwich-Plumstead Branch of the Anti-War Congress.

He had also joined a less public and even more exclusive club, as an agent for Soviet military intelligence.

In part to antagonise his patrician parents, Ivor Montagu had from an early age displayed a keen 'enthusiasm for all things Russian', and a penchant for radical politics. In 1927, the twenty-three-year-old Ivor was contacted by Bob Stewart, a founder member of the British Communist Party and a recruiter of Soviet agents in Britain. Stewart told Montagu: 'We have had a request from the Communist International for you to go at once to Moscow. How soon can you leave?' In Moscow, Ivor was fêted and flattered: he played table tennis in the Comintern building with 'the keenest players in Moscow', went to the Bolshoi, and watched the revolutionary parade from a VIP stand in Red Square. Someone in the upper reaches of the Soviet state was taking good care of Ivor Montagu.

Back in Europe, Ivor's film career blossomed, as did his interests in table tennis, small rodents and Soviet movies. At the same time, his commitment to communism deepened. In 1929, he began to correspond with Leon Trotsky, the Bolshevik revolutionary expelled from the Communist Party and now living in exile on the Turkish island of Prinkipio.

'Dear Comrade Trotsky,' Ivor wrote on 1 July. 'Allow me to volunteer to be of service . . . I should be glad to be of assistance in any way possible.'

Trotsky replied, in friendly vein, and a most unlikely correspondence ensued. Ivor made plans to meet the exiled Soviet revolutionary in person. He would frame his trip to Prinkipio as the innocent journey of a young idealist studying the splits in Russian communism. It seems more likely that he was sent by Moscow to gain Trotsky's confidence, and report back on his activities. Ivor arrived in Istanbul in the pouring rain, 'like Edinburgh at its worst', and hired a boat to take him to the island. 'Two Turkish policemen were guarding the villa. Mrs Trotsky, a short motherly woman with an air of distress, made me welcome. Trotsky appeared and we settled down to talk.'

They talked deep into the night, about Trotsky's frustrations, his friends exiled to Siberia and his desire to make contact with Christian Rakovsky, the Bulgarian Bolshevik who would eventually perish at the hands of Stalin's executioners. At the end of the evening Ivor was handed a loaded pistol 'to put under my pillow as a precaution against assassins'. (Trotsky would be assassinated in Mexico in 1940.) Ivor could not sleep. 'I did not know what precautions to take against the revolver, and was terrified.'

The next morning, Trotsky and Ivor went fishing in the

Sea of Marmara. The Turkish bodyguards rowed. The political conversation continued. The weather was atrocious. They caught nothing. 'The memory I shall always retain of him,' wrote Ivor, 'is of our little boat, perilously poised at the top of a wave, ready to crash down on top of a monstrous rock, Trotsky himself perched aquiline in the stern and in a voice and with an authority that might have commanded an army, repeating the Turkish equivalent of "in-out in-out" as the policemen rowed for dear life.'

The meeting with Trotsky marked a turning point. Ivor Montagu was attracted to this 'fascinating and commanding personality' but 'repelled by his self-admiration', the raw ambition of the revolutionary in exile: 'I felt I understood now why he was impossible in a party, that his personality swamped his judgement.' Ivor was not yet thirty, but he was already a party disciplinarian, and a fully committed Stalinist. Trotsky knew that Ivor was a willing tool of the Soviet regime. In 1932, he wrote: 'Ivor Montagu has, or had, some personal sympathy for me, but now he is even on that small scale paralysed by his adherence to the party.'

That adherence was now absolute, and permanent: he gave speeches, wrote pamphlets and made films in support of communism. The more covert, and more dangerous, manifestations of that party obedience remained secret for the rest of his life.

MI5 had started to take an interest in the Hon. Ivor Montagu back in 1926, after intercepting a letter he had written to a member of a visiting Soviet trade delegation requesting permission to visit Moscow. The snoopers immediately began to open Ivor's mail and follow his movements, reporting that 'Montagu has for some time been known to associate with the inner ring of the Communist Party'. His behaviour was distinctly suspicious: he attended radical meetings, played table tennis, translated French plays, mixed with left-wing film actors and directors, wore a long Mongolian leather coat, and distributed Soviet films. The correspondence with Trotsky was copied, and added to Ivor's growing MI5 files. A report by Special Branch in 1931 was tinged with anti-semitism: 'Montagu has dark curly hair and is of distinctly Jewish appearance. His eyes are dark brown and his complexion is pale. He is generally rather dirty and untidy.'

By the outbreak of war, Ivor Montagu had all but severed contact with his family, with the exception of Ewen. While his older brother continued to enjoy the services of the family butler at Kensington Court, Ivor lived in Brixton, sharing a grotty flat with a mongrel from Battersea Dogs Home called Betsy, his wife Hell, her daughter Rowna, and his mother-in-law, who was addicted to cheese and pickles even though these gave her chronic indigestion. 'What is the use of living if you cannot eat cheese and pickles?' she asked. As co-founder of the Cheese Eaters' League, Ivor thought she had a point. The brothers Montagu could not have been more different personalities, nor have entertained more opposed political views, yet they continued to meet throughout the war.

Ewen Montagu sent Iris regular bulletins on Ivor's activities, mocking but affectionate. 'Last night Ivor came to dinner after the Prom at the Albert Hall,' he wrote in June 1942. 'He is simply enormous, almost all tummy. Hell is well and digging for victory, which she hasn't found yet.' He regarded Ivor's politics as a harmless obsession. 'Ivor is really bad on this war,' he told his wife. 'He is busy working for the Russian government on Russian propaganda [and] writing anti-war or Communist letters to the papers.'

MI5 was well aware that one of the country's most senior intelligence officers – a man who, by his own account, 'knew in advance practically every secret of the war, including the atom bomb' – was in regular contact with a brother who was a known Soviet sympathiser, corresponded with Russian revolutionaries and opposed the war. By 1939, MI5 had started referring to 'that particularly unpleasant communist, the Hon. Ivor'. Ivor represented a major security risk. Ewen knew that there was an

MI5 dossier on Ivor, but had no idea that, by 1943, it extended to three volumes and hundreds of pages.

In Ivor Montagu's MI5 files, any explicit reference to Ewen has been weeded out, but as the older brother's intelligence career developed and his responsibilities grew, so surveillance of the younger brother intensified. MI5 questioned Ivor's neighbours, infiltrated the meetings he addressed, and analysed his writings and speeches, yet they could find no hard evidence against him. That would take another two decades.

Between 1940 and 1948, American cryptanalysts intercepted copies of thousands of telegrams passing between Moscow and its diplomatic missions abroad, written in a code that was theoretically unbreakable. Over the next forty years, Allied codebreakers struggled to unpick the Soviet code in an operation initially known as 'the Russian problem' and later codenamed 'Venona', a project so secret that the CIA remained unaware of its existence until 1952. Large swaths of the correspondence were, and are still, unreadable, but finally some 2,900 messages were translated, a tiny fraction of the whole but an astonishing glimpse into Soviet espionage.

These decrypted intercepts included 178 sent to and from the London office of the GRU, the military branch of Soviet intelligence, between March 1940 and April 1942.

The messages are partial and fragmentary, and many are missing, but they revealed something quite remarkable: for at least two years, the Soviet Union had run an undetected British spy ring codenamed 'X Group' (*Gruppa iks*) under the leadership of an individual codenamed 'Intelligentsia'.

Soviet spies, like their British and German counterparts, seemed to take perverse delight in selecting codenames containing the most unsubtle hints. The Venona code for France was 'Gastronomica'; the Germans were 'Sausage Dealers' (*Kolbasniki*). The codename chosen for the spy in control of X Group was no exception. Agent Intelligentsia was the intellectually inclined Ivor Montagu.

On 25 July 1940, Simon Davidovitch Kremer, secretary to the Soviet military attaché in London and a GRU spy handler, sent a message under the codename 'Barch' to 'Director' in Moscow:

> I have met representatives of the X GROUP. This is IVOR MONTAGU (brother of Lord Montagu), the well-known local communist, journalist and lecturer. He has [*unintelligible*] contacts through his influential relatives. He reported that he had been detailed to organise work with me, but that he had not yet obtained a single contact. I came to an agreement with him about the work and pointed out the importance of speed.

The report went on to relay Ivor's analysis of Hitler's 'Last Appeal to Reason', his 'peace offer' to Britain. Ivor, correctly, thought a peace deal unlikely: 'Intelligentsia considers there is an anti-Sausage Dealer mood in the army.' The reference to Ivor's 'influential relatives' suggests that the GRU knew of Ewen Montagu's senior status within British intelligence.

Ewen and Ivor Montagu were now, in effect, spying for opposite sides in the war. Since 1939, under the Molotov-Ribbentrop pact, the Soviet Union and Nazi Germany had been bound together in a formal non-aggression agreement, and until Hitler ruptured the pact in June 1941, information passed to Soviet intelligence could find its way into the hands of the Gestapo.

Initially, Ivor Montagu's Soviet spymasters were unimpressed:

> Intelligentsia has not yet found the people in the military finance department. He has promised to deliver documentary material from Professor Haldane who is working on an admiralty assignment concerned with submarines and their operation. We need a man of a different calibre and one who is bolder than INTELLIGENTSIA.

Professor J. B. S. Haldane was one of the most celebrated scientists in Britain. A pioneering and broad-ranging thinker, he developed a mathematical theory of population genetics, predicted that hydrogen-producing windmills would replace fossil fuel, explained nuclear fission, and suffered a perforated eardrum while testing a homemade decompression chamber: 'Although one is somewhat deaf, one can blow tobacco smoke out of the ear in question, which is a social accomplishment.' Haldane was a dedicated atheist and communist: 'I think that Marxism is true,' he declared in 1938.

Ivor Montagu and Jack Haldane had become friends at Cambridge, and soon after the outbreak of war, Ivor recruited the scientist into X Group. In 1940, Haldane was working at the Navy's underwater research establishment at Gosport, and in July he submitted a secret paper to the Admiralty entitled *Report on Effects of High Pressure, Carbon Dioxide and Cold*, a study of long-term submersion in submarines. Two months later, Kremer reported: 'Intelligentsia has handed over a copy of Professor Haldane's report to the Admiralty on his experiments relating to the length of time a man can stay underwater.'

Under Kremer's nagging guidance, Ivor Montagu's X Group slowly expanded, and the quality of intelligence improved. By the autumn of 1940, Ivor had recruited 'three military sources', and an agent codenamed 'Baron', probably a senior officer in the secret service of the Czechoslovakian government in exile, who furnished copious information on German forces in Czechoslovakia. MI5 later speculated that another of Ivor's recruits, codenamed 'Bob', was the future trade union leader Jack Jones. In October 1940, Ivor 'reported that a girl working in a government establishment noticed in one document that the British had broken some Soviet code or other'. Kremer told Ivor 'that this was a matter of exceptional importance and he should put to the [X] Group the business of developing this report'.

By the end of 1940, X Group had become so productive that

the handling of Ivor Montagu was taken over by the top GRU officer in London, Colonel Ivan Sklyarov, the Soviet military and air attaché, codenamed 'Brion'. The surviving X Group messages reveal a steady stream of military intelligence passing to Moscow, including troop movements, air raid damage, technical information obtained from 'an officer of the air ministry', tank production and weapons, and reports on British preparations for a possible German invasion. 'The coastal defence is based on a network of blockhouses that are weak in design with no allowance made for the manoeuvrability of strong artillery and tank equipment of the Sausage Dealers.' Such information was of great interest to Moscow, but it would have been of even greater importance to the Germans, then actively planning Operation Sealion, the invasion of Britain.

Ivor Montagu's most valuable information was passed to Moscow on 16 October 1940, following an air raid on an aircraft factory near Bristol: '30 Sausage Dealer bombers and 30 fighters used a radio beam to fly from Northern France'.

The aim of the Luftwaffe bombers had been steadily improving in recent months, prompting suspicion that the Germans had developed some sort of sophisticated guiding apparatus using radio beams. This was the so-called 'Knickebein' system: the German bombers followed a radio beam broadcast from France until the beam was intersected by another over the target, at which point the bombs were released. Churchill had formed a secret committee to try to discover how the system worked, and how it might be countered. The problem was codenamed 'Headache'; the countermeasures, inevitably, were codenamed 'Aspirin'. In time, the RAF developed a technique for 'bending' the radio beams to redirect the Luftwaffe's bombs away from the intended targets: Headache was cured. But in October 1940, Headache was a highly classified secret, known only to a handful of intelligence chiefs, senior RAF officers and government scientists. X Group was now gathering intelligence from the very highest levels.

Ivor Montagu was an idealist, but his actions were treasonable.

He was not merely passing important military secrets to a foreign power, but to one that was bound in a friendly pact with the enemy. Ivor was a committed anti-fascist, and would have been appalled at the accusation that he was aiding Nazism, but his commitment to the cause of communism was absolute, though naïve. If caught, he would certainly have been arrested and prosecuted under the Treason Act.

Some of Ivor's information may have come, inadvertently, from his older brother. Ewen Montagu was aware of his brother's politics ('he still seems to be going on with his meetings', he told his wife) but was entirely in the dark about his espionage activities. He had no idea how closely his sibling was being monitored by his own colleagues in MI5. Ivor, on the other hand, was aware that his brother worked in Naval Intelligence at a senior level, and was undoubtedly interested in the contents of his locked briefcase. Did Ivor's slavish adherence to the party, as noted by Trotsky, outweigh his brotherly affection?

We will probably never know whether Ivor spied on his brother, because at the end of 1942 the Venona intercepts come to an abrupt halt. The traffic between the London *rezidentura* and Moscow continued unabated, but was henceforth unreadable. The last translated report from Brion reads: 'Intelligentsia has reported that his friend, a serviceman in a Liverpool regiment has handed over [*unintellgible*] German exercise, with dive bombers taking part [*unintelligible*] between Liverpool and Manchester everything – industry . . .' This was the last decipherable word from Agent Intelligentsia.

By 1943, Nazi Germany and the Soviet Union were locked in mortal conflict, and there was now little danger that information from X Group would be passed on to Berlin. But Ivor undoubtedly remained immersed in the spying game. Germany had spies operating within Soviet intelligence. Ewen had spent months planning the most elaborate deception of the war. The person most likely to blow Operation Mincemeat, if he should ever discover it, was his own brother.

The Butterfly Collector

Cholmondeley and Montagu were convinced that they had created a fully credible character in William Martin. 'We felt that we knew him just as one knows one's best friend,' wrote Montagu. 'We had come to feel that we had known Bill Martin from his earliest childhood, his every thought and his probable reaction to any event that might occur in his life.'

It is hardly surprising that Montagu and Cholmondeley felt they knew Bill Martin as well as they knew themselves, for in a way the personality they had created was their combined alter ego, the person they would have liked to be. One contemporary described Cholmondeley as 'an incurable romantic of the old cloak and dagger school'. In Bill Martin, he found an imaginary figure who could wear the cloak and wield the dagger on his behalf. Where Cholmondeley was earthbound by his eyesight and deskbound by his job, Bill Martin was a young officer on the front line, heading to war with a girl waiting for him at home. Montagu once wrote that he 'joined up to go to sea, to use my seamanship experience, and to fight'. Bill Martin was the active naval officer that he was not. But Montagu took the identification with Bill Martin a stage further.

'Ewen *lived* the part,' according to Jean Leslie. 'He *was* Willie Martin and I was Pam. He had the sort of mind that worked that way.' Ewen (as Bill) began to pay court to Jean (as Pam) in earnest. He took her to clubs, films and out to dinner. He gave her presents, jewellery, and a Royal Marines shirt collar, as a memento of 'Bill'.

'He wrote me endless letters, *from Bill*.' Jean kept some of these letters from her imaginary fiancé. They are an extraordinary testament to one of the oddest love affairs imaginable, to the way that fiction was eliding into fact in an entirely unexpected way. Jean Leslie was not, it seems, averse to Montagu's advances or, perhaps more accurately, to those of Bill Martin. She had a copy of the bathing photograph enlarged, and wrote on it: 'Till death us do part, Your loving Pam', and gave it to Montagu.

Montagu wrote back:

Pam dearest,

I just loved the photograph – so much so that I couldn't bear the idea of anything happening to it and I have left it in the care of my best friend – I know you'll like him a lot – he has done everything for me and made me what I am today.

This sounds as if I have a foreboding – I have, and from your inscription on the photo I think you have the same fear.

In case I don't come back you may not like to wear the ring I gave you so I hope you will like this brooch. You can still wear that even if, as I hope you will, you meet someone worthier than me – I know he will understand if he is the sort of man you'll like.

Ever yours,

Bill

P.S. Try the RNVR next time.

Ewen Montagu, of course, was in the RNVR, the Royal Naval Volunteer Reserve. He placed Pam's photograph on his dressing table at Kensington Court.

Montagu had been apart from his wife since 1940, with only one, brief, reunion in America in 1941, when he was sent out to liaise with the FBI. In letters to his wife, Ewen referred openly to his dates with a young woman with lodgings in the Elms in Hampstead, although he never identified Jean Leslie by name.

'The girl from the Elms is one of Tar Robertson's secretaries and is a very nice, very intelligent girl (22-24?),' he told Iris. 'One of her appealing virtues [is] she is such a good listener.' He added: 'She has been much connected with one side of my doings.' Iris had already broached the subject of whether she and the children should return to Britain. On 15 March 1943, Ewen wrote to her: 'I took the girl from the Elms to dinner and we went to see "Desert Victory" at the Astoria.' In the very same letter he observed: 'I feel definitely that you ought not to come back yet.'

If Iris was suspicious of Ewen's relationship with this unnamed woman connected with her husband's 'doings', she was not alone. Montagu later claimed he had placed 'Pam's' photograph, with its loving inscription, on his dressing table at Kensington Court to see whether his inquisitive mother would react to it, or even remove it. 'If Mother did touch my things it would be the last straw. It is the only irritating thing she doesn't do so far.' Lady Swaythling duly spotted the picture, and demanded an explanation. 'I told her truthfully that it was a souvenir of something I had been doing . . . I'm not entirely sure what she thought I meant by that!!'

Montagu's mother began sending coded warnings to her daughter-in-law in New York, 'writing in her letters that she felt that [Iris] should come home as soon as [her] job allowed it'.

The relationship between Ewen Montagu and Jean Leslie may have been mere romantic play-acting, nothing more than flirtatious, joking banter. But when Iris later saw the photograph with its passionate dedication, Montagu insisted that it was a joke, part of a wartime operation, and that nothing had gone on between him (and his alter ego) and Jean (and hers). His wife may have believed him. He may have been telling the truth.

Forging the character of Major William Martin, and flirting with his fiancée, had been a most pleasurable challenge. Far more taxing – and more important – was the task of creating documentary evidence to be planted on the body. If the faked intelligence was too obvious, the Germans would spot the hoax; if it was too subtle, they might miss the clues altogether. At what level should the disinformation be pitched? Major Martin was supposed to be a serving officer whose plane had crashed en route from Britain to Gibraltar. He could not simply carry operational orders or battle plans, since these would never have been entrusted to a single messenger, but instead sent by diplomatic bag. Moreover, if a message contained highly classified information, it would tend to be transmitted by encrypted wireless message. The false information, it was decided, would have to be conveyed in the form of private letters between individual officers, of sufficiently elevated rank to ensure the enemy took the information seriously. These had to be names the Germans would recognise. A communication from some minor member of the planning staff in London to a counterpart in Algiers 'would not carry enough weight'. The job, as Montagu saw it, was 'to fake documents of a sufficiently high level to have strategic effect, even after prolonged study and consideration by suspicious and highly trained minds which would be reluctant to believe them'. Even more problematic was the question of how, exactly, to phrase the disinformation. If Sicily was identified as the cover target but the Germans somehow rumbled the trick, then that would reveal Sicily as the real target. Instead of the enemy being misled, he would be tipped off.

Montagu approached the forging of the letters as if he was in court, briefing his opposing counsel with selective, invented evidence. It was, he later reflected, 'a crooked lawyer's dream of heaven'. He set out three basic principles on which the letter or letters should be drafted:

1. That the planted target [i.e. Greece, Sardinia, or both] should be casually but definitively identified.

2. That two other places should be identified as cover, that one of these should be Sicily itself and the other thrown in so that, if the Germans grasped that the document was a plant, Sicily should not be pinpointed.

3. That the letter should be 'off the record' and of the type that would go by the hand of an officer but not in an official bag; it would have to have personal remarks and evidence of a personal discussion or arrangement which would prevent the message being sent by signal.

Montagu knocked out a first draft: a letter from General Sir Archibald 'Archie' Nye, Vice Chief of the Imperial General Staff (VCIGS), to General Sir Harold Alexander in Tunisia. Nye was privy to all military operations. Alexander was in command of an army under General Dwight Eisenhower at 18th Army Group Headquarters. The two British generals knew one another fairly well, and were senior enough to be fully apprised of the battle plans. Harold Alexander had fought with distinction in the First World War, but was widely perceived as not too bright. Indeed, one colleague unfairly described him as 'bone from the neck up'. Still, he was the epitome of British martial uprightness, ramrod stiff, and always looking 'as if he had just had a steam bath, a massage, a good breakfast and a letter from home'. More importantly, he was probably Britain's most famous soldier after Montgomery, and destined to become Eisenhower's commander of ground forces in Sicily. The Germans would know instantly who, and how important, he was.

Montagu's rough draft was a chatty, chummy letter between two members of the top brass, making no obvious reference to Allied intentions but dropping clues that no careful reader could miss. It implied a debate over whether Sicily or Marseilles should be the cover target; it referred to a choice of landing spots in Sardinia; it contained some apparently idle chat about the American allies ('Will Eisenhower go ahead at his own speed?'), salutations from a mutual friend ('So and so [naming a general] sends his best') and some light-hearted ribbing of Montgomery, the victor of El Alamein, for his big-headedness.

Montagu thought his draft hit the perfect note, with just the right mix of 'personal and "off the record"' information. He was very pleased with it. His immediate bosses, however, were not. The planners at the London Controlling Section (LCS), the committee in overall command of deception, suggested a less ambitious plan, arguing that 'the contents of such a letter should be of the nuts-and-bolts variety and not on a high level'. On 11 March, Johnnie Bevan, the head of the LCS, flew to Algiers for a meeting with Dudley Wrangel Clarke, the officer in command of deception for Operation Husky, the assault on Sicily. Clarke also believed that Operation Mincemeat was aiming too high. He suggested that the letter should merely give a false indication of the date of a planned invasion, without pin-pointing where this would take place.

Over the next month, the letter would be repeatedly revised, redrafted and rewritten, as senior intelligence officers, the Chiefs of Staff and others, added their pennyworth to the plan. One of the hazards of having a good idea is that intelligent people tend to realise it is a good idea, and seek to play a part. Like most novelists, Montagu did not like the editing process. He did not like the way Operation Mincemeat was being watered down. He did not like senior officers pulling rank and tinkering with a project in which he had invested so much of his time, energy and personality. But most of all, he did not like Johnnie Bevan.

Montagu had once been a supporter of Bevan, the smooth, patrician chief of the London Controlling Section. But tensions rose quickly in the cramped and strained atmosphere of wartime deception planning. Soon after Bevan was appointed, they began to spar, which led to disagreements, and culminated in a titanic personality clash. Bevan took malicious pleasure in ordering Montagu about; Montagu responded with withering contempt. Early in March, in the midst of discussions over the form of Operation Mincemeat, Montagu mounted a full-scale assault on Bevan, accusing him of being incompetent, mendacious, inefficient, and 'almost completely ignorant of the German Intelligence Service, how they work and what they are likely to believe'.

When Montagu got the bit between his teeth, he was not easily reined in. Bevan, he protested, 'is almost completely inexperienced in any form of deception work. He has a pleasant and likeable personality and can "sell himself" well. He has not got a first-grade brain. He can expound imposing platitudes such as "we want to contain the Germans in the West" with great impressiveness . . . I am sure he will not improve with experience. The remainder of the staff of the London Controlling Section are either unsuited to this sort of work (in which they are all wholly inexperienced) or are third-rate brains.'

The rant continued for several more pages. Montagu's character assassination of Bevan was completely over the top. It was also wrong, because Bevan possessed a brain quite as supple as that of Ewen Montagu. The memo attacking Bevan was internally circulated to the chiefs of Naval Intelligence, but Montagu's colleagues seem to have realised he was merely blowing off steam, and the document did not leave NID – which was just as well, for if Montagu's complaints had reached the ears of Churchill, who had complete faith in Bevan, then he might well have been sacked. Some saw Montagu's attitude towards Bevan as evidence of thwarted ambition and backstabbing. More likely, it was the overreaction of an obsessive perfectionist, frustrated at the way his pièce de résistance was being tampered with, and deeply alarmed by what he saw as the leaden response to developments in the Mediterranean.

At the end of February, Bletchley Park deciphered a message from the Nazi high command to the German command in Tunisia, assessing the situation in the Mediterranean. 'From reports coming out about Anglo-American landing intentions it is apparent that the enemy is practising deception on a large scale. In spite of this, a landing on a fairly large scale can be expected in March. It is thought the Mediterranean is the most probable theatre of operations and the first operation to be an attack against one of the large islands, the order of probability being Sicily first, Crete second, and Sardinia or Corsica third.'

The Germans not only anticipated a deception operation, but had correctly divined the intended target, and time was running out to change their minds. 'Sicily has now been allowed to become our most probable target and will be hard to remove from the enemy's minds,' warned Montagu. 'It is much easier to persuade the Germans that we will attack X than it is to dissuade them from an appreciation already formed by them that we will attack Y.' Bevan seemed to be doing nothing: 'He still has no deception plan for Husky . . . why, even now, weeks after HUSKY has been laid on, have we got no deception plan drafted, much less approved and started?' Mincemeat was pushing ahead, but if it did not work, there would be a 'complete failure to deceive the Germans by any action of ours'. The Allies were on the verge of attacking a target that the Germans expected to be attacked. Britain and her allies, Montagu warned, were 'now in a highly dangerous situation'.

He wrote another letter to 'Tar' Robertson, more temperate this time but flatly rejecting Bevan's idea that a 'nuts-and-bolts' letter would be sufficient: 'It would be a very great pity if we used a letter on a low level. I do not feel that such a letter would impress either the Abwehr or the operational authorities.'

While Montagu fought it out with Bevan, and the wrangling continued over the contents of the letters, a separate debate was underway to determine where the body should be floated ashore. After briefly toying with Portugal, or the south coast of France, the planners had settled once more on Spain. Both Britain and Germany maintained embassies in Madrid, but pro-German and anti-British sentiment was rife, particularly within the armed forces and Spanish bureaucracy. As one MI5 officer observed, parts of the Spanish state were effectively in German employ: 'Spanish police records and officers of the Seguridad [the Spanish Security Service] were instructed to facilitate the Germans in all they required, passports to Spanish nationals were issued on German recommendation, or refused on their instructions. The Spanish press and radio services were under German control. The Spanish general staff was collaborating to the maximum. The use of Spanish diplomatic bags was theirs for the asking.' If the misleading documents could be put into the right Spanish hands, then they would almost certainly be passed on to the Germans. But Spain was unpredictable, and there were plenty of Spaniards fundamentally opposed to the Nazis. The worst outcome would be if the body and its papers ended up with a British sympathiser, and were then handed back intact and unread. Where, then, was the most pro-German part of the Spanish coast?

A cable was sent to Captain Alan Hillgarth, the naval attaché at the Madrid embassy and Churchill's intelligence chief in Spain, asking him to send a trusted lieutenant to London for an urgent conference. Salvador Augustus Gómez-Beare, assistant naval attaché at the British Embassy in Madrid, duly presented himself at the Admiralty, fresh off the plane from Madrid, and was ushered into Room 13.

Gómez-Beare, universally known by his nickname 'Don', was an Anglo-Spaniard from Gibraltar who perfectly straddled the two cultures. He was a British citizen, enjoyed a large private income, spoke pure upper-class English, and displayed impeccable English manners and habits as only someone who is not English can. He played bridge with Ian Fleming at the Portland Club, and golf all year round. But in Spain, he was Spanish, brown-skinned, speaking with a southern accent, and invisible. In 1914, as a medical student in Philadelphia, he had volunteered to join the British Army, and spend two years in the trenches before joining the Royal Flying Corps. During the Spanish civil war he had 'worked in military intelligence for

Franco's army'. Gómez-Beare could reach places no Englishman could penetrate, 'a Spaniard to Spaniards and an Englishman to the English, who served England with an intensity and thoroughness that no mere Anglo-Saxon could attain'. Hillgarth had recruited him in 1939, initially suggesting that he be given the rank of captain in the Royal Marines, 'because of his enormous RAF moustache'. He was given the rank of lieutenant commander in the RNVR on condition he shaved and despite having 'no more than a smattering of sea experience'. From the start of the war, Gómez-Beare could be found 'padding about Madrid, driving up to San Sebastian, flitting over to Barcelona, hovering about Gibraltar, and smuggling British airmen out of France'. When Airey Neave escaped from Colditz in 1942, it was Gómez-Beare who smuggled him across the border to Gibraltar. He had a villa in Seville, a flat in Madrid, and spies in every corner of the Spanish establishment, society, and the underworld. Gómez-Beare was Hillgarth's primary recruiter and runner of secret agents.

Alan Hillgarth, as a senior member of the embassy staff in a neutral country, could not be seen to engage directly in espionage or recruit spies, but Gómez-Beare was under no such constraints. In Hillgarth's words, he was 'exceptionally favoured by character and linguistic attainments to cultivate such people, and in the majority of cases his contacts would not have agreed to work with anyone else'. Gómez-Beare's spies ran through the Spanish bureaucracy like veins through marble: he had agents in the Spanish police, the Security Service, the Ministry of the Interior, the Spanish general staff and every branch of the military. He had informants in high society and low, from the salons of Madrid to the docks of Cadiz. These spies never met one another, and only ever made contact through Gómez-Beare himself. 'He was invaluable,' said Hillgarth. 'It was he who handled our special contacts. His loyalty and discretion are unequalled and the Spaniards, particularly the Spanish Navy, love him.'

The Germans, by contrast, did not love Don Gómez-Beare. Britain's assistant naval attaché narrowly escaped being blown up by a car bomb during a clandestine visit to Lisbon. His chauffeur, in German pay, loosened the wheels on his car before his boss went driving in the mountains of Despeñaperros. Gómez-Beare spotted the assassination attempt just in time. Madrid was a festering nest of espionage and counterespionage, and for four years a fierce war had raged between British spies and German spies in Spain, undeclared, unofficial and unrelenting. Both sides deployed bribery and corruption on a lavish scale. Abwehr agents spied on the British counterparts, who responded in kind; the Spaniards spied on both sides, rather inefficiently. At first, the odds seemed stacked against the British. The Germans simply had too many advantages, with numerous 'privileges and facilities (of course unofficially)' provided by willing Spanish collaborators. The Abwehr infiltrated all branches of the civil service, police, government and even business. But with time, the contest had levelled out, as Hillgarth and Gómez-Beare extended their web of informants through a combination of charm, bribery and skulduggery. 'Spain contained a large number of German agents and plenty of Spaniards in German pay,' wrote Hillgarth. 'They had some ingenious ideas. We did our best to learn their plans, and to some extent succeeded.' In this febrile atmosphere, it was impossible to be sure who was spying for whom. 'Madrid was full of spies,' wrote Hillgarth, 'no one is watched all the time, but everyone is watched some of the time.'

And no one was watched more closely, or better at watching, than Don Gómez-Beare.

Once tea had been served in Room 13, Cholmondeley and Montagu laid out their plans before the Gibraltarian. Where, they asked, would be the best place to launch a dead body with false information into German hands? Gómez-Beare considered the problem. If the body washed up close to Cadiz, then it might simply be handed over to the British authorities in Gibraltar, which would scupper the plan at the outset. There was also, he explained, a 'danger of the body being recovered and/or dealt with by the Spanish Navy who might not cooperate with the Germans'. The navy, owing in part to the efforts of Gómez-Beare, was far more sympathetic to Britain than other branches of the military, so if possible the body and its contents should be kept out of naval hands.

The ideal place, Gómez-Beare finally declared, would be somewhere near Huelva, the fishing port on Spain's coast where the River Tinto flows into the Atlantic. 'German influence in Huelva is very strong,' explained Gómez-Beare; the town was home to a large and patriotic German community. The British consul in Huelva, Francis Haselden, was 'a reliable and helpful man', whose assistance would be needed for the ruse to succeed. Huelva also had a 'very pro-German chief of police [who] would give the Germans access to anything of interest found on the body'.

But most importantly Huelva was the home turf of a particular – and particularly troublesome – German spy. The agent in question was 'active and influential' across the region, as well as highly efficient, well connected and perfectly ruthless. It would not merely be desirable to stitch this man up, Gómez-Beare observed, but a positive pleasure.

Adolf Clauss collected butterflies. The walls of his large home were covered with cases of butterflies, each one carefully pinned and identified. He spent his days with butterfly net, binoculars and camera on the cliffs at Rabida, where the Odiel and the Tinto meet and flow into the sea, the spot from which Christopher Columbus prepared to set sail for the New World. Clauss owned a large farm at Rabida, where he grew enormous tomatoes and beetroots. He painted, played tennis in the evenings, and smoked filterless cigarettes whenever he was awake. He constructed elaborate wooden chairs which fell apart when you sat on them. Adolf was an extraordinary-looking man. A bout of malaria picked up while travelling in the Congo had rendered him cadaverously thin, and as the disease recurred, he grew ever more emaciated. His large ears stuck out at right angles; he looked like a corpse with two saucers attached. His tendency to appear at your shoulder, silently and without warning, had earned him the nickname 'The Shadow'. At forty-six, Clauss was said to have retired, although quite what he had retired from was a mystery.

The Clauss family was the richest in Huelva. Adolf's father, Ludwig, was an industrialist and entrepreneur who had moved from Leipzig to Spain at the end of the nineteenth century. With his partner, Bruno Wetzig, Ludwig set up a company processing agricultural products, selling fish to the Madrid markets, and supplying food and other material to the workers in the British-owned Rio Tinto mines. Clauss and Wetzig made a fortune. With this, Ludwig purchased land outside Huelva, built himself a large walled compound, and became Germany's honorary consul.

The German community was matched by the equally large, and even richer British community. If the Clauss family ruled over the Germans of Huelva, then the Rio Tinto Company ruled everyone else, employing more than 10,000 workers and running the town like a corporate fiefdom. The mines were 100 kilometres inland, and the copper and pyrite were brought to the dock at Huelva by a specially constructed railway. The company bosses rode around on horseback, and were referred to as 'the viceroys', so arrogant and regal was their bearing. The richer Spaniards aped British colonial manners, taking tea at five and playing bridge. Privately, the British were loathed, and resented for extracting so much money from Spanish soil: 'First the Romans mined it, then the British, then the Spanish, by which time there was nothing left.'

Like many colonists, the British and Germans tended to exaggerate their cultural distinctiveness. The British built a reproduction English village, which they called Queen Victoria

Barrio, with gabled cottages and a village green. The Germans sent their children to be educated in Germany, and maintained German traditions: Spain was home, but Germany was the Fatherland. Before the war, the two communities had mixed on terms of social equality, playing golf and tennis together and attending one another's functions. With the outbreak of war, all social contact ceased.

Spanish opinion in Huelva was divided on Adolf Clauss, Ludwig's younger son. Some said he was 'the black sheep', because he never seemed to do any work. Others reckoned he was 'the only clever one in the family', again because he never seemed to do any work. Clauss was very clever indeed, and he was also probably working harder than anyone else in Huelva, spying for Hitler's Reich.

Adolf Clauss had trained as an architect and industrial engineer in Germany, and at the age of seventeen, with the outbreak of the First World War, he joined the army, and volunteered for secret service work. Speaking impeccable Spanish, he was sent on a mission by submarine to blow up British factories in Cartagena. The rubber dinghy he set off in had sunk, owing to the weight of explosives on board, and Clauss was finally picked up by the Spanish navy after treading water for eight hours. He was briefly imprisoned, and then sent back to Germany. The incident, oddly, seemed only to increase Clauss's appetite for cloak and dagger work, and by 1920, although theoretically working as an agricultural technician, he was already the chief Abwehr agent in Huelva.

His marriage, during the 1930s, to the daughter of a senior Spanish army officer gave Clauss an entrée into the fascist Falange movement. When civil war erupted, he immediately enlisted as a captain in the Condor Legion, the German volunteer unit fighting for the Nationalists under General Franco. Most infamously, pilots of the Condor Legion carried out the bombing of the Basque town of Guernica on 26 April 1937, an act of brutality immortalised in Pablo Picasso's painting of that name. For most of the conflict, Clauss acted as the personal interpreter for Colonel Wilhelm von Thoma, commander of the Condor Legion's ground contingent. When Madrid fell to the Nationalists, Captain Clauss proudly rode into the captured capital on his tank. He was awarded the Red Cross for Military Merit by a grateful Franco regime, to add to the Iron Cross already awarded for his service to Germany in the First World War. He later earned another Iron Cross from Hitler's Third Reich. Clauss would later claim, as many did, that he had fought for Germany, not for Hitler. But there is no evidence he ever questioned Nazi policy. A number of Abwehr officers shrank from Hitler's barbarism. Clauss was not one of these. When war broke out he was happy to offer his well-honed espionage talents, his high-level Spanish contacts and his almost limitless energies to the Nazi cause.

By 1943, Adolf Clauss was running the largest and most efficient spy ring on the Spanish coast. Huelva, situated between the Portuguese frontier and Gibraltar, was of vital strategic importance in the war. From here, British merchant ships headed into the Atlantic, heavily laden with raw materials from the mines. From his farm, ideally situated on the coast, Clauss monitored every ship leaving port, and every ship coming in. His informants up and down the coast completed the picture. Sometimes he would take photographs using a Minox camera and a long-distance lens. The information was then relayed to Berlin by a team of Abwehr wireless operators, working out of the German consulate at 51 Avenida de Italia. Adolf's older brother, Luis, was an equally enthusiastic supporter of Nazism. Since their father Ludwig Clauss, the honorary German consul, was now in his eighties and almost stone deaf, consular duties were delegated to Luis. Both sons were named as vice consuls, and the consulate was placed at the disposal of the Abwehr. Luis had a fleet of fishing vessels with onboard radios to relay shipping movements.

The other main function of the Abwehr chief in Huelva,

in addition to sabotage and target-spotting for U-boats, was bribery. Every evening, thin-faced Adolf Clauss could be found at the Café del Palma, a bar near the port, buying drinks but drinking little, meeting and massaging his contacts, and discreetly distributing large quantities of cash. Clauss bribed everyone who mattered, and many who did not. He bribed the harbour master and the stevedores, the officers of the Guardìa Civil and the police chief. Word soon got out that Don Adolfo was prepared to pay handsomely for information on the movement of shipping, the activities of the British in Huelva, and the comings and goings of Spanish officials. Nothing could be said, nothing could be whispered in Huelva, without news eventually reaching the preternaturally large ears of Adolf Clauss, who faithfully relayed everything he heard back to his Abwehr bosses in Madrid.

Gaunt, introverted, and unsociable, Adolf Clauss nonetheless possessed the spy's essential talent for listening. 'He didn't dispute; if you thought you had the right argument, he always let you have the last word.' But even his family found him 'cold, distant and silent'. He started work at six in the morning and never took a siesta. He seldom drank alcohol. He almost never smiled. His was the mind of the collector, the perfectionist. He liked to collate the different sorts of information from his intelligence network, and then to pin it down, in different compartments, like butterflies.

The British authorities in Huelva knew what the odd-looking German lepidopterist was up to, for the British had their own spies and informers. In Huelva's peaceful, orange-tree-lined streets, another spy contest was underway, a smaller but no less intense echo of the espionage battle taking place in Madrid. The Clauss spy network was a menace to British shipping. Countless lives had already been forfeited on account of his activities, yet Clauss was an elusive adversary. As one British intelligence officer put it: 'He was an active and intelligent person. It was impossible for any of our agents to watch him and keep tabs on him. He was sharper and gave the slip to anyone who followed him.'

Don Gómez-Beare described the Clauss network to Montagu and Cholmondeley. Some of what he said was familiar. The decoding of Abwehr messages had revealed, early in the war, the existence in Huelva of this 'very efficient German agent who had the majority of Spanish officials there working for him, either for pay or for fascist ideology'. For more than three years, Montagu had monitored the steady build-up of German espionage activity in southern Spain, the use of Spanish territorial waters by German U-boats, and the activities of what he called this 'super-super efficient agent' in Huelva with 'first-rate' sources, who seemed to own the town: 'No ship can move without being seen, named and reported by W/T [wireless telegraphy]. The Germans get reports from lighthouse keepers, fishing boats, pilots and navy vessels, and agents in neutral fishing boats.' When the Germans began building an infrared spotting system to track ships passing through the Strait of Gibraltar at night, Churchill briefly considered launching a commando raid against the installation. Only the most vigorous diplomatic objections from the British government persuaded the Spanish to intervene and have it removed. For the most part, the Spanish government quietly tolerated, or actively condoned, the German espionage and sabotage of British and Allied ships.

Gibraltar, just fifty miles south of Huelva, was Britain's key to the Mediterranean, 'one of the most difficult and complicated places on the map', in John Masterman's words. The Rock guarded the gateway to the sea, a pivotal British outpost on the Spanish coast, and a magnet for spies. As MI5's senior officer on the island wrote, in a burst of lyricism: Gibraltar was 'the tiniest jewel in the imperial crown . . . this strategic dot on the world's map is not only a colony: it is also a garrison town, a naval base, a commercial port, a civil and military aerodrome, and a shop window for Britain in Europe'. The Abwehr funnelled money to willing Spanish saboteurs in Gibraltar and the surrounding region through one Colonel Rubio Sánchez, codenamed 'Burma', the chief of military intelligence in the Algeciras region. Sánchez was distributing 5,000 pesetas a month to saboteurs in and around Gibraltar. So far, the damage was limited since, as the MI5 chief in Gibraltar pointed out, the saboteurs' 'mercenary instincts were more outstanding than either their efficiency or their enthusiasm'. Montagu believed that special intelligence had successfully foiled several sabotage attempts, but the threat from German espionage in southern Spain was growing. In the month that Operation Mincemeat was born, Montagu warned that German sabotage had 'increased and spread' and was now being actively pursued by the Nazis and their collaborators 'in all Spanish and Spanish-owned ports'.

Adolf Clauss had, so far, enjoyed a most pleasant and productive war. In Madrid and Berlin he was held in high esteem, as 'one of the most important, active and intelligent German agents in the South of Europe'. Even NID and MI6 had a healthy respect for his manipulative skills. His network of spies and informers extended from Valencia to Seville. If anything of importance or interest washed up within fifty miles of the Café del Palma, let alone a body carrying documents, then Clauss would surely hear of it. The German spy's industriousness would be used against him. Later, if the operation worked, the proof of Clauss's espionage activities would be so blatant that it could be used to ignite a diplomatic row, and, with luck, 'sufficient evidence can be obtained to get the Spaniards to eject him'. It was agreed: Huelva was the target, and if the unpleasant Clauss could be undermined, made to look a fool and thrown out of Spain as a result, then so much the better.

A memo was sent to the Royal Navy's hydrographer, the official repository of technical maritime information, with a veiled enquiry: if an object was dropped off the Spanish coast near Huelva, would the tides and prevailing winds bring it ashore? At the same time, Gómez-Beare was instructed to fly to

Gibraltar and inform the flag officer there, and his staff officer in charge of intelligence, of the plan's broad outlines. 'They would have to be in the picture,' Montagu explained, 'in case the body or documents should by any chance find their way to Gibraltar.' Before returning to Madrid, Gómez-Beare should visit the British consuls at Seville, Cadiz and Huelva and instruct them that 'the washing ashore of any body in their area was to be reported only to NA Madrid [naval attaché Alan Hillgarth] and to no other British authority'. Francis Haselden, the consul in Huelva, 'was to be told the outline of the plan without, of course, any description of its object'. Gómez-Beare should then return to Madrid and fully brief his boss.

Captain Alan Hillgarth would stage-manage the Spanish end of the operation, and there was no one better suited to the task.

9

My Dear Alex

Even Charles Cholmondeley's elastic mind was having trouble wrapping itself around the problem of how to transport a corpse from London to Spain, and then drop it in the sea, without being spotted, in such a way that it would appear to be the victim of an air crash. There were, he reckoned, four possible methods of shipping Major Martin to his destination. The body could be transported aboard a surface ship, most easily on one of the naval escorts accompanying merchant vessels in and out of Huelva port. This option was rejected, 'owing to the need for placing the body close inshore'; nothing was more likely to attract the attention of Adolf Clauss and his spies than a Royal Navy ship lingering in shallow waters. An alternative would be to take the body by plane, and simply open the door and throw it out at the right spot. The problem, however, was that 'if the body were dropped in this way it might be smashed to pieces on landing', particularly if it had already started to decompose. A seaplane, such as a Catalina, might be able to land if the conditions were right, and slip the body into the water more gently. Cholmondeley drew up a possible scenario: the seaplane and its cargo would 'come in from out at sea simulating engine trouble, drop a bomb to simulate the crash, go out to sea as quickly as possible, return (as if it were a second flying boat) and drop a flare as if searching down the first aircraft, land, and then while ostensibly searching for survivors, drop the body etc., and then take off again'. On examination, this plan seemed far too elaborate. Any number of things could go wrong, including a real plane crash.

A submarine would be better. The drop could be carried out at night, and if there was insufficient depth of water, then a rubber dinghy could be used to take the body closer inshore. The submarine captain could monitor the winds and tides in order to surface and drop the body at the optimum moment. 'After the body has been planted it would help the illusion if a "set piece" giving a flare and explosion with delayed action fuse could be left to give the impression of an aircraft crash.' The only problem, as Cholmondeley delicately put it, was the 'technical difficulties in keeping the body fresh during the passage'. Submariners were a notoriously hardy bunch, able to withstand long periods underwater in the most foetid and cramped conditions. But even submariners would surely object to having a rotting corpse as a shipmate. Moreover, the operation was top secret: the presence of a dead body on a submarine would not remain secret very long. 'Of these methods,' Cholmondeley concluded, 'a submarine is the best (if the necessary preservation of the body can be achieved).'

There is no easy way to smuggle a dead body aboard a submarine, let alone prevent it from rotting in the warm, fuggy atmosphere of a submarine hold. For help, Cholmondeley turned to Charles Fraser-Smith of 'Q-Branch', chief supplier of gadgets to the Secret Service. A former missionary in Morocco, Fraser-Smith was officially a bureaucrat in the Ministry of Supply's Clothing and Textile Unit; his real job was to furnish secret agents, saboteurs, and prisoners of war with an array of wartime gizmos, such as miniature cameras, invisible ink, hidden weaponry and concealed compasses. (Fraser-Smith provided Ian Fleming with equipment for some of his more outlandish plans, and he doubtless helped to inform the character of 'Q', the eccentric inventor in the James Bond films.)

Fraser-Smith possessed a wildly ingenious but supremely practical mind. He invented garlic-flavoured chocolate to be

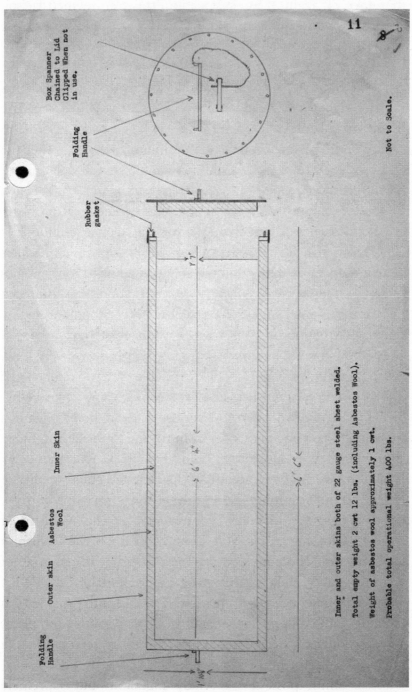

Box Spanner
Chained to Lid
Clipped When not
in use.

Folding
Handle

11

Not to Scale.

Rubber
gasket

Inner Skin

Asbestos
Wool

Outer skin

Folding
Handle

Inner and outer skins both of 22 gauge steel sheet welded.

Total empty weight 2 cwt 12 lbs. (including Asbestos Wool).

Weight of asbestos wool approximately 1 cwt.

Probable total operational weight 400 lbs.

The National Archives

consumed by agents parachuting into France in order that their breath should smell appropriately Gallic as soon as they landed; he made shoelaces containing a vicious steel garrotte; he created a compass hidden in a button which unscrewed clockwise, based on the impeccable theory that the 'unswerving logic of the German mind' would never guess that something might unscrew the wrong way.

With the help of Fraser-Smith, Cholmondeley drew up a blueprint for the world's first underwater corpse transporter. This was a tubular canister, six feet six inches long and almost two feet in diameter, with a double skin made from 22-gauge steel, the space between the skins packed with asbestos wool. One end would be welded closed, while the other had an airtight steel lid, which was screwed on to a rubber gasket with sixteen bolts. A folding handle was attached to either end, and a box spanner was clipped to the lid for easy removal. With the body inside, Cholmondeley estimated the entire package would weigh about 400lb, and would fit snugly into the pressure hull of a submarine. Sir Bernard Spilsbury was consulted once more. Oxygen, he explained, was the cause of rapid decomposition. But 'if most of the oxygen had previously been excluded' from the tube with dry ice, and if the canister was completely airtight, and if the body was carefully packed around with dry ice, then the corpse would 'keep perfectly satisfactorily', and remain as cold as it had been inside the morgue. Fraser-Smith's task, then, was to design 'an enormous Thermos flask', thin enough to fit down the torpedo hatch. The Ministry of Aircraft Production was given the plans, and instructed to build this container as fast as possible, without being told what it was for. On the outside of the canister should be stencilled the words: 'HANDLE WITH CARE – OPTICAL INSTRUMENTS – FOR SPECIAL FOS SHIPMENT.'

Montagu, meanwhile, contacted Admiral Sir Claude Barry, the Flag Officer in command of Submarines (FOS), to find out which submarine might best be used for the mission. Barry replied that British submarines passed Huelva frequently, en route to Malta; indeed, HM Submarine *Seraph* was currently in Scotland, docked at Holy Loch on the Clyde and preparing to return to the Mediterranean in April. The *Seraph* was commanded by Lieutenant Bill Jewell, a young captain who had already carried out several secret assignments and who could be relied on for complete discretion. Montagu drew up some draft operational orders for Jewell, and arranged to meet the submarine officer in London and give him a full briefing on his new mission.

The hydrographer at the Admiralty submitted his report on the winds and tides off the coast at Huelva. As befits a man immersed in the vagaries of marine conditions, he was distinctly non-committal, pointing out that 'the Spaniards and Portuguese publish practically nothing about tides, tidal streams and currents off their coasts'. Moreover, 'the tides in that area run mainly up and down the coast'. If the object was dropped in the right place, in the right conditions, 'wind between S[outh] and W[est] might set it towards the head of the bight near P. Huelva'. However, if the body did wash up on the shore, there was no guarantee it would stay there because 'if it did not strand, it would be carried out again on the ebb'. This was less than perfect, but not discouraging enough to call off the operation. In any case, Montagu reflected, the 'object' in question was a man in a life jacket, rather larger than the object the hydrographer had been asked to speculate about, and might be expected to catch an onshore wind and drift landwards. He concluded: 'The currents on the coast are unhelpful at any point but the prevailing southwest wind will bring the body ashore if Jewell can ditch it near enough to the coast.'

In the last week of March, Montagu drew up a seven-point progress report for Johnnie Bevan, who had just returned from North Africa, where he had coordinated plans for Operation Barclay with Lieutenant Colonel Dudley Clarke. Relations between Montagu and Bevan remained tense. 'I am not quite clear as to who is in sole charge of administrative arrangements in connection with this operation,' Bevan wrote to Montagu, in a note calculated to rile him. 'I think we all agree that there are quite a number of things that might go wrong.' Montagu was fully aware of the dangers and in no doubt whatever that he was in sole charge of the operation, even if Bevan did not see it that way. Privately, Montagu accused Bevan of 'thinking it couldn't come off and disclaiming all responsibility'.

Montagu's report laid out the state of play: the body was almost ready, with Major Martin's uniform and accoutrements selected; the canister was under construction; Gómez-Beare and Hillgarth were standing by in Spain. And there was now a deadline. 'Mincemeat will be taken out as an inside passenger in HMS *Seraph* leaving the northwest coast of this country probably on the 10th April.' That left just two weeks to complete preparations. Montagu and Cholmondeley had deliberately sought to arrange everything before obtaining final approval for the operation, on the assumption that senior officers were far less likely to meddle when presented with a *fait* very nearly *accompli*. But there was now little time to finalise the last, and by far the most important, piece of the puzzle. Montagu's letter to Bevan ended on a note of exasperation: 'All the details are now "buttoned up",' he wrote. 'All that is required are the official documents.'

The debate about what should, or should not, be contained in Major Martin's official letters had already taken up more than a month. It is doubtful whether any documents in the war were subjected to closer scrutiny, or more revisions. Draft after draft was proposed by Montagu and Cholmondeley, revised by more senior officers and committees, scrawled over, retyped, sent off for approval, and then modified, amended, rejected, and rewritten all over again. There was general agreement that, as Montagu had originally envisaged, the main plank of the deception should be a personal letter from General Nye to General Alexander. It was also agreed that the letter should identify Greece as the target of the next Allied assault, and Sicily as the cover target. Beyond this, there was very little agreement about anything at all.

Almost everyone who read the letter thought it could do with 'alteration and improvement'. Everyone, and every official body concerned, from the Twenty Committee to the Chiefs of Staff, had a different idea about how this should be achieved. The Admiralty thought it needed to be 'more personal'. The Air Ministry insisted the letter should clearly indicate the bombing of Sicilian airfields was in preparation for invading Greece, and not a prelude to an attack on Sicily itself. The Chief of the Imperial General Staff and Chairman of the Chiefs of Staff, General Sir Alan Brooke, wanted 'a letter in answer to one from General Alexander'. The Director of Plans thought the operation was premature, and 'should not be undertaken earlier than two months before the real operation', in case the real plans changed. Bevan wondered whether the draft letter sounded 'rather too official', and insisted 'we must get Dudley Clarke's approval as it's his theatre'. Clarke himself, in a flurry of cables from Algiers, warned of the 'danger of overloading this communication', and stuck to the view that it was 'a mistake to play for high deception stakes'.

Bevan remained anxious: 'If anything miscarries and the Germans appreciate that the letter is a plant they would no doubt realise that we intend to attack Sicily.' Clarke framed his own draft, further enraging Montagu, who regarded this effort as 'merely a lowish grade innuendo at the target of the type that has often been, and could always be, put over by a double agent'. The Director of Plans agreed that 'Mincemeat should be capable of much greater things'. Bevan then also tried his hand at a letter, which again Montagu dismissed as 'of a type which could have been sent by signal and would not have appeared genuine to the Germans if carried in the way this document would be'. There was even a brief but fierce debate over how to spell the Greek city 'Kalamata'. The operation seemed to be running into a swamp of detail.

Typically, Montagu tried to insert some tongue-in-cheek

jokes into the letter. He wanted Nye to write: 'If it isn't too much trouble, I wonder whether you could ask one of your ADCs to send me a case of oranges or lemons. One misses fresh fruit terribly, especially this time of year when there is really nothing to buy.' The Chiefs of Staff excised this: General Nye could not be made to look like a scrounger. Even to the Germans. Especially to the Germans. So Montagu tried another line: 'How are you getting on with Eisenhower? I gather he is not bad to work with . . .' That was also removed: too flippant for a general. Next Montagu attempted a quip at the expense of the notoriously big-headed General Montgomery: 'Do you still take the same size in hats, or do you need a couple of sizes larger like Monty?' That, too, was censored. Finally, Montagu managed to squeeze a tiny half-joke in at the end, relating to Montgomery's much-mocked habit of issuing orders every day. 'What is wrong with Monty? He hasn't issued an order of the day for at least forty-eight hours.' That stayed in, for now.

Montagu's temper, never slow to ignite, began smouldering dangerously as the deadline neared and the key letter was tweaked and poked, polished and moulded. And then scrapped, and restarted. Page after page of drafts went into the files, covered with Montagu's increasingly enraged squiggles and remarks.

Finally, the Chiefs of Staff came up with a good suggestion: why not have General Nye draft the letter himself since this would be 'the best way of giving it an authentic touch'? Archie Nye was no wordsmith, but he knew General Alexander fairly well, and he knew the sound of his own voice. Nye read all the earlier drafts, and then put the letter into his own words. The key passage referred to General Sir Henry 'Jumbo' Wilson, then Commander-in-Chief of the Middle East, making it appear that he would be spearheading an attack on Greece; it indicated, falsely, that Sicily was being set up as a cover target for a simultaneous assault in another part of the Mediterranean; it referred to some run-of-the-mill army matters, which also happened to be authentic, such as the appointment of a new commander of the Guards Brigade and an offer from the Americans to award Purple Hearts to British soldiers serving alongside American troops. Above all, it sounded right. Montagu, after so many weeks spent trying to pull off the forgery himself, admitted that Nye's letter was 'ideally suited to the purpose'. The false targets were 'not blatantly mentioned although very clearly indicated', allowing the enemy to put two and two together, making at least six.

Bevan wrote to Nye, asking him to have the letter typed up, and then to sign it in non-waterproof ink, since a waterproof signature might raise suspicions. 'Your signature in ink might become illegible owing to contact with sea water and consequently it would be advisable to type your full title and name underneath the actual signature.'

Bevan had one final tweak. 'General Wilson is referred to three times, as "Jumbo", "Jumbo Wilson" and "Wilson". I wonder whether it would not be more plausible to refer to him on the first occasion as "Jumbo Wilson" and "Jumbo" thereafter.'

Nye replied: 'I referred to him variously intentionally (and committed a couple of – almost – grammatical errors) so as not to be guilty of too meticulous a letter. In fact, in dictating letters, which one normally does, these things occur and I think to leave them in makes it more realistic.' At the last moment, Nye dropped the joke about Monty. 'I would never have written such a thing . . . it wouldn't be me. It might have struck a false note and, if so, did one really gain anything by taking such a risk?' The general toyed with a joke of his own: 'P.S. We saw you on the cinema the other night and Colleen thought you looked uncommonly like Haile Selassie!' General Alexander *did* look a little like the Ethiopian Emperor, and Nye thought this remark 'might help to strike the right note of informality'. On the other hand, General Nye had no sense of humour, and was enough of a realist to know it. His final letter was entirely joke-free. He sent it back with a note and a flourish: 'Now I hope your friends will ensure delivery.' It was, in Montagu's words, 'a truly magnificent letter'.

Telephone: Whitehall 9400
Chief of the Imperial General Staff
War Office
Whitehall
London S.W.1.

23rd April 1943

Personal and Most Secret

My Dear Alex,

I am taking advantage of sending you a personal letter
by hand of one of Mountbatten's officers, to give you the
inside history of our recent exchanges of cables about
Mediterranean operations and their attendant cover plans.
You may have felt our decisions were somewhat arbitrary,
but I can assure you that the C.O.S. Committee gave the
most careful consideration both to your recommendation
and to Jumbo's.

We have had recent information that the Boche have been
reinforcing and strengthening their defences in Greece
and Crete, and C.I.G.S. felt that our forces for the
assault were insufficient. It was agreed by the Chiefs
of Staff that the 5th Division should be reinforced by
one Brigade Group for the assault on the beach south of
CAPE ARAXOS and that a similar reinforcement should be
made for 56th Division at KALAMATA. We are earmarking the
necessary forces and shipping.

Jumbo Wilson had proposed to select SICILY as the
cover target for 'HUSKY', but we had already chosen
it as cover for operation 'BRIMSTONE'. The C.O.S.
Committee went into the whole question exhaustively
again and came to the conclusion that in view of the
preparations in Algeria, the amphibious training which
will be taking place on the Tunisian coast and the
heavy bombardment which will be put down to neutralise
the Sicilian airfields, we should stick to our plan
for making it the cover for 'BRIMSTONE' - indeed, we
stand a very good chance of making him think we will go
for Sicily - it is an obvious objective and one about
which he must be nervous. On the other hand, they felt
there wasn't much hope of persuading the Boche that

the extensive preparations in the Eastern Mediterranean were also directed at Sicily. For this reason they have told Wilson his cover plan should be something nearer the spot i.e. the Dodecanese. Since our relations with Turkey are now so obviously closer, the Italians must be pretty apprehensive about these islands.

I imagine you will agree with these arguments. I know you will have your hands more than full at the moment and you haven't much chance of discussing future operations with Eisenhower. But if, by any chance, you do want to support Wilson's proposal, I hope you will let us know soon, because we can't delay much longer.

I am very sorry we weren't able to meet your wishes about the new commander of the Guards Brigade. Your own nominee was down with a bad attack of the 'flu and not likely to be really fit for another few weeks. No doubt, however, you know Forster personally; he has done extremely well in command of a brigade at home, and is, I think, the best fellow available.

You must be about as fed up as we are with the whole question of war medals and 'Purple Hearts'. We all agree with you that we don't want to offend our American friends, but there is a good deal more to it than that. If our troops who happen to be serving in one particular theatre are to get extra decorations merely because the Americans happen to be serving there too, we will be faced with a good deal of discontent among those troops fighting elsewhere perhaps just as bitterly – perhaps more so. My own feeling is that we should thank the Americans for their kind offer, but say firmly it would cause too many anomalies and we are sorry we can't accept. But it is on the agenda for the next Military Members Meeting, and I hope you will have a decision very soon.

Best of Luck

Yours ever,

Archie Nye

General the Hon Sir Harold R.L.G. Alexander, G.C.B., C.S.I, D.S.O., M.C.

Headquarters, 18th Army Group

The letter twanged every chord. It indicated that there was not one assault planned, but two: General Wilson's army under Montgomery would attack two points in Greece under the codename 'Husky'; General Alexander, under Eisenhower's command, was preparing to launch a separate attack in the western Mediterranean, codenamed 'Brimstone'. The cover target for this latter operation was Sicily. The letter openly stated the intention to deceive the Germans into believing an attack on Sicily was imminent, pointing out that amphibious training in North Africa and the bombardment of Sicilian airfields would tend to support that impression. The training and bombing were, of course, preparations for the real attack on Sicily. Husky was the genuine codename for that invasion; if the Germans came across any allusion to Husky in the future, having read Nye's letter, they would, with luck, assume that this referred to the attack on Greece.

Nye's letter hinted at a second assault in the western Mediterranean, but did not say where the fictional Operation Brimstone would be aimed. Nor did it explain why such an important letter was being carried by this particular officer. There was nothing to explain what Major Martin was doing in North Africa, on the eve of a major invasion. A second letter was called for. Since Martin was on the staff of Combined Operations, Colonel Neville of the Royal Marines, who had been consulted on Major Martin's uniform, drafted a letter to be signed by Lord Louis Mountbatten, Chief of Combined Operations, and addressed it to Admiral Sir Andrew Cunningham, commander-in-chief in the Mediterranean. Cunningham was Eisenhower's naval deputy, a hard-grained Scot with red-rimmed eyes who had been in uniform ever since the Boer War. Like Alexander, his name and seniority would be well known to the Germans; unlike Alexander, there was nothing smooth and refined about Admiral Cunningham, who preferred the cut and thrust of battle to the comforts and trappings of high rank. His favourite expression, when things seemed to be going too well, was: 'It's too velvety-arsed and Rolls-Royce for me.'

The letter clearly indicated that Martin, a trusted expert on landing craft, was coming out to help Admiral Cunningham with preparations for the next amphibious assault.

```
                In reply quote: S.R. 1924/43
                  Combined Operations Headquarters
                            1A Richmond Terrace
                            Whitehall, S.W.1


                                    21st April


Dear Admiral of the Fleet,
  I promised VCIGS that Major Martin would arrange with
you for the onward transmission of the letter he has
with him for General Alexander. It is very urgent and
very 'hot' and as there are some remarks in it that
could not be seen by others in the War Office, it could
not go by signal. I feel sure that you will see that it
goes on safely and without delay.
  I think you will find Martin the man you want. He is
quiet and shy at first, but he really knows his stuff.
He was more accurate than some of us about the probable
run of events at Dieppe and he has been well in on the
experiments with the latest barges and equipment which
took place in Scotland.
  Let me have him back, please, as soon as the assault
is over. He might bring some sardines with him - they
are 'on points' here!
  Yours sincerely,
  Louis Mountbatten


Admiral of the Fleet Sir A.B. Cunningham G.C.B., D.S.O.
Commander-in-Chief Mediterranean
Allied Forces HQ
Algiers
```

The most crucial element of the letter was the last paragraph, clearly indicating that the assault on which Martin would advise was to be on the home of the sardine. Operation Brimstone, therefore, must be aimed at Sardinia. It was, Montagu admitted, a 'laboured' witticism. Like many Britons, Montagu found the German sense of humour somewhat leaden. 'I thought that that sort of joke would appeal to the Germans.'

The Germans might or might not be amused, but would they be taken in? This second letter contained some dangerous flaws. It appeared to indicate that Mountbatten knew the contents of Nye's letter, which, in reality, was exceedingly unlikely. Would the Chief of Combined Operations have needed to explain why the information was not being sent by cable? The sardines joke smelled fishy. Louis Mountbatten was a member of the royal family, and hardly constrained by rationing. If anyone could get sardines whenever he wanted them, it was surely Lord Louis. The reference looked dangerously like an artificial attempt to crowbar the word 'sardines' into the letter.

There was one final letter to add to the cache. This had no military significance whatever, and was included to literally make weight. If Martin was carrying only two letters, he would most probably have put them in an inside pocket for safety. But in that case, they might be overlooked by the Spanish or Germans, as had happened with the body of Lieutenant Turner in 1942. 'Papers actually on the body would run a grave risk of never being found at all due to the Roman Catholic prejudice against tampering with corpses.' A briefcase would be much harder to miss, but if Martin were to carry a briefcase, then he would need something bulkier than a couple of letters to put in it. Hilary Saunders, the House of Commons librarian and the husband of Montagu's colleague Joan Saunders, had just written a pamphlet on the history of the Commandos, a tub-thumping story of derring-do to boost public morale. It was decided that in addition to the other letters, Martin's briefcase would contain proofs of this worthy book, together with another letter from Mountbatten, asking General Eisenhower to write a puff for the American edition.

In reply quote: S.R. 1989/43
Combined Operations Headquarters
1A Richmond Terrace
Whitehall, S.W.1
22nd April

Dear General,

I am sending you herewith two copies of the pamphlet which has been prepared describing the activities of my Command; I have also enclosed copies of the photographs which are to be included in the pamphlet.

The book has been written by Hilary St. George Saunders, the English author of Battle of Britain, Bomber Command, and other pamphlets which have had a great success both in this country and in yours.

The edition which is to be published in the States has already enjoyed pre-publication sales of nearly a million and a half, and I understand the American authorities will distribute the book widely throughout the U.S. Army.

I understand from the British Information Service in Washington that they would like a 'message' from you for use in the advertising for the pamphlet, and that they have asked you direct, through Washington, for such a message.

I am sending the proofs by hand of my Staff Officer, Major W. Martin of the Royal Marines. I need not say how honoured we shall all be if you will give such a message. I fully realise what a lot is being asked of you at a time when you are so fully occupied with infinitely more important matters. But I hope you may find a few minutes' time to provide the pamphlet with an expression of your invaluable approval so that it will be read widely and given every chance to bring its message of co-operation to our two peoples.

We are watching your splendid progress with admiration and pleasure and all wish we could be with you.

```
    You may speak freely to Major Martin in this as well
as any other matters since he has my entire confidence.
    Yours sincerely,
    Louis Mountbatten

    General Dwight Eisenhower
    Allied Forces H.Q.
    Algiers
```

Both letters were written on the same typewriter, and signed by Mountbatten himself, who was told the letters were needed for a secret mission. The only element now missing was the seal of approval from on high.

At 10.30 in the morning on 13 April, the Chiefs of Staff Committee gathered for its seventy-sixth meeting. Presided over by the Chief of the Imperial General Staff, the First Sea Lord and the Chief of the Air Staff, the committee included eight other senior officers from the different services. Item 10 on the agenda was Operation Mincemeat. The letters were approved, and Lieutenant General Sir Hastings 'Pug' Ismay was told to inform Johnnie Bevan of the decision, with instructions to make an appointment with the Prime Minister in order to obtain final approval for the operation to commence. Ismay dropped Churchill a note, advising him that 'the Chiefs of Staff have approved, subject to your consent, a somewhat startling cover plan in connection with HUSKY. May the Controlling Officer see you for five minutes within the next day or two, to explain what is proposed?' The note came back with 'yes', scrawled in Churchill's hand. '10.15 on Thursday.'

Two days later, Bevan found himself sitting on Winston Churchill's bed, and explaining Operation Mincemeat to a Prime Minister wearing his pyjamas and dressing gown, and puffing on a large cigar. Large wine cellars that had once served a stately home opposite St James's Park had been transformed into a fortified network of chambers, tunnels, offices, and dormitories known as the Cabinet War Rooms, the operational nerve centre. Above the war rooms was the Number Ten

Annexe, including the private flat where Churchill usually slept. Britain's wartime Prime Minister tended to work late, whisky in hand, and rise at a commensurate hour.

Bevan had arrived for the meeting in full uniform, at ten o'clock sharp. 'To my surprise I was ushered into his bedroom in the annexe where I found him in bed smoking a cigar. He was surrounded with papers and black and red cabinet boxes.' Churchill loved deception plans, the more startling the better, and relished the seamy, glamorous trade of espionage. 'In the higher ranges of Secret Service work, the actual facts of many cases were in every respect equal to the most fantastic inventions of romance and melodrama,' Churchill wrote after the war.

Bevan handed over a single sheet of foolscap paper, outlining the plan, and Churchill read it through. Bevan felt he had better say something: 'Of course there's a possibility that the Spaniards might find out this dead man was in fact not drowned at all from a crashed aircraft, but was a gardener in Wales who's killed himself with weedkiller.' Bevan had left the details to Montagu and Cholmondeley, and now found himself trying to explain the pathology of chemical poisoning to a Prime Minister in his nightwear, and scrambling the facts in the process. 'Weedkiller goes into the lungs and is very difficult to diagnose,' he bluffed. 'Apparently it would take you three weeks to a month just to find out what it was.'

Churchill 'took much interest' in the scheme, so much so that Bevan felt obliged to warn him that it could go spectacularly wrong. 'I pointed out that there was of course a chance that the plan might miscarry and that we would be found out. Furthermore that the body might never get washed up or that if it did, the Spaniards might hand it over to the local British authority without having taken the crucial papers.'

The Prime Minister's response was characteristically pithy. 'In that case, we shall have to get the body back and give it another swim.'

Churchill was on board. But he had one stipulation: before Operation Mincemeat could go ahead, agreement must be obtained from General Eisenhower, whose invasion of Sicily would be profoundly affected by its success or failure. Leaving Churchill to finish his cigar in bed, Bevan returned to the London Controlling Section offices and dashed off a Most Secret Cypher Telegram, under the codename 'Chaucer', to Eisenhower at Advance Headquarters in Algiers. The response arrived within hours: 'General Eisenhower gives full approval MINCEMEAT.'

Table Tennis Traitor

There was discreet rejoicing among the handful of people privy to the secret. Montagu's dark mood lifted: 'I get more and more optimistic,' he told Iris. 'We ought, by the time you get this, to have exposed Hitler's weak spot (Italy) to attack and the Ities ought not to last too much longer.' Astonishingly, this overt reference to war plans passed the censor. 'Mincemeat is in the making,' Guy Liddell, MI5's head of counterespionage, wrote in his secret diary. 'Plan Mincemeat has been approved by the Prime Minister. The documents are extremely well faked.'

Liddell was in overall command of 'B' Section, that branch of the Security Service dedicated to rooting out enemy spies and suspected agents: he monitored defectors, suspect refugees, Nazi agents, double agents, Soviet sympathisers and, among many others, Ivor Montagu. For while the Hon. Ewen was about to launch a most elaborate feat of espionage, concern about the behaviour of the Hon. Ivor had been steadily growing within both MI5 and MI6.

In May 1942 MI5 noted that Ivor was 'in close touch with many Russians in this country, including members of the embassy, the Trade Delegation and the TASS [news] agency'. Agents introduced into the audience during anti-war rallies, at which Ivor was a regular speaker, reported that he was 'an incurable anti-nationalist'. One P. Wimsey (possibly his real name) filed a report stating that on 16 December 1942, Ivor Montagu addressed a meeting of the Friends of the Soviet Union and stated that 'facilities for sport were far greater in Russia than in England'. Ivor was spotted having lunch with Constantine Zinchenko, Second Secretary at the Soviet Embassy, and consorting with 'men of decidedly foreign appearance, possibly Russian'. A minor scare was set off when he was seen hanging around a secret Royal Observer Corps installation in Watford, but the informant added that he 'did not think Montagu would get anything secret unless he got inside the station'. Given 'his association with the Russians in this country', MI5 concluded, 'any information of importance that came into his possession would undoubtedly be passed on'. Mr Aiken Sneath (again, surely, a name too implausible not to be real) informed MI5, without producing any evidence, that Montagu was 'an active Fifth Columnist'. His neighbours were encouraged to spy on him. They reported that 'he is always very keen to listen to the foreign news' on the radio, and 'has a wooden hut at the bottom of the garden and it is well stocked with books'. Ivor's wife Hell shared his politics, and was also viewed as a potential subversive. It is probable that Hell knew of Ivor's covert activities, and may have contributed to them. If so, MI5 could find no proof.

In 1940 Ivor had applied for a travel permit to visit the USSR as a journalist accredited to the *Daily Worker*. The application was turned down at the urging of MI5. 'It does not seem desirable to allow the Communist Party to have a courier travelling from this country to Moscow. . . a Communist Party member of his standing should not be allowed to leave the country. It is one thing to allow the *Daily Worker* to conduct its war propaganda in this country, but it is another thing to give such a newspaper special facilities for sending correspondents abroad for the purpose of facilitating propaganda.' Ivor complained about his failed application to a left-wing MP, who raised the matter in Parliament, demanding to know 'whether this refusal is personal to Mr Montagu, whether I should be allowed to go, or whether it indicates hostility to Russia?'

Ivor had openly and vehemently opposed the war, but once the Soviet Union became locked in battle with Germany he had declared his willingness to fight. 'I myself have registered and am ready to join up and I hope if I get in shall make a ruddy good soldier,' he told the Woolwich-Plumstead Branch of the Anti-War Congress, words that were immediately channelled back to MI5. Ivor was called up in 1941, but his call-up papers were immediately rescinded, it being 'most undesirable that he should be allowed to serve in HM armed forces'.

'I expect they've checked up on you,' one of his communist friends joked, and was overheard by the MI5 phone-tapper. Ivor had, by this time, moved with his family to the village of Bucks Hill in Hertfordshire, much to the annoyance of his Soviet handler: 'INTELLIGENTSIA lives in the provinces and it is difficult to contact him.'

Ivor Montagu was overdrawn and dishevelled. He once met Sylvia Pankhurst, the suffragette; he listened to the foreign news, denigrated British sporting facilities, promoted Soviet films, mixed with left-wing actors and directors, and read books. He had a German woman living in his house, Elfriede Stoecker, a Jewish refugee. From MI5's point of view, this was all most suspicious. Britain's counterespionage officers saw signs of treachery in everything Ivor Montagu did: they saw it in his friends, his appearance, his opinions, and his behaviour. But above all, they saw it in his passionate, and dubious, love of table tennis.

Suspicion that Ivor's interest in ping pong must disguise some darker purpose was the legacy of Colonel Valentine Vivian, the foremost communist spy hunter in the British Secret Service. Vivian headed Section V, MI6's counterintelligence unit, before going on to become Deputy Chief of SIS in charge of MI6's war station at Bletchley Park. Throughout his long intelligence career most of Vivian's energies, and those of Section V, were directed against British communists and the Comintern, which he regarded 'as a criminal conspiracy rather than a clandestine political movement'. He had become deeply, even fanatically, obsessed with the activities of Ivor Montagu, suspecting, quite rightly, that this son of privilege was more than merely a fellow traveller. But years of intense surveillance – opening Ivor's letters, eavesdropping on his conversations, trailing and photographing him – had so far produced only circumstantial evidence of skulduggery. Colonel Vivian had convinced himself that Ivor Montagu's enthusiasm for ping pong was a cover for something very much more sinister.

Many of Ivor's intercepted letters – a suspiciously large number, in the eyes of the interceptors – referred to the supply of table-tennis equipment from foreign parts. Two Bulgarians, Zoltan Mechlovitz and Igor Bodanszky, wrote to him repeatedly, ostensibly about arcane aspects of the game, the spin potential of different types of ball, and the optimal weight of bat. Vivian gave instructions that the Bulgarians should be investigated to find out if they are 'known to be queer in any other way'. (The word 'other' is most telling.) To the MI6 man in Sofia, Vivian wrote: 'The reason for our tentative interest in these people will appear to you rather quaint. They write interminably to Ivor Montagu about table tennis and the trying out of table-tennis balls. Montagu is, of course, known as a Ping Pong enthusiast well at the heart of the Table Tennis International, but even in England, which is not noted for sanity in this respect, we find it hard to believe that a gentleman can spend weeks upon weeks testing tennis balls.'

The reply from Bulgaria was disappointing: 'Bulgarian police authorities have nothing on their records . . . in a superficial way one would judge that Mechlovitz and Bodanszky are perfectly solid individuals who spend their time testing table-tennis balls.' Even more worrying was Ivor's correspondence, before the war, with Fritz Zinn, treasurer of the German Table Tennis Association. The letters went back and forth, discussing something called the 'Hanno-ball' and 'certain net-stretchers'. There were also hints that Zinn was getting a divorce, and

Ewen Montagu, naval intelligence officer, lawyer, angler, and the principal organiser of Operation Mincemeat.

Charles Cholmondeley, the RAF officer seconded to MI5 whose 'corkscrew mind' first alighted on the idea of using a dead body to deceive the Germans.

Sir Bernard Spilsbury, the senior pathologist at the Home Office and pioneer of forensics who knew more about death than any man alive.

Bentley Purchase, the cheerful coroner of St Pancras.

Iris Montagu, wife of Ewen.

Admiral John Godfrey, the irascible Director of Naval Intelligence and model for 'M' in the Bond novels, whose 'Trout Memo' written in 1939 inspired the deception plan.

Ian Fleming, wartime naval officer and the creator of James Bond, seen here in Room 39 of the Admiralty, the nerve centre of British naval intelligence.

Ivor Montagu, film-maker, communist, table tennis pioneer and Soviet spy, with his wife Hell.

Ewen Montagu at work in Room 13, c. 1943.

Cartoon by Robert Bartlett depicting Ewen Montagu in Room 13. Montagu tended to shout on the scrambler telephone; the telephonist is telling him to hush.

Jean Leslie, the attractive
MI5 secretary whose
photograph would be
used to depict 'Pam',
the fictional fiancée of
'William Martin'.

The staff of Section 17M in Room 13 in the Admiralty basement: Ewen Montagu,
front row, seated second right; Joan Saunders, back row third right; Juliette
Ponsonby to her right; Patricia Trehearne to her left.

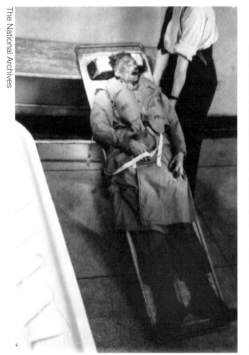

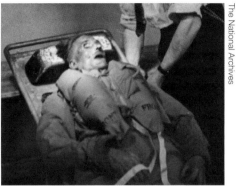

Glyndwr Michael, dressed as Major William Martin, on the Hackney mortuary gurney. His clenched hand and discoloured upper face are evidence of phosphorus poisoning. The figure on the right is PC Glyndon May, the coroner's officer.

Charles Fraser-Smith, the inventor who designed the canister to transport the body.

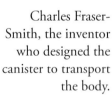

Cholmondeley and Montagu posing outside the van at Langbank on the River Clyde, at dawn on Sunday, 18 April 1943, a few hours before delivering the body to the submarine.

The racing driver Jock Horsfall, enjoying a cup of tea in the back of the van taking the body to Scotland. 'William Martin' is inside the canister.

Salvador Augustus 'Don' Gómez-Beare, Assistant Naval Attaché, First World War flying ace and agent-runner.

The crew of HM Submarine *Seraph* posing in the conning tower. Lieutenant Bill Jewell is at the helm (*left*); his second-in-command, First Lieutenant David Scott, is standing, centre.

'suspected of running an illegal gaming club'. Was the 'Hanno-ball' code for some secret weapon? Was Ivor Montagu sending secret messages to his Bulgarian and German contacts under the seemingly innocent guise of sport? Could Montagu and these shadowy foreigners 'be using the channel of international table tennis for this curious piece of domestic espionage'? Vivian was determined to break up the mysterious table-tennis conspiracy. 'I know this all seems very trivial,' he wrote, 'but when one looks at it closely it is also puzzling.'

Vivian was not alone in thinking that a man who spent so much time discussing table tennis was probably a spy. When he was first inducted into the inner circle of British intelligence, Ewen Montagu had expected that MI5 would make a thorough check of his background, and thus would know about Ivor and his communist politics. 'I had no great faith in the records of MI5. I felt that they were likely to confuse me with my younger and communist brother.' He was half-right. One day, apparently apropos of nothing, John Masterman leaned across the table during a Twenty Committee meeting and asked Montagu in an offhand way: 'How is the table tennis going?' Masterman had clearly been making his own enquiries into the Montagu brothers, and had read up on Colonel Vivian's investigation into the international table-tennis fraternity. 'That's my communist younger brother,' Montagu replied. 'He's the progenitor of table tennis, not me.' Montagu assumed Masterman had simply made a mistake, mixing up the two brothers. But the precise Oxford don did not make mistakes: he was probing, to see if his colleague on the Twenty Committee might just be part of this sinister table-tennis connection.

Vivian was right, of course, but also profoundly wrong. Ivor Montagu *was* spying for the Soviet Union, as Agent Intelligentsia, and would continue to do so for the rest for the war, undetected and unrepentant. On the other hand, his interest in table tennis was neither puzzling nor malign. He just liked table tennis. Sometimes even MI5 officers can go slightly mad looking at the same spot, and imagine shadows where none exist. As Freud once said, when asked about the significance of his ever-present pipe: 'Sometimes a pipe is just a pipe.' And sometimes a table-tennis ball is just a table-tennis ball.

As the launch date for Operation Mincemeat approached, Cholmondeley and Montagu raced around London, attempting to tie up loose ends. The Prime Minister had approved the plan, and HMS *Seraph* was waiting, so the operation was now unstoppable, yet a number of serious problems remained: solutions would be found for all of them, though none was entirely satisfactory.

Nye was instructed to fold the key letter once, but only once. The 'special examiners' at the Censor's Department, responsible for investigating wartime postal communication, then took close-up photographs of the fold using a camera with a microscopic lens. That way, it might be possible to determine whether the letter had been opened and replaced in the envelope. In a final, rather melodramatic demonstration of spycraft, a single dark eyelash was placed in the fold of the paper. If this was still in place if and when the letter was retrieved, it would suggest the letters had not been read, but 'if the eyelash was gone, it would be a simple way of knowing whether the letter had been opened'. Montagu was somewhat coy about the measures taken to detect whether the letters had been tampered with. To his lawyerly mind, the presence or absence of a single eyelash was not the sort of evidence that would stand up in court.

The key letter was placed in an envelope, and then sealed, twice, with the formal wax seal of the VCIGS, depicting the heraldic arms of the War Office. Once again the Censor's Department photographed the ragged edges of the wax seals, to ensure that any tampering could be traced. Mountbatten's letters were also sealed, and the seals photographed in close-up. Once the letters were in his hands, Montagu ensured that he, and only he, handled them. The same went for Martin's other possessions. Montagu kept Pam's letters in his own wallet, unfolding and folding them repeatedly, as a newly engaged man might. The Germans, if they were suspicious and had the opportunity, might well dust the letters for fingerprints: 'Mine were used for Major Martin's throughout,' he wrote. This was a sensible precaution, but hardly a foolproof one. If the Germans compared the fingerprints on the letters to those of the dead man, they would easily spot the difference.

The letters and proofs of the Commandos pamphlet would be placed inside 'an ordinary black Government briefcase with the Royal cipher' embossed on the flap. The key to the lock was placed on Major Martin's key chain. But here arose another issue. The Spaniards would be more likely to notice, and pass to the Germans, an official-looking briefcase, but how to ensure that the briefcase and body arrived in Spain together? The case might be placed in the dead man's hand, but it was highly unlikely that rigor mortis alone would ensure that the body drifted ashore still clutching the case. The man was supposed to have died in an air crash, so the most realistic alternative would simply be to put the body and case into the water simultaneously but separately, and hope both floated ashore. But as the Hydrographer's Department had made clear, the winds and tides off Huelva were highly unpredictable. A body held up by a life jacket would behave quite differently from a soggy leather briefcase filled with paper. The case might sink, or wash up in Portugal. The solution, it was agreed, would be to attach the briefcase to Major Martin using a leather-covered chain of the sort used by bank messengers, passing up the right sleeve and fastened to the belt by a dog-lead clip, with a similar clip at the other end attached to the case handle. The case and corpse would then float ashore chained together. This might serve to underline the value and importance of the contents in the case. The only snag was that British military officers never used this method to transport and safeguard documents.

The chain seemed 'horribly phoney' to Montagu's mind. Cholmondeley was equally dubious. After a meeting with the other planners, he wrote, 'the use of a chain to the bag from the body [is] too doubtful and might endanger the whole operation'. But there seemed little alternative.

From the Air Ministry, Cholmondeley requisitioned a rubber dinghy and oars, of the type used on Catalinas. The original plan had been to distribute debris out at sea and have this float ashore with the body, but further research revealed that 'little or no wreckage floated from a normal aircraft' after a crash, so it was agreed that 'for simplification and for security with the submarine crew, nothing should be released except the rubber dinghy'.

Most frustrating was the apparent impossibility of finding a lookalike to pose for Bill Martin's identity card. Two fellow officers had agreed to be photographed. Neither closely resembled Glyndwr Michael, but time was running out. In late March, Montagu attended a meeting at B1A to discuss the case of Eddie Chapman, the double agent 'Zigzag'. Chapman, a career criminal, had been parachuted into Britain after being trained as a saboteur in a secret spy camp in occupied France, and Montagu was on the committee debating what to do with him. Sitting across the table was Chapman's case officer, Ronnie Reed, a former BBC technician and radio expert. Reed's resemblance to the man in the morgue was striking. Montagu would later assert that he 'might have been the twin brother' of the dead man. He certainly had the same sharp chin and narrow face as Glyndwr Michael, though his hair was thicker and darker. Reed was four years older than the dead man, and wore a small moustache. But he would do. Reed was duly photographed, the epaulettes of the Royal Marines battledress clearly showing on his shoulders. Montagu believed Major Martin's identity card looked 'far more like [him] even after his death than mine was like me'. The only official photograph of William Martin shows a thin-faced man wearing a small, sly smile.

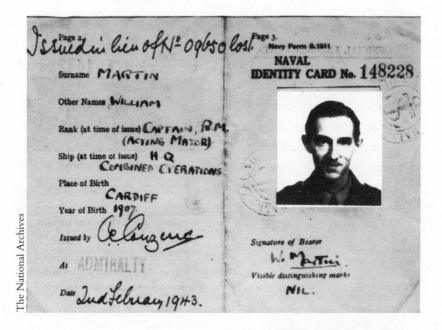

Issued in lien of Nº 09650 lost.

Page 2.

Page 3.

Navy Form S.1511

**NAVAL
IDENTITY CARD No. 148228**

Surname **MARTIN**

Other Names **WILLIAM**

Rank (at time of issue) **CAPTAIN, R.M.
(ACTING MAJOR)**

Ship (at time of issue) **H Q
COMBINED OPERATIONS**

Place of Birth **CARDIFF**

Year of Birth **1907**

Issued by

At **ADMIRALTY**

Date **2nd February 1943.**

Signature of Bearer

W. Martin.

Visible distinguishing marks

NIL.

Bill Martin now had a face that fitted, and a uniform, which might not. They decided to return to St Pancras mortuary and try on the clothes Cholmondeley had broken in. A last-minute discovery that the trousers were too short, or that the shirt did not fit, would be disastrous. Stripping and then dressing the dead body – starting with the late Warden Fisher's underwear and ending with the trench coat – was a task they 'heartily disliked'. Montagu suffered an 'odd psychological reaction' on seeing the corpse lying stiff on the mortuary slab, gradually being transformed into someone he almost knew by the clothes, and the personality, they had fashioned for it. The uniform fitted well. It was decided to leave him in battledress inside the refrigerator, and put the boots on later.

Ronnie Reed, the MI5 case officer who 'might have been the twin brother' of Glyndwr Michael.

HMS *Seraph* had spent five months in the Mediterranean in close underwater combat with the enemy, before returning to Britain for repairs at Blyth dockyard. The submarine had then sailed around Scotland to the River Clyde, where she worked up under realistic conditions, preparing for her next sortie. She was now lying alongside the submarine depot ship HMS *Forth* at Holy Loch on the west coast of Scotland, and ready to return to battle. Her departure date was delayed by a week, and her commander, Lieutenant Bill Jewell, was 'told to report to the intelligence side of the Admiralty' while the remaining officers and crew continued 'normal final training' at Holy Loch. The delay offered an additional week to complete the finishing touches, and ensure that both Alan Hillgarth in Spain and Dudley Clarke in Algiers were fully prepared. Bevan sent a coded telegram to Clarke: 'Mincemeat sails 19th April and operation probably takes place 28th April.'

The later date would also 'enable the operation to be carried out with a waning moon in a reasonably dark period (approximately 28th–29th April)'. Jewell arrived at Submarine Headquarters, a block of flats requisitioned in Swiss Cottage, north London, where Rear Admiral Barry told him to go to an address in St James's. There he was greeted by Montagu, Cholmondeley, Captain Raw, Chief Staff Officer to Admiral Submarines, and a set of operational orders laying out his mission.

Lieutenant Norman Limbury Auchinleck Jewell was thirty years old, with a cheerful grin and bright blue eyes. Understated and charming, Bill Jewell, as he was known, was also tough as teak, ruthless, occasionally reckless, and entirely fearless. He had seen fierce action in the Mediterranean and Atlantic. His submarine had been depth-charged, torpedoed, machine-gunned and mistakenly shot at by the RAF; he had spent seventy-eight hours, slowly suffocating with his crew, in a half-crippled submarine at the bottom of the sea; he had taken part in several clandestine operations which, had they been intercepted, might have led to espionage charges and, possibly, a German firing squad. In four years of watery war, Jewell had seen so much secrecy, strangeness and violence that the request to deposit a dead body in the sea off Spain did not remotely faze him. 'In wartime, any plan that saved lives was worth trying,' he reflected.

Jewell was never informed of the identity of the body, or the exact nature of the papers he was carrying, and he hardly needed to be told of 'the vital need for secrecy'. The tall man with the extravagant moustache was introduced as 'a squadron leader for RAF intelligence'. The body, Cholmondeley explained, would be brought to him in Scotland, 'packed, fully clothed and ready', inside a large steel tube. This canister could be lifted by two men, but should on no account be dragged by a single handle, 'as the steel is made of light gauge to keep the weight as low as possible', and it might give way if roughly handled. The possibility of the container breaking and the body falling out was too awful to contemplate. The canister would fit down the torpedo hatch, and could then be hidden below decks. Jewell would also receive a rubber dinghy in a separate package, a locked briefcase with chain attached, and three separate identity cards for William Martin, with three different photographs. In idle moments, Montagu had taken to rubbing Martin's fake identity cards on his trouser leg to give them the patina of use.

What, Jewell asked, should he tell the men under his command about this large object on his small ship? Montagu explained that the lieutenant could take his officers into his confidence once underway, but that the rest of the crew should be told only that the container 'held a super-secret automatic meteorological reporting apparatus, and that it was essential that its existence and position should not be given away or it would be removed by the Spaniards and the Germans would learn of its construction'.

Jewell pointed out that if the weather was rough, the officers might need the help of the crew to get the canister up on deck. If a member of the crew spotted the body, he should be told that 'we suspected the Germans of getting at papers on bodies washed ashore and therefore this body was going to be watched: if our suspicions were right the Spaniards would be asked to remove the Germans concerned'. This cover story could also be told to the officers, but 'Lt Jewell was to impress on [them] that they would never hear the result and that if anything leaked out about this operation not only would the dangerous German agents not be removed, but the lives of those watching what occurred would be endangered'.

Upon reaching a position 'between Portil Pillar and Punta Umbria just west of the mouth of the Rio Tinto River', Jewell should assess the weather conditions. 'Every effort should be made to choose a period with an onshore wind.' Jewell studied the charts and estimated 'the submarine could probably bring the body close enough inshore to obviate the need to use a rubber dinghy'. Cholmondeley had originally envisaged setting off an explosion out at sea to simulate an air crash, but after some discussion 'the proposed use of a flare was dropped'. There was no point in attracting any unnecessary attention.

Under cover of darkness, the canister should be brought up through the torpedo hatch 'on specially prepared slides and lashed to the rail of the gun platform'. Any crew members should then be sent below, leaving only the officers on deck. 'The container should then be opened on deck as the "dry-ice" will give off carbon dioxide.' It would also smell terrible.

Montagu and Cholmondeley had given a great deal of thought to exactly how the briefcase should be attached to Major Martin. No one, even the most assiduous officer, would sit on a long flight with an uncomfortable chain running down his arm. 'When the body is removed from the container all that will be necessary will be to fasten the chain attached to the briefcase through the belt of the trench coat which will be the outer garment of the body . . . as if the officer has slipped the chain off for comfort in the aircraft, but has nevertheless kept it attached to him so that the bag should not either be forgotten or slide away from him in the aircraft.' Jewell should decide which of the three identity cards most closely resembled the dead man in his current state, and put this in his pocket. The body, with life jacket fully inflated, should then be slipped over the side. The inflated dinghy should also be dropped, and perhaps an oar, 'near the body but not too near if that is possible'. Jewell's final task would be to reseal the canister, sail into deep water, and then sink it.

If, for any reason, the operation had to be abandoned, then 'the body and container should be sunk in deep water', and if it was necessary to open the canister to let water in, 'care must be taken that the body does not escape'. A signal should be sent with the words: 'Cancel Mincemeat'. If the drop was successful, then another message should be sent: 'Mincemeat completed'.

Jewell noted that the two intelligence officers seemed utterly absorbed by the project, and had obviously had 'a pleasant time building up a character'. Before the meeting broke up, Montagu asked the young submariner if he would like to contribute, in a small way, to 'making a life for the Major of Marines'. A nightclub ticket was needed for the dead man's wallet. Would Lieutenant Jewell care to spend a night on the town, and then send over the documentary evidence? 'I had the enjoyment of going around London nightclubs on his ticket,' said Jewell. 'It was an enjoyable period.'

While Jewell returned north with his new operational orders and a slight hangover, another telegram was despatched to General Eisenhower in Algiers. 'Mincemeat sails 19th April and operation probably takes place 28th April but could if necessary be cancelled on any day up to and including 26th April.'

If all went according to plan, Major Martin would wash up in Spain on or soon after 28 April, where an extraordinary reception was being prepared for him by Captain Alan Hugh Hillgarth: naval attaché in Madrid, spy, former gold prospector and, perhaps inevitably, successful novelist.

Gold Prospector

In his six novels, Alan Hillgarth hankered for a lost age of personal valour, chivalry and self-reliance. 'Adventure was once a noble appellation borne proudly by men such as Raleigh and Drake,' he wrote in *The War Maker*, but it is now 'reserved for the better-dressed members of the criminal classes'. Hillgarth's own life read like something out of the *Boy's Own Paper*, or the pages of Rider Haggard.

The son of a Harley Street ear, nose and throat surgeon, Hillgarth had entered the Royal Naval College at the age of thirteen, fought in the First World War as a fourteen-year-old midshipman (his first task was to assist the ship's doctor during the Battle of Heligoland Bight by throwing amputated limbs overboard) and skewered his first Turk, with a bayonet, before his sixteenth birthday. At Gallipoli he found himself in charge of landing craft, as all the other officers had been killed. He was shot in the head and leg, and spent the recovery time learning languages and cultivating a passion for literature. Hillgarth was small and fiery, with dense bushy eyebrows and an inexhaustible supply of energy. He was also an arborphile: he loved trees, and was never happier than in forest or jungle.

In 1927, Evelyn Waugh recalled his first meeting with 'a young man called Alan Hillgarth, very sure of himself, writes shockers, ex-sailor'. By this time, Hillgarth had embarked on a second career as a novelist, a third, as adviser to the Spanish Foreign

Legion during the uprising of the Rif tribes in Morocco, and a fourth, as a 'King's Messenger', carrying confidential messages on behalf of the government. But it was Hillgarth's fifth career, as a treasure hunter, that defined the rest of his life, and the next stage of Operation Mincemeat.

In 1928, Hillgarth met Dr Edgar Sanders, a Swiss adventurer born in Russia and living in London, who told him a most intriguing story. Sanders had travelled to the interior of Bolivia in 1924, lured by legends of a vast hoard of gold, the treasure of Sacambaya, mined by the Jesuits, and hidden before they were expelled from South America in the eighteenth century. Sanders showed Hillgarth a document, given to him by a Boer War veteran and rubber tapper, who claimed to have obtained it from the family of an elderly Jesuit priest. The document identified the hiding place of the gold in a network of underground caverns 'that took five hundred men two and one half years to hollow out'.

Sanders claimed to have found the site amid the ruins of a once-great Jesuit colony deep in the remote Quimsa Cruz range of the eastern Andes.

A 'squarish man with conspicuously high cheekbones and hard slate eyes', Sanders was fanatical in his quest, and utterly convincing. He believed the Jesuits had created the underground cavern by tunnelling from the river bank but the water table had since risen: getting to the entrance would require large pumps, digging equipment, a lot of money, and a great deal of sweat. Sanders invited Hillgarth to join him in what promised to be the greatest treasure hunt of all time. The twenty-eight-year-old accepted without hesitation.

The Sacambaya Exploration Company was duly formed. On the eve of the Great Crash, money could be minted from dreams, and investors flocked to a project promising returns of 48,000 per cent.

Hillgarth and Sanders set about recruiting 'men who had had considerable experience of harsh conditions', which were described in detail. 'Sacambaya is a poisonous place, a dark, dirty valley, shut in by hills that rise almost immediately to 4,000 feet. It is either very dry or you are flooded out. It is generally very hot by day and pretty near freezing at night. It abounds in bugs, fleas, flies, ants, mosquitoes, sand flies, rattlesnakes and other kinds of snakes. It is famous among Indians as a plague spot of Malaria. There are also skunks.' There were also bandits, no certainty of success, and a high probability of death. But this was an age that revered Shackleton and Scott. Some twenty-three men were chosen on the basis of expertise, resilience and amusement value, including a photographer, a doctor, a Serbian miner and an American engineer named Julius Nolte.

On 1 March 1928, the expedition set sail from Liverpool on the first stage of the 9,000-mile journey from England to Sacambaya. The 40 tons of equipment stashed in the hold included two Morris six-wheel tractors, four vast compressors to drive the pneumatic hoists, picks, spades and drills, two pumps, six cranes, a petrol motor, winches, electric light plants, forges, tents, mosquito nets, and a circular saw to cut wood for the railway that would have to be built at the other end. Dr P. B. P. Mellows, of St Bartholomew's Hospital, brought, in addition to the usual medical supplies, 28,000 quinine tablets to fight malaria and 5,000 aspirin. Hillgarth purchased twenty rifles and twenty automatic pistols, four shotguns, two automatic rifles and enough ammunition to start a small war.

From the port of Arica in Chile, the expedition chartered a train to take them the 330 miles to La Paz, then south, as far as a station called Eucalyptus, where the line stopped. From here the road, such as it was, went as far as Pongo, a one-eyed mining town built to service the Guggenheim mines and presided over by a formidable American woman named Alicia O'Reardon Overbeck, whom the team nicknamed 'Mrs Starbird'. Sacambaya was still forty-five miles distant, along a track partly washed away by rains. Now the hard work began.

The smaller machinery was packed into loads of up to 500lb, and strapped on to reluctant mules, while the largest items, including the compressors each weighing 1½ tons, had to be dragged along the mountain tracks using manpower and oxen.

'This,' said Hillgarth, with echoing understatement, 'was quite an undertaking.' In some places the track had to be rebuilt, cut out of the solid rock. In others, the heavy machinery had to be lowered with a block and tackle. One compressor, two oxen and several men hurtled over the edge, and were saved only by becoming entangled in trees thirty feet below. Hillgarth, five other white men, and twenty Indians, successfully transferred all the equipment to Sacambaya in five weeks and four days. Total losses en route amounted to 'one case containing 200lb of macaroni'.

That was the last piece of good news.

Armed with modern technology and an ancient document, the Sacambaya Exploration Company now set about picking, drilling, pumping and blasting its way '100 feet into the hillside' in pursuit of Jesuit gold. For ten hours a day, six days a week, from June to October, the men hacked into the mountain. Some 37,000 tons of rock were removed to create an enormous hole.

Conditions at Sacambaya were quite as nasty as advertised. Within weeks, three-quarters of the men had jiggers – small worms that burrow into the feet. 'A complete absence of fresh fruit and vegetables from our dietary [sic] has brought on chronic constipation, but a great range of purges varying in propulsive powers have catered for all tastes,' Dr Mellows reported cheerily. The mules and oxen came under attack from vampire bats, which were also partial to human gore if they could get it. 'One of our party awakened the other night and was startled to find a vampire bat tearing at his mosquito net.' Mellows identified a new ailment, which he named *Sacambayaitis*: 'Claustrophobia brought on by being shut up in an unhealthy valley between high mountains for month after month, working hard, living on a monotonous diet, with no diversions, subject to constant fear of possible attack by bandits.'

The only member of the team immune to Sacambayaitis was Alan Hillgarth. The photographs of the expedition show him fresh-faced and happy: digging, grinning, never without a tie, even when helping to perform a rustic appendectomy on a colleague.

It was not the jiggers, the claustrophobia, the constipation, bats, or bandits that finally did for the Sacambaya Exploration Company, but water. It poured from the sky in sheets, and bubbled up from the ground in gouts, filling every hole as soon as it was dug, despite the panting efforts of the pumps. Finally, even Hillgarth had to admit defeat, despite believing that the cave wall might be just fifteen feet away.

The expedition had been an unmitigated, magnificent disaster. The company went spectacularly bust. Two of the team headed into the interior and were never seen again. The chief engineer was left behind in Pongo. 'He has fallen seriously in love with Mrs Starbird, and apparently does not intend to leave.' The Serbian miner was poisoned in La Paz, 'either by the hotel people or the police'.

Sanders was flung into a Bolivian jail. Some months earlier, he realised the Bolivian police were intercepting his mail, so he had planted a fake letter referring to a shipment of mustard gas, to see if this would flush them out. The Bolivian authorities took the letter at face value: Sanders was accused of planning a coup against the Bolivian government, and charged with smuggling arms into the country, including fifty machine guns and 100 tons of poison gas.

Hillgarth returned to Britain to face the wrath of his investors, and the realisation that he had been thoroughly and comprehensively duped. Sanders's documents, it transpired, were fakes. The words on them had not even been written by a Spanish speaker, since they contained numerous grammatical errors and modern English idioms directly translated into Spanish.

The Sacambaya debacle had been a salutary experience. A very large hole in the Bolivian jungle was testament to the heroic pointlessness of that achievement, but it was also a lesson that Hillgarth would never forget: otherwise entirely sensible people could be persuaded to believe, passionately, what they already wanted to believe. All it required was a few, carefully forged documents, and some profoundly wishful thinking on the part of the reader. The Sacambaya trip formed the basis for Hillgarth's fifth and most successful novel, *The Black Mountain*, published in 1933 to acclaim from, among others, Graham Greene.

By then, Hillgarth had settled in Majorca with his wife Mary and three children, becoming honorary British vice consul, and then consul, in Palma. At the same time, 'he doubled up as a spy'. On the eve of the Spanish Civil War, Winston Churchill met Hillgarth in Majorca, on his way to a holiday in Marrakesh. They got on famously. When Clementine Churchill complained about the smell of the drains at their hotel, Hillgarth invited the Churchills to stay at his picturesque villa, Son Torella.

Hillgarth played a pivotal role as a go-between during the Spanish Civil War, helping to arrange prisoner swaps between the two sides, and successfully ensuring the bloodless handover of Minorca to Franco's forces in 1939. The commander of Nationalist forces in the Balearic Islands was Rear Admiral Salvador Moreno Fernández, and it was through him that Hillgarth arranged for the Republican forces to leave the island, thus averting, in Hillgarth's words, 'an intense bombardment which could have caused some 20,000 deaths'. Hillgarth's prolonged negotiations with Moreno, a convivial and subtle politician, marked the start of a most fruitful partnership. When Captain John Godfrey of HMS *Repulse* wanted to dock in Barcelona, it was Hillgarth who ensured, through his navy contacts with Franco's regime, that the British ship did not come under air attack.

As the newly appointed Director of Naval Intelligence at the start of the war, Godfrey remembered Hillgarth, and recommended his promotion to naval attaché in Madrid. It was an inspired appointment, to a most difficult and sensitive job. Spain was pivotal to British interests, the key to the Mediterranean and Gibraltar. With the fall of France, there were German troops on Spain's border. Franco was in debt to both Italy and Germany for arms. Would he side with the Axis powers, and if he did not, and Spain remained non-belligerent, would Hitler invade? Hillgarth's role would be to combat Nazi influence, stymie German sabotage efforts, prevent U-boats refuelling and resupplying at Spanish ports, and countering the pro-Axis Falange within Franco's government. With Ian Fleming, he helped to plan the campaign of sabotage and guerrilla war that would erupt if Spain was invaded, codenamed 'Operation Goldeneye' (the name that Fleming would eventually bestow on his Caribbean home). British policy required a nuanced approach, and Hillgarth's reports showed how well he understood that delicate balance: Franco was anxious to preserve his neutrality and freedom of action, Hillgarth reported, but 'a decisive German victory over Russia might enable the Falange to take complete control [and] Spain would probably throw in her lot with Germany'.

Sir Samuel Hoare, a former Chamberlain loyalist appointed ambassador in Madrid by Churchill, played this tricky game at the diplomatic level. Hillgarth did so at a subterranean level, while simultaneously coordinating the operations of MI6, SOE and his own network of agents. In all of this, Hillgarth had the personal backing of Winston Churchill (they were distinctly similar characters), who regarded him as a 'very good' man 'equipped with a profound knowledge of Spanish affairs'. The Prime Minister instructed Hillgarth to write to him 'privately about anything interesting'. Ian Fleming shared Churchill's high opinion of Hillgarth, describing him as a 'useful petard and a good war-winner'. Despite contrasting personalities, Hoare and Hillgarth got on well, and cooperated closely. The ambassador called him 'the embodiment of drive'. By contrast

Kim Philby, who ran counterintelligence on the Iberian desk at MI6 and was later revealed as a Soviet spy, disliked Hillgarth intensely, believing that Churchill's support, the 'secret funds that were made available to him for undercover activity', and his direct access to 'C', Stewart Menzies, the head of MI6, had all 'helped to feed the gallant officer's illusions of grandeur'. Philby was particularly irked by Hillgarth's choice of 'Armada' as a codename, which he considered self-inflating.

It is hard to say which reflected better on Hillgarth: the admiration of Fleming and Churchill, or Philby's animosity. Philby would have been even angrier had he known the extent of funds available to Hillgarth, for the purposes of bribery, on a staggering scale. Adolf Clauss bribed policemen and dock workers; Gómez-Beare paid off 'local police, dock watchmen and stevedores'. But Hillgarth bribed generals.

The Spanish armed forces contained many patriotic monarchists opposed to the fascist Falange, who had no desire to become 'expendable parts of Hitler's war machine'. Such officers, Hillgarth calculated, needed only a little financial encouragement to lobby Franco against an alliance with Hitler, and keep Spain out of the war. The money was channelled to the generals through Juan March, a Majorcan businessman whom Hillgarth had known for many years. March had made a fortune in tobacco, worked for British intelligence in the First World War, helped to finance Franco's rebellion in 1936, and purchased twelve bombers for Mussolini. He was small, thin, greedy, clever, morally void and monstrously bent. March 'took corruption for granted, and used it casually and openly'. He had been imprisoned for bribery, escaped to France, and by 1939 he was the richest, and dodgiest, man in Spain, nicknamed 'the last pirate of the Mediterranean', with a fortune that extended to shipping, oil, banks and newspapers. 'It would be a mistake to trust him an inch,' Hillgarth reported cheerfully. But March was also prepared to back Britain and that, as far as Hillgarth was concerned, was all that mattered: 'He has already had two

German agents shot in Iviza [Ibiza], though I did not ask him to do so . . .' March was the ideal conduit for bribing the generals. The money would have no British fingerprints on it, and if word ever leaked that March was involved, no one would be remotely surprised.

In the first phase of the scheme, with Churchill's approval, $10 million was released by the Treasury, and deposited in a Swiss bank in New York. From this, selected Spanish generals were invited to make withdrawals, in pesetas, with the balance to be paid after the war. Some $2 million is thought to have been funnelled to General Antonio Aranda Mata, who was expected to take over the army if Franco should fall. Another happy beneficiary was General Luis Orgaz y Yaldi, the commander of Spanish Morocco. (Orgaz was being rewarded by both sides: the Abwehr promised him 'an amphibious car'.) It is probable that Admiral Moreno, the man who had negotiated the surrender of Minorca with Hillgarth and had since been promoted to Navy Minister in Franco's government, was also on the payroll. The admiral had long opposed Spanish involvement in the war: he kept Hillgarth abreast of the mood in Francoist government circles, reassuring him that if Germany ever invaded Spain there would be a general uprising: 'There was not a Spaniard who would not wish to fight if the Germans came in,' he told Hillgarth.

Hillgarth poured money into the pockets of sympathetic officers. 'The Cavalry of St George have been charging,' noted Hugh Dalton, head of SOE and Minister for Economic Warfare. This was an oblique reference to the image of St George slaying the dragon on the British gold sovereign. In September 1941, the scheme hit a snag. The Swiss account in New York was locked, as part of the American freeze on European assets, but Hillgarth urgently needed reinforcements from St George's cavalry. 'We must not lose them now, after all we have spent – and gained,' wrote Churchill, who sent an urgent appeal, via Henry Morgenthau, the US Treasury Secretary, to Roosevelt, urging him to unfreeze the New York account. The sluice gates reopened. There is no documentary evidence that Roosevelt backed this campaign of corruption and subversion but, as the historian David Stafford notes, 'his approval can safely be assumed'.

The bribery scheme continued up to 1943, but whether the 'Cavalry of St George' achieved anything is open to question. Many Spanish officers were already disinclined to become entangled in the war and naturally opposed to the fascists, fearing that 'German victory would mean servitude for Spain, and an end to the individual freedom which is as necessary as air to most Spaniards'. Even Hillgarth acknowledged, with the sort of generalisation beloved of certain Englishmen, that 'the Spaniard is xenophobic and suspicious and wants to keep clear of other peoples' quarrels'. The money may simply have made the generals rich – and Juan March even richer – but it certainly reaffirmed Churchill's faith in his Madrid spymaster, and pay-master: 'I am finding Hillgarth a great prop,' he said.

Hillgarth possessed, by his own account, 'a natural sympathy' for Spain. 'Handling Spaniards is a special technique,' he wrote. 'Everything in Spain is on a personal basis.' He cultivated his contacts like an expert forester planting trees, propagating and nourishing them, metaphorically and literally, with large and lavish dinners. An intelligence officer, he once remarked, 'will be at a very definite disadvantage if he is a teetotaller. A good digestion is also important.' Charming, polished, and speaking perfect Spanish, Hillgarth moved effortlessly through the Madrid elite, making contacts with generals, admirals, diplomats, and foreign newspaper correspondents. 'Even during the worst of the war, I had little difficulty in maintaining old friendships and making new ones.'

Hillgarth could call in (or buy in) favours from every level of Spanish officialdom. But perhaps his most useful agent, whom he ran in tandem with MI6, was 'Agent Andros', a senior officer in the Spanish navy. Andros has never been identified. More than sixty years later, MI6 will not divulge the name of the 'very reliable and well-placed straight agent called ANDROS who obtained information of great value'. Andros would also demonstrate his value as a double agent. In 1943 he was approached in Madrid by a senior officer of the SD, the Sicherheitsdienst, the feared intelligence service of the SS, named Eugene Messig, who asked him 'to supply intelligence which he would send straight to Berlin (i.e. not through the German intelligence HQ in Madrid)'. The SD and the Abwehr were mutually suspicious rivals. 'C' was initially dubious, fearing that this 'might compromise a very valuable agent', but Hillgarth was keen to open a channel of disinformation into the SS. Andros accepted Messig's invitation, and began feeding him nuggets of false information, selected by Hillgarth: 'The items were so chosen that the Germans would be bound to draw the deductions that we wanted.' Andros, who also went by the codename 'Blind', proved a brilliant double agent, successfully passing on information indicating that the Spanish navy had learned, through its own sources, that U-boats were liable to attack from British planes and submarines in Spanish waters: 'Messig swallowed the stories whole, was extremely pleased, and continually pressed for more.'

In order to mislead Messig, Andros must have had genuine access to top-grade Spanish intelligence. 'It was a delicate job. However, Andros was in a particularly good position to inform Messig.' The admission that Andros was in 'a particularly good position' to misinform the Germans suggests that he may have been highly placed within Spanish naval intelligence. Whoever Andros was, Hillgarth trusted him completely.

The British and German spies circled one another, spitting like cats. Hillgarth knew that 'copies of all our telegrams were given to the Germans', and that his telephone was tapped: 'It seemed the listening in was done by an Abwehr member, but it might have been done by a Spanish telephone operator.' 'Only by naval ciphers can really safe messages be sent,' he reported.

One of the guards at the British Embassy was 'suborned by a woman in German pay', but was intercepted before he could do much damage. Even so, he knew that the Germans 'kept lists of everyone who went in and out of the British embassy'.

Hillgarth relished the contest – 'the Germans would have someone following him, and he would have someone following the Germans' – and found the constant surveillance, by both Spanish and German spies, quite amusing since these were usually 'very amateurish and inefficient'. Occasionally he would bump into Abwehr officers at official functions. 'Our deportment towards the German diplomats was to behave as if they did not exist. If we met them at a party, we ignored them. They did exactly the same to us.'

Madrid was the crucible of European espionage, and as the chief among the British spies, Hillgarth found himself fielding some odd customers from the intelligence world.

Dudley Wrangel Clarke was the master of 'A' Force, based in Cairo, the unit devoted to deception operations in the Mediterranean. As the intelligence officer in overall command of deception for Operation Husky, Clarke had been involved at every stage in the build-up to Operation Mincemeat. But Hillgarth had already come across him in a very different guise. In October 1941 he had bailed Dudley Clarke out of a Spanish jail. There was nothing so odd in that: Hillgarth was often bailing people out of jail. What made the occasion special, and acutely embarrassing, was Colonel Clarke's outfit: he was dressed as a woman. A Spanish police photograph shows this master of deception in high heels, lipstick, pearls, and a chic cloche hat, his hands, in long opera gloves, demurely folded on his lap. He was not supposed to even be in Spain, but in Egypt. In spite of the colonel's predicament, in the photo he seems thoroughly comfortable, even insouciant.

His fellow spy chiefs were not. Guy Liddell of MI5 noted: 'The circumstances of his release were to say the least of it peculiar. At the time he was dressed as a woman complete with brassiere, etc.' It is the 'brassiere etc.' that gives it away. What on earth was the blighter thinking of? A chap might go in disguise, if needed, but in a brassiere? The Spanish authorities seemed to find the incident equally amusing, and put out a propaganda leaflet announcing that a man named 'Wrangal Craker' who claimed to be *The Times*'s correspondent in Madrid had been arrested, dressed as a woman.

Having helped to get Clarke out of prison, Hillgarth obtained the photographs of his colleague, both in and out of drag, and gleefully sent them to Churchill's personal assistant, Charles 'Tommy' Thompson, who showed them to the Prime Minister. Hillgarth attached a deadpan note: 'Herewith some photographs of Mr Dudley Wrangel Clarke as he was when arrested and after he had been allowed to change.' The 'after' photograph showed Clarke in his more usual bow tie and jacket. 'PM has seen,' said a note scrawled on Hillgarth's letter. Sadly, history does not relate Churchill's reaction to what he had seen. Word of the photographs spread around Whitehall: some wondered whether Clarke was 'sound in mind', while the more sympathetic explanation was that 'he is just the type who imagines himself as the super secret service agent'. It did his career no long-term damage, but Dudley Clarke's strange episode of cross-dressing remains an enduring mystery.

By the spring of 1943, following the successful North African campaign, the danger than Spain might join the Axis had receded, and after more than three years of playing cat and mouse with the Germans, Hillgarth was keen to counterattack. In February 1943 he sent a letter to the Director of Naval Intelligence, declaring: 'It is time to pass from the defensive to the offensive. It is time to get tough.' Axis submarines were still using Spanish waters; Spanish fishing vessels were being used to spot U-boat targets; German and German-paid saboteurs were preying on British shipping, and the Spanish port authorities were supplying the Abwehr with 'more or less any naval intelligence they obtain'. All of this was in direct violation of

Spanish neutrality. Despite repeated British protests, Hillgarth pointed out, the Axis was 'allowed with little or no interference from the Spanish authorities, and in spite of constant British representations, to establish and maintain observation and reporting stations at vantage points along the Spanish coast'. Hillgarth specifically cited the activities of Adolf Clauss's older brother Luis in Huelva.

The solution Hillgarth proposed was simple and dramatic: 'I have found a good man prepared to stick a limpet bomb on one of the larger German ships from a fishing boat, on a dark night with rain.' The cost of the operation would be 50,000 pesetas, 5,000 before and 45,000 on completion. The bomb would be timed to go off after the enemy ship left harbour. The Foreign Office should not be involved. 'All operations are, if I may say so, better left to me,' wrote Hillgarth. 'If anything goes wrong there is a perfectly good comeback by referring to German sabotage in Spain, and I could always be disowned and officially sacrificed. I am happy to stand the rub, as I feel so strongly that the situation now warrants action of this kind.' All Hillgarth wanted was a nod of approval, and a bomb.

The request was turned down flat. If the Spaniards got wind that the British naval attaché was sticking limpet mines to boats, there would be a diplomatic explosion, possibly undoing all Hillgarth's good work to date. 'You and your staff have shown that you are quite able to take care of yourselves, but I am not prepared to take the chance of anything going wrong,' wrote Commodore Rushbrooke, the new Director of Naval Intelligence, adding that an attack on German shipping in Spanish waters was both 'undesirable and unnecessary'. Kim Philby, looking back, reckoned that a campaign of British sabotage would have sparked a 'James Bond style free-for-all in Spain'.

Hillgarth was deeply frustrated, itching to land a blow on his German adversaries, but held in check. The Cavalry of St George had disbanded. He was getting bored. At the very moment Hillgarth's sabotage plan was scuppered, Gómez-Beare reappeared in Madrid, fresh from his briefing on Operation Mincemeat and with new instructions for his boss: once the body was delivered by HMS *Seraph*, it would be up to Hillgarth to coordinate its reception in Spain, find out where and when it landed, and what happened to the documents, and maintain the essential fiction that a crucial batch of secrets had gone missing.

Hillgarth the naval novelist would now write the second chapter of Operation Mincemeat. He would take the role of hero; Gómez-Beare would play second lead; Adolf Clauss in Huelva would, with luck, act as the helpful receptionist.

And in Madrid, at the very centre of the web of German intelligence, was a man who might have been typecast as the leading villain of the piece.

The Spy Who Baked Cakes

The Abwehr's agents and informants in Spain came not as single spies, but in battalions; Spanish collaboration with the Germans, as one MI5 officer put it, was 'ubiquitous'. Of the 391 people employed in the German Embassy in Madrid, 220 were Abwehr officers, divided into sections for espionage, sabotage and counterespionage, deploying some 1,500 agents throughout Spain, many of them German émigrés. These, in turn, recruited their own subagents in a vast and sprawling network: 'All classes were represented from Cabinet Ministers to unnamed stewards of cargo ships', according to a wartime intelligence assessment. 'In the higher ranks there was undoubtedly a genuine ideological sympathy but at a lower level the transaction was mainly financial and in a country where so many live at starvation level, recruiting was fairly easy.' The quantity of intelligence pouring into the Abwehr's Madrid headquarters, which adjoined the embassy, was so enormous that it required thirty-four radio operators, ten secretaries (including Adolf Clauss's cousin, Elsa) and maintained a direct teletype link with Berlin, via Paris.

Thanks to one of his agents, a senior officer in the Dirección General de Seguridad, the Spanish security service, Alan Hillgarth knew the name, rank, role and in most cases the codename, of virtually every Abwehr agent of importance. At Hillgarth's behest, this agent had set up a special section to monitor German espionage. Ostensibly this was to ensure that the Spanish Ministry of the Interior was kept informed of covert German activities. 'Indeed, the reports went to the Ministry of the Interior,' wrote Hillgarth, 'but they also came to us.' This same informer provided Hillgarth with a complete list of Abwehr personnel in Spain, with 'particulars on each'. Menzies, the head of MI6, authorised Hillgarth to buy the list 'for a very large sum'. Back in London, Philby carped that the price paid by 'Armada' to this 'precious source' was 'very high indeed'; 'I had to fight to get an extra £5 a month for agents who produced regular, if less spectacular, intelligence!' he complained. But it was worth every peseta, providing British intelligence with a detailed picture of the Abwehr power structure in Spain: know thine enemy, and then work out how to deceive him.

At the head of the Abwehr station in Spain stood Wilhelm Leissner, honorary attaché at the German Embassy, who used the codenames 'Heidelberg' and 'Juan'. A small, soft-voiced figure and Condor Legion veteran, Leissner had stayed on in Spain, where he ran an import-export firm under the pseudonym Gustav Lenz. Beneath Leissner were Hans Gude, in charge of naval intelligence, Fritz Knappe-Ratey, an agent runner codenamed 'Federico', and George Helmut Lang, known as 'Emilio'. Since the autumn of 1942, the Abwehr's ranks in Spain had also included Major Fritz Baumann, a former policeman seconded by the German army to the sabotage branch of the Abwehr. Baumann was in charge of coordinating attacks on Allied shipping, but he was also an experienced pathologist who had studied forensic medicine at Hamburg Police Academy before the war. An expert in determining 'the cause of death and the extent of injuries', Baumann had 'examined hundreds of corpses' both before and during the war.

But the Abwehr officer who most intrigued Hillgarth was Major Karl-Erich Kuhlenthal. The MI5 file on this man is three inches thick; more was known about him than any other German spy in Spain. Kuhlenthal's father had been a distinguished soldier, rising to the rank of general and serving as Germany's military attaché in Paris and Madrid. The Kuhlenthal family was wealthy and well connected. Admiral Wilhelm Canaris, the head of the Abwehr, was a relative, which helped to explain Kuhlenthal's rapid rise through the ranks of the intelligence service. Like Clauss, Kuhlenthal had served in the Condor Legion, as secretary to Joachim Rohleder, the unit's chief of intelligence. After the civil war, he returned to Germany for a while, working for an uncle in the wine trade, and then for his father-in-law in the Dienz clothing firm. He travelled to London, Paris and Barcelona; he spoke good English and perfect Spanish. By 1938 he was back in Spain, ostensibly running a radio business while continuing his undercover work. At the outbreak of war, he was appointed adjutant general to Leissner, but soon distinguished himself by his raw ambition and drive.

In 1943, at the age of thirty-seven, Kuhlenthal was head of the Abwehr's espionage section in Madrid, coordinating political and military intelligence and operating under the codename 'Carlos' or, more usually, 'Felipe'. In the bars and cafés of Madrid, he was known as 'Don Pablo'. Kuhlenthal's spy network extended to every corner of the country, but his speciality was recruiting agents in neutral Spain to work overseas, in North Africa, Portugal, Gibraltar and, most importantly, Britain and America. In Britain alone, the so-called 'Felipe network' included dozens of undercover agents, sending back huge volumes of top-grade information. 'Nothing happened in the Abwehr station without him knowing about it,' said a fellow officer. Kuhlenthal cut a dandyish figure in the streets of Madrid. Tall and aristocratic, he wore his hair swept back, had 'fleshy, boneless cheeks', a 'curved hawk-like' nose and 'blue piercing eyes'. He wore elegant double-breasted suits, and drove 'a dark brown French four-seater coupé, using different number plates'. His fingernails were always 'carefully manicured'. He played tennis beautifully. MI5 assessed him as 'a very efficient, ambitious and dangerous man with an enormous capacity for work'. He was promoted, awarded the War Service Cross, and gradually 'contrived to push Leissner out of all positions of authority' until the nominal head of the Abwehr 'became a mere figurehead'.

By 1943, Kuhlenthal was in charge: 'He was an extremely able man and carried in his head all that went on in the office and became so essential that he became virtually the head of the office.' Inevitably, his Abwehr colleagues were envious of 'the esteem and reputation which Kuhlenthal seems to enjoy with the High Chiefs'. As the protégé of Canaris, he could do no wrong. A confidential file from 1943 described him as 'by far the best man in Group I [espionage] in Spain and very reliable from the political point of view'. Himmler himself 'sent a personal message of appreciation to Felipe in Madrid for the work achieved by his network in England'. In the eyes of the German high command, Kuhlenthal was the golden boy of the Madrid Abwehr.

The reality was rather different. So far from being a master spy, Kuhlenthal was a one-man espionage disaster area who had already fallen victim to one of the most elaborate hoaxes ever mounted. Instead of winning the spy war, Kuhlenthal was helping Germany to lose it in the most dramatic fashion.

In May 1941 a Spaniard named Juan Pujol García presented himself to the Abwehr in Madrid and explained that he intended to travel to Britain, and wished to spy for the Germans when he got there. Kuhlenthal was initially unenthusiastic, telling Pujol he was 'extremely busy and that his visit was inconvenient'. Pujol was bald, bearded, short-sighted and distinctly odd. But the Spaniard seemed to nurse a genuine hatred of the British, and a profound admiration for Hitler. He told Kuhlenthal he had good contacts within the Spanish security service and Foreign Office. Eventually, Kuhlenthal agreed to take him on. Pujol was instructed on writing in secret ink, and told to forward information through the Spanish military attaché in London. The Spaniard was sent off with a wad of English money, a number of cover addresses in Britain, and some advice from Kuhlenthal, who told his new recruit to be 'careful not to underestimate the

British as they were a formidable enemy'. Pujol could expect to stay in Britain indefinitely since this, Kuhlenthal predicted, 'would be a very long war'.

On 19 July, Kuhlenthal received a letter from Pujol, written in the secret ink, informing him that he had arrived safely in England, and had recruited a courier working for a civilian airline, who had agreed to carry his letters at £1 a time and post them in Lisbon, thus circumventing the British censor.

In fact, Pujol had not reached Britain and was still in Portugal: this was the first of a long and fantastic stream of lies he would feed to Kuhlenthal. Pujol was no Nazi-sympathiser. Born in 1912 to a liberal middle-class Catalan family, he had somehow contrived to fight for both sides in the Spanish Civil War, though he never fired a gun, deserted, and emerged with a ferocious hatred of fascism. By 1941 he had resolved to fight the war in his own way. Three times he approached the British authorities in Madrid, offering to spy for Britain. Repeatedly rejected, he offered himself instead to the Abwehr, intent on betraying them.

From Lisbon, Pujol began sending fictitious reports to the Germans, pretending to be in Britain. His information was culled from guide books and magazines borrowed at the public library, an old map of Britain, newsreels, a Portuguese publication entitled *The British Fleet* and a vocabulary of English military terms. Pujol had never set foot in Britain, and it showed. His reports were full of elementary mistakes. He could never get his head around the pre-decimal currency. He confidently asserted that: 'There are people in Glasgow who will do anything for a litre of wine', whereas most Glaswegians, at the time, would never have consented to drink wine, even if it had been served in litres.

Kuhlenthal, however, believed every word.

Meanwhile, Pujol's messages were being deciphered by Britain's codebreakers, to the consternation of MI5. Who was this German agent, operating undetected in Britain, who seemed to know nothing about the place?

Finally, early in 1942, after Pujol's wife approached the US legation in Lisbon, the self-made spy was identified and Allied intelligence realised, belatedly, that they had an espionage gem in their hands. Pujol was whisked to Britain, installed in a safehouse in Hendon, north London, and put to work as a double agent. His first codename, 'Bovril', was soon changed to the more respectful 'Garbo', in recognition of his astonishing acting talents.

Over the next three years, Agent Garbo sent 1,399 messages and 423 letters to his handlers in Spain. Three full-time MI5 case officers were needed to handle his traffic, and the twenty-seven fictional characters in the Garbo network. Garbo's subagents were British, Greek, American, South African, Portuguese, Venezuelan and Spanish; some were officials, such as his mole in the Spanish Ministry of Information, some were disgruntled soldiers or pilots, and at least five were seamen recruited from different ports around Britain. Other recruits included a commercial traveller, housewives, office workers, a wireless mechanic, and an Indian poet named Rags who was part of a strange Aryan organisation operating in Wales. Garbo's agents had nothing in common except for the fact that they did not exist. The information they sent to Madrid was a careful concoction of non-dangerous truths, half-truths and untruths, and Kuhlenthal happily passed it all on to Berlin, never once suspecting that he was being duped. 'We have absolute trust in you,' he told his star spy, massaging the ego of the agent whose success was ensuring his own rapid promotion: 'Your last efforts are all magnificent . . .'

Pujol's messages to his Nazi handler were flights of pompous poetry. He never used one word where eight, very long ones, would do, and he showered Kuhlenthal with a combination of flattery and Nazi bombast. 'My dear friend and comrade,' Pujol wrote in a typical effusion, 'we are two friends who share the same ideals and are fighting for the same ends. I have always had a very strong feeling of respect and admiration for your advice, full of good sense and calm . . . These things can only be dealt with between men of spirit and tenacity, and by people who follow a doctrine, by fighting men and bold combatants. The unfolding of confidences can only be made between comrades. Thus the great Germany has become what it is. Thus it has been able to deposit such great confidence in the man who governs it, knowing that he is not a democratic despot but a man of low birth who has only followed an ideal . . .'

For page after page, Garbo railed against 'the democratic-Jewish-Masonic ideology', urged the Germans to attack Britain ('England must be taken by arms, she must be fallen upon, destroyed, dominated . . .'), his letters peppered with Nazi jingoism: 'With a raised arm I end this letter with a pious remembrance for all our dead.'

Kuhlenthal swallowed the lot. 'His characteristic German lack of sense of humour, in such serious circumstances as these, blinded him to the absurdities of the story we were unfolding.' The Abwehr officer openly boasted of his talented spy, codenamed 'Arabel', who was sending top-secret information from the heart of Britain. When Canaris, the Abwehr chief, visited Spain, Kuhlenthal was 'the star turn', and amused his boss with one story in particular. In March 1943, Agent Arabel had obtained a valuable handbook on RAF planes, which he had wrapped inside greaseproof paper, and baked into a cake. On the top, in chocolate icing, he had inscribed: 'With good wishes to Odette'. Enclosed with the cake was a letter to make it seem that the gift came from a British seaman to a girlfriend in Lisbon. Kuhlenthal explained to Canaris that the cake had been dropped off at a safehouse in Lisbon, along with a covering note from Pujol which he read to his delighted audience: 'I did the lettering myself. I had to use several rationed products which I have given in a good cause . . . Good Appetite.' Kuhlenthal ended his performance with a lumbering joke, pointing out that although his agent 'made cakes which were unpleasant in taste, their contents were excellent'.

Canaris was impressed. Kuhlenthal's reputation went up another notch. (The cake, in fact, had been baked by Garbo's wife, sent to Lisbon by diplomatic bag, and dropped off by an MI6 agent. The RAF pamphlet was out of date, and British intelligence knew the Abwehr had it already.)

The high point of Garbo's career would come with the Allied invasion of Normandy in 1944. The deception plan covering the invasion was codenamed 'Fortitude'; its aim was to persuade the Nazis that instead of attacking Normandy, the main thrust would come in the Pas de Calais. To this end, a vast fake US army was 'assembled' in Kent, wireless traffic was confected, and hints were dropped to less than reliable 'neutral' diplomats. Many strands of deception were woven into Operation Fortitude, but none was more important than the double-agent system, and of these agents none was more vital than Garbo. From the safehouse in Crespigny Road, Hendon, Pujol fired off more than 500 radio messages between January 1944 and D-Day, a fantastic web of deceit from his posse of bogus 'agents', tiny elements in a jigsaw which would only make sense once completed by the Germans. The deception was astonishingly successful. Six weeks after D-Day, Pujol was awarded the Iron Cross by order of the Führer for 'extraordinary services' to the Third Reich. He was also appointed MBE, in secret.

By 1943, Karl-Erich Kuhlenthal, the star of the Madrid Abwehr, was eating out of Garbo's hand, and was voracious for more. A separate office was set up to handle the 'vast information' coming in, and running the 'Felipe network' had become his principal job: 'As a keen and efficient officer he did everything in his power to supply Garbo with ciphers, secret inks, and addresses of the highest grade to ensure his greater security. He was also forthcoming with considerable funds.' Through radio interceptions, the British watched with pleasure as Kuhlenthal grew steadily more dependent on Garbo, and his stock rose in Berlin. 'We had the satisfaction of knowing through MSS [Most Secret Sources, principally Ultra material] that all GARBO material was being given priority and that every military report which reached Madrid from the GARBO network was immediately retransmitted to Berlin.' Garbo's British handlers were amazed how readily Kuhlenthal believed 'the many incredible things we ask them to believe'. Indeed, 'the more sensational the reports, the more certain could we be of Madrid retransmitting them to headquarters'. Sometimes Kuhlenthal seemed to pass on Garbo's information without even reading, let alone questioning it. 'In some cases where messages appeared to be of extreme urgency they were retransmitted to Berlin with approximately one hour's delay in Madrid.' Through Garbo and Kuhlenthal, British intelligence was speaking directly to Berlin: 'Felipe had become our mouthpiece.' Here, then, was 'an invaluable channel through which we would be able to deceive the enemy'.

As they combed through Kuhlenthal's messages to Berlin, the British codebreakers noticed something rather odd. Garbo's intelligence was already sensational enough, but Kuhlenthal was spicing it up still further, to lend extra weight. He was not above inventing his own subagents, and adding them to the pot. Many of his elaborations were either wrong, or meaningless. He also made some hilarious mistakes, including his 'conviction that the Isle of Man is in the North of Ireland'. The added extras, MI5 concluded, were 'invented by Felipe himself'. Kuhlenthal was deceiving his Abwehr bosses, by passing on invented intelligence, along with the information he fervently believed to be true, which was not. 'The information provided by his organisation up to date has been either untrue, useless, or provided by MI5 through the double agents under its control.' Guy Liddell of MI5 considered Kuhlenthal to be 'one of the people who make up most of their information'. He may also have been embezzling. Some within the Abwehr certainly thought so. According to one intercepted message, Kuhlenthal was said to be running a very expensive agent in London, a Yugoslav diplomat, who had cost the Abwehr £400 over two years. 'There are officers in Spain who are convinced that K is making half-part business, i.e. splitting the monthly allowances between his and the Diplomat's pocket.'

There was one other factor that made Garbo's German spymaster ideally suited to receive the Mincemeat hoax: Karl-Erich Kuhlenthal was Jewish.

The Abwehr officer had a Jewish grandmother, though Kuhlenthal did not consider himself Jewish. Marriage to a half-Jewish woman had not impeded his father's military career. But that was before the rise of the Nazis. Under Hitler's brutal racial policies, the one quarter of Jewish blood in Kuhlenthal was enough to mark him out for discrimination, persecution, or worse. Kuhlenthal would later claim that anti-semitism had forced him to flee Germany, 'leaving a good job as manager of a large champagne and wine cellar owned by his uncle'. His brother, an army officer, had left Germany for the same reason, winding up in Chile. It was Canaris who had intervened on behalf of his relative (the Abwehr chief had a record of helping Jews), and arranged for him to take up the post in Spain, since 'he could not serve in the Army being a half-blood Jew'. In Madrid, he was farther from Gestapo persecution, though hardly safe.

In 1941, Canaris had his protégé 'Aryanised', and formally declared to be of good German stock. Leissner, the chief of the Abwehr station, confirmed that Kuhlenthal was now officially racially pure. In the minds of hard-line Nazis, however, either a person had Jewish blood, and was thereby corrupt and dangerous, or they did not. The attempt to tinker with Hitler's race laws provoked a rebuke from Berlin: 'He has been created an Aryan at the instigation of his station. A formulation of this nature is out of touch of all reality. Can JUAN [Leissner] state the legal foundation for such acts of state?' The Spanish branch of the SD, the SS intelligence organisation, also questioned how Kuhlenthal could simply be declared Aryan, 'since there appeared to be no authority for such an act'. Canaris again intervened, and the SD in Madrid was instructed 'to let the matter drop'. Kuhlenthal's colleagues in Spain knew of his Jewish ancestry, and the attempt to expunge it. For some, this was prima facie evidence of treachery. Major Helm, the head of counterespionage in Spain, sent a confidential report to Canaris accusing Kuhlenthal of being 'in the pay of the British Secret Service'. The Abwehr chief 'refused to take the report seriously'. Helm was transferred to another Abwehr station.

The British spies tracking Kuhlenthal had noted that he seemed 'cold and reserved', but also deeply uneasy. 'Appearance: nervous, uncertain. Peculiarity: shifty eyes,' read one surveillance report. Kuhlenthal had every reason to be anxious. His stock in Berlin was high, thanks to Pujol and the Felipe network, but if Canaris should fall from power or cease to defend him, or if something went wrong with his organisation, then his anti-semitic enemies would pounce. Kuhlenthal was deeply, and understandably, paranoid. Failure might well prove fatal. As one informer told British intelligence: 'Kuhlenthal is trembling to keep his position so as not to have to return to Germany and he is doing his utmost to please his superiors.'

Kuhlenthal had already fallen for the elaborate con trick that was Agent Garbo. He was the ideal target for Operation Mincemeat: deeply gullible, but admired and trusted by his bosses, including Himmler and Canaris; ambitious and determined, but also frantically eager to please, ready to pass on anything that might consolidate his reputation, and save him from the fate suffered by others of Jewish blood; he was also vain, possibly corrupt, and prepared to deceive those of higher rank to enhance his own standing. Kuhlenthal perfectly exemplified the qualities that John Godfrey had identified as the two most dangerous flaws in a spy: 'wishfulness' and 'yesmanship'. He would believe anything he was fed, and he would do whatever he could to suck up to the boss and preserve his own skin.

To succeed, Operation Mincemeat needed to reach Hitler himself. The best way of doing that, Alan Hillgarth knew, was to get the information to Adolf Clauss in Huelva, from whom it was certain to pass into the hands of Karl-Erich Kuhlenthal, and then, with the blessing of that favoured but gullible officer, up the German chain of command. Clauss was the perfect recipient, because he was such an efficient spy. Kuhlenthal was the ideal spy to pass the information on, because he was worse than useless.

Mincemeat Sets Sail

Leverton & Sons, undertakers and funeral directors, began making coffins in the St Pancras area of London around the time of the French Revolution. For two hundred years the business was passed from father to son, along with the severe and formal cast of countenance required of officials in the death business.

By 1943 the custodian of this long tradition, six generations on, was Ivor Leverton. His older brother Derrick was serving as a major with the Royal Artillery in North Africa, and about to take part in the invasion of Europe everyone knew was coming. Ivor had breathing difficulties and was declared medically unfit for military service, and therefore was left to run the family business. Although only twenty-nine, Ivor took the traditions of the firm very seriously, ensuring that all clients, rich or poor, were treated with the same solemnity and dignity. But beneath that decorous exterior, like most undertakers, Ivor Leverton was a man of unflappable temperament, and a bone-dry sense of humour. He felt a lingering guilt over being unable to fight on the front line. The closest he had come to seeing action was in 1941 when he went to collect a dead body from the Temperance Hospital in Euston and a Luftwaffe bomb came down the chimney, blasting shards of glass through his black 'Anthony Eden' hat. Ivor longed to play his part. He was only too pleased, therefore, to be asked to transport a body, in the middle of the night, in deadly secrecy, as a task of 'national importance'.

The request came from PC Glyndon May, an officer working for Bentley Purchase, the St Pancras coroner. Leverton & Sons did regular business with the coroner, but had never been presented with a job quite like this. 'I was not to divulge what I was told, under the Official Secrets Act, not even to my own family,' Ivor wrote in his diary. 'No record would be made, and we would not be paid a penny.' May's request arrived on April Fool's Day, and for a moment Ivor Leverton wondered whether the 'phone call from St Pancras Coroner's Court might be dismissed as a hoax'. But Constable May was entirely serious: Ivor should get a coffin, and take it to the mortuary behind the coroner's office, where May would meet him at 1.00 a.m. on the morning of Saturday, 17 April. He should act entirely alone, and carry the coffin himself. 'I was still in fairly good shape,' grumbled Ivor, 'but this was really asking a bit much.'

Soon after midnight, Ivor Leverton tiptoed downstairs from the flat above the funeral parlour in Eversholt Street, taking care not to wake his wife, and retrieved a hearse from the company garage in Crawley Mews. He then drove to the front of the parlour, and manhandled one of the firm's wood and zinc-lined 'removal coffins' into the back, hoping Pat, their most inquisitive neighbour, would not wake up and spot him wrestling with a heavy coffin in the dark. Glyn May was waiting at the coroner's court. Together, with some difficulty, they heaved the body into the coffin. The dead man was wearing a khaki military uniform, but no shoes. Leverton was struck by his height. Leverton & Sons' standard coffins measured six foot two inside, but the dead man 'must have stood six foot four inches tall' and could not be made to lie flat. 'By adjustment to the knees and setting the very large feet at an angle, we were just able to manage.'

After an uneventful drive through the deserted city streets to Hackney, Leverton helped May unload the coffin, 'left our passenger' in one of the mortuary refrigerators, and returned home. His wife, pregnant with one of the next generation of Leverton undertakers, was still asleep.

Hackney had been selected by Bentley Purchase because it was run by 'a mortuary-keeper on whom he could rely not to talk'. Later that day, at six in the evening, Purchase met Cholmondeley and Montagu at the mortuary, with Glyn May. The body of Glyndwr Michael was removed from the refrigerator and placed on a mortuary gurney. Nearly three months had now elapsed since Michael's death, and during the long period of refrigeration his eyes had sunk into their sockets; the skin was yellow from the poison-induced jaundice, otherwise the body appeared to be in a reasonable state of preservation. A 'Mae West' military life jacket was put over his head and tied around his waist (Mae West being rhyming slang for 'breasts': when fully inflated, the rubber jacket gave the wearer a distinctly busty look – reminiscent, if you happened to be a sex-starved soldier, of the curvaceous film star). The chain was looped around his shoulder, outside the coat and under the Mae West, and securely tied to the belt of the trench coat. It had been assumed that the briefcase would be given to Lieutenant Jewell to clip to the chain at the last moment, but it was found that the canister could accommodate both case and body. The handle of the case was fastened to the end of the chain, and the case placed on top of the body. Jewell would now only have to insert the documents and tip the body into the water, thus ensuring it would arrive on shore in a way that 'made it as easy as possible for the Spaniards or the Germans to remove the bag and chain without trace'. The watch, with the winder run down, was set to 2.59, and fastened to the left wrist: with luck, the Germans should assume that the watch had stopped when the imagined Catalina crashed into the sea.

All Major Martin now needed to complete his outfit was footwear. But getting him into his boots proved to be the most difficult aspect of the entire dressing operation. In the extra-cold refrigerator, the feet had frozen solid, with the ankles at right angles to the leg. Even when the laces were fully undone, the boots refused to go on. Bentley Purchase came up with a solution. 'I've got it,' said the coroner. 'We'll get an electric fire and thaw out the feet only. As soon as the boots are on we'll pop him back in the refrigerator again and refreeze him.'

PC May went to fetch the single-bar electric heater from the lodge of the coroner's office. There then followed a truly macabre scene, as Montagu attempted to defrost the dead man's feet, and Cholmondeley tried to lever on the boots. Finally, the ankles defrosted sufficiently, and the boots went on, followed by gaiters. Thawing and refreezing was certain to hasten decomposition, but with the gaiters securely buckled, his feet would probably not fall off. It was, said Montagu with feeling, 'the least pleasant part of our work'.

Major Martin's wallet, containing the letters from Pam and Father, were slipped into his inside breast pocket. His remaining pockets were filled with all the 'litter' that made up a complete personality: pencil, loose change, keys and, in an inspired last-minute addition, two ticket stubs for *Strike A New Note*, a variety show at the Prince of Wales Theatre starring the music-hall comedian Sid Field. This was another of Cholmondeley's brainwaves. HMS *Seraph* would depart from Holy Loch on Monday, 19 April, and take ten or eleven days to reach Huelva. The Germans, however, needed to be persuaded that the body had washed up after no more than a week at sea, following an air crash. If the body was found on, say, 28 April, then there must be something in his pockets indicating that he was still in London on 24 April. This was where Sid Field could play his part. Cholmondeley purchased four tickets for his new show at the Prince of Wales Theatre on 22 April, tore off the dated counterfoils of the two in the middle, and put them in the pocket of Major Martin's trench coat. 'We decided Bill Martin and Pam should have a farewell party before he left.' This would be their last evening together, before the young officer headed to North Africa, and certain death. The stubs would offer incontrovertible 'proof' that the only way he could have reached Spain by the 28th was by aircraft.

Close examination of the letters and pocket litter would offer a detailed itinerary of Major Martin's last, poignant days in London:

18 April – Check in to the Naval and Military Club

19 April – Receive bill from S. J. Phillips of New Bond Street for diamond ring

21 April – Lunch with Father and Gwatkin, the solicitor, at the Carlton Grill; Pam attends dance with Jock and Hazel

22 April – To the theatre with Pam, followed by a nightclub

24 April – Check out of Naval and Military Club, pay bill in cash (£1. 10s); collect letters from Combined Operations HQ and War Office; board flight to Gibraltar; 1459 hours, crash in the Gulf of Cadiz.

The body was photographed twice on the mortuary gurney. Only the torso of the man holding the trolley is visible, but this was almost certainly PC May, the coroner's officer. The mouth of the corpse has fallen open. The skin around the nose has sunk, and the upper part of the face is discoloured. The fingers of the left hand are bent, as if clawing in pain. These are the only known pictures of Glyndwr Michael, a man whom no one bothered to photograph when he was alive.

The already visible decomposition of the face raised another potential complication. The body would now have to be driven 400 miles to Scotland, then loaded into a cramped submarine and taken on a ten-day sea voyage that might encounter rough weather. If the canister was jolted about, the face would surely suffer further damage from chafing against the sides of the canister. Again, Bentley Purchase came up with a solution: 'Get an army blanket. Wrap the face and neck in it, and there will be no friction.' The body was rolled up in a blanket, and 'lightly tied with tape'. Following Bernard Spilsbury's instructions, 21lb of dry ice had already been placed in the canister to expel the oxygen. The body was now 'reverently' inserted into the homemade carrying case, and packed around with more dry ice before the lid was screwed tightly in place. The body now needed to get to Scotland, fast.

Waiting in the Hackney mortuary car park was a Fordson BBE van, with two seats in front, fitted with a customised V8 engine. At the wheel was a small man with a neat moustache, wearing civilian clothes. His name was St John 'Jock' Horsfall, an MI5 chauffeur who also happened to be one of the most famous racing drivers in the country.

St John Ratcliffe Stewart Horsfall, born in 1910 into a family of car fanatics, acquired his first Aston Martin at the age of twenty-three. Between 1933 and the outbreak of war, he won trophy after trophy on the racing circuit, including the Dunlop Outer Circuit Handicap at over 100 mph. Horsfall was short-sighted and astigmatic, but declined to use spectacles. He seldom wore racing leathers or a crash helmet, preferring to race in 'a shirt and tie, with either a bomber jacket or a sleeveless sweater'. He drove at staggering speed, and suffered a number of serious accidents, including a trial run at Brooklands when his car 'went berserk [and] tried to hurl itself over the top of the banking'. On another occasion, the throttle stuck open, forcing the engine up to 10,000 rpm until the clutch exploded, sending 'potentially lethal pieces of metal' bursting through the bell housing at his feet.

At the start of the war Horsfall had been recruited into the Security Service by Eric Holt-Wilson, the deputy director of MI5, who had employed the racing driver's mother as a staff car driver during the First World War. Horsfall's primary job was driving MI5 and MI6 officers and agents, double agents, and captured enemy spies from one place to another, very fast. He was also involved in testing the security of naval sites and airfields, and privy to a good deal of highly classified information.

Horsfall knew only that he was to transport to the west of Scotland a canister containing a dead body, which would be used to play a humiliating trick on the Germans. Horsfall was fond of practical jokes. He once wired up a loo seat to a battery and waited for a girlfriend to use it. 'The scream that Kath gave when the magneto was turned on was most satisfying.' He even wrote a poem to commemorate the occasion.

> *I gave her time to start her piddle*
> *Then gave the thing a violent twiddle*
> *Before I could complete a turn*
> *She closed the circuit with her stern,*
> *And shooting off the wooden seat*
> *Emitted a most piercing shriek.*

Though the idea of carrying a dead body through the night in order to bamboozle the Germans appealed strongly to Jock Horsfall's sense of humour, he never told anyone of this, perhaps the most significant drive of his life. Reckless behind the wheel, outside a motorised vehicle Jock Horsfall was discretion personified. MI5 had a fleet of cars and vans, but for this operation Horsfall had selected one of his own, a six-year-old 30cwt Fordson van, customised to accommodate an Aston Martin in the back, with a souped-up engine in which 'he claimed to have done 100 mph in the Mall'. It was past midnight when Ewen Montagu, Charles Cholmondeley and Jock Horsfall loaded the canister into the back.

The trio paused for a brief pit stop at Cholmondeley's mews flat off the Cromwell Road, where they ate a light meal, with 'one of us sitting in the window to make sure that no one stole Major Martin from the van (even if he was not worth much to the thief, he was valuable to us)'. It was, Cholmondeley later said, the first time he had ever 'had supper with a corpse parked in his garage'. Cholmondeley's sister, Victoria, prepared some cheese sandwiches and a vacuum flask of hot tea, and at around two in the morning, the party set off, heading north. Jewell had requested that the additional passenger be brought aboard HMS *Seraph* no later than midday on 18 April. Horsfall was racing against the clock, his second favourite occupation.

Operation Mincemeat almost came to a premature and embarrassing end before they had left London. On passing a local cinema, where a spy film was showing, Jock Horsfall remarked on the 'much better story' they were currently engaged in, became paralysed with giggles, and nearly drove into a tram stop. A little later, the myopic racing driver failed to see a roundabout until too late and shot over the grass circle in the middle. This is what driving with Jock Horsfall was like; an experience rendered yet more alarming by the need to drive with masked headlights during the blackout. Luckily there were few other cars about. Montagu and Cholmondeley took it in turns to lie in the back and try to sleep. This was the closest either came to death in action during the war.

South of the village of Langbank, on the road between Glasgow and Greenock along the west side of the River Clyde, they stopped to stretch, and eat Dottie's sandwiches. In the pallid dawn light of the Highlands, they posed for photographs beside the van. Jock Horsfall climbed into the back, and was photographed drinking a cup of tea perched on the canister.

At Greenock Dock a launch waited to meet them. With the help of half a dozen seamen and some rope, the 400lb canister was carefully lowered into the boat, followed by the dinghy and the oars. It took only a few minutes to motor to HMS *Forth*, the depot ship with the submarine lying alongside. The officers of the ship were 'partially "in the know"', but the arrival of the canister provoked no suspicion or comment among the crew, 'being accepted as merely being a more than usually urgent and breakable FOS shipment'. Montagu and Cholmondeley were greeted warmly by Jewell, who gave orders for the special shipment to be lowered on to the submarine the following morning, along with a large supply of gin, sherry and whisky he was transporting to refresh the 8th Flotilla in Algiers. This cargo was also kept secret from the crew.

Jewell now received his final instructions from Montagu and Cholmondeley, and a large buff envelope containing the documents. This would be securely stashed in the submarine safe until the body was ready to be launched. In the ship's log, the operation was referred to as '191435B', the code number of Jewell's secret operational orders. At the last moment, Montagu decided to keep one of the dinghy oars as a souvenir. If the forty-four-man crew of the *Seraph* thought it strange to be taking on a dinghy with only one oar, no one said so.

After three months in the imaginary company of Bill Martin, Montagu and Cholmondeley headed for home. There was something oddly touching in the leave-taking. 'By this time Major Martin had become a completely living person to us,' wrote Montagu, who would never have come across a man like Glyndwr Michael in his normal life. The fictional creation had taken on a form of reality. 'We felt that we knew him just as one knows one's best friend . . . we had come to feel that we had known Bill Martin from his early childhood and were taking a genuine and personal interest in the progress of his courtship and financial troubles.'

Montagu wrote in excitement to Iris, relaying his 'news such as can be written': 'I had to go up to Scotland last weekend. It was great fun as I and another couple had to drive up in a lorry. It was a lovely moonlit night, so wasn't too bad even with wartime headlights and it was quite like old times to go for a long drive. I had two days on board a ship (stationary . . . I haven't been to sea yet!!). It was great fun as they were a grand lot on board. When I got back things were very hectic as I had to button up the job I had been on.'

On board the *Seraph*, First Lieutenant David Scott, second-in-command, was instructed by Jewell to take extra care when bringing aboard the canister marked 'Optical Instruments'. 'I was to see that this package was treated with every precaution to ensure that it was not bumped while being embarked through the torpedo loading hatch.' One torpedo was left behind, to make room for the canister in the reload rack. Like most wartime submarines, the *Seraph* did not have enough bunks to accommodate all the crew, and so they took turns to sleep in the forward torpedo room. For the next ten days, they would be sleeping alongside Bill Martin.

At 1600 hours on 19 April, HMS *Seraph* slipped her moorings, and sailed out of Holy Loch into the Clyde. Montagu sent word to the Admiralty that Operation Mincemeat was underway. 'It was a real thrill,' he reflected. Yet the excitement was tinged with real anxiety. 'Would it work?'

The *Seraph* ploughed towards the sea in the gloaming. 'Spring was on the way,' wrote Scott, 'but there was little sign of it in the wooded slopes of the hills on our port side. To starboard lay Dunoon, its outlines softened by a light mist and the smoke from wood and coal fires rising from the chimneys of its dour, grey houses.' Out in the broad Clyde, the *Seraph* linked up with her escort, a minesweeper, whose principal task was to ward off possible attacks from British aircraft, which tended to assume submarines were hostile unless there was clear evidence otherwise.

Abreast of the Isle of Arran, the *Seraph* performed a 'trim dive' to ensure that the submarine was correctly balanced, and then headed into the Irish Sea. South of the Scilly Isles, the minesweeper departed, having taken aboard a canvas bag of the crew's last letters. 'A final exchange of "Good Luck" signals passed by light and we headed out into the Atlantic swell, diving shortly afterwards.' The *Seraph* was alone. The weather was fine, and with only a light sea running, the ship settled into the strange, half-lit world of a long submarine journey, compounded in equal parts of boredom, anticipation and fear. By day, the submarine would travel submerged; at night she would resurface and continue by diesel, to recharge her batteries, and then dive again as dawn broke. If they were not attacked or otherwise diverted, covering 130 miles a day, the passage to Huelva should take ten days.

It was stuffy below decks. The crew and officers were on watch for two hours, and then off for four, twenty-four hours a day, seven days a week. 'Monotony never really set in, because at the back of our minds was the determination to survive, which demanded constant alertness.' By wartime standards, the food on the *Seraph* was excellent and plentiful. 'We were never short of meat, butter, sugar or eggs. We even had luxuries like chocolate biscuits and honey . . . we were lucky enough to have a chef who could bake good bread.' No one shaved, and everyone slept in their clothes. A few days out of Holy Loch, and the smell of unwashed bodies and engine oil suffused the ship.

Lieutenant Scott lay on his bunk, attempting to read *War and Peace*, and trying not to think about death. He admired Jewell, considering him the 'epitome of what a submarine captain should be: quite fearless, he was invariably cool and calculating'. Yet however brave and astute his commanding officer, Scott knew that he was quite likely to die before his twenty-third birthday. 'At that time, the chances of returning home from a Mediterranean-based submarine were 50/50.' Before joining the *Seraph,* Scott had spent a week in London. On the last day of his leave, his Uncle Jack and recently widowed mother took him to lunch in an expensive restaurant. When the time came to say goodbye, both mother and uncle had tears in their eyes. 'I realised with a bit of a shock that they were thinking they might not see me again.'

A few feet away, in his own bunk, the commander of the *Seraph*, Lieutenant Jewell, was not thinking about death. Indeed, in more than three years of the most ferocious submarine combat and several irregular and exceptionally dangerous missions, the thought of dying seems never to have crossed his mind.

Jewell had been born in the Seychelles, where his father, a doctor, was in the Colonial Service. He volunteered for submarine work in 1936. The war was already two years old when the young lieutenant qualified for command of the newly launched *Seraph*, an S-class submarine. Shortly after taking command, Jewell fell down the hatch. In 1946, a doctor pointed out that Jewell had broken two vertebrae: he fought the entire war with a broken neck.

His first patrol, in July 1942, had set the pattern for what followed: extreme danger, a narrow escape, and a certain amount of farce. The *Seraph* was fired on by an RAF plane, but escaped serious damage. Then, in the waters off Norway, Jewell spotted a U-boat, and blew it to pieces with a single torpedo. The *Seraph*'s first kill turned out to be a whale.

In October 1942, during the run-up to Operation Torch, the invasion of North Africa, Bill Jewell was given his first secret mission: transporting the American General Mark Clark, Eisenhower's deputy, to the Algerian coast, for secret negotiations with the French commanders there. The invasion, led by General Patton, was already underway, and the neutrality of the Vichy forces in French Algeria was considered critical if it was to succeed. Many Vichy officers were deeply hostile to the British following the sinking of much of the French fleet at Mers-el-Kebir. Clark faced an extremely delicate situation. Jewell had the equally tricky task of getting him ashore without being spotted. On 19 October, the *Seraph* and her American passengers arrived at the designated spot, a remote coastal villa some fifty miles west of Algiers. Soon after midnight, Jewell brought the submarine to within 500 yards of the shore, and the American negotiating party disembarked in four collapsible canoes, accompanied by a protection squad of three British Marines of the Special Boat Service, led by Roger 'Jumbo' Courtney, a former big-game hunter with a 'bashed-in sort of face and a blunt no-nonsense manner'.

The all-night negotiations went well, but at one point the visitors were forced to hide in a dusty cellar to avoid an impromptu visit from the gendarmes. Courtney suffered a coughing fit, which threatened to give them away. General Clark passed the choking commando some chewing gum.

'Your American gum has so little taste,' whispered Courtney, once the spasm subsided.

'Yes,' said Clark. 'I've already used it.'

When the time came to pick up the party, Jewell brought the *Seraph* perilously close to shore, until she was almost aground. Clark appears to have been betrayed, and moments ahead of a French raiding party, the general and his party dashed for the boats, paddled through the surf, and scrambled aboard the *Seraph*. Jewell gave the order to turn tail, and then dive. Sir Andrew Cunningham, the addressee of one of the Mincemeat letters and Royal Navy commander-in-chief in the Mediterranean, described the joint Anglo-American adventure as 'a happy augury for the future'.

Jewell's unflappability had marked him out for secret work, and his next assignment was even stranger: to pick up, from the south coast of France, General Henri Honoré Giraud. A charismatic, self-important, and popular veteran of the Great War, the sixty-three-year-old French general was seen as the only officer able to deliver French North African forces to the Allies. Giraud was hiding out with the French resistance after escaping from the Germans. Allied command decided that Giraud could be an important figurehead to galvanise Vichy opposition to the Germans, if he could be safely collected. The mission was codenamed 'Operation Kingpin'. The only problem was that the crusty general, like De Gaulle, was said to entertain a hearty loathing for the British, and had insisted that if he were to be rescued, the Americans must do it. The *Seraph*, therefore, would briefly have to adopt a new nationality. An American captain, Jerauld Wright, was placed in nominal command.

Flying the Stars and Stripes, the *Seraph* duly waited off Le Lavandou, until Jewell spotted the light signals from the shore, and sent a boat to pick up Giraud. The French general managed to miss his footing while transferring to the submarine, and was hauled aboard dripping wet. To maintain the charade, the crew of the *Seraph* had attempted to adopt American accents, and spent the rest of the voyage imitating Clark Gable and Jimmy Stewart. General Giraud, it turned out, spoke English, and was not remotely fooled. But he was far too proud to acknowledge the trick.

In the wake of the North African invasion, the *Seraph* roamed the Mediterranean, conducting more traditional submarine operations, and attacking any and every enemy vessel. In the space of a few weeks, she sank four cargo ships destined to supply Rommel's army, and disabled an Italian destroyer. Back in Algiers harbour, the piratical Jewell raised the Jolly Roger. Late in December 1942, the *Seraph* was assigned to another secret mission: the reconnaissance of the Mediterranean island of Galita, eighty miles north of the African coast. The island was occupied by German and Italian troops and was used as a lookout post to monitor the movements of Allied ships. Jewell's mission – codenamed 'Operation Peashooter' – was to reconnoitre the island in secret, and establish whether it could be successfully attacked by a commando force led by an American, Colonel William Orlando Darby of the US Rangers. On 17 December, Jewell had set off for Galita, with Bill Darby as his passenger.

The two Bills struck up an immediate friendship, which was hardly surprising, since Darby was, in Jewell's words, 'a two-fisted fighting man', with a taste for danger that matched Jewell's own. The 1st Ranger Battalion, an elite and highly trained assault force (the counterpart to the Royal Marine Commandos) had been formed under Darby's leadership in 1942. They had already distinguished themselves in North Africa by their courage and devotion to their leader: 'We'll fight an army on a dare, we'll follow Darby anywhere . . .' At thirty-one-years old, 'El Darbo', as his troops called him, gave the impression of having been hewn out of Arkansas granite: three times in his career, he spurned promotion in order to stay at the head of his troops, a varied crew that included a jazz trumpeter, a hotel detective, a gambler and several toughened coalminers. At Arzew in North Africa, Darby had led the 1st Ranger Battalion into battle, hurling hand grenades in the face of heavy machine-gun fire, 'always conspicuously at the head of his troops'.

On the way to Galita, Darby regaled Jewell and his crew with ribald stories. For two days, the *Seraph* prowled around the island charting possible landing spots, while the American took photographs. 'I think we can do it,' declared Darby. Eventually, it was ruled that no troops could be spared for the assault on Galita, and Operation Peashooter was called off, but not before Darby got a taste of Jewell's methods. All friendly forces had been cleared from the operational area, and Jewell's orders invited him to 'sink on sight any vessel'. On the way back to Algiers, Jewell rammed one U-boat underwater, and attacked another with three torpedoes, one of which failed to detonate on impact while the other two veered off target owing to the damage sustained in the earlier collision. Even the unshakable Darby found the experience of underwater combat alarming, telling Jewell: 'Put me ashore, give me a gun and there isn't anyone or anything I won't face. But, gee, Bill, I haven't been so scared in my life as in the last two days.'

The *Seraph* had sustained serious damage to her bows, and her crew was suffering from the 'constant strain', as became apparent when two former friends fell out and 'one grabbed a large, evil-looking carving knife from the galley and tried to stab the other in the back'. The *Seraph* was ordered to return home for rest, recuperation and repairs. On the return journey, the submarine was attacked, once again, by a flight of Allied bombers.

The repairs at Blyth dockyard had reset the submarine's 'broken nose', giving the *Seraph* 'a lithe, graceful look'. A cartoon of Ferdinand the Bull had been painted on her conning tower – a reference to the children's story about the bull who shunned the bullring, and a nickname reflecting the fact that *Seraph* spent more time on special missions than operational patrols.

As the *Seraph* made towards Huelva, Jewell was itching for another scrap, but knew he must avoid contact with the enemy if possible. 'We were told that we were not going to be required to attack anything, as this was more important.' The RAF had issued strict instructions to aircraft not to attack any submarines on the route, and naval intelligence confirmed that there were no known enemy vessels in the Gulf of Cadiz. But then, west of Brest, about midway through the voyage, the submariners heard a noise they all knew, and dreaded: 'The unmistakable sounds of a submarine being depth-charged.' Somewhere, very close at hand, a duel was underway. 'We knew that at least one of our boats was in the vicinity,' wrote Lieutenant Scott, 'and as each series of explosions hit our pressure hull like a hammer, despite the distance, we feared for the safety of our friends.' Jewell had his orders, and the *Seraph* continued south. Scott returned to *War and Peace*.

At the precise moment Bill Jewell was uncharacteristically turning his back on a fight, Ewen Montagu and Jean Leslie were in London preparing to go out to the theatre and dinner, for the last time, as Bill Martin and his fiancée Pam.

Bill's Farewell

Ewen Montagu had been planning 'Bill Martin's Farewell Party' for some time, but did not tell Jean Leslie until the afternoon of 22 April. He sent a note from 'Bill' inviting 'Pam' to see the variety star Sid Field in *Strike A New Note* at the Prince of Wales Theatre, to be followed by dinner at the Gargoyle Club. The MI5 secretary was thrilled by the invitation from her office admirer: 'I rushed home, changed out of office clothes, and threw on some makeup.' Cholmondeley had bought four tickets for the evening performance – that way they could demonstrate that the tickets had been bought in a block, even though the counterfoils of the two in the middle were missing, and already en route to Spain in the dead man's pocket. Wasting the tickets, Montagu later wrote, would have been 'absurd'. Besides, it was an ideal opportunity to continue the courtship of his imaginary fiancée. Charles Cholmondeley's date for the evening was Avril Gordon, another young secretary in the office who had helped Hester Leggett compose 'Pam's' letters. Both women were 'in the loop' on Operation Mincemeat, although ignorant of its details.

Montagu remained firmly in character. The death of Bill Martin, presumed drowned at sea following an air crash, would shortly be announced, but in the meantime Montagu composed a personal tribute to him, to be published in *The Times* in due course. The ruse would have to be maintained and reinforced long after Mincemeat had landed.

The notice described the life of a deskbound literary genius who had insisted on fulfilling his patriotic duty, only to die tragically.

Bill Martin's death 'on active service' came as a complete surprise to many of his friends when it was announced in your columns. Few of them knew that he had for some time been serving with the Commandos where hitherto unsuspected qualities had been revealed.

Martin was a unique personality and his loss is tragic. An ever-growing number of his more discerning contemporaries were convinced that he had genius. He made little mark at school where he was more interested in his own reading and music than in the normal work and athletics of his friends. After a university career during which he impressed with his literary talents and qualities of leadership a small circle of dons and college friends, he retired into the country to farm, fish and write.

On the outbreak of war, Martin, who had already been profoundly stirred by the growing menace to all that he loved most deeply, hastened to offer his services to his country. He found himself placed in an office job, and although it was an important one and well suited to his talents, the determined, if unorthodox, efforts which he made to escape and prepare himself for more active and dangerous work, were ultimately successful.

As to others of an imaginative and artistic temperament, Martin's experiences with the Commandos had brought a new meaning into life, an immense stimulus to creative activity. He had refused, until the war was over, to publish any of his work. We will therefore have to wait some time before a wider public can appreciate his rare talent.

The fake obituary was never published, but it gives a fascinating insight into the spymaster's level of emotional involvement.

The two couples made an attractive sight as they entered the Prince of Wales Theatre, the men in full uniform, the women in their best dresses and heels. Montagu handed the tickets to an usherette. 'We were terribly agitated when she tore the tickets,' said Jean. 'Would she notice that two were missing?' She did, and summoned the manager, who accepted that the middle counterfoils had been torn off 'as a joke'.

The lights dimmed, and the four settled into the plush seats of the circle to watch Sid Field open his new show. A veteran performer, Field had toured the provincial music halls for thirty years, singing, dancing and performing comic skits. He had recently broken into the big time, playing the part of 'Slasher Green', a cockney spiv. *Strike A New Note* was his first West End appearance, and he was supported by a group of young theatrical hopefuls 'gathered from every part of the country', performing together as 'George Black and the Rising Generation'. Black, a theatrical impresario, is today as obscure in public memory as Sid Field, but some of the rising generation rose very high indeed. Among the cast were two unknowns, Eric Morecambe and Ernie Wise, aged sixteen and seventeen respectively.

Strike A New Note had opened to rave reviews a month earlier: *The Times* hailed Field as 'definitely "a find"'; the *Daily Mail* noted 'the loudest laughter we have heard in years'; the *Daily Telegraph* was gratified that 'all his jokes are clean'. By April the show was playing to packed houses. Sid danced, told jokes, performed sketches and sang:

> *I'm going to get pickled when they light up Piccadilly,*
> *I'm going to get pickled like I've never been before.*

In fact, Sid was already well pickled, since he never went on stage without 'an adequate ration of gin'. *Strike A New Note* was tailor-made escapism for wartime theatregoers. Many in the audience were American GIs, and the satires on Anglo-

American relations raised the loudest cheers. The war seemed impossibly distant, even irrelevant. A note on the back of the programme read: 'If an Air Raid Warning should be received during the performance the audience will be informed. Those desiring to leave the theatre may do so, but the performance will continue.' The show ended with Sid's fan song:

> *When you feel unhappy*
> *And if you're looking blue*
> *We recommend*
> *Sid Field to you.*

Even the cast seemed a little bemused by the rapturous audience reception. Jerry Desmonde, Sid Field's straight-man sidekick, wrote: 'The laughs came like the waves of a rough sea, breaking on a shingle beach, and when they came they lasted. They lasted a long, long time.'

Eight hundred miles away, far out at sea, Lieutenant Scott stood on the deck of the *Seraph*, listening to the waves breaking, and peered through the darkness towards the coast of Portugal. 'The weather was warm at last, and it was a delight to keep a watch on the bridge at night beneath a cloudless sky.'

Submarine crews develop a sixth sense for the peculiar. Long periods spent underwater, in close proximity with little to do, when the faintest noise or smallest mistake can mean death, render submariners acutely sensitive to anything out of the ordinary. Bill Jewell firmly believed he was the only person aboard with an inkling of the additional passenger, but at least some members of the crew suspected that the strange tubular canister in the forward torpedo room did not contain optical or meteorological instruments. It was a telltale length, and oddly heavy. When the submarine lurched, a faint sloshing noise could be heard inside. Crewmen began joking about 'John Brown's Body' mouldering in the torpedo rack, and 'our pal Charlie the weatherman coming for a ride'. Jewell himself had no idea of the identity of the body, real or fictional. In his mind he, too, had begun to refer to his passenger as 'Charlie'.

Jean Leslie left the theatre on Montagu's arm, high with excitement, her ears ringing with the applause. Bill Martin's farewell party continued at the Gargoyle, the raffish rooftop club above Meard Street in Soho. Founded in 1925, the Gargoyle was the haunt of artists, writers and actors, the epitome of decadent glamour. It could only be reached by a tiny, rickety lift, the dimensions of which 'were such that strangers entering it left as intimate friends at the top'. The interior was decorated in Moorish style, the walls adorned with mirrored shards of eighteenth-century glass inspired by Henri Matisse, who was a member, as were Noël Coward, Augustus John and Tallulah Bankhead. Spies, including Guy Burgess and Donald Maclean, were drawn to its dark corners and air of secret assignation. The Gargoyle was half-lit, avant-garde, and slightly louche. The film-maker Michael Luke described the atmosphere inside this den as 'mystery suffused with a tender eroticism'. Jean Leslie had never been anywhere like this before. Her mother would have been scandalised.

It was a 'very cheerful evening', Montagu recalled. It was also distinctly flirtatious. The foursome was shown to a corner table, with a banquette and two chairs. Montagu suggested that the women sit together on the banquette. Getting into the dramatic spirit, Avril Gordon remarked playfully: 'Considering Bill and Pam are engaged, they are the least affectionate couple I know. They don't even want to sit together at his farewell party before he goes abroad.' An American couple eavesdropping at the next table looked round sharply. Warming to his own role, and sensing they were being overheard, Montagu replied that he had only known Pam for a few days before getting engaged to her. 'It would be different if Pam and I knew one another better,' he said loudly. 'My boss has said in a letter that although I am quiet and shy at first, I really do know my stuff' – a reference to Mountbatten's fake letter to Admiral Cunningham, in which he used these words to describe Major Martin. It was also a deliberate double entendre.

The couple looked daggers at this naval officer, engaged to a young woman on such brief acquaintance, and now joking about his own romantic prowess. The man was clearly a cad. Registering strong disapproval, they got up to dance. Still, if they did not like that sort of suggestive conversation, they should not have come to the Gargoyle Club. The foursome spent the evening drinking and dancing. Cholmondeley proposed a toast 'to Bill', and they clinked glasses. The men were relaxed and plainly enjoying themselves, but Jean sensed an undercurrent of tension. 'They kept looking at their watches and saying things like: "I wonder if he's afloat now."' She noticed that Ewen Montagu seemed anxious, as if his life was about to change.

The next morning, Montagu wrote to Iris as usual, in a tone of forced indifference: 'I had to go and take someone officially to the theatre. We went to see a new comedian who has been a lot in the North but hadn't been in London before. He was called Sid Field and is frightfully funny. A thoroughly good evening.'

In a few days, the engagement of Pam and Bill would come to its predestined end, and so would the strange parallel bond between a naval officer and his secretary. Montagu, who had been so 'smitten' in the early days of the fantasy, was never quite as flirtatious after the farewell dinner. Lady Swaythling's report to Montagu's wife about the suspicious signed photograph on his dressing table had had its intended effect. The letter from Iris demanding an explanation has not survived, but it is not hard to imagine what was in it. Montagu asked a colleague, who happened to be passing through New York, to visit his wife and clarify matters on his behalf. Iris seems to have accepted his explanation. 'I am glad that Verel told you about my doings,' he wrote. 'I was more nervous of what you might think about the photo and its compromising inscription than what Mother might think!!!' 'Pam' and 'The Girl from the Elms' disappeared from Montagu's life. But nearly half a century later, he was still writing to Jean as 'Pam', and signing himself 'Bill'.

As the *Seraph* neared the drop point, the anxiety levels in Room 13 rose steadily. 'We were all very excited, but also worried, and we couldn't tell anyone outside the room what was happening,' Pat Trehearne recalled. Any number of things might go wrong, and the stakes could hardly have been higher.

Operation Barclay was to be, in Clarke's words, 'the peak of the deception effort in the Mediterranean'. Although never formally integrated into Operation Barclay, the Mincemeat plan was a key element in the expanding operation to deceive the Germans into believing that the next blow would fall simultaneously in Sardinia and Greece, as a prelude to a major campaign in the Balkans. To keep as many German troops as possible away from Sicily and the Central Mediterranean, the plans devised by Johnnie Bevan in London and Dudley Clarke of 'A' Force now encompassed double agents, Greek partisans, false rumours and the imaginary British 12th Army, poised to invade the Balkans.

The host assembled at Cyrenaica in Libya, within range of German reconnaissance planes, consisted of dummy landing craft, dummy gliders and dummy tanks, as well as real anti-aircraft batteries and fighters to be scrambled at the first sign of enemy aircraft, reinforcing the lie. A genuine sabotage operation was planned to concentrate German attention on Greece. Hints of an impending Greek invasion were dropped at diplomatic dinner parties in neutral countries, in the hope that these would filter back to Germany. Greek troops underwent amphibious training in Egypt, calls for Greek speakers were sent out, and Greek drachmas were bought on the Cairo foreign exchange. 'One patriotic Greek managed to remain with a British unit and was no doubt amazed to find himself landing in Sicily instead of his homeland.' Leaflets were distributed on 'hygiene in the Balkans'. Similar, though less intensive, efforts were made to indicate an impending assault on Sardinia at the other end of the Mediterranean: fishermen in Algeria were quizzed on their knowledge of Sardinian waters.

At the same time, preparations for the real invasion of Sicily were progressing swiftly, with troops assembling at North African ports. If Mincemeat and Barclay worked, then the Germans would see those preparations as elements of Brimstone, the fake plan for attacking Sardinia, and the supposed attacks on Greece. The airfields in Sicily would have to be bombed, since, in Montagu's words, 'no major operation could be launched, maintained, or supplied until the enemy airfields and other bases in Sicily had been neutralised'. If the plan succeeded, the bombing would be seen as supporting action for the invasions in the eastern and western Mediterranean, and not as a prelude to what they were: a full-scale assault on Sicily itself. Various false dates for an imminent invasion were spread through numerous channels, and then 'postponed'. The false dates were selected to coincide with the darkest lunar periods. That way, it was hoped, the enemy might assume a dark night was the only time to fear an attack, and relax its guard when the moon was high.

Operation Mincemeat was just one cog in the deception machine, but it was a pivotal one. If it failed, then all the other elements of the deception might be revealed as part of an enormous fraud, allowing the Germans to reinforce Sicily and see the preparations for invading Greece as the sham they were. As Montagu had warned at the outset, 'if they should suspect that the papers are a "plant" it might have far-reaching consequences of great magnitude'. The responsibility weighed heavily on Montagu's shoulders. 'I had to carry the can (and have it on my conscience) if anything happened to *Seraph*.'

There would be no second chance. John Godfrey, the former boss of Naval Intelligence, had always insisted that deception was a dish best served piping hot: 'Intelligence, like food, soon gets stale, smelly, cold, soggy and indigestible, and when it has gone bad does more harm than good. If it ever gets into one of these revolting conditions, do not try to warm it up. Withdraw the offending morsel, and start again.' Once Mincemeat went bad, it would have to be discarded. Jewell was under no illusions: the smallest hitch, and the operation would be aborted, the body taken to Gibraltar, and the documents handed to the Staff Officer (Intelligence) 'with instructions to burn the contents unopened'. Contingency plans were also laid in case matters went awry after the body was launched.

On 22 April, a coded message was sent to the senior intelligence officer in Gibraltar: 'Operation known as Mincemeat repeat Mincemeat has been mounted . . . If body is sent to Gibraltar with documents in despatch case please advise Robertson MI5 immediately and give opinion whether such documents have or have not been tampered with. If such documents come into your hands they are to be sent complete with seals intact by direct weighted air bag addressed Colonel Robertson MI5.'

On the evening of 28 April, the *Seraph* rounded Cape St Vincent, and headed for Huelva. Jewell summoned his officers to the wardroom. Seated around the table, in addition to Jewell and his second-in-command, David Scott, were Lieutenants Dickie Sutton, John Davis and Ralph Norris. Taking a large envelope from the safe, Jewell proceeded to describe the gist of Operation Mincemeat. As Scott remarked, the contents of the canister came as 'something of a shock'. What seemed to upset him most was the thought that 'sailors had been sleeping alongside it, possibly using part of it as a pillow'. The officers nodded and asked no questions. After dropping off a genial American general in one part of the Mediterranean, picking up a grumpy French one in another, blowing up a whale and becoming, briefly, an American submarine, their new mission was just about par for the course. Jewell stressed 'the vital need for absolute secrecy'. Submariners are notoriously superstitious. When Jewell was out of earshot, one of the officers remarked: 'Isn't it pretty unlucky carting dead bodies around?'

At dawn the next day, just off Punta Umbria, Jewell gave the order to dive. For the next few hours, he and Scott carried out 'a close-range reconnaissance of the beach, making sure we knew every landmark'. The place seemed all but deserted, with just a handful of fishing huts and a few boats drawn up on the sand. This mission, Scott reflected, wrongly, was going to be 'easy, even enjoyable'. The only impediment was a strong offshore wind. Their orders were clear: 'The operation had to be carried out as near as we could manage to the time of low water' with 'an onshore wind, or no wind at all'. Jewell decided to wait.

'The next day turned out to be ideal,' Scott wrote. 'The wind was light and Southerly and the sky overcast.' The *Seraph* withdrew twelve miles off the coast, to recharge her batteries, and waited for low tide and complete darkness. In London, the Admiralty requested the Air Ministry to 'arrange total bombing restrictions' in the area. Naval Intelligence reported: 'No known defensive dangers' near Huelva.

At 0100 hours on 30 April, the submerged submarine stealthily approached the shore once more. Two hours later, the *Seraph* reached the prearranged spot, 148 degrees off Portil Pilar, and some eight cables, a little under one mile, from the beach. 'We were just about to surface,' Jewell described, 'when the fishing fleet went over the top of us, going out to collect sardines.' Waiting until the boats were well clear, the *Seraph* surfaced and Jewell surveyed the area with his binoculars. 'A large number of small fishing boats were working in the bay. The closest about a mile off' – too far, he calculated, to be able to spot the dark submarine. The sky was overcast with low clouds and patchy visibility, and the wind was picking up.

The crew had been told that the officers were 'landing some pseudo-secret instruments on the beach in order to try to trap a German agent known to be operating in the vicinity of Huelva, and that we hoped enough evidence against him could be gathered to result in his expulsion from neutral Spain'. Three of the ratings hauled the canister through the torpedo hatch, which would usually only be opened in harbour. The metal tube was laid on the forecasing, and the crewmen ordered to return below. Scott manned the bridge, while Lieutenant Norris acted as lookout. Lieutenants Sutton and Davis set to work, unscrewing the bolts in the canister lid. Scott ran the echo sounder, which showed almost two fathoms of water beneath the keel. 'We crept in a little closer to the beach.'

Major Martin was lifted out of the steel tube at 0415 hours. There was, as Jewell put it with his usual understatement, 'some little stink'.

Perhaps through oxygen trapped in the dead man's uniform and blanket, decomposition had accelerated during the passage from Scotland. Several of the officers recoiled. They had seen the worst of wartime underwater combat, but as Jewell observed, 'I doubt if any of them had seen a dead body at that time.' Jewell himself was sublimely unconcerned. 'I had seen bodies before. My father was a doctor, a surgeon. My brothers were doctors. I wasn't that worried by it.' Jewell's official report described the extent of the decay: 'The blanket was opened up and the body examined. The briefcase was found to be securely attached. The face was heavily tanned and the whole of the lower half from the eyes down covered with mould. The skin had started to break away on the nose and cheek bones. The body was very high.'

Working quickly, Jewell inflated the Mae West, transferred the documents from envelope to briefcase, locked it, and placed the keys in the pocket of the corpse. He then selected the identity card picturing Ronnie Reed, and added that to the pocket. Up on the bridge, Lieutenant Scott was becoming steadily more anxious. It was now 0430, and a glimmer of dawn light was spreading over the water. More worryingly, the wind was strengthening and the submarine was drifting closer to the shore. 'We seemed to be practically on the beach.' The *Seraph*'s draft was 6.4 metres. The depth at low water in her current position was just 4.5 metres. The tide was almost out, and the submarine was very nearly aground.

Bill Jewell straightened, took off his officer's cap and, bending his head, briefly recited 'what I could remember of the funeral service' – a fragment of the 39th Psalm. The choice was oddly appropriate, given the extreme secrecy of their mission: 'I will keep my mouth as if it were with a bridle: while the ungodly is in my sight. Held my tongue, and spake nothing: I kept silence, yea, even from good words; but it was pain and grief to me.'

The three officers then picked up the body, and gently slipped it into the sea. Jewell turned to Scott on the bridge and gave the thumbs-up sign. 'With some relief', Scott jammed the submarine full speed astern. 'The wash of the screws helped Major Martin on his way.' As the submarine headed seawards, Scott could just make out the grey shape, drifting towards the shore. In the official report on the operation, Jewell was praised for steering so close to the beach, even though the submarine had almost grounded: 'He virtually assured success by approaching as close inshore as he did.'

A half-mile south, the partially inflated rubber dinghy and oar were thrown overboard, while the officers stuffed the blankets, tapes, and dinghy packaging inside the canister. Still on the surface, powered by the quieter electric motor, Scott steered the submarine into deep, open water. Twelve miles out, the *Seraph* stopped for the last time, and the canister was thrown overboard. The seafloor here was 200 fathoms down. The canister would never be found. If, that is, it could be made to sink. Charles Fraser-Smith had made Major Martin's capsule too well. 'Because it had been designed to keep the ice from melting, it had pockets of air all the way around it.' The double skin acted as an inbuilt buoyancy tank.

A Vickers gun was brought up from below, and the canister was 'riddled by fire'. Still it would not go down and, worse, it was drifting towards the shore. Jewell then handed Scott a .455 service revolver, and instructed him to stand on the foreplanes, while he manoeuvred the submarine until the canister was directly below him. 'He did this with his usual skill, and I fired all six shots into the top of the canister.' Still the steel tube bobbed defiantly on the surface. It was, Jewell reflected, 'a hell of a time', and time was now running out. 'Daylight was fast approaching, and we could see some fishing boats not far off.' Jewell opted for radical measures. The steel tube, now resembling a large colander with some 200 bullet holes in it, was hauled back on to the casing, and packed with plastic explosive, inside and out. The fuse was lit, the canister lowered overboard, and the submarine hastened to get out of the way. The resulting explosion was exceptionally loud. In Jewell's laconic epitaph: 'It then disappeared, finally.' Jewell was relieved, but he knew he had taken a risk. His orders were to sink the canister in one piece, not to blow it to smithereens. Fragments of the casing, or even bits of blanket and tape, might now wash ashore. Perhaps these would be assumed to be debris from the downed aircraft, but not necessarily. Moreover, even if the Spanish fishermen in the bay had not spotted the submarine setting off the explosion, they would surely have seen the flash and heard the sound echoing through the still dawn. In his final report, Jewell made no mention of having to explode the canister, merely observing that after being shot full of holes, 'it was seen to sink'. Indeed, he did not tell anyone how the canister had been blown to shreds until 1991, when he was seventy-seven years old.

'We dived and set course for Gibraltar,' wrote Scott. 'Breakfast tasted wonderful, and so was the deep sleep into which I fell immediately afterwards.'

At 0715 hours, Lieutenant Bill Jewell of HMS *Seraph* sent a wireless message to the Admiralty in London: 'Mincemeat Completed.' Back on land in Gibraltar, Jewell scribbled a postcard, which he posted to Montagu: 'Parcel delivered safely.'

15

Dulce et Decorum

All morning the body lay in the dunes, beneath the pines, where the fisherman José Antonio Rey María had carried it. As the sun rose, the sand grew hotter, and the smell grew worse. A series of important visitors came to look at the dead man.

The officer in command of the 1st Company of the 2nd Battalion of the 72nd Infantry Regiment (in charge of coastal defence around Huelva), who had been drilling his men on the beach before the body was brought ashore, sent word to the police at Punta Umbria. The police duly informed the port authority at Huelva that a drowned soldier had washed up on the beach at La Bota. The case therefore came under the military jurisdiction of the port. In late morning, the rotund figure of navy lieutenant Mariano Pascual del Pobil Bensusan, second in command of the port and acting military judge, appeared at the beach in a canoe, paddled by two Spanish seamen. Lieutenant Pascual del Pobil was sweating profusely, very hot, and he wanted his lunch. With some distaste, he made a cursory examination of the body, noting the military uniform, and the briefcase with the crest 'G VI R and the royal crown' attached to the dead man by a chain 'which had penetrated the muscles of the neck as a result of the swelling'. He also extracted the wallet, and noted down Major Martin's name from his identity card. Pascual del Pobil then unclipped the locked case from its chain, ordered that the body be taken to Huelva, and climbed back into his boat, taking the case with him. He did not think to look in the dead man's pocket for a key. The next to arrive, on foot, was a local doctor, José Pablo Vázquez Pérez, who came to certify that the body was really dead. The stench wafting from under the pines suggested this was not strictly necessary.

There was no road to the dock at Punta Umbria, merely a sandy track winding five miles through the dunes. The body was loaded on to a donkey, which set off, led by a child, through the sweet afternoon scent of wild rosemary and jacaranda. The two infantrymen followed behind. In the late afternoon, the grim little procession arrived at the infantry headquarters by the dock, too late to arrange transport of the body across the estuary mouth. The corpse was placed in an outhouse, ready to be taken over to Huelva in the morning.

Lieutenant Pascual del Pobil had by now sent word to the British consulate that a dead British soldier, found on La Bota beach, would be arriving by motor launch at Huelva dock the next morning. Francis Haselden was profoundly relieved. For the last forty-eight hours the British vice consul had been waiting anxiously, unaware that the delivery of the body had been delayed by the weather.

Gómez-Beare had left Haselden with very specific instructions: as soon as he received word that the body had come ashore, the vice consul 'should telephone him at Madrid and inform him of the finding of the body, its particulars, etc.'. Gómez-Beare would then verbally instruct Haselden to arrange the burial while he notified London. A few days later, 'when a signal from London might be expected to have reached him', Gómez-Beare would call again to ask if anything had washed ashore with the body. The assistant naval attaché 'would say that he could not talk on the 'phone but would come down to Huelva. He would then do so and make discreet inquiries whether any bag or paper had been washed ashore.' Gómez-Beare knew that the telephones at the Madrid embassy were bugged. It was likely that Adolf Clauss also had spies inside the consulate, and that anything said on the telephone there would be reported back to the Germans. At the same time, Alan Hillgarth in Madrid would send cables to Huelva backing up the story, again in the knowledge that these would be intercepted at source, and relayed to Karl-Erich Kuhlenthal and his colleagues at Abwehr headquarters in Madrid. The entire performance was for German benefit: London, and the embassy in Madrid, should appear to be increasingly agitated about the loss of top-secret documents. Parallel to these 'breakable' messages, Hillgarth would despatch 'a separate series in his personal cipher, keeping London in the picture of what was going on'.

Haselden must play the part of a harassed official under mounting pressure from his bosses to trace a missing briefcase. The role required nuance. Haselden would have to make inquiries, with increasing urgency, for the missing papers, but he must not do so too 'energetically', as this might lead to the documents actually being returned before they reached the Germans. In that case, Operation Mincemeat would have failed.

Here lay an additional, but crucial, consideration. The British *did* want to get the documents back, intact, once the Germans had had a good look at them. Under international law, as a neutral country, Spain was obliged to return any property belonging to a British national who had died in Spain. The precedent of Lieutenant Turner suggested that the briefcase would, eventually, be returned by the Spaniards. But in reality if top-secret plans really had fallen into enemy hands, and the breach of security was detected, then those plans might well be abandoned, or at least substantially altered. The Germans must be made to believe that they had gained access to the documents undetected; they should be made to assume that the British believed the Spaniards had returned the documents unopened, and unread. Operation Mincemeat would only work if the Germans could be fooled into believing that the British had been fooled. All of this would require the most careful stage management.

Francis Haselden was not an actor. Nor was he a spy, novelist or fly fisherman. He did not even particularly want to be a vice consul, but had inherited the post after the sudden death of his predecessor in 1940. He was a gentle, civilised, sixty-two-year-old mining engineer and businessman, who had settled in Huelva two decades earlier, and might reasonably have expected to spend the rest of his life playing golf and running his mine supplies company, a pillar of the community in a small and sunny British outpost. War had made a new man of Haselden: he now ran an underground network helping escaped prisoners of war, harboured downed Allied pilots, monitored the nefarious doings of Adolf Clauss and his agents, and did everything he could to help the Allied secret services respond in kind. In most parts of Spain, Franco was content simply to monitor the espionage battle between the Germans and the British, and leave the two sides to get on with it. But in Huelva the civilian governor, Joaquín Miranda González, was a keen member of the fascist Falange, strongly pro-German, and keen to help his friend Clauss root out British spies. To Haselden's annoyance, three members of Huelva's British community had already been expelled on suspicion of spying, including Montagu Brown, the head of a local railway company. Here, then, was Haselden's opportunity to strike back at Clauss and his Spanish allies, by playing – but not overplaying – the part of a worthy functionary looking after the interests of a dead British officer. He rose to the occasion magnificently.

Emilio Morales Candela, Huelva's undertaker, was waiting at the jetty when the ferry from Punta Umbria pulled in the following morning, carrying a handful of passengers and one dead body. Beside him stood Francis Haselden, who had asked Candela to transport the body to the cemetery. The vice consul had also, as instructed, made the first telephone call to Gómez-Beare in Madrid informing him that a dead British soldier had washed ashore. The body was lifted into a wooden coffin, and loaded on to the horse-drawn cart provided by 'La Magdalena' funeral services of Huelva (it would be another decade before the town had its own motorised hearse). Pulled by an ancient horse and steered by Candela, the square wooden funeral carriage, locally known as the 'Soup Bowl' (La Sopera), set off up the hill towards the cemetery, with Haselden following in his car. The route to Nuestra Señora de la Soledad cemetery led through the area of Huelva known as Concepción, little more than a cluster of fishing huts surrounding the ancient Torre de Vigilancia, one of the circular brick watch towers built in the sixteenth century to spot pirates.

News spreads fast in a small town, and word that a dead British soldier had been found at La Bota travelled well ahead of the slow-moving cortège. A small knot of people gathered outside the Church of Nuestra Señora de Lourdes to watch it pass. Several made the sign of the cross. The priest, Father José Manuel Romero Bernal, muttered a prayer. The carriage continued through the centre of the town, and past the Teatro Mora, which was showing *Pygmalion* starring Leslie Howard. The sun was already baking.

The cemetery of Nuestra Señora de la Soledad sits on a small hill just outside Huelva, a high-walled compound surrounded by fields of sunflowers. Alongside it is the much smaller British cemetery, in which members of the Protestant German community, in a strange alliance of religion in defiance of politics, were also interred. The horse was sweating by the time the lumbering funeral carriage reached the cemetery. Waiting at the gates were Lieutenant Pascual del Pobil, the naval judge, with the briefcase under one arm. Alongside him stood Dr Eduardo Fernández del Torno, and his son, Dr Eduardo Fernández Contioso, who would together carry out an autopsy. The final member of the reception committee was a young American pilot called Willie Watkins.

Three days before the body was brought ashore, an American P-39 Airacobra plane crash-landed in a field in Punta Umbria. The pilot was Watkins, a twenty-six-year-old

from Corpus Christi, Texas, who had been flying from North
Africa to Portugal when his plane ran out of fuel. Unable to
open the cockpit cover, Watkins had come down with his
plane, escaping with only minor injuries. He had been taken
into custody by the infantry detachment guarding the coast,
briefly lodged at the Hotel La Granadina in Huelva, and then
transferred to the home of Francis Haselden, the refuge of
all Allied soldiers since there was no American consulate in
Huelva. Lieutenant Pascual del Pobil had requested that the
American pilot be brought to the cemetery in case the dead
body and the downed plane were connected in some way, and
Watkins might be able to identify the body.

The coffin was carried to the small building on the edge
of the cemetery that served as a morgue. Glyndwr Michael's
body was lifted out, and placed on the raised marble slab.
Methodically, the mortuary attendant went through the
pockets, extracted the contents, and laid them out on the
table: cash, sodden cigarettes, matches, keys, receipts, identity
card, wallet, stamps, and theatre ticket counterfoils. Pascual del
Pobil barely glanced at these. Lunch was already beckoning.
Haselden did his best to seem uninterested. The Spanish
officer now turned his attention to the briefcase, which he
unlocked with one of the dead man's keys. The contents
were soaked, but the writing on the envelopes was still clearly
legible. Pascual del Pobil carefully 'examined the names on the
envelopes', and motioned Haselden over to look. Haselden
had been told only the outline of Operation Mincemeat. But
from the red seals and embossed envelopes, these were clearly
confidential military letters. Pascual del Pobil also seems to
have registered their importance, for he now did exactly what
Montagu and Cholmondeley had hoped would not happen.
He gestured towards the case, and asked Haselden if he would
like to take it. Since these items would have to be returned
to the British eventually, would the vice consul like to take
custody now? Pascual del Pobil liked the English vice consul;

he believed he was doing Haselden a favour; and he wanted his lunch and siesta.

Haselden knew he had to 'react swiftly'. Indeed, he had mentally prepared himself for the possibility that Pascual del Pobil would cut corners, and simply hand over the briefcase. With as much nonchalance as he could muster, he said: 'Well, your superior might not like that, so perhaps you should deliver it to him, and then bring it back to me, following the official route.' Pascual del Pobil shrugged, and closed the briefcase.

Willie Watkins had observed this exchange. Although he spoke little Spanish, it was clear what was going on. Haselden's 'attitude, in refusing the briefcase, struck him as odd'. The American pilot was now beckoned over by Pascual del Pobil, and asked if he could identify the dead man. Needless to say, he could not, and said so. The dead man's lifebelt, he pointed out, was 'of an English pattern, whereas he himself had flown an American plane, which carried a completely different type of lifebelt'. Pascual del Pobil stated the obvious: 'There are clearly two completely unconnected accidents.'

Packing up the briefcase, wallet, and other possessions, the naval judge explained that these would be formally handed over to his commanding officer, the naval commander of the port of Huelva. The tubby Spanish officer departed, taking the case and other items with him. Haselden casually announced that he would stay to watch the autopsy. If it seemed odd to Watkins that the British vice consul should decline the offer of the briefcase, it was surely even odder that he should choose to remain in a broiling hut with a tin roof while two Spanish doctors cut up a half-rotted corpse. The American pilot was only too happy to escape the foetid room with its stench of death, and smoke a cigarette in the shade of the willow tree outside.

The autopsy would usually have been carried out by a military pathologist, but since he was away, the task fell to Dr Fernández, the civilian forensic pathologist, and his son Eduardo, a recent medical graduate. Contrary to Spilsbury's dismissive remark about the poor state of Spanish forensic expertise, Fernández was a good and experienced pathologist. A native of Seville, he had studied medicine at Seville University, and then spent many years working as the company doctor for a large mining concern. Since 1921 he had been senior pathologist for the Huelva area. Fernández may not have been in Spilsbury's forensic league, but he had a wide practical knowledge of dead bodies in general and, given his coastal location, of drowning victims in particular.

Haselden later described the autopsy. 'On the first incision being made, there was a minor explosion, for while the body externally was in good preservation, the inside had deteriorated badly.' The lungs were filled with fluid, but given the state of decomposition and without further tests, Dr Fernández would have been unable to say whether this was sea water. He examined the ears and hair of the corpse, and its strangely discoloured skin. Haselden knew nothing of the real circumstances surrounding the body, but he knew enough of the plot to realise that the more detailed the autopsy, the more likely it was that the pathologist would find some clue to the real cause of death. The British vice consul was friendly with the Spanish doctor. The stench of putrefaction in the room was now almost overwhelming. With what was later described as 'remarkable presence of mind', he decided to intervene. 'Since it was obvious the heat had done its worst,' he said, there was no need for a detailed autopsy. 'On receiving this assurance from the VC that he was quite satisfied, the doctor, not without relief perhaps, agreed to call it a day and issued the necessary certificate.'

The postmortem verdict was straightforward: 'The young British officer fell in the water while still alive, showed no evidence of bruising, and drowned through asphyxia caused by submersion. The body had been in the water between eight and ten days.'

The body was returned to its plain wooden coffin, and formally transferred into the care of the British vice consul.

Fernández had missed the telltale discolouration of the skin, indicating phosphorus poisoning. He made only a cursory examination of the lungs, and took no samples from the lungs, liver or kidneys for testing. Yet there were other aspects of the case that troubled him. The doctor had examined hundreds of drowned fishermen over the years. In every case, there was evidence of 'nibbling and bites by fish and crabs on the earlobes and other fleshy parts'. The ears of the British officer were untouched. On bodies that have been in sea water for more than a week, the hair on the head becomes dull and brittle. 'The shininess of the hair did not correspond to the time which he had supposedly spent in the water', and there was also, in Fernández's mind, some 'doubt over the nature of the liquid in the man's lungs'. Privately, Fernández also noted something peculiar about the clothing. The man's uniform was waterlogged, but it had not attained the shapeless, soggy form of clothing that has been in sea water for a week. 'He seemed very well dressed to be in the water for so many days,' the doctor reflected. The two doctors had also compared the photograph on the identity card with the dead man, but concluded that these were 'identical'. Yet even here, there was room for doubt, for the father and son medical team noted 'that a bald patch on the temples was more pronounced than in the photograph'. The William Martin in the photograph had a thick head of hair, but the one on the mortuary slab was thinning on top. Fernández concluded that 'either the photograph was taken some two or three years ago or the baldness on the temples was due to the action of sea water'. This was an odd conclusion: sea water has many effects on the human body, but male-pattern baldness is not one of them.

It is impossible to know how many of Fernández's doubts found their way into his final report: the autopsy was passed to the port authority, filed in the archives by Pascual del Pobil, and then destroyed in a fire in 1976.

There was one additional, far more glaring inconsistency, which Fernández did spot, although he did not realise its significance. The degree of decomposition, according to Fernández, indicated that the body had been at sea for a minimum of eight days, or possibly longer. According to the evidence in Major Martin's pocket, he flew from London late on 24 April; and the body was retrieved in the early hours of 30 April. The decayed state of the body was simply inconsistent with a body submerged in cold sea water for only a little over five days. Fernández, of course, was unaware of the supposed timing of Major Martin's death. That evidence was contained in his wallet, which was now in the possession of Captain Francisco Elvira Alvárez, commander of the port of Huelva and, as it happened, the best friend of Ludwig Clauss, Huelva's elderly German consul.

At 8.30 that evening, Francis Haselden sent a cable to assistant naval attaché Don Gómez-Beare in Madrid: 'With reference to my phone message today, body is identified as Major W. Martin R. M. identity card 148228 dated 2nd Feb. 1943 Cardiff. Naval judge has taken possession of all papers. Death due to drowning probably 8 to 10 days at sea. I am having funeral Sunday noon.'

Normally, in such circumstances, the naval attaché would have sent a message to the Admiralty in London, with the name and rank of the dead man. In this case, no such Royal Marines officer existed, and if the cable was distributed through normal channels someone in London might well spot the anomaly. Hillgarth had arranged that just before he was ready to send the telegram reporting the death of Major Martin, he would send a separate message, in code, to 'C' at MI6, 'so that the action for suppressing it could be taken'. The plan went wrong. The message to 'C' duly arrived, but by the time MI6 got around to acting on it, the signal from Hillgarth had already begun to be distributed to various Admiralty departments: one of these might well be conversant with the names of Royal Marines officers, and start making embarrassing enquiries. A flurry of telephone calls to the heads of the departments that had received the message ordered 'the suppression of the signal on the excuse that the individual in question was not a naval officer, but had, with the authority of the First Sea Lord, been given the cover of rank in the Royal Marines when he was setting out on a secret and very special mission abroad . . . the secrecy of his task rendered it necessary that the signal should be suppressed and no action taken on it'. In a way, the excuse was true.

Haselden's message was addressed to 'Sadok', Gómez-Beare's cable name, but its intended recipient was Adolf Clauss, the senior Abwehr officer in Huelva and the man identified by Montagu as the 'super-super-efficient agent' most likely to intercept the documents. Clauss was living up to his billing, for he was already fully aware that the body of a British officer carrying letters had washed up in his bailiwick. It may have been Lieutenant Pascual del Pobil himself who told the German agent about the body and its accompanying briefcase, or the harbour master, or the mortuary attendant, or even Dr Fernández, who had conducted the autopsy. Whoever it was, by the time the British vice consul informed Madrid that the papers had arrived, Clauss had already mobilised his extensive spy network to intercept them.

This was proving rather difficult, for the briefcase and its contents had fallen, from the point of view of both the British and the Germans, into the wrong hands. Had the case simply been handed over to the Huelva police, as the British intended, then Clauss would have obtained it within hours. The same thing would have happened had the documents ended up in the possession of Huelva's civilian governor, the harbour master, or the army authorities, for these, too, were in the pay of Clauss. Instead, the Spanish navy had them, and this was an altogether trickier nut for German espionage to crack. Montagu himself later admitted that the fact that the documents had been 'taken into naval custody' very nearly derailed the entire operation. Many Spanish naval officers were pro-British, and there was a tradition of mutual respect between the British and Spanish navies. The Navy Minister, Admiral Moreno, was a personal friend of Alan Hillgarth, who had made a point of cultivating naval officers: 'The Spanish navy is <u>not</u> in German hands,' he wrote.

Clauss's first approach was the most direct one: he instructed his father, the consul, Ludwig Clauss, to ask his friend and golfing partner, Captain Francisco Elvira Alvárez, to hand over the documents. Captain Elvira refused. Politely, he explained that these documents were now locked away in his safe at the Navy Office at 17 Avenida de Italia, where they would remain until he received orders from Cadiz about what should be done with them. Elvira was a cheerful, garrulous and sociable man. He liked Clauss, was happy to eat the dinners laid on by the German consul, and the hospitality he provided at Huelva Golf Club. But there is no evidence he was on Clauss's payroll. Elvira was also a stickler for the rules, 'a rigid disciplinarian', and a firm believer in hierarchy. He would await instructions from above.

At midday on 2 May 1943, a group of mourners, official and unofficial, public and secret, gathered for the funeral and burial of Major William Martin. It was a day of 'suffocating heat', according to the local newspaper, yet the turnout was impressive. Representing Britain were Francis Haselden, the vice consul, and Lancelot Shutte, a British mining company executive who had been expelled from Spain once already by Governor Miranda on suspicion of espionage. Here, too, was the Frenchman Pierre Desbrest, a Gaullist and close friend of Haselden. Officially, Desbrest was the representative in Spain of a French-owned pyrites company. Less officially, he organised an underground route for Free French forces from occupied France through Spain to North Africa, and conspired with Haselden against the Germans. The port commander, Elvira, and the naval judge, Pascual del Pobil, attended in full naval uniform. The military governor of Huelva was in Seville, meeting General Franco, but sent an army lieutenant to represent the Spanish armed forces.

Glyndwr Michael had died without a single mourner. His funeral, as someone completely different, was carried out with full military honours, and all the ceremony and solemnity Huelva could muster. In addition to the officials and military brass, a small crowd of civilians also gathered at Nuestra Señora de la Soledad cemetery: the curious, the pious, and the clandestine. Haselden does not seem to have spotted the tall, cadaverous figure of Adolf Clauss among the crowd. Clauss would later claim that he had only come to the funeral in his capacity as German vice consul, 'as a mark of respect to the fallen soldier'. In truth, of course, he was there to observe, to see if he might pick up any useful information about the dead man, and his intriguing briefcase.

The death certificate, filled out by funeral director Candela, formally marked the passing of 'W. Martin, aged between thirty-five and forty, native of Cardiff (England) [sic], officer of the British marines, found on the beach known as "La Bota" at half past nine on 30 April 1943. Death by drowning.' After a brief funeral service in the cemetery chapel, the coffin was carried along a cobbled path, down a neat avenue of cypresses, to the section of the cemetery known as San Marco. Swallows dipped and dived among the palm trees, and the strong scent of jasmine trees rose in the midday heat. The funeral procession passed the large and imposing mausoleums of Huelva's wealthiest Spanish families, marble tombs surrounded by iron railings. Here was the grave of Huelva's most famous son, Miguel Biez, 'El Litri', a bullfighter famously gored to death in 1929. Litri's huge and ostentatious tomb depicted the matador wearing the 'suit of lights'.

As the procession neared the northwest corner of the cemetery, the graves grew smaller and humbler. The San Marco section was where the poor and ordinary folk of Huelva were buried. Haselden had ordered a 'Class Five' burial, the cheapest available: total cost, including coffin, being just 250 pesetas. The British consulate contracted to pay the cost of renting and maintaining the grave in perpetuity. Major Martin was not the first tenant of grave number 46, in the fourteenth avenue of the

San Marco section, backing up to the cemetery wall. In 1938, a ten-year-old girl named Rosario Vilches had been buried there, but her parents had been unable to keep up payments on the plot, and two months earlier the body had been removed and reburied elsewhere.

At half past twelve, the coffin was lowered into the grave. Of the official mourners, only Francis Haselden knew that the man inside had not died at sea, and even he was ignorant of the full scale of the imposture taking place: a Welsh Baptist in a Spanish Catholic grave, a derelict who had never worn uniform accorded rank and honour, a man with no relatives (at least none who seemed to care) invested with a parent to mourn him, and buried with full military pomp by a grateful nation. Glyndwr Michael had probably killed himself on the spur of the moment, or through insanity, or by accident. The fatal dose of poison had carried him 500 miles, into another country, and another personality. The inscription on his tomb would eventually read: *Dulce et decorum est pro patria mori*, the line from Horace's *Odes*: 'It is sweet and fitting to die for your country.' There was nothing remotely decorous or patriotic about the way Glyndwr Michael died. Yet in a way, the epitaph was apt: Michael had, indeed, given his death, if not his life, to his country, even if he was given no choice about it.

The officials climbed into their hot cars, the gravediggers began to fill in the hole, and the mourners trailed away down the hill towards the town. Adolf Clauss watched them leave, and then headed back to the German consulate on foot. He did not sign the mourners' book, and he spoke to no one, but his presence did not go unremarked. Among the other mourners was an innocuous-looking middle-aged man in a nondescript suit. The Spaniards had assumed he must be part of the official delegation. The officials assumed he was a local Spaniard. From the shade of a Cyprus tree, Don Gómez-Beare watched Adolf Clauss leave the cemetery, and then quietly slipped out, and followed him down the hill.

Spanish Trails

Clauss had much to occupy his mind. His attempts to obtain the
briefcase had so far failed. The Spanish naval authorities were
proving vigorously uncooperative. Perhaps they would be more
amenable to an approach from a fellow Spaniard. Frustrated, the
German spy resolved to try a more indirect approach. Lieutenant
Colonel Santiago Garrigos was commander of the Guardia Civil,
the Spanish paramilitary police, for the Huelva district, and an
enthusiastic recipient of German largesse. Clauss instructed Garrigos
to 'do everything necessary to obtain copies of the documents
which were found in the briefcase'. Garrigos may have been a
keen collaborator, but he was also a coward, and knew that if he
asked Elvira or Pascual del Pobil to show him the documents, they
would conclude that he was on the German payroll, and send him
packing. 'Notwithstanding his great desire to serve the Germans,
this Lt Colonel apparently did not have the courage to approach
the naval judge' and simply demand that he open the letters.

Garrigos did, however, persuade someone in the naval office
to tell him what was in the briefcase. He sent the list to Clauss:

a) Three British Operation bulletins
b) Two plans
c) 33 photographs
d) Three envelopes addressed to Cunningham, General
Eisenhower and General Alexander.

Helpfully, but unnecessarily, Garrigos added: 'These three persons are in command of the Allied troops in North Africa.'

Clauss knew that whatever was in that briefcase must be extremely interesting. Heavier guns were mobilised. The German consul, Ludwig Clauss, was once again wheeled out, and asked by his son to approach his 'intimate friend' Joaquín Miranda González, the civilian governor of Huelva and head of the provincial Falange. A keen fascist, Miranda 'nursed a profound antipathy towards the British, in common with the sentiment among most officials, and maintained excellent relations with the German consulate . . . he treated the Germans with favouritism and the British with a heavy hand'. Miranda was anxious to help, and made discreet enquiries at the naval office, but he too stopped short of demanding that the letters be opened. 'This gentleman,' reported one of Hillgarth's agents, 'did not dare to ask the naval judge for copies of the documents.' Clauss received this fresh rebuff with mounting frustration and growing curiosity. He had spent a small fortune bribing the local officials. 'In Huelva, Don Adolfo can open every door,' it was said. Yet the door to Captain Elvira's safe remained firmly shut. A bag full of secret British documents had been sitting in Huelva for three days, and, so far, these had been 'neither copied nor photographed [and] were only seen and read in the naval judge's office'. The three envelopes, which Clauss knew must contain the most important information, were still sealed.

Back in London, Cholmondeley and Montagu were equally frustrated that the information appeared to have reached its target, only to become lodged in the annoyingly honest hands of the Spanish navy. They decided to give the pot a stir.

Alan Hillgarth sent a cable to London, unencrypted, reporting that Major Martin of the Royal Marines had been laid to rest with due decorum: 'I am glad to say the naval and military authorities were well represented and extremely sympathetic.' Two days after the funeral – enough time, it was estimated, for news of Major Martin's death to filter through the British military bureaucracy – the Naval Intelligence Department in London sent a much less casual-sounding cable to Hillgarth in Madrid, numbered '04132'. It was marked 'Top Secret' but intended for German eyes, and carefully flavoured with rising anxiety. 'Some papers Major Martin had in his possession are of great importance and secrecy. Make formal demand for all papers and notify me by personal signal immediately of addressees of any official letters recovered. Such letters should be returned addressed to Commodore Rushbrooke, Personal, by fastest safe route and should not repetition not be opened or tampered with in any way. If no official letters are recovered make searching but discreet inquiries at Huelva and Madrid to find whether they were washed ashore and if so what has happened to them.'

At the same time, Montagu sent a separate message to Hillgarth, using the secret personal cipher that was the only safe method of communication with the spy-riddled embassy in Madrid. 'Carry out instructions in my Naval Signal as this is necessary cover but lack of success is desirable.' The message merely confirmed what Hillgarth already knew. The novelist-naval attaché would be creating a fiction especially for Kuhlenthal and his informants but, once again, this would need to be done with extreme subtlety. The Germans knew British diplomatic methods by now: if a bag full of secrets really had been lost, the British would still not rush in and demand its return, as this would tip off the Spanish to its importance. Hillgarth must start with an apparently routine enquiry, and then gradually give the impression of greater and greater urgency. It was a tricky balancing act, since enquiries must be 'kept on such a plane as (theoretically) not to arouse Spanish suspicions that we were really frightened that someone might get those documents, but in fact making it plain to them that we were so frightened'.

Hillgarth passed on London's message to Haselden in Huelva, instructing him to make a 'searching but discreet' investigation into the whereabouts of these important and secret papers. At the same time, he set the first cog of Madrid's mighty rumour

mill grinding into action. In wartime Spain, practically the
only commodity freely available everywhere was gossip: spies
traded in it, the government was saturated with it and just
about everyone, from Franco down, indulged in it. Gossip was
currency. Gossip was power. 'Rumours are extremely easy
to spread in Spain,' wrote Hillgarth. 'The country lives on
word-of-mouth stories. A casual word in a club or café is often
enough.' To get a rumour flying, he told London, all he need
do was 'select from among his acquaintance the most inveterate
gossips and, taking into account their connections, use them
accordingly'. Hillgarth quietly began to spread word that the
British were searching for an important set of documents in
Huelva: he knew that, like any game of Chinese whispers,
the story would be mangled and inflated as it passed from one
gossip to the next, and with any luck, it would soon reach the
Germans, who would react accordingly.

The British naval attaché also made an unobtrusive approach
to Rear Admiral Moreno, the Navy Minister. Hillgarth liked
Moreno, believing him to be 'sincerely anti-war'. The two
men were friends, although perfectly happy to use their
friendship for mutual manipulation. On an earlier occasion,
Hillgarth recalled, 'I managed to make the Minister of Marine
so sorry for me because he could not do what I wanted that
in the end he did it, at considerable hazard to himself, just
because he felt he was letting a friend down if he didn't.'
Through a contact in the Spanish navy, Hillgarth sent word to
the admiral, asking for assistance in securing the return of the
briefcase. Hillgarth was careful to make the request a verbal
one, and commit nothing to paper. Moreno was a reliable and
well-informed source, and almost certainly one of the prime
recipients of British gold. But Hillgarth also knew that the
Spanish Minister of Marine, while professing his attachment
to Britain, and Hillgarth personally, was in close contact with
the German Embassy, and spoke frequently to the German
ambassador, Hans-Heinrich Dieckhoff. Moreno was the ideal

conduit: he was the government minister in command of the navy, and thus likely to see the documents sooner rather than later; he would make strenuous efforts to retrieve them and return them to Britain; but he could also be relied upon to pass on the information to the Germans, or at least enable access to the documents, thus ensuring the continued goodwill of both sides.

Four days after the funeral of Major Martin, Hillgarth secretly reported to London 'that the Minister of Marine, who knew nothing of the papers or effects, was expecting an early report' from naval authorities in the south, and had pledged to keep him abreast of developments. Hillgarth gave Moreno no indication of what might be in the briefcase, and was careful to avoid any impression of undue anxiety.

Finally, Hillgarth mobilised his most trusted informant, the senior Spanish naval officer codenamed 'Agent Andros', and asked him to keep track of what happened to the briefcase and its contents. To judge from results, Andros was perfectly placed to do this, reinforcing suspicion that he may have been the chief of Spanish naval intelligence. The report he subsequently sent to Hillgarth and MI6 was astonishingly detailed, an almost daily account of the fate of Major Martin's briefcase.

Hillgarth's rumour-mongering paid swift dividends. On 5 May, Captain Elvira, the senior navy officer in Huelva, informed Vice Consul Haselden that he had been ordered to pass the dead man's effects, under guard, to his superior officer in San Fernando, Cadiz, who would arrange for their onward transfer to the Ministry of Marine in Madrid. He also shared this information with the German vice consul, Adolf Clauss. Haselden passed the information on to Hillgarth, who sent a telegram to London through the normal, permeable channels:

Vice Consul Huelva saw body. Postmortem performed. Verdict drowning several days previously. Funeral attended by representative military and naval officers.

1. Pocket book containing private letters
2. Identity disc
3. Identity papers
4. Medal and crucifix
5. Black leather documents case, locked and attached to strap. By lifting flap envelope could be seen inside. Presumably this is what is referred to in your [telegram] 041321

Vice Consul was informed all effects must be sent C in C, Cadiz (who is unfortunately pro-German). In due course they will reach Ministry of Marine and be handed to me. Vice Consul had no (repeat no) chance of obtaining possession of the case. Am trying everything possible, but fear too much display of interest will only increase official curiosity, which is already aroused.

Montagu and Cholmondeley sent back a message in kind, subtly infused with the flutter of rising panic: 'Secret papers probably in black briefcase. Earliest possible information required whether this came ashore. If so, it should be recovered at once. Care should be taken it does not get into undesirable hands if it comes ashore later.'

At the same time, they sent a separate message, by 'Most Secret Special Route', urging Hillgarth to maintain the guise of a harassed official being asked to perform the impossible. 'Normally you would be getting frantic messages asking you to get the secret documents at once, and to hurry the Spaniards. You must adjust your actions to achieve desired results and maintain normal appearance.' Hillgarth needed no stage directions: 'Understood and acted on throughout,' he replied.

While Hillgarth played the part of a spy under pressure, there was nothing remotely fake about the strain Adolf Clauss was now under. The German spy had sent word to Abwehr headquarters in Madrid as soon as the body was discovered. When he learned that a briefcase containing British documents had also come ashore, he confidently told Madrid that he would be able to copy the contents within days. The messages flying between London and Madrid had been picked up by the Germans' eavesdroppers, as predicted, and the Abwehr spy chiefs in Madrid were now thoroughly alerted to the existence of a cache of secret documents that the British were desperate to retrieve. What had seemed, at first, to be a golden intelligence opportunity was turning into a nightmare for the Abwehr's man in Huelva. Clauss had 'promised to obtain copies of the documents, but was unable to keep his promise'. Gómez-Beare was also in Huelva, making 'discreet inquiries whether any bag or paper had been washed ashore'. The presence of the Gibraltarian was undoubtedly communicated to Clauss, ratcheting up the strain another notch.

Agent Andros reported: 'As the local Germans were not able to obtain copies of these documents, to which they attached the utmost importance, the matter was taken up in Madrid by either Leissner personally, or by Kuhlenthal.' The ambitious Karl-Erich Kuhlenthal saw an opportunity to add another feather to his espionage cap.

Clauss's reputation was at stake, and to make matters worse, his colleagues and bosses were muscling in. Through its own informants, the Abwehr in Portugal had got wind of what was happening, and offered to help. Clauss was 'summoned to Villarreal de San Antonio [in nearby Ayamonte] for a conference' on what to do about the situation. The full might of the German secret services on the Iberian peninsula was now unleashed in an effort to obtain the British documents that the British, with equal determination, were trying to put into their hands.

Clauss insisted he could still get the documents through his Spanish contacts. He instructed the willing Colonel Santiago Garrigós to go immediately to Seville and make contact with a fellow member of the Guardia Civil, Major Luis Canis, a man described by Agent Andros as 'very pro-German and in German pay'. Canis was probably Clauss's most important contact. 'This individual,' Hillgarth's spy reported, 'who is under complete German control, is in charge of the contra-espionage services in the Seville Captain General's headquarters and therefore of all Andalucia.' In theory, Canis was responsible for tracking espionage activities aimed at Spain; in reality, he was an employee of the German Abwehr. Garrigós explained the situation to Canis, and instructed him, on behalf of Clauss, 'to do everything possible to obtain copies of the documents, availing himself of his official position'. The head of counterespionage for the region might reasonably claim an interest in anything of intelligence value washing up on the coast. Canis selected one of his junior officers from the counterespionage unit, and told him to go to San Fernando, where Major Martin's effects were now lodged with the Cadiz naval authorities. 'Urging him to use the utmost discretion', Canis told this officer to sniff around the naval headquarters, talk to the naval commander there, and obtain, by whatever means necessary, 'accurate information regarding the contents of the documents'.

He very nearly succeeded. Someone in the naval office in Cadiz agreed to photograph the contents of the briefcase: the letters, photographs, and the proofs of Hilary Saunders's book about the commandos. This person, however, flatly refused to open the letters, 'either because they were afraid to break the seals lest the Minister of Marine should disapprove, or more probably because they had no experience in opening them without leaving a trace'. Admiral Moreno was known to be sympathetic to the British; if he found out that someone had opened official letters without the highest authorisation, the minister would hit the roof. The naval commander in Cadiz, it transpired, was not quite as pro-German as the British thought. He refused to hand over the letters, and Canis's officer trailed home with a flea in his ear, and a handful of photographs of no intelligence value whatever. 'Either because of the junior rank of his envoy, or because this person acted with excessive discretion or perhaps because this is the usual procedure in the navy, he had to return to Seville and confess that he had not been able to obtain any information whatever and stated that he had been told by the naval authorities that if the Captain General of Seville wanted any information about the documents he should address himself to the Ministry of War in Madrid.' Furious and embarrassed, Canis prepared to head to Cadiz and confront the naval authorities in person. But it was already too late.

Admiral Moreno, the Minister of Marine, had sent explicit orders that the briefcase and its contents must be 'forwarded, unopened, to the Admiralty, Madrid' and they were now en route, in the custody of an official from the Marine Commandant's Office in Cadiz. Adolf Clauss had failed to intercept the documents in Huelva; his agent Luis Canis has failed to obtain them in Cadiz; it was now up to Karl-Erich Kuhlenthal to try to snare them in Madrid, and quickly. The items belonging to Major Martin had been in Spanish custody for more than a week. The British were apparently agitating to get them back, and sooner or later the Spanish authorities would have to comply in order to avoid a major diplomatic row, even though this was the very last thing the British wanted.

Back in London, Johnnie Bevan sent a progress report to the Chiefs of Staff. There was, he warned, 'only scanty information' so far. 'Mincemeat was found by the Spaniards washed ashore at Huelva on 1 May . . . It seems that certain documents were taken from him by Spaniards and that these have been passed back to the Spanish authorities in Madrid.'

For Montagu and Cholmondeley, the slow progress was worrying, and the uncertainty agonising. Agent Andros's report describing German efforts to obtain the papers would not reach London for many weeks. All they knew for certain was that Major Martin's effects had been passed to the navy, the least pro-German of the Spanish services. Hillgarth had laid an obvious trail for the Germans to follow, but had they picked up the scent? The codebreakers at Bletchley Park combed the messages passing between the Abwehr stations in Huelva, Madrid and Berlin, but found nothing to indicate that the Germans were aware of the documents' existence, much less of their contents. Mincemeat, it seemed, might simply work its way through Spanish military bureaucracy and back to Britain without ever reaching the Germans.

The operation organisers reacted to the tension in different ways. Cholmondeley went for long walks around St James's, a tall, gangling figure, plunged in thought. He spent hours in his garage at Queen's Gate Mews, tinkering with the Bentley he was restoring. Montagu's primary reaction to tension was irritation. Reality's stubborn refusal to conform to his expectations made him peevish. With the fraud apparently in stasis, he complained bitterly, largely about little things. 'We sweat away, eleven of us, in far too small and low a room, with often foul potted air and five typewriters often all going at once, jaded and headachy from the conditions. By giving up many of my days off, by coming in after dinner, I have managed to keep up with essential work although I am usually too tired in the evening to do anything but go to bed straight after dinner. No one has any idea, or will even consider, how hard pressed we are.'

With the departure of Bill Martin, his alter ego, and stuck once more behind a desk, Montagu appears to have turned in on himself, wondering if the complex ruse he had created would prove an abject and potentially calamitous failure. The strain brought out his sarcasm. Bitterly, he reflected that the Abwehr chiefs were more appreciative of his work than his own bosses, since the Germans, at least, sent money and praise to the double agents, real and invented, that he was helping to run. He wrote a half-joking letter of resignation: 'It is requested that I may be given permission to relinquish my commission in the RNVR in order to be free to join the German navy. The reason for this request is that my services are appreciated more highly by Admiral Canaris than they appear to be by their Lordships.

The former has just awarded me a special bonus and has agreed to my pay being increased. Signed, E. S. Montagu Failed-Commander RNVR.' He never sent the letter. Montagu knew he sounded petty – 'I always was a selfish shit' – but could not help himself. Cholmondeley was the ideas man, content to see his inspirations float away, in this case literally, to whatever outcome fate intended. But Montagu was a perfectionist, and a workaholic: 'I have never been able to half-do a job,' he wrote, 'even if it means working to a standstill.'

At the forefront of Montagu's mind was the knowledge that thousands of Allied soldiers were massing on the coast of North Africa, whose future depended on a ruse that had once seemed like a jolly game, but was now a matter of life and death on a massive scale. 'If I had made a slip in the preparation and devising of Mincemeat,' Montagu reflected, 'I could have ballsed-up Husky.'

That anxiety would have been at least partially relieved, had he been able to witness the frantic scenes taking place at Abwehr headquarters in Madrid, where Leissner, Kuhlenthal and the other German spies were now focused on a single task: getting inside Major Martin's briefcase. A week after the funeral, the documents had arrived at the Admiralty in Madrid, and passed immediately into the hands of Admiral Moreno himself. Then they seemed to vanish into the labyrinth of Spanish military officialdom. The Germans were desperate to get them; the British were equally determined that they should do so; the only obstacle was Spanish bureaucracy, inefficient, self-important and leisurely in the extreme. 'Official procedure is always slow,' Hillgarth had warned. In this case, it appeared to have ground to a halt.

Major Kuhlenthal was tying himself in knots trying to find out where the papers might be, and whom he needed to bribe in order to get them. Admiral Moreno, it seemed, had taken receipt of the briefcase personally, and then handed over everything to the Alto Estado Mayor, the Supreme General

Staff. Kuhlenthal had several high-level contacts within the General Staff, but when enquiries were made there, the Abwehr was 'informed that they had not received the documents or copies of them and in fact that they knew nothing at all about the matter'. Next stop was the Spanish Ministry of War, but the response was the same. The Abwehr now turned to the Gestapo, which maintained a permanent office in Spain. The Gestapo chief in Spain was asked to get in touch with his informants in the Dirección General de Seguridad, or DGS, the state security apparatus, and get them working on the case. 'Again they failed, as nothing was known about the matter.' The last person known to have had the package was Admiral Moreno, who received it from 'an official of the [Cadiz] Marine Commandant's Office'; but no one seemed to know whom he had passed it to, and the Germans 'did not dare approach the Ministry of Marine' to ask him, as Moreno would almost certainly tip off the British to the hunt.

For help, the Germans turned to one of their most trusted spies, a Spanish air force officer named Captain Groizar, 'an assiduous worker for the Germans', in the words of Agent Andros, with wide-ranging military contacts. Groizar reported 'that he had heard about the body and documents being washed ashore and promised to get into touch with the Army General Staff'. Groizar appears to have worked, in some undefined capacity, for Spanish intelligence, enjoying 'many privileges and facilities to investigate anything in which he may be interested'. The Spanish captain went first to the General Staff, without success; he then applied to the DGS, but was 'unable to obtain any fresh information'; then he made contact with 'certain high officials in the police', with the same negative result. Groizar's enquiries produced nothing, but by poking sticks into every corner of the Spanish military hierarchy, the Germans stirred up a swarm of speculation surrounding the missing briefcase. 'Great interest was aroused in these documents,' Andros later reported. 'Groizar fostered this interest to such an extent that eventually Lt Colonel Barrón, Secretary General of the Directorate General of Security, took a personal interest in the matter.'

This was the turning point. Colonel José López Barrón Cerruti was Spain's most senior secret policeman, a keen fascist and an exceptionally tough cookie. He had fought in the Blue Division, the Spanish volunteer unit sent to the Russian front to fight alongside Hitler's troops, and he now ran Franco's security service with ruthlessness and guile. The Blue Division, formed in 1941 and so called for the colour of its Falangist shirt, represented the high-water mark of Spanish military collaboration with Nazi Germany. If the Condor Legion, in which both Adolf Clauss and Kuhlenthal had served, was Germany's gift to Franco, then the Blue Division was Spain's gift to Hitler. No other non-belligerent country raised an entire division to fight in the war. Some 45,000 Spaniards volunteered to fight for fascism, and Barrón was among the first. Like all members of the division, he had sworn a personal military oath to Hitler. The Blue Division had fought fiercely on the Eastern Front in appalling conditions for over two years, leaving 5,000 dead. 'One can't imagine more fearless fellows,' declared SS General Sepp Dietrich. Hitler had been so impressed by the division that he ordered a special medal for its members.

The unit was formally disbanded in 1943. By then, José Barrón had become Franco's head of security. Hillgarth had his own spies within the state security apparatus, but the prevailing attitude in the DGS was vigorously pro-German. Under Barrón, the unit actively worked to gather information for the Germans, and ordered provincial governors to compile files on every Jew in Spain. Colonel Barrón, then, was a battle-hardened fascist veteran, an avowed Germanophile presiding over a secret police force riddled with spies and German sympathisers. Once Colonel Barrón was on the scent, it was only a matter of time before the documents were located, and made available to the Germans.

Karl-Erich Kuhlenthal, ambitious and paranoid, was becoming frantic. He was now in the same uncomfortable position in which he had placed Adolf Clauss, under growing pressure from above to produce documents he had promised but could not deliver. Word of the elusive British briefcase had by now reached the upper echelons in Berlin, most notably Wilhelm Canaris, the head of the Abwehr. Canaris had close links with the Spanish government, dating back to the First World War, when he had worked as a secret agent in Spain under civilian cover, gathering naval intelligence. In 1925 Canaris had established a German intelligence network in Spain. He spoke fluent Spanish, and cultivated close relations with the nationalists, including General Franco himself and Martínez Campos, his intelligence chief. It was almost certainly Kuhlenthal, the Abwehr chief's protégé, who informed Canaris of the so-far fruitless hunt for the documents, 'in the hope that he will come to Spain where they think he will be able to obtain copies because of his great friendship with many high military officers, especially General Vigon, Minister for Air, and General Asensio, Minister for War'.

Juan Vigón, former head of the Supreme General Staff, had personally negotiated with Hitler, on behalf of Franco, in the early days of the war. Carlos Asensio was keenly pro-German, and had long argued that Spain should enter the war in support of Hitler. According to a British intelligence report, 'approaches were made by the Germans' to both men, but in the end, the aid of these two powerful generals, and the intercession of Canaris, proved unnecessary.

Nine days after arriving in Spain, the faked letters landed in the Germans' lap.

Kuhlenthal's Coup

British intelligence would not discover the name of the man who had handed over the Mincemeat papers to the Germans for another two years. In April 1945, as the Nazis retreated, a group of British naval intelligence commandos, a unit set up by none other than Ian Fleming, captured the entire German admiralty archives at Tambach Castle near Coburg. Fleming himself travelled to Germany to supervise the unit he referred to as his 'Red Indians', and ensure the safe return of the German files to Britain.

Among the documents were several relating to Operation Mincemeat, including one revealing the identity of the officer on the Spanish General Staff who had presented the documents to the Abwehr: this was a Lieutenant Colonel Ramón Pardo Suárez, described by the Germans as 'a Spanish Staff Officer with well-established connections' and an informant 'with whom we have been in contact for many years'. Years later, Wilhelm Leissner was still covering up Pardo's identity, describing him merely as 'my Spanish agent in the General Staff'. Pardo's brother, José, was Civil Governor of Zaragoza and Madrid, and a senior figure in the Franco regime. Ramón Pardo would go on to become a general, Governor of the Spanish Sahara and, finally, General Director of the Spanish Department of Public Health.

Ramón Pardo was not acting alone, and German documents clearly indicate he was under instructions from a higher authority, and may even have been assigned as 'case officer' to liaise between the General Staff and the Germans. Agent Andros indicates, though he does not state explicitly, that pressure from the security chief Colonel Barrón brought about the decision to pass over the documents. It may well have been agents of Barrón's security service who successfully extracted the letters from their envelopes, and then replaced them, leaving barely a trace.

The British later worked out exactly how the Spanish had performed this delicate and difficult task. The letters had been stuck down with gum, and then secured with oval wax seals. 'Those seals held the envelopes closed as all the gum had washed off.' By pressing on the top and bottom of the envelope, the lower flap of the envelope, which was larger than the top one, could be bent open. Inserting a thin metal double prong with a blunt metal hook into the gap, the Spanish spies snagged the bottom edge of the letter, wound the still-damp paper tightly around the probe into a cylindrical shape, and then pulled it out through the hole in the bottom half. Even the British, normally so dismissive of the espionage efforts of others, were impressed by the Spaniards' ingenuity: 'It was possible to extract all the letters through the envelopes by twisting them out [leaving] the seals intact and untampered with.'

The letters were then carefully dried with a heat lamp. No one, needless to say, noticed a microscopic eyelash falling out of the unfolded sheet of notepaper. The letters were then almost certainly copied by the Spanish officials, although no copies have ever come to light. 'The Spaniards had, very intelligently, not bothered to supply photographs of the letter to Eisenhower, which only dealt with the pamphlet on Combined Operations, and was mere padding.' The two other letters, however, were clearly very significant indeed.

These letters were taken by Colonel Pardo of the General Staff to the German Embassy and handed, in person, to Leissner, the Abwehr chief in Spain, who was told he had one hour to do whatever he wanted with them. Leissner understood English, while Kuhlenthal spoke and read the language fluently. The Germans immediately realised that they had stumbled on something explosive, an impression doubtless compounded by the difficulties they had encountered in obtaining the documents. 'They seemed to me to be of the highest importance,' Leissner later recalled. The letters not only indicated an imminent Allied landing in Greece, and possibly Sardinia too, but specifically identified Sicily as a decoy target.

'A short white-haired man with a birdlike brightness of eye', Leissner 'gave more the impression of a diplomat than an intelligence officer'. By 1943 he had been all but supplanted by the energetic Kuhlenthal, but he was no fool. Even on this first, swift reading, something about the documents struck him as odd: 'These letters mentioned the operational name "Husky". That stuck in my memory, because it seemed to me a dangerous thing to name the codeword in the same document as discussed the possible destinations.' He was also cautious about drawing firm conclusions from a single letter, and considered 'the strategic considerations not definite enough to suggest an already fixed target on the North Mediterranean coast . . . the final choice seemed to be left to General Alexander'. Kuhlenthal, by contrast, with the mixture of eagerness and gullibility that defined him, seems to have entertained no such doubts. Just as he had run the Garbo network for years without once questioning its veracity, so he believed the Mincemeat letters, instantly and unquestioningly.

The German spies moved quickly, knowing that the documents must be returned within the hour. 'I took them to the basement of the German Embassy,' Leissner later recalled, 'and had my photographer photocopy them there. I even stood over him while he worked, so that he could not read the documents.' Leissner informed Dieckhoff, the German ambassador to Spain, of the discovery, and described the contents of the letters to him.

The original documents were now returned to Colonel Pardo, who took them back to the offices of the General Staff, accompanied by Kuhlenthal. The German spy observed as the Spanish technicians reinserted the letters into the envelopes, reversing the method used to extract them. It is hard enough to remove a damp letter from an envelope this way, but harder still to get one back in without creasing the paper, leaving telltale marks or breaking the seals. The Spanish spy responsible must have been astonishingly dextrous, for, to the naked eye, 'there was no trace whatever' to show that the letters had left their envelopes. The letters were then placed in salt water, and soaked for twenty-four hours, to return them to their damp condition. Finally, the envelopes and book proofs were replaced in the briefcase, which was relocked, and then passed back to the Spanish Ministry of Marine, along with Major Martin's wallet and other personal property. The entire process – opening the letters, transferring them to the Germans, the copying, resealing and restitution – was completed in less than two days. But even before the documents were back in Spanish hands, the copies were winging their way to Berlin.

The letters had been handed over to Leissner, as head of the Abwehr in Spain, but it was Karl-Erich Kuhlenthal who bore them back in triumph to Germany. The copied documents were far too secret and significant to be sent by wireless or telegram. As Leissner later observed, the decision to send Kuhlenthal in person was a measure of 'the importance attached to them'. It appears that Berlin may already have been informed that the documents had been intercepted, and summoned the wunderkind of the Madrid station to bring them by hand. He, and only he, should present this new intelligence coup to the high command and, since it came from Kuhlenthal, it was far more likely to be believed. From the British point of view, this was ideal. The credibility of intelligence often depends less on its intrinsic value than on who finds it, and who passes it on. Presentation is critical and, from the British point of view, Major Martin's documents were now in the hands of the ideal courier.

Colonel Pardo of the Spanish General Staff was interviewed once more, in order to obtain more details about how and when the body and its hoard of secrets had been found. This information, written up some time later, would go into a long report entitled 'Drowned English Courier picked up at Huelva':

On the 10th May, 1943, a further conversation with the case officer clarified the following questions:

1. The courier carried, clutched in his hand, an ordinary briefcase which contained the following documents:

a) An ordinary white paper as a cover for the letters addressed to General Alexander and Admiral Cunningham. This white paper carried no address.

The letters were contained each in its own envelope with the usual superscription and addressed personally to the recipients, and apparently sealed with the private seal of the sender (signet ring). The seals were intact. The letters themselves, which I have already had replaced in their original envelopes, are in good condition. For the purposes of reproduction they were dried by artificial heat by the Spaniards, and thereafter were again placed for some 24 hours in salt water, without which their condition would undoubtedly have been altered.

b) In the portfolio there were also the proofs of the pamphlet on the functions of Combined Operations Command referred to by Mountbatten in his letter of the 22nd April, 1943, as also the photographs mentioned in the letter. The proofs are in excellent condition, but the photographs are completely ruined.

2. In addition the courier carried in his breast pocket a letter case containing personal papers, among them his military papers with photographs. (These papers connect up with Mountbatten's reference to Major Martin in his letter of 22nd April.) There were, too, a letter to Major Martin from his fiancée and another from his Father, also a London night-club bill dated 27th April.

Therefore Major Martin left London on the forenoon of the 28th April and during the afternoon of the same day the aircraft met with an accident in the neighbourhood of Huelva.

3. The British Consul was present at the discovery and knows all about it. On the pretext that anything found on the corpse, including all documents, must be made available to competent Spanish authorities, we anticipated representations which the British Consul would probably have made for the immediate delivery of the documents. All the documents were, after reproduction, replaced in their original condition in such a way that even I would have been convinced, and definitely give the impression that they have not been opened. In the course of the next few days they will be handed back to the British by the Spanish Foreign Office.

Enquiries regarding the remains of the pilot of the aircraft, presumably wounded in the crash, and interrogation of the same concerning other passengers, are already being put in hand by the Spanish General Staff.

The report was unsigned, but the phrase 'even I would have been convinced' was typical of Kuhlenthal's braggadocio. Equally characteristic were the mistakes and exaggerations, the over-egging that was his Achilles heel. He implied that a pilot had been found and was being interrogated; he claimed to have overseen the reinsertion of the letters, a process at which he was merely an observer; he described the seals as personal signet-ring seals, when they were standard military seals; he made no mention of the chain attaching the briefcase to the body, but instead added the melodramatic (and inaccurate) detail that the corpse had been found clutching the briefcase. Describing the theatre tickets as nightclub receipts was an easy mistake to make, but getting the date wrong was not. The date on these was 22 April, not 27 April. The body was discovered on 30 April. According to Kuhlenthal's report, the body had been immersed for less than three days when it was picked up, a timescale flatly contradicted by the state of decomposition and the autopsy, which estimated that death had occurred at least eight days earlier.

Bletchley Park intercepted a message indicating that Kuhlenthal 'left Madrid hurriedly for Berlin in order to consult at the latter's request with Oblt von Dewitz, the evaluator of KO [Abwehr] Spain's reports at the Luftwaffenführungsstab'. Kuhlenthal was booked into the Adlon Hotel in Berlin, but apparently travelled directly to Abwehr headquarters, south of the city. On 9 May he presented his delighted bosses with the greatest intelligence feat of his career.

Oddly, the significance of Kuhlenthal rushing to Berlin does not seem to have been picked up at the time. The intercept may have been accidentally backdated, or decoded too late to be of use, and the dates in Kuhlenthal's MI5 files are contradictory. Montagu and Cholmondeley remained unaware that Kuhlenthal had flown to Germany in a hurry: as far as they knew, the documents were still marooned somewhere in the byzantine Spanish bureaucracy.

On 11 May, Admiral Alfonso Arriago Adam, the Spanish Chief of Naval Staff, arrived at the British Embassy carrying a black briefcase and a buff envelope, and asked to see the naval attaché, Alan Hillgarth. The Spanish officer explained that the Spanish Naval Minister, Rear Admiral Moreno was currently away in Valencia, but had given him instructions to hand over to Hillgarth in person 'all the effects and papers' found on the body of the British officer. 'They are all there,' said Admiral Arriago, with a knowing look. The key, removed from Major Martin's keyring, was in the briefcase lock, and the case was unlocked. 'From his manner it was obvious the Chief of Naval Staff knew something [of the] contents,' wrote Hillgarth. 'While expressing gratitude I showed both relief and concern. Neither [the] secretary nor I showed any wish to discuss [the] matter further.' Having handed over the envelope containing the wallet and other items, the Spanish admiral saluted crisply, and departed.

Locking his office door, Hillgarth gingerly opened the case and peered inside. This was his first glimpse of the hard evidence he had worked so strenuously to pass to the Germans. He was under strict instructions not to open the letters or rearrange the contents in any way, since these would need to be microscopically studied back in London. The Spaniards did not disguise that the case had been opened. 'It is obvious [that the] contents of bag have been examined though some of the documents appear to be stuck together by sea water,' Hillgarth reported to London. He wrapped the case and other effects in paper, addressed the parcel to Ewen Montagu, Naval Intelligence Department, Whitehall, and sent a telegram explaining that the package would be included in the sealed diplomatic bag on the first flight to London, leaving Madrid on 14 May. Hillgarth was convinced that the Spanish Chief of Naval Staff knew what was in the case, but added: 'While I do not believe he will divulge his knowledge to the enemy it is clear [a] number of other people are in [on the] secret. It is to say the least extremely probable that it has been communicated to [the] enemy. In any case notes or copies have certainly been made.' Hillgarth also requested permission to ask the SIS head of station to try to find out through whose hands the documents had passed. 'If you concur I will ask 23000 to discover through his channels whether Germans have got them as he can do if they get to

Combined General Staff (which they almost certainly will).' In fact, of course, the letters had come back to the naval authorities *from* the General Staff.

Hillgarth's telegram was the first solidly good news since the body had come ashore, yet it did not amount to hard evidence that the Germans had obtained the documents, and still less that they believed the contents.

Unbeknown to anyone on the British side, by the time the letters were back in British hands, the Germans had been poring over them for at least forty-eight hours. On 9 May, the Abwehr forwarded the letters to the German high command, with an accompanying message stating that 'the genuineness of the report is held as possible', though that note of caution would swiftly evaporate. The task of authenticating the letters would fall to the intelligence branch of the German army's high command, Fremde Heere West (Foreign Armies West) or FHW, the linchpin of German military intelligence.

At its headquarters in a two-storey bunker in Zossen, south of Berlin, FHW received and evaluated all intelligence connected to the Allied war effort. The unit was run by professional officers from the General Staff, but also staffed by reserve personnel, journalists, businessmen and bankers with the ability to think beyond structured military ideas. At FHW, every scrap of intelligence was subjected to scrutiny and analysis: Abwehr reports, communications intercepts, prisoner interrogations, reconnaissance data, and captured documents. FHW issued long-range assessments of enemy planning and, every two weeks, a detailed survey of the Allied armies and their dispositions, the order of battle. These top-secret documents were distributed not only to Hitler and the Supreme Command of the Armed Forces, the Oberkommando der Wehrmacht (OKW) under Field Marshal Wilhelm Keitel, but also to German commanders in the field. Daily situation reports assessing Allied strength and intentions were sent directly to the Führer himself, together with information on troop movements, enemy activity, and any newly discovered intelligence. The FHW reports represented the cream of German intelligence, and the most direct access route into Hitler's mind.

The Führer was in need of some good news. In four months, Hitler had lost one-eighth of his fighting men on the battlefields of North Africa and the Eastern Front. Fleets of bombers were tearing German cities and industries to shreds. Germany was now losing the underwater war: forty-seven U-boats had been sunk in May, and triple that number in March, thanks to the codebreakers pinpointing the 'wolfpacks'. Hitler blamed his military leaders. 'He is absolutely sick of the generals,' Joseph Goebbels noted in his diary. 'All generals lie. All generals are disloyal.' Hitler needed to be told something he could believe in, to counter the lies of his generals, to bolster the mad myth of his own invincibility. The German intelligence service would now oblige.

Presiding over FHW was Lieutenant Colonel Alexis Baron von Roenne, a small, bespectacled aristocrat whose family had once ruled swaths of Baltic Germany. Von Roenne was a former banker, and still looked like one: he was meticulous, pedantic, snobbish, intensely Christian and glintingly intelligent. 'Behind his rimless spectacles and compressed lips there worked a brain as clear as glass.' Von Roenne had volunteered to fight on the Eastern Front, suffered a serious wound, and been transferred back to military intelligence, where he ascended rapidly, developing his own intelligence technique which involved piecing together a picture of the enemy, a *Feinbild*, from tiny fragments of information. As a result he enjoyed an almost mystical reputation for divining and predicting Allied intentions. The myth of Von Roenne's infallibility was largely undeserved but, critically, it was believed by Hitler, who held Von Roenne in the highest regard: when the command of FHW fell vacant in the spring of 1943, the Führer personally ordered the appointment of the small, clever Latvian-born aristocrat. Von Roenne had been in control of the western intelligence arm of the German army for just two months when the Mincemeat letters landed on his desk at Zossen.

Montagu had rightly predicted that the Germans would examine such a trove of information with profound suspicion and extreme caution. The Spaniards had handed over the two crucial letters, but the Germans had also obtained a full inventory and description of every item in the briefcase, wallet and pockets of the dead man: 'The Germans studied each phrase of the material letters with great care and also were fully informed about the documentary build-up of Major Martin's personality.'

The first full German intelligence assessment of the documents was written on 11 May, and signed by Baron von Roenne himself. It was addressed to the OKW Operations Staff, or Wehrmachtführungsstab, headed by General Alfred Jodl, and entitled, portentously, 'Discovery of the English Courier'. It began: 'On the corpse of an English courier which was found on the Spanish coast, were three letters from senior British officers to high Allied officers in North Africa . . . They give information concerning the decisions taken on the 23 April 1943, regarding Anglo-American strategy for the conduct of the war in the Mediterranean after the conclusion of the Tunisian campaign.' Major Martin is described as 'an experienced specialist in amphibious operations'.

Von Roenne went on to lay out, point by point, the misinformation prepared by Cholmondeley and Montagu. 'Large-scale amphibious operations in both the western and eastern Mediterranean are intended. The proposed operation in the eastern Mediterranean, under the command of General Wilson, is to be made on the coast round Kalamata, and the section of the coast south of Cape Araxos. The codename for the landings on the Peloponnesus is "Husky" . . . The operation to be conducted in the Western Mediterranean by General Alexander was mentioned, but without naming any objective.' Von Roenne, however, had picked up on the reference to sardines. 'A jocular remark in this letter refers to Sardinia,' he wrote. 'The codename for this operation is "Brimstone".' The attack on Sardinia, he surmised, must be 'a minor "commando type"' since Mountbatten had requested the return of Major Martin after the operation. 'This indication points to the invasion of an island rather than of a major undertaking . . . This is another point in favour of Sardinia.'

Just as importantly, Von Roenne relayed the news that Sicily was not a real target for the Allies, but a decoy: 'The proposed cover operation for "Brimstone" is Sicily.' That lie would sit, immovably, at the centre of German strategic thinking over the coming months: the attacks would come in the East, in Greece, and the West, most probably Sardinia; evidence of any planned assault on Sicily could safely be dismissed as a hoax. The only uncertainty, Von Roenne warned, was that of timing. If the two divisions identified in Nye's letter – the 56th Infantry attacking Kalamata and the 5th Infantry Division aimed at Cape Araxos – were deployed at less than full strength, then the 'operation could be mounted immediately', and the offensive might start at any time. However, the 56th Division, Von Roenne noted, had two brigades 'still in action' at Enfidaville. If the entire division was to be used in the assault, these troops 'must first be rested and then embarked. This possibility, which necessitates a certain time lag before the launching of the operation, is, judging by the form of the letters, the most likely.' In Von Roenne's mature estimation, Germany still had 'at least two or three weeks' to reinforce the Greek coast before the attack.

That was also enough time for the British to change their plans, which they might well do if they knew the information had reached the Germans. Von Roenne now turned to this important consideration. 'It is known to the British Staff that the courier's despatches to [sic] Major Martin fell into Spanish hands,' he wrote, '[but] it is not perhaps known to the British General Staff that these letters came to our notice, since an English Consul was present at the examination of the letters by Spanish officials.' The letters had been reinserted in the envelopes and returned to the British, and a senior officer of the Madrid Abwehr station had personally inspected the resealed envelopes before they were returned to Alan Hillgarth. The British might suspect, but would have no proof, that the letters had been read, let alone passed to the Germans and copied. 'It is, therefore, to be hoped that the British General Staff will continue with these projected operations and thereby make possible a resounding Abwehr success.' In order to convince the British that their secrets were still safe, Von Roenne suggested that the Germans mount their own deception: they should give no indication that they feared simultaneous attacks in the East and West Mediterranean, and instead 'initiate a misleading plan of action which will deceive the enemy by painting a picture of growing Axis concern regarding Sicily'. The Germans should pretend to reinforce Sicily, while doing nothing of the sort.

Von Roenne ended with a security warning. 'News of this discovery will be treated with the greatest secrecy, and knowledge of it confined to as few as possible.' The Baron's assessment was remarkable in many ways: it hauled on board every single aspect of the deception, and even launched a corresponding deception plan to reinforce it. But perhaps most astonishing of all was the ringing endorsement that accompanied the appraisal: 'The circumstances of the discovery, together with the form and contents of the despatches, are absolutely convincing proof of the reliability of the letters.' The army's chief intelligence analyst, from the outset, utterly dismissed the possibility of a plant.

This was, to say the least, strange. The analysts of FHW usually distrusted uncorroborated information emanating directly from the Abwehr, knowing the inefficiency and corruption of that organisation, and tended to be sceptical of Abwehr revelations 'unless these were clearly corroborated by more tangible evidence'. Von Roenne's natural scepticism seemed to have deserted him. He knew only what the Madrid Abwehr station had told him about the discovery of the body, which was second-hand information derived through Adolf Clauss. The report detailing the results of the second meeting with Pardo on

10 May had not yet reached Berlin. No additional checks had been made, the body had not been examined, and the original documents had remained in German hands for only one hour, far too short a time for forensic testing. And yet he chose to describe the documents as incontrovertibly genuine.

Deception is a sort of seduction. In love and war, adultery and espionage, deceit can only succeed if the deceived party is willing, in some way, to be deceived. The betrayed lover sees only the signs of love, and blocks out the evidence of faithlessness, however glaring. This unconscious willingness to see the lie as truth – 'wishfulness' was Admiral Godfrey's word for it – comes in many forms: Adolf Clauss in Huelva wanted to believe the false documents because his reputation depended on believing them; for Karl-Erich Kuhlenthal, any intelligence breakthrough to his credit, no matter how fantastic, made him safer, a Jew among anti-semitic killers. Von Roenne, however, may have chosen to believe in the fake documents for an entirely different reason: because he loathed Hitler, wanted to undermine the Nazi war effort and was intent on passing false information to the high command in the certain knowledge that it was wholly false, and extremely damaging.

It is quite possible that Lieutenant Colonel Alexis Baron von Roenne did not believe the Mincemeat deception for an instant.

Mincemeat Digested

Alexis Baron von Roenne appeared, on the outside, to be the consummate Nazi intelligence officer: a veteran of the First World War, a wounded war hero, holder of the Iron Cross, loyal to his oath, and the Führer's favourite intelligence analyst. 'Hitler had implicit faith in Von Roenne and in his reasoning ability, and seems to have liked him personally.' The aristocratic former banker had fought in the celebrated Potsdam Regiment, attended the War Academy, and demonstrated his intellectual mettle from the outset of the war. In 1939 he had been entrusted with the task of assessing whether Britain and France would come to Poland's aid if Germany attacked that country, and had sent a special report to Hitler, predicting that 'the Western allies would protest a German attack, but would take no military action'. Von Roenne's prediction was 'exactly what Hitler wanted to hear'; he was exceptionally attuned to what the Führer wanted to hear. 'Hitler was greatly impressed by Von Roenne's intuition, as well as by the accuracy of his evaluation'.

Again, in 1940, Von Roenne predicted that the Maginot Line, supposedly protecting France's eastern border, could be circumvented, enabling a successful German assault. Again, he was correct. By May 1943, Von Roenne had become Hitler's most trusted reader of the intelligence runes – a fearsome responsibility. 'It was his mission to produce for the high command the definitive intelligence they needed . . . It was at his desk that the buck-passing ended.'

Colleagues described Von Roenne as cold and distant, 'an intellectual but aloof person, impossible to make friends with'. Von Roenne's unapproachable manner was, perhaps, unsurprising, for there was another side to him, the obverse of the prim fascist functionary, of which his Nazi colleagues – and, most importantly, Hitler – knew nothing whatsoever. Von Roenne was a secret but committed opponent of Nazism, living a double life. He detested Hitler and the uncouth thugs surrounding him. His was an old-fashioned, monarchist, military cast of mind, steeped in feudal tradition and the belief that certain people (like himself) 'because of their origins, have title to be a higher class among the people'. His Christian conscience had been outraged by the appalling SS terror unleashed in Poland. Quietly, but with absolute conviction, he had turned against the Nazi regime.

From 1943 onwards, he deliberately and consistently inflated the Allied order of battle, overstating the strength of the British and American armies in a successful effort to mislead Hitler and his generals. His precise motive is still uncertain. Von Roenne may simply have been compensating for the tendency of his superiors to deflate military numbers. He may have been trying to impress his bosses. He was a fanatical opponent of Bolshevism, which threatened to destroy the class system to which he was heir, and he may have calculated, in common with other German anti-communists, that 'if Germany should give in to superior force in the West the Allies would help hold back the Soviets: and inflating Allied strength was a means to that end'. Perhaps, like other German anti-Nazi conspirators, he just wanted Germany to lose the war as swiftly as possible, to avoid further bloodletting and remove Hitler and his repellent circle from power. Whatever his reasons, and despite his reputation as an intelligence guru, by 1943 Von Roenne was deliberately passing information he knew to be false, directly to Hitler's desk.

Von Roenne's finest hour would come with the invasion of Normandy in 1944. In the build-up to D-Day, he faithfully passed on every deception ruse fed to him, accepted the existence of every bogus unit regardless of evidence, and inflated forty-four divisions in Britain to an astonishing eighty-nine. Without Von Roenne's willing connivance, the entire elaborate net of deception woven for D-Day might have unravelled. In the words of one historian, 'his way of fighting the Nazi war machine was to inflate estimates of Allied troop strength in England and convince Hitler and OKW that the main attack would be at Calais', when he may well have known that the real attack was aimed at Normandy. His determination to be deceived played a crucial part in the last chapter of the war.

Von Roenne was not directly involved in the failed plot, led by Claus von Stauffenberg, to assassinate Hitler in July 1944. But he was close friends with Stauffenberg and the other conspirators of the Schwarze Kapelle, the Black Orchestra, and his links with the planned rebellion were sufficient to ensure a grim fate in the ferocious Gestapo reprisals that followed. Hitler's revenge was breathtakingly brutal. A month after the July plot, Von Roenne was arrested, tried, and sentenced to death after a show trial by the 'People's Court'. In his own defence, Von Roenne simply declared that Nazi race policies were inconsistent with Christian values. On 11 October 1944, with other alleged conspirators, he was bound hand and foot in Berlin-Plötzensee prison, hanged on a meat hook by his throat, and left to die slowly. In an additional exercise in barbarity, Hitler ordered some of the executions to be filmed for his viewing pleasure. On the eve of his death, Von Roenne wrote a martyr's epitaph to his wife: 'In a moment now I shall be going home to our Lord in complete calm and in the certainty of salvation.' Von Roenne undoubtedly helped the Allies to win the war, but his precise reasons for doing so are an enduring mystery. If Kuhlenthal was losing the intelligence war by accident, then Von Roenne seemed to be losing it by design.

In May 1943, the allegation that Colonel von Roenne was

an anti-Nazi conspirator, working to undermine Hitler, would have been unthinkable, even treasonable. The diminutive baron was still Hitler's favourite intelligence analyst, and if he declared that there was 'absolutely convincing proof of the reliability' of this 'resounding Abwehr success', then that is what Hitler was most likely to believe.

For two weeks, during the wait for news from Spain, the atmosphere in Room 13 had been 'frousty, peevish and petulant'. Montagu's grumbling had intensified; he complained that 'he had to duck each time he had to go under the air duct, and approach Room 13 in a stooping position'. Given the pressure, he muttered, it was 'surprising that we only have five breakdowns among the female staff'.

On 14 May, the very day that Hillgarth reported the safe return of the briefcase, Juliette Ponsonby, the secretary of Section 17M, went to collect the latest Bletchley Park despatches from the teleprinter room in the Admiralty. Montagu began leafing through the printouts, and then suddenly uttered a loud whoop, and banged the table so hard his coffee cup flew off the desk. That morning, the interceptors had picked up a wireless message sent by General Alfred Jodl, the OKW Chief of the Operations Staff responsible for all strategic, executive, and war-operations planning, stating that 'an enemy landing on a large scale is projected in the near future in both the East and West Mediterranean'. The information, sent to the senior German commanders Southeast and South, with copies to the Naval Staff Operations Division and Air Force Operations Staff, was described by Jodl as coming from 'a source which may be regarded as being absolutely reliable'. The message then furnished full details of the planned attack on Greece, precisely as described in Nye's letter. Jodl himself gave his seal of approval to the documents: 'It is very unusual for an intelligence report to be passed on in operational traffic or by someone of [such] seniority with so high a recommendation of reliability,' wrote Montagu, who had studied thousands of such signals. 'So far as I can recollect it is almost unknown that such a thing should happen.'

The mood in the Admiralty basement changed instantly with the arrival of Most Secret Source message 2571. 'Everyone jumped up and down. We were so thrilled,' recalled Pat Trehearne. The ladies hugged one another. The gentlemen shook hands. The fly had been taken, and the tension seemed to vanish.

No corresponding message relating to the fake assault in the west on Sardinia was picked up, but the British concluded it was 'almost certain' that German commanders in the western theatre had received by teleprinter 'similar details from the letter which concerned that area'. Jodl's message was only the hors d'oeuvre. From this moment on, evidence steadily accumulated showing that 'the Germans were reinforcing our imaginary invasion areas in Greece . . . and at the same time spreading their available forces into Sardinia'. These were, in Montagu's words, 'wonderful days'.

Winston Churchill was in Washington for the war conference codenamed 'Trident', working on plans with Roosevelt for the invasion of Italy, the bombing of Germany and the Pacific War. A telegram was immediately despatched to the Prime Minister, stating cryptically that 'Mincemeat' had reached 'the right people and from best information they look like acting on it'.

Cholmondeley was quietly jubilant. Montagu scribbled a celebratory note on a postcard and sent it to Bill Jewell of HMS *Seraph*: 'You will be pleased to learn that the Major is now very comfortable.' He also wrote to Iris in New York: 'Friday was almost too good to be true. I had marvellous news of the success of a job that I was doing (it was so good that I feel a snag must arise).' Montagu was deeply relieved, yet he remained cautious, knowing that the deception was still at an early stage. The Abwehr in Madrid had fallen for the hoax, and so, it seemed, had the intelligence analysts in Berlin. The initial messages, wrote Montagu, 'proved that we had convinced <u>them</u>. Now would <u>they</u> convince the general staff?'

He had no cause to fret, for back in Germany the Mincemeat

lie was building up steam. On the day Jodl's cable was sent to Germany's Mediterranean commanders, Hans-Heinrich Dieckhoff, the German ambassador in Madrid, sent a telegram to the Foreign Office in Berlin: 'According to information just received from a wholly reliable source, the English and Americans will launch their big attack on southern Europe in the next fortnight. The plan, as our informant was able to establish from English secret documents, is to launch two sham attacks on Sicily and the Dodecanese, while the real offensive is directed in two main thrusts against Crete and the Peloponnese.'

Dieckhoff was clearly writing without the benefit of Von Roenne's analysis, for he missed the reference to Sardinia. An hour later, Dieckhoff sent another message, reporting that Francisco Gómez-Jordana y Souza, the Spanish Foreign Minister, had told him 'in strict confidence' that Allied attacks should be expected in Greece and the western Mediterranean. The secret was now streaming through the upper echelons of the Spanish government, and being fed back to the Germans. 'Jordana begged me not to mention his name,' reported Dieckhoff, 'especially as he wanted to exchange further information with me in the future. He considered the information wholly trustworthy, and felt it his duty to pass it on.'

The Mincemeat letters were now, finally, homing in on the ultimate target. Three weeks, and 3,000 miles, after their journey began, the forgeries finally landed on the desk of the man for whose eyes they had always been intended, the only person whose opinion really mattered.

Hitler's initial response was sceptical. Turning to General Eckhardt Christian of the Luftwaffe, he remarked: 'Christian, couldn't this be a corpse they have deliberately planted on our hands?' General Christian's response is not recorded, but by 12 May, the day after Von Roenne's enthusiastic report, any doubts in Hitler's mind had evaporated. That day, the Führer issued a general military directive: 'It is to be expected that the Anglo-Americans will try to continue the operations in the Mediterranean in quick succession. The following are most endangered: in the Western Med, Sardinia, Corsica and Sicily; in the Eastern Med, the Peloponnese and the Dodecanese . . . Measures regarding Sardinia and the Peloponnese take precedence over everything else.' The orders reflected a dramatic shift in priorities since, as Montagu observed, 'the original German appreciation had been that Sicily was more likely to be invaded than Sardinia'. Sicily now appeared to be, in German thinking, the least vulnerable of the Mediterranean islands, with the focus firmly trained on Greece and Sardinia. Hitler ordered 'all German commands in the Mediterranean to utilise all forces and equipment to strengthen as much as possible the defences of these particularly endangered areas during the short time which is probably left to us'.

In Washington DC, Roosevelt and Churchill were hammering out the next stage of the war, looking beyond Operation Husky. 'Where do we go from Sicily?' the President asked. The Americans favoured assembling a mighty army in Britain to attack across the Channel, as soon as possible. Churchill and his advisers preferred an invasion of the Italian mainland itself, disembowelling the soft underbelly. 'The main task which lies before us,' the British argued, 'is the elimination of Italy' – this would force Hitler to divert troops from elsewhere and undermine German strength on both the Eastern and Western Fronts. After three days in the presidential retreat in the mountains of Maryland, later named Camp David, Churchill addressed a joint session of Congress: 'War is full of mysteries and surprises,' he said. 'By singleness of purpose, by steadfastness of conduct, by tenacity and endurance – such as we have so far displayed – by this and only this can we discharge our duty to the future of the world and to the destiny of man.' The Anglo-American conference broke up with the agreement that Eisenhower would continue the fight in the south of Europe, while a great cross-Channel offensive would be prepared for the following May. But first, Sicily.

At the press conference ending the Trident meeting, Churchill was asked: 'What [do] you think is going on in

Hitler's mind?' There was laughter, and Churchill replied: 'Appetite unbridled. Ambition unmeasured – all the world!' But secretly, Churchill now knew that in one corner of Hitler's mind another conviction had settled: that the Allied armies in North Africa were aiming at Greece in the east and Sardinia in the west, while Sicily would be left alone.

With the effects of Operation Mincemeat appearing in intercepted German messages, a security issue arose. If someone outside the secret saw reports referring 'to a document that had been captured from a dead body' there would be a serious 'security flap', and questions would be asked about why top-secret documents had been carried abroad in this way, in defiance of wartime regulations. Bletchley Park had been instructed to ensure that any messages referring to the intercepted Mincemeat documents were initially sent only to 'C', the head of MI6, and to Montagu himself. 'Arrangements could then be made to warn recipients or to limit the distribution.'

Von Roenne had chosen to accept the documents at face value, and his analysis was now hurtling up the German power structure. Not everyone was entirely convinced. Major Percy Ernst Schramm, who kept the OKW war diary, recalled the intense discussion among senior officers over whether the letters might be forged: 'We earnestly debated the question "Genuine or not? Perhaps genuine? Corsica, Sardinia, Sicily, the Peloponnese?"' On 13 May, a sceptical officer at FHW in Zossen, identified by the codename 'Erizo', sent a message to the Abwehr in Madrid demanding more details about the discovery of the documents. 'The evaluation office attach special importance to a more detailed statement of the circumstances under which the material was found. Particular points of interest are: when the body was washed ashore, when and where the crash is presumed to have taken place. Whether aircraft and further bodies were observed, and other details. Urgent Reply by W/T if necessary.'

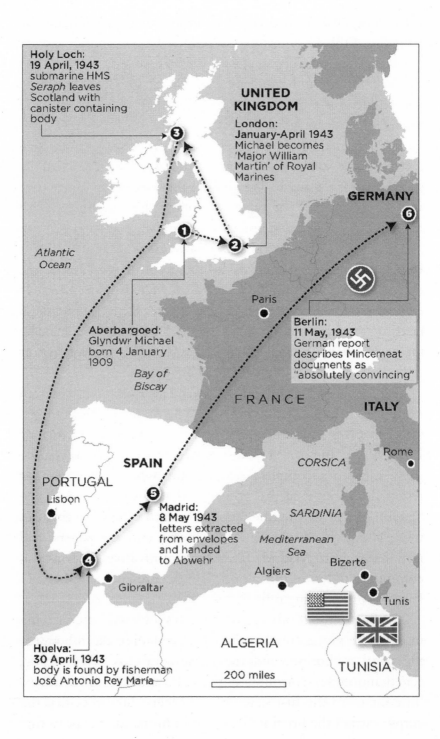

Holy Loch:
19 April, 1943
submarine HMS
Seraph leaves
Scotland with
canister containing
body

**UNITED
KINGDOM**

London:
January-April 1943
Michael becomes
'Major William
Martin' of Royal
Marines

GERMANY

*Atlantic
Ocean*

Berlin:
11 May, 1943
German report
describes Mincemeat
documents as
"absolutely convincing"

Aberbargoed:
**Glyndwr Michael
born 4 January
1909**

*Bay of
Biscay*

Paris

F R A N C E

ITALY

SPAIN

CORSICA

Rome

PORTUGAL

Lisbon

Madrid:
8 May 1943
letters extracted
from envelopes
and handed
to Abwehr

SARDINIA

*Mediterranean
Sea*

Bizerte

Algiers

Gibraltar

Tunis

**Huelva:
30 April, 1943**
body is found by fisherman
José Antonio Rey María

ALGERIA

200 miles

TUNISIA

German analysts had now spent several days studying the letters, and the accompanying reports. The demand for greater detail on the discovery suggests that the inconsistency between the postmortem, indicating at least eight days of decomposition, and Kuhlenthal's timing of just three days between crash and discovery, had not gone unnoticed. The FHW also appears to have questioned how a decomposing corpse, at sea for more than a week, could still be holding a full briefcase when it reached the shore. And if a plane had crashed in the Mediterranean, where was the wreckage? The cable was followed by a telephone call from FHW, again pressing for more details.

The Madrid Abwehr office replied, somewhat huffily, that it had already requested, four days earlier, a detailed report on the discovery from the Spanish General Staff: 'The latter immediately despatched an officer to the spot. The results of the officer's findings partly differ in detail from the facts of the case as first represented by the general staff. Detailed report will arrive at Tempelhof [airport in Berlin] on evening of 15/5. Have it collected.'

Kuhlenthal had clearly picked up the new note of scepticism in Berlin, and, as he always did when under pressure, he simultaneously covered his back and passed the buck: 'Oberst Lt Pardo on the 10 May was emphatic that the answers he gave us were a complete story of the whole affair without reservations, but it seems, however, that this was not so.' The Spanish officer sent by the General Staff to Huelva to find out more about the discovery of the body, and the papers, had now returned to Madrid. 'The result of his investigations was communicated to us this morning in the presence of Oberst Lt Pardo's commanding officer.'

The Spanish staff officer had done his job well, interviewing most of the protagonists in the story, including the fishermen, the naval authorities and the pathologist: his verbal report added numerous corroborating details, and corrected others. 'In contrast to the first statement of Oberst Lt Pardo, that the corpse carried the briefcase clutched in his hand, it appears that the above mentioned briefcase was secured to the corpse by a strap around the waist. The briefcase was fastened to this strap by a hook.'

The new report, sent from the Abwehr office in Spain to Colonel Von Roenne at FHW as well as the Abwehr chiefs, accurately described how the papers and briefcase had travelled up the Spanish chain of command, from Huelva to Cadiz to Madrid, before being presented to Admiral Moreno himself. 'He [the Minister for Marine] handed the whole collection – the courier's briefcase, together with all papers found in his breast pocket – to AEM [Alto Estado Mayor, the Spanish General Staff] who undertook the opening, reproduction and resealing, and then returned them to him. He then gave the whole collection to the British naval attaché in Madrid.' The British plane carrying the courier seemed to have vanished into the sea without a trace, at least none that Adolf Clauss and his agents in Huelva could find. 'A search for the remains of Major Martin's aircraft and also for the corpses of any other passengers in this plane was unsuccessful.' But, as ever, Kuhlenthal had an excuse: 'The fishermen state that in the area where the corpse was found there are strong currents and other corpses together with parts of the aircraft might later on be found in other places.'

Far harder to explain away was how the body had so thoroughly decomposed in such a short time. But Kuhlenthal was up to the task:

A medical examination of the corpse showed that there were no apparent wounds or marks which could have resulted from a blow or stab. According to medical evidence, death was due to drowning (lit: the swallowing of sea water). The corpse carried an English pattern lifebelt and was in an advanced state of decomposition. According to medical opinion, it had been in the water from five to eight days. This contradicts the evidence provided by the discovery of a nightclub bill on the corpse dated 27th April, and the discovery of the corpse at 9.30 in the morning of the 30th April. It is, however, considered possible that the effect of the sun's rays on the floating corpse accelerated the rate of decomposition. The doctors also stated that the corpse was identical with the photographs in its military papers with the sole exception that a bald patch on the temples was more pronounced than in the photographs. Either the photograph of Major Martin had been taken some two or three years ago or the baldness on the temples was due to the action of sea water.

Here was a classic example of willingness to believe, blended with self-deception and outright falsification. The earlier report had got the date of the theatre tickets wrong, but rather than correct the error, this report fudged the time gap. The Spanish pathologists had concluded that death took place at least eight days before 30 April, but in order to fit in with his own (erroneous) timing, Kuhlenthal changed this to between five and eight days. Two spurious but plausible-sounding scientific explanations were adduced to explain why the corpse was rotting, and why Major Martin looked substantially older than his photograph. The Abwehr had decided, from the outset, that the discovery was genuine, and moulded the evidence, despite obvious flaws, towards that belief. Kuhlenthal stood by his intelligence coup. With the information now swirling around the upper reaches of the Nazi war machine, he had no choice.

In the foetid basement of the Admiralty, Montagu and Cholmondeley were sweating over an entirely unforeseen development that would have been funny, had it not been so deeply alarming: Major Martin's briefcase had disappeared, again. Hillgarth had taken receipt of the case and other personal effects on 11 May, and promised to send them in the diplomatic bag to London on 14 May. By 18 May, the package had still not arrived at Room 13, and the Mincemeat team was starting to panic. That evening, Hillgarth received a telegram in secret cipher: 'Bag not yet arrived. Urgent that letters should be received earliest possible. Was bag sent by air or sea?' Hillgarth immediately replied that the items, packed in 'a small, sealed bag', had left Madrid for Lisbon, as planned, and should have arrived by air, addressed personally to Ewen Montagu. For months, they had been working to get the bag into the wrong hands, as if by accident. Now it might very well have fallen into the wrong hands, by accident.

In the same telegram, Montagu asked whether the rubber dinghy set adrift by the *Seraph* had ever washed up. He also passed on the news that initial signs seemed to show that Mincemeat was working: 'Evidence that operation successful but vital that no suspicion should be aroused.' Hillgarth replied that there was no trace of the dinghy, which had almost certainly been appropriated by the fishermen of Punta Umbria.

From his own discreet investigations, Hillgarth already knew that the deception was taking satisfactory shape. Agent Andros had 'reported that there was great excitement over some official documents found on the body of a British officer at Huelva'. The rumour mill was grinding away: 'I naturally asked him to find out what he could.' A few days later, Hillgarth ran into Admiral Moreno at a cocktail party for foreign diplomats. The Minister of Marine brought up the subject of the documents without prompting, and 'said that immediately he heard they had reached Madrid (he was in Valencia) he gave Chief [of] Naval Staff orders to hand over to me at once'. This was a bald lie. German documents show that Moreno took personal custody of the papers, and then handed them, unopened, to the General Staff.

There then followed a most revealing conversation between Hillgarth and his Spanish friend:

'Why did you go to so much trouble?' Hillgarth asked nonchalantly.

'I was anxious no one should have an unauthorised look at them,' Moreno replied. 'Which might be a serious matter.'

Moreno had tripped himself up. Hillgarth had requested the return of the case through a third party, but had never indicated that this was anything other than a routine matter, let alone that the contents were secret and should be kept from 'unauthorised' eyes. 'He obviously did not know the exact terms of my request which was verbal and could never alone have led him to say what he did,' Hillgarth reported to London. 'It can be taken as a certainty that Spanish government know contents of documents. I am not so certain they have [reached] enemy. Yet they were more than a week in Huelva and Cadiz.'

The Spanish admiral was playing a dangerous double game. On 19 May, the German ambassador, Dieckhoff, sent another message to Berlin, describing a meeting with Moreno: 'He told me that all his information indicated that strong forces would be concentrated in preparation for an attack on Greece and Italy . . . The Navy Minister regards an attack on Greece as especially likely.' While reassuring the British that their secrets were safe, Moreno was simultaneously passing those secrets to the Germans. The duplicitous Spanish admiral would make a very useful tool for reinforcing the deception. 'The operation has given conclusive proof of the extent to which the Spaniards will go in assistance to the Axis.'

On 21 May, to the intense relief of the Mincemeat team, the package containing Major Martin's briefcase and other effects finally arrived in London. No satisfactory explanation was offered for its week-long, heart-stopping disappearance. Spanish bureaucracy was not alone in moving in mysterious ways. The letters were immediately sent to the Special Examiners ('Censorship') for microscopic analysis. First they inspected the wax seals, and found that despite all that had happened over the preceding weeks, these were still perfectly intact. 'The seals were photographed and marked by us before they were despatched, and they have been photographed also after their return. They have not been altered in any way.'

Imperial War Museum

FIGURE 1.

Left-hand seal
before despatch

FIGURE 2.

Left-hand seal
after return.

But that was only part of the story. 'Although we can say that there has been no tampering with the seals [it is] quite possible that the letters have been rolled out, from under the bottom flaps . . . as the bottom flap was very much deeper than the upper, there was plenty of room for the contents to be taken out.' The eyelash was missing from each envelope, but the examiners had laid another, rather more scientific trap. Before being placed in the briefcase, back in April, each letter was folded into three, symmetrically, just once. A letter when folded dry creates a crease that is noticeably 'sharper than one made in it when it was well soaked and soft, more like that which would be made in a piece of cloth'. Under the microscope, it was revealed that at least one of the letters had been folded twice, 'once symmetrically and secondly irregularly . . . while the letter was wet'. Thus the examiners deduced that when the Spaniards closed up the key letter, 'it was not done on <u>exactly</u> the same folds and there were damaged fibres in the paper minutely separate from the new folds'.

There was one other test. To extract the letters, the paper must have been tightly wound around a metal prong. The letters had been soaked again before being replaced inside the envelopes, and despite the delayed journey from Spain, they were still slightly damp. A piece of paper rolled up when wet will tend to curl up when dried out. The censors extracted the letters and then carefully watched to see whether or not the paper would lie flat. Sure enough, 'as the letter began to dry naturally, outside the envelope, the edges began to curve upward, that is to say as they would if the letter had been rolled out of the back of the envelope'. Moreover, the rolling up must have happened when the letter was folded in three, since the examiners noted that 'when the letter is folded up, it all curves the same way'. Here was solid physical proof that the letters had been opened, corroborating the evidence now appearing in the intercepted wireless messages.

The Germans would be expecting the British to examine the returned letters carefully to see if they had been tampered with. The deception would be reinforced if the Germans could be made to believe that such an examination had been carried out and that the British scientists were satisfied the letters had never been opened. The best person to pass on that message would be the fickle Admiral Moreno.

A message was drafted to Captain Hillgarth, referring to his earlier conversation with the admiral. 'Inform Minister of Marine as soon as possible that sealed envelopes have been tested by experts and there was no trace of opening or tampering before they reached care of Spanish navy and that you are instructed to express our deep appreciation for the efficiency and promptitude with which Spanish navy took charge of all documents before any evilly disposed person could get at them. You should say that you may tell him in confidence that one of the letters was of the greatest importance and secrecy and the appreciation expressed at this token of friendship is most sincere.' This message was not sent in cipher, but by naval cable. A second, secret cable informed Hillgarth that the 'letters [were] in fact opened', but he should spread the word to anyone 'likely to pass it on' that the British were confident the letters were never read in Spain. 'Important there should be no repetition no suspicion that we believe letters were read so that present success may not be endangered.'

Despite the misgivings of some at FHW, and Kuhlenthal's blustering excuses for the gaps and contradictions in the story, the lie had by now firmly embedded itself in German strategic thinking, and was beginning to metastasise, spreading out through the veins of Axis intelligence. Important and exciting information, whether true or false, develops its own momentum. So far from being questioned, the expected attacks in Greece and Sardinia were fast becoming accepted wisdom.

Hitler Loses Sleep

Four days after Von Roenne's initial analysis, one Captain Ullrich, an officer on the German General Staff, offered a fresh assessment of the intelligence. This report, dated 14 May, 'consisted of comments for the perusal of Admiral Doenitz'. Ullrich was, if anything, even more wildly enthusiastic about the Mincemeat information than Von Roenne.

'No further doubts remain regarding the reliability of the captured documents. Examination as to whether they were intentionally put into our hands shows that this is most unlikely.' It is not clear what examination, if any, had been made in order to clear up 'remaining doubts'. No new evidence had been found, and no formal investigation had been undertaken. Yet the impetus of wishful thinking was unstoppable.

Captain Ullrich next addressed the question of 'whether the enemy is aware of the interception by us of these documents or whether he is only aware of the loss of a plane over the sea'. The analyst was confident that Germany now had the upper hand. 'It is possible that the enemy knows nothing of the capture of these documents but it is certain that he will know they have not reached their destination. Whether the enemy intend to alter the operations they have planned or accelerate the timing is not known but remains improbable.' The letter from Nye to Alexander was 'urgent'; Alexander had been asked to 'reply immediately "since we cannot postpone the matter any longer"'.

On the other hand, there had been sufficient time to send the letter by air courier, rather than by wireless, and to await a response. 'It is the opinion of the German General Staff that sufficient time remains for alteration in the planning of both the eastern and western Mediterranean operations.'

With Germanic precision, Ullrich laid out his conclusions: the attacks in the east and west would be simultaneous 'since only in this case would Sicily be unsuitable as cover for both'; the troops attacking Greece would probably leave from Tobruk, in northeastern Libya; Alexandria would not be used as an embarkation point, since it would be 'absurd' to pretend that such forces could reach Sicily, in conformity with the cover plan. ('This shows how wrong a staff can be, as Sicily was invaded from Alexandria,' Montagu remarked, when Captain Ullrich's report was eventually recovered.) It was possible, thought Ullrich, that the 5th and 56th Divisions would 'comprise the whole of the assault forces' in the Peloponnese. As for the decoy attack on Sicily, this might be a brief commando-style assault followed by an immediate retreat, but it could also 'be continued after the launching of the actual operation'. The report concluded by stressing that the German defensive focus should shift, emphatically, to Greece. 'It must be especially emphasised that this document indicated extensive preparations in the eastern Mediterranean. This is especially important because from that area, on account of the geographical situation, there has, up to this time, been considerably less news about preparations than from the area of Algiers.' There was, of course, another very good reason why the Germans had less evidence of an attack in the east: the Allies, in reality, had no plans to launch one. Once again, when the truth did not fit, the Germans willingly manoeuvred the facts in favour of the deception.

Grand Admiral Karl Doenitz, who had been made commander-in-chief of the German navy three months earlier, undoubtedly read Captain Ullrich's analysis, since he wrote on it. Among the documents seized at Tambach in 1945 was Ullrich's original report: in the margin, Doenitz's 'personal squiggle' is clearly visible, the initials indicating that he had read it, and absorbed its contents. Doenitz was one of Hitler's most trusted decision makers, and would become his heir: his influence was critical.

Benito Mussolini had long believed that the next Allied attack would be aimed at Sicily, the key strategic point for a full-scale assault on Italy. His German allies now set about convincing him otherwise. Doenitz returned from Rome and sent a report of his meeting with Mussolini to Hitler. In his official war diary for 14 May, the German admiral noted: 'The Führer does not agree with the Duce that the most likely invasion point is Sicily. Furthermore, he agrees that the discovered Anglo-Saxon order confirms the assumption that the planned attack will be directed mainly against Sardinia and the Peloponnesus.' A few days later, Hitler wrote to Mussolini: 'It is also clear from documents which have been found that they intend to invade the Peloponnese and will in fact do so . . . if the British attempts are to be prevented, as they must be at all costs, this can only be done by a German division.' Hitler's faith in his Italian ally was fading fast, and Italian troops could not be relied on to do the job. 'Within the next few days or weeks, a large number of German divisions must be sent immediately to the Peloponnese.' With regard to the Balkan threat, the Nye letter had not changed Hitler's mind; it had merely bolstered what he already, wrongly, believed. As one intelligence historian wrote in his assessment of Operation Mincemeat: 'It is very unusual and very difficult for deception to create new concepts for an enemy. It is much easier and more effective to reinforce those which already exist.'

Corroborative titbits flooded in from all sides, as Mincemeat's false information spread through German sources, official and unofficial. Ernst Kaltenbrunner, chief of the RSHA – the Reichssicherheitshauptamt, Reich Security Main Office – the organisation formed by Himmler combining the Security Service and Gestapo, told the Foreign Minister, Joachim von Ribbentrop, that his spies in the British and American embassies in Madrid confirmed that 'targets of enemy operation [are] Italy and her islands as well as Greece'. The Turkish embassies in London and Washington picked up the news, and reported to Germany that 'the Allies wanted to advance into the Balkans via Greece'. General Jodl was overheard on the telephone telling German commanders in Rome: 'You can forget Sicily, we know it's Greece.'

Additional Ultra intercepts showed that the German Abwehr station in Rhodes, citing the Italian high command as its source, reported 'that the Allied attack would be directed against Cape Araxos and Kalamata', and added a little embroidery of its own: 'Allied submarines had received orders to assemble at an unknown assembly point for massed operations.' The warning was passed from Athens to German commanders in the Aegean and Crete, the army commander in southern Greece, and the Abwehr in Salonika, which 'forwarded it to Belgrade and Sofia'. The deception was reinforcing itself, to London's delight: 'The reports coming from opposite quarters seemed to confirm each other and have evidently, for the time being at least, been accepted as true.'

The information had all originated in the same place, but having trickled out in the form of gossip, rumour and information passed from source to source, it now filtered back to Germany, confirming itself like an echo growing ever louder.

On 19 May, Hitler held a military conference in which he referred to the expected assault on Greece and the thrust up through the Balkans. The Führer's 'congenital obsession about the Balkans', stoked by the Mincemeat letters, was keeping him awake. 'In the last few days, and particularly last night, I have again been giving much thought to the consequences which would follow if we lost the Balkans, and there is no doubt that the results must be very serious.' The ravenous German war machine could not survive without raw materials from the Balkans and Romania, the source of half its oil, all its chrome, and three-fifths of its bauxite. German commanders had emphasised the threat of an Allied offensive in Greece since the previous winter, and discussions between the Axis allies in February had concluded that Greece was vulnerable. The documents had crystallised Hitler's pre-existing anxieties: 'the danger is that they will establish themselves in the Peloponnese'; he now proposed 'as a precaution to take a further preventive measure against an eventual attack on the Peloponnese'. Partisan activity was increasing in the German-held Balkans, and from Hitler's perspective the area seemed, in his own words, the 'natural' target. Greece was the thin end of an exceedingly sharp wedge: 'If a landing takes place in the Balkans, let us say the Peloponnese, then in a foreseeable time Crete will go,' he told his generals at the conference on 19 May. 'I have therefore decided whatever happens to transfer one armoured division to the Peloponnese.'

While the fake letter from General Nye concentrated Hitler's mind on Greece, Montagu's joke about sardines focused German attention on Sardinia. 'Sardinia is particularly threatened,' observed General Walter Warlimont, Deputy Chief of the Operations Staff. 'In the event of the loss of Sardinia, the threat to Northern Italy is extremely acute. This is the key point for the whole of Italy.' German fears for the vulnerability of Greece and the Balkans were mirrored by Hitler's anxiety over Sardinia: 'He foresaw that from Sardinia the enemy could threaten Rome and the main ports of Genoa and Leghorn, strike simultaneously through upper Italy and at southern France, and strike at the heart of the European fortress.'

A British spy within Italian government circles, meanwhile, reported that the Mincemeat information had reached Rome, 'through the Spaniards and not directly through the Germans' – confirmation that the Spanish General Staff had made its own copies of the documents, and passed these on to the Italians. 'The Italian high command have the details of the letter and have accepted it as genuine.' The Italian ambassador in Madrid told the Germans that he had obtained 'information from an absolutely unimpeachable source that the enemy intend landing operations in Greece in the very near future'. The German ambassador in Rome passed on the news, now no longer new, to Berlin. It is an intriguing comment on the state of the Axis alliance that the Italians delivered this high-grade information to the Germans, but the Germans, who had known it for considerably longer, felt no such obligation to share intelligence with its Italian ally.

Fragments of corroborative information were swirling around the diplomatic world. British intelligence discovered that the German ambassador in Ankara had informed the Turkish minister in Budapest that the German army would soon be reinforcing its military stance in Greece, but that it had no hostile intention towards neutral Turkey: 'There would be troop and transport movements towards the south which will affect Greece but that the Turkish government should not be worried in any way as these were not aimed against Turkey.' As always with Chinese whispers of gossip, the information tended to get mangled in transition. From Madrid, Hillgarth reported wryly: 'German circles here have a story that they have obtained warning of our plans through papers found on a British officer in Tunis.'

Soon after, Hillgarth received a report from Agent Andros describing, in minute detail, how the documents had reached German hands. 'The degree of Spanish complicity' was laid bare: 'This exchange of information with the Germans in fact took place at the highest levels in Madrid.' Andros confirmed that Leissner and Kuhlenthal, the two most senior Abwehr officers, had been directly involved in obtaining the documents from the Spaniards, and the entire episode, as Montagu wrote to 'C', was 'adding to our knowledge of German intrigues in Spain'.

Months later, shards of the false intelligence continued to ricochet from one source to another, breaking up in the process. A spy in Stockholm reported that the local Germans had information from a British aircraft shot down in the

Mediterranean, with battle orders showing 'simultaneous landings in Sardinia and the Peloponnese', and a secondary attack on Sicily. Almost every other detail in the report was inaccurate, but it was plain that it had come, as the report put it, from 'our refrigerated friend'.

One by one, Hitler's key advisers were being drawn into the deception, either by access to the documents themselves, or through independent 'confirmation', as the same intelligence arrived by other routes: Canaris, Jodl, Kaltenbrunner, Warlimont, Von Roenne. By 20 May, Mussolini 'had come round to the same view'. A collective willingness to believe seems to have gripped the upper reaches of the Nazi war apparatus, driven by Hitler's own belief. It takes a brave man to stand up to the boss in such circumstances. The men surrounding Hitler were not made of such stuff.

Nazi confidence was in dire need of reinforcement: with the Axis powers defeated in North Africa, bogged down in blood on the Eastern Front, facing an increasingly confident Allied enemy, before the arrival of the Mincemeat letters, the entire southern coast of Europe had appeared vulnerable. Now, instead of waiting for the Allied armies to attack, somewhere, anywhere, the Germans and their Italian allies could lie in wait at Kalamata, Cape Araxos and Sardinia, and then hurl the British and Americans back into the sea. The papers washed up in Spain represented more than just an intelligence coup: here was a real chance to strike back. The tide of war was turning, but here, floating in on the waves, was an opportunity to reverse the current. Fate was smiling on Germany. No wonder they chose to believe.

There was one man in Hitler's circle who remained sceptical. Joseph Goebbels was alone among the Nazi elite in wondering whether the letters that had so conveniently arrived in German hands at this opportune moment were nothing more than 'camouflage', an elaborate effort by the British to put Germany off the scent. The Nazi propaganda minister knew better than most that reality, in war, is a malleable and fickle substance. 'The truth is whatever helps bring victory,' he wrote. Goebbels had no faith in the Abwehr, which made such extravagant claims for its spy networks but produced so little of real use. 'Despite all the assertions, our political and military intelligence just stinks,' he complained. Having bungled and blustered its way through four years of war, the Abwehr was now trumpeting a 'resounding' success, with a set of letters that revealed Allied planning down to a comma. Goebbels thought he knew the British mind. He had *The Times* translated for him daily, and complained about the newspaper exactly as if he was a retired general living in the Home Counties, rather than the master of Nazi propaganda. '*The Times* has once again sunk so low as to publish an almost pro-Bolshevik article,' he harrumphed. 'It praised the Bolshevik revolution and used words that make one blush with shame.' Doctor Goebbels may have been one of the most repulsive creatures in the bestiary of Nazism, but he had a sensitive nose for a lie, and the British letters smelled wrong. To use the favourite expression of Admiral Cunningham, one of the notional recipients, something about the letters was just too 'velvety-arsed and Rolls-Royce'.

'I had a long discussion with Admiral Canaris about the data available for forecasting English intentions,' Goebbels wrote in his diary for 25 May 1943. 'Canaris has gained possession of a letter written by the English general staff to General Alexander. This letter is extremely informative and reveals English plans almost to the dotting of an "i". I don't know whether the letter is merely camouflage – Canaris denies this energetically – or whether it actually corresponds to the facts.' Unlike most of Hitler's advisers, and Hitler himself, Goebbels tried to test the reality presented in the letters against what he knew of British strategic thinking. 'The general outline of English plans for this summer revealed here seems on the whole to tally. According to it, the English and Americans are planning several sham attacks during the coming months: one in the west, on Sicily, and one on the Dodecanese islands. These attacks are to immobilise our troops stationed there, thus enabling English forces to undertake other and more serious operations. These operations are to involve Sardinia and the Peloponnesus. On the whole, this line of reasoning seems to be right. Hence, if the letter to General Alexander is the real thing, we shall have to prepare to repel a number of attacks which are partly serious and partly sham.' No other senior Nazi wondered if the letter was the real thing. Goebbels kept his doubts to himself, and his diary.

The trickiest aspect to lying is maintaining the lie. Telling an untruth is easy, but continuing and reinforcing a lie is far harder. The natural human tendency is to deploy another lie to bolster the initial mendacity. Deceptions – in the war room, boardroom, and bedroom – usually unravel because the deceiver lets down his guard, and makes the simple mistake of telling, or revealing, the truth.

The invasion of Sicily was planned for 10 July. That left a gap of two months in which the elaborate fabrication had to be protected, buttressed and fortified. For weeks, Allied deception planners had built up the fictional '12th Army' in Cairo, the dummy force apparently poised to strike at the Peloponnese, by spreading modern Greek myths: recruiting Greek fishermen familiar with the coast, distributing Greek maps to Allied troops, employing Greek interpreters.

On 7 June, Karl-Erich Kuhlenthal sent a message to Juan Pujol, asking his star spy to find out whether the British were recruiting Greek soldiers in preparation for the assault. The First Canadian Division was already training in Scotland, and preparing to embark for Sicily. Kuhlenthal assumed they were heading for Greece. 'Try to find out if Greek troops are stationed close to the First Canadian Army or elsewhere in the South of England, and if so, which Greek troops are these?' wrote Kuhlenthal. 'It is of greatest importance to discover the next operation.' Garbo told his handler that Agent No. 5, a wealthy Venezuelan student, would immediately head to Scotland 'to investigate the presence of Greek troops'. The Greek troops did not exist, of course; but then, neither did Agent No. 5.

The Germans had clearly taken the bait, but they would also be watching closely for any evidence confirming or disproving what they now believed. Dudley Clarke sent a message suggesting that 'the only serious danger' of the deception being rumbled would be a 'legal or illegal exhumation with a view to more thorough autopsy' on the body in Huelva cemetery. Montagu arranged another meeting with the St Pancras coroner Bentley Purchase, who reassured him that an autopsy at this late stage would probably be inconclusive. 'By the time that he had been buried for a short period his internal organs must have been, according to the coroner, in a very mixed up condition [and] the lungs would probably have been liquefied', making it even harder to establish death by drowning. Montagu sent a message to Bevan: 'Although no one in this world can be certain of anything it does not seem that the fear that the Germans may learn anything from a disinterment and subsequent autopsy is well founded.'

Still, a large slab of engraved marble might help to discourage any grave-robbing, while giving William Martin the sort of dignified gravestone he deserved. On 21 May, Alan Hillgarth received an encoded message from London: 'Suggest unless unusual that a medium-priced tombstone should be erected on grave with inscription such as quote William Martin, born 29 March 1907 died 24 repetition 24 April 1943 beloved son of John Glyndwyr repetition Glyndwyr Martin and the late Antonia Martin of Cardiff, Wales. *Dulce et Decorum Est Pro Patria Mori*. RIP. end quote.'

Montagu spelled Glyndwr Michael's first name wrong in his cable: the error was duly transferred to the stone. For a moment, the spies had second thoughts. Would a large marble gravestone look suspicious? 'This to be done unless restrictions on making payment from England to Spain or other wartime difficulties would have made it too difficult for a father to get this done in normal circumstances.' Hillgarth replied immediately: 'Please send me ordinary cipher signal saying that relations would like this stone put up telling me to get on with it I will then get exchange in normal way and proceed immediately.'

Germany's spies within the British Embassy could be relied on to pick up the message, and relay it to the Abwehr in the usual way. In a final element of stage design, the Mincemeat team wrote: 'Suggest Consul place wreath now with card marked quote From Father and Pam end quote.' Mario Toscana, the Huelva gravestone carver, was instructed to make the stone 'as fast as possible'. Francis Haselden sent the wreath, as well as several bouquets picked from the garden of the Casa Colón, the headquarters of the Rio Tinto Company. 'The purpose of this was not only to carry out what would probably have occurred in real life, but also to enable the grave to be visited often enough to discourage any chance of a secret and illicit disinterment for further autopsy.' Lancelot Shutte, Haselden's sidekick, would make a daily pilgrimage to the graveside, ostensibly as an official mourner, in reality to see if the flowers had been moved and the grave disturbed.

Hillgarth composed and dictated a letter, addressed to 'John G. Martin ESQ' but for the attention of Kuhlenthal and his spies:

Sir,

In accordance with instructions from the Admiralty, I have now arranged for a gravestone for your son's grave. It will be a simple white marble slab with the inscription which you sent to me through the Admiralty, and the cost will be 900 pesetas.

The grave itself cost 500 pesetas, and, as I think you know, it is in the Roman Catholic cemetery.

A wreath with a card on it with the message you asked for has been laid on the grave. The flowers came from the garden of an English mining company in Huelva.

```
    I have taken the liberty of thanking the Vice Consul,
Huelva, on your behalf for all he has done.
    May I express my deep sympathy with you and your son's
fiancée in your great sorrow?
    I am, Sir, Your obedient servant,
    Alan Hillgarth
```

At the same time, Montagu sent a message to Hillgarth, with the same audience in mind: 'I have been asked by Major Martin's father, fiancée and friends, to thank you for the trouble you and the vice consul have taken in connection with his funeral and to say how much they appreciate the promptitude with which you returned his personal effects. Few though they were, as Major Martin was an only son and just engaged to be married, they will be greatly treasured.' Here was confirmation for the Germans that all Martin's accoutrements were safely back in Britain. 'Could you possibly procure for him a photograph of the grave after the tombstone has been erected?' Hillgarth duly obliged.

As far as the Germans knew, the British authorities were deeply relieved to get their valuable documents back intact. Another small outlay by Hillgarth would bolster that impression, by way of local gossip: 'A reasonable reward of not more than £25 should be given to the person who handed the papers to the safe custody of naval authorities. It is left to your judgement whether this should be done by you through naval authorities or by Consul Huelva direct.' The sum of £25 was a small fortune in wartime Huelva: José Rey's fishing trip would turn out to be the most lucrative of his life.

While 'Pam' and 'Father' grieved in private, the news of Major William Martin's death now needed relaying to a wider, public audience. The Germans had access to the British casualty lists, and if Martin's name failed to appear on them, suspicions might be aroused. At least equal suspicion might be provoked among Royal Marines officers if one of their number was suddenly declared dead without warning. A letter, marked 'Most Secret and Personal', was sent to the commanders of the three Royal Marines Divisions, as well as the colonel who edited the *Globe and Laurel*, the Marines' official newsletter: 'No action is to be taken in respect of the notification of the death of Major William Martin. This officer was detached on special service and no mention will be made in General Orders.' The casualty section received a curt order: 'Insert the following entry in the next suitable casualty list "Tempy Captain, (Acting Major) William Martin, R.M." This should appear at the earliest possible moment.' But it was not so easy to slip a false death past the authorities. The department of the Medical Director-General later demanded to know whether Major Martin had died in action, and if so, how. The Navy's legal department wanted to know if the gallant major had left a will, 'and, if so, where was it?' Both departments were politely, but firmly, told to mind their own business.

The announcement of Major William Martin's death on active service duly appeared in *The Times* on Friday, 4 June 1943. By pure chance, the names of two other real naval officers, whose death in an aircraft accident had previously been reported in the newspaper, appeared on the same list. The Germans, Montagu speculated, might link the reported death of Martin with that accident. The death of Leslie Howard, 'distinguished film and stage actor', was reported in a news story alongside the Roll of Honour featuring W. Martin. The civilian plane carrying the actor had been shot down by a German fighter over the Bay of Biscay. Somewhat eerily, an Abwehr informant may have mistaken Howard for Winston Churchill, who had recently visited Algiers and Tunis. It is safe to assume that more public attention was paid to this 'severe loss to the British theatre and to British films' than to the obscure death of an officer whom no one, bar a few spies, had ever heard of.

The Times was the place all important people wanted to be seen dead in, and it is not possible to be deader than in the death columns of Britain's most venerable newspaper. That said, several people have been pronounced dead in the press while being very much alive, including Robert Graves, Ernest Hemingway, Mark Twain (twice) and Samuel Taylor Coleridge. In July 1900, George Morrison, the Peking correspondent of *The Times*, read of his own death in his own newspaper after he was believed to have perished during the Boxer Rebellion. (The obituary described him as devoted and fearless. A friend remarked: 'The only decent thing they can do now is double your salary.' They didn't.) This, however, was the first time in the newspaper's history that a person was formally pronounced dead without ever having been alive.

At the end of May, the Director of Naval Intelligence noted in his secret diary that 'the first German Panzer Division (strength about 18,000 men) is being transferred from France to the Salonika region'. The information was graded 'A1'. This was the first indication of a major troop movement in response to the Mincemeat papers. An intercepted message added further details of the 'arrangements for the passage through Greece to Tripolis, in the Peloponnese, of the 1 German Panzer Division'. The movement seemed directly linked to the information in Nye's letter, since Tripolis, Montagu noted, was a 'strategic position well suited to resist our invasion of Kalamata and Cape Araxos'. The 1st Panzer Division, with eighty-three tanks, had seen fierce action in Russia, but was now 'completely reequipped'. Last located by British intelligence in Brittany, the Panzer division was a formidable, hardened force, and it was now being rolled from one end of Europe to the other, to counter an illusion.

On 8 June, Montagu wrote an interim report on the progress of Operation Mincemeat. 'It is now about half way between the time when the documents in MINCEMEAT reached the Germans and the present D-Day for Operation HUSKY, and I have therefore considered the state of the Germans' mind in so far as we have evidence.' Montagu summarised the intercepted messages, known troop movements, diplomatic gossip, and the double agent feedback, all of which suggested the most 'gratifying' progress. 'The present situation is summed up in the [7 June] message to Garbo which to my mind indicates the Germans are still accepting the probability of an attack in Greece, and are still anxiously searching for the target we foreshadowed in the Western Mediterranean.' Whatever suspicions there may have been on the German side now seemed to be allayed: 'They raised (but did not pursue) the question [of] whether it was a plot.'

'Mincemeat has already resulted in some dispersal of the enemy's effort and forces. It is to be hoped that, as visible signs in the eastern Mediterranean increase, the story we have put over may be "confirmed" and lead the enemy to take their eye off Sicily still more, although they obviously cannot entirely neglect the re-inforcement [sic] of so vulnerable and imminently threatened a point. It already appears to be having the desired effect on the enemy and (as the preparations for Husky grow) its effect may become cumulative.'

There was still time for Mincemeat to go horribly wrong, but so far, Major Martin's secret mission was going swimmingly. Montagu's interim report declared: 'I think that at this halfway stage Mincemeat can still be regarded as achieving the objective for which we hoped.'

Seraph and Husky

Bill Jewell steered the *Seraph* towards the jagged silhouette of the coastline, as the wind whipped and wailed around the conning tower. It was past ten o'clock, and curtains of thick fog draped an irritable sea, the rearguard of a nasty summer storm. Jewell shivered inside his sou'wester. The weather, he reflected, was 'moderately vile', but the reduced visibility would work to his advantage.

Once again, the *Seraph* was creeping towards the southern coast of Europe in the darkness, to drop off an important item. Once again, she had been entrusted with a mission of profound secrecy and extreme danger, and the lives of thousands depended on her success. The difference between this mission, and the one successfully executed three months earlier, was that the canister in the hold really did contain scientific instruments, a homing beacon to guide the largest invasion force ever assembled to the shores of Sicily. Having played her part in the secret build-up to 'Husky', the *Seraph* had been selected to lead in the invasion itself.

A week earlier, Jewell had been summoned to Submarine HQ, Algiers, where he was briefed by his commanding officer, Captain Barney Fawkes: 'You are to act as a guide and beacon submarine for the Army's invasion of Sicily.' The *Seraph*'s mission would be to drop a new type of buoy containing a radar beacon 1,000 yards off the beach at Gela on the island's south coast, just a few hours before D–Day: 10 July, 0400 hours. Destroyers leading flotillas of landing craft carrying the troops of America's 45th Infantry Division would lock on to the homing beacon, and the assault troops would then storm ashore in the early hours of the Sicilian morning. The *Seraph* should remain in position as a visible beacon 'for the first waves of the invasion force', and retire once the attack was underway. The submarine would act as the spearhead for a mighty host, an armada of Homeric proportions comprising more than 3,000 freighters, frigates, tankers, transports, minesweepers and landing craft carrying 1,800 heavy guns, 400 tanks, and an invasion force of 160,000 Allied soldiers made up from the United States's 7th Army under General George Patton and Montgomery's British 8th Army.

Sicily may be the most thoroughly invaded place on earth. From the eighth century BC, the island had been attacked, occupied, plundered and fought over by successive waves of invaders: Greeks, Romans, Vandals, Phoenicians, Carthaginians, Ostrogoths, Byzantines, Saracens, Normans, Spaniards and British. But never had Sicily witnessed an invasion on this scale. If Operation Mincemeat had succeeded, then the Allied troops would face only limited resistance. Jewell had no idea whether his strange cargo had ever reached the coast of Huelva, but as he absorbed his new orders, he found himself wondering whether the dead body 'had delivered his false information to the Germans and whether, as a result, the thousands of troops preparing to assault the island would meet less resistance'. If the ruse had failed, and tipped off the Axis powers to the real target of Operation Husky, then the *Seraph* might be leading the vast floating host into catastrophe.

After receiving his orders, Jewell had reported to the 7th Army headquarters for a briefing from General Patton himself. Swaggering, foul-mouthed and inspirational, Patton was a born leader of men, and a deeply divisive figure. Jewell detested him on sight. With a pearl-handled revolver on each hip, the general

strode around the briefing room, barking orders at Jewell and
the two other British submarine commanders who would help
to guide in the American ground troops. 'His force was to land
in three parts, each on its own beach; he wanted reconnaissance
checked and the submarines allocated to the beaches to stay in
their position over the beacon buoys to ensure that the right
forces landed on the right beaches.' The briefing lasted all of ten
minutes. 'He was really very short with us, somewhat conceited
and very rudely outspoken,' Jewell recalled.

Outside the conference room, Jewell heard a loud American
voice call his name, and turned to find Colonel Bill Darby of the
US Rangers, his friend from the earlier Galita reconnaissance.
Darby explained that he would be leading his troops ashore
in the *Seraph*'s wake, at the head of Force X, made up of two
crack Ranger battalions. 'Do as good a job for us as you did
at Galita,' said Darby, 'and we'll be mighty grateful.' Jewell
promised to do his best. Yet the submarine commander was
privately apprehensive. If the enemy spotted the *Seraph* laying
the beacon buoy, they would certainly realise that an invasion
was imminent, and rush reinforcements to that section of the
coast. 'Discovery,' Jewell reflected, 'would throw the whole
Husky plan into jeopardy.' Eisenhower himself had warned that
if the Germans were tipped off, the attack on Sicily would fail.
The American general told Churchill: 'If substantial German
ground troops should be placed in the region prior to the attack,
the chances for success become practically nil and the project
should be abandoned.' Even a few hours' warning would be
paid for in greatly increased bloodshed. Surprise was essential;
lack of it was potentially suicidal. Patton's closing remark also
stuck in Jewell's mind, both irritating and alarming him: 'The
submarines would be less than a mile from the enemy, but come
what may they must stay there until the Task Force with the
army arrived, no matter how late.' The *Seraph,* codenamed
'Cent', would be left on the surface as the sun rose, isolated and
defenceless, a sitting duck for the Italian guns ranged along the

coast. This was undoubtedly Jewell's most dangerous mission, with every probability that it might also be his last.

Jewell was sublimely indifferent to his own safety. He had faced danger and discomfort on an extravagant scale in a gruesome war. Time after time he had demonstrated his willingness to die. But now he had something new to live for. Bill Jewell had fallen in love.

After performing his part in Operation Mincemeat, Jewell had returned to Algiers for some well-earned shore leave. Among the new arrivals at Allied Headquarters in the city was Rosemary Galloway, a young officer in the Wrens, the Women's Royal Naval Service. Rosemary was a cipher clerk, coding and decoding the messages passing in and out of Allied Headquarters, and thus was privy to secret and sensitive information. She was vivacious, intelligent and exceedingly attractive. Jewell and Rosemary had met once before, in Britain, and in the sultry heat of wartime Algiers that acquaintance rapidly bloomed into romance. Once Bill Jewell had spotted Rosemary on his emotional periscope, he pursued her with unswerving determination. She proved a most cooperative quarry. There were limited opportunities for courtship in wartime Algiers, and Jewell seized all of them.

At Sidi Barouk, just outside the city, the American forces had created a rest camp that was the nearest thing in Algeria to an American country club, with bar, restaurant, tennis court and swimming pool. Jewell recalled: 'The American High Command had taken possession of a strip of beach and olive grove and converted it into an Arabian Night's dream – barring the houris, of course!' (Actually, these were available too.) An evening at Sidi Barouk was, in Jewell's words, 'a really de luxe experience'. Jewell's friendly relations with senior American officers earned him access to this 'most exclusive spot', and even the use of an American driver, one Private Bocciccio, a Brooklyn native, who drove with one leg permanently hanging out of his jeep. When Bocciccio was unavailable, Jewell squired

Rosemary around town in an ancient Hillman acquired by the 8th Flotilla and known as 'The Wren Trap', less for its romantic allure, which was zero, than its captive potential: 'None of the doors opened from the inside and, no matter how urgent the need for fresh air, Wrens who accepted the risk had to rely on the chivalry of their companions to release them.' Bocciccio, who had picked up some fruity British slang, was scathing about the Wren Trap, and what went on in it: 'Bloody heap ain't got no springs left.'

The Hotel St George was the best hotel in Algiers, and Eisenhower's headquarters. Built on the site of an ancient Moorish palace, it was surrounded by botanical gardens with hibiscus, roses and flowering cacti; in both war and peace, visitors sipped cocktails in the shade of vast umbrellas beneath the palms and banana trees, served by Algerian waiters in starched uniforms with epaulettes. The hotel chef, in Jewell's estimation, 'could turn out a meal, even in the depleted Algiers of that day, in keeping with the finest traditions of French cuisine'. Rudyard Kipling, André Gide, Simone de Beauvoir, and King George V had all stayed at the St George. On 7 June 1943, the hotel hosted the crucial conference at which Churchill and Eisenhower finalised plans for the Allied invasion of Sicily. That same month, it was the setting for the culmination of Jewell's campaign to win Rosemary Galloway. For two joyful weeks, he had wooed her with every weapon at his disposal: French food, an American swimming pool and a British car with doors that wouldn't open. Rosemary was in no mind to resist, and at the end of this sustained bombardment she had sunk, unresistingly, into Lieutenant Jewell's arms.

It was therefore with even more than his usual alertness that Jewell scanned the foggy seas off the Sicilian coast at midnight on 9 July: he had captured Rosemary Galloway's heart and he did not intend to lose his prize by getting killed. If Mincemeat had failed – or worse, had backfired – then Jewell, his crew, and the thousands of British and American troops steaming into battle behind him might not live through the next few hours. If the plan had worked, and he survived, then perhaps he would see Rosemary again. Jewell, who had never paid much attention to his own mortality, was surprised at how much this mattered to him.

The crew of the *Seraph* had already laid out a trail of small marker buoys, each primed with a fuse that would set off simultaneous blinker lights in exactly four hours, to lead the flotilla to shore. The heavier beacon buoy was brought up on deck, and the submarine slowly edged towards the drop point. Jewell was about to give the order to lower the buoy, when the lookout's hushed voice cut through the darkness. 'E-boat on port quarter, Sir.'

The German *Schnellboot*, known to the Allies as the E-boat, was a motor torpedo launch with three 2,000-horsepower Daimler-Benz engines, carrying four torpedoes, two 20mm-cannon, and six machine guns. It was better armed, and three times faster, than the *Seraph*. And it was about 400 yards away, motionless, 'a clearly visible silhouette standing out blackly against the dark blueness of the night'. The E-boat had also spotted the British submarine, and was attempting to determine whether it was friend or foe. 'It was a ticklish moment,' wrote Jewell. 'That Nazi, I knew, was faster than we and much better armed. I knew her gunners were at battle stations, manning their weapons and waiting for the word to fire.' For seconds that passed like minutes, Jewell 'waited tensely for the E-boat to make its move'. At a whispered order, the submarine's gun crews and torpedo men moved to action stations. If the German attacked, the *Seraph* would have to try to fight it out. Even if he won that duel, the coastal defenders would be alerted to what was coming over the dark horizon.

The British submarine lay low in the water; the swirling fog made identification doubly difficult. The German captain was plainly 'undecided about her identity, expecting only friendly submarines so near his coast'. Suddenly, he flashed his navigation lights. 'I knew that would be a recognition signal of some sort that I'd be expected to answer immediately.' The German captain's challenge gave Jewell the vital few seconds he needed. The decks were cleared, the buoy manhandled below, the hatch slammed shut, and Jewell barked the order to dive. 'Down she went in a few seconds. To the enemy she must have seemed literally to vanish.' With luck, reflected Jewell, the encounter would not tip off the defenders to the impending invasion: 'The captain of the E-boat would still be victim to his own indecision [and] so long as he couldn't be sure whether we were friend or enemy it was not likely the Germans would take alarm.' But time was short. The buoy would have to be laid within the next hour, for the mighty Allied army of invasion was now only a few hours away, strung out in a vast flotilla just over the horizon to the south.

The broad plan for the invasion of Sicily had been agreed at Casablanca back in January, but the process of working out the specifics of Operation Husky had turned into a dogfight, with intense disagreements among commanders, and rising tensions between the British and American allies. Patton found Montgomery 'wonderfully conceited' and noted that Alexander, the commander of Allied ground forces, had 'an exceptionally small head'. This from a man whose big-headedness was legendary. Montgomery said of Eisenhower: 'His knowledge of how to make war, or to fight battles, is definitely nil.' The British general flatly refused to accept Eisenhower's initial battle plans, which called for an American invasion in the west of Sicily aimed at Palermo, while the British took Augusta and Syracuse on the southeast coast. Monty insisted that he knew better, which he did, and predicted a 'military disaster' if the plan was not scrapped. Montgomery was adept at tactical manoeuvres: he finally got his way after cornering Major General Walter Bedell Smith, Eisenhower's Chief of Staff, in the toilets at Allied Forces HQ in Algiers. First at the urinal, then by drawing a map of Sicily on the steamy mirror above the hand basin, Montgomery laid out his alternative plan: a consolidated assault on the southeast coast by both armies.

Agreement was reached. Before dawn on 10 July, Patton's 7th Army would assault the coast at the Gulf of Gela, while Montgomery's 8th Army would storm ashore farther east at the Gulf of Noto and Cassibile. In all, some twenty-six beaches would be attacked along a hundred miles of Sicily's southern coast, by troops assembled in the ports of Algeria, Tunisia, Libya and Egypt. The invasion would be preceded by intensive bombing of Sicilian airfields. Immediately before the assault, paratroopers would drop behind enemy lines to sever communications, forestall counterattacks, secure vital road junctions and confuse the enemy. The Combined Chiefs approved the plan for Husky on 12 May, the very day that London intercepted the first message indicating that Hitler had seen, and believed, the documents in Major Martin's briefcase.

The logistics of the operation would have boggled most minds: the American contingent alone called for 6.6 million sets of rations, 5,000 crated aeroplanes, 5,000 carrier pigeons and accompanying pigeoneers, and a somewhat unambitious 144,000 condoms, fewer than two each. The task of assembling this plethora of kit was rendered yet more complex by the need for absolute secrecy. Amphibious landings are notoriously hard, as Gallipoli and Dieppe attested. They are all but impossible if the defenders are ready and waiting. Eisenhower was insistent on the paramount importance of surprise, predicting that the operation would fail if more than two divisions were waiting, and the defenders put up strong resistance. The Germans could hardly fail to spot the 160,000 soldiers and 3,000 boats assembling on the north coast of Africa: the key would be to keep them guessing as to where, exactly, the attack might come.

Once the offensive was underway, a secondary deception plan, Operation Derrick, would try to convince the enemy that the assault on the south was diversionary, and the real attack would still come in the west of Sicily, keeping more troops out of the battle zone. Maps of Sicily were kept under lock and key. The soldiers of the invasion force would not be told where they were going until the task force was at sea. Letters home were strictly censored to ensure that the intended target remained secret, with officers only half-joking when they instructed their men that when writing home: 'You cannot, you must not, be interesting.'

Yet word, inevitably, had leaked out, on to the docks of North Africa. *The Soldier's Guide to Sicily* was accidentally distributed too early. A British officer in Cairo sent his uniform to be cleaned with the Husky battle plans in the pocket. The papers were retrieved, but not before several pages had been used to write out customer invoices: somewhere in Cairo was a person with clean clothes, and the Allies' most secret plans. Still more alarmingly, an officer of the British 1st Airborne Division accidentally left a top-secret cable on the terrace of Shepheard's Hotel in Cairo. The document not only gave the date and time of the Sicily invasion, but also the timing for dropping paratroops and even 'the availability of aircraft and gliders for such operations'. The paper was missing for at least two days before the hotel manager returned it to the military authorities. Dudley Clarke was confident, however, that if it had fallen into enemy hands through such an obvious and 'gross breach of security' then it would probably be dismissed as a plant, pointing to Sicily as the cover target in accordance with Mincemeat. He concluded that 'the accident may well have assisted rather than hindered us'.

Operation Barclay, the overall deception plan to disguise Allied intentions and keep as many Axis forces as possible away from Sicily, reached a climax in the days leading up to 10 July. Submarines had dropped men on the coasts of Sardinia and the Greek island of Zante, to leave behind unmistakable signs of reconnaissance for the Germans to find, as if in preparation for major assaults. 'Operation Waterfall', simulating the gathering of an army in the eastern Mediterranean as if to invade the

Balkans, assembled huge numbers of dummy tanks and planes. SOE organised a genuine sabotage operation by Greek resistance fighters, codenamed 'Animals', to suggest increased partisan activity in the Greek target area.

Double agents were used to bolster the deception, most notably André Latham, a dodgy, high-living French aristocrat and career army officer with a rabid loathing for communism, who had been recruited by the Abwehr in Paris in 1942. Latham was introduced to the rest of his spy team in the Elizabeth Arden Beauty Parlour on Faubourg St Honoré: a playboy called Dutey-Marisse (or possibly Duthey Harispe), a former French naval officer named Blondeau, and a pimp and saboteur called Duteil who, unbeknown to Latham, had orders from the Germans to kill him if he showed any sign of betrayal. The team had headed to Tunis, with orders to gather information for the Abwehr. On 8 May, as the preparations for Sicily were gathering pace, Latham – 'athletic, middle-aged, of medium height, with grey hair and military moustache' – presented himself to the head of French intelligence in North Africa, and declared his intention to spy against the Germans. He was given the codename 'Gilbert' and put to work sending false information to his German spymasters, who considered him 'an agent of very high class'. Gilbert reported that a large invasion force was assembling at the Tunisian port of Bizerte, which was in fact composed of dummy landing craft, to divert attention from the genuine preparations.

The Garbo network was deployed to muddy the waters still further: Agent 6 in Garbo's stable was Dick, an anti-communist South African recruited in 1942 by Pujol, 'who had promised him an important post in the New World Order after the war' if he would spy for Germany. Dick had been taken on by the War Office 'on account of his linguistic abilities', and sent to Allied Headquarters in Algiers. Pujol supplied him with secret ink, and the South African was soon reporting back via Garbo to Kuhlenthal in Spain on preparations for the coming assault.

The Germans were 'delighted with their new agent'. To draw attention away from Sicily, and further disperse the available German forces, Agent 6 'speculated that on account of certain documents which had come to his notice whilst working in the Intelligence Section at Headquarters the landing would probably be made in Nice and Corsica'. Soon after, Dick managed to 'steal some documents relating to the impending invasion' and promised to forward these to Pujol hidden in a packet of fruit.

On 5 July, however, Garbo relayed sad news to Kuhlenthal: Dick's 'unmarried wife', Dorothy, had informed him that Agent 6 had been killed in an air crash in North Africa. The Germans had lost a key spy just as he was getting into his stride. This small tragedy was, of course, entirely fictitious. Dick and Dorothy did not exist. The invented spy had been terminated because of a real death: the 'officer who had been acting as scribe for Agent No. 6 met with a fatal air accident whilst returning from leave in Scotland'. Dick had had distinctive handwriting. MI5 debated whether to 'pretend that the agent had damaged his right hand and was therefore obliged to write with his left, or to attempt to forge his handwriting'. Neither option seemed safe, so Dick, the South African spy who never was, was summarily put to death.

Despite the tight security surrounding the Sicilian campaign, and the vast clouds of disinformation thrown up by Operation Barclay and the double agents, German and Italian intelligence could hardly fail to spot the signs of an imminent invasion: the hospital ships assembled at Gibraltar; the 8 million leaflets dropped over Sicily warning that Hitler was a fickle ally: 'Germany will fight to the last Italian.' Even more significantly, the fortified island of Pantelleria, sixty miles southwest of Sicily, surrendered on 11 June after a three-week bombardment in which 6,400 bombs were dropped. The assault on Pantelleria, 'Operation Corkscrew', was the obvious prelude to a full-scale invasion of Sicily itself, since its capture would furnish the Allies with an airbase within range of the larger island. In London it was feared that the successful capture of the island 'would give the game away altogether'. Double agent Gilbert told his controllers 'not to be alarmed as the attack on Pantelleria was merely a feint', and the real attack would come elsewhere.

Even so, some on the German side correctly anticipated what was to come, and German messages deciphered at Bletchley Park suggested that the Germans were increasingly concerned about Sicily. Even Karl-Erich Kuhlenthal, watching from Spain, began to wonder whether the plans detailed in the intercepted letters had changed. After the capture of Pantelleria, Kuhlenthal 'received increasing reports that Sicily would be the next invasion goal. Numerous reports to that effect were sent to Berlin, but Berlin discounted the validity of such information.' Field Marshal Albert Kesselring, the canny German commander in the Mediterranean, had believed for six weeks before D-Day that the most likely point of attack would be Sicily. Yet for the most part, the German high command appeared wedded to the belief that the main assaults would come in the eastern and western Mediterranean, while the assault on Sicily might still be a feint.

The false picture of Allied strength painted by Mincemeat and the other deception operations had left Germany attempting to mount defences across an impossibly wide front. 'Operation Cascade' successfully convinced the Germans that the Allies had some forty divisions available to participate in the offensive – almost twice the real figure – and could therefore easily mount two or more attacks simultaneously. In truth, the Allies never had enough landing craft for more than one operation. In the same way, the Allies' strategic thinking rejected the launching of an amphibious assault without adequate air cover: realistically, this ruled out Sardinia and Greece as objectives for major landings. The two targets identified by Mincemeat were simply not on the genuine Allied agenda. The Germans never realised this.

German intelligence was quite unable to tell the high command where or when the main attack would come. Confusion and hesitation reigned, as the Germans struggled to see through the murk of deception, and their own flawed and limited sources of intelligence. The agenda of possible landing sites included not only Sardinia and Greece, but also Corsica, southern France, and even Spain, while Hitler's fear for the Balkans coloured his every strategic move. In Sardinia, which the Japanese chargé d'affaires in Rome reported 'was still regarded as the favourite target', troop strength was doubled to more than 10,000 men by the end of June, and bolstered with additional fighter aircraft. At the critical moment in the Kursk tank battle on the Eastern Front in July, two more German armoured divisions were placed on alert to go to the Balkans. German torpedo boats were ordered from Sicily to the Aegean; shore batteries were installed in Greece, and three new minefields were laid off its coasts. Between March and July 1943, the number of German divisions in the Balkans was increased from eight to eighteen, while the forces defending Greece increased from one division to eight.

Despite Italian intelligence warnings that an attack on Sicily was coming, and urgent Italian calls for German reinforcements, 'no measures were taken to reinforce the island'. As the official assessment of Operation Mincemeat later noted, 'it was never possible for the Germans to cease reinforcements and fortifications of Sicily altogether, as we might have changed our plans and it was always too vulnerable a target'. Yet the Germans clearly continued to believe that Sicily, if it were attacked at all, would not face a full Allied onslaught. At the end of May, an Ultra intercept from Kesselring's quartermaster revealed how chronically underprepared the Germany forces were: rations for just three months, and less than 9,000 tons of fuel. Confidence that Mincemeat was doing its job rose higher still. 'Compared with the forces employed in Tunisia, this was a tiny garrison.' Four days before the invasion, Kesselring reported that his troops in Sicily had 'only half the supplies they needed'. Eisenhower's fears of meeting 'well-armed and fully organised German forces' on the shores of Sicily were unfounded. Germany simply did not know what was coming, or where, and by the time it became clear that Sicily was the real target after all, it was too late.

The Allies, by contrast, had a clear-cut idea of Sicily's defences, and the Axis failure to reinforce them. The British and American invaders would face some 300,000 enemy troops defending 600 miles of coastline. More than two-thirds of the defenders were Italian, poorly equipped and ill-trained. Many were Sicilian conscripts, men with little stomach for this fight, old, unfit, unenthusiastic and, in some cases, armed with ancient weapons dating back to the previous war. The Italian coastal defence troops, according to one Allied intelligence report, suffered from 'an almost unbelievably low standard of morale, training and discipline'. The German forces, some 40,000 men in two divisions, were made of more motivated material. The newly rebuilt Hermann Goering Armoured Division, three battalions of infantry, had seen hard fighting in Tunisia, and had been transferred to Sicily by Kesselring after the seizure of Pantelleria. The 15th Panzer Grenadier Division was a battle-scarred, war-toughened unit with 160 tanks and 140 field artillery guns. The Italian defenders would probably put up little resistance, it was predicted, but the Germans would be 'hot mustard'.

'It will be a hard and very bloody fight,' Montgomery gloomily predicted. 'We must expect heavy losses.' Bill Darby was also expecting the worst, and rather looking forward to it: 'If casualties are high, it will not be a reflection of your leadership,' the Ranger commander told his officers. 'May God be with you.'

A Nice Cup of Tea

The weather forecast was grim, and the weather deteriorating, as the great invasion force set sail. In Malta, Admiral Sir Andrew Cunningham, naval commander in the Mediterranean and the recipient of the second Mincemeat letter, received the news that the flotilla had set off with more resignation than hope. The admiral had recorded a message for the troops, to be broadcast on loudspeakers once the task force was underway: 'We are about to embark on the most momentous enterprise of the war, striking for the first time at the enemy in his own land.' The upbeat tone contrasted with Cunningham's gloomy feelings, as the flotilla set off into 'all the winds of heaven', with every possiblility that the entire force might perish at sea. 'The die was cast. We were committed to the assault. There was nothing more we could do for the time being.' Over dinner in the Malta headquarters, Admiral Lord Louis Mountbatten, the signatory of two Mincemeat letters, was even gloomier: 'It doesn't look too good.'

The weather steadily deteriorated, and the wind began to bellow, creeping up to gale force 7. The troop ships lurched and bucked through the 'breakers and boiling surf, whipped into needle spray'. Landing craft tore free of their davits and smashed into the decks. Cables snapped. The gale – some called it 'Mussolini's wind' – screamed louder. Some soldiers prayed or cursed, but most 'lay in their hammocks, green and groaning', surrounded by the stench of vomit and fear.

While all around him retched, Major Derrick Leverton of the 12th Light Anti-Aircraft Regiment of the Royal Artillery, jovial heir to a long line of British undertakers, played another hand of bridge with himself in the officers' mess and happily munched the latest rations: 'We are now getting Cadbury's-filled blocks,' he told his mother. 'I had a Peppermint Crème and a Caramello – very nice.' Derrick, known to all as 'Drick', was thoroughly enjoying 'the show', as he referred to the invasion. He would have been happier still had he known of the small but important part played by his brother Ivor in paving the way for the invasion, by ferrying a dead body to Hackney mortuary in the middle of the night. Like Ivor, Drick had an irrepressible talent for looking on the bright side of everything, the consequence of being brought up in a family dedicated to dealing with death. 'It was a most excellent cruise,' he wrote, describing the hellish trip to Sicily. 'Once we were clear of land, everyone was told the whole plan: date, time and everything. We had maps, plans, models, a copy of *A Soldier's Guide to Sicily* and a copy of Monty's message each.' Drick was particularly impressed by the naval officer who briefed the troops on the strategic importance of Sicily. 'He was excellent. He looked like a masculine edition of Noël Coward.' Major Leverton's task would be to set up his field battery on the beach and shoot down any enemy planes attacking the invasion forces.

Leverton could not sleep. 'I went up on deck just before the sun set and could see the Sicilian mountains quite clearly in the distance.' The wind was now dropping. 'The sea had been wickedly rough all afternoon, but it had now calmed down. I definitely believe it was a miracle.' The soldiers had already set to work with chalk on the landing craft, on which were scrawled a variety of joking messages: 'Day Trips to the Continent' and 'See Naples and Die'. Shortly before midnight, Leverton watched the heavy bombers passing overhead, followed by towed gliders, packed with troops for the assault.

'I was standing up on deck by myself then. I had previously often wondered what my feelings would be when the party started. I was disappointed to find that I had absolutely none. Although I was perfectly conscious that quite a lot of people I knew were about to be killed and that I might be just about to kick the bucket myself, I wasn't really interested. I didn't feel excited or heroic or anything like that. I seemed to be watching a play.'

Drick trotted below for a final hand of bridge ('rather a nice small slam') and another Cadbury's Caramello.

At the same moment, just a few miles ahead, in the darkness, Bill Jewell was setting the stage for the next act of the play. Submerged, the crew had heard the noise of the E-boat propellers fade as the torpedo attack vessel moved off. After twenty more minutes of listening, the *Seraph* cautiously resurfaced. The German boat was nowhere to be seen. Perhaps she was lying in wait for an ambush. If so, the two vessels would have to fight it out. The deadline was now less than an hour away. 'There could be no more diving – this time the buoy had to be laid.' The wind had dropped, but the sea was still choppy, making the task of dropping the homing buoy 'three times as difficult as it should have been'. Just after midnight, the buoy was hauled back on deck for a second time, and dropped at the precise spot indicated, 1,000 yards offshore. Jewell now heard, for the first time, the low, thickening drone in the skies above, hitherto masked by the wind. 'Unseen planes, hundreds of them, were roaring through the dark skies overhead. The vanguard of the invasion! "Invasion!" That electrifying word.'

For the first time, Jewell wondered if victory might finally be in sight: 'The invasion of Sicily would be a long stride in the direction of Europe, and at least a short step on the road to Berlin,' he reflected. If it succeeded. The same thoughts were echoed among the assault troops. An American journalist sailing with the 5th Division wrote: 'Many of the men on this ship believe that the operation will determine whether this war will end in stalemate or whether it will be fought to a clear-cut decision.'

Jewell heard a series of loud explosions and, looking back towards the land, he could see 'great fires springing up in every direction'. Those paratroopers who had survived the flight and the drop were now at work. At the same time, above the echo of detonations and the drone of aircraft, Jewell picked up another noise. The wind had now dropped completely, as it often does in the Mediterranean, and he could now hear 'the faint throb of approaching engines'. Italian coastal radar had also picked up the shape of the advancing fleet. Seconds later, a battery of searchlights from the shore turned night to day, and the British submarine found herself in the limelight. 'Their blindingly brilliant beams cut across the water and blended into a dazzling ball of light concentrated on *Seraph*.' In normal circumstances, this would have been the cue to dive, but Jewell's orders were to stay put until the flotilla arrived. The shore guns opened fire, and for the next ten minutes – 'a nerve-tightening, shell-packed eternity' – the *Seraph* sat immobile, as hell exploded all around her. The cook, crouched behind a machine gun, cursed eloquently. Each shell sent up a plume of water, and the lookouts huddled into the sides of the conning tower, 'as much to avoid the cascading water as to find protection from flying shrapnel'. Between explosions, the 'throbbing beat' grew louder.

Then, out of the gloom, came 'a flicker of light from the leading destroyer of the mighty invasion fleet'. Moments later the ships took on form, as 'dark shapes emerged slowly from the shadows'. Forgetting the shells dropping around him, Jewell thought he had never seen anything so lovely. 'The English language needs a new descriptive noun to replace the hackneyed word *armada*,' he wrote. 'As far as my night glasses would carry, I saw hundreds of ships following in orderly fashion.' The destroyer searchlights now picked out the gun emplacements on shore, 'like footlights on a stage', and opened fire. 'Shells whistled high overhead.' Enemy planes screamed over, dropping flares to aid the onshore gunners.

Out at sea, Derrick Leverton admired the flak pouring into the sky 'with different coloured tracer', and the shimmering light in the sky as the dry wheat fields above the beaches ignited. It was horribly beautiful. 'With flares, searchlights and blazing fires, plus the vivid chromatic effects of bomb bursts and shell explosions, all of Sicily so far as the eye could reach was like nothing in the world so much as a huge pyrotechnical show.' The first destroyer passed the *Seraph*, her American crew 'cheering the stubborn little submarine'. Moments later, a small landing craft approached, with an American naval captain standing in the stern. Above the noise, he shouted: 'Ahoy *Seraph*! The Admiral has sent me over to thank you for a great job of work.' Jewell gave what he later admitted was 'a slightly astonished salute'. But the captain had not finished his peroration. 'You know, those boys who landed are going to remember for a long time how you guided 'em in . . .'

This was the moment for the *Seraph* to 'slide warily back into the protective darkness'. Jewell took a last look back at the shore, where 'tiny, darting flashes marked the progress of the assault force as the tommy guns blazed a path through the defenders'. Bill Darby's US Rangers had hit the beach at Gela. Jewell 'hoped the friendly, ever-joking colonel would do nothing foolhardy'.

Leading from the front, since he knew no other place to lead from, Bill Darby stormed up the beach like a man possessed, which he was; through the defences, and straight on to the town of Gela, much of which had already been demolished by the naval guns. Italian troops of the Livorno Division attempted to make a stand at the town's cathedral, and were swiftly overwhelmed by the Rangers. Darby personally held off an Italian counterattack by light Renault tanks, armed only with a .30-calibre machine gun mounted on his jeep. Realising that something more substantial was needed, he ran back to the beach, obtained a 37mm anti-tank gun, opened its ammunition box with an axe, and then, with the help of a captain, used it to blow up another Italian tank as it bore down on his command post. For good measure, he popped a grenade on the tank hatch. Its terrified Italian crew immediately surrendered.

Some twelve hours into the invasion, Darby took a rolled-up American flag from his backpack and nailed it to the door of the Fascist Party headquarters in Gela's main square. After the battle of Gela, Patton awarded Darby the Distinguished Service Cross, and a promotion to full colonel. He accepted the medal, and turned down the promotion, again. 'Darby is really a great soldier,' marvelled Patton.

To the east, Major Derrick Leverton was taking the invasion at a more leisurely pace. Having 'wished my chaps good luck. All perfectly normal and matter-of-fact', the undertaker waited on deck to be called to the landing craft. 'As there was still a bit of time in hand, I went to sleep.' Leverton holds the distinction of being the only man to doze off in the middle of the biggest seaborne invasion man had yet staged. There was, he recalled, 'quite a bit of banging about going on in the background', but Derrick had no problem dropping off. As acts of heroism go, this very nearly compares to the exploits of Colonel Darby.

'It was getting close to dawn, and the hills could just be seen in silhouette' when Leverton clambered into the landing craft. In a few minutes he was ashore, after wading through the wreckage of gliders that had made 'slightly premature landings'. Two dead paratroopers lay on the beach. Leverton was the last man to be upset by the sight of dead bodies ('The first thing I was conscious of was the delicious smell of crushed thyme'). He and his men headed to the spot chosen for the gun emplacement, straight through a minefield. 'Occasional mines went off, making a hell of a row and a lot of black smoke.' While his guns were unloaded, Leverton decided it was time for a cup of tea. His rations, he was delighted to find, contained 'tea-sugar-and-milk powder', which could be brewed simply by adding hot water. 'Most nourishing, appetising and intelligent,' thought Drick. Then he was dive-bombed.

This, he told his mother in a letter, 'added zest to the party'. 'As the bombs came down, I hopped down beside a stone wall. A lot of dust and stuff flew about, and when I got up I found a bit of stone as big as a football had been blown out of the wall a few feet from my head.' Only an incurable optimist like Leverton could see the bright side of being bombed. 'Another bomb fell in the sea and splashed us with nice cool water.' In case of further attacks, the undertaker instructed his men to dig 'little graves about three feet deep which were most comfortable'. The guns had still not been unloaded, so Leverton tucked himself up in his foxhole, and went back to sleep. Unlike his nourishing kip on the boat, this sleep was less restful. 'I had rather an awful sort of dream of dive bombing and so forth and I woke up with a glorious sort of feeling that it was only a dream, when I realised it wasn't a dream and the blighters were just above me in their dive.' The bombs caused only minor damage, although, as he wrote to his parents, 'the concussion in my grave jarred a bit'.

By nightfall, the guns were assembled, and in action. To Leverton's satisfaction, one dive-bomber was shot down on the first day. Over the next six weeks, eleven more kills would follow, 'plus quite a lot of "possibles" and "damaged"'. Leverton was happy. 'Our chaps are very bucked at knowing we were the first battery to go into action in Europe since Dunkirk.'

It was hot on the beach, and organising the guns in long drill slacks and gaiters was sweaty work. 'I didn't feel I was suitably dressed for the job,' wrote Major Leverton. 'I therefore designed myself a utility invasion suit, consisting of a thin shirt, my blue Jantzen swimming shorts, a pair of blue gym shoes and a tin hat. An excellent and highly recommended costume.'

Lieutenant Colonel Alexis Baron von Roenne, chief German intelligence analyst and anti-Nazi conspirator.

Wilhelm Leissner, alias Gustav Lenz, codename 'Heidelberg', head of German military intelligence in Spain.

Adolf Clauss, butterfly collector and the senior Abwehr officer in Huelva.

Alan Hillgarth: spy-master in Madrid (*above*), gold-hunter in South America (*top right*), novelist in his spare time and, in the words of Ian Fleming, a 'war-winner'.

Francis Haselden, Britain's vice consul in Huelva.

Two photographs taken by the Spanish police of Lieutenant Colonel Dudley Wrangel Clarke, the officer in command of deception for Operation Husky. Clarke was arrested in women's clothes in Madrid. He was then allowed to change into more conventional attire before being photographed again.

Juan Pujol García, Agent Garbo, the most celebrated double agent of the Second World War.

Colonel José López Barrón Cerruti, the Spanish security chief who played a key role in obtaining the documents.

Lieutenant Mariano Pascual del Pobil Bensusan, the Spanish naval officer and acting judge in Huelva.

Dr Eduardo Fernández del Torno, the Spanish pathologist who carried out the autopsy.

Lieutenant Bill Jewell, commander of the *Seraph*

Rosemary Galloway, fiancée of Bill Jewell

Churchill and his senior officers plan the invasion of Sicily at the George Hotel in Algiers. Admiral Andrew Cunningham and General Sir Harold Alexander, the two intended 'recipients' of the Mincemeat letters, are standing behind Churchill, centre and right; the addressee of the third letter, General Dwight Eisenhower, is seated right. General Bernard Montgomery is standing far right.

General Sir Harold Alexander, the commander of Allied ground forces, who usually looked 'as if he had just had a steam bath, a massage, a good breakfast and a letter from home'.

Admiral Wilhelm Canaris, the formidable chief of the Abwehr, German military intelligence.

Derrick Leverton, undertaker, gunnery officer and unsung hero of the Sicilian invasion.

The invasion flotilla steaming towards Sicily.

The tanks roll ashore on the south coast of Sicily.

British soldiers pass shells ashore.

Sicilians greet the Allied invaders as liberators.

Alexis von Roenne on trial before the Nazi People's Court, accused of plotting against Hitler. He was found guilty, inevitably, and hanged in Berlin-Plötzensee prison on 11 October 1944.

Charles Cholmondeley hunting locusts in the Middle East in Bedouin costume.

A still from the 1956 film *The Man Who Never Was*: Ewen Montagu, right, plays an air vice marshal; the American actor Clifton Webb, left, plays Montagu.

And so, as the bombs fell around him, this heroic British undertaker sat in his own grave, wearing his swimming trunks and a helmet, drinking a nice cup of tea.

He looked ridiculous and, at the same time, bloody magnificent.

Mussolini was woken by an army colonel at six in the morning, to be told that the invasion of Sicily was underway. Il Duce was bullish: 'Throw them back into the sea, or at least nail them to the shore.' He had been right all along: Sicily was the obvious target. 'I'm convinced our men will resist, and besides, the Germans are sending reinforcements,' he said. 'We must be confident.'

Never was confidence more misplaced. By the end of the day, more than 100,000 Allied troops were ashore, with 10,000 vehicles. The Italian defenders surrendered in large numbers, often simply stripping off their uniforms and walking away, or running. Sicilian cheers, not bullets, greeted the invaders in many places. The British 8th Army had expected some 10,000 casualties in the first week of the invasion; just one-seventh of that number were killed or wounded. The Navy had anticipated the loss of up to 300 ships in the first two days; barely a dozen were sunk.

At 11.00 the previous evening, André Latham, Agent Gilbert, had sent a wireless message to his German handlers: 'Most important. Have learned from reliable source that large force now on its way to Sicily. Invasion may be expected hourly.' He was only telling the defenders what they already knew, for the first major alert had reached Italian coastal units several hours before Jewell dropped his homing buoy. By then, it was far too late for the defenders to make adequate preparations, and the bombing of the Sicilian telephone network ensured that many units remained unaware of the attack until it was well underway. Some went to bed, assuming the enemy would not be so rash as to attack in the middle of a storm. The Italian commander in Sicily was fully expecting an attack – indeed, the Italian intelligence services were never as taken in by the deception as their German counterparts – yet owing in part to Operation Derrick, the secondary deception, the assault was expected in the west, not the south.

As predicted, the response of the German divisions, stationed inland, was more vigorous. But by the time the Germans counterattacked on Sunday, 11 July, crucial time had been lost, and the Allied beachhead was firmly in place. Spitfires attacked the Luftwaffe's Sicilian headquarters, disorientating what remained of German air defences at the crucial moment. Field Marshal Kesselring had sent the 15th Panzer Division to intercept the expected invasion in the west of the island, leaving the Hermann Goering Panzers to absorb the brunt of the assault. The Germans did nothing to hide their disgust as the Italian troops melted away, and the coastal defences collapsed like sandcastles in a hurricane. A message to Berlin, sent on the day after the landings, reported the 'complete failure of coastal defence' and noted sourly that 'on enemy penetration many of the local police and civil authorities fled. In Syracuse, the enemy landings gave rise to plundering and rioting by the population, who accepted the landings with indifference.' So many Italians surrendered in the first two days that the long lines of prisoners impeded the advancing troops. Kesselring complained that 'half-clothed Italian soldiers were careering around the countryside in stolen lorries'.

At 5.15 on the afternoon of D-Day, Kesselring ordered the Hermann Goering Division: 'at once and with all forces attack and destroy whatever opposes the division. The Führer has ordered all forces to be brought into operation immediately in order to prevent the enemy from establishing itself.' The German tanks could not break through. Some forty-three were destroyed, in bitter and bloody combat. The commander of the Goering Division conceded: 'The counterattack against hostile landings has failed.' The German tanks rumbled north, to continue the fight inland. General Patton, screeching around the battlefield in his jeep, called it 'the shortest Blitzkrieg in history'. Montgomery agreed with him on this, if nothing else. 'The German in Sicily is doomed. Absolutely doomed. He won't get away.'

The conquest of the island was just beginning, more ferocious fighting was to come, but the Sicilian D-Day was over, and won.

Hook, Line and Sinker

A loud cheer erupted from Room 13 as the news of success in Sicily broke. Cholmondeley performed a shuffling dance, and a strange ululation. 'Auntie' Joan Saunders wiped her eyes.

The strain of waiting had been almost unbearable. As the success of Operation Mincemeat became clear, Montagu privately feared his part in the war might be coming to an end. 'Even if I have once brought off something really important and worthwhile . . . I'm never going to be allowed to do anything of the kind again.' The pressure had left the planners hollow-eyed and, in Montagu's words, 'too keyed-up to read a book or to get to sleep'.

Looking back, Montagu recalled the flooding relief as the Allies surged through Sicily. 'It is really impossible to describe the feeling of joy and satisfaction at knowing that the team must have saved the lives of hundreds of Allied soldiers during the invasion – a feeling mixed with the delight that we had managed to do what we said we could do and what so many of our seniors had said was impossible – and what I have always thought even Churchill really thought was only worth trying as a desperate measure.' For Montagu, a special pleasure lay in the subsequent discovery that Hitler himself had fallen for the phoney documents: 'Joy of joys to anyone, and particularly a Jew, the satisfaction of knowing that they had directly and specifically fooled that monster.'

The deception had succeeded beyond every expectation, and Montagu was jubilant: 'We fooled those of the Spaniards who assisted the Germans, we fooled the German intelligence service both in Spain and in Berlin, we fooled the German operational staff and supreme command, we fooled Keitel, and, finally, we fooled Hitler himself, and kept him fooled right up to the end of July.' The operation was also gratifyingly economical: 'One specially made canister, one battledress uniform, some dry ice, the time of a few officers, a van drive to Scotland and back, about sixty miles added to HMS *Seraph*'s passage and a few sundries: about £200 at most.'

There was no grand celebration over the success of Operation Mincemeat, no return to the Gargoyle Club with Montagu and Jean Leslie playing the parts of Bill Martin and his beloved Pam. Montagu's wife, Iris, perhaps prompted by the dark hints from her mother-in-law, had announced that she was returning from America with the children. Montagu knew that Hitler was still planning to unleash pilotless flying bombs on London, and that the capital remained deeply unsafe. Since this information came from Ultra, however, he could not tell Iris. 'The most I could do was make vague references to Hitler's last fling. But this made no impression on her.' It was probably not Hitler's fling that worried her. Iris and the children returned to London while the invasion of Sicily was underway. The reunion was a joyful one. The photograph of Pam in her bathing suit, lovingly signed, was swiftly removed from Montagu's dressing table. Montagu could not yet explain what that was all about. Perhaps this was just as well.

Secret messages of congratulation flooded in from those who had touched, or been touched by, Operation Mincemeat. Dudley Clarke, the cross-dressing maverick behind 'A' Force, wrote: 'I do congratulate you most warmly on the success of your "M" operation. It was very remarkable and a fine piece of organisation and whatever the developments may be you have achieved 100 per cent success.' General Nye also applauded the planners: 'It is a most interesting story, and it seems it was swallowed [whole].' Frank Foley, the celebrated MI6 officer who had helped thousands of Jews to escape from Germany before the war, told Montagu that the operation had been 'the greatest achievement in the [deception] line ever brought off'. In his diary, Guy Liddell celebrated: 'Mincemeat has been an outstanding success.'

There was already talk of medals for the framers of Operation Mincemeat. Johnnie Bevan and Ewen Montagu had spent months at loggerheads, but to Bevan's great credit he insisted that both Montagu and Cholmondeley deserved formal recognition, albeit secretly. 'From evidence at present available it appears that a certain deception operation proved a considerable success and influenced German dispositions with all-important strategical and operational results. The fact that it achieved such very successful results must be attributed in large measure to the ingenuity and tireless energy on the part of these two officers.' Montagu had pushed the operation through by force of personality, while Cholmondeley 'was the originator of this ingenious scheme and was responsible, in conjunction with a certain naval officer, for the detailed execution of the operation'. Both men, Bevan recommended, 'should receive a similar decoration, since each seems to have played equally vital parts on the plot'.

Montagu was so delighted by the success of Mincemeat that he proposed a sequel. A plane carrying the Polish Prime Minister in exile, Władysław Sikorski, had crashed on take-off from Gibraltar on 4 July. Six days later, on Sicilian D-Day, Montagu sent a note to Bevan pointing out that 'papers from Sikorski's aircraft are still washing up and likely to reach the Spanish shore', and suggesting that this might be an opportunity to plant some false documents among the debris. The object would be 'to show that Mincemeat was genuine and that we are going to attack Greece, etc., and that we only delayed it and switched from Brimstone [Sardinia] to Sicily because we suspected that the Spaniards might have shown the papers in

Mincemeat to the Germans'. Mincemeat Mark II was vetoed by Commodore Rushbrooke, the Director of Naval Intelligence, because the Germans could not be expected to fall for the same ruse twice. 'Not worth trying. The Spaniards will know that everything of importance has been recovered, and a valuable secret "wash up" could have no verisimilitude.'

The success of the Sicily invasion could not, of course, be attributed to Operation Mincemeat alone. To an important degree, the deception plan reinforced what the Germans already believed. Every element of Operation Barclay – of which Mincemeat was but one strand – tended to back up that misperception. Moreover, the comparative weakness of German forces in Sicily reflected Hitler's mounting doubts about Italy's commitment to the war. Sicily was a strategic jewel, but it was also an island, physically separated from the rest of the Axis forces. If large numbers of German troops were committed to defend it, but Italy dropped out of the war, they would be isolated, and Sicily would become, in Kesselring's words, a 'mousetrap for all German and Italian forces fighting down there'.

Yet up to, and even after, the invasion of Sicily, the effects of Mincemeat lingered on in German tactical planning, slewing attention to east and west. The night before the attack, Keitel had distributed a 'Most Immediate' analysis of Allied intentions, predicting a major Allied landing in Greece, and a joint attack on Sardinia and Sicily: 'Western assault forces appear to be ready for an immediate attack while the eastern forces appear to be still forming up,' he wrote. 'A subsequent landing on the Italian mainland is less probable than one on the Greek mainland.' Half the Allied troops available in North Africa, Keitel predicted, would be used 'to reinforce the bridgehead which . . . would be established in Greece'.

Ultra intercepts showed that four hours after the landings, twenty-one ground-attack aircraft took off from Sicily, which was now under attack, heading for Sardinia, which was not. The same day, the Abwehr in Berlin sent a message to its

Spanish office 'stating that the High Command in Berlin were particularly anxious that a sharp lookout should be kept for convoys passing through the straits of Gibraltar which might be going to attack Sardinia. It gave as a reason for these orders that the high command appreciated that the attack on Sicily was possibly only a feint and that the main attack was going to be elsewhere.' That assessment, Naval Intelligence noted with satisfaction, was 'entirely consistent with the Mincemeat story'.

The same effects were visible at the other end of the Mediterranean, where the fictional attack on Greece was directly undermining Germany's ability to repel the genuine attack on Sicily. The 'R-boats', or *Räumboote*, were 150-ton minesweepers and a key component of German naval strength, used to pick up mines but also for convoy escort, coastal patrol, mine-laying and rescuing downed air crews. On 12 July, Sicilian D-Day +2, the commander of German naval forces in Italy sent a cable to headquarters 'complaining that the departure of the 1st R-boat Group, sent to the Aegean for the defence of Greece, had prejudiced the defence of Sicily, as the Gela barrages were no longer effective, the shortage of escort vessels was "chronic", and the departure of any more boats, as ordered, would have a serious effect.' Yet the belief in an impending Greek attack remained rooted: in late July, Rommel was despatched by Hitler to Salonika to take command of the defence of Greece if and when the Allies attacked. The Abwehr laid intricate plans in anticipation of the expected assault on Greece, including teams of secret agents and saboteurs to be left behind if the Germans were forced to withdraw.

The recriminations on the Axis side started almost immediately after the invasion. When he heard that the Italian coastal defenders had failed to repulse the attack, Goebbels muttered darkly about 'macaroni-eaters', but refrained from pointing out that he had never quite believed in the Abwehr's great intelligence coup. Hitler never admitted he had been fooled, but his military response to the invasion was proof enough that he knew he had made a major strategic error in failing to reinforce Sicily. 'Hitler's own reaction was immediate. He ordered two more German formations, 1st Parachute and 29th Panzer Grenadier Division to be hurried to Sicily to throw the invaders into the sea.' Again, it was too late.

Others within the German hierarchy realised they had been sold a fantastic and extremely damaging lie, and responded with fury. Joachim von Ribbentrop, the Nazi Foreign Minister, demanded a full explanation of why Major Martin's documents indicating that the attack on Sicily was a decoy had been so blithely accepted as genuine: 'This report has been proved to be false, since the operation directed by the English and Americans against Sicily, far from being a sham attack, was of course one of their planned major offensives in the Mediterranean ... The report from "a wholly reliable source" was deliberately allowed by the enemy to fall into Spanish hands in order to mislead us.' Von Ribbentrop suspected that the Spaniards were in on the ruse all along, and ordered his ambassador in Madrid, Dieckhoff, to conduct a full-scale witch-hunt: 'Undertake a most careful reappraisal of the whole matter and consider in so doing whether the persons from whom the information emanated are directly in the pay of the enemy, or whether they are hostile to us for other reasons.' Dieckhoff blustered, and tried to swerve out of the way: 'The documents had been found on the body of a shot-down English officer, and handed over in the original to our counterintelligence here by the Spanish general staff. The documents were investigated by the Abwehr and I have not heard their investigations cast any doubt on their authenticity.' Rather weakly, Dieckhoff argued that the enemy must have altered their plans after losing the documents. 'The English and Americans had every intention of acting in the way laid down in the documents. Only later did they change their minds, possibly regarding the plans as compromised by the shooting down of the English bearer.'

Von Ribbentrop was having none of it. 'The British Secret Service is quite capable of causing forged documents to reach the Spaniards,' he insisted. The deception had been intended to persuade Germany 'that we should not adopt any defensive measures . . . or that we should adopt only inadequate ones'. With the Allies storming through Sicily, he wanted names, and he wanted heads to roll. 'It is practically certain that the English purposely fabricated these misleading documents and allowed them to fall into Spanish hands so that they might reach us by this indirect route. The only question is whether the Spaniards saw through this game, or whether they were themselves taken in.' The finger of suspicion pointed at Admiral Moreno, the double-dealing Minister of Marine, and at Adolf Clauss and his Spanish spies. Further up the chain of command, it cast a shadow over the Abwehr in Spain, and the intelligence analysts in Berlin who had verified the fakes. 'Who originally circulated the information?' demanded Von Ribbentrop. 'Are they directly in the pay of our enemies?'

Karl-Erich Kuhlenthal was also in the firing line. 'After the invasion of Italy had actually taken place, Berlin reprimanded [the Abwehr office in] Spain for having failed to submit adequate data.' Kuhlenthal, as adept at escaping blame as he was skilled at gathering credit, kept his head down until the storm passed. He must have known that the documents passed to Berlin back in May had been proven entirely misleading, but he said nothing. Kuhlenthal watched the invasion of Sicily with mounting consternation, but at least one of his fellow intelligence experts, who had played an equal role in facilitating the fraud, may have witnessed the unfolding of events with secret satisfaction. Not until 26 July, more than a fortnight after the landings in Sicily, did Alexis von Roenne, the head of Foreign Armies West (FHW) and secret anti-Nazi conspirator, issue a report stating, 'at present at any rate, the attack planned against the Peloponnese had been given up'. Von Roenne was too canny to acknowledge that the letters were fakes; he merely asserted, like Dieckhoff, that the plans had changed. In Hitler's world there was no room for an honest mistake.

The most significant victim in the fallout, on the Axis side, was Mussolini himself. From the first Allied footfall in Sicily,

Il Duce was doomed, though he refused to acknowledge it. Goebbels noted: 'The only thing certain in this war is that Italy will lose it.' The Pact of Steel was cracking up. By 18 July, the Allied front line had moved halfway up Sicily. That day, Mussolini sent an almost defiant cable to Hitler: 'The sacrifice of my country cannot have as its principal purpose that of delaying a direct attack on Germany.' The Führer summoned him to an urgent meeting. Il Duce did not care to be summoned anywhere, but went meekly.

The two fascist leaders met in Feltre, fifty miles from Venice, where Hitler launched into a long harangue, lambasting the 'inept and cowardly' Italian troops in Sicily and insisting: 'What has happened now in Sicily must not be allowed to happen again.' In the midst of the tirade, an aide interrupted to inform Mussolini that Rome was under massive air attack, the first time the capital had been targeted. Mussolini sat impassively through the two-hour monologue. The great Italian bull seemed to be fatally gored, diminished and distant. At the end of the excruciating meeting, he said simply: 'We are fighting for a common cause, Führer.' It sounded more like an epitaph than a statement of solidarity.

On 22 July, Palermo fell to Patton's American troops. Three days later, Mussolini was outvoted by the Fascist Grand Council, summoned by King Victor Emmanuel III to a private audience, and toppled. 'It can't go on any longer,' said the King: Mussolini must resign at once, to be replaced by Marshal Pietro Badoglio, the former chief of the armed forces. Italy's deposed dictator left the royal Villa Savoia hidden in an ambulance, and the new government in Rome began the secret task of extracting Italy from the war, and Hitler's poisonous embrace. In Badoglio's words: 'Fascism fell, as was fitting, like a rotten pear.' The next day, Rommel was recalled from Greece to defend northern Italy.

Would it have fallen so fast, or rotted so quickly, without Operation Mincemeat? The invasion of Sicily was a far from perfect military operation, bedevilled by poor planning and personal rivalries between selfish and powerful men. The airborne landings were horrifically costly: only 12 out of 147 British gliders landed on target, and 67 crashed into the sea. A relatively small contingent of German troops successfully held up the advance of an Allied host seven times larger, and then evacuated the island to continue the battle up mainland Italy. The fight for Sicily was grim and bitter. But how much worse would it have been had the Nazi high command been prepared for it? What if, say, the full-strength, battle-tempered First Panzer Division, instead of being despatched to Greece to await an imaginary invasion, had been deployed along the coast at Gela?

It is impossible to calculate how many lives, on both sides of the conflict, were saved by Operation Mincemeat, nor exactly how much it contributed to hastening the end of the war and the defeat of Hitler. The Allies had expected it would take ninety days to conquer Sicily. The occupation was completed on 17 August, thirty-eight days after the invasion began. Looking back after the war, Professor Percy Ernst Schramm, keeper of the OKW war diary, left no doubt that the fake documents had played a critical role: 'It is well known that under the influence of the letters, Hitler moved troops to Sardinia and southern Greece, thereby preventing them from taking part in the defence against [Husky].' In September, Italy formally surrendered, although the war in Italy would not end until May 1945.

The impact of the Sicilian invasion was felt 1,500 miles away on the blood-soaked Eastern Front, and most importantly around the Russian city of Kursk. On 4 July, Hitler had launched Operation Citadel, his massive, long-awaited offensive against the Red Army following the German defeat at Stalingrad. The Battle of Kursk would be history's largest tank battle, the most costly day of aerial warfare yet fought, and Germany's last major strategic offensive in the east. With 900,000 troops and 3,000 tanks, Field Marshal Erich von Manstein planned to eliminate the bulge in the lines known as the Kursk salient, encircle the Soviets, and then head south to reconquer more lost territory.

Repeated delays, and excellent Soviet intelligence, ensured that the Red Army had a good idea of what was coming. Like Sicily, Kursk was an obvious target; unlike Sicily, by the time the attack came, it was massively fortified, with layered, in-depth lines of defence, a million mines, 3,000 miles of trenches, and an army of 1.3 million men, with reserves strategically placed to strike back when German troops were exhausted. After five days of furious combat, the battle still hung in the balance. The German blitzkrieg in the north of the battlefront had stalled, with terrible losses on both sides, but in the south the German forces, although heavily depleted, pushed on. By 12 July, the German forces had broken through the first two Soviet lines of defence, and believed that the final breakthrough was at hand.

But by now, events in the Mediterranean had changed the strategic picture, and the cast of Hitler's mind. Three days after the invasion of Sicily, the Führer summoned Von Manstein to the Wolf's Lair, his headquarters in East Prussia, and announced that he was suspending Operation Citadel. The Field Marshal insisted that the Red Army was tottering, and the German offensive was at a critical stage: 'On no account should we let go of the enemy until the mobile reserves which he had committed were decisively beaten.' But Hitler had made up his mind. 'Inescapably faced with the dilemma of deciding where to make his main effort, he gave the Mediterranean preference over Russia.' One week after Allied troops landed on the shores of Sicily, Hitler cancelled the Eastern Front offensive, and ordered the transfer of the SS Panzer Korps to Italy. Hitler's decision to call off the attack, partly in order to divert forces to threatened Italy and the still-feared threat to the Balkans, marked the turning of the tide. For the first time, a blitzkrieg attack had failed before breaking through enemy lines. The Red Army launched a devastating counterattack, taking first Belgorod and Orel and then, on 11 August, the city of Kharkov. By November, Kiev itself would be liberated. The Third Reich never recovered from the failure of Operation Citadel, and from now until the end of the war, the German armies in the east were on the defensive as the Red Army rolled, inexorably, towards Berlin. 'With the failure of *Zitadelle* we have suffered a decisive defeat,' wrote General Heinz Guderian, the foremost German theorist of tank combat. 'From now on, the enemy was in undisputed possession of the initiative.'

Unsurprisingly, those involved in the planning and execution of Mincemeat were unanimous in their self-congratulation. A 'top secret' assessment of the operation, written shortly before the end of the war, described it as 'a small classic of deception, brilliantly elaborate in detail, completely successful in operation . . . The Germans took many actions, to their own prejudice, as a result of Mincemeat.' At the very least, the deception had encouraged Hitler to do what he already wanted to do, which was exactly what the Allies wanted him to do. The German defences in southern Europe had been spread 'as widely and thinly as possible', by stoking fears of multiple assaults, instead of the one, massive attack on southern Sicily. 'There can be no doubt that Mincemeat succeeded in the desired effect [and] caused the dispersal of the German effort at a crucial time . . . it was largely responsible for the fact that the east end of Sicily, where we landed, was much less defended both by troops and fortifications.' Even more gratifying, the progress of the lie had been tracked at every stage: 'Special intelligence enabled us to know that the enemy was deceived by it.' In one of his last private messages to Churchill from Madrid, Alan Hillgarth described how the success of the Sicilian campaign had transformed public and official opinion in Spain: 'Sicily has impressed everyone and delighted most. Mussolini's resignation and what it presages has stunned opponents.' The fear that Franco might side with the Axis was now over, and so was Hillgarth's role in Spain.

Bill Jewell often wondered, in later years, how much Operation Mincemeat 'really affected the outcome in Sicily'. He was told that this was 'impossible to estimate'. Deception may not be measured in battlefield yards won, or soldiers lost, but it can be gauged in other ways, large and small: in the toppling of Mussolini and the buttressing of Hitler's fixation with the Balkans; in the thin defences on Sicily's coast that allowed the Allied army ashore with so little bloodshed; in the Axis troops tied up in Sardinia and the Peloponnese, and the great retreat at Kursk; in the Panzers, waiting on the shores of Greece for an attack that never came; in Derrick Leverton, sitting unscathed in his foxhole, as the German counterattack petered out.

Later historians have been equally convinced that the deception not only worked, but succeeded dramatically, and with a profound impact. Hugh Trevor-Roper called Operation Mincemeat 'the most spectacular single episode in the history of deception'. The official history of Second World War deception described it as 'perhaps the most successful single deception of the entire war'. It was also the luckiest. The deception depended on skill, timing and judgement, but it would never have succeeded without an astonishing run of good fortune.

Wars are won by men like Bill Darby, storming up the beach with all guns blazing, and by men like Leverton, sipping his tea as the bombs fall. They are won by planners, correctly calculating how many rations and contraceptives an invading force will need; by tacticians, laying out grand strategy; by generals, inspiring the men they command; by politicians, galvanising the will to fight; and by writers, putting war into words. They are won by acts of strength, bravery and guile. But they are also won by feats of imagination. Amateur, unpublished novelists, the framers of Operation Mincemeat, dreamed up the most unlikely concatenation of events, rendered them believable, and sent them off to war, changing reality through lateral thinking, and proving that it is possible to win a battle fought in the mind, from behind a desk, and from beyond the grave. Operation Mincemeat was pure make-believe; and it made Hitler believe something that changed the course of history.

This strange story was conceived in the mind of a writer, and put into action by a fisherman, who cast his fly on the water with no certainty of success but an angler's innate optimism and guile. The most fitting, and aptly fishy, tribute to the operation was contained in a telegram, sent to Winston Churchill on the day the Germans took the bait: 'Mincemeat swallowed rod, line and sinker.'

Mincemeat Revealed

Ewen Montagu began lobbying the British government for permission to reveal Operation Mincemeat before the war had even ended. In 1945 he was offered the 'considerable sum' of £750 to reveal the story, although who made the offer, and how they learned of Operation Mincemeat, is unclear. Montagu wrote to the War Cabinet Office asking to be allowed to publish his account of what had happened. 'I am a prejudiced party, but I feel strongly that no harm could result and good might well be obtained,' he wrote, adding that the story had already 'leaked fairly widely'. Anticipating the objection that the operation would reveal how Britain had partly lied its way to victory, he argued: 'It would pay to release Mincemeat as a specialised ad hoc operation to draw attention away from the fact that deception was a normal operation.'

Montagu's request was turned down flat. Guy Liddell of MI5 told him 'the Foreign Office would never allow publication in any form in view of the inevitable effect on our relationship with Spain'. Yet it was true that the story was starting to leak. Indeed, a copy of the report on Operation Mincemeat, one of only three made, had gone missing in March 1945. Another remained in Montagu's possession, apparently with Guy Liddell's blessing, 'in case the embargo should eventually be lifted'.

Two months after the Normandy landings, a British radio journalist named Sydney Moseley picked up the scent from a contact in British intelligence. Moseley had worked for the *Daily Express* and the *New York Times*; he was also John Logie Baird's business manager and a tireless promoter of the new technology of television. And he knew a good story when he heard one. In August 1944, Moseley broadcast an item on the Mutual Broadcasting System radio network in America: 'Our intelligence obtained over in England the body of a patient that had died, and dressed it up in the uniform of a senior officer. In due course this body . . . floated across the Channel to the enemy-occupied coast where, as was hoped, it was picked up. As a result of a set of faked documents, orders, and plans, the Nazis actually did concentrate their forces elsewhere, and when we made the big move into Normandy, they still regarded it as a feint.' Moseley concluded his report: 'I believe this story is the greatest of the war.' Moseley had the wrong location, and the wrong D-Day, but his story was close enough to the truth to put a gale-force wind up the Secret Service.

'Tar' Robertson wrote to Bevan, pointing out that while the Official Secrets Act could silence the inquisitive in Britain, it had no power in the US: 'Unless some action is taken fairly soon, this, being such an attractive subject, will produce sooner or later, a flood of stories in America, some of which will be true, others invented.' On the other hand, if the journalist was approached and urged to keep quiet, that would show that 'there was in fact some truth behind what Moseley says'. It would be better to ignore the story, and 'leave the American authorities and Moseley in ignorance on this whole question'. Even so, it was only a matter of time before others came hunting. Britain's spymasters were adamant: 'We should do our utmost to stop the true story getting out.'

The story, when it finally emerged, came not from an inquisitive journalist, but from Winston Churchill himself. In October 1949, Alfred Duff Cooper, later Viscount Norwich, the wartime Minister for Information, began work on a novel based on the story of Operation Mincemeat. *Operation Heartbreak* tells the story of 'William Maryngton', a man unable to serve his country in life, but deployed in death in a way that was equally unmistakable. The last chapter reads:

Dawn had not broken, but was about to do so, when the submarine came to the surface. The crew were thankful to breathe the cool, fresh air, and they were still more thankful to be rid of their cargo. The wrappings were removed, and the Lieutenant stood to attention and saluted as they laid the body of the officer in uniform as gently as possible on the face of the waters. A light breeze was blowing shoreward, and the tide was running in the same direction. So Willie went to war at last, the insignia of field rank on his shoulders, and a letter from his beloved lying close to his quiet heart.

Operation Heartbreak is a charming fiction, quite obviously based on fact.

Duff Cooper had learned of the case in March 1943, while head of the Security Executive, but he must also have obtained access to the Mincemeat file itself after the war was over. Montagu believed 'Duff Cooper learned of Mincemeat from Churchill in one of his expansive "after-dinner" moods and then was (I'm pretty sure, but my evidence doesn't amount to proof) shown a copy of the report by someone I won't name.' It is just possible that Montagu himself showed Duff Cooper the file, as a way of bringing pressure on the Government to allow him to tell the non-fiction version. Churchill may well have wanted the story to be told. When the other Operation Mincemeat – a simple minefield-laying operation – was revealed in the 1950s, Alan Brooke, former Chief of the Imperial General Staff, apparently got his Mincemeats confused and wrote: 'Sir W always wanted to hear this story told.'

The authorities in 1950, however, most emphatically did not want the story told, and when Whitehall got word of the contents of *Operation Heartbreak*, Duff Cooper came under intense pressure – possibly from the Prime Minister, Clement Attlee, himself – not to publish. The story, it was pointed out, might damage Anglo-Spanish relations, and British intelligence might want to use the same ruse in the future. Duff Cooper 'considered the objections to be ridiculous'. According to Charles Cholmondeley, Cooper threatened to say that he had learned the story 'direct from Churchill if prosecuted'. *Operation Heartbreak* was published on 10 November 1950, prompting a ripple of critical acclaim and 'consternation in security quarters'. It sold 40,000 copies.

The cat was now out of the bag, at least in fictional form, and Montagu renewed his demand to be allowed to publish, since 'there could not be one law for a Cabinet minister and a different one for the blokes who do the work'. He wrote to Emanuel 'Manny' Shinwell, the Defence Secretary, demanding to know whether Cooper would be prosecuted for breaching the Official Secrets Act and, if not, whether there was any reason why he should not now publish his own, non-fiction account. Again, the authorities resisted. Publication of the facts would be 'wholly contrary to the public interest', wrote Sir Harold Parker, Permanent Secretary to the Minister of Defence. 'Any true account would have to show how the law was manipulated to secure possession of a corpse, the forgery of documents from well-known firms (whether with their consent or not) and the use made of beliefs of Catholics' as part of the plot. Sir Harold also ordered Montagu to return the Mincemeat files, since 'there is no longer any reason for you to retain a copy of the record of the operation'.

Montagu immediately fired back: 'One would not think even the most ardent Catholic would be offended that a man of unknown religious belief was buried as a Catholic to save thousands of lives and render the invasion of Sicily more certain of success.' The Mincemeat files would remain firmly in his possession until the minister saw sense: 'I see no reason why I should hand over my copy.'

After months of wrangling, the authorities partly relented. In a later letter to John Godfrey, Montagu wrote: 'I forced Shinwell to agree that, if they did not prosecute Duff Cooper, they must give me permission to publish . . . Shinwell gave me a clear consent.'

The deal came with strings attached: Montagu must write an outline of what he planned to write, submit the finished manuscript for vetting, and 'sympathetically consider advice as to modification'. He began writing immediately. Initially he envisaged an extended magazine article, and contacted the editor of *Life* magazine, who was wildly enthusiastic. By April 1951, a first draft outline was completed. Now he hesitated, wondering whether 'it would be wrong to publish'.

Meanwhile an enterprising journalist named Ian Colvin, who had worked in Berlin before the war and would go on to become deputy editor of the *Daily Telegraph*, had picked up rumours that there was more to *Operation Heartbreak* than fiction, and went digging. In 1952, the diaries of Erwin Rommel were published, in which the Field Marshal described being sent to Greece soon after the invasion of Sicily to resist an expected attack. A footnote, written by Basil Liddell Hart, hinted at the connection to the story told in *Operation Heartbreak*. Ian Colvin, in Montagu's words, 'shot off to Spain' and began asking questions. When Britain's ambassador to Spain learned what the journalist was up to, he 'cabled back in a frenzy', fearful of a major breach in Anglo-Spanish relations. 'The Foreign Office's chief worry was that Colvin had been told by our ex vice-consul in Huelva that he had been in the know and had taken part in deceiving the Spanish government.' The Foreign Office took a dim view of 'using diplomats to lie and deceive their host government'.

The Foreign Office was not the only branch of the British government fearful of what Colvin might find, and urged the Joint Intelligence Committee to intervene. 'Further pressure was applied by the Home Office who were very worried lest it became known that a coroner had handed over a corpse with no one's permission.'

The Joint Intelligence Committee decided on a pre-emptive strike. Colvin had already been commissioned by the *Sunday Express*, and was getting close to the truth in Spain. A spoiling operation was launched. Montagu was told he should now write his account as long as he did not reveal any information on 'the true means by which the corpse was obtained and any details from which the man's real identity could be inferred'. He would have to do so very fast. He was 'rushed round to the *Sunday Express* who had first claim on Colvin's work and they said they would consider it if they got the story written by Monday so that they could decide before they got Colvin's'. This was an underhand trick. Colvin had worked hard on the story for two years: the Government, and the newspaper that had commissioned him, were now conniving to scoop him.

Montagu later wrote, disingenuously, that government permission to write his account had been 'wholly unexpected' and that permission to do so had been unsolicited. 'The request not to publish, which I had accepted, was altered to a request that I should write the true story and publish it as soon as possible so as to kill these dangerous untruths.' The reason given for the volte-face was that Colvin's account was likely to be 'so wildly inaccurate as to be dangerous'. The reverse was true: the danger of Colvin's account was its probable accuracy, in particular the fear that it would reveal the way British diplomats had deceived the Spanish government, and how Bentley Purchase had simply conjured up a corpse to order. The guardians of official secrecy knew they could edit and mould what Montagu might write. This would be a 'controlled version, in which delicate points could be modified', whereas Colvin, in Montagu's own words, was 'someone not under any control or influence'. If the story of Operation Mincemeat must be told, it would be told in a way that would not upset the Spanish, and conceal how the body was obtained.

Writing to John Godfrey, Montagu was quite explicit about the terms of his deal with the intelligence censors: he would not reveal secret information, most importantly the Ultra intercepts, and he would write nothing that could embarrass the Foreign or Home Offices. 'The return that the country got was therefore not only the protection of "our sources", but also the other two quite important points' – concealing the roles of Haselden and Hillgarth in Spain, and Purchase in London. The newspaper could edit the serialisation, but the final version would need to be approved by the Secret Service before publication: 'The *Express* will submit and get passed anything that they may add or any alterations that they may make.' The story of Operation Mincemeat would be an official publication in all but name.

Montagu claimed to have written his authorised account in the space of forty-eight hours 'with much black coffee and no sleep' in order to get it to the newspaper's offices by Monday, 24 January. In fact, a draft was complete, and had already been approved by the authorities and sent to the *Sunday Express*, at least three weeks before the newspaper's deadline. On 8 January, Montagu wrote to Jean Gerard Leigh ('or should it be "Pam"?'), warning her that his book was about to be published: 'The powers that be have decided that an accurate story by me "under control" would be less dangerous than an inaccurate one which might lead anywhere.' Montagu asked Jean for permission to use her photograph as 'Pam': 'We don't want to alter anything of that kind as we want to be able to say "this is true".' Montagu assured her that she would be identified only as 'a girl working in my section'. Montagu sent a simultaneous letter to Bill Jewell, informing him that 'Mincemeat is soon going to be published', and that his draft had been approved by Whitehall. 'My account has been vetted and passed,' he wrote. 'I felt that you ought not to be taken by surprise.'

Jewell raised no objection, but Jean was concerned: 'I was most interested to hear that parts of your and Bill's doubtful past are to be revealed to the unsuspecting public,' she wrote.

'But what should my answer be if someone sees through the ravages of time and identifies me with Pam!? . . . Perhaps you would come and have a drink one evening and put me "in the picture" if it is not too late.' Montagu suggested that if anyone made the connection and asked what she had done during the war, she should 'merely say that you were working in a branch of the War Office'.

Charles Cholmondeley wanted nothing to do with the project. As an MI5 officer, he refused to be named, but his natural reticence would have prevented his participation in any case. Montagu had first raised the idea of writing a book together two years earlier, after the appearance of *Operation Heartbreak*. He now offered to cut his former partner in on the deal, with a 25 per cent share of the profits from 'book, film rights, or other uses to which the story might be put'. Cholmondeley's response was typically polite, but firm. 'As you will recall, when you originally broached the subject in 1951, I felt, due to my position, that I could not take part in it.' In the interim, Cholmondeley had left MI5. 'Whilst the general situation has changed considerably,' he wrote, 'I do not feel that my own rather peculiar position has done so and therefore I must reaffirm my decision to take no part and accept no benefit from this publication. I am sure you will appreciate this difference in our positions, but reaching this decision has not been easy and believe me I am not less appreciative of your very generous offer.'

The first instalment of the story, proclaiming 'The war's most fantastic secret disclosed for the first time', appeared in the *Sunday Express* on 1 February, under the headline 'The Man Who Never Was' – the title was the inspiration of the news editor, Jack Garbutt. This was followed by two more instalments. Ian Colvin was understandably furious at being elbowed out of the story, but as a sop he was allowed to write an introduction and analysis to the pieces. His own book of the story – necessarily incomplete, but nonetheless a remarkable piece of investigation – appeared later that year under the title *The Unknown Courier.*

Montagu's book, *The Man Who Never Was*, was published a few months later by Evans Brothers, with the image of a faceless Marine on the cover (wrongly wearing service dress). It was an instant bestseller, and went on to sell more than 3 million copies. It has never been out of print.

Opinion among Montagu's former colleagues in the intelligence world was sharply divided over the decision to reveal Operation Mincemeat. Charles Cholmondeley made no comment on the contents, but was generous, as ever: 'I shall look forward to a gripping and soul-searing saga on the silver screen at some future date.' Mountbatten gave qualified support: 'Although I heartily disapproved of *Operation Heartbreak*, and told the author so when I saw him, once the beans had been spilt in that way I think it was probably a good thing that the true story should be told.' However, Archie Nye, the author of the plot's centrepiece, was sharply critical, telling Montagu that he would need 'a good deal of persuasion that the merits of publication exceeded the drawbacks'. John Masterman was also opposed. 'You and I don't agree on the wisdom of publishing Mincemeat in this form,' he wrote. 'I always thought that a good deal could be published with advantage but I also thought that such publication should be anonymous and with official sanction.' (Such scruples did not endure. In 1972, Masterman would publish his own account of the Double Cross System, under his own name, and in the teeth of strong official opposition.) The most trenchant criticism came from Admiral John Godfrey. 'Uncle John blitzed me on the phone in quite the old way,' Montagu told another former denizen of Room 13. The old admiral testily pointed out that the book claimed to be non-fiction, while withholding key truths: 'Your admirable *Man Who Never Was* covers up the real final secret – how did we know that the <u>Germans</u> had access to the despatches?'

The Man Who Never Was remains a classic of postwar literature. With a lawyer's precision, Montagu laid out the plot in careful steps, to reveal 'an exploit more astonishing than any story in war fiction'. More than half a century later it is still gripping, a tour de force of reconstruction.

Yet the book is – and was always intended to be – partial, in both senses. In some ways, it fulfilled the demands of postwar propaganda. In Montagu's telling, the British planners made no mistakes, and the Germans were duped without the slightest hint that anything might go wrong. Montagu can be forgiven for presenting himself as the hero of his own drama – many of those involved could or would not be identified – but in so doing, he made Operation Mincemeat appear to be a one-man show. Cholmondeley appears fleetingly in the book, under the pseudonym 'George'. The others who played roles, large or small – Alan Hillgarth, Gómez-Beare, Johnnie Bevan, Charles Fraser-Smith, Juan Pujol, Jean Leslie and many others – were not only unnamed, but in some cases simply excised from the story. The Ultra secret would not be revealed until the 1970s, so Montagu was unable to describe how the success of the operation had been tracked. The book was carefully vetted, and contained nothing that might embarrass the government: the extent to which British diplomatic officials had cooperated in deceiving the Spanish was glossed over, as was the level of Spanish collaboration with the Germans; the way the body had been obtained was made to seem entirely official and above board. Partly for dramatic effect, partly in obedience to the guardians of official secrecy, and partly because that is the way he was, Montagu 'managed to give the impression', wrote one detractor, 'that he was single-handedly responsible for the entire deception scheme'.

As for Glyndwr Michael, he was removed from the story, permanently, or so Montagu believed. In a first draft of *The Man Who Never Was*, he concocted a story in which the 'real' identity of the dead man was hinted at, misleadingly, as 'an only son, an officer of one of the services, from an old service family'. He wrote: 'His parents were then alive and we decided to take a chance on their agreeing to our plan. We could not tell them the whole story but we felt we could not in decency keep them completely in the dark. They did not like the idea – who would? – but they agreed on the strict condition that neither the real name nor any identifying particulars of their son would ever come out.'

In the final version of the book, however, he opted for an even vaguer explanation, claiming that relatives of the dead man had been asked for permission to use the body 'without saying what we proposed to do with it and why', and that 'permission, for which our indebtedness was great, was obtained on condition that I should never let it be known whose corpse it was'. Montagu couched his refusal to divulge the name as a matter of honour, since he had given his word to the relatives of the dead man. In 1977 he claimed that all those relatives had since died: 'I gave a solemn promise never to reveal whose body it was and, as there is no one alive from whom I can get a release, I can say no more.' The truth, of course, was that none of Michael's few relatives had ever been contacted, let alone asked for permission to use his body. This was a cover-up, to spare the blushes of the British government, and to avoid the admission that the body had been obtained by falsifying a legal certificate indicating burial outside the country, and used entirely without permission.

While not exactly a white lie, this untruth was surely an excusable shade of grey. In the midst of a ferocious war, Montagu and Cholmondeley had persuaded a coroner to bend the law in the national interest. Bentley Purchase had done so on the understanding that he would not be later called to account. The Joint Intelligence Committee would never have allowed Montagu to publish a book revealing that the body of Glyndwr Michael had, in effect, been seized illegally by government intelligence officers: that would have provoked a scandal, as well as undermining the moral high ground upon which *The Man Who Never Was* rested. If the identity had been revealed, then Glyndwr Michael's relatives might, with some reason, have kicked up an almighty stink. So Montagu hid the truth with another deception, and continued to hide it for the rest of his life.

During the war, Montagu had complained: 'My work is such that I will never be able to mention its importance and people will merely say "Oh, he didn't do much good in the war". I will therefore go down as someone who was a failure when tested in the war.' The publication of *The Man Who Never Was* turned him, almost overnight, into a celebrity. He toured the US, gave lectures, and appeared on American television alongside a chimpanzee named J. Fred Muggs. Hollywood swiftly came calling, as Cholmondeley had predicted, and a vigorous auction ensued. The film rights were finally purchased by 20th Century Fox.

The film of *The Man Who Never Was*, an Anglo-American Technicolor Cinemascope production directed by Ronald Neame, opened with a royal premiere attended by the Duchess of Kent, on 14 March 1956. Shot in Britain and Huelva, it starred the American actor Clifton Webb playing Montagu, and Gloria Grahame as 'Lucy', his secretary's fictional flatmate. André Morell played Sir Bernard Spilsbury. The screenplay, by Nigel Balchin, used the truth where convenient, and made up the rest, including an Irishman spying for the Nazis, played by Stephen Boyd, tasked with verifying the body's identity. Montagu declared himself entirely happy with the 'thrilling incidents which, although they did not happen, <u>might</u> have happened'. Mountbatten got an early look at the script, and complained that it made him 'appear to be grudging and rather "Old Blimpish"'. 'I would like to make it clear that I was the most enthusiastic supporter of this idea from the beginning.' He even tried to insert a line to make his character more appealing: 'I would have no objection to the addition of a phrase like "Nice of Mountbatten to take a dead man on his Staff."'

Among those on set during filming was a tall, ungainly man with an extravagant Air Force moustache, who was described as a 'technical adviser' and known only as 'George'. He did not appear in the credits. Even Ronald Neame never knew that George was Charles Cholmondeley, content, as ever, to organise matters anonymously, from the wings.

In the film, Montagu makes a cameo appearance as an air vice marshal with doubts about the plan's feasibility. At one point, Montagu leans over to Webb, looks him in the eye, and declares: 'I suppose you realise, Montagu, that, if the Germans see through this, it will pinpoint Sicily.' This was a wonderfully surreal moment: the real Montagu addressing his fictional persona, in a work of filmic fiction, based on reality, which had originated in fiction.

The film was a box-office and critical success, winning a Bafta for best British screenplay. Perhaps the ultimate accolade, the sign that Operation Mincemeat had truly and permanently entered British culture, came in 1956, when *The Goon Show* devoted an entire episode to the story. Monty saw the film in Holland and, rather missing the point, complained that Archie Nye had looked quite different. Adolf Clauss went to see *The Man Who Never Was* in Huelva's Teatro Mora. He told his son: 'There's nothing true in it. It was nothing like that.' Someone tipped off the press to the identity of 'Pam'. Jean Gerard Leigh was besieged by journalists, and denied everything.

Montagu had hoped that by framing his refusal to identify the body as a promise he could never break, he would end all attempts to attach a name to it. The very title of his book seemed to imply that the corpse had no previous existence worthy of mention. But there *was* a man, and the runaway success of the book and film ensured that the speculation over whom he might have been started immediately. The body was variously identified as 'a derelict alcoholic found beneath the arches of Charing Cross Bridge', a professional soldier, and 'the wastrel brother of an MP'. Numerous candidates were put forward, with evidence ranging from possible to wishful to fanciful. The conspiracy theories continue to this day.

Aftermath

Three weeks after the invasion of Sicily, Lieutenant Bill Jewell was reunited with Rosemary Galloway in Algiers: they immediately became engaged. While Rosemary went on to serve at Allied Headquarters in Italy, Jewell continued to attack enemy shipping in the Mediterranean, eastern Atlantic and Norwegian Sea. At the Normandy landings in June 1944, the *Seraph* once again guided the invading forces ashore. The same month, Bill Jewell and Rosemary were wed in a ceremony in Pinner. They remained married, and 'absolutely devoted to one another', for the next fifty-three years. Jewell was awarded the DSC and the American Legion of Merit, and appointed MBE, for his part in Operation Husky, along with the French Croix de Guerre. He rose to the rank of captain in command of a submarine flotilla, and died in 2004 at the age of ninety.

HMS *Seraph* also remained on active service. In recognition of her role in the run-up to the invasion of North Africa, a brass plaque was nailed to the door of the submarine toilet: 'General Mark Wayne Clark, Deputy Supreme Commander in North Africa, sat here.' She served as a training ship at Holy Loch on the Clyde, the port from which she had set off for Huelva in 1943. The submarine was decommissioned in 1963, twenty-one years to the day after her launch, and finally scrapped at Briton Ferry in South Wales, close to the birthplace of Glyndwr Michael. The *Seraph*'s conning tower, forward torpedo hatch and periscope were all preserved and erected as a memorial to Anglo-American cooperation during the Second World War at the Citadel, the American military training college in South Carolina. US and British flags fly jointly over the memorial, the only place in America permitted to fly the white ensign.

Lieutenant David Scott of the *Seraph* finished reading *War and Peace* shortly before the end of the war. He served on ten submarines, in war and peace, commanding five of them, and was promoted to Rear Admiral in 1971.

Derrick Leverton fought through the Italian campaign, was mentioned in despatches, took over command of his artillery regiment, and then returned to Britain to resume his rightful place, alongside his brother Ivor, in the family funeral business. Ivor Leverton would boast that he had 'played a tiny part in ending the war'; he liked to tease Drick that he had saved his life on the beach at Sicily by taking a dead body to Hackney in the middle of the night. In a quiet way, he felt 'redeemed' by the part he had played. Ivor's sons took over the business, and have since passed it on to an eighth generation of undertakers.

Colonel Bill Darby of the US Rangers was killed in northern Italy, two days before the final German surrender in Italy. As Darby was giving orders to cut off the German retreat, an 88mm shell burst outside his command post, killing him instantly. He was thirty-four. Darby was unable to turn down the promotion to brigadier general which was awarded to him posthumously. James Garner played Darby in the 1958 film *Darby's Rangers*.

With the success of Operation Mincemeat, and the Mediterranean under Allied control, Alan Hillgarth looked to new pastures. At the end of 1943 he was transferred to Ceylon as chief of intelligence for the Eastern Fleet, going on to become head of Naval Intelligence for the entire eastern theatre. There he 'developed an intelligence organisation [that] materially aided the Allied war effort at sea against Japan', and once more his intelligence advice was sent directly to Churchill.

The war won, he retired from the Navy, and purchased an estate in Ireland, where he planted a forest. 'He walked several miles a day, inspecting his trees.' But he also continued to cultivate exotic human flora, most notably Juan March, the dubious financier who had helped to bribe the Spanish generals, and Winston Churchill. Through a series of questionable financial manoeuvres, March's fortune and notoriety expanded in tandem: by 1952 he was the seventh richest man in the world. Hillgarth had once described Juan March as 'the most unscrupulous man in Spain', but his own scruples did not prevent him from becoming director of the Helvetia Finance Company, March's nominee business in London. It has been suggested that Hillgarth and MI6 may have helped smooth over March's business dealings as payback for his help in paying off the Cavalry of St George. March was killed in a car accident outside Madrid in 1962.

While looking after March's business interests, Hillgarth continued to act as Churchill's unofficial adviser on intelligence. Between the end of the war and Churchill's return to Downing Street in 1951, Hillgarth met regularly with the once and future Prime Minister, at Chartwell, at his Hyde Park Gate apartment, and in Switzerland. Mining his intelligence and diplomatic contacts, Hillgarth briefed Churchill on Spanish affairs, American plans for atomic warfare and, above all, the threat of Soviet espionage in Britain, which he described as a 'quiet, cold-blooded war of brains in the background'. The Soviet codes would be far harder to crack than the German Enigma, Hillgarth warned: 'The Russians are cleverer than the Germans.' Hillgarth's secret correspondence with Churchill in opposition, disguised under the codename 'Sturdee', lasted six years and played a crucial part in framing Churchill's attitude in the early years of the Cold War.

A few years after the war, Hillgarth received a letter from Edgar Sanders, his partner in the disastrous Sacambaya expedition, adding a postscript to that fiasco: according to Sanders, the American engineer, Julius Nolte, had spotted an entrance to the treasure cavern while everyone else was digging the huge hole, but did not share his discovery with the others. Nolte had returned to Sacambaya in 1938 with an American team of explorers and heavy digging equipment, extracted $8 million worth of gold, and then retired to California, where he built himself a castle. 'Thus ends the story of the Sacambaya treasure,' wrote Sanders, who had visited Nolte and tried, unsuccessfully, to extract some money from him. 'Crazy Nolte is rich, while you and I are poor, at least I am, certainly. Hell! Let's have another drink.'

Hillgarth had no idea whether to credit a word Sanders wrote. He had long ago learned not to believe what one reads in letters.

Alan Hillgarth remained a close friend of Churchill, converted to Catholicism, never breathed a word about his wartime and postwar intelligence activities, and died in 1978 at Illannanagh in County Tipperary, surrounded by mystery, and trees.

Don Gómez-Beare was appointed OBE, although quite what for was never fully explained. He spent his retirement in Seville and Madrid, playing bridge and golf. When a British journalist asked him what he had done during the war, he responded with exquisite politeness: 'I am sorry, but I am not free to discuss some subjects.'

On 16 December 1947, Sir Bernard Spilsbury, the great forensic scientist, dined alone at the Junior Carlton Club, then went to his rooms in University College London, locked the door, turned on the Bunsen burner tap, and gassed himself to death. Spilsbury had become increasingly conscious that his mental faculties were deserting him; he was making mistakes, and Sir Bernard did not tolerate mistakes. The scientist, who had studied, investigated and catalogued so many thousands of deaths, left no note to explain his own. His friend Bentley Purchase, the coroner, examined Spilsbury's body and pronounced a verdict of suicide: 'His mind was not as it used to be.'

The cheerful coroner was appointed CBE in 1949 and knighted in 1958. Purchase retired the following year, to look after his pigs and listen to Gilbert and Sullivan. He resisted writing his memoirs: 'Every time I tell a story I am likely to rattle a skeleton in someone's cupboard.' This applied particularly to his role in Operation Mincemeat. Sir Bentley Purchase died in 1961, after falling off his roof while fixing a television aerial. Having performed some 20,000 inquests himself, Sir Bentley, typically, left behind a small postmortem mystery: the coroner in his case could not tell whether he had suffered a fatal heart attack before or after falling off the roof.

Adolf Clauss, the Huelva spy, also declined to discuss his wartime work, although for rather different reasons. At the end of the war, retribution against Germans who had been active in espionage was unevenly applied. Luis Clauss was accused of spying because his fishing fleet had been used to track Allied shipping, and spent two dreary years under house arrest in the little village of Caldes de Malavella in northeast Spain. Don Adolfo, although far more senior in the Abwehr, was never punished. 'His wife was the daughter of a powerful Spanish general, and so he was protected.' Clauss went back to collecting butterflies, and building chairs that still broke if you sat on them. Years later, when the truth about Operation Mincemeat began to emerge, like the super-spy he was, Clauss invented a new version of reality. His son still insists: 'He was always suspicious because the papers came into his hands too easily. He immediately realised it was a trick, and warned his superiors in Berlin and Madrid, but they refused to believe him. He thought the people in Berlin were useless for failing to realise they were being duped.' Gustav Leissner, alias Lenz, the Abwehr chief in Madrid, was more honest in defeat. He was arrested and interrogated by the Americans in 1946, but then permitted to return to Spain. When presented with the evidence of what British intelligence had done, ten years later, he 'admitted the possibility with a long-drawn "*Schön!* Ach, if that is so, I really must congratulate them . . . I take off my hat".'

Karl-Erich Kuhlenthal, the linchpin of the Abwehr in Spain, was far too busy trying to save his own skin to worry about keeping up appearances, or admitting his own errors.

As the Nazi power structure crumbled, Juan Pujol,

Kuhlenthal's Agent Arabel and Britain's Agent Garbo, kept up a steady stream of Nazi jingoism in messages to his German spymaster. In response to a letter from Kuhlenthal bemoaning 'the heroic death of our beloved Führer', Garbo wrote with typical bombast: 'News of the death of our dear chief shook our profound faith in the destiny which awaits our poor Europe, but his deeds and the story of his sacrifice will save the world . . . the noble struggle will be revived which was started by him to save us from chaotic barbarism.'

Kuhlenthal told his star spy that he intended to go into hiding. Their roles had reversed. 'If you find yourself in any danger let me know,' Pujol wrote. 'Do not hesitate in confiding your difficulties fully in me. I only regret not being at your side to give you real help. Our struggle will not terminate with the present phase. We are entering a world civil war which will result in the disintegration of our enemies.' This was all part of an elaborate ruse to find out if remnants of the German intelligence service might be planning to re-establish some sort of underground Nazi network after the war. In the wake of the German defeat, Kuhlenthal fled Madrid, having systematically destroyed the Abwehr's records, and took refuge under an assumed name in Ávila, west of the capital. Britain's MI5 despatched Pujol to track him down and find out what the former golden boy of the Abwehr was planning to do next. Pujol traced Kuhlenthal to Ávila, and knocked on his door. 'Kuhlenthal was overcome with emotion when he welcomed Garbo into his sitting room.' The two men talked for three hours, with Pujol studiously maintaining his guise as a Nazi fanatic. 'Kuhlenthal made it abundantly clear, not only that he still believed in the genuineness of Garbo but that he looked upon him as a superman.'

Kuhlenthal explained that Pujol had been awarded the Iron Cross in recognition of his work for the Third Reich, and that Hitler had 'personally ordered that the medal should be granted. Unfortunately the certificate in evidence of this had not reached

Madrid prior to the German collapse.' Still, it is the thought that counts. As for himself, Kuhlenthal explained that he was desperate to escape Spain, and would not consider returning to Germany, where he was sure to be arrested. Pujol told Kuhlenthal to 'remain patiently in his hideout until Garbo could evolve a plan to facilitate his escape'. Pujol was stern, telling his former spymaster 'he should obey instructions to the letter if he wished to save himself . . . This Kuhlenthal promised to do.' The Spanish spy explained that he planned to get to South America, via Portugal, and solemnly pledged to work for Germany again, should the Abwehr ever be restored. When Kuhlenthal asked him how he intended to get out of the country, Pujol replied, truthfully, with one word: 'Clandestinely'.

MI5 concluded that Karl–Erich Kuhlenthal was no threat to the postwar world. The former Abwehr chief waited, paranoid but patient, for word from his former protégé, but no message came. Like Clauss, he later put a rather different gloss on the past. He had stayed in Spain, he explained, because the country was 'a melting pot of many races, conveying an atmosphere of tolerance and understanding of human nature'. In truth, he was too terrified to budge, waiting for a message from the spy who had double-crossed him so spectacularly. Kuhlenthal's wife, Ellen, was heiress to the Dienz clothing company in Germany, and before 1939 Karl-Erich had worked in his wife's family business. The company premises were bombed at the end of the war, but the business was slowly rebuilt. In 1950, the couple slipped back to Germany, moved into a house in Koblenz, and took over running the clothing company. Kuhlenthal turned out to be much better at buying and selling clothes than buying and selling secrets. The House of Dienz prospered. In 1971, the former spy was elected president of the Federal Association of German Textile Retailers, representing about 95 per cent of German textile retailers, with a purchasing power of about 390 billion deutschmarks. He inaugurated the first pedestrian shopping zone in Koblenz. He gave long, dull speeches on the subject of tax reform, business promotion, and parking in his hometown. No one ever enquired about his past. A more solid member of the German establishment it would be impossible to imagine, worthy, dependable and predictable. The German spy and textile magnate died in 1975 still wondering, perhaps, whether his star agent would reappear from the past. The most interesting thing his obituary could find to say was that 'he always tried to dress correctly as an example to his colleagues'.

Kuhlenthal's life perfectly exemplified what Juan Pujol, Alexis von Roenne and Glyndwr Michael had already proven: it is possible to fit at least two people into one life.

Agent Garbo went to ground. With a gratuity of £15,000 from MI5 and an MBE, he moved to Venezuela, and vanished. After he was tracked down by the spy writer Rupert Allason (Nigel West), he re-emerged, briefly, to accept formal recognition at Buckingham Palace of the debt owed to him. He then disappeared into obscurity again. Garbo wanted to be alone. He died in Carácas in 1988.

With victory, the denizens of Room 13 emerged, blinking, into the light. An anonymous poet in Section 17M marked the occasion with a verse entitled 'De Profundibus'.

> In the depths of the fusty dungeons,
> In the bowels of NID
> Where wild surmise or blatant lies
> Are digested for those at sea,
> The in-trays are all empty,
> The dreary toil is done,
> And with mental daze and bleary gaze
> The Troglodytes see the sun.

The year after the war ended, Jean Leslie married a soldier, an officer in the Life Guards named William Gerard Leigh, a dashing and handsome polo player with a reputation as a 'bold man to hounds'. He, too, had gone ashore at Sicily, and then 'fought through Italy', the unknowing beneficiary of a plot in which his future wife had played a crucial part. Gerard Leigh, known as 'G', was brave, upright, and utterly correct, not entirely unlike the gallant and doomed William Martin.

Jock Horsfall, the chauffeur on the night drive to Scotland, returned to motor racing after the war. He won the Belgian Grand Prix, and then took second place in the British Empire Trophy Race in the Isle of Man. In 1947 he joined Aston Martin as a test driver, and in 1949 he entered the Spa 24-Hour Race, and finished fourth out of a field of thirty-eight, covering 1,821 miles at an average speed of over 73 mph. On 20 August 1949, he entered the *Daily Express* International Trophy Race at Silverstone: on the thirteenth lap, at the notorious Stowe Corner, the car left the track, hit a line of straw bales intended as a buffer, and flipped over. Horsfall's neck was broken and he died at once. The St John Horsfall Memorial Trophy, a race open only to Aston Martins, is awarded at Silverstone every year, in his memory.

Ivor Montagu listed his activities in *Who's Who* as 'washing up, pottering about, sleeping through television'. This was not quite accurate, for 'pottering' was never Ivor's style: frenetic activity in multiple causes, both public and secret, was closer to the mark. In 1948 he co-wrote the film *Scott of the Antarctic* with Walter Meade; he translated plays, novels and films by a new generation of Soviet writers and film-makers; he travelled extensively in Europe, China and Mongolia; he wrote polemical pamphlets attacking capitalism, and a book about Eisenstein; he championed cricket, Southampton United, and the Zoological Society, but his two greatest passions remained communism and table tennis, a dual obsession that earned him the lifelong suspicion of MI5. He was awarded the Lenin Peace Prize by the Soviet Union in 1959.

Ivor Montagu was never publicly exposed as Agent Intelligentsia. The Venona transcripts cease abruptly in 1942. Whether Montagu learned of Operation Mincemeat, and whether he passed on what he knew to Moscow, will never be known for sure unless the files of the Soviet secret services are finally opened to scrutiny.

What is certain is that Moscow knew all about Operation Mincemeat and, very probably, obtained its information before the operation took place. A secret report by the NKVD, Stalin's intelligence service, dated May 1944 and entitled *Deception during the Current War*, provided an astonishingly detailed account of the operation, its codename, planning, execution and success. The Soviet report described the precise contents of the letters, the exact location of the dummy attacks in Greece, and noted that the operation had been 'somewhat complicated by the fact that the papers ended up with the [Spanish] general staff'. The author of the report also provided a description of the role of Ewen Montagu within British intelligence, and his position on the Twenty Committee: 'Captain [sic] Montagu is in charge of the dissemination of misinformation through intelligence channels. He is also engaged in researching special intelligence sources.' Moscow's spymasters were in no doubt that Operation Mincemeat had worked: 'The German general staff apparently were convinced that the documents themselves were genuine,' the report concluded. 'When the [invasion] was launched, it was clear that the German and Italian commands were somewhat taken by surprise and ill-prepared to repel the attack.'

Much of the information on Operation Mincemeat was supplied to the Soviets by Anthony Blunt, the MI5 officer tasked with overseeing the illegal XXX (Triplex) Operation to extract material from the diplomatic bags of neutral missions in London. Blunt was recruited by the NKVD in 1934, and between 1940 and 1945 he passed huge volumes of secret material to his Soviet handlers. Two other members of the 'Cambridge Five' spy ring probably supplied additional intelligence on the Sicily deception: John Cairncross, who had access to the Ultra decrypts at Bletchley Park, and Kim Philby, the most notorious Soviet mole of all, who headed the Iberian subsection of MI6's counterintelligence branch. Some of the material in Soviet intelligence files on Operation Mincemeat may have come from Ivor Montagu.

MI5 and MI6 continued to watch him and Hell closely. Kim Philby was partly responsible for coordinating reports on the shambolic figure of Ivor Montagu, as he trailed through Vienna, Bucharest and Budapest in 1946. In one report, Philby described Montagu as 'intelligent and agreeable, and an expert at ping-pong'. Philby almost certainly knew more about Montagu than he let on. Montagu's handler, the Soviet air attaché in London, Colonel Sklyarov, alias 'Brion', left London that year. Did Ivor Montagu continue to supply intelligence to the Soviet Union? If so, MI5 could find no hard evidence, although in 1948 it was reported that 'information from secret sources shows that Montagu has recently been in touch with the Soviet embassy'.

By the time the Venona transcripts were decoded in the mid-1960s, and agent 'Intelligentsia' was identified as Ivor Montagu, it was impossible to do anything about him. Venona was simply too secret and too valuable to be revealed in court, and the spies it had unmasked could not be prosecuted. In spite of the many fruitless years spent trying to establish a link between table tennis and Soviet espionage, MI5 had been right all along. Montagu never knew he had been rumbled, and took his role as Agent Intelligentsia to the grave, another double life concealed. Ivor Montagu died in Watford in 1984, leaving behind a clutch of Soviet decorations, his correspondence with Trotsky and the unpublished second volume of his autobiography misleadingly entitled *Like It Was*, which avoided any mention of his activities as a secret agent.

The second half of Charles Cholmondeley's life was, perhaps, the most mysterious of all. The last reference made to him by Guy Liddell of MI5 noted that he was 'somewhere in the Middle East, chasing locusts'. This was an accurate, although partial, description of what Cholmondeley was up to. In October 1945, he joined the 'Middle East Anti-Locust Unit' as 'First Locust

Officer', a job that involved chasing swarms of locusts all over the Arab states, and feeding them bran laced with insecticide.

Another English locust hunter, named George Walford, met Cholmondeley in the desert in 1948, and described a man obsessed: 'His objective was the destruction, at almost any price, of all living locusts in Arabia. It was an impossible task. Only a person with a rare combination of patience, tact and strength of purpose could have achieved any success at all.' The qualities that had served Cholmondeley so well as a wartime intelligence officer were now put to work waging war on the locust. For months on end, he would simply vanish into the desert, disguised as a Bedouin. In the Yemen, he visited villages so remote that when he arrived, women came out with hay offering to feed his jeep. From Arabia, he moved on, in 1949, to the International Council for the Control of the Red Locust in Rhodesia. Cholmondeley was certainly keen on killing locusts ('they are loathsome insects'). Equally certainly, he was still working for the British Secret Service, using his cover as a locust officer for more clandestine work, although quite what this might have been has never been revealed.

Cholmondeley was appointed MBE in 1948, and two years later he signed up with the RAF for a five-year commission on 'intelligence duties'. By December of that year he was in Malaya, using his 'wide experience of deception work' to coordinate with MI5 and Special Branch on bamboozling a rather different enemy – the guerrillas of the Malayan National Liberation Army.

Charles Cholmondeley left MI5 in 1952. He moved to the West Country, married, and set up a business selling horticultural machinery. He regarded the vow of secrecy he had made on joining MI5 as a blood oath, and he never broke it. In the words of his wife, Alison, 'He would not give information to anyone who did not "need to know". Infuriatingly I found this included me.' He still enjoyed shooting with a handgun, although his deteriorating eyesight made this extremely hazardous, except for the birds. 'He would take a revolver when we walked up partridges,' recalled his friend John Otter. 'I never saw him hit one.' No one in the Somerset town of Wells had a clue that the tall, short-sighted, courtly gentleman who sold lawnmowers had once been an officer with the Secret Service, and the inspiration behind the most audacious deception of the war. When the story of Operation Mincemeat finally emerged, he refused to be identified or accept any public credit. Cholmondeley died in June 1982. He never wanted to be recognised, let alone celebrated. Even his headstone is discreet and understated, simply bearing the initials 'CCC'. An obituary letter written to *The Times* by Ewen Montagu drew attention to his 'invaluable work during the war . . . work which, through circumstances and his innate modesty is not adequately known'. As Montagu observed: 'Many who landed in Sicily owe their lives to Charles Cholmondeley.'

Ewen Montagu was appointed OBE for his part in Operation Mincemeat. He returned to the law, as he had always intended, and in 1945 he was appointed Judge Advocate of the Fleet, responsible for administering the court-martial system in the Royal Navy. He would hold that post for the next eighteen years, while also serving as a judge in Hampshire and Middlesex, and Recorder, successively, of Devizes and Southampton. Montagu lived a double life: alongside the feared judge and pillar of Anglo-Jewish society was another Ewen Montagu: the dashing wartime intelligence officer with an extraordinary story to tell.

As a judge, Montagu proved scrupulously fair, wonderfully rude and almost always embroiled in one controversy or another. The press nicknamed him 'The Turbulent Judge'. In 1957, he remarked in court, while trying a merchant seaman: 'Half the scum of England are going into the Merchant Navy to escape military service.' He apologised. Four years later, he told an audience of Rotarians: 'A boy crook should have his trousers taken down and should be spanked by a policewoman with a hairbrush.' He apologised again. When deliberations in court displeased or bored him, he would groan, sigh, roll his eyes and crack inappropriate jokes. Barristers complained often about his offensive behaviour. He apologised, and carried on. His corrosive humour was usually misunderstood; his wit was so sharp and sarcastic it could humble the most arrogant barrister, and did so, frequently. In 1967, a pimp appealed against his conviction, arguing that Montagu had been so rude to his lawyer that he deserved a retrial. The appeal was rejected on the grounds that 'discourtesy, even gross discourtesy, to counsel, however regrettable, could not be a ground for quashing a conviction'.

Often he would impose a lenient sentence on an offender, acting on a hunch that the man or woman genuinely planned to go straight. His hunches were seldom wrong. 'If a man can't have a stroke of luck once in his life, it's not much of a life.' But to those who should know better, or seemed incorrigible, he was merciless. Sentencing the actor Trevor Howard for drinking at least eight double whiskies and then driving into a lamppost, he said: 'The public needs protecting from you, you are a man who drinks vast quantities, every night, yet you have so little care for your fellow citizens that you are willing to drive.'

Summing up Montagu's career, one contemporary wrote: 'Few judges have trodden so hard on the corns of so many people's dignity as this tall, witty, testy, wartime naval commander with the sensitive face and the turbulent tongue. But few judges have been so quick to apologise with the air of a boxer shaking hands after a fight.' Montagu was aware of his own shortcomings. 'Perhaps I should have been more patient,' he once said. 'It is fair, I think, to say that I don't suffer fools gladly.' In truth, he did become more patient and tolerant with age. He also became more devout, plunged into numerous charitable works, and became President of the United Synagogue.

Montagu had lived an extraordinary life, as a lawyer, intelligence officer, and writer: a judge of deep seriousness, he had also retained a boyish side, and a talent for self-mockery. Without his combination of 'extreme caution and extreme daring', Operation Mincemeat could never have happened. The entire plan was, in a way, a reflection of his sense of the ridiculous, and his love of the macabre, of playing a part. In 1980, a photograph of Jean Gerard Leigh appeared in *The Times* after her husband was made CBE. 'Dear "Pam",' wrote Montagu, now seventy-nine years old. 'It was a voice from the past to see you in today's papers and I can't resist being another such voice and sending you congratulations. Ever yours, Ewen (alias Major William Martin).'

Shortly before his death, Montagu received a letter from the father of two young Canadian girls, who had read of his wartime exploits, requesting a memento. He immediately replied, enclosing 'one of the buttons I wore when carrying out Operation Mincemeat', along with some advice: 'Keep a real sense of humour. By real I don't mean just to be able to see a joke, but to be able to really and truly laugh at oneself.'

Ewen Montagu died in 1985, at the age of eighty-four, believing he had successfully hidden, for all time, the identity of the body used in Operation Mincemeat.

Roger Morgan, a council planning officer in London and an indefatigable amateur historian, began researching the story of Operation Mincemeat in 1980. He wrote to Montagu, and later met him, and like every other would-be sleuth, received a response that was as courteous as it was unhelpful. Like most others, Morgan concluded that the secret of Major Martin's identity had died with Montagu: the man who never was would never be. But then, in 1996, Morgan was leafing through a newly declassified batch of government files, when he came across a three-volume report on Ewen Montagu's wartime activities, including a copy of the official account of Operation Mincemeat, written just before the end of the war. 'There, at the end of the last volume, staring out at him was the answer to many sleepless nights.' The official censor, perhaps unaware of the extraordinary efforts of concealment made over the preceding half-century, had failed to redact a name. 'On 28

January there had died a labourer of no fixed abode. His name was Glyndwr Michael and he was thirty-four years old.'

Nuestra Señora de la Soledad cemetery is a ghostly but tranquil place at dusk. Swallows swoop over the cobbled paths, and the cypresses stand sentry. Far out in the bay, you can see the fishing boats, bringing in the sardines. As the sun sinks and the dusk settles, the graves seem to merge into one long field of engraved marble, stories of lives long and short, full and empty. One of the gravestones is different. It tells of a double life, one brief, sad and real, the other a little longer, entirely invented, and oddly heroic. The body in this grave washed ashore wearing a fake uniform and the underwear of a dead Oxford don, with a love letter from a girl he had never known pressed to his long-dead heart. No one in this story was quite who they seemed to be. The Montagu brothers, Charles Cholmondeley, Jean Leslie, Alan Hillgarth, Karl-Erich Kuhlenthal and Juan Pujol – each was born into one existence, and imagined themselves into a life quite different.

Grave number 1886 in Huelva's cemetery was taken over by the Commonwealth War Graves Commission in 1977. In a small local armistice, it is now maintained, on behalf of Britain, by the German consulate in Huelva. Every year, in April, an Englishwoman from the town lays flowers on the gravestone.

In 1997, half a century after Operation Mincemeat, the British government added a carved postscript to the marble slab:

Glyndwr Michael
served as
Major William Martin, RN

WILLIAM MARTIN
BORN 29TH MARCH 1907
DIED 24TH APRIL 1943
BELOVED SON OF JOHN
GLYNDWYR MARTIN
AND THE LATE ANTONIA MARTIN OF
CARDIFF, WALES
DULCE ET DECORUM EST PRO PATRIA MORI
R. I. P.
Vª DE M. TOSCANO.

Appendix

COPY

OPERATION MINCEMEAT

1. Object

To cause a brief-case containing documents to drift ashore as near as possible to HUELVA in Spain in such circumstances that it will be thought to have been washed ashore from an aircraft which crashed at sea when the case was being taken by an officer from the U.K. to Allied Force H.Q. in North Africa.

2. Method

A dead body dressed in the battle-dress uniform of a Major, Royal Marines, and wearing a "Mae West" will be taken out in a submarine, together with the brief case and a rubber dinghy.

The body will be packed fully clothed and ready (and wrapped in a blanket to prevent friction) in a tubular air-tight container (which will be labelled as "Optical Instruments").

The container is just under 6' 6" long and just under 2' in diameter and has no excrescences of any kind on the sides. The end which opens has a flush fitting lid which is held tightly in position by a number of nuts and has fitted on its exterior in clips a box-spanner with a permanent tommy-bar which is chained to the lid.

Both ends are fitted with handles which fold down flat. It will be possible to lift the container by using both handles or even by using the handle in the lid alone, but it would be better not to take the whole weight on the handle at the other end as the steel of which the container is made is of light gauge to keep the weight as low as possible. The approximate total weight when the container is full will be 400 lbs.

When the container is closed the body will be packed round with a certain amount of "dry-ice". The container should therefore be opened on deck as the "dry-ice" will give off carbon dioxide.

3. Position

The body should be put into the water as close inshore as prudently possible and as near to HUELVA as possible, preferably to the North West of the river mouth.

According to the Hydrographic Department the tides in that area run mainly up and down the coast, and every effort should therefore be made to choose a period with an on-shore wind. South Westerly winds are in fact the prevailing winds in that area at this time of year.

The latest information about the tidal streams in that area, as obtained from the Superintendant of Tides is attached.

4. Delivery of the Package.

The package will be brought up to the port of departure by road on whatever day is desired, preferably as close to the sailing day as possible. The brief case will handed over at the same time to the Captain of the submarine. The rubber dinghy will also be a separate parcel.

/3.

5. Disposal of the body

When the body is removed from the container all that will be necessary will be to fasten the chain attached to the brief case through the belt of the trench-coat which will be the outer garment on the body. The chain is of the type worn under the coat, round the chest and out through the sleeve. At the end is a "dog-lead" type of clip for attaching to the handle of the brief case and a similar clip for forming the loop round the chest. It is this loop that should be made through the belt of the trench coat as if the officer has slipped the chain off for comfort in the aircraft, but has nevertheless kept it attached to him so that the bag should not either be forgotten or slide away from him in the aircraft.

The body should then be deposited in the water, as should also be the rubber dinghy. As this should drift at a different speed from the body the exact position at which it is released is unimportant, but it should be near the body but not too near if that is possible.

6. Those in the know at Gibraltar

Steps have been taken to inform F.O.I.C. Gibraltar and his S.O.(I). No one else there will be in the picture

7. Signals

If the operation is successfully carried out a signal should be made "MINCEMEAT completed". If that is made from Gibraltar the S.O.(I) should be asked to send it addressed to D.N.I. (PERSONAL). If it can be made earlier it should be made in accordance with orders from F.O.S.

8. Cancellation

If the operation has to be cancelled a signal will be made "Cancel MINCEMEAT". In that case the body and container should be sunk in deep water; as the container may have positive buoyancy it may either have to be weighted or water may have to be allowed to enter. In the latter case care must be taken that the body does not escape. The brief case should be handed to the S.O.(I). at Gibraltar, with instructions to burn the contents unopened, if there is no possibility of taking that course earlier. The rubber dinghy should be handed to the S.O.(I) for disposal.

9. Abandonment

If the operation has to be abandoned a signal should be made "MINCEMEAT abandoned" as soon as possible (See para 7 above).

10. Cover

This is a matter for consideration. Until the operation actually takes place it is thought that the labelling of the container "Optical Instruments" will provide sufficient cover. It is suggested that the cover after the operation has been completed should be that it is hoped to trap a very active German agent in this neighbourhood and it is hoped that sufficient evidence can be obtained by this means to get the Spaniards to eject him.

/The

The importance of dealing with this man should be impressed on the
crew together with the fact that any leakage that may **ever** take place
about this will compromise our power to get the Spaniards to act in
such cases; also that they will never learn whether we were
successful in this objective as the whole matter will have to be
conducted in secrecy with the Spaniards or we won't be able to get
them to act.

It is in fact most important that the Germans and
Spaniards should accept these papers in accordance with para 1. If
they should suspect that the papers are a "plant" it might have far-
reaching consequences of great magnitude.

(Sgd) E.E.S. Montagu,
Lt. Cdr. R.N.V.R.

31.3.43.

Appendix

I am afraid there is nothing to add to the remarks in S.D.'s
"West Coasts of Spain & Portugal Pilot" page 13, lines 31-39.
There would be a probability that an object freed near Cape St.
Vincent would drift towards the Straits of Gibraltar, while winds
between S and W might set it towards the head of the bight near P.
Huelva.   If it was drifting off the port at L.W. Lisbon it would
probably be carried inwards by the flood stream, but if it did not
strand it would be carried out again on the ebb.

The Spaniards and Portuguese publish practically nothing
about tides, tidal streams and currents off their coasts.

(Initialled)

22.3.43.

PERSONAL DOCUMENTS AND ARTICLES IN POCKETS

Identity discs (2)   "Major W. MARTIN, R.M., R/C"
                     attached to braces.

Silver cross on Silver chain round neck.

Watch, wrist.

Wallet, containing:-

        Photograph of Fiancee
        Book of stamps (2 used)
        2 letters from Fiancee
        St. Christopher plaque
        Invitation to Cabaret Club
        C.C.O. Pass   In cellophane
        Admiralty Identity Card   container
        Torn off top of letter.
        1 £5 note - March 5th 1942 $\frac{C}{227}$ 45827

        3 £1 notes   X 34 D   527008
                   W 21 D   029293
                   X 66 D   443119

1 Half crown

2 Shillings

2 six pences

4 pennies

Letter from "Father"

Letter from "Father" to McKenna & Co., Solicitors

Letter from Lloyds Bank

Bill (receipted) from Naval & Military Club

Bill (cash) from Gieves Ltd.

Bill for engagement ring

2 bus tickets

2 counterfoil stubs of tickets for Prince of Wales' Theatre 22.4.43

Box of matches

Packet of Cigarettes

Bunch of keys

Pencil Stub

Letter from McKenna & Co. Solicitors.

BLACK LION HOTEL.
MOLD.
N. WALES.
13th April 1943

My dear William,

I cannot say that the hotel is any longer as comfortable as I remember it to have been in pre war days. I am, however, staying here as the only alternative to imposing myself once upon an aunt whose depleted staff & strict regard for fuel economy (which I agree to be necessary in war time) has made the house almost uninhabitable to a guest, at least one of my age. I propose to be in town by the night of the 20th & 21st of April when no doubt we shall have an opportunity to meet. I enclose the copy of a letter which I have written to Stratton & McKenna's about your affairs. You will see that I have asked him to lunch with me at the Carlton Grill (which I understand still to be open)

at a quarter to one on Wednesday the 21st. I should be glad if you would make it possible to join us. We shall not however wait lunch for you, so I trust that, if you are able to come, you will make a point of being punctual.

Mrs John cowan Priscilla has asked I be remembered to you. She has grown into a sensible girl though I cannot say that her work for the Land Army has done much to improve her looks. In that respect I am afraid that she will take after her father's side of the family.

Your affectionate
father.

COMBINED OPERATIONS HEADQUARTERS,

1A, RICHMOND TERRACE,

WHITEHALL. S.W.I.

Telephone:
Whitehall 9777

21st April,
1 9 4 3.

Dear Admiral of the Fleet,

    I promised V.C.I.G.S. that Major Martin would
arrange with you for the onward transmission of a
letter he has with him for General Alexander. It is
very urgent and very "hot" and as there are some
remarks in it that could not be seen by others in the
War Office, it could not go by signal. I feel sure
that you will see that it goes on safely and without
delay.

    I think you will find Martin the man you want.
He is quiet and shy at first, but he really knows his
stuff. He was more accurate than some of us about the
probable run of events at Dieppe and he has been well
in on the experiments with the latest barges and
equipment which took place up in Scotland.

    Let me have him back, please, as soon as the
assault is over. He might bring some sardines with him -
they are "on points" here!

        Yours sincerely,

        Louis Mountbatten

Admiral of the Fleet Sir A.B. Cunningham, G.C.B.,D.S.O.,
Commander in Chief Mediterranean,
Allied Force H.Q.,
Algiers.

THE MANOR HOUSE
OGBOURNE ST. GEORGE
MARLBOROUGH
WILTSHIRE
TELEPHONE OGBOURNE ST. GEORGE 243

Sunday 18th

31

MOST SECRET

From The Commanding Officer, H.M. Submarine "SERAPH".

Date: 30th April, 1943.

To Director of Naval Intelligence.

    Copy to F.O.S.

    (for Lt. Cdr. The Hon. E.E.S. Montagu.R.N.V.R.) personal.

OPERATION MINCEMEAT

Weather: The wind was variable altering between SW and SE, force 2.
It was expected that the sea breeze would spring up in the
morning, close inshore, as it had on the previous morning
in similar conditions.
Sea and swell - 2.0. - Sky overcast with very low clouds -
visibility was patchy, 1 to 2 miles - Barometer 1016.

2.**Fishing boats:** A large number of small fishing boats were working in
the bay. The closest was left, about a mile off,
and it is not thought that the submarine was observed
by them.

3.**Operation:** The time of 0430 was chosen as being the nearest to Low Water
Lisbon, (0731) which would allow the submarine to be well
clear by dawn. The Cannister was opened at 0415 and the body
extracted. The blanket was opened up and the body examined. The
brief case was found to be securely attached. The face was heavily
tanned and the whole of the lower half from the eyes down covered
with mould. The skin had started to break away on the nose and
cheek bones. The body was very high. The Mae West was blown up
very hard and no further air was needed. The body was placed in
the water at 0430 in a position 148° Portil Pillar 1.3 miles
approximately eight cables from the beach and started to drift
inshore. This was aided by the wash of the screws going full
speed astern. The rubber dinghy was placed in the water blown
up and upside down about half a mile further south of this
position. The submarine then withdrew to seaward and the
cannister, filled with water, and containing the blanket, tapes
and also the rubber dinghy's container was pushed over the side in
position 36°37'30 North 07°18'00 West in 310 fathoms of water by
sounding machine. The container would not at first submerge but
after being riddled by fire from Vickers gun and also .455 revolver
at very short range was seen to sink.
Signal reporting operation complete was passed at 0715.
A sample of the water close inshore is attached.

                                  N. L. A. JEWELL.

                                  Lieutenant-in-Command.

Postscript

The story of Operation Mincemeat is far from over. The events themselves took place sixty-six years ago, and all but a handful of those involved in the planning and execution of the operation are now gone. Yet the story continues to grow, as new information, new memories, and new documents come to light.

The Black Lion

A week after publication, I received the sort of telephone call writers of non-fiction routinely receive, and usually dread. 'I believe you have got something wrong...' said a polite voice. My heart sank a little. The voice continued: 'In Chapter Seven you wrote, "The plot would never have stood up to scrutiny if German spies in Britain had made even the most cursory checks on it ... A glance at the hotel register for the Black Lion Hotel would have showed that no J. G. Martin had stayed there on the night of 13 April."' I braced myself. I had indeed written that the letter supposedly written by Bill Martin's 'Father' at a specific hotel on a specific date was a dangerous hostage to fortune. 'Well, I happen to have the old register for the Black Lion open in front of me. And if you look at the page for April, 1943, you will clearly see the name J. G. Martin.'

I was flabbergasted, and my respect for the planners of Operation Mincemeat rose another notch. They had thought of everything: they had even despatched someone to Mold, in North Wales, to stay at the hotel and pose as the fictional father of a fictional officer, simply to ensure that the hotel register would look correct if anyone came snooping afterwards. That was true spycraft.

When the caller sent me a photograph of the page from the register, I studied it carefully. The handwriting appeared to be that of Charles Cholmondeley, the originator and co-creator of Operation Mincemeat. The false address given for 'J. G. Martin' was Scotts House, Eynsham, in Oxfordshire (now a day care centre).

The faked letter in Major Martin's pocket clearly indicated that 'Father' had been staying at the hotel for some time ('the only alternative to imposing myself once more on your aunt'). According to the register, he had arrived at the hotel on 9 April, and checked out on 20 April, in time for the fake meeting with his son in London. So far, so convincing.

But closer examination revealed something very odd. The name and signature of J. G. Martin did not appear in the correct date sequence, but was added in the space at the bottom of the page. It was clearly an afterthought, written in at a later date; and possibly much later. To even the most casual investigator this would have set off loud alarm bells: far from covering up the mistake, Cholmondeley had compounded it, by drawing attention to the fact that there was something distinctly out of the ordinary about John Martin and his sojourn at the Black Lion.

One can speculate about what must have happened. As Operation Mincemeat got underway, the planners began to realise that it was working far more effectively than they had dared to hope. They began to wonder and worry about possible loose ends. The coroner, Bentley Purchase, was contacted again and quizzed over whether, if the Germans exhumed the body and carried out another post mortem, they would be able discover that he had died of poisoning, rather than drowning. (The cheery coroner, ever optimistic, was confident they would not.) They also, I suspect, took another look at the letters, and despatched Cholmondeley to Mold to doctor the record. The result was not a cover-up, but a giveaway. A register without the name J. G. Martin would merely have presented a mystery; a register with the name so obviously added in was patently a botched attempt to deceive.

In the end, it did not matter. There is no evidence that the Germans ever carried out any checks in Britain on the Bill Martin backstory. Had they attempted to do so, this would almost certainly have been picked up by British intelligence since the entire German espionage system in the UK was effectively controlled by MI5. Once the lie was embedded in German strategic thinking, no effort was made to disprove it.

Still, it is a sobering thought, that if a single German agent had travelled to Mold to examine the register of the Black Lion, he would surely have spotted the obvious subsequent addition of 'J. G. Martin', realised there was something fishy going on, and warned the Germans before the invasion of Sicily, with incalculable consequences. That single register entry could have changed the course of the Second World War.

The planners deliberately placed John Martin in a hotel to ensure there was no home address for the Martins that a German spy might be able to investigate. To his credit, Montagu felt rather guilty for casting aspersions on the hotel in the fake letter: 'I cannot say that this hotel is any longer as comfortable as I remember it to have been in pre-war days'. Even so, 'Father' may have had a point. The Black Lion went out of business after the war. It is now the Halifax bank.

The help of the Post Office

A letter from another reader drew my attention to a different anomaly. The letter from the bank manager to Bill Martin was addressed to him at the Army and Navy Club, yet all the other documents, including a bill from the club itself, clearly showed that he had been staying at the Naval and Military Club, an entirely different establishment. This looked like a glaring error. Whoever typed up the letter from the bank had, it seemed, mixed up the two armed forces clubs. Why had Cholmondeley and Montagu, usually so meticulous and entirely absorbed in the fictional character and habits of their creation, failed to spot the mistake? Why, for that matter, had the Germans missed this clear proof that these were not genuine documents, but fabrications?

But when I went back to the archives, I discovered that so far from being a mistake, the wrongly addressed letter was part of the plan. The envelope containing the bank manager's dunning letter was indeed addressed to Martin at the Army and Navy Club, but the club name had been crossed out – scrawled below were the words 'Not known at this address. Try Naval and Military Club, 94 Piccadilly'. The envelope had even been postmarked twice: the first time 14 April, and the second, when it was forwarded to the correct address, 18 April – the very day that Bill Martin supposedly checked in.

Far from being a mistake, the wrongly addressed letter was yet another way to bolster the apparent genuineness of the documents, a tiny, subtle twist to the story. If the Germans spotted it, it would only serve to show that Bill Martin was a real person, with a real bank manager, who made a real (though unimportant) mistake when demanding that he pay off his overdraft. And if Bill Martin was real, then his official documents would also seem the more believable.

I can't help thinking that the wrongly addressed envelope was also a sly joke, of the sort that serving officers might appreciate, at the expense of Ernest Whitley Jones, the pompous Joint General Manager of Lloyds Bank. Bank managers may be most efficient, even peremptory, in demanding that we pay off an overdraft, but they don't know the difference between one services club and the other.

Out of date

There is one other oddity in Bill Martin's 'wallet litter' that was brought to my attention after publication. The Major's pass for Combined Operations Headquarters was out of date, since it clearly states 'Not Valid after March 31st, 1943'. Here was yet another reinforcement of the character – disorganised, dreamy and inclined to overlook details. His photographic identity card also underlined this aspect of his personality, since it was 'issued in lieu of No. 09650 lost'. This would also allay the suspicions of any German intelligence officer who wondered why the identity card seemed so new (despite Montagu's attempts to give it the patina of wear). Major Martin was simply the sort of person who spent £53 on a diamond ring despite a thumping overdraft, lost his identity card, and forgot to renew his official pass. But the expired pass poses a small mystery: if the fictional Major Martin could not get into Combined Operations Headquarters, how did he manage to pick up the letters from Lord Mountbatten? We will never know because, of course, no such thing ever happened.

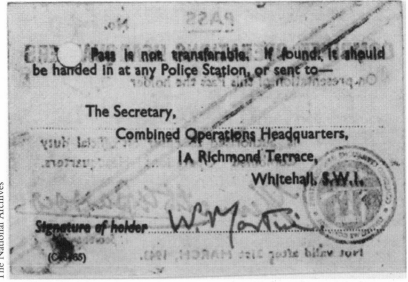

The name Martin was chosen partly because there were several Martins in the Royal Marines, and also because the real William Martin was the right age, rank and far enough away not to make trouble. William Hynd Norrie Martin's son, Peter Martin, wrote to me explaining that in 1943 his father was 'the

Assistant Superintendent of British Air Training at Quonset Point, Rhode Island, in charge of training and converting British aircrews to Avenger and Vought Corsair aircraft'. But the name was also chosen because it began with 'M'. Montagu knew – through the Ultra intercepts passed on by Bletchley Park – that the Germans only had the first volume of the Navy List, covering letters A to L. If they tried to check up on the identity, they would have to obtain the second volume, or use intermediaries who had access to it, and any such attempt at verification would probably appear in the intercepts.

Dudley Clarke

After the war, Colonel Clarke, the chief of deception in the Mediterranean, was unstinting in his praise for Operation Mincemeat. 'Preparation of the body had called for infinite pains and untold ingenuity: not the smallest detail had been overlooked and every conceivable contingency had been provided for. It was a masterpiece of planning and stage-management'.

Yet the mystery of Clarke's own transvestite brush with the Spanish police was one detail of the story that many readers seemed to find particularly intriguing. Several went to the trouble of digging up more details on this episode.

Clarke was arrested on 18 October 1943, on a street in Madrid. He was apparently in Spain to recruit agents to help with his deception work, although the specifics of his mission remain tantalisingly vague. Whether he was arrested on suspicion of espionage, or because he looked like a man in women's clothes, is not revealed. He first told the Spanish police that he was a novelist and 'wanted to study the reactions of men to women in the streets'. He then changed his story, insisting he was 'taking the feminine garments to a lady in Gibraltar' and thought that he would 'try them on for a prank'.

The British embassy was sceptical, pointing out, in a telegram that could hardly contain its mirth, that the shoes fitted him perfectly, and he had 'unusually big feet'. The police decided that Clarke must be a 'homosexualist'; the Gestapo in Spain concluded he must be a spy. His colleagues could not work out *what* he was.

Once liberated from jail by Alan Hillgarth, Clarke played down the whole incident with magnificent nerve. Indeed, he brazenly asserted that the affair had been intentional, and had helped to reinforce his cover as a correspondent for *The Times* – although as a former foreign correspondent of *The Times* myself, I am not sure how flattered I am by this line of argument.

The incident even merited a small footnote in the most famous spy scandal of all. On 31 October 1941, Kim Philby, in a message that can only have reinforced the KGB's belief in Western decadence, reported to his Moscow handlers: 'So far, no reason has reached London as to why he was found in women's clothes.'

Franco's hand in the matter

I had always suspected that General Franco must have known about the Mincemeat documents, but with the publication of *Deathly Deception* by Denis Smyth (Oxford University Press, 2010), came proof. According to Smyth, an authority on Spanish history, the documents were translated into Spanish and forwarded to the *Caudillo*. Franco himself must therefore have approved the appointment of Colonel Pardo as a go-between, and then personally authorised the passing on of the secret documents in direct contravention of Spain's supposed neutrality.

Professor Smyth also sheds additional light on the route the information took to Berlin. On 8 May, soon after the documents had been extracted from their envelopes but before handing them over to the Germans, a Spanish officer (almost certainly Pardo) briefed an Abwehr officer (either Leissner or

Kuhlenthal) on the gist of the Nye letter. This information was written up in a 'Most Secret Letter', and taken by hand to Berlin by Kurt von Rohrscheidt of the Madrid Abwehr counter-espionage section, who had no idea of its contents. According to this timetable, Alexis Von Roenne, the head of FHW, gave his initial seal of approval to the intelligence contained in this letter before he had even seen the photographs of the original documents – yet more evidence of his determination to believe them, without question or investigation. A few days later, with Berlin's appetite thoroughly wetted, Kuhlenthal arrived bearing copies of the letters themselves.

Fisher's knickers

The use of H. A. L. Fisher's underwear to clothe the dead man prompted a remarkable correspondence in *The Times*. Unlike other types of clothing, underwear was available only with ration coupons, and could not simply be bought in a shop. None of the officers, understandably, was willing to surrender his own.

On 14 January 2010 *The Times* published a letter from Harry Judge, fellow of Brasenose College, Oxford, and an authority on the life of Fisher, under the headline 'Upper-class unmentionables – No upper-class corpse would be convincing without appropriate underwear.' Garments that had previously belonged to Fisher were given by his widow to her nephew, Courtenay. He handed them over to intelligence officers (in circumstances that are not clear), who wisely removed the Cash's name tapes. I was first told of this unlikely detail by [the historian] Hugh Trevor-Roper in 1978 and, doubting it, secured confirmation from Fisher's late daughter, at that time the Principal of St Hilda's College.'

Courtenay Young, an intelligence colleague of John Masterman, appears to have obtained the underwear from his aunt Lettice, Fisher's widow, in response to a request from

Masterman himself. Lettice does not seem to have found the request remotely odd. As her nephew, Robin Ilbert, wrote: 'She was indeed a remarkable combination of keen intellect and common sense, needing to spend a portion of each day either gardening and being a keen hen wife, or playing her violin. Household economics, and household economy, were in her bones. Add that to "Make Do and Mend" and clothes rationing during the war, and you will find it entirely credible that Lettice should, after Herbert's death, post Herbert's clothes to Courtenay. And then the presence of mind to remove the then ubiquitous Cash's name tapes!' In fact, the planners of Operation Mincemeat carefully had the underwear laundered again, to make sure the laundry marks were the same as those on the rest of Bill Martin's clothing.

Mr Judge's letter triggered the sort of exchange that could only take place in the letters page of *The Times*. Stanley Martin, author of *The Order of Merit*, an account of Fisher's life, wrote to report that in the 1980s the story of the underwear was part of New College folklore. Alistair Cooke wrote from London: 'Sir, H. A. L. Fisher, Warden of New College, Oxford, from 1925 to 1940, was not the kind of man who would have wanted his underwear to end up on a dead young tramp to help to deceive the Germans. He followed his godfather, the Prince Consort, in reserving his approval for "anything that he found exalted". He had no time for life's failures. As Lloyd George's Minister for Education, his one objective was to help "young ambition starving for knowledge and stinted in opportunities". Nor would the destruction of Germany have appealed to him. His last published article, which appeared in February 1940, expressed the hope that "a *modus vivendi* with the Germans" would be found. A contribution to Operation Mincemeat should have been sought from the clothes closet of Oxford's most zealous supporter of the war, A. L. Rowse, of All Souls.'

Here, then, was the sort of debate that John Masterman, don

and spy, would have relished: which Oxford academic would most willingly have surrendered his underwear to confound Hitler?

'Animals'

The SOE operation in Greece to bolster the deception was codenamed 'Animals' (p. 281), and it played a crucial role in maintaining German focus on the Eastern Mediterranean, long after it became obvious that Sicily would be attacked by the Allies. After parachuting into Northern Greece, Lieutenant Colonel Eddie Myers and Captain Monty Woodhouse were ordered to launch a coordinated campaign of sabotage, starting in late June 1943 and continuing throughout the invasion period. The intention was quite specific, according to a memo written by Woodhouse now in the National Archives: 'To create the utmost havoc in the enemy's communications throughout the length and breadth of Greece, in order to deceive the enemy into thinking that this was the preliminary to the invasion of Greece'.

On 21 June 1943, a six-man sabotage team destroyed the railway viaduct at Asopos, after scaling down a cliff and through a waterfall. Across the country, roads were blown up, railways ruptured and telephone lines cut. With the viaduct down, the 1st German Panzer division was effectively trapped. The guerrilla campaign made it practically impossible to reinforce Sicily with troops from Greece, but more importantly it redoubled the German conviction, sown by the Mincemeat deception and Operation Barclay, that Greece was facing imminent Allied attack.

Cholmondely's romance

The most touching letter I received in the wake of publication came from a former girlfriend of Charles Cholmondely, who also worked in intelligence during the war.

Courtesy of Tom Cholmondely

'I am so glad that Charles Cholmondeley has at last been given the credit due for his idea. I knew him when he was in MI5 and I worked in MI6. I inadvertently sent him some wrong papers in the diplomatic bag. He met me to return the papers and took me to the Piccadilly Hotel to dinner. He was a charming and modest companion, almost ashamed of being "chairborne" instead of "airborne". And if he was eccentric – well, so were a lot of others in MI6. He had a little car which he drove with the sunroof open and his head almost poking through and he unflatteringly described himself as "like toothpaste squeezed out of a tube", but I was used to tall men as my father was 6 ft 4 in. He gave me an opal ring which he had made himself, saying "It is not an engagement ring". He didn't want to settle down, as his life was too full of adventure. He loved the film *The Third Man* and we often danced to the signature tune. It

might have been the start of a beautiful romance ... thank you
for reminding me of him and of London during the war.'

The flirtatious aspect of Ewen Montagu's character is
clear from his letters to 'Pam'. Here was the correspondingly
romantic side of his partner, the self-effacing, self-mocking, and
chairborne Charles Cholmondeley.

Something in the words of his girlfriend – recalling him
so fondly, so many years later – reminded me of the fictional
relationship between 'Pam' and 'Bill', the doomed wartime love
affair that never was.

Ben Macintyre, June 2010

Courtesy of Judith Kuhlenthal

Karl Erich Kuhlenthal is standing second from left in a family photograph. Blurred as it is, this is the only surviving image of the German intelligence officer from the time he was working in Spain as head of the Abwehr's espionage section.

Courtesy of Patricia Davies

Patricia Trehearne, working in Room 13. Miss Trehearne addressed the envelopes of the official letters: the only other person to handle the documents was Ewen Montagu. Too many sets of fingerprints might have alerted the Germans that these were no routine letters.

Courtesy of Lawrence and Wisam

Ivor Montagu, table tennis aficionado, film maker and vole-expert. In this photograph Ivor looks indisputably (and somewhat self-consciously) like the Soviet spy he was.

Courtesy of Jeremy Montagu

Ewen Montagu smoking his pipe. In the cramped confinement of Room 13, which housed fourteen people without windows or ventilation, no one ever forgot the smell of Montagu's pipe.

Notes

Epigraph

'Who in war will not have . . .' Winston Churchill, *The Second World War*, Vol. V *Closing the Ring* (London, 1951), p. 91.

Preface

'some memoranda which . . .' Ewen Montagu, *Beyond Top Secret Ultra* (London, 1977), p. 14.

Chapter 1: The Sardine Spotter

'lump' Cited in Jesús Ramírez Copeiro del Villar, *Huelva en la II Guerra Mundial* (Huelva 1996), p. 408.
'no-one wanted . . .' Ibid., p. 409.

Chapter 2: Corkscrew Minds

'The Trout Fisher' TNA ADM 223/478.
'marked flair' Cited in Ben Macintyre, *For Your Eyes Only: Ian Fleming and James Bond* (London, 2008), p. 42.
'romantic Red Indian daydreams' Ibid., p. 43.
'deception, ruses de guerre' TNA ADM 223/478.
'At first sight' Ibid.
'The business of deception' John Godfrey, 'Afterthoughts', TNA ADM 223/619, p. 51.
'pushing quicksilver' Ibid.
'treasure ship' TNA ADM 223/478.
'an unimpeachable and immaculate' Ibid.
'with instructions on the' Ibid.

'A Suggestion (not a very nice one)' Ibid.

'research' *Time* magazine, 'The Thomson Case', 18 Jan 1926.

'I know the stuff' Basil Thomson, *The Milliner's Hat Mystery* (London, 1937), p. 64.

'offers us far more' Godfrey, 'Afterthoughts', TNA ADM 223/619 p. 26.

'the target date' David Kahn, *Hitler's Spies: German Military Intelligence in World War II* (New York, 2000), p. 471.

'extremely worried' *After the Battle*, 54, 1986.

'not been tampered with' Kahn, *Hitler's Spies*, p. 471.

'quite legible' Ibid.

'It was highly unlikely' Ibid.

'All the documents' TNA CAB 163/1.

'no greater importance' Kahn, *Hitler's Spies*, p. 471.

'documents had likely' Frank J. Stech, 'Outguessed and One-Behind: The Real Story of The Man Who Never Was,' paper presented to conference, University of Wolverhampton, Jul 2004.

'This suggested that' TNA ADM 223/794.

'lifting his toes as he walked' Interview with Jean Gerard Leigh (JGL), 5 Mar 2008

'This was a terrible' Interview with Tom Cholmondeley, 1 Oct 2007.

'ideas man' Thaddeus Holt, *The Deceivers: Allied Military Deception in the Second World War* (London, 2004), p. 370.

'extraordinary and delightful' Ibid.

'one of those subtle' Ewen Montagu, *The Man Who Never Was* (Oxford, 1996), p. 116.

'a plan for introducing documents' IWM 97/45/1, folder #2.

'A body is obtained from one' Ibid.

'the drop' Ibid.

'double for an actual officer' Ibid.

'and injuries inflicted after death' Montagu, *Man*, p. 116.

'a full and capable postmortem' Memo to XX Committee, 4 Feb 1943, IWM 97/45/1 folder #2.

'Of these, Spain was clearly' Ibid.

'Meinertzhagen knew no half measures' T. E. Lawrence, *Seven Pillars of Wisdom* (London, 1991), p. 452.

'Good-bye, my darling!' John Lord, *Duty, Honour, Empire* (London, 1971) p. 332.

'easy, reliable and inexpensive' Meinertzhagen, *Army Diary*, cited in ibid., p. 336.

'fair going' Holt, *The Deceivers*, p. 95.

'there was never any evidence' Ibid., p. 297.

Chapter 3: Room 13

'The Germans, having cause to regret' Jimmy Burns, *Papa Spy: Love, Faith and Betrayal in Wartime Spain* (London, 2009), p. 233.

'strongly supported' Draft of report on Operation Mincemeat, 29 May 1943, IWM 97/45/1 folder #2.

'go into the question' Ibid.

'fertile brain' Montagu, *Man*, p. 108.

'My memory is of' Ewen Montagu, Untitled, unpublished autobiography in manuscript, in Montagu Papers, courtesy of Jeremy Montagu. Henceforth Ewen Montagu, *Autobiography*.

'*Montagu, first Baron Swaythling he*' Ivor Montagu, *The Youngest Son: Autobiographical Chapters* (London, 1970), p. 18.

'exquisite chandelier' Ewen Montagu, *Autobiography*.
'Statesmen (British and world)' Ibid.
'like a very animated piece' Ibid.
'It was a *servants'* lift' Montagu, *Younger Son*, p. 14.
'Born as I was' Ewen Montagu, *Autobiography*.
'idiotic' Ibid.
'the sort of American social life' Ibid.
'I felt a great debt' Ibid.
'The 'spread' among us three' Ibid.
'already had a banker's attitude' Ibid.
'He and I were much' Ibid.
'we had nothing to do' Ibid.
'I advised him to choose' Ibid.
'Our great ambition was' Ibid.
'to study something' Ibid.
'I put it in my pocket' Ibid.
'one of the best fly-fisherman' Anthony Cave Brown, *Bodyguard of Lies*, Vol. I
    (London, 1975), p. 278.
'never better than a mediocre' Ewen Montagu, *Autobiography*.
'the thrill of the strike' Ibid.
'an exceedingly primitive vole' Montagu, *Younger Son*, p. 283.
'Baron's Son Weds Secretary' *Evening News*, 23 Mar 1927.
'Dear Gladys, I feel for you' Obituary of Lord Swaythling, *Daily Telegraph*, 4 Jul
    1998.
'remarkably obscene curse' Ivor Montagu, *Like it Was*, unpublished, undated
    autobiography, manuscript in Montagu Collection, Labour History Archive
    and Study Centre (People's History Museum), Manchester. Henceforth Ivor
    Montagu, *Autobiography*.
'a certain sympathy with rogue characters' Montagu, *Ultra*, p. 9.
'see the point of view' Ibid.
'gentle manners' M. R. D. Foot, entry in *Oxford Dictionary of National Biography*
'If he could see a really artistic lie' Ewen Montagu, *Autobiography*.
'looking out to sea' Ibid.
'It is quite useless' TNA ADM 223/478.
'two stockbrokers, a schoolmaster' Godfrey, 'Afterthoughts', TNA ADM 223/619
    p. 26.
'The permanent inhabitants' Ibid.
'worked like ants' Ibid.
'learning a new language' Ewen Montagu, 'History of Section 17M (now
    section 12Z)', 26 Oct 1942, courtesy of Jeremy Montagu. Henceforth Montagu
    Papers.
'the cream of all intelligence' TNA ADM 223/792.
'The Germans have a passion' Ewen Montagu, 'History of Section 17M', Montagu
    Papers.
'to do the detailed work' Ibid.
'Auntie' Interview with Pat Davies (née Trehearne), 4 Oct 2009.
'She is extraordinarily good' EM to Iris Montagu (IM), 31 Jan 1941, courtesy of
    Rachel Montagu. Henceforth Montagu Letters.
'watchkeepers' TNA ADM 223/792.
'far too small' Montagu, *Ultra*, p. 51.
'which made everyone' Interview with Pat Davies (née Trehearne), 5 Oct 2009.
'were not supposed to listen to' TNA ADM 223/792.

'a brilliant band of . . .' John Godfrey (JG) to EM, 13 Sep 1964, Montagu Papers.
'began to regard some almost as friends' 'History of Section 17M', Montagu Papers.
'They were so kind to us unconsciously' Montagu, *Ultra*, p. 52.
'in the racket too' EM to Vera Ruth Filby, 3 Feb 1979, Montagu Papers.
'The most fascinating job' Montagu, *Ultra*, p. 50.
'If I am killed there are' EM to IM, 17 Aug 1941, Montagu Letters.
'very entertaining but useless' 'History of Section 17M', Montagu Papers.
'A great number who' Montagu, *Ultra*, p. 36.
'it might be an indication' Naval Intelligence Department memo, 12/13 Sep 1945
    TNA ADM 223/794.
'Though I have kept' Victor Rothschild to EM, 13 Nov 1941, TNA ADM 223/794.
'had heard and believed the propaganda' TNA ADM 223/794.
'I thought you had realised' Montagu, *Ultra*, p. 59.
'an out and out traitor' TNA ADM 223/794.
'a four-letter man' EM to IM, 13 Nov 1942, Montagu Letters.
'Fleming is charming' Ibid.
'The bare idea of the dead airman' JG to EM, 13 Sep 1964, Montagu Papers.
'I quite honestly don't remember' EM to JG, 19 Sep 1964, Montagu Papers.

Chapter 4: Target Sicily

'underbelly of the Axis' Churchill speech, 11 Nov 1942.
'no major operation could be' Ewen Montagu, unpublished critique of Constantine
    Fitzgibbon, *Secret Intelligence in the Twentieth Century* (London, 1976), Montagu Papers.
'and might be the beginning' Cited in Rick Atkinson, *The Day of Battle: The War in
    Sicily and Italy 1943–1945* (London, 2007), p. 7.
'Everyone but a bloody fool' Montagu, *Ultra*, p. 143.
'prepare deception plans' Christopher Andrew, *The Defence of the Realm: The
    Authorized History of MI5* (London 2009), p. 284.
'When things were looking pretty' Holt, *The Deceivers*, p. 184.
'an ingenious imagination' Nicholas Rankin, *Churchill's Wizards: The British Genius
    for Deception 1914–1945* (London, 2008), p. 178.
'fourteen of the biggest Nigerians' Ibid., p. 181.
'special section of intelligence' Ibid., p. 253.
'The idea of knocking' 'Future Anglo Saxon Operative Possibilities', FHW of
    OKW 8/2/43, cited in Ralph Bennett, *Ultra and Mediterranean Strategy 1941–
    1945* (London, 1989), p. 227.
'wishfulness' and 'yesmanship' Godfrey, 'Afterthoughts', TNA ADM 223/619, p. 10.
'If the authorities were clamouring' Ibid.
'inclined to believe the one' Ibid., p. 12.
'He could achieve single-handed' Colin Evans, *The Father of Forensics: How Sir
    Bernard Spilsbury Invented Modern CSI* (London, 2009), p. 122.
'He formed his opinion' Ibid., p. 27.
'just carried on' Ewen Montagu, *Autobiography*.
'England's modern Sherlock Holmes' *Washington Post*, 30 Mar 1938, p. 3.
'haughty, aristocratic bearing' Evans, *The Father of Forensics*, p. 5.
'unlucky sixteen' *After the Battle*, 11, Nov 2006.
'that extraordinary man' Montagu, *Man*, p. 122.
'wanted the Germans and Spaniards' Ibid.
'never once did he ask why' Ibid.
'clear, resonant, without any trace' Evans, *The Father of Forensics*, p. 27.

'Many die from exposure' Montagu, *Man*, p. 122.

'doing a Burke and Hare' Ibid.

'A depressing job?' Robert Jackson, *Coroner: The Biography of Sir Bentley Purchase* (London, 1963), p. 5.

'They were found in Auntie's bag' Ibid., p. 260.

'rugged in appearance and character' Ibid., p. 15.

'an impish sense of humour' Ibid.

'an old friend from my barrister days' EM to Roger Morgan, 19 Apr 1982, Montagu Papers.

'An alternative means of getting' Bentley Purchase to EM , 25 Aug 1953, Montagu Papers.

'conspicuous gallantry and devotion to duty' Jackson, *Coroner*, p. 28.

'aching to get into the war' Ibid., p. 104.

'distort the truth in the service of security' Roger Morgan in *After the Battle*, 54, 1986.

'cursory in the extreme' Ibid.

'a warlike operation' Jackson, *Coroner*, p. 148.

'did not wish to disclose why a body' Ibid.

'You can't get bodies just' Ibid.

'of national importance' Ibid.

'public confidence in coroners' Ibid.

'At what level has this scheme . . .' Ibid.

'The Prime Minister's' Ibid.

'well-developed sense of comedy' Ibid., p. 313.

'absolute discretion' EM to JG, 19 Sep 1964, Montagu Papers.

'A coroner' Ibid.

'remained unidentified' Jackson, *Coroner*, p. 196.

'After one or two possible corpses' Ibid., p. 148.

'the inevitable misery of separation' Montagu, *Ultra,* p. 65.

'I miss you most frightfully' EM to IM, 11 Aug 1941, Montagu Letters.

'In a way it was like a mixture' Montagu, *Ultra*, p. 61.

'It was lovely . . .' EM to IM, 11 Jun 1941, Montagu Letters.

'super-secret papers' Montagu, *Ultra*, p. 68.

'as long as I always wore' Ibid.

'one of the best cooks in London' Ibid., p. 28.

'Mother is too awful' EM, 11 Aug 1941, Montagu Letters.

'crossword puzzles' Montagu, *Ultra*, p. 61.

'who had been in the family' Ewen Montagu, *Autobiography*.

Chapter 5: The Man Who Was

'senile decay' Medical records of Angelton Mental Hospital, Bridgend, 11 Dec 1924, Glamorgan Record Office.

'melancholic' Ibid., 12 Dec 1924.

'confused and very depressed' Ibid.

'deep mental depression' Ibid.

'Hair is grey and thin' Ibid.

'a hectic temperature' Ibid., 28 Mar 1925.

'on condition that the scale' House of Commons Debate, 6 Jul 1926, Hansard, Vol. 197.

'led men and women to London' Jackson, *Coroner*, p. 196.

'It still surprised him' Ibid.

'a common lodging house' Draft of report on Operation Mincemeat, 29 May 1943, IWM 97/45/1 folder #2.

'kept in suitable cold storage' Montagu, *Man,* p. 123.

'lunatic' Glyndwr Michael, death certificate.

'labourer, no fixed abode' Ibid.

'phosphorus poisoning' Ibid.

'removed out of England' Draft of report on Operation Mincemeat, 29 May 1943, IWM 97/45/1 folder #2.

'a minimal dose' EM to J. H. Bevan (JHB), 28 May 1943, TNA CAB 154/67.

'This dose was not sufficient' Ibid.

'phosphorus is not one of' Ibid.

'except possibly faint' Draft of report on Operation Mincemeat, 29 May 1943, IWM 97/45/1 folder #2.

'a highly skilled medico-criminal' EM to JHB, 28 May 1943, TNA CAB 154/67.

'bet heavily against anyone' Ibid.

'You have nothing to fear' Montagu, *Man,* p. 123.

'I am a martyr to Spilsburyism' Andrew Rose, *Lethal Witness: Sir Bernard Spilsbury, the Honorary Pathologist* (London, 2008), p. 139.

'died from pneumonia after exposure' Montagu, *Man,* p. 123.

'really worthwhile purpose' Ibid.

'on condition that I should never' Ibid.

'feverish enquiries into his past' Ibid.

'The most careful possible' Draft MS of *Man,* IWM 97/45/2.

'a ne'er do well, and his relatives' EM to Billy Bob Crim, 26 Dec 1981, Montagu Papers

'extra-cold refrigerator' TNA ADM 223/794, p. 450.

'would have to be used within' Minutes of XX Committee, 4 Feb 1943, IWM 97/45/1 folder #2.

'They ought not to be given names' Winston Churchill to General 'Pug' Ismay, minute, 8 Aug 1943.

'stupidity' Montagu, *Ultra,* p. 52.

'no deductions could be' Ibid.

'sense of humour' Montagu, *Man,* p. 125.

'good omen' Ibid.

'This Operation is proposed' Memo to XX Committee, 4 Feb 1943, IWM 97/45/1 folder #2.

'a courier carrying important' Ibid.

'the real target is omitted from' Ibid.

'the Germans will be looking' Ibid.

'The body must be dropped' Ibid.

'find out a suitable position' Minutes of XX Committee, 4 Feb 1943, IWM 97/45/1 folder #2.

'into the question of providing' Ibid.

'so he will be able to cope' Ibid.

'continue with preparations' Ibid.

Chapter 6: A Novel Approach

'active and well-distributed team' J. C. Masterman, *The Double Cross System in the War 1939–1945* (London, 1972), p. 119.

'The one-man band of Lisbon' Ibid., p. 146.

'for deception, "notional"' Ibid., p. 33.
'The Germans could seldom resist' Ibid., p. 21.
'How difficult it was' Montagu, *Ultra*, p. 43.
'must *never* step out of character' Ibid.
'The more real he appeared' Montagu, *Man*, p. 149.
'Would the ink of the manuscript' Manuscript of 'Post Script' to Montagu, *Man*, p. 4, Montagu Papers.
'give the game away' Ibid.
'Many inks on a freshly written' Ibid., p. 6.
'We talked about him until' Montagu, *Man*, p. 149.
'He does not have to look like' Ibid. p. 123.
'complete failure' Ibid., p. 140.
'appearance that would have' Ibid., p. 141.
'rudely staring at anyone' Ibid.
'almost the same build' Ibid., p. 146.
'The difficulty of obtaining' Masterman, *Double Cross*, p. 137.
'one enormous mausoleum' Michael Ignatieff, *Isaiah Berlin*, p. 60.
'brilliant' 'Obituary' of William Martin, TNA CAB 154/67.
'Keen for more active and dangerous' Ibid.
'a thoroughly good chap' Undated note in CAB 154/67.
'could sometimes come from head' EM to Miss Winton, Lloyds Bank, 29 Feb 1978, Montagu Papers.
'a father of the old school' Montagu, *Man,* p. 154.
'a brilliant tour de force' Ibid.
' . . . at the last moment' TNA, WO 106-5921-15.
'effort to find a flaw in' Montagu, *Man*, p. 149.
'We decided that a' Ibid., p. 150.

Chapter 7: Pam

'What on earth are we going to do' Interview with JGL, 5 Mar 2008.
'glaring inconsistencies' Ibid.
'I was frightfully willing' Ibid.
'Don't run, Miss Leslie!' Ibid.
'In fact, he was trailing me' Ibid.
'charming' Montagu, *Man*, p. 152.
'very attractive' Draft of Operation Mincemeat report EM and CC, 27 April 1943, IWM 97/45/1 folder #2.
'The more attractive girls in' Montagu, *Man*, p. 152.
'I think he had every intention' Interview with JGL, 5 Mar 2008.
'The swimming there was horrible' Ibid.
'quite a collection' Montagu, *Man*, p. 152.
'Uncle John gave specific orders' Interview with Pat Davies (née Trehearne), 4 Oct 2009.
'We were all rather jealous' Ibid.
'I knew it was going to be planted' Interview with JGL, 5 Mar 2008.
'Has anybody else got that' Ibid.
'I never realised how lonely' EM to IM, 17 Aug 1941, Montagu Letters.
'How ultra-happy our life was' EM to IM, 30 Dec 1940, Montagu Letters.
'Bugger Hitler' Ibid.
'You must have gone off' EM to IM, 2 Dec 1940, Montagu Letters.

'I am always the gooseberry' EM to IM, 28 Sep 1941, Montagu Letters.
'It was a question of whether' EM to IM, 22 Dec 1940, Montagu Letters.
'I took a girl from the office' EM to IM, 19 Apr 1942, Montagu Letters.
'no German could resist the "Englishness"' Montagu, *Man,* p. 152.
'achieved the thrill and pathos' Ibid.
'P.L. from W.M. 14.4.43' TNA, WO 106-5921-19.
'We will insert the legacy of £50' Montagu, *Man,* p. 156.
'since the wife's family will not' Ibid.
'The nearer the approach' John Godfrey, 'Afterthoughts' TNA ADM 223/619.
'He is very old' EM to IM, 13 Nov 1942, Montagu Letters.
'He was the world's prize shit' EM to Captain A. N. Grey, 12 Dec 1980, IWM
    97/45/1 folder #5.
'the unhoped-for benefit' EM to 'Ginger', 6 Jul 1943, Montagu Papers.
'preparation and devising' Ibid.
'was entirely unsupervised' Ibid.
'How will that argument' Montagu, *Ultra,* p. 90.
'There was almost complete' TNA ADM 223/794.
'Masterman raised the question' Ibid.
'execution subcommittee' Ibid.
'the only deceptioneer' Ibid.
'enthusiasm for all things Russian' TNA KV2/598.
'attracted by Marxism' Ivor Montagu, *Autobiography.*
'We have had a request' Ibid.
'the keenest players' Ibid.
'Dear Comrade Trotsky' Ivor Montagu to Leon Trotsky, 1 Jul 1929, in Montagu
    Collection, Labour History Archive and Study Centre (People's History Museum).
'able, even brilliant' Ivor Montagu, *Autobiography.*
'allowed this quality to divorce' Ibid.
'like Edinburgh at its worst' Ibid.
'Two Turkish policemen' Ibid.
'to put under my pillow' Ibid.
'I did not know what precautions' Ibid.
'The memory I shall always . . .' Ibid.
'fascinating and commanding' Ibid.
'repelled by his self-admiration' Ibid.
'I felt I understood' Ibid.
'Ivor Montagu has' Leon Trotsky to Reg Groves, 13 Jul 1932, KV2/598.
'Montagu has for some time' Memo, 10 May 1926, KV2/598.
'Montagu has dark curly hair' Ibid.
'What is the use of living' Ivor Montagu, *Autobiography.*
'Last night Ivor came dinner' EM to IM, 30 Jun 1942, Montagu Letters.
'Hell is digging for victory' EM to IM, 4 Aug 1940, Montagu Letters.
'Ivor is really bad' EM to IM, 2 Dec 1940, Montagu Letters.
'He is busy working for the Russian' EM to IM, 30 Jun 1942, Montagu Letters.
'knew in advance practically' Montagu, *Ultra,* p. 30.
'that particularly unpleasant' RHH to DP, MI5 report, 3 Mar 1942, TNA KV2/599.
'I have met representatives' TNA HW 15/43.
'Intelligentsia considers there is' Ibid.
'removed from the leadership' Ibid.
'secret parliamentary session' Ibid.
'influential relatives' TNA HW 15/43.
'Intelligentsia has not yet found' Ibid.

'Although one is somewhat deaf' J. B. S. Haldane, *What is Life* (London, 1949), p. 32.

'I think that Marxism' J. B. S. Haldane, *The Marxist Philosophy and the Sciences*, (New York, 1939) p. 4.

'Intelligentsia has handed over' TNA HW 15/43.

'three military sources' Ibid.

'that this was a matter' Ibid.

'I promised to bring' Ibid.

'reported that a girl' Ibid.

'an officer of the air ministry' Ibid.

'the organisational structure' Ibid.

'The coastal defence is' Ibid.

'30 Sausage Dealer bombers' Ibid.

'he still seems to be going on with . . .' EM to IM, 11 Jun 1941, Montagu Letters

'Intelligentsia has reported' TNA HW 15/43.

Chapter 8: The Butterfly Collector

'We felt that we knew' Montagu, *Man,* p. 160.

'joined up to go to sea' Montagu, *Ultra,* p. 20.

'an incurable romantic' Andrew, *Defence of the Realm,* p. 285.

'Ewen *lived* the part' Interview with JGL, 5 Mar 2008.

'He wrote me endless letters' Ibid.

'Till death us do part' Montagu, *Man,* p. 168.

'Pam dearest' EM to Jean Leslie, undated letter, courtesy of Jean Gerard Leigh.

'The girl from the Elms' EM to IM, 9 Jan 1943, Montagu Letters.

'One of her appealing virtues' EM to IM, 29 Jun 1943, Montagu Letters.

'She has been much connected' EM to IM, 15 Apr 1943, Montagu Letters.

'I took the girl from the Elms' Ibid.

'I feel definitely that you ought' Ibid.

'If Mother did touch my things' EM to IM, 29 Jun 1943, Montagu Letters.

'I told her truthfully that it was' Ibid.

'writing in her letters' Montagu, *Man,* p. 168.

'would not carry enough weight' TNA ADM 223/794 p. 442.

'to fake documents of a sufficiently' EM to Thomas Thibeault, 18 Mar 1980, Montagu Papers.

'a crooked lawyer's dream of heaven' Montagu, *Ultra,* p. 150.

'bone from the neck up' Atkinson, *Day of Battle,* p. 130.

'as if he had just had a steam bath' Ibid., pp. 130–31.

'Will Eisenhower go ahead' EM, first draft, 16 Feb 1943, TNA CAB 154/67.

'So and so [naming a general]' Ibid.

'personal and "off the record"' Ibid.

'the contents of such a letter' JHB report to T. A. Robertson (TAR), TNA CO/43/66, 12 Feb 1943.

'almost completely ignorant' EM memo, 5 Mar 1943, TNA ADM 223/794.

'is almost completely inexperienced' Ibid.

'From reports coming out' German high command to command in Tunisia, 26 Feb 1943, MSS 2180/T.28 IWM 97/4/1 folder #1.

'Sicily has now been allowed' EM memo, 5 Mar 1943, TNA ADM 223/794.

'It is much easier' Ibid.

'He still has no deception' Ibid.

'now in a highly dangerous situation' Ibid.

'It would be a very great pity' EM to TAR, 16 Feb 1943.

'Spanish police records' Tomas Harris, *Garbo: The Spy Who Saved D-Day* (London, 2004), p. 38.

'worked in military intelligence' Burns, *Papa Spy*, p. 232.

'a Spaniard to Spaniards' Ian Colvin, *The Unknown Courier* (London, 1953), pp. 98–9.

'because of his enormous' Hector Licudi, *Gibraltar Chronicle*, Aug 1989.

'no more than a smattering of' TNA ADM 223/490.

'padding about Madrid' Colvin, *Unknown Courier,* p. 98.

'exceptionally favoured by character' TNA ADM 223/490.

'He was invaluable' TNA ADM 223/490.

'privileges and facilities' Ibid.

'Spain contained a large' Ibid.

'Madrid was full of spies' Ibid.

'danger of the body' TNA ADM 223/794, p. 444.

'German influence in Huelva' Ibid.

'a reliable and helpful man' Ibid.

'very pro-German chief of police' Cyril Mills to EM, 8 Nov 1983, Montagu Papers.

'active and influential' TNA ADM 223/794, p. 444.

'The Shadow' Copeiro, *Huelva*, p. 306

'the viceroys' Interview with Jesús Ramírez Copeiro del Vilar, 3 Jun 2009.

'First the Romans' Ibid.

'the black sheep' Interview with Isabel Naylor, 3 Jun 2009.

'the only clever one in the family' Ibid.

'He didn't dispute' Interview with Federico Clauss, 2 Jun 2009.

'cold, distant and silent' Interview with Jesús Ramírez Copeiro del Vilar, 3 Jun 2009.

'He was an active and intelligent' Copeiro, *Huelva*, p. 306.

'very efficient German agent' EM to Lynne Gladstone-Miller, 1 Nov 1983, Montagu papers.

'a super-super efficient agent' 'History of section 17M', Montagu Papers.

'first rate' EM to Lynne Gladstone-Miller, 1 Nov 1983, Montagu Papers.

'No ship can move without being' 'History of section 17M', Montagu Papers.

'one of the most difficult' J. C. Masterman, cited in David Stafford, *Roosevelt and Churchill: Men of Secrets* (London 1999), p. 94.

'the tiniest jewel in the imperial' TNA KV4/260.

'increased and spread' 'History of section 17M', Montagu Papers.

'in all Spanish and Spanish owned ports' Ibid.

'one of the most important' Copeiro, *Huelva*, p. 306.

'sufficient evidence can be obtained' Draft of Operation Mincemeat Report, EM and CC, 27 April 1943, IWM 97/45/1 folder #2.

'They would have to' Ibid.

'the washing ashore of any' Ibid.

'was to be told the outline of the plan' Ibid.

Chapter 9: My Dear Alex

'owing to the need for placing' Charles Cholmondeley (CC), memo, 6a, TNA WO 106/5921.

'if the body were dropped in this way' Ibid.

'come in from out at sea' Ibid.

'After the body has been' Ibid.

'technical difficulties in keeping' Ibid.

'Of these methods' Ibid.

'unswerving logic of the German' Macintyre, *For Your Eyes Only*, p. 108.

'if most of the oxygen had previously' TNA ADM 223/794, p. 446.

'keep perfectly satisfactorily' EM to JHB, 26 Mar 1943, TNA ADM 223/464.

'an enormous Thermos flask' Montagu, *Man*, p. 126.

'HANDLE WITH CARE' TNA ADM 223/794, p. 445.

'the Spaniards and Portuguese' N. L. A. Jewell (NLAJ) operational orders, 31 Mar 1943, TNA ADM 223/464.

'the tides in that area' Ibid.

'wind between S and W' Hydrographer's Report, 22 Mar 1943, TNA W0 106/5921

'if it did not strand' Ibid.

'The currents on the coast' EM to JHB, 26 Mar 1943, TNA CAB 154/67.

'I am not quite clear as to who' JHB to EM, 1 Mar 1943, TNA CAB 154/67.

'thinking it couldn't come off' EM to 'Ginger', 6 Jul 1943, Montagu Papers.

'Mincemeat will be taken out' EM to JHB, 26 Mar 1943, TNA ADM 223/464.

'All the details are now 'buttoned up'' Ibid.

'alteration and improvement' Ibid.

'more personal' JHB to A. Nye (AN), 8 Apr 1943, TNA CAB 154/67.

'a letter in answer to one from' EM draft, 6 Apr 1943, TNA CAB 154/67.

'should not be undertaken' Admiralty amendment to official report, 3 Jun 1945, TNA CAB 154/67.

'rather too official' JHB to AN, 10 Apr 1943, TNA CAB 154/67.

'we must get Dudley Clarke's' JHB memo TNA CAB 154/67.

'danger of overloading' Dudley Clarke to JHB, 2 Apr 1943, TNA CAB 154/67.

'a mistake to play for high' Admiralty amendment to official report, 3 Jun 1945, TNA CAB 154/67.

'If anything miscarries' JHB, memo 12 Apr 1943, TNA CAB 154/67.

'merely a lowish grade innuendo' Excised paragraph 13 in 'Draft history of Operation Mincemeat', 29 May 1943, IWM 97/45/1 folder #2.

'Mincemeat should be capable' Admiralty amendment to official report, 3 Jun 1945, TNA CAB 154/67.

'of a type which could have' Excised paragraph 14 in 'Draft history of Operation Mincemeat', 29 May 1943, IWM 97/45/1 folder #2.

'If it isn't too much trouble' EM, undated draft letter, TNA CAB 154/67.

'How are you getting on' Ibid.

'Do you still take the same size' Ibid.

'What is wrong with Monty?' Ibid.

'the best way of giving it' EM, draft letter, 6 Apr 1943, TNA CAB 154/67.

'ideally suited to the purpose' Ibid.

'not blatantly mentioned' EM memo, 4 Apr 1943, TNA CAB 154/67.

'Your signature in ink might' JHB to AN, 8 Apr 1943, TNA CAB 154/67.

'General Wilson is referred to' Ibid.

'I referred to him variously' AN to JHB, 14 Apr 1943, TNA CAB 154/67.

'I would never have written' AN to EM, 26 Apr 1954, Montagu Papers.

'P.S. we saw you on the cinema' Ibid.

'Now I hope your friends' AN to JHB, 14 Apr 1943, TNA CAB 154/67.

'a truly magnificent letter' Montagu, *Man*, p. 135.

'It's too velvety-arsed and Rolls-Royce' Atkinson, *Day of Battle*, p. 52.

'laboured' Montagu, *Man*, p. 143.

'I thought that that sort of joke' Ibid.

'Papers actually on the body' CC, memo, 10 Feb 1943, TNA CAB 154/67 p. 229.

'the Chiefs of Staff have approved' TNA CAB 154/67.

'To my surprise I was ushered' JHB handwritten account, undated [15 Apr 1943], TNA CAB 154/67.

'In the higher ranges of Secret Service' Cited in Macintyre, *For Your Eyes Only*, p. 58.

'Of course there's a possibility' From conversation recalled by Randolph Churchill in conversation with JHB, recorded in Martin Gilbert, *Road to Victory* (London, 1981), p. 389.

'Weed-killer goes into the lungs' Ibid.

'took much interest' JHB handwritten account, undated [15 Apr 1943], TNA CAB 154/67.

'I pointed out that there' Ibid.

'In that case, we shall' Ibid.

'General Eisenhower gives full' IZ 1416, received 1620, 17 Apr 1943, Freedom Algiers to Air Ministry, TNA CAB 154/67.

Chapter 10: Table Tennis Traitor

'I get more and more optimistic' EM to IM, 24 Jan 1943, Montagu Letters.

'We ought, by the time' EM to IM, 13 Nov 1942, Montagu Letters.

Mincemeat is in the making' Guy Liddell, *The Guy Liddell Diaries, 1939–1945,* Vol. II (London, 2005), p. 45.

'Plan Mincemeat has been approved' Ibid., p. 67.

'in close touch with many Russians' TNA KV2 599.

'an incurable anti-nationalist' Ibid.

'facilities for sport were far greater' Ibid.

'men of decidedly foreign' Ibid.

'did not think Montagu would get' Ibid.

'his association with the Russians' Ibid.

'an active Fifth Columnist' Ibid.

'he is always very keen' Ibid.

'has a wooden hut' Ibid.

'It does not seem desirable' Ibid.

'whether this refusal is' *Hansard* 357, no 23, 14 Mar 1940.

'I myself have registered' TNA KV2 599.

'most undesirable that he should' Ibid.

'as a criminal conspiracy' Ibid.

'known to be queer in any other way' Ibid.

'The reason for our tentative interest' Ibid.

'Hanno-ball' Ibid.

'certain net-stretchers' Ibid.

'suspected of running an illegal' Ibid.

'be using the channel of international' Ibid.

'I know this all seems very trivial' Ibid.

'I had no great faith in the records' Montagu, *Ultra*, p. 48.

'How is the table tennis going?' Ibid. p. 49.

'That's my communist' Ibid.

'special examiners' History of Operation Mincemeat, 10 Apr 1945, CAB 154/67.

'if the eyelash was gone' Copeiro, *Huelva*, p. 426.

'Mine were used for Major Martin's' Montagu, *Ultra*, p. 149.

'an ordinary black Government' TNA ADM 223/794, p. 449.

'horribly phoney' Montagu, *Man*, p. 145.
'the use of a chain to the bag' CC, memo 10 Feb 1943, TNA CAB 154/67,
    p. 229.
'little or no wreckage floated' TNA ADM 223/794, p. 445.
'for simplification and for security' Ibid.
'might have been the twin brother' Montagu, *Man*, p. 141.
'far more like' Draft manuscript, *Man*, IWM 97/45/2.
'heartily disliked' Montagu, *Man*, p. 160.
'odd psychological reaction' Ibid.
'told to report to the intelligence' Interview with N. L. A. Jewell, 1991, IWM
    Sound Archive 12278.
'normal final training' TNA ADM 223/794, p. 445.
'Mincemeat sails 19th April' TNA CAB 154/67.
'enable the operation to be carried' TNA ADM 223/794, p. 445.
'In wartime, any plan that saved' Interview with N. L. A. Jewell, IWM 12278.
'the vital need for secrecy' TNA ADM 223/794, p. 450.
'packed, fully clothed and ready' NLAJ operational orders, TNA ADM 223/464.
'as the steel is made of light gauge' Memo, 31 Mar 1943, TNA ADM 223/464.
'held a super-secret automatic' TNA ADM 223/794, p. 450.
'we suspected the Germans' Ibid.
'Lt Jewell was to impress' Ibid.
'between Portil Pillar and Punta Umbria' Ibid., p. 445.
'Every effort should be made' NLAJ operational orders, TNA ADM 223/464.
'the submarine could probably' TNA ADM 223/794, p. 445.
'the proposed use of a flare was dropped' Ibid.
'on specially prepared slides' NLAJ operational orders, TNA ADM 223/464.
'The container should then be opened' Ibid.
'When the body is removed' Ibid.
'near the body but not too near' Ibid.
'the body and container' Ibid.
'care must be taken that' Ibid.
'Cancel Mincemeat' Ibid.
'Mincemeat completed' Ibid.
'a pleasant time building up' Interview with N. L. A. Jewell, IWM 12278.
'making a life for the Major of Marines' Ibid.
'I had the enjoyment' Ibid.
'Mincemeat sails' 'Chaucer' to Goldbranson, 15 Apr 1943, TNA CAB 154/67.

Chapter 11: Gold Prospector

'Adventure was once a noble' Alan Hillgarth, *Men of War* (London, 1926).
'a young man called Alan Hillgarth' Evelyn Waugh, *Diaries* (London, 1995), 1 Jul 1927.
'that took five hundred men' Daniel Buck, 'Americas', Vol. 52, May 2000.
'squarish man with conspicuously' Ibid.
'men who had had considerable' Report of Sacambaya Company, 23 Apr 1929.
'Sacambaya is a poisonous place' Ibid.
'This was quite an undertaking' Ibid.
'one case containing 200lbs' Ibid.
'100 feet into the hillside proper' Ibid.
'A complete absence of fresh fruit' P. B. P. Mellows, *St Barts Journal*, January 1929,
    p. 59.

'One of our party awakened' Ibid.

'Claustrophobia brought on by' Ibid.

'He has fallen seriously in love' Edgar Sanders to Alan Hillgarth, 5 Jan 1929, courtesy of Tristan Hillgarth.

'either by the hotel people or the police.' Ibid.

'he doubled up as spy' Burns, *Papa Spy*, p. 22.

'an intense bombardment which' Note on the surrender of Menorca written by Captain Alan Hillgarth, then British Consul in Palma, translated from Catalan by Tristan Hillgarth.

'a decisive German victory over Russia' Alan Hillgarth memo, 13 Jul 1942, TNA ADM 223/478.

'very good' Cited by Denis Smyth, *Oxford Dictionary of National Biography*.

'equipped with a profound knowledge' Ibid.

'privately about anything interesting' Alan Hillgarth memo, TNA ADM 223/490.

'useful petard and a good war-winner' Cited in Andrew Lycett, *Ian Fleming* (London, 1996), p. 158.

'the embodiment of drive' Stafford, *Roosevelt and Churchill*, p. 110.

'secret funds that were made available' Kim Philby, *My Secret War: The Autobiography of a Spy* (London, 1968), p. 54.

'helped to feed the gallant' Ibid.

'local police, dock watchmen and stevedores' Alan Hillgarth Report, TNA ADM 223/490.

'expendable parts of Hitler's war machine' Stafford, *Roosevelt and Churchill*, p. 92.

'took corruption for granted' John Brooks, 'Annals of Finance', *New Yorker*, 21 May 1979.

'the last pirate of the Mediterranean' Ibid.

'It would be a mistake to trust him an inch' Stafford, *Roosevelt and Churchill*, p. 90.

'He has already had two German agents shot' Ibid.

'an amphibious car' 'Spanish help to the Germans', Records of NID12, TNA ADM 223/490.

'There was not a Spaniard who would not' Alan Hillgarth report, TNA ADM 223/490.

'The Cavalry of St George' Stafford, *Roosevelt and Churchill*, p. 93.

'We must not lose them now' Ibid., p. 96.

'his approval can safely be assumed' Ibid., p. 100.

'German victory would mean servitude' Donald McLachlan, *Room 39: Naval Intelligence in Action 1939–45* (London, 1968), p. 194.

'the Spaniard is xenophobic and suspicious' Alan Hillgarth report, TNA ADM 223/490.

'I am finding Hillgarth a great prop' Stafford, *Roosevelt and Churchill*, p. 96.

'a natural sympathy' Alan Hillgarth report, TNA ADM 223/490.

'Handling Spaniards is a special' Ibid.

'will be at a very definite' Ibid.

'Even during the worst of the war' Ibid.

'very reliable and well placed' EM report, 21 Aug 1945, TNA ADM 223/794.

'to supply intelligence which' Ibid.

'might compromise a very' Ibid.

'The items were so chosen' Ibid.

'Messig swallowed the stories' Ibid.

'It was a delicate job' Ibid.

'It seemed the listening' Montagu, *Ultra*, p. 121.

'Only by naval ciphers' Alan Hillgarth report, TNA ADM 223/490.

'suborned by a woman in German pay' Ibid.
'kept lists of everyone' Burns, *Papa Spy*, p.190.
'the Germans would have someone' Interview with Tristan Hillgarth, 13 Jan 2009.
'very amateurish and inefficient' Alan Hillgarth report, TNA ADM 223/490.
'Our deportment towards the German' Ibid.
'The circumstances of his release' Rankin, *Churchill's Wizards*, p. 346.
'Wrangal Craker' Terry Crowdy, *Deceiving Hitler: Double Cross and Deception in World War II* (London 2008), p. 142.
'Herewith some photographs' Rankin, *Churchill's Wizards*, p. 349.
'sound in mind' Crowdy, *Deceiving Hitler*, p. 143.
'he is just the type who imagines' Ibid.
'It is time to pass from the defensive' Memo, Alan Hillgarth to Edmund Rushbrooke, TNA ADM 223/490.
'more or less any naval intelligence' Ibid.
'was allowed with little' Ibid.
'I have found a good man' Ibid.
'All operations are, if I may say so' Ibid.
'You and your staff have shown' Rushbrooke to Hillgarth, TNA ADM 223/490.
'undesirable and unnecessary' Ibid.
'James Bond style free-for-all in Spain' Philby, *My Secret War*, pp. 54–5.

Chapter 12: The Spy Who Baked Cakes

'ubiquitous' Harris, *Garbo*, p. 18.
'All classes were represented' 'Spanish help to the Germans', Records of NID12, TNA ADM 223/490.
'In the higher ranks there' Ibid.
'Indeed, the reports went' TNA ADM 223/490.
'particulars on each' Philby, *My Secret War*, pp. 54–5.
'for a very large sum' Ibid.
'precious source' Ibid.
'very high indeed' Ibid.
'I had to fight to get an extra £5' Ibid.
'the cause of death' Colvin, *Unknown Courier*, p. 42.
'examined hundreds of corpses' Ibid., p. 41.
'Nothing happened in the Abwehr station' Interrogation of Hans Joachim Rudolph, Kuhlenthal MI5, TNA KV2/102.
'fleshy, boneless cheeks' Ibid.
'curved hawk-like' Ibid.
'blue piercing eyes' Ibid.
'a dark brown French four-seater' Ibid.
'carefully manicured' Ibid.
'a very efficient, ambitious' Harris, *Garbo*, p. 69.
'contrived to push Leissner' TNA KV2/102.
'became a mere figurehead' Ibid.
'He was an extremely able man' Ibid.
'the esteem and reputation' Ibid.
'by far the best man in Group I' Ibid.
'sent a personal message' Harris, *Garbo*, p. 74.
'extremely busy and that his visit' Ibid., p. 46.
'careful not to underestimate' Ibid., p. 50.

'would be a very long war' Ibid.

'There are people in Glasgow' Ibid., p. 58.

'We have absolute trust in you' Ibid., p. 250.

'My dear friend and comrade' Ibid., p. 257.

'the democratic-Jewish-Masonic' Ibid.

'England must be taken by arms' Ibid., p. 137.

'With a raised arm I end this letter' Ibid.

'His characteristic German lack' Ibid., p. 70.

'the star turn' Ibid., p. 128.

'With good wishes to Odette' Ibid.

'I did the lettering myself' Ibid.

'made cakes which were unpleasant' Ibid.

'extraordinary services' Ibid., p. 261.

'As a keen and efficient officer' Ibid., p. 69.

'We had the satisfaction of knowing' Ibid.

'the many incredible things we ask' Ibid. p. 95.

'the more sensational the reports' Ibid., p. 146.

'In some cases where messages' Ibid.

'Felipe had become our mouthpiece' Ibid., p. 72.

'an invaluable channel' Ibid.

'conviction that the Isle of Man' MSS report, TNA KV2/102.

'invented by Felipe himself' Ibid.

'The information provided' Ibid.

'one of the people who make up' Liddell, Diaries, 10 Mar 1944, p. 179.

'There are officers in Spain' Statement of Josef Ledebur-Wichelin, 25 Nov 1944, at Camp 020, TNA KV2/102.

'leaving a good job as manager' Ibid.

'he could not serve in the Army' Ibid.

'Aryanised' Ibid.

'He has been created an Aryan' Telegram Berlin to Madrid 18 Jul 1941 TNA KV2/102.

'since there appeared to be no' Ibid.

'to let the matter drop' MSS 5.11.41 TNA KV2/102.

'in the pay of British Secret Service' Ibid.

'refused to take the report seriously' Ibid.

'cold and reserved' Ibid.

'Appearance: nervous, uncertain' Ibid.

'Kuhlenthal is trembling to keep' Statement of Josef Ledebur-Wichelin, 25 Nov 1944, at Camp 020, TNA KV2/102.

Chapter 13: Mincemeat Sets Sail

'national importance' Interview with Basil Leverton, 8 Sep 2009.

'I was not to divulge' Ivor Leverton, unpublished diary, courtesy of Andrew Leverton.

'I was still in fairly good shape' Ibid.

'removal coffins' Interview with Andrew Leverton, 27 Jan 2009.

'must have stood 6'4" inches tall' Ivor Leverton, Letter to Daily Telegraph, 13 Aug 2002.

'left our passenger' Ivor Leverton, unpublished diary.

'a mortuary-keeper on whom' EM to JG, 19 Sep 1964, Montagu Papers.

'made it as easy as possible' TNA ADM 223/794, p. 450.

'I've got it' Jackson, *Coroner*, p. 149.

'the least pleasant part of our work' Montagu, *Man*, p. 160.

'We decided Bill Martin and Pam' Ibid., p. 162.

'Get an army blanket.' Jackson, *Coroner*, p. 149.

'lightly tied with tape' Ibid.

'reverently' Montagu, *Man*, p. 162.

'a shirt and tie' Ian Girling, *Aston Martin Magazine*, Vol. 33, No. 142, Spring 1999, 'The Horsfall Story: A Tribute'.

'went berserk' Ibid.

'potentially lethal pieces of metal' Ibid.

'The scream that Kath gave' Ibid.

'*I gave her time to start her piddle*' Ibid.

'he claimed to have done 100 mph' John Otter, letter to *Daily Telegraph*, 15 Aug 2002.

'one of us sitting in the window' Draft manuscript of *The Man*, IWM 97/45/2.

'had supper with a corpse parked' John Otter, letter to *Daily Telegraph* 15 Aug 2002.

'much better story' Montagu, *Man*, p. 163.

'partially 'in the know'' TNA ADM 223/794, p. 450.

'being accepted as merely being' Ibid.

'By this time Major Martin' Montagu, *Man*, p. 160.

'We felt that we knew him' Ibid.

'news such as can be written' EM to IM, 24 Apr 1943, Montagu Letters.

'I had to go up to Scotland' Ibid.

'I was to see that this package' David Scott, 'The Man That Never Was: Operation Mincemeat'; Reminiscences of Sir David Scott, Churchill Archives, DKNS II, p. 2.

'It was a real thrill' EM, unpublished account, 7 Oct 1976, Montagu Papers.

'Spring was on the way' Scott, *Reminiscences*, p. 3.

'trim dive' Ibid.

'A final exchange of 'Good Luck'' Ibid.

'Monotony never really set in' Ibid.

'We were never short of meat' Ibid.

'epitome of what a submarine captain' Ibid., p. 4.

'At that time, the chances of returning' Ibid.

'I realised with a bit of a shock' Ibid.

'bashed-in sort of face' John Parker, *SBS: The Story of the Special Boat Service* (London 1997), p. 19.

'Your American gum' Terence Robertson, *The Ship with Two Captains: The Story of the 'Secret Mission Submarine'* (London, 1957), p. 92.

'a happy augury for the future' Ibid.

'a two-fisted fighting man' NLAJ , as told to Cecil Carnes, *Secret Mission Submarine: Action Report of the HMS Seraph* (London, 1944), p. 101.

'We'll fight an army on a dare' Atkinson, *Day of Battle*, p. 82.

'always conspicuously' Citation for Distinguished Service Cross.

'I think we can do it' Robertson, *The Ship with Two Captains*, p. 106.

'sink on sight any vessel' Ibid.

'Put me ashore, give me a gun' Ibid., p. 110.

'constant strain' Ibid., p. 112.

'one grabbed a large' Ibid.

'broken nose' Ibid.

'a lithe, graceful look' Ibid., p. 124.
'We were told that we were not' Interview with N. L. A. Jewell, IWM 12278.
'The unmistakable sounds' Scott, *Reminiscences*, p. 5.
'We knew that at least' Ibid.

Chapter 14: Bill's Farewell

'I rushed home' Interview with JGL, 5 Mar 2008.
'absurd' Montagu, *Man*, p. 167.
'Bill Martin's death' TNA CAB 154/67.
'We were terribly agitated' Interview with JGL, 5 Mar 2008.
'as a joke' Montagu, *Man*, p. 167.
'gathered from every part' John Fisher, *What a Performance: The Life of Sid Field* (London, 1975), p. 85.
'definitely "a find" ' Cited in Fisher, *What a Performance*, p. 99.
'the loudest laughter we' Ibid., p. 100.
'all his jokes are clean' Ibid.
'*I'm going to get pickled*' Ibid., p. 96.
'an adequate ration of gin' Ibid., p. 85.
'If an Air Raid Warning' Ibid.
'*When you feel unhappy*' Ibid., p. 103.
'The laughs came like the waves' Ibid., p. 88.
'The weather was warm at last' Scott, *Reminiscences*, p. 3.
'John Brown's Body' Montagu, *Man*, p. 169.
'our pal Charlie' Robertson, *The Ship with Two Captains,* p. 124.
'were such that strangers' *Independent*, Obituary of Michael Luke, 19 Apr 2005.
'mystery suffused with a tender' Ibid.
'very cheerful evening' Montagu, *Man*, p. 167.
'Considering Bill and Pam are engaged' Ibid.
'It would be different' Ibid.
'They kept looking at their watches' Interview with JGL, 5 Mar 2008.
'I had to go and take' EM to IM, 23 Apr 1943, Montagu Letters.
'smitten' Interview with JGL, 5 Mar 2008.
'I am glad Verel' EM to IM, 29 Jun 1943, Montagu Letters.
'the peak of the Deception effort' Holt, *The Deceivers*, p. 366.
'One patriotic Greek managed' Holt, *The Deceivers*, p. 368.
'hygiene in the Balkans' Ibid.
'no major operation could be' Ewen Montagu, unpublished critique of Constantine Fitzgibbon, *Secret Intelligence in the Twentieth Century* (London, 1976), Montagu Papers.
'if they should suspect that the' EM, 31 Mar 1943, TNA WO 106/5921.
'I had to carry the can' EM to 'Ginger', 6 Jul 1943, Montagu Papers.
'Intelligence, like food' Godfrey 'Afterthoughts' TNA ADM 223/619, p. 91.
'with instructions to burn' NLAJ operational orders, TNA ADM 223/464.
Operation known as Mincemeat' Telegram to DSO Gibraltar, 22 Apr 1943, TNA CAB 154/67.
'something of a shock' Scott, *Reminiscences*, p. 4.
'sailors had been sleeping' Ibid.
'the vital need for absolute secrecy' TNA ADM 223/794, p. 451.
'Isn't it pretty unlucky' Montagu, *Man*, p. 170.
'a close-range reconnaissance' Scott, *Reminiscences*, p. 4.

'easy, even enjoyable' Ibid.
'The operation had to be carried' NLAJ operational orders, TNA ADM 223/464.
'an onshore wind' Ibid.
'The next day turned out to be ideal' Scott, *Reminiscences*, p. 4.
'arrange total bombing restrictions' Memo, 15 Apr 1943, IWM 97/45/1 folder #1.
'No known defensive dangers' TNA ADM 223/794, p. 445.
'We were just about to surface' Interview with N. L. A. Jewell, IWM 12278.
'A large number of small fishing boats' NLAJ Report, 30 April 1943, cited in
    Montagu, *Man*, p. 168.
'landing some pseudo-secret instruments' NLAJ Operation orders, TNA ADM
    223/464.
'We crept in a little closer' Scott, *Reminiscences*, p. 4.
'some little stink' Interview with N. L. A. Jewell, IWM 12278.
'I doubt if any of them' Ibid.
'I had seen bodies before' Ibid.
'The blanket was opened up' TNA 223/794.
'We seemed to be practically' Scott, *Reminiscences*, p. 5.
'what I could remember' Interview with N. L. A. Jewell, IWM 12278.
'With some relief' Scott, *Reminiscences*, p. 5.
'He virtually assured success' TNA ADM 223/794, p. 453.
'Because it had been designed' Ibid.
'riddled by fire' Ibid.
'He did this with his usual skill' Scott, *Reminiscences*, p. 5.
'a hell of a time' Interview with N. L. A. Jewell, IWM 12278.
'Daylight was fast approaching' Scott, *Reminiscences*, p. 5.
'It then disappeared, finally' Interview with N. L. A. Jewell, IWM 12278.
'it was seen to sink' NLAJ Report, 30 April 1943, cited in Montagu, *Man*, p. 168.
'We dived and set course for Gibraltar' Scott, *Reminiscences*, p. 5.
'Mincemeat Completed' TNA ADM 223/794.
'Parcel delivered safely' Robertson, *The Ship with Two Captains*, p. 117.

Chapter 15: Dulce et Decorum

'G VI R and the royal crown' IWM, 97/45/1 folder #2.
'which had penetrated the muscles' Ibid.
'should telephone to him at Madrid' TNA ADM 223/794, p. 445.
'would say that he could not talk' Ibid.
'a separate series in his personal cipher' EM to Fitzroy McLean, 30 Mar 1977, IWM
    97/45/1 folder #5.
'energetically' TNA ADM 223/794, p. 445.
'Soup Bowl' Copeiro, *Huelva*, p. 411.
'examined the names on the envelopes' Appendix III, in IWM 97/45/1 folder #2.
'react swiftly' Copeiro, *Huelva*, p. 422.
'Well, your superior might not like' Ibid.
'attitude, in refusing the briefcase' Ibid.
'of an English pattern' Telegram to Von Roenne, 22 May 1943, TNA ADM
    223/794, p. 207.
'There are clearly two' Ibid.
'On the first incision being made' Edward Smith, former head of Reporting
    Organisation Section, NID, to EM, 6 May 1969, IWM.
'remarkable presence of mind' Ibid.

'Since it was obvious the heat' Ibid.

'On receiving this assurance' Ibid.

'The young British officer fell in the water' Copeiro, *Huelva*, p. 414.

'nibbling and bites by fish' Ibid.

'The shininess of the hair' Ibid.

'doubt over the nature of the liquid' Ibid.

'He seemed very well dressed' Interview with Isabel Naylor, Huelva, 3 Jun 2009.

'identical' Telegram to Von Roenne, 22 May 1943, TNA ADM 223/794, p. 207.

'that a bald patch on the temples' Ibid.

'either the photograph was taken' Ibid.

'With reference to my phone message' Telegram 012210 sent at 2030 on 1 May TNA ADM 223/794.

'so that the action for suppressing' TNA ADM 223/794, p. 457.

'the suppression of the signal' Ibid.

'taken into naval custody' EM to Cyril Mills, 11 Nov 1983, Montagu Papers.

'The Spanish navy is <u>not</u> in German' EM to C, 21 Jun 1943, IWM 97/45/1/folder #2.

'a rigid disciplinarian' Copeiro, *Huelva*, p. 422.

'suffocating heat' Ibid., p. 414.

'as a mark of respect' Interview with Federico Clauss, 2 Jun 2009.

'W. Martin, aged between thirty-five and forty' Copeiro, *Huelva*, p. 420.

'Class Five' Ibid.

Chapter 16: Spanish Trails

'do everything necessary' Andros report, IWM, 97/45/1 folder #2.

'Notwithstanding his great desire' Ibid.

'These three persons are in command' Ibid.

'intimate friend' Ibid.

'nursed a profound antipathy' Copeiro, *Huelva*, p. 286.

'did not dare to ask this gentleman' Andros report, IWM, 97/45/1 folder #2.

'In Huelva, Don Adolfo' Interview with Federico Clauss, Seville, 2 Jun 2009.

'neither copied nor photographed' Andros report, IWM, 97/45/1 folder #2.

'I am glad to say the naval' Alan Hillgarth to EM, 9 Jun 1943, IWM 97/45/1 folder #1.

'Some papers Major Martin' Telegram 04132, 4 May 1943; Director Naval Intelligence (DNI) to Naval Attaché (NA), 4 May 1943, W0106/5921, p. 32.

'Carry out instructions' Telegram 869, 4 May 1943, IWM 97/45/1 folder #1.

'kept on such a plane' Ewen Montagu, 'Draft proposal for compiler of MI5 history', 24 Jul 1945, IWM 97/45/1 folder #1.

'searching but discreet' Ibid.

'Rumours are extremely easy' Alan Hillgarth report, TNA ADM 223/478.

'select from among his acquaintance' Ibid.

'sincerely anti-war' TNA ADM 223/876.

'I managed to make the Minister' Alan Hillgarth report, TNA ADM 223/490.

'that the Minster of Marine' Alan Hillgarth, 5 May 1943, IWM 97/45/1 folder #2.

'Vice Consul Huelva saw body' NA to DNI, 5 May 1943, 1823, IWM 97/45/1 folder #2.

'Secret papers probably in black' DNI to NA, telegram #071216, 7 May 1943, W0 106/5921, p. 33.

'Normally you would be getting' EM to NA, Madrid, telegram 870, 6 May 1943, IWM 97/45/1 folder #1.

'Understood and acted on throughout' IWM 97/45/1 folder #1.
'promised to obtain copies' Andros report, IWM, 97/45/1 folder #2.
'discreet inquiries whether any' AH Memo, IWM, 97/45/1.
'As the local Germans' Andros report, IWM, 97/45/1 folder #2.
'summoned to Villarreal de San Antonio' Ibid.
'very pro-German and in German pay' Ibid.
'This individual' Ibid.
'to do everything possible to obtain' Ibid.
'Urging him to use the utmost' Ibid.
'accurate information regarding' Ibid.
'either because they were afraid' Ibid.
'Either because of the junior rank' Ibid.
'forwarded, unopened' ABW 2282/43 TNA CAB 154/101.
'only scanty information' JHB memo, 3 May 1943, TNA CAB 154/67.
'Mincemeat was found by' Ibid.
'We sweat away, 11 of us' EM to 'Ginger', 6 Jul 1943, Montagu Papers.
'It is requested that I may' Undated note in Montagu Papers.
'I always was a selfish shit' EM to 'Ginger', 6 Jul 1943, Montagu Papers.
'I have never been able' Ibid.
'If I had made a slip in the preparation' Ibid.
'Official procedure is always' NA to DNI, 5 May 1943, 1823. IWM 97/45/1 folder #2.
'informed that they had not' Andros report, IWM, 97/45/1 folder #2.
'Again they failed' Ibid.
'an official of the [Cadiz] Marine' ABW 2282/43 TNA CAB 154/101.
'did not dare approach' Andros report, IWM, 97/45/1 folder #2.
'an assiduous worker for the Germans' Ibid.
'that he had heard about the body' Ibid.
'many privileges and facilities' Ibid.
'unable to obtain any fresh' Ibid.
'certain high officials in the police' Ibid.
'Great interest was aroused' Ibid.
'Groizar fostered this interest' Ibid.
'One can't imagine' Stanley G. Payne, *Franco and Hitler: Spain, Germany and World War II* (London, 2008), p. 150.
'in the hope that he will come to Spain' Andros report, IWM, 97/45/1 folder #2
'approaches were made by the Germans' Ibid.

Chapter 17: Kuhlenthal's Coup

'Red Indians' Macintyre, *For Your Eyes Only*, p. 32.
'a Spanish Staff Officer' Abw Nr 2282/43, Spain to FHW, 15 May 1943, TNA CAB 154/101, p. 203.
'with whom we have been in contact' Appendix to Operation Mincemeat, TNA ADM 223/794, p. 459.
'my Spanish agent in the General Staff' Colvin, *Unknown Courier*, p. 95.
'case officer' Abw Nr 2282/43, Spain to FHW, 15.5.43., TNA CAB 154/101, p. 203.
'Those seals held the envelopes' TNA ADM 223/794, p. 453.
'It was possible to extract' Report of Special Examiners, 21 May 1943, IWM 97/45/1 folder #5.

'The Spaniards had, very intelligently' Appendix to Operation Mincemeat, TNA
    ADM 223/794, p. 459.
'They seemed to me to be of the' Colvin, *Unknown Courier*, p. 95.
'A short white-haired man' Ibid., p. 34.
'These letters mentioned' Ibid., p. 95.
'the strategic considerations' Ibid.
'I took them to the basement' Ibid.
'there was no trace whatever' TNA ADM 223/794 p. 453.
'the importance attached to them' Colvin, *Unknown Courier*, p. 96.
'left Madrid hurriedly for Berlin' MSS message 7 Apr 1943, TNA KV2/102.
'all the effects and papers' TNA ADM 223/794, p. 453.
'They are all there' NA Madrid to DNI, Telegram 111925, 12 May 1943, IWM
    97/45/1 folder #1.
'From his manner it was obvious' Ibid.
'It is obvious contents of bag' Ibid.
'While I do not believe' Ibid.
'If you concur I will ask' Ibid.
'the genuineness of the report' Atkinson, *Day of Battle*, p. 6.
'All generals lie. All generals are disloyal' Ibid.
'Behind his rimless spectacles' Kahn, *Hitler's Spies*, p. 424.
'The Germans studied each phrase' Ewen Montagu, 'Draft proposal for compiler of
    MI5 history', 24 Jul 1945, IWM 97/45/1 folder #1.
'Discovery of the English Courier' TNA CAB 154/101, p. 200.
'On the corpse of an English courier' Ibid.
'the Germans studied each phrase' Ewen Montagu, 'Draft proposal for compiler of
    MI5 history', 24 Jul 1945, IWM 97/45/1 folder #1.
'an experienced specialist' Ibid.
'Large-scale amphibious operations' Ibid.
'A jocular remark in this letter' Ibid.
'The proposed cover operation' Ibid.
'operation could be mounted' Ibid.
'still in action' Ibid.
'must first be rested' Ibid.
'at least two or three weeks' Ibid.
'It is known to the British Staff' Ibid.
'It is, therefore, to be hoped' Ibid.
'initiate a misleading plan' Ibid.
'News of this discovery will' Ibid.
'The circumstances of the discovery' Ibid.
'unless these were clearly' Holt, *The Deceivers*, p. 102.
'wishfulness' Godfrey 'Afterthoughts' TNA ADM 223/619, p. 10.

Chapter 18: Mincemeat Digested

'Hitler had implicit faith' David Alan Johnson, *Righteous Deception: German Officers
    Against Hitler* (Westport, Connecticut, 2001), p. 77.
'the Western allies would protest' Ibid.
'exactly what Hitler wanted to hear' Ibid.
'Hitler was greatly impressed' Ibid.
'It was his mission to produce' Ibid., p. 78.
'because of their origins' Kahn, *Hitler's Spies*, p. 426.

'if Germany should give in to' Holt, *The Deceivers*, p. 101.

'his way of fighting the Nazi war' Johnson, *Righteous Deception*, p. 126.

'In a moment now I shall be going' Cited in Albert Edward Day, *Dialogue and Destiny* (New York, 1981) p. 91.

'absolutely convincing proof' TNA CAB 154/101, p. 200.

'resounding Abwehr success' Ibid.

'frousty, peevish and petulant' Godfrey, 'Afterthoughts' TNA ADM 223/619, p. 63.

'he had to duck each time he had' TNA ADM 223/792.

'surprising that we only have five' Ibid.

'an enemy landing on a large scale' MSS 2571/T4, cited in TNA ADM 223/794, p. 456.

'a source which may be regarded' Ibid.

'It is very unusual for an intelligence' NID 12 report, 2 Sep 1943, IWM, 97/45/1 folder #2.

'So far as I can recollect' Ibid.

'Everyone jumped up and down' Interview with Pat Davies (née Trehearne), 4 Oct 2009.

'almost certain' MSS 2571/T4, cited in TNA ADM 223/794, p. 456.

'similar details from the letter' Ibid.

'the Germans were reinforcing' Unpublished note, 7 Oct 1976, in IWM 97/45/1 folder #4.

'wonderful days' Ibid.

'the right people and from best' Michael Howard, *Grand Strategy* (London 1972), p. 370.

'You will be pleased to learn' Montagu, *Man,* p. 176.

'Friday was almost too good' EM to IM, 16 May 1943, Montagu Letters.

'proved that we had convinced them' Ewen Montagu, unpublished, undated account, IWM, 97/45/1 folder #2.

'According to information' F. W. Deakin, *The Brutal Friendship: Mussolini, Hitler and the Fall of Italian Fascism* (London, 1962), p. 376.

'in strict confidence' Ibid., p. 377.

'Jordana begged me not to' Ibid.

'especially as he wanted' Ibid.

'Christian, couldn't this be a corpse' David Irving, *Hitler's War* (London, 1977), p. 586.

'It is to be expected that' Deakin, *The Brutal Friendship*, p. 377.

'the original German appreciation' TNA ADM 223/794, p. 457.

'all German commands' Deakin, *The Brutal Friendship,* p. 377.

'Where do we go from Sicily?' Atkinson, *Day of Battle*, p. 14.

'The main task which lies before us' Ibid., p. 15.

'War is full of mysteries and surprises' Ibid., p. 22.

'What [do] you think is going' Ibid., p. 25.

'Appetite unbridled' Ibid.

'to a document that had been' TNA ADM 223/794, p. 457.

'security flap' Ibid.

'Arrangements could then be made' Ibid.

'We earnestly debated' Bennett, *Ultra and Mediterranean Strategy*, p. 227.

'The evaluation office attach special' TNA CAB 154/67.

'The latter immediately despatched' MSS 13 May 1943, 1837, 'Berlin to Madrid No 117 for Samoza. Ref your most secret of 9/5/43' CAB 154/67.

'Oberst Lt. Pardo on the 10th May' ABW 2282/43 TNA CAB 154/101.

'The result of his investigations' Ibid.
'In contrast to the first statement' Ibid.
'He (the Minister for Marine)' Ibid.
'A search for the remains' Ibid.
'The fishermen state' Ibid.
'A medical examination' Ibid.
'Bag not yet arrived' Telegram 877, 18 May 1943, TNA CAB 154/67.
'a small, sealed bag' Ibid.
'Evidence that operation successful' Ibid.
'reported that there was great excitement' AH Memo, undated, IWM 97/45/1 folder #2.
'I naturally asked him to find out' Ibid.
'said that immediately he heard' Part one of telegram 171914, TNA CAB 154/67.
'Why did you go to so much trouble?' Ibid.
'I was anxious no one should have' Ibid.
'He obviously did not know' Telegram 171811, TNA CAB 154/67.
'It can be taken as a certainty' Ibid.
'He told me that all his information' Deakin, *The Brutal Friendship*, pp. 377–8.
'The operation has given conclusive' Ewen Montagu report, 29 May 1943, IWM, 97/45/1 folder #2.
'The seals were photographed' Report of Special Examiners, 21 May 1943, IWM 97/45/1, folder #5.
'Although we can say that there' Ibid.
'sharper than one made in it when' Ibid.
'once symmetrically and secondly' Ibid.
'it was not done on exactly' EM, letter to producer of *The Secret War*, IWM 97/45/1 folder #5.
'as the letter began to dry' Report of Special Examiners, 21 May 1943., IWM 97/45/1, folder #5.
'when the letter is folded up' Ibid.
'Inform Minister of Marine as soon' DNI to NA Madrid, undated notes, TNA CAB 154/67 (possibly not sent).
'letters [were] in fact opened' TNA CAB 154/67.
'likely to pass it on' Ibid.
'Important there should be no' Ibid.

Chapter 19: Hitler Loses Sleep

'consisted of comments' TNA ADM 223/794, p. 459.
'No further doubts remain' Telegrame SSDMBBZ 725, TNA CAB 154/101.
'whether the enemy' Ibid.
'urgent' Ibid.
'reply immediately "since we' Ibid.
'It is the opinion' Ibid.
'since only in this case' Ibid.
'absurd' Ibid.
'This shows how wrong a staff' TNA ADM 223/794, p. 459.
'personal squiggle' Montagu, *Man*, p. 184.
'The Führer does not agree' Deakin, *The Brutal Friendship*, p. 379.
'It is also clear from documents' Ibid., p. 383.
'Within the next few days' Ibid. p. 383.

'It is very unusual and very difficult' Michael I. Handel, *War Strategy and Intelligence* (London 1989), p. 436.

'targets of enemy operation' Deakin, *The Brutal Friendship*, p. 378.

'the Allies wanted to advance' Ibid., p. 379.

'You can forget Sicily' Bennett, *Ultra and Mediterranean Strategy*, p. 227.

'that the Allied attack' TNA CAB 154/67, p. 64.

'Allied submarines had received' Ibid.

'forwarded it to Belgrade and Sofia' Ibid.

'The reports coming from' Ibid., p. 64.

'congenital obsession about the Balkans' Howard, *Grand Strategy*, p. 92.

'In the last few days' Deakin, *The Brutal Friendship*, p. 379.

'the danger is that they will establish' Ibid., p. 380.

'as a precaution to take a further' Ibid.

'natural' Ibid., p. 381.

'If a landing takes place' Ibid.

'I have therefore decided' Ibid.

'Sardinia is particularly threatened' Ibid.

'In the event of the loss' Ibid.

'He foresaw that from Sardinia' Ibid., p. 375.

'through the Spaniards and not directly' IWM, 97/45/1 folder #2.

'The Italian High Command' IWM, 97/45/1 folder #2.

'information from an absolutely' Deakin, *The Brutal Friendship*, p. 386.

'There would be troop and transport' EM to JHB et al, 8 Jun 1943, TNA CAB 154/67 p. 64.

'German circles here have a story' AH to DNI, 1 Jun 1943, TNA CAB 154/67.

'The degree of Spanish complicity' Undated draft letter, IWM, 97/45/1 folder #2.

'adding to our knowledge of German' EM to 'C', 21 Jun 1943, IWM, 97/45/1 folder #2.

'simultaneous landings in Sardinia' Crichton to JHB, 4 Aug 1943, TNA CAB 154/67.

'our refrigerated friend' Ibid.

'had come round to the same view.' Holt, *The Deceivers*, p. 378.

'camouflage' Goebbel *Diaries*, 25 June 1943.

'The truth is whatever helps bring victory,' Irving, *Goebbels*, p. 437.

'Despite all the assertions' Ibid., p. 433.

'resounding' TNA CAB 154/101, p. 200.

'*The Times* has once again sunk' Irving, *Goebbels*, p. 421.

'velvety-arsed and Rolls-Royce' Atkinson, *Day of Battle*, p. 52.

'I had a long discussion with' *The Goebbels Diaries*, 25 Jun 1943 (London, 1948).

'The general outline of English plans' Ibid.

'Try to find out if Greek troops' MSS received 7 Jun 1943, CAB 154/67.

'to investigate the presence' Harris, *Garbo*, p. 135.

'the only serious danger' 'Dowager' (Clarke) to 'Chaucer', 20 May 1943, TNA CAB 154/67.

'legal or illegal exhumation' Ibid.

'By the time that he had been' EM to JHB, 28 May 1943, TNA CAB 154/67.

'Although no one in this world' Ibid.

'Suggest unless unusual' Telegram 878, 21 May 1943, TNA CAB 154/67.

'This to be done unless restrictions' Telegram 879 TNA CAB 154/67.

'Please send me ordinary cipher' Telegram, 23 May 1943 TNA CAB 154/67.

'Suggest Consul place wreath' Telegram 878, 21 May 1943, TNA CAB 154/67.

'as fast as possible' Ibid.

'The purpose of this was not only' TNA ADM 223/794, p. 452.

'Sir, In accordance with instructions' 9 Jun 1943, IWM 97/45/1 folder #1.
'Could you possibly procure' EM to Alan Hillgarth, 26 May 1943, IWM 97/45/1 folder #1.
'A reasonable reward of not more' Telegram 880, 23 May 1943, TNA CAB 154/67.
'No action is to be taken' TNA ADM 223/794, p. 457.
'Insert the following entry' Note to casualty section, 20 May 1943, IWM 97/45/1 folder #1.
'and, if so, where was it?' Montagu, *Man*, p. 178.
'distinguished film and stage actor' *The Times*, 4 Jun 1943.
'severe loss to the British theatre' Ibid.
'The only decent thing they can do' Ben Macintyre, *The Times*, 30 Dec 2008.
'the first German Panzer Division' DNI notes 31 May 1943, TNA ADM 223/353.
'arrangements for the passage' EM to JHB et al, 8 Jun 1943, TNA CAB 154/67 p. 64.
'strategic position well suited' Ibid.
'completely reequipped' Bennett, *Ultra and Mediterranean Strategy*, p. 224.
'It is now about half way between' EM to JHB et al, 8 Jun 1943, TNA CAB 154/67 p. 64.
'The present situation is summed' Ibid.
'They raised (but did not pursue)' Ibid.
'Mincemeat has already resulted' EM, report 29 May 1943, IWM, 97/45/1 folder #2.
'I think that at this half way stage' EM, 'Draft proposal for compiler of MI5 history', 24 Jul 1945, IWM 97/45/1 folder #1.

Chapter 20: *Seraph* and **Husky**

'You are to act as guide and beacon' Robertson, *The Ship with Two Captains*, p. 124.
'had delivered his false information' Ibid., p. 126.
'His force was to land in three parts' Ibid., p. 124.
'He was really very short with us' Interview with N. L. A. Jewell, IWM 12278.
'Do as good a job for us' Robertson, *The Ship with Two Captains*, p. 125.
'Discovery' Ibid., p. 127.
'If substantial German ground troops' Dwight Eisenhower to Winston Churchill, 28 Mar 1943, cited in Handel, *War Strategy*, p. 437.
'The submarines would be less' Robertson, *The Ship with Two Captains*, p. 125.
'The American High Command' Jewell, *Secret Mission Submarine*, p. 106.
'a really de luxe experience' Ibid.
'most exclusive spot' Ibid.
'The Wren Trap' Ibid.
'None of the doors opened' Robertson, *The Ship with Two Captains*, p. 139.
'Bloody heap ain't got no springs' Ibid.
'could turn out a meal' Jewell, *Secret Mission Submarine*, p. 100.
'E-boat on port quarter, Sir' Robertson, *The Ship with Two Captains*, p. 126.
'a clearly visible silhouette' Ibid., p. 127.
'It was a ticklish moment' Jewell, *Secret Mission Submarine*, p. 111.
'undecided about her identity' Ibid.
'I knew that would be a recognition' Ibid.
'Down she went in a few seconds' Robertson, *The Ship with Two Captains*, p. 127.
'The captain of the E-boat' Ibid.
'wonderfully conceived' John Follain, *Mussolini's Island: The Untold Story of the Invasion of Italy* (London, 2005), p. 14.

'an exceptionally small head' Atkinson, *Day of Battle*, p. 131.
'His knowledge of how to' Follain, *Mussolini's Island*, p. 13.
'military disaster' Atkinson, *Day of Battle*, p. 53.
'You cannot, you must not, be interesting' Atkinson, *Day of Battle*, p. 34.
'the availability of aircraft and gliders' Wilson to CIGS, 16 May 1943, TNA CAB 154/67.
'gross breach of security' Ibid.
'athletic, middle-aged, of medium height' Crowdy, *Deceiving Hitler,* p. 196.
'an agent of very high class' Holt, *The Deceivers*, p. 360.
'who had promised him an' Harris, *Garbo*, p. 316.
'on account of his linguistic abilities' Ibid., p. 130.
'delighted with their new agent' Ibid.
'speculated that on account' Ibid.
'steal some documents relating' Ibid., p. 131.
'unmarried wife' Ibid.
'officer who had been' Ibid.
'pretend that the agent' Ibid.
'would give the game away altogether' Howard, *Grand Strategy*, p. 91.
'not to be alarmed as the attack' Crowdy, *Deceiving Hitler*, p. 206.
'received increasing reports' Interrogation of Joachim Canaris in Kuhlenthal file, TNA KV2/102.
'was still regarded as the favourite' Howard, *Grand Strategy*, p. 92.
'no measures were taken to reinforce the island' Ibid.
'it was never possible for the Germans' TNA ADM 223/794, p. 455.
'Compared with the forces employed' Bennett, *Ultra and Mediterranean Strategy*. p. 225.
'only half the supplies they needed' Ibid., p. 231.
'well armed and fully organised' Atkinson, *Day of Battle*, p. 53.
'an almost unbelievably' G2 Intelligence notes, No. 18, 1 Aug 1943, WO 204/983.
'hot mustard' Atkinson, *The Day of Battle*, p. 54.
'It will be a hard and very bloody' Follain, *Mussolini's Island*, p. 37.
'If casualties are high' Atkinson, *Day of Battle*, p. 71.
'May God be with you' Ibid.

Chapter 21: A Nice Cup of Tea

'We are about to embark' Follain, *Mussolini's Island*, p. 69.
'all the winds of heaven' Atkinson, *Day of Battle*, p. 67.
'The die was cast' Follain, *Mussolini's Island*, p. 69.
'It doesn't look too good' Atkinson, *Day of Battle*, p. 67.
'breakers and boiling surf' Jewell, *Secret Mission Submarine*, p. 112.
'lay in their hammocks, green' Atkinson, *Day of Battle*, p. 65.
'We are now getting Cadbury's' Derrick Leverton, letter to mother and father, 29 Nov 1943, courtesy of Andrew Leverton.
'It was a most excellent cruise' Ibid.
'He was excellent' Ibid.
'I went up on deck' Ibid.
'The sea had been wickedly rough' Ibid.
'Day Trips to the Continent' Ibid.
'I was standing up on deck' Ibid.
'rather a nice small slam' Ibid.

'There could be no more diving' Robertson, *The Ship with Two Captains*, p. 127.

'three times as difficult' Jewell, *Secret Mission Submarine*, p. 112.

'Unseen planes, hundreds of them' Ibid.

'The invasion of Sicily would be' Ibid., p. 109.

'Many of the men on this ship' Atkinson, *Day of Battle*, p. 36.

'great fires springing up' Jewell, *Secret Mission Submarine*, p. 112.

'the faint throb of approaching' Ibid.

'Their blindingly brilliant beams' Robertson, *The Ship with Two Captains*, p. 128.

'a nerve-tightening, shell-packed' Ibid.

'as much to avoid the cascading' Ibid.

'throbbing beat' Ibid., p. 129.

'a flicker of light from' Jewell, *Secret Mission Submarine*, p. 113.

'dark shapes emerged slowly' Robertson, *The Ship with Two Captains*, p. 129.

'The English language needs' Jewell, *Secret Mission Submarine*, p. 114.

'like footlights on a stage' Robertson, *The Ship with Two Captains*, p. 129.

'Shells whistled high overhead' Ibid., p. 128.

'with different coloured tracer' Ibid.

'With flares, searchlights' Jewell, *Secret Mission Submarine*, p. 114.

'cheering the stubborn little submarine' Robertson, *The Ship with Two Captains*, p. 129.

'Ahoy *Seraph*' Ibid.

'a slightly astonished salute' Ibid.

'You know, those boys' Ibid.

'slide warily back into' Ibid.

'tiny, darting flashes marked the progress Ibid.

'hoped the friendly, ever-joking' Ibid.

'Darby is really a great soldier' Carlo D'Este, *Bitter Victory: The Battle for Sicily 1943* (London 1988), p. 275.

'wished my chaps good luck' Derrick Leverton, letter, 29 Nov 1943.

'As there was still a bit of time' Ibid.

'quite a bit of banging about' Ibid.

'It was getting close to dawn' Ibid.

'slightly premature landings' Ibid.

'The first thing I was conscious' Ibid.

'Occasional mines went off' Ibid.

'tea-sugar-and-milk powder' Ibid.

'Most nourishing, appetising' Ibid.

'added zest to the party' Ibid.

'As the bombs came down' Ibid.

'Another bomb fell in the sea' Ibid.

'little graves about three feet deep' Ibid.

'I had rather an awful sort of dream' Ibid.

'the concussion in my grave' Ibid.

'our chaps are very bucked' Ibid.

'plus quite a lot of "possibles"' Ibid.

'I didn't feel I was suitably dressed' Ibid.

'I therefore designed myself' Ibid.

'Throw them back into the sea' Follain, *Mussolini's Island*, p. 85.

'I'm convinced our men will resist' Ibid., p. 84.

'We must be confident' Ibid.

'Most important' Holt, *The Deceivers*, p. 381

'complete failure of coastal defence' Message Rome to Berlin 2124 11/7/43, TNA ADM 223/147.

'on enemy penetration many' Ibid.
'half-clothed Italian soldiers' Bennett, *Ultra and Mediterranean Strategy*, p. 225.
'At once and with all forces attack' TNA ADM 223/147.
'The counterattack against hostile' Atkinson, *Day of Battle*, p. 103.
'the shortest Blitzkrieg in history' Follain, *Mussolini's Island*, p. 310.
'The German in Sicily is doomed' Atkinson, *Day of Battle*, p. 123.

Chapter 22: Hook, Line and Sinker

'Even if I have once brought off' EM to 'Ginger', 6 Jul 1943, Montagu Papers.
'too keyed-up to read a book' Ibid.
'It is really impossible to describe' Unpublished note, 7 Oct 1976, in IWM 97/45/1 folder #4.
'Joy of joys to anyone' Ibid.
'We fooled those of the Spaniards' Montagu, *Man*, p. 196.
'One specially made canister' Ewen Montagu, unpublished critique of Constantine Fitzgibbon, *Secret Intelligence in the Twentieth Century* (London, 1976), Montagu Papers.
'The most I could do was make' Montagu, *Ultra*, p. 166.
'I do congratulate you most warmly' Dudley Clarke to EM, note dated 14 May 1943, TNA CAB 154/67.
'It is a most interesting story' AN to JHB, note dated 20 Jul 1945, TNA CAB 154/67.
'the greatest achievement' EM to 'Ginger', 6 Jul 1943, Montagu Papers.
'Mincemeat has been' Liddell, *Diaries*, 20 May 1931.
'From evidence at present available' JHB to Inglis, 4 Oct 1943, TNA CAB 154/67.
'was the originator of this ingenious' JHB to Lamplough, 21 Aug 1943, TNA CAB 154/67.
'papers from Sikorski's aircraft' EM to JHB, 10 Jul 1943, TNA CAB 154/6.
'to show that Mincemeat was' Ibid.
'Not worth trying' Note attached to Ewen Montagu, JHB, 10 Jul 1943, TNA CAB 154/6, initials illegible.
'mousetrap for all German' Cited in Follain, *Mussolini's Island*, p. 311.
'Most Immediate' Signal Keitel to C in C Med, 9 Jul 1943, translation accompanying Rushbrooke report 19 Jul 1943, IWM, 97/45/1 folder #2.
'Western assault forces appear' Ibid.
'A subsequent landing' Ibid.
'stating that the High Command' TNA ADM 223/794, p. 456.
'entirely consistent with the' Ibid.
'complaining that the departure' Ibid., pp. 460–1.
'macaroni-eaters' Cited in Irving, *Goebbels*, p. 437.
'Hitler's own reaction was' Howard, *Grand Strategy*, p. 368.
'This report has been proved' Deakin, *Brutal Friendship*, p. 417.
'Undertake a most careful reappraisal' Ribbentrop to Dieckhoff in Madrid: 29 July 1943, Deakin, *Brutal Friendship*, p. 417.
'The documents had been found' Ibid.
'The English and Americans had' Ibid.
'The British Secret Service is quite' Ibid.
'that we should not adopt any' Ibid., p. 418.
'It is practically certain that' Ibid.
'Who originally circulated' Ibid.

'After the invasion of Italy' Interrogation of Joachim Canaris in MI5 Kuhlenthal file, TNA KV2/102.

'at present at any rate' MI 14/522/2 Kurze Feind Beurteilung West, 982 of 25 Jul 1943.

'The only thing certain in this war' Goebbels, *Diaries*, p. 437.

'The sacrifice of my country' Cited in Deakin, *Brutal Friendship*, p. 417.

'inept and cowardly' Ibid.

'We are fighting for a common' Atkinson, *Day of Battle*, p. 140.

'It can't go on any longer' Cited in Follain, *Mussolini's Island*, p. 240.

'Fascism fell, as was fitting' Atkinson, *Day of Battle*, p. 142.

'It is well known that under' OKW/KTB iv. 1797, cited in Bennett, *Ultra and Mediterranean Strategy*, p. 227.

'On no account should we let go' Alan Clark, *Barbarossa: The Russian–German Conflict 1941–45* (London, 1966) p. 337.

'Inescapably faced with the dilemma' Bennett, *Ultra and Mediterranean Strategy*, p. 222.

'With the failure of *Zitadelle*' Christer Bergström, *Kursk: The Air Battle of July 1943* (London, 2007), p. 58.

'a small classic of deception' TNA ADM 223/794, p. 442.

'as widely and thinly as possible' Bennett, *Ultra and Mediterranean Strategy*, p. 227.

'There can be no doubt' TNA ADM 223/794, p. 455.

'Special intelligence enabled us' Ibid., p. 442.

'Sicily has impressed everyone' Stafford, *Roosevelt and Churchill*, p. 107.

'really affected the outcome' Robertson, *The Ship with Two Captains*, p. 132.

'impossible to estimate' Ibid.

'the most spectacular single episode' Foreword to Montagu, *Ultra*, p. 10.

'perhaps the most successful single' Howard, *British Intelligence in The Second World War*, Vol. V: *Strategic Deception*, p. 89.

'Mincemeat swallowed rod' Howard, *Grand Strategy*, p. 370.

Chapter 23: Mincemeat Revealed

'considerable sum' EM to Shinwell, 7 Jan 1951, IWM 97/45/2.

'I am a prejudiced party' EM to Colonel Patavel at War Cabinet Office, 9 Jul 1945, IWM folder #1, 97/45/1.

'It would pay to release Mincemeat' Ibid.

'the Foreign Office would' EM to John Drew, 7 Nov 1950, IWM 97/45/2.

'in case the embargo' Ibid.

'Our intelligence obtained' Radio Monitoring report, 6 Aug 1944, IWM 97/45/1 folder #1.

'I believe this story is the greatest' Ibid.

'Unless some action is taken' TAR to JHB, 31 Aug 1944, TNA CAB 154/67.

'there was in fact some truth' Ibid.

'leave the American authorities' Ibid.

'We should do our utmost to stop' JHB to TAR, 21 Aug 1944, TNA CAB 154/67.

'Dawn had not broken' Alfred Duff Cooper, *Operation Heartbreak* (London, 2007) p. 103.

'Duff Cooper learned of Mincemeat' EM to Roger Morgan, 19 Apr 1982, IWM 97/45/1 folder #5.

'Sir W always wanted to hear this' *After the Battle*, 54, 1986.

'considered the objections' John Julius Norwich, in introduction to Montagu, *Man*, p. xi.

'direct from Churchill if prosecuted' R. V. Jones, *Most Secret War* (London, 1978) p. 217.

'consternation in security quarters' Ewen Montagu 'Postscript', Montagu Papers.

'there could not be one law for' EM to JG, 19 Sep 1964, Montagu Papers.

'wholly contrary to public' Sir Harold Parker to EM, 20 Dec 1950, IWM 97/45/2.

'One would not think even' EM to Sir Harold Parker, 7 Nov 1950, IWM 97/45/2.

'I forced Shinwell to agree that' EM to John Godfrey, 19 Sep 1964, Montagu Papers.

'sympathetically consider advice' EM to Sir Harold Parker, 2 Apr 1951, IWM 97/45/2.

'it would be wrong to publish' Ewen Montagu 'Postscript', Montagu Papers.

'shot off to Spain' EM to JG, 19 Sep 1964, Montagu Papers.

'cabled back in a frenzy' Ibid.

'The Foreign Office's chief worry' Ibid.

'using diplomats to lie' Ibid.

'Further pressure was applied' Ibid.

'the true means by which' Roger Morgan, *Beyond the Battle*, 146, Nov 2009.

'rushed round to the *Sunday Express*' Ibid.

'wholly unexpected' Montagu, *Ultra*, p. 12.

'The request not to publish' Ewen Montagu 'Postscript', Montagu Papers.

'so wildly inaccurate as to be' Ibid.

'controlled version' Morgan, *Beyond the Battle*, 146, Nov 2009.

'someone not under any control' EM to NLAJ, 11 Jan 1953, Montagu Papers.

'The return that the country got' EM to JG, 19 Sep 1964, Montagu Papers.

'The *Express* will submit and get' EM to NLAJ, 11 Jan 1953, Montagu Papers.

'with much black coffee and no' Ewen Montagu 'Postscript', Montagu Papers.

'or should it be "Pam"' EM to JGL, 8 Jan 1953, Montagu Papers.

'The powers that be have decided' Ibid.

'We don't want to alter anything' Ibid.

'a girl working in my section' Ibid.

'Mincemeat is soon going to be' EM to NLAJ, 11 Jan 1953, Montagu Papers.

'My account has been vetted' Ibid.

'I felt that you ought not to be' Ibid.

'I was most interested to hear' JGL to EM, 14 Jan 1954, Montagu Papers.

'merely say that you were working' EM to JGL, 21 Jan 1953, Montagu Papers.

'book, film rights, or other uses' CC to EM, 3 Mar 1954, Montagu Papers.

'As you will recall' Ibid.

'Whilst the general situation' Ibid.

'I do not feel that my own' Ibid.

'The war's most fantastic secret' *Sunday Express*, 1 Feb 1953.

'Although I heartily disapproved' Lord Mountbatten to EM, 31 Aug 1953, Montagu Papers.

'a good deal of persuasion that' AN to EM, 26 Apr 1954, Montagu Papers.

'You and I don't agree' J. C. Masterman to EM, 31 Aug 1954, Montagu Papers.

'Uncle John blitzed me' EM to Margery Boxall, 30 Oct 1950, courtesy of Fiona Mason.

'Your admirable *Man Who Never Was*' JG to EM, 13 Sep 1964, Montagu Papers.

'an exploit more astonishing' *Sunday Express*, 1 Feb 1953.

'managed to give the impression' Holt, *The Deceivers*, p. 370.

'an only son, an officer of' First draft of manuscript, IWM 97/45/1 folder #5.

'His parents were then' Ibid.

'without saying what we proposed' Montagu, *Man*, p. 123.

'I gave a solemn promise never' Montagu, *Ultra*, p. 145.

'My work is such that I will never' EM to 'Ginger', 6 Jul 1943, Montagu Papers.

'thrilling incidents which' EM 'Postscript', Montagu Papers.

'appear to be grudging' Lord Mountbattten to Ronald Neame, 29 Apr 1955, IWM 97/45/1 folder #4.

'I would like to make it clear' Ibid.

'I would have no objection' Ibid.

'There's nothing true in it' Interview with Federico Clauss, 2 Jun 2009.

'a derelict alcoholic found' Cave Brown, *Bodyguard of Lies*, p. 282.

'the wastrel brother of an MP' Ibid.

I have not explored the theory that the body was a victim of the HMS *Daster* explosion, since this is most effectively demolished by Roger Morgan in his essay 'Mincemeat Revisted', *Beyond the Battle*, 146, Nov 2009.

Chapter 24: Aftermath

'absolutely devoted to one another' Interview with Nicholas Jewell, 24 Jun 2008.

'General Mark Wayne Clark' Robertson, *The Ship with Two Captains*, p. 175.

'played a tiny part in ending the war' Ivor Leverton, letter to *Daily Telegraph*, 13 Aug 2002.

'redeemed' Interview with Basil Leverton, 8 Sep 2009.

'developed an intelligence' Denis Smyth, *Oxford Dictionary of National Biography*

'He walked several miles a day' Ibid.

'the most unscrupulous man in Spain' Stafford, *Roosevelt and Churchill*, p. 109.

'quiet, cold-blooded war of brains' Ibid., p. 373.

'The Russians are cleverer than' Ibid., p. 378.

'Thus ends the story' Edwin Sanders to Alan Hillgarth, 28 Jun 1948, collection of Tristan Hillgarth.

'Crazy Nolte is rich' Ibid.

'I am sorry, but I am not free' Colvin, *Unknown Courier*, p. 101.

'His mind was not as it used to be' Jackson, *Coroner*, p. 192.

'Every time I tell a story' Ibid., p. 201.

'His wife was the daughter of' Interview with Federico Clauss, 2 Jun 2009.

'He was always suspicious' Ibid.

'admitted the possibility' Colvin, *Unknown Courier*, p. 96.

'I take off my hat' Ian Colvin, *Sunday Express*, 8 Mar 1953.

'the heroic death of our beloved Führer' Harris, *Garbo*, p. 278.

'News of the death of our dear chief' Ibid., p. 280.

'If you find yourself in any danger' Ibid., p. 277.

'Kuhlenthal was overcome' Ibid., p. 285.

'Kuhlenthal made it abundantly' Ibid., p. 285.

'personally ordered that the medal' Ibid., p. 286.

'remain patiently in his hideout until' Ibid., p. 287.

'he should obey instructions to the letter' Ibid.

'Clandestinely' Ibid., p. 288.

'a melting pot' Dienz Website, http://www.dienz.de/Inhalt/karl-erichkuhlen.html

'he always tried to dress correctly' Ibid.

'De Profundibus' IWM 97/45/2.

'bold man to hounds' Obituary of John Gerard Leigh, *Daily Telegraph*, 1 Oct 2008.

'fought through Italy' Ibid.

'washing up, pottering about' Cited in *Oxford Dictionary of National Biography*.

'somewhat complicated by the fact' Nigel West and Oleg Tsarev, *Triplex: Secrets from the Cambridge Five* (Yale, 2009), p. 288.

'Captain [sic] Montagu is in charge' Ibid., pp. 277–8.

'The German General Staff' Ibid., p. 288.

'When the [invasion] was launched' Ibid.

'intelligent and agreeable' Philby to unnamed recipient MI5, 26 Nov 1946, TNA KV2/598.

'information from secret sources' TNA KV2/600.

'Middle East Anti-Locust Unit' Interview with Tom Cholmondeley, 1 Oct 2007.

'His objective was the destruction' G. F. Walford, *Arabian Locust Hunter* (London 1963) p. 32.

'they are loathsome insects' Ibid., p. 11.

'International Council for the Control' Interview with Tom Cholmondeley, 1 Oct 2007.

'intelligence duties' Ibid.

'wide experience of deception work' Ibid.

'He would not give information' Alison Cholmondeley, letter to the author 8 May 2008.

'He would take a revolver' John Otter, letter to *Daily Telegraph*, 15 Aug 2002.

'invaluable work during the war' EM, letter to *The Times*, 23 Jun 1982.

'The Turbulent Judge' *Sunday Mirror*, 5 Jul 1964.

'Half the scum of England' *Daily Telegraph*, 1 Feb, 1957.

'A boy crook should have' *Sunday Mirror*, 5 Jul 1964.

'discourtesy, even gross discourtesy' *The Times*, 24 Oct 1967.

'If a man can't have a stroke of luck' *Sun*, 2 Aug 1969.

'The public needs protecting from' *The Times*, 26 Sep 1962.

'Few judges have trodden so hard' *Sun*, 2 Aug 1969.

'Perhaps I should have been more' Henry Stenhope, *The Times*, 2 Aug 1969.

'extreme caution and extreme daring' M. R. D. Foot, *Oxford Dictionary of National Biography*.

'Dear "Pam"' EM to JGL, 31 Dec 1980, courtesy of Jean Gerard Leigh.

'one of the buttons I wore' EM to John F. Meek, undated, IWM 97/45/1 folder #5

'Keep a real sense of humour' Ibid.

'There, at the end of the last volume' *Beyond the Battle*, 94, 1995.

'On 28 January there had died' TNA ADM 223/794, p. 442.

'Glyndwr Michael' Inscription on gravestone, Huelva cemetery.

Select Bibliography

Archives

National Archives, Kew (TNA).
Imperial War Museum Archives (IWM).
Bundesarchiv-Militärarchiv, Freiburg.
National Archives, Washington DC.
British Library Newspaper Archive, Colindale.
Churchill Archives Centre (CA).
Mountbatten Papers, University of Southampton.
Labour History Archive and Study Centre (People's History Museum), Manchester (PHM.)

Printed Sources

Andrew, Christopher, *Secret Service: The Making of the British Intelligence Community* (London, 1985).

————*The Defence of the Realm: The Authorized History of MI5* (London, 2009).

Atkinson, Rick, *The Day of Battle: The War in Sicily and Italy 1943–1945* (London, 2007).

Beesly, Patrick, *Very Special Admiral: The Life of Admiral J. H. Godfrey* (London, 1980).

Bennett, Gill, *Churchill's Man of Mystery: Desmond Morton and the World of Intelligence* (London, 2007).

Bennett, Ralph, *Behind the Battle: Intelligence in the War with Germany 1939–45* (London, 1999).

————*Ultra and Mediterranean Strategy 1941–1945* (London, 1989)

Burns, Jimmy, *Papa Spy: Love, Faith and Betrayal in Wartime Spain* (London, 2009).

Cave Brown, Anthony, *Bodyguard of Lies*, Vol. I (London, 1975).

Carter, Miranda, *Anthony Blunt: His Lives* (London, 2001).

Colvin, Ian, *The Unknown Courier* (London, 1953).

Copeiro del Villar, Jesús Ramírez, *Huelva en la II Guerra Mundial* (Huelva, 1996).

Crowdy, Terry, *Deceiving Hitler: Double Cross and Deception in World War II* (London, 2008).

Curry, J., *The Security Service 1908–1945: The Official History* (London, 1999).

Day, Albert Edward, *Dialogue and Destiny* (New York, 1981).

Deakin, F. W., *The Brutal Friendship: Mussolini, Hitler and the Fall of Italian Fascism* (London, 1962).

D'Este, Carlo, *Bitter Victory: The Battle for Sicily 1943* (London, 1988).

Evans, Colin, *The Father of Forensics: How Sir Bernard Spilsbury Invented Modern CSI* (London, 2009).

Farago, Ladislas, *The Game of the Foxes: The Untold Story of German Espionage in the US and Great Britain during World War Two* (New York, London, 1972).

Fisher, John, *What a Performance: A Life of Sid Field* (London, 1975).

Follain, John, *Mussolini's Island: The Untold Story of the Invasion of Italy* (London, 2005).

Foot, M. R. D., *SOE: The Special Operations Executive 1940–1946* (London, 1999).

Gilbert, Martin, *Winston S. Churchill*, Vol. 6: *Finest Hour, 1939–1941* (London, 1983).

Handel, Michael I., *War Strategy and Intelligence* (London, 1989).

Harris, Tomas, *Garbo: The Spy Who Saved D-Day*; Introduction by Mark Seaman (London, 2004).

Hastings, Max, *Finest Years: Churchill as Warlord 1940–45* (London, 2009).

Hinsley, F. H., *British Intelligence in the Second World War: Its Influence on Strategy and Operations*, Vol. I (London, 1979).

Hinsley, F. H. and Simkins, C. A. G., *British Intelligence in the Second World War: Security and Counter-Intelligence*, Vol. IV (London, 1990).

Holmes, Richard, *Churchill's Bunker: The Secret Headquarters at the Heart of Britain's Victory* (London, 2009).

Holt, Thaddeus, *The Deceivers: Allied Military Deception in the Second World War* (London, 2004).

Howard, Michael, *Grand Strategy* (London, 1972).

————British Intelligence in the Second World War, Vol. V: Strategic Deception (London 1990).

Irving, David, Hitler's War (London, 1977).

Jackson, Robert, Coroner: The Biography of Sir Bentley Purchase (London, 1963).

Jewell, Lt N. L. A., as told to Cecil Carnes, Secret Mission Submarine: Action Report of the HMS Seraph (London, 1944).

Johnson, David Alan, Righteous Deception: German Officers Against Hitler (Westport, Connecticut, 2001).

Kahn, David, Hitler's Spies: German Military Intelligence in World War II (New York, 2000).

Knightley, Philip, The Second Oldest Profession (London, 1986).

Lawrence, T. E., Seven Pillars of Wisdom (London, 1991).

Liddell, Guy, The Guy Liddell Diaries, 1939–1945, Vols. I and II; edited by Nigel West (London, 2005).

Lord, John, Duty, Honour, Empire (London, 1971).

Macintyre, Ben, For Your Eyes Only: Ian Fleming and James Bond (London, 2008).

Masterman, J. C., The Double Cross System in the War 1939–1945 (London, 1972).

————On the Chariot Wheel: An Autobiography (Oxford, 1975).

McLachlan, Donald, Room 39: Naval Intelligence in Action 1939–45 (London, 1968).

Miller, Russell, Codename Tricycle: The True Story of the Second World War's Most Extraordinary Double Agent (London, 2005).

Montagu, Ewen, Beyond Top Secret Ultra (London, 1977).

————The Man Who Never Was (Oxford, 1996).

Montagu, Ivor, The Youngest Son: Autobiographical Chapters (London, 1970)

Mure, David, Practise to Deceive (London, 1997).

Paine, Lauran, The Abwehr: German Military Intelligence in World War II (London, 1984).

Payne, Stanley G., Franco and Hitler: Spain, Germany and World War II (London, 2008).

Philby, Kim, My Silent War: The Autobiography of a Spy (London, 1968)

Popov, Dusko, Spy/Counterspy (New York, 1974).

Rankin, Nicholas, Churchill's Wizards: The British Genius for Deception 1914–1945 (London, 2008.)

Robertson, Terence, The Ship with Two Captains: The Story of the 'Secret Mission Submarine' (London, 1957).

Rose, Andrew, *Lethal Witness: Sir Bernard Spilsbury, the Honorary Pathologist* (London, 2008).

Rose, Kenneth, *Elusive Rothschild: The Life of Victor, Third Baron* (London, 2003).

Sebag-Montefiore, Hugh, *Enigma: The Battle for the Code* (London, 2000).

Smyth, Denis, *Diplomacy and Strategy of Survival: British Policy and Franco's Spain 1940–41* (Cambridge, 1986).

Stafford, David, *Churchill and the Secret Service* (London, 1997).

————*Roosevelt and Churchill: Men of Secrets* (London, 1999).

Stephens, R. 'Tin Eye', *Camp 020: MI5 and the Nazi Spies*; Introduction by Oliver Hoare (London, 2000).

Stephenson, William, *A Man Called Intrepid: the Secret War of 1939–45* (London, 1976).

Thomson, Sir Basil, *The Milliner's Hat Mystery* (London, 1937).

Walford, G. F., *Arabian Locust Hunter* (London, 1963).

Waller, John H., *The Unseen War in Europe: Espionage and Conspiracy in the Second World War* (New York, London, 1996).

West, Nigel, *MI5: British Security Service Operations 1909–45* (London, 1981).

————At Her Majesty's Secret Service: The Chiefs of Britain's Intelligence Agency, MI6 (London, 2006).

————*Mask: MI5's Penetration of the Communist Party of Great Britain* (London, 2005).

————*Venona: The Greatest Secret of the Cold War* (London, 1999)

West, Nigel and Tsarev, Oleg (eds), *Triplex: Secrets from the Cambridge Five* (Yale, 2009).

Wilson, Emily Jane, *The War in the Dark: The Security Service and the Abwehr 1940–1944*, PhD thesis (Cambridge, 2003).

Winterbotham, F. W., *The Ultra Secret* (London, 1974).

Acknowledgments

I am hugely indebted to the scores of people in five countries who have helped me in the writing of this book. In Britain, Germany and Spain, the families of the participants in Operation Mincemeat have been extraordinarily generous with their time, memories and documentary material: Jeremy Montagu, Jennifer Montagu, Rachel Montagu, Sarah Montagu, Tom Cholmondeley, Alison Cholmondeley, Jean Gerard Leigh, John Gerard Leigh, Carolyn Benson, John Michael, Paul Jewell, Nicholas Jewell, Tristan Hillgarth, Jocelyn Hillgarth, Juliette Kuhlenthal, Federico Clauss, Andrew Leverton, Basil Leverton, Yvette Bourguignon and Sir Alan Urwick. Many others, either directly or indirectly involved, willingly contributed additional material: the late Joan Bright-Astley, Gill Drake, Lady Victoire Ridsdale, Peggy Harmer, Patricia Davies, John Julius Norwich, Eve Streatfeild, Nicholas Reed, Isabelle Naylor and Selina Fraser-Smith. Still others offered useful advice and contacts: Annabel Merullo, Sam Merullo, Emma Crichton, Guy Liardet, Jack Baer, James Owen, Jan Dalley, John Scarlett, Ian Brunskill, Robert Hands, Fiona and Peter Mason, Stephen Walker, Sally George, Phil Reed and Robin Hunt. To the other individuals who have asked not to be named: my covert but heartfelt gratitude.

I am grateful to numerous experts in various fields for their advice and guidance: Dr Sacha Kolar on forensic pathology; Neil Cooke on Whitehall geography; Mary Teviot for her genealogical sleuthing; Pedro J. Ramírez, Julio Martín Alarcón and the staff of *El Mundo* in Spain; Jesús Copeiro for sharing his local knowledge and for a fascinating guided tour of Huelva and Punta Umbria; Paul Bryant; Graham Keeley for his work in Spain and Jo Carlill and Paul Bellshaw for their help with pictures.

Numerous historians and writers have also helped me to shape the book: Christopher Andrew, Michael Foot, Frank Stech, Andrew Rose, Roger Morgan, Tim Cottingham, John Follain, Sarah Street, Thomas Boghardt, Andrew Lycett, and Martin Gilbert. I am particularly grateful to Peter Martland, Mark Seaman and Terry Charman for reading the manuscript, and saving me from some toe-curling errors. The remaining mistakes are all my own.

This book has involved many hours of archive research, and I have been helped immeasurably by a number of brilliant and dedicated archivists: Rod Suddaby of the Imperial War Museum; Howard Davies, Hugh Alexander and the staff of the National Archives; James Beckett of the Formula One Archives; Neil F. Murray of the Aston Martin Club; Lesley Hall of the Wellcome Trust; Darren Treadwell of the People's History Museum, and Caroline Herbert of the Churchill Archives Centre.

My friends and colleagues on *The Times* have been, as always, unstinting in their help and advice. I have Duncan Stewart to thank, once again, for the fine maps.

My thanks to Michael Fishwick, Kate Johnson and the team at Bloomsbury for all their enthusiasm, professionalism and patience. Ed Victor has been my rock for each of my last seven books. My thanks and apologies to the friends and family who have put up with me banging on about Operation Mincemeat for three years. And to Kate, as ever, all my love.

Index

Figures in bold refer to illustrations.